SAP PRESS Books: Always on hand

Print or e-book, Kindle or iPad, workplace or airplane: Choose where and how to read your SAP PRESS books! You can now get all our titles as e-books, too:

▶ By download and online access
▶ For all popular devices
▶ And, of course, DRM-free

Convinced? Then go to www.sap-press.com and get your e-book today.

Demand and Supply Planning with SAP® APO

PRESS

SAP PRESS is a joint initiative of SAP and Galileo Press. The know-how offered by SAP specialists combined with the expertise of the Galileo Press publishing house offers the reader expert books in the field. SAP PRESS features first-hand information and expert advice, and provides useful skills for professional decision-making.

SAP PRESS offers a variety of books on technical and business-related topics for the SAP user. For further information, please visit our website: *www.sap-press.com*.

Sandeep Pradhan and Pavan Verma
Global Available-to-Promise with SAP: Functionality and Configuration
2012, 349 pp., hardcover
ISBN 978-1-59229-385-8

Jochen Balla and Frank Layer
Production Planning with SAP APO (2nd Edition)
2011, 402 pp., hardcover
ISBN 978-1-59229-354-4

Balaji Gaddam
Capable to Match (CTM) with SAP APO
2009, 273 pp., hardcover
ISBN 978-1-59229-244-8

Marc Hoppe
Inventory Optimization with SAP
2008, 705 pp., hardcover
ISBN 978-1-59229-205-9

Sandeep Pradhan

Demand and Supply Planning with SAP® APO

Bonn • Boston

Galileo Press is named after the Italian physicist, mathematician, and philosopher Galileo Galilei (1564–1642). He is known as one of the founders of modern science and an advocate of our contemporary, heliocentric worldview. His words *Eppur si muove* (And yet it moves) have become legendary. The Galileo Press logo depicts Jupiter orbited by the four Galilean moons, which were discovered by Galileo in 1610.

Editor Laura Korslund
Technical Reviewer Frank Layer
Copyeditor Miranda Martin
Cover Design Graham Geary
Photo Credit iStockphoto.com/TMSK
Layout Design Vera Brauner
Production Graham Geary
Typesetting Publishers' Design and Production Services, Inc.
Printed and bound in the United States of America, on paper from sustainable sources

ISBN 978-1-59229-423-7
© 2013 by Galileo Press Inc., Boston (MA)
1st edition 2013

Library of Congress Cataloging-in-Publication Data
Pradhan, Sandeep.
Demand and supply planning with SAP APO / Sandeep Pradhan. — 1st ed.
p. cm.
ISBN 978-1-59229-423-7 — ISBN 1-59229-423-5 1. APO. 2. SAP ERP. 3.
Inventory control—Computer programs. 4. Inventory control—Data
processing. 5. Production planning—Data processing. 6. Production
control—Data processing. I. Title.
TS160.P73 2013
658.5—dc23
2012036369

Contents at a Glance

Dear Reader,

What you hold in your hands is much more than just a book on supply and demand planning, and even more than a book on SAP APO. While each topic within this book is strongly connected to the SAP APO Demand Planning and Supply Network Planning functionalities, this book can't be merely defined as something that will help you set up processes in SAP APO. What you hold in your hands is a tool that will give you an understanding of the intricacies of working with SAP APO on a grander scale. Find insight on how SAP APO can transform your entire supply chain, and what resources you need to make that happen. From information on SAP APO implementation, configuration of its different functionalities, and integration with SAP and non-SAP tools, you'll find what you need to get you started with transforming the way you think about and manage your supply chain.

Of course, such an all-encompassing book could not be successfully completed without a seasoned and expert author. It has been my pleasuring working with Sandeep for the second time, and on what is now his third book with SAP PRESS. It's been a long time coming to establish our flagship title on the demand and supply planning functions of SAP APO, and we're thrilled to be able to present this book to you!

We at SAP PRESS are always eager to hear your opinion. What do you think about *Demand and Supply Planning with SAP APO*? As your comments and suggestions are our most useful tools to help us make our books the best they can be, we encourage you to visit our website at *www.sap-press.com* and share your feedback.

Thank you for purchasing a book from SAP PRESS!

Laura Korslund
Editor, SAP PRESS

Galileo Press
Boston, MA

laura.korslund@galileo-press.com
www.sap-press.com

Contents

Introduction

SAP Advanced Planning & Optimization (SAP APO) is one of the key modules within SAP Supply Chain Management (SAP SCM), which has come a long way in gaining Advanced Planning and Scheduling (APS) market maturity and popularity. The tool provides the capability to support a company's sales and operations planning process with a set of functions that balance market demand with supply chain constraints. The Demand Planning (which we'll refer to throughout the book as APO-DP) functionality within SAP APO provides advanced forecasting and demand planning tools that enable companies to capture changes in demand signal and patterns as early as possible. Similarly, Supply Network Planning (which we'll refer to as APO-SNP) provides tactical supply planning capabilities with integration to purchasing, manufacturing, distribution, and transportation and creates a feasible plan in a constraint supply network environment. The objective of this book is to provide an in-depth introduction to the APO-DP and APO-SNP functions, applications, and customizations.

This book is written based on the current SAP SCM 7.02 (containing SAP APO 7.0 with Enhancement Pack 2) release and provides coverage in using APO-DP and APO-SNP functionalities for basic and advanced planning concepts. While the basic planning focuses on how to configure and model the demand and supply planning cycle in SAP APO, the advanced planning provides insight into enhanced functionalities (seasonal planning, subcontracting, etc.), which support unique business scenarios. SAP APO, a user-decision support tool, is best explained with a business case study, which is the approach this book has adopted, using a fictitious company example. The book demonstrates how a fictitious computer manufacturing company named ABC Technology goes about initiating a supply chain transformation project to improve its supply chain planning process with APO-DP and APO-SNP capabilities. Throughout the book, a constant balance of theory and practice is adapted to ensure that you have a good grasp of the discussed topics. Besides explaining the functional and technical aspects of APO-DP and APO-SNP, the book also devotes some time to data conversion activities and an implementation approach for a typical SAP APO project.

The overall goals of this book are to:

▶ Explain the industry best practices for demand and supply planning business processes

▶ Introduce SAP APO in the form of APO-DP and APO-SNP as a planning tool for business planners

▶ Explain the basic planning concepts and teach readers how to configure and model the planning process in SAP APO

▶ Deep-dive on the real-life business scenarios that will flush out the SAP APO functionalities (APO-DP and APO-SNP)

▶ Use a case study example to explain difficult topics

▶ Explain technical operational concepts in SAP APO

▶ Discuss an implementation approach for SAP APO

Who This Book Is For

This book is aimed at supply chain practitioners who are concerned with learning the concept of demand and supply planning and would like to implement and configure SAP APO Demand Planning and Supply Network Planning functionalities. The target audience for this book is the supply chain managers, supply chain planners, project managers, and consultants who are interested in this topic.

Basic knowledge of the supply chain management processes and a sound understanding of the supply chain planning, material management, production planning, and transportation business processes is required to understand the business scenarios explained in this book.

What This Book Covers

The book can be broadly divided into three sections. The first section (Chapter 1 through Chapter 7) explains how APO-DP and APO-SNP can fit in the company's sales and operations planning process by supporting weekly and monthly planning cycles. This section explains how to model your supply chain and configure and set up the system. The second section (Chapter 8 through Chapter 14) touches on cross-functional areas, such as inventory planning, optimization engines, reporting, collaboration, and industry solutions, which are integral parts of SAP APO. The final section (Chapter 15 and Chapter 16) explains the SAP APO Core Interface

(CIF) and technical concepts and provides some data conversion guidelines for SAP APO project success.

The chapters can be further broken down as follows:

- **Chapter 1**

  This chapter provides a theoretical introduction to supply chain planning based on various literatures. It also discusses leading practices for the sales and operations planning process and uses the Supply Chain Council's supply chain operation reference (SCOR) model to articulate the demand and supply planning business process decomposition. An introduction is provided to the fictitious company that's faced with current planning challenges. An overview of SAP Supply Chain Performance Management is also provided to formulate a company's supply chain scorecard metrics.

- **Chapter 2**

  This chapter starts by describing the Advanced Planning and Scheduling (APS) concepts and then introduces SAP Advanced Planning & Optimization (SAP APO). A brief overview of SAP APO Demand Planning (APO-DP) and SAP APO Supply Network Planning (APO-SNP) is provided, along with key functions and planning characteristics. The chapter ends with technical architecture and a brief explanation of SAP liveCache technology.

- **Chapter 3**

  This chapter provides practical guidelines for implementing the SAP APO package. Besides highlighting the implementation methodology (with the example of global template rollout), the chapter also focuses on explaining the importance of change management, business benefits, and business readiness towards steering a successful SAP APO implementation.

- **Chapter 4**

  This chapter teaches you basic customization and master data modeling steps in APO-DP and APO-SNP. Besides showing how we can design planning books for business users, this chapter also provides detailed information on the statistical forecasting process and supply chain modeling steps for supply network planning.

- **Chapter 5**

  This chapter is devoted to explaining the basic interactive planning activities for performing demand and supply planning cycle activities in APO-DP and APO-SNP. The focus of this chapter is on providing the building blocks for the business user to start navigating the system and using basic SAP APO functionalities (for example, forecasting, supply planning runs, simulation, and alerts) in an interactive manner for preparing demand and supply plans.

▶ **Chapter 6**
This chapter demonstrates the advanced functionalities in SAP APO Demand Planning. You will learn how promotion planning, lifecycle management, seasonal planning, bill of material (BOM) forecasting, product and customer segmentation, customer forecast management, and demand alerts can be customized and set up in APO-DP.

▶ **Chapter 7**
This chapter demonstrates the advanced functionalities in Supply Network Planning and explains how APO-SNP can be customized and modeled to solve many complex supply chain business scenarios. Various APO-SNP functionalities that support tactical (i.e., safety stock planning, interchangeability, subcontracting, direct shipment, shelf life, and aggregated planning) and operational (i.e., Transport Load Builder (TLB), stock balancing, and warehouse capacity evaluation) planning processes are explained in both theory and practice (i.e., customization and setup).

▶ **Chapter 8**
This chapter describes the collaborative planning process setup between internal and external business partners to reach a consensus on balance demand and supply plans. Using the examples of Vendor Managed Inventory (VMI) and collaborative planning, forecast, and replenishment (CPFR), this chapter shows how SAP APO collaborative planning capabilities can be modeled in the system for effective demand and supply collaborations.

▶ **Chapter 9**
This chapter provides comprehensive information regarding the SAP APO's internal SAP NetWeaver Business Warehouse (BW) staging, extracting, transformation, and reporting processes. It also explains the BW data model for demand and supply planning and outlines how SAP NetWeaver BW business content can be leveraged to activate some of the SAP standard reporting in the areas of forecast accuracy, global inventory, and global capacity.

▶ **Chapter 10**
This chapter demonstrates how we can configure APO-SNP optimizer to solve complex supply chain optimization problems. The chapter provides an explanation of how mathematical models (i.e., linear and mixed integer programming)

can be formulated in the APO-SNP optimizer planning engine to solve typical distribution and allocation supply chain problems.

▶ **Chapter 11**

This chapter explains the capable-to-match (CTM) functionality in APO-SNP for demand and supply matching in the supply chain. It also explains the customization and master data steps required for setting up the CTM planning engine to respect business rules around demand and supply priorities.

▶ **Chapter 12**

This chapter focuses on designing inventory modeling in SAP APO for supply chain optimization. The chapter outlines a methodology for setting up different inventory models and demonstrates various tools in SAP ERP and SAP APO for effective inventory management.

▶ **Chapter 13**

This chapter provides an introduction to characteristics-based planning in SAP APO and explains the concept with detailed customization and master data setup in the SAP ERP and SAP SCM systems. It also describes how we can perform characteristics-based forecasting and supply planning. The functionality of SAP APO Production Planning and Detailed Scheduling (PP/DS) is also highlighted in this chapter as it forms a part of the integrated solution in SAP APO.

▶ **Chapter 14**

This chapter provides an example of SAP APO integration with an SAP industry solution and uses an Apparel and Footwear (AFS) example to demonstrate how the complexity of the industry can be matched with an integrated solution of SAP ERP AFS and SAP APO. It also describes how SAP APO functionalities, such as seasonal planning and aggregated planning, can be used to support AFS industry business requirements.

▶ **Chapter 15**

This chapter explains the technical concepts within SAP APO, beginning with Core Interface (CIF), which provides the interface foundation of keeping the execution (SAP ERP) and planning (SAP SCM) systems synchronized. The chapter guides the audience in setting up CIF and monitoring and troubleshooting errors.

The second part of the chapter examines various stages of the upgrade process and some of the key functional activities that need to be performed to bring the system back to its original state. The chapter also describes the process chain for scheduling routine background jobs.

► **Chapter 16**

This chapter explains the SAP APO technical concepts in the form of data conversion activities using the Legacy System Migration Workbench (LSMW) and various technical enhancements. Examples are provided to show that we can use LSMW for master data and transactional data integration. This chapter also provides numerous business scenarios and technical enhancement solutions, where SAP APO native functionality needs to be enhanced to support unique business requirements.

The **Appendix** contains a glossary of the acronyms used in the book. In the beginning of each chapter, a supplementary mind map diagram is presented to depict the learning objective of the topic.

Acknowledgements

I would like to offer my special thanks to my wife, Imelda Linggawidjaja; my daughter, Jessica Anna; and my parents, for giving me the time and encouragement to write this book.

Finally, I would also like to convey my sincere thanks to editor Laura Korslund and the Galileo Press team with whom I have now worked on three amazing projects. Also, my special thanks to Frank Layer (author of *Production Planning with SAP APO*, SAP PRESS 2010) for becoming the technical reviewer for this book and providing valuable corrections and comments.

Sandeep Pradhan
Denver, Colorado – October 2012

This chapter provides introduction to theoretical background on supply chain planning concepts. Using the Supply Chain Operation Reference (SCOR) model, you will understand the business process decomposition within the demand and supply planning business process.

1   Introduction to Supply Chain Planning

SAP Supply Chain Management (SAP SCM) uses a functionality call *supply chain planning*, which helps businesses balance demand and supply. Businesses choose to implement supply chain planning primarily because of the market volatility in an extended supply chain environment where the supply chain extends beyond the company's wall toward customers and suppliers. This in turn requires organizations to not only effectively plan their resources internally, but also collaborate with external business partners to proactively react to any market supply chain situations. In today's global economy, companies are differentiating their business operating models by integrating and coordinating with their internal and external business partners to fulfill customer demands.

In this chapter we will learn five distinct topics related to supply chain planning (see Figure 1.1). We will discuss the sales and operations planning process and then explain how the SCOR (Supply Chain Operation Reference) model supports the supply chain planning process. Then we will discuss different types of supply chains in the context of our fictitious company, ABC Technology, before breaking down the processes for demand and supply planning. We'll end the chapter with a brief overview on supply chain maturity.

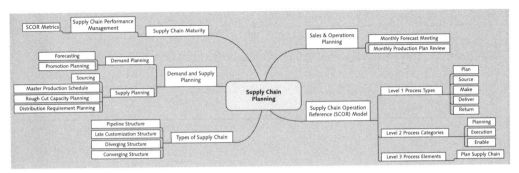

Figure 1.1 Learning Points for the Chapter (Mind Map)

To better understand what supply chain planning is and how it works, we need to break down the concepts a little more: A *supply chain* is referred to as an integrated system that synchronizes a series of interrelated business processes in order to accomplish the following:

▶ Procure raw materials

▶ Transform these raw materials to finished products

▶ Add value to the finished products

▶ Promote and distribute the finished products to its customers

The main objectives of a supply chain are to enhance operational efficiency, increase profitability, and improve on its competitive position in the marketplace. Typically, a supply chain consists of multiple end-to-end business processes, as shown in Figure 1.2:

▶ **Inbound logistics**
Supports the procurement of raw material from supplier, internal control of the production process, and warehouse storage. The process is also called *purchase to receipt* upon bringing the products from suppliers for further manufacturing processes or distribution.

▶ **Order management and inter-faculty movements**
Consists of capturing customer orders and fulfillment. The process may require transfers of inventory within the network to meet customer orders. The process is also called order-to-cash, which begins with order capture and ends with customer billing.

▶ **Outbound logistics**

Relates to the physical distribution of outbound logistics activities: customer order receipt and processing, inventory deployment, storage and handling, and order consolidation. This process can also form part of order-to-delivery, with primary focus on transportation.

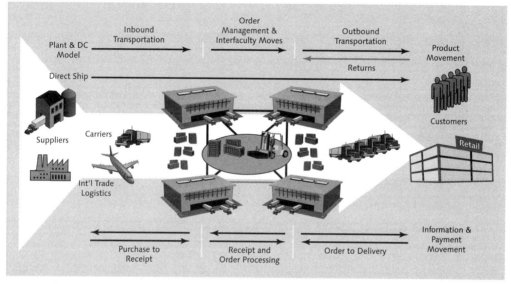

Figure 1.2 Company's Supply Chain: Physical Goods and Information Flows

Combining these business processes, the supply chain consists of a web of multiple network and business relationships among partners. The successful integration of an entire supply chain depends heavily on proper supply chain planning and execution of business processes:

▶ *Supply chain planning (SCP)* consists of predicting future requirements to balance supply and market demands.

▶ *Supply chain execution (SCE)* consists of the flow of tasks involved in the supply chain, such as order fulfillment, procurement, warehousing, and transporting. Since this book is focused on SCP, we will only be discussing the SCE integration points further in relevant chapters and sections.

This chapter looks at demand and supply software components that constitute supply chain planning and provide a planning framework using the Supply Chain Operation Reference (SCOR) model. The chapter also highlights the importance of the sales and operation planning process and SAP Supply Chain Performance Management for an organization to progress in the supply chain maturity curve. We'll lay a theoretical foundational background on supply chain planning concepts before introducing you to the SAP Advanced Planning & Optimization component (which we'll refer to throughout the book as SAP APO).

> **Note**
>
> Please note that the terminology we use in this chapter primarily relates to the industry terms in general, and not necessarily a specific SAP application unless otherwise indicated.

Our first point of business is to understand that supply chain planning is a cross-functional effort in an organization where sales, marketing, finance, and operations collaborate towards a consensus-based demand and supply plan. This will help you understand the different types of supply chains that exist, and why each has its own unique needs. This collaborative planning process within the organization is called *sales and operations planning,* which we'll explain in the next section.

1.1   Sales and Operations Planning

In general, sales and operations planning is a monthly business process that enables a company to determine the one plan that will allow the organization to meet its operational, sales, and financial goals. The process is typically the responsibility of a specific sales and operations planning team, which includes the company's decision makers and line managers in marketing, sales, finance, operations, and customer service functions.

The sales and operations planning process enables the company to effectively manage the demand of its customers with the capacity of its operations. Sales and operations planning generates a uniform and agreed-to set of numbers used to drive the business. It specifically integrates strategic, tactical, and operational planning.

> **A Typical Example of Sales and Operations Planning Horizons**
>
> A company's planning horizon consists of short-, medium-, and long-term periods:
>
> ► **Strategic company planning**
> One to five years, reviewed yearly. Sets the company's strategic direction for future growth. The strategic planning processes set the timing and key strategies for the plan period and strategically allocate resources.

- ▶ **Tactical planning**
  Eighteen months, reviewed quarterly. An output of strategic planning. Tactical planning identifies the material requirements and resources to translate medium-term plans into a short-term operational plan and execution.
- ▶ **Operational planning**
  Rolling twelve months, reviewed monthly. Translates tactical plans into specific objectives and confirms activities and timings through short-term plans and execution.

In the following sections, we'll explain the sales and operations planning goal, and provide a case study example to help illustrate its importance.

1.1.1 Goal of Sales and Operations Planning

The primary goal of the sales and operations planning process is to facilitate the flow of information between master planning (supply) and demand planning. *Master planning* is concerned with coordinating the supply side of the organization and seeks efficient and economical ways to fulfill market demands by creating purchasing, manufacturing, and distribution plans. The process of *demand planning* focuses on generating future forecast estimates based on historical customer sales order patterns. Sales and marketing campaigns further enrich the baseline forecast. The process itself is fairly simple and comprises the following five essential steps:

1. Create a demand plan.
2. Create a supply plan.
3. Compare the demand and supply plans.
4. Reconcile the demand and supply plans with the financial plan.
5. Update the sales and operations plan.

Figure 1.3 shows a typical monthly cycle for sales and operations planning. The demand review is performed first, followed by the supply review with possible supply chain constraints (for example, reduced capacity) before the sales and operations planning meeting is conducted. The example shows that the sales, marketing, planning, and finance teams reached a demand planning consensus during the first week of the monthly cycle. The second week focuses on supply planners' efforts to balance the unconstrained demand with the constrained supply planning. Meetings are held before the official sales and operations planning meeting to resolve any demand and supply imbalances with alternative supply chain options.

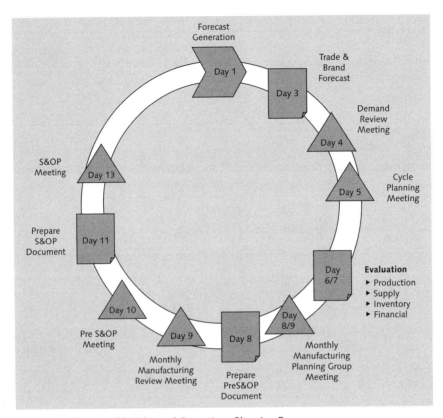

Figure 1.3 The Monthly Sales and Operations Planning Process

Next, let's look at a case study from a manufacturing and distribution company selling consumer electronics goods. The company acts as a great example in the sales and operations planning process with clear definitions of roles and responsibilities.

1.1.2 Sales and Operations Planning Case Study: Manufacturing and Distribution

A consumer goods company markets its electronics products in North America. Since its product offering has less product differentiation in the market than its competitors', the company depends heavily on promotions and direct consumer selling marketing strategy. The company recently received Class A accreditation and provides example as industry best practice organization. The company sets example in the industry by integrating their sales and operations planning with their core business process, building a rich data, and working on an exception-driven decision making process, which ensures demand and supply plans are proactively balanced.

Table 1.1 shows the business criteria and business activities on which the organization that's following industry best practices differs from other common organizations on the sales and operations planning capability matrix.

	Common	Progressive	World Class
Decision-making meeting structure	Ad hoc meetings between key impacted functions held in a reactive or fire-fighting mode	Proactive formal meetings between core functional teams.	Proactive formal meetings with all functional teams across the extended supply chain.
Underlying technology and data support	Data is maintained and reported using desktop-based tools such as MS Excel and ad hoc MS Access applications.	Data is maintained and sourced from ERP applications and reported using a mix of desktop tools and ERP reporting tools.	Data is maintained and sourced from ERP applications and reported using a web-enabled integrated planning workbench.
Organizational integration	No integrated planning capability to integrate into the organization.	Integrated planning seen as an essential addition to business as usual.	Integrated planning embedded into organizational operating processes to the extent that it is part of business as usual.
Analysis capability	All analysis is conducted manually using spreadsheet-based tools. No what-if analysis capability.	Scenario and what-if analysis capabilities are used, based mainly on cost and gross sales drivers.	Scenario, what-if, and optimization analysis capabilities are used, based on profit and similar drivers.

Table 1.1   Sales and Operations Planning Capability Matrix

	Common	Progressive	World Class
Segmentation approach	Supply chain capability is seen as a one-size-fits-all solution with little differentiation of capability based on customer value.	Some segmentation of supply chain capability, but requires extensive manual intervention to enable.	Supply chain capability is fully segmented based on customer value. Systems enable this capability.
One-number production and adherence	Multiple operating plans are used to drive business activities and actions.	One-number plan agreed to drive business activities; however, some functions still use additional plans.	All business activities are driven off the integrated planning one number—with no other plans developed or tracked.

Table 1.1 Sales and Operations Planning Capability Matrix (Cont.)

The consumer goods electronics company uses a formal, cyclical set of exception-driven sales and operations planning meetings to conduct integrated planning over a rolling eighteen-month horizon in a mix of weekly and monthly buckets.

> **Note**
>
> *Time buckets* are defined as periods or horizons of time in which the receipts (for example, an incoming purchase order), requirements (for example, an outgoing sales order), and stocks (inventory) are cumulated.

Figure 1.4 shows the participants, format, and result that come out of the weekly and monthly meetings. The collaboration leads to better demand and supply matching with proactive measures to meet market demands.

The sales and operations planning process for the consumer electronics company results in a one-number plan that is then distributed in functional-specific formats of sales, supply, distribution, inventory, and financial plans, as shown in Figure 1.5.

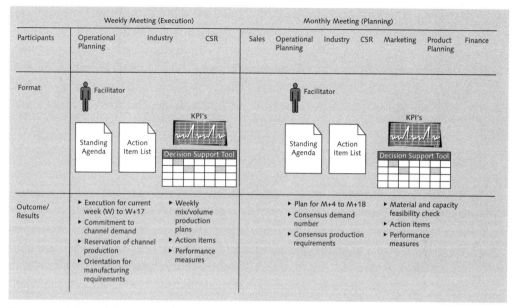

Figure 1.4 Sales and Operations Planning Tactical and Operational Meetings

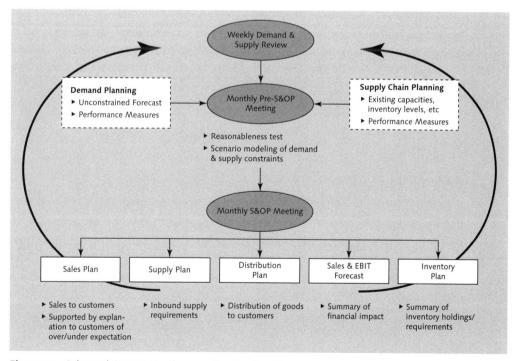

Figure 1.5 Sales and Operations Planning Meeting Results

Implementation of sales and operations planning in an organization requires a framework that links business processes, metrics, best practices, and technology features into a unified structure to support communication among supply chain partners and to improve the effectiveness of supply chain management and related supply chain improvement activities. The Supply Chain Operations Reference model, which we'll explain in the next section, provides this form of framework.

1.2 Supply Chain Operations Reference Model

The Supply Chain Operations Reference (SCOR) model is a process reference model that was developed by the management consulting firm PRTM and AMR Research. SCOR is endorsed by the Supply Chain Council (*www.supply-chain.org*) as the cross-industry, *de facto,* standard diagnostic tool for supply chain management. SCOR enables users to address, improve, and communicate supply chain practices within and among all interested parties in an extended enterprise. SCOR is a management tool, spanning from customer to supplier, and has been developed to describe the business activities associated with all phases of satisfying customer demand.

The SCOR model is designed and maintained to support supply chains of various complexities and across multiple industries. As Figure 1.6 shows, the model focuses on three process levels, which are primarily on the business process side and do not attempt to prescribe the systems/information flow. For example, a company that performs process improvements using the SCOR model will need to extend the model to Level 4 (workflow) and Level 5 (transactions) during the implementation.

We'll explain the three main levels of the SCOR model in the following sections.

1.2.1 Level 1: Process Types

SCOR provides standard business process definitions, terminology, and metrics. It enables companies to benchmark themselves against others and influence future application development to improve business processes in five distinct functional areas: plan, source, make, deliver, and return (see Figure 1.7). The five distinct management processes link together (the chain in supply-chain) seamlessly from supplier to customer:

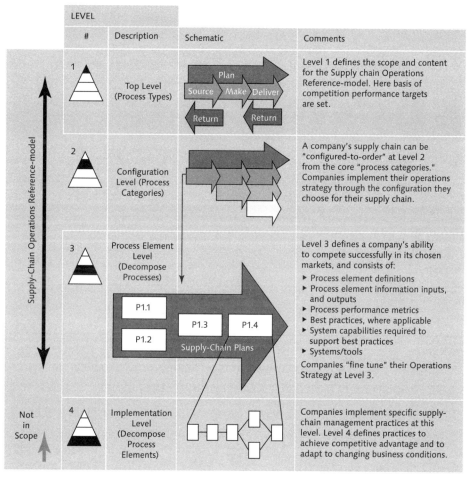

Figure 1.6 SCOR Model Process Levels

1. **Plan**

   Processes that balance aggregate demand and supply to develop a course of action that best meets sourcing, production, and delivery requirements.

2. **Source**

   Processes that procure goods and services to meet planned or actual demand.

3. **Make**

   Processes that transform products to a finished state to meet planned or actual demand.

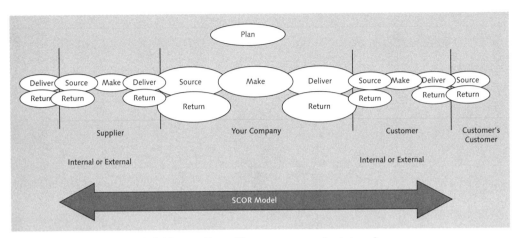

Figure 1.7 SCOR Model Process Types (Source: *www.supply-chain.org*)

4. **Deliver**

   Processes that provide finished goods and services to meet planned or actual demand, typically including order management, transportation management, and distribution management.

5. **Return**

   Processes associated with returning or receiving returned products for any reason, extending into post-delivery customer support.

SCOR provides a list of Level 1 performance metrics for supply chain diagnostics measurements the company can measure to identify process improvement areas in its business. Table 1.2 lists the performance attributes and the corresponding metrics for measurement.

Performance Attribute	Performance Attribute Definition	Level 1 Metric
Supply chain delivery reliability	The performance of the supply chain in delivering the correct product, to the correct place, at the correct time, in the correct condition and packaging, in the correct quantity, with the correct documentation, to the correct customer.	▶ Delivery performance ▶ Fill rates ▶ Perfect order fulfillment

Table 1.2 SCOR Performance Metrics for Level 1 Process Types

Performance Attribute	Performance Attribute Definition	Level 1 Metric
Supply chain responsiveness	The rate at which a supply chain provides products to the customer.	Order fulfillment lead times
Supply chain flexibility	The agility of a supply chain in responding to marketplace changes to gain or maintain a competitive advantage.	▸ Supply chain response time ▸ Production flexibility
Supply chain costs	The costs associated with operating the supply chain.	▸ Cost of goods sold ▸ Total supply chain management costs ▸ Value-added productivity ▸ Warranty/returns processing costs
Supply chain asset management efficiency	The effectiveness of an organization in managing assets to support demand satisfaction, including the management of all assets: fixed and working capital.	Cash-to-cash cycle time

Table 1.2 SCOR Performance Metrics for Level 1 Process Types (Cont.)

1.2.2 Level 2: Process Categories

The five basic management processes (plan, source, make, deliver, return) that provide the organizational structure of the SCOR model are further classified into three main process types in the model: planning, executing, and enabling.

▸ **Planning**
A planning element is a process that aligns expected resources to meet expected demand requirements. Planning processes balance aggregated demand across a consistent planning horizon. Planning processes generally occur at regular intervals and can contribute to supply chain response time.

▸ **Executing**
The execution processes consists of source, make, and deliver. Planned or actual demand that changes the state of products triggers these processes. They include scheduling and sequencing, transforming materials and services, and moving product.

▶ **Enabling**
The enabling processes prepare, maintain, and manage information or relationships upon which the planning and execution processes rely.

The SCOR model further breaks down these three process types into different business models:

▶ **Stocked product**
This type of model is used by businesses to match their consumer demand with the production forecast. Inventory drives this business model, which has a standard material order, high order fill rate, and short turnaround. It is commonly seen in the consumer goods market, where stable demand is both seasonal and non-seasonal.

▶ **Make-to-Order product**
This is a business production strategy that typically allows consumers to purchase products customized to their specifications. Customer orders drive this business model, which has configurable materials and longer turnaround times. This is commonly seen with computer assembly companies that customize products based on customer configuration requirements.

▶ **Engineer-to-Order product**
A manufacturing philosophy whereby finished goods are built to unique customer specifications. Assemblies and raw materials may be stocked but are not assembled into the finished good until a customer order is received and the part is designed. Customer requirements drive this business model, which sources new materials and has long lead times and a low fill rate. This business model is seen commonly in engineering and construction companies where a project schedule drives different phases of the project.

1.2.3 Level 3: Process Elements

In this section, we'll look at how SCOR defines the process element for the plan supply chain. SCOR defines all the supply chain planning process in four basic steps (Figure 1.8):

1. Gathering requirements (Px.1)
2. Gathering resources (Px.2)
3. Balancing resources with requirements (Px.3)
4. Establishing and publishing the plan (Px.4)

> **Note**
>
> Px stands for PLAN SCOR element.

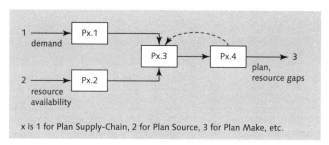

x is 1 for Plan Supply-Chain, 2 for Plan Source, 3 for Plan Make, etc.

Figure 1.8 SCOR Plan Processes

The following tables provide the SCOR definition of the core processes and the leading practice around each. Table 1.3 provides the SCOR definition of the core planning process.

Process Category: Plan Supply Chain	Process Number: P1 (Plan)
Process Category Definition	
The development and establishment of courses of action over specified time periods that represent a projected appropriation of supply chain resources to meet supply chain requirements.	
Best Practices	**Application Features**
Supply/demand process is highly integrated from customer data gathering to order receipt, through production to supplier request.	Integrated supply chain planning system with interfaces to all supply/demand data sources through public and private digitally enabled supply networks
Re-balancing of full-stream supply/demand on a daily basis, including source-make-deliver resources and requirements from "customers' customer to suppliers' supplier."	▸ Enterprise-wide planning system ▸ Customer relationship systems
Capability to run "simulated" full-stream supply/demand balancing for "what-if" scenarios.	Supply chain modeling and visualization system

Table 1.3 SCOR Definition on Plan Supply Chain (Source: SCOR [*www.supply-chain.org*])

Process Category: Plan Supply Chain	Process Number: P1 (Plan)
A change in the demand signal instantaneously reconfigures the production and supply plans.	Event-driven supply chain re-planning
Responsiveness and flexibility are emphasized by developing expertise in making business processes re-programmable, re-configurable, and continuously changeable.	Integrated process modeling and software reconfiguration tools
Supply chain is designed to have supply flexibility equal to demand volatility.	None identified
On-line visibility of all supply-chain demand requirements and resources, both currently available and committed (pegged).	▶ Enterprise resource planning system ▶ Customer relationship management system
Tools support balanced decision making (e.g., tradeoff between service level and inventory investment).	Supply chain planning optimization system
All functions and organizations understand their impact on supply/demand balancing, including sales, marketing, product management, manufacturing, customers, suppliers, materials management, and product development.	None identified

Table 1.3 SCOR Definition on Plan Supply Chain (Source: SCOR [*www.supply-chain.org*]) (Cont.)

The planning process begins with demand requirements in the form of forecasts, customer orders, or customer backorders. Table 1.4 lists the SCOR definition for identifying, prioritizing, and aggregating these supply chain requirements in the form of forecast.

Process Element: Identify, Prioritize and Aggregate Supply Chain Requirements	Process Element Number: P1.1
Process Category Definition	
The process of identifying, aggregating, and prioritizing all sources of demand for the integrated supply chain of a product or service at the appropriate level, horizon, and interval.	

Table 1.4 SCOR Definition on Plan—Gathering Requirements (Source: SCOR [*www.supply-chain.org*])

Process Element: Identify, Prioritize and Aggregate Supply Chain Requirements	Process Element Number: P1.1

The sales forecast is composed of the following concepts: sales forecasting level, time horizon, and time interval. The sales forecasting level is the focal point in the corporate hierarchy, where the forecast is needed at the most generic level, i.e., corporate forecast, divisional forecast, product line forecast, stock keeping unit (SKU), and SKU by location. The sales forecasting time horizon generally coincides with the timeframe of the plan for which it was developed, i.e., every one to five years, annually, every one to six months, monthly, weekly, or daily. The sales forecasting time interval generally coincides with how often the plan is updated, i.e., daily, weekly, monthly, or quarterly.

Best Practices	Application Features
Collaboration among supply chain partners extends outward to customers, spanning the supply chain planning.	None identified
Collaboration among operations strategy team.	▶ Supply chain advanced planning systems ▶ Supply chain integration systems ▶ Integration between supply chain advanced planning and ERP execution systems ▶ Supply chain capacity planning systems ▶ B2B integration and application server systems
Digital links (XML based, EDI, etc.) among supply chain members.	▶ Real-time exchange of supply chain information between supply chain members ▶ Collaborative planning systems, internet trading exchanges, B2B integration, and application server systems
Joint service agreements (JSA).	Collaborative planning systems

Table 1.4 SCOR Definition on Plan—Gathering Requirements (Source: SCOR [*www.supply-chain. org*]) (Cont.)

Process Element: Identify, Prioritize and Aggregate Supply Chain Requirements	Process Element Number: P1.1
Push-based forecasts are replaced with customer-replenishment pull-based signals.	▶ Standards-based (Rosetta Net, XML, OAGI, etc.) B2B integration tools and systems ▶ Systems support accurate on-line visibility of full-stream demand requirements and priorities. ▶ Advance planning and scheduling system ▶ Supply chain event management software

Table 1.4 SCOR Definition on Plan—Gathering Requirements (Source: SCOR [*www.supply-chain.org*]) (Cont.)

Next, the supply planning process, in the form of sourcing, manufacturing, inventory targets, and capacities, are collected to feed into the supply chain model. Table 1.5 lists the SCOR definition for identifying, prioritizing, and aggregating these supply chain resources.

Process Element: Identify, Prioritize and Aggregate Supply Chain Resources	Process Element Number: P1.2
Process Category Definition	
The process of identifying, prioritizing, and aggregating, as a whole with constituent parts, all required supply sources that add value in the supply chain of a product or service at the appropriate level, horizon, and interval.	
Best Practices	**Application Features**
Collaborative planning, forecasting, and replenishment (CPFR)	▶ Business process modeling ▶ Workflow systems ▶ Collaboration tools ▶ Advanced planning optimization ▶ Constraint-based planning ▶ Integrated resource and material plan ▶ B2B integration and application server systems

Table 1.5 SCOR Definition on Plan—Gathering Resources (Source: SCOR [*www.supply-chain.org*])

Process Element: Identify, Prioritize and Aggregate Supply Chain Resources	Process Element Number: P1.2
Joint service agreements (JSA)	Collaborative planning systems
Digital links (Internet, EDI, etc.) among supply chain members	▶ Real-time exchange of supply chain information among supply chain members ▶ Collaborative planning systems, Internet trading exchanges
Lead times updated monthly	None identified
Categorize 100% of total inventory (active, usable, excess, and obsolete) for appropriate action	None identified
Review product profitability	ABC classification (ranking system for identifying and grouping important items) and cost modeling

Table 1.5 SCOR Definition on Plan—Gathering Resources (Source: SCOR [*www.supply-chain.org*]) (Cont.)

The process of demand and supply balancing occurs next. This process looks at inventory policies, supply chain performance, and planning decision rules to determine how the volume gaps can be closed. Table 1.6 lists the SCOR definition of the process of balancing supply chain resources with supply chain requirements.

Process Element: Balance Supply Chain Resources with Supply Chain Requirements	Process Element Number: P1.3
Process Category Definition	
The process of identifying and measuring the gaps and imbalances between demand and resources in order to determine how to best resolve the variances through marketing, pricing, packaging, warehousing, outsource planning, or some other action that will optimize service, flexibility, costs, assets, or other supply chain inconsistencies in an iterative and collaborative environment.	

Table 1.6 SCOR Definition of Plan—Balancing Resources with Requirements (Source: SCOR [*www.supply-chain.org*])

Process Element: Balance Supply Chain Resources with Supply Chain Requirements	Process Element Number: P1.3
Best Practices	**Application Features**
Demand planning and demand flow leadership	Software that provides multiple data models, including business rules and metrics for the entire supply chain planning process. Algorithms use the business rules and metrics as drivers for the planning engine.
Collaborative planning, forecasting, and replenishment (CPFR)	Supply chain planning systems and communication technologies, as well as newly defined standards that reflect the CPFR model and participate in the entire planning process.
Business intelligence (BI)	A data warehouse or data mart is the source of all planning (master) data, business rules, and transaction data. Analytical tools enable ongoing maintenance and improvement of business rules based on actual data.
Customer relationship management (CRM)	Software that provides customer input and keeps the customer informed about the planning of the production and delivery processes. CRM does this by managing all contacts and communications with the customer thorough all channels, including Internet and traditional sales and customer service channels.

Table 1.6 SCOR Definition of Plan—Balancing Resources with Requirements (Source: SCOR [*www.supply-chain.org*]) (Cont.)

The last process in the SCOR model involves establishing and communicating the supply chain plans. Table 1.7 lists the SCOR definition for this process.

Process Element: Establish and Communicate Supply Chain Plans	Process Element Number: P1.4

Process Element Definition

Establishing and communicating courses of action over the appropriate time-defined (long-term, annual, monthly, weekly) planning horizon and interval, representing a projected appropriation of supply chain resources to meet supply chain requirements.

Best Practices	Application Features
Collaboration among supply chain partners extends outward to suppliers and customers, spanning the supply chain planning.	► Supply chain advanced planning systems ► Supply chain integration systems ► Integration between supply chain Advanced Planning and ERP execution systems ► Supply chain capacity planning systems
Collaboration among operations strategy team.	► Supply chain advanced planning systems ► Supply chain integration systems ► Integration between supply chain advanced planning and ERP execution systems ► Supply chain capacity planning systems
Joint service agreements (JSA).	Collaborative planning systems
Digital links (Internet, EDI, etc.) connecting supply chain members.	► Real-time exchange of supply chain information between supply chain members ► Collaborative planning systems, Internet trading exchanges.
Systems support accurate on-line visibility of full-stream demand requirements and priorities, as well as resource utilization and availability.	Advance planning and scheduling system

Table 1.7 SCOR Definition of Plan—Establishing and Publishing the Plan (Source: SCOR [*www.supply-chain.org*])

> **Note**
>
> You can find additional information on SCOR model metrics in Chapter 9, Section 9.6.3.

To better understand the planning process, it's important to look at various types of supply chain business models. Depending on the characteristics of these supply chain models, an organization can better organize its planning processes. In the next section, we'll look at varying types of supply chains.

1.3   Types of Supply Chains

Supply chains exist for both manufacturing and service businesses, and depending on the sequence of business activities, we can categorize supply chains into various structures, such as pipelined, late customization, divergent, and convergent.[1] Each of these supply chain types needs to be modeled during the analysis to understand current supply chain planning challenges and issues. Each of the four defined supply chain structures may require its own unique supply chain modeling and master data maintenance in SAP applications. We'll talk about each structure in the following sections.

1.3.1   Pipeline Structure

The product goes through a series of production/assembly stages as in mass production or continuous manufacturing. Continuous production is characterized by streams of products such as laundry soap, food products, paper products, general materials production, and other products produced in bulk and made into discrete products during the packaging process.

1.3.2   Late-Customization Structure

The initial stages will produce standard items assembled and customized to specific requirements either in local plants or during the distribution process. Personal computers, integrated circuits (IC) chips, disk drives, laser printers, and electronic gadgets fall into this category. Here, the product variety is obtained in late stages of manufacturing/assembly. Inventories are maintained at the subassembly level,

---

1 Y. Narahari and S. Biswas, Indian Institute of Science whitepaper, Supply Chain Management (2000).

and customization facilities or plants will assemble these or rapidly configure them into desired products. The success of this business model is achieved by proactively developing product families with modular product architecture, implementing flow manufacturing to achieve production batch run, and an agile supply chain around sourcing and order fulfillment.

1.3.3   Diverging Structure

Customization starts early in the production phases. A wide variety of finished products are produced from a limited number of raw materials or components. Examples of such supply chains include electro-mechanical systems such as motors, textiles, metal fabrications, and chemicals.

1.3.4   Converging Structure

The fourth type is the converging structure, in which a series of assembly operations are carried out to obtain the final product. Examples include aircrafts and construction machinery.

In the next section, we'll show how we can use SCOR and value stream mapping methodology to model the supply chain for a case study company.

1.4   Case Study: A Supply Chain Dilemma

Throughout this book, we'll be using a fictional company to help illustrate how to connect the business theories and practices to a more technical application using SAP APO. Our case study company is ABC Technology, a US-based corporation with headquarters in Silicon Valley, California. The company manufactures and distributes several product lines of desktop and laptop personal computers positioned for home users (consumer channel) and for business customers (commercial channel). The products are sold to the consumer channel via large retailers, while the commercial channel is supplied through major distributors. ABC Technology sells its products to retailers and distributors via a direct sales force.

In the following sections, we'll explain the existing supply and demand issues, as well as their supply chain processes and SCOR applications.

1.4.1 Business Situation

Currently, ABC Technology's executives are increasingly alarmed with the company's frequent inability to fulfill customer orders, while inventory levels continue to rise. The company bases its plans on the market forecast, and while the production schedule can be adjusted based on actual market demand, a significant portion of the supply chain is locked for three months in advance. The primary reason for this is long lead times from the supplier for critical components (for example, memory chips), which demand that material be ordered well in advance of planned shipment dates. As a result, most products are built according to the sales forecast. The build-to-forecast strategy means that unless the customer order stream is consistent with the forecast, many orders are queued until the production schedule can be adjusted and the correct product manufactured. Customer orders are not released for shipment until product is available in inventory. In the meantime, inventory levels of finished goods for over-forecasted products continue to grow.

Recently, the company has been encountering several product shortage situations that resulted in near loss of large customer orders. Retailers are willing to switch to other suppliers based on pricing and product availability; one missed shipment could result in loss of major chain business for a year or more. The management found on one of the recent near misses that the ordered stock-keeping unit (SKU) was in stock, except the larger hard drive ordered. The order was delayed because the configuration was not forecasted, even though there were enough larger hard drives in stock.

In the next sections, we'll see some areas where ABC Technology has room for improvement in the different functional areas with the help of demand and supply planning application capabilities. We'll also see how we can use the SCOR model to visualize the company's processes.

1.4.2 Sourcing

ABC Technology sources most raw materials at the plant level. The exceptions are CPUs and hard drives, for which commodity managers negotiate annual contracts, and deliveries are made to purchase orders. ABC Technology buys the following components for its products:

- CPU chips developed and produced by Intel
- CD drives and laptop screens from other US suppliers (lead times of up to three months)
- Production of circuit boards outsourced to Gamma CB for assembly

Supplier performance is not tracked, but the sourcing department estimated on-time delivery at no more than 80%. Nearly 95% of all components are inspected when delivered at the plant because yields can be as low as 60%. Production stoppages due to stockouts are frequent on the shop floor, with downtime ranging from several hours to several days.

> **Advanced Planning and Scheduling System Goals**
>
> ABC Technology has identified that it needs to improve its supply planning process in the area of procurement to make critical components available on time for production.

1.4.3 Manufacturing

The company has three manufacturing locations for laptop, desktop, and monitor production. The facilities use traditional assembly lines to build and test products, with each technician working in an individual manufacturing cell. Cycle time at each assembly line is approximately 45–60 seconds. Daily production schedules are set based on a master schedule, which is based primarily on the sales forecast. Material availability is checked before the work orders are released. A minimum batch run for the laptop facility is 400 units. The kitting and quality verification takes additional four to five hours.

After assembly is completed each day, an inventory backflush is performed to record the consumption and provide an up-to-date inventory of raw materials. Work orders remain open until all units have been packaged and transferred to finished goods inventory. Some work orders remain open for several weeks as units cycle through the repair/rework process. Each plant is currently running at 65% to 75% capacity utilization.

> **Advanced Planning and Scheduling System Goals**
>
> ABC Technology has identified that it also needs to improve its master production schedule with a proper outlook on material availability and capacity utilization.

1.4.4   Order Management

All customer orders are processed at the company's headquarters in Silicon Valley. The company provides the value-added service to customers of the next-day delivery promise for both their forecasted and custom laptops and desktop products. However, orders with no available inventory are not released until all required inventory becomes available. Outstanding orders are reviewed four times a day in all the plants, and efforts are made to fulfill them as early as possible. Also, during new product launch, the company uses an allocation mechanism for customer orders to distribute its products to retailers and distributors based on business priorities.

Advanced Planning and Scheduling System Goals

ABC Technology has realized that its master production schedule plan, in the form of production planning, is not currently integrated with customer allocation planning for distribution, often resulting in incorrect product availability promises to customers. In many situations, larger customer orders take the inventory promised earlier for smaller orders.

1.4.5   Distribution

The company has three distribution centers that handle respective orders for laptops, desktops, and monitor products. The majority of the orders are dispatched from these distribution centers. The laptop distribution center also receives products from one of the semiconductor distributors.

1.4.6   Modeling the Company with the SCOR Model

We'll now model ABC Technology's supply chain using SCOR methodology. Modeling in SCOR provides an opportunity for ABC Technology to look at its distribution strategy and planning for lead times. Let's go over the seven steps as recommended:[2]

1. Select the business entity to be modeled (geography, product set, organization). In our business scenario we are modeling ABC Technology's laptop and desktop products sold in North America for both its manufacturing and distribution business processes.

---

2   SCOR, Supply Chain Council

2. Map the physical locations of the following:

   ▶ Production facilities (Make)

   ▶ Distribution activities (Deliver)

   ABC Technology has three production bases in Seattle (laptops), New Jersey (desktops), and Atlanta (monitors). Upon production, the goods are send to the three respective distribution centers for order fulfillment. The distribution centers are located in Salt Lake City (laptops), Raleigh (desktops), and Tampa (monitors). Besides manufacturing and distribution facilities, the company also has a semiconductor distributor in New Mexico and an overseas supplier of peripherals in Taiwan.

3. Map out the primary point-to-point material flow using the solid-line arrows. Figure 1.9 shows the material flow across different locations.

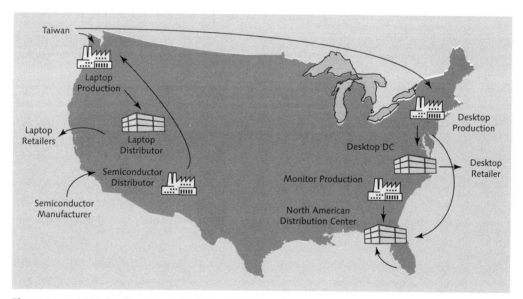

Figure 1.9 ABC Technology Supply Chain for North America

4. As we discussed, SCOR defines three execution process categories in the form of source, deliver and make. The *source* is primarily for procurement, *deliver* for distribution, and *make* for manufacturing. Place the most appropriate Level 2 (refer back to Section 1.2.2) execution process categories to describe activities at each location activity. Figure 1.10 shows the Level 2 execution process categories for each location activity.

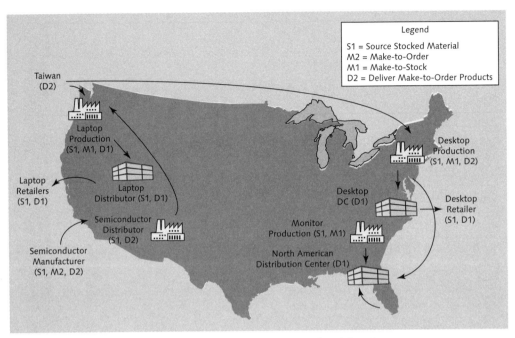

Figure 1.10   Level 2 Execution Process Categories Mapped with Locations

5. Describe each distinct supply chain thread. A *supply chain thread* ties together the set of source-make-deliver supply chain processes that a given product family flows through.

   Develop each thread separately to understand common and distinct execution and return process categories. Consider end-to-end threads in the inter-company case. Figure 1.11 shows the thread link for ABC Technology supply chain processes.

6. The supply chain execution process categories (source, make, deliver) are shown for each individual supply chain partner. The process category defines the process activities for the specific location. Next, we place planning process categories where applicable, using dashed lines to show links with execution processes

7. The planning activities are represented by nomenclature P-Plan. We place P1, if appropriate, on the supply chain thread diagram drawn in our earlier steps.

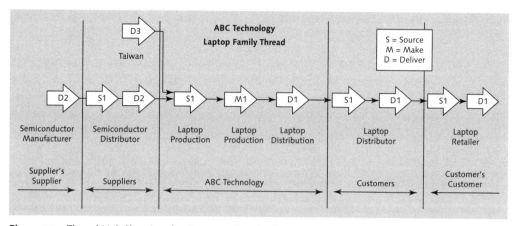

Figure 1.11 Thread Link Showing the Company Supply Chain

Nomenclature

P1- Plan supply chain aggregates outputs from P2, P3, and P4.

Figure 1.12 shows the planning process integrated into the supply chain thread.

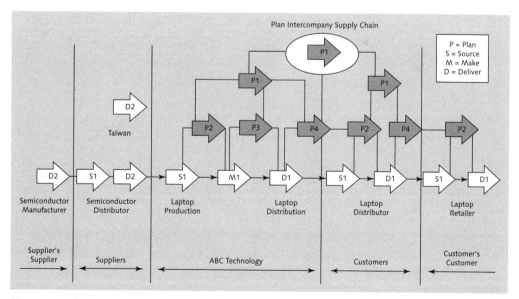

Figure 1.12 Planning Processes Integrated into the Supply Chain

1.4.7 Value Stream Mapping

Another supply chain methodology is *value stream mapping* (VSM), which can be performed after developing the SCOR model. VSM is a lean manufacturing technique used to analyze and design the flow of materials and information required to bring a product or service to a consumer. This method can be applied in a logistics environment as well. The use of VSM allows ABC Technology to correctly map its lead times and identify any process bottlenecks in its supply chain. The VSM steps are as follows:

1. Identify the target product, product family, or service. Specific to our business case study will be ABC Technology's products (laptops, desktops, and monitors).

2. Draw a current state value stream map while on the shop floor, which shows the current steps, delays, and information flows required to deliver the target product or service. This may be a production flow (raw materials to consumer) or a design flow (concept to launch). There are "standard" symbols for representing supply chain entities. ABC Technology will first draw the supply chain network with lead times and then decompose the logsitics activities (i.e., receiving, storing, manufacturing, and shipping) for each facility.

3. Assess the current state value stream map in terms of creating flow by eliminating waste. Identify the ABC Technology supply chain activities that take more cycle time than average and are in the critical path of the supply chain.

4. Draw a future state value stream map. Identify the improvement initiatives that can improve the supply chain bottlenecks.

5. Work toward the future state condition.

An example of VSM mapped for the supply chain using a VSM-specific software is shown in Figure 1.13. The VSM software helps to construct and analyze the value stream maps. Besides mapping the business process, the VSM software also helps perform additional calculation (take time, inventory, and value-added time) on the maps.

After detailed analysis, ABC Technology recognizes that it needs to improve its supply chain planning process in the areas of demand and supply. The next section provides overview of demand and supply planning process definition.

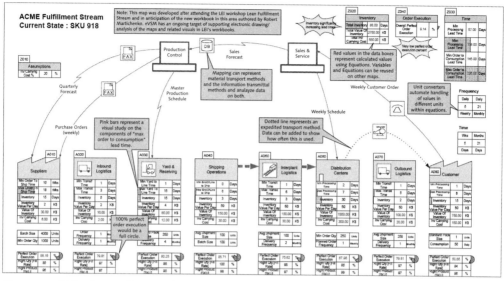

Figure 1.13   Value Stream Mapping (Source: *www.evsm.com*)

1.5   Demand and Supply Planning Overview

The process of demand and supply planning enables companies to understand their customers' buying patterns and adapt to fluctuating market demands. The SCOR model provides industry planning framework for companies looking for process improvements in this area.

ABC Technology currently does not have any streamlined tactical or operational planning process and is looking to improve. Demand and supply planning ensures a profitable match of market demand and supply to increase the company's revenue. The purpose of demand planning is to predict customer buying behavior, which no company can control. However, the purpose of supply planning is to take the demand planning as input and schedule product to arrive in advance, when the demand is likely to occur. The overall objectives of demand and supply planning are to ensure the availability of finished goods per agreed customer service levels and to minimize supply chain costs.

In market economics, the term *equilibrium* is used to suggest a state of balance between supply forces and demand forces. As seen in Figure 1.14, at any price above *P*, supply exceeds demand, while at a price below *P*, demand exceeds supply.

In other words, prices at which demand and supply are out of balance are termed points of disequilibrium, creating shortages or oversupply. Changes in the conditions of demand or supply will shift the demand or supply curves. This will cause changes in the equilibrium price and quantity in the market.

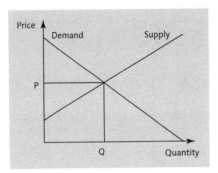

Figure 1.14 Economics Equilibrium (Source: Hal R. Varian, *Microeconomic Analysis*, 3rd Ed. Norton, New York, 1992)

To study the economics further, we'll look at demand planning and supply planning in more detail in the following sections.

1.5.1 Demand Planning

The objective of demand planning is to ensure that the best possible estimate of true customer demand is released on a weekly basis to drive supply, sales, and financial planning processes. Figure 1.15 shows the different functions that combine to form a consensus demand plan in the company. The plan is created by coming to a consensus within the sales, marketing, and planning functions. While the sales team is more focussed on the customer channels, the marketing team works on pricing, branding, and consumer promotions to increase the company's profit margin. The planning team looks at historical sales patterns to predict the future forecast based on a time series or casual forecasting model.

Next we'll look at the demand planning process decomposition. Figure 1.16 shows the process decomposition with a planning horizon of 24 months. The demand planning process is generally performed on a monthly basis (or fiscal period) and consists of two short-term and medium-term planning processes. The short term is a rolling 12-week period and primarily aims to achieve the sales target. The medium term consists of monthly buckets beyond those 12 weeks, and focuses on statistical forecast generation and adding a market intelligence component to the demand plan. The following list explains the sub-processes in more detail.

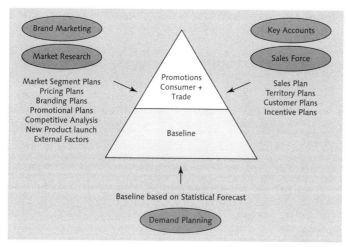

Figure 1.15   Team Interactions Towards Forming the Consensus Demand Plan

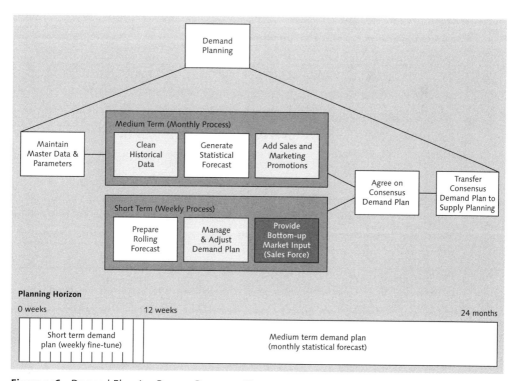

Figure 1.16   Demand Planning Process Decomposition

59

1. **Maintain master data and parameters**

   Though forecasting is primarily driven by historical data, there is master data that helps establish a more accurate forecast. One example of master data are characteristics-value combinations: every time a new product is launched or a customer or customer group starts buying a product they did not buy in the past, a new characteristic combination needs to be created. Another example for parameters can be a forecast profile, which contains the logic or forecasting model for a specific product or group of products.

2. **Clean historical data**

   The purpose of this process is to clean the history from the effect of any extraordinary events such as sales and marketing promotions, special deals, weather fluctuations, and stock outs. The goal here is to capture the true market demand and clean any outliers driven by the company's own actions or any other external factors.

3. **Generate statistical forecast**

   The statistical forecast is primarily performed once a month on a monthly time bucket. The monthly baseline forecast is further split into weekly buckets based on historical proportions.

4. **Add sales and marketing promotions**

   The purpose of this process is to close the gap between the baseline forecast and the yearly budget plan. While the sales team will add promotions more on channel, the trade marketing promotions are more consumer-focused.

5. **Prepare rolling forecast**

   This process refers to the rollover of forecast from the medium-term plan to the short-term plan. Time disaggregation will split the monthly bucket to weekly buckets.

6. **Manage and adjust demand**

   This process refers to the weekly review of demand plans for the short-term horizon. The demand planner uses sales input and alerts to identify exceptions management and primarily focuses on Category A products.

7. **Provide bottom-up market input**

   In this process, the sales team provides bottom-up market input to the demand planner. A collaborative process may be established with key customers to get their forecast inputs.

8. **Agree on consensus demand plan**
   This process refers to the monthly forecast review meeting among sales, marketing, and the supply chain (demand management) to agree on an unconstrained demand plan. The meeting usually occurs during the first two weeks of the month and provides key input for the sales and operations planning meeting. While the meeting might just focus on the horizon where the promotions are planned, the yearly demand outlook versus budget is also discussed.

9. **Transfer consensus demand plan to supply planning**
   Once the final number is agreed upon in the monthly demand planning meeting among the teams, the unconstrained demand plan is released to supply planning functionality for a feasibility check on the plan. The supply planning team performs the rough-cut capacity check on the unconstrained demand plan to identify any capacity issues.

The whole supply chain planning process starts with demand forecasting, which we'll explain in the next section.

Forecasting

Forecasting is an important component of business planning. The forecast is defined as a future estimation or predication based on some mathematical method or techniques. The forecast methods can be broadly classified into two categories: qualitative and quantitative methods:

► *Qualitative* forecasting techniques are subjective, based on the opinion and judgment of consumers and experts. They are appropriate when past data is not available and are usually applied to intermediate- to long-range decisions. The following are examples of qualitative forecasting methods:

  ► Informed opinion and judgment
  ► Delphi method
  ► Market research
  ► Historical life cycle analogy

► *Quantitative* forecasting models are used to estimate future demands as a function of past data and are appropriate when past data is available. They are usually applied to short- to intermediate-range decisions. The following are examples of quantitative forecasting methods:

- Last-period demand
- Arithmetic average
- Simple moving average (N-period)
- Weighted moving average (N-period)
- Simple exponential smoothing
- Multiplicative seasonal indexes

The quantitative forecasting technique is more broadly used and can be further divided into two types:

1. **Intrinsic forecasting technique**
   Focuses on data about demand, such as historical sales. These techniques are called *time series models* because they collect during set intervals of time: days, weeks, months, etc. The time series based on sales data seldom form straight lines, but instead form a combination of the following patterns:

   - **Trends**: A steady movement up or down represents a trend in the data.
   - **Seasonality**: Changes correlate with the seasons of the year.
   - **Cycles**: Cyclical movements with long-term upward or downward movements correlate with business performance cycles.
   - **Sporadic**: Variations occur randomly and can neither be predicted nor explained after the fact. These random changes are short term, mere bumps and dips on the trend line.

2. **Extrinsic forecasting technique**
   Also called casual/econometric, these methods base their predictions on factors that are related to demand. Some forecasting methods use the assumption that it is possible to identify the underlying factors that might influence the variable that is being forecast. For example, including information about weather conditions might improve the ability of a model to predict umbrella sales. This is a model of seasonality, which shows a regular pattern of fluctuations. Another example that can influence the sales is price, which can be combined with historical sales. The technique is best illustrated by a simple linear relationship, or a complex regression analysis that includes a large group of methods to predict future values of a variable using information about other variables.

Case Study: ABC Technology's Approach to Demand Planning

During the implementation of the supply chain planning process, ABC Technology has realized that a close integration of their business processes and IT system is required. The following subsections detail some key lessons from ABC Technology's implementation of demand planning.[3]

Getting the Process Right

Demand planning is a sub-process within sales and operations planning or integrated business planning, not a stand-alone activity. ABC Technology must create an integrated business plan that is a cross-functional and aligned with company's goal on growth.

Decide what Demand Planning Levels Make Sense for Your Business

Some companies analyze and plan demand at the product family level, customer level or geographic level. The way that ABC Technology forecasts and plans demand is unique to their business. ABC Technology plans to forecast at product family and location aggregation level.

Tips & Tricks
Don't be dictated by limitations of your IT technologies, and be prepared to change how you plan demand according to changes in your business.

A Collaborative Process, Not a Test of Statistical Algorithms

The statistical forecast based on algorithms will provide the baseline forecast, which needs to be further enriched by human analysis. The final forecast needs to be derived by internal collaboration between supply chain, sales, and marketing and finance process teams along with possible external collaboration with customers. ABC Technology needs to recognize that the closer you get to the true demand signal, the better the forecast will be.

Demand Planning is Not Just Forecasting

Forecasting is a component of demand planning, and using historical pattern and forecasting model projects the future estimate. ABC Technology needs to constantly challenge the forecast (and the integrated business plan) and seek opportunities

---

3   White paper by Dave Blanchard, Industry Week 2008

to influence total demand through marketing events and promotions to bring the final forecast aligned with the company's annual budget plan.

Control What You Measure
ABC Technology needs to put the right set of linked supply chain KPIs in place and measure regularly against these. Measurement of forecast accuracy (planned forecast versus actual sales) is a good KPI to identify whether the selected forecasting model is proposing correct results.

Educate before Training
The demand planner needs to be trained in statistical forecasting and techniques to make revisions. Also, other cross-functional members involved in the process need to be provided with system training for better performance.

Cleanse the Data
Demand planning processes require historical sales orders data for estimating the future forecast. This data needs to be cleansed to only reflect the true customer demand. ABC Technology plans to deploy an automatic outlier correction mechanism to cleanse their historical sales orders.

Trust the Numbers and Manage by Exception
80% of your return can be achieved by reviewing 20% of the items. Identify the market segmentation using Pareto principle.[4]

Use the Error in Your Forecast to Positive Effect
The accuracy of the forecast is best judged by the forecast error. The lowest the forecast error the more the forecasting model has used the historical pattern for the product. Better forecasting will reduce the safety stock (buffer) ABC Technology plan to store to manage market demand and supply fluctuations. With better inventory management the customer service level for ABC Technology will improve as well.

Deploy a Best-in-Class Solution
An Aberdeen study shows that companies that excel in demand management—reporting higher forecast accuracies and lower inventories—are two-and-a-half times as likely to have implemented a best-in-class demand planning system.[5]

---

4   Tague, Nancy R., *The Quality Toolbox*. (Milwaukee, WI, ASQ Quality Press, 2004)
5   Global Supply Chain Benchmark Report 2006

Implementing a better demand planning system allows the business planners to analyze and fine tune the planning data more efficiently.

Next we'll look at supply planning, which performs the material availability and capacity checks on the unconstrained demand.

1.5.2 Supply Planning

The supply planning process takes the unconstrained demand plan and proposes replenishment and distribution plan for the network of distribution centers. Based on the inventory policy of each distribution center, the supply planning team makes decisions about what to produce when, where, and in what quantity. The main objectives of supply planning are the following:

▶ Determine the stock requirements in supply network locations to meet objectives based on stock policies and demand plans

▶ Calculate replenishment plans to bring distribution center inventory to target levels

▶ Plan distribution of stock and future manufacturing to meet the net requirements

▶ Review and modify automated plans based on any changes in demand plan

▶ Identify and resolve supply exceptions

▶ Perform the collaborative replenishment planning process with business partners

The supply planning process decomposition consists of the following sub-processes (see Figure 1.17):

1. **Set up supply chain model and inventory models**
   In this process, the master data and parameters are maintained for the supply network. The physical locations are connected with transportation lanes to identify material flow in the network with various planning parameters (e.g., lot size or lead times). Besides the basic planning parameters, various inventory models are also identified for safety stock calculation.

2. **Determine unconstrained supply requirements**
   In this process, the safety stock is calculated first, based on inventory models. Next, the unconstrained demand is netted with current supply and inventory to determine the net supply requirements from other sources. The unconstrained net requirements are given to the source location based on lead times and other planning parameters.

65

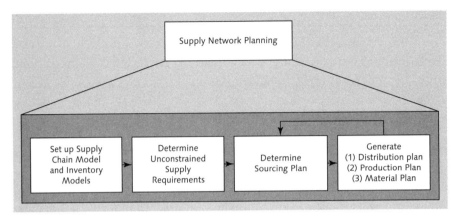

Figure 1.17 Supply Planning Process Decomposition

3. **Determine sourcing plan**

   This process provides the best available source to fulfill the unconstrained supply requirements based on production and transportation costs. It also looks at capacity availability.

4. **Generate production plan**

   This process is often referred to as the master production schedule. It takes the input from the sales and operations planning process, where the demand and supply balancing is done at an aggregated level, projecting volumes for product families rather than individual products. The master production schedule process disaggregates the plan into individual products at weekly buckets. Upon the creation of a production plan, a rough cut capacity check is performed to check the production feasibility with current resources, labor, and materials. A capacity leveling may be performed for bottleneck resources to balance out the supply plan.

5. **Generate material plan**

   Also known as *material requirements planning* (MRP), this process focuses on the critical planning for procurement of raw materials with long lead times at the medium-term planning horizon. The MRP process is based at the plant level and not multiple networks as planned by advanced planning and scheduling (APS) systems. The material plan schedules dependent demand of finished goods and performs a bill-of-material explosion to identify the raw materials required for finished goods manufacturing. The material plan takes input from the master production schedule of finished goods, bill of materials, current inventory, and production lead times. The process also adheres to the vendor minimums, which can be ordering quantity or price.

6. **Generate distribution plan**

   The distribution requirement planning process is performed in two sub-processes. The first process uses demand (forecast and internal supply network transfers) to develop a stock replenishment program that works throughout the network. The unconstrained requirements are propagated over the complete supply chain network from the destination to source locations. Once the master production schedule plan is calculated and rough-cut capacity performed, the second process, called deployment or load planning, creates distribution or transportation loads with the proper allocation of supply. This allows supply planning team to identify the supply shortages and number of days of supply in inventory at the receiving location for any proactive business actions (e.g., stock balancing).

During the supply planning process, the dilemma every supply chain manager faces is the *push versus pull distribution* decision.[6]

Push Supply Chains

In a push supply chain, the distribution and manufacturing is based on forecast. The manufacturing plans the production based on the forecast. Once the production is completed, the inventory is pushed to the distribution center for sales. There is always variation between the demand and supply planning and companies buffer the inventory with safety stock to manage the fluctuations.

The push supply chain routinely experiences the bullwhip effect, which suggests that variability of orders received from retailers and warehouses is much larger than variability in customer demand. This increase in variability is directly related to supply chain lead time — the longer the lead time, the larger the increase in variability.

Pull Supply Chains

In a pull supply chain, the distribution and manufacturing are based on customers' orders. The manufacturing produces the product once the customer orders are received. This method reduces the bullwhip effect but is not viable if there are long lead-times for raw materials. Additionally, planning consolidation on the manufacturing and distribution makes it difficult to achieve economies of scale.

---

6 Terry P. Harrison, Hau Leung Lee, and John J. Neale, *The Practice of Supply Chain Management* (Medford, MA: Springer, 2008).

These advantages and disadvantages of push and pull supply chains have led companies to look for a new supply chain strategy that takes advantage of the best of both worlds. Enter a hybrid of the two systems: push-pull supply chain systems.

Push-Pull Supply Chains

In a push-pull strategy, the distribution and manufacturing follows the combination of the pull and push method. The manufacturing plans its long lead time components based on forecast but produces the final product based only of customer orders. Dell Computers is an excellent example of the impact the push-pull system on supply chain performance. Dell Computers uses the push technique for its procurement cycle in keeping critical components as inventory. The pull technique is seen on the customer order and manufacturing cycle where the custom products are assembled after the customer orders places the orders. While Dell relies upon immediate turnaround times on parts and materials from its vendors, the basic approach is to have the product semi-finished and then finish the rest of once the customer orders. Delivery times are minimized and inventory costs reduced.

> **Example**
>
> In our case study, ABC Technology has decided to apply a push-pull supply chain strategy that will allow the procurement to plan its key components based on the forecast. The production will only commence based on the customer orders and will either be shipped directly to the customer or retailers.

After studying the demand and supply planning concept, let's look at the supply chain maturity model.

1.5.3 Supply Chain Maturity Model

The concept of process maturity proposes that a process has a lifecycle gauged by the extent to which the company business process is defined, managed, measured, and controlled. Supply chain maturity can be defined by four major levels, as shown in Figure 1.18.

▶ **Level 1 is informal**

A company doing business and deals but without formalised procedures or processes. Management is characterised by fire fighting. The lack of formalized policies/processes and basic operations management results in unpredictable quality and supply.

- ► Keywords: no formal plans, no forecast, no balancing of supply and demand

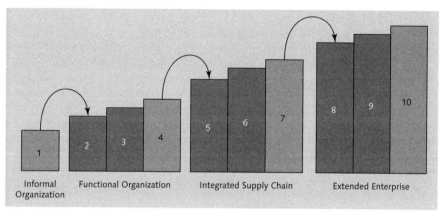

Figure 1.18 Supply Chain Management: Four Levels of Maturity

- ► **Level 4 is functional**
  A company with good functional management that is optimizing the performance of its own function without reference to what is happening in other areas of the business. Processes are typically carried out sequentially with information being passed "over the wall" from one function to the next. Functional orientation sub-optimizes enterprise performance in asset management, cost, and customer satisfaction.

  - ► Keywords: cost driven, reactive, monthly processes, push, standard services

- ► **Level 7 is the integrated supply chain**
  Processes are cross functional and optimized for the whole organization. Processes are carried out in parallel by cross-functional teams, and information flows freely around the organization. There is some integration with major suppliers and customers. With alignment across all sub-processes and levels of management, operations processes are integrated and display world-class, continuous performance and continuous improvement.

  - ► Keywords: flexibility, responsiveness, pro-active, weekly/daily, pull, differentiated services, cross-functional decision making

▶ **Level 10 is the extended enterprise**
This level indicates a company that's on the leading edge of all emerging practices. It is highly internally and externally integrated, working with enterprises ranging from suppliers' suppliers to customers' customers. There is internal and external process integration, allowing each enterprise to focus on its customers and core competencies and create value.

▶ Keywords: real time full visibility, event driven, JIT, joint optimization, customized services

Levels 2, 3, 5, 6, 8, and 9 are transition stages.

1.5.4 Supply Chain Performance Management

In today's competing market environment, manufacturing, and distribution companies are going through increasing requirements for better customer service, new products, and quicker delivery of products to the customer. Everyone in the supply chain needs to help reduce cost, streamline production, and speed up delivery in order to help their company compete and remain profitable. To achieve these goals, companies are turning to the *supply chain performance management* (SCPM) concept to improve their supply chains.

Supply chain performance management is the practice of managing the effectiveness and value of an organization's supply chain by aligning the trading partners, service providers, employees, processes, and systems to a common set of goals and objectives. The concept of supply chain performance management helps companies improve supply chain effectiveness by focusing on actionable, operational process metrics that impact supply chain performance. The capabilities of SCPM is best explained when it is built around industry-recognized SCOR metrics, which work on the assess, diagnose, and correct mechanism (assess whether your supply chain is healthy, then find out where the problem lies, and finally correct the problem).

The performance of any company's supply chain improves when it looks at a holistic view instead of just measuring departmental metrics. The leading practices call for aligning the operational and geographical key performance indicators (KPI) with enterprise-strategic KPI. Any company should use the KPI metrics as a starting point for identifying the root problems in the supply chain for corrective actions. Figure 1.19 depicts the pyramid of a global company operating with multiple ERP systems that consolidates all its supply chain operations in the form of KPIs and metrics. While the metrics measure the business processes of different business units, the KPI provides the holistic view of business performance across the company's business units.

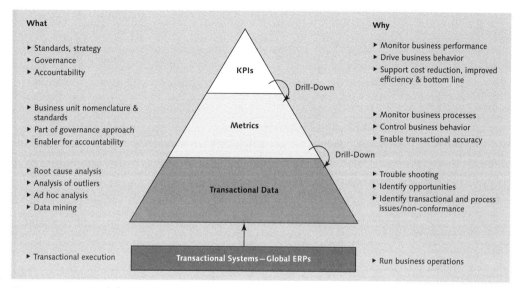

Figure 1.19 Pyramid Showing Consolidation of KPI and Metrics

Key Supply Chain Metrics toward SCPM

It's important to recognize that supply chain performance is not just a measurement process. Cross-functional, balanced metrics are necessary, but not sufficient. Instead, SCPM is a cycle consisting of identifying the problems, understanding the root causes, responding to problems with corrective actions, and continuously validating the data, processes, and actions at stake.

The following list illustrates seven key SCOR scorecard metrics that help in translating company strategic goals into measurable targets, measure effectiveness across end-to-end business processes, and proactively identify bottlenecks and pinpoint root causes:

▶ **Perfect order fulfillment**

  A *perfect order* is defined as an order that meets all the following five business process standards:

- ▶ **Percent order delivered in full**

  An order is considered complete if the products ordered are the products provided and the quantities ordered match the quantities provided.

- ▶ **Delivery performance to customer by commit date**

  An order is considered on time if the location, specified customer entity, and delivery time are met upon receipt.

- ▶ **Perfect condition**

  An order is considered to be in perfect condition if the products delivered have no manufacturing or packaging errors and are accepted by the customer.

- ▶ **Shipment transaction accuracy**

  An order is considered to have shipment transaction accuracy if all the shipment documentation related to the order is accurate, complete (with the correct price and quantity), and on time.

- ▶ **EDI transaction accuracy**

  An order is considered to have EDI transaction accuracy if the customer-facing EDIs 810, 855, and 859 run error free.

▶ **Order management cycle time**

The *order fulfillment cycle time* is defined as the time taken from customer authorization of a sales order to customer receipt of the product. The major segments of time include order entry, manufacturing, distribution, and transportation.

▶ **Demand management accuracy**

Demand management accuracy is the percentage of how accurately sales figures are forecasted. The *mean absolute percentage error* (MAPE) is the industry-wide accepted tool to measure supply chain forecast accuracy.

▶ **Up-side supply chain flexibility**

Up-side supply chain flexibility measures the amount of time it takes the supply chain to respond to an unplanned increase in demand from the forecast without incurring any service or cost penalty. It measures the total time taken (in days) from generating the manufacturing order to its shipment.

▶ **Inventory turns**

Inventory turns measure how many times the company inventory is sold or replaced during a financial year. Since inventory (both finished goods and components) has low liquidity, a high inventory turnover ratio would measure that the company is using its inventory assets well. It is the ratio of cost of goods sold to average inventory.

- **Total supply chain management cost**

  The total supply chain management cost measures controllable and uncontrollable costs associated with the plan, source, make, deliver, and return processes of the supply chain.

- **Return on working capital**

  A measurement comparing the depletion of working capital (cash in hand) to the generation of sales over a given period. This provides some useful information about how effectively a company is using its working capital to generate sales.

Steps for Successful Implementation of SCPM

Follow this methodology to successfully implement SCPM:

- Start by defining the business objectives you are trying to achieve through improved SCPM.
- Define a balanced mix of measures between leading and lagging indicators, between operational and financial measures, and between customer-focused and internally focused measures.
- Focus on gaining organizational understanding and buy-in to the key performance measures.
- Carefully define the hierarchy of underlying business intelligence, including data, reports, and cubes that will enable drill-down capability and more specific insights into performance.
- Be diligent about the precise source and definition of the data and calculations required to accurately represent supply chain performance.
- Select a software application that will support your business and technical requirements, including the ability to scale to other functional areas.

Supply Chain Performance Management Application

The SCPM application helps you manage, monitor, and measure the performance of your company's supply chain. The SCPM application provides supply chain executives with a holistic view of their entire supply chain, including planning, sourcing, manufacturing, operations, and logistics. The application allows organizations to measure and monitor various supply chain metrics and, more importantly, to understand the correlation between these metrics and how changing one metric impacts the others in a positive or negative way.

Companies that implement the SCPM application should benefit from gaining overall visibility and enhanced collaboration across their supply chain, increased supply chain flexibility and responsiveness, and overall improved process efficiency. The SCPM application provides the following capabilities:

▶ **Strategy management**
To develop and define a supply chain strategy and to manage, monitor, and measure its progress.

▶ **Impact analysis**
To understand the relationship between metrics and their impact on each other.

▶ **What-if analysis**
To simulate different business scenarios and to find possible business impacts on operations and finance.

▶ **Operational analysis**
To provide end-to-end visibility into all supply chain functions and perform root-cause analysis.

1.6   Summary

In recent years, many companies have improved their supply chain operations with proper supply chain planning. This has been achieved largely by restructuring on the business processes to work in an integrated way.

To summarize what we have learned in this chapter, the SCOR model provides a supply chain framework toward industry best practices in the demand and supply planning processes. The SCOR framework, along with types of supply chain and sales and operations planning, determines the demand and supply planning business process.

This chapter detailed the business decomposition within demand and supply planning. Improving the supply chain planning processes provides the path toward the supply chain maturity, which in turn improves the company's supply chain performance.

The next chapter introduces SAP technology in the form of SAP Advanced Planning & Optimization (which we'll refer to throughout the book as SAP APO), which serves as a decision-support tool for business planners for supply chain planning. The chapter explains the SAP product capabilities supporting different business scenarios and how the software meets customer-specific supply chain planning requirements.

In this chapter, we'll introduce you to SAP Advanced Planning & Optimization (SAP APO), a great advanced planning and scheduling component you can use in a multi-plant network. More specifically, we'll focus on the Demand Planning and Supply Network Planning modules within SAP APO.

2 Introduction to SAP APO as an Advanced Planning and Scheduling (APS) Tool

With increased globalization and market competition, companies are eagerly adopting the concepts of advanced planning and scheduling (which we'll refer to throughout the book as APS). While traditional material requirement planning is more focused on single-plant optimization, APS looks at the global network and constraints during supply chain planning. The planning approach of network versus plant allows companies to react proactively on any downstream or upstream supply chain situation.

By implementing an APS system, companies have the benefits of lower inventory levels, increased customer satisfaction, and increased sales revenue. SAP Supply Chain Management (SAP SCM) provides SAP Advanced Planning & Optimization (which we'll refer to throughout the book as SAP APO), which is a component that works on the concepts and principles of APS.

In this chapter we will learn six distinct topics related to SAP APO as an APS tool. The chapter will start with highlighting the APS concepts and then introduce SAP APO. After briefly explaining the core planning functions, we give an overview on the APO-Demand Planning (which we'll refer to as APO-DP) and APO-Supply Network Planning (which we'll refer to as APO-SNP) core functionalities. The chapter closes by introducing the SAP APO technical architecture with specific mention of SAP liveCache technology. Refer to Figure 2.1 for a map of this chapter.

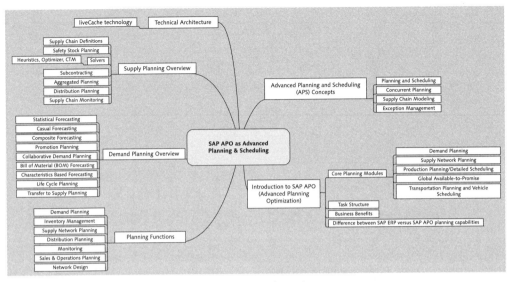

Figure 2.1 Learning Points for the Chapter (Mind Map)

> **Note**
>
> Although SAP APO offers many planning modules, the focus of this chapter is only on APO-DP and APO-SNP.

2.1 Advanced Planning and Scheduling Concepts

APS is defined by a manufacturing management concept for which the material and supply chain resource capacities are simultaneously planned and optimally allocated to meet market demands, thus increasing a company's profitability. The goal of the APS system is to create a feasible strategic, tactical plan and pass it back to the execution system as an operational plan. As shown in Figure 2.2, the APS system pulls the master data and transaction data from the execution layer. Then the APS layer provides the operating and tactical decisions (how much to produce, sourcing, etc.) back to the execution layer.

In the following sections, we'll study the key characteristics and concepts behind APS and how it is applied across different industries. We'll focus on three industries: consumer goods, computer hardware, and retail distribution. Each of these industries presents its own unique characteristics; we'll help you understand how APS uses different modeling techniques to balance demand and supply.

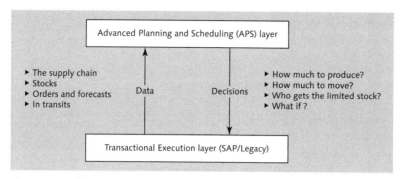

Figure 2.2 Information Exchange between APS and Execution Layers

2.1.1 Planning and Scheduling

APS comes with mathematical logic for both planning and scheduling. We'll go over each activity in the following subsections.

Planning

Planning focuses more on the strategic and tactical side. Planning functionality focuses on optimizing the network with balanced demand and supply planning.

Planning is primarily concerned with the following:

▶ What products to make

▶ When and where to make the products

▶ Working with product families and groups

▶ Key supply chain capacities, rates and constraints, and inventory targets

▶ Campaign and seasonal planning

▶ Balancing resource usage meeting stock and replenishment targets

▶ Budget planning

Depending on the industry, the supply chain constraints can vary in the APS model. In consumer goods, for example, the resource capacities to meet market changing demands will always be an issue, which is not the case for computer hardware. For the latter industry, the main constraint lies in the raw material availability having long lead times and not much on resource capacity. Retail distribution has its own challenge of ensuring product mix availability at the right place and right time. Retail distribution works on the value proposition of shorter delivery dates, and ensuring correct inventory levels is of the utmost importance. All these business dimensions and priorities need to be identified before implementing an APS solution.

Scheduling

Scheduling, on the other hand, is inclined toward the operational side with a focus on optimizing manufacturing business processes. It ensures that the plant is utilizing all its supply chain resources with economies of scale. Scheduling is mainly concerned with the following:

- ▶ Meeting due dates of production
- ▶ Detailed products and recipes
- ▶ Routing (how best to make a product)
- ▶ Synchronizing activities across resources to minimize downtime
- ▶ Handling priorities and constraints
- ▶ Monitoring shop floor execution

A business example for scheduling is shop floor scheduling, whereby the machine and labor capacities need to be modeled along with material availability and differing throughput rates.

Both planning and scheduling look at *time buckets* (defined in Chapter 1), which are defined as periods or horizons of time in which the receipts (for example, an incoming purchase order), requirements (for example, an outgoing sales order), and stocks (inventory) are cumulated. One example is forecasting that's done on a weekly time bucket with no distinction on which daily time bucket of the week the forecast will fall. APS provides the ability to aggregate and disaggregate at multi-horizon visibility across time dimensions. The term *planning* relates to the time modeled in buckets, while the term *scheduling* relates more to the exact day and time.

2.1.2 Concurrent Planning

APS combines rough-cut capacity and constrained planning and provides planner solvers for concurrent planning across the supply chain network. Planning in this manner ensures that the material availability and resource capacity are both planned at the same time.

Another feature of APS is the ability to effectively perform constraint management during the concurrent planning process. By this, we mean that APS seeks to identify the bottleneck in the supply chain and model the throughput to align the limitations of this bottleneck. APS systems are designed to handle situations when multiple bottlenecks exist and also when the bottleneck locations change over time. This is a common business scenario for consumer goods, when the resource capacity constraint leads to identifying multiple sourcing options. Since APS plans the complete supply chain network, this leads to global optimization. All our business case study companies aim to provide global optimization by harmonizing common business processes, data, and systems across multiple business units in the global supply chain network.

APS also provides opportunities to not only collaborate internally, but also provide a platform for customer and vendor collaboration. Companies can exchange planning information seamlessly via web collaboration on nearly a real-time basis.

2.1.3 Modeling

The backbone of APS is supply chain modeling, in which all the physical entities in the supply chain are connected together in the form of nodes and arcs, as shown in Figure 2.3. While the node represents different physical locations, the arc (also known as transportation lanes) defines the material flow within the supply chain network. Besides connecting the nodes, the product planning parameters (e.g., lot size and lead time) are also defined for each location.

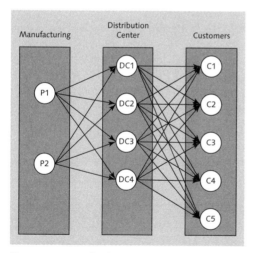

Figure 2.3 Supply Chain Modeling in APS

APS turns all these logical relationships into a data model for a mathematical equation calculation during the processing.

ABC Technology has both manufacturing and distribution locations in its supply chain structure. Depending on their product group (laptop, desktop, or monitor) the number of distribution warehouses vary.

Once the model is formulated in APS, the solvers that serve as a mathematical engine do various calculations to facilitate decisions in the supply chain planning business process. One example is a statistical method (e.g., exponential smoothing or linear regression), which derives the statistical forecasting. Supply planning optimization is done primarily by a heuristics algorithm or linear and mixed integer programming. Depending on the business model, different solvers can be identified to perform demand and supply planning steps.

While the APS solver does background calculations, the graphical user interface (GUI) is the frontend interface allowing business users to analyze and interpret the planning results. The GUI has a spreadsheet-like display with graphs and alert notifications that help the users to quickly identify, diagnose, and solve supply chain problems that might occur, enhancing the decision-support functionality.

2.1.4   Exception Management Using the Alert Mechanism

Exception management is an action that must take place after an unplanned supply chain situation has occurred (for example, a stock out, production breakdown, material delay, etc.). In these business scenarios, the business planners need to react based on APS capabilities to identify alternative options to resolve such a situation. APS provides real-time visibility on any demand and supply imbalance, allowing business users to react proactively. Different alerts can be configured to highlight material- (stock outs), capacity- (overload), or demand- (late or short orders) related problems.

This feature really helps the retail distribution planners at ABC Technology who have to work on large number of SKUs. Using the alerts, the planners can prioritize their work activities and effectively plan procurement and replenishments for their products.

Also important for the consumer goods and computer hardware company is the APS ability of *re-plan*, which allows the company to react on any upstream or downstream changes in the supply chain. This helps the business make alternative plans for fulfilling the order commitments to customers. On any unplanned supply chain situations, the planner can perform a re-planning run to identify the next best optimal sourcing to fulfill customer orders. The retail distribution planner can look at the regional inventory situation and may perform stock balancing to fulfill any sales backorders.

Another area of importance is the difference between enterprise resource planning (ERP) and APS using MRPII/DRP (Manufacturing Resource Planning and Distribution Requirement Planning) logic and APS. It is important for businesses to identify the difference between outputs run by traditional material requirements planning (MRP) and APS planning during the implementation analysis phase. Table 2.1 highlights the difference between these two concepts.

Functions	ERP	APS
Material and capacity planning	Sequential	Concurrent
Time buckets	Separate	Continuous
Planning approach	Planning per function	Integrated planning
Allocate supply to customers	Unable	Able
Constraints	Soft constraints	Hard and soft constraints
Available-to-promise due date quoting	Static based on pre-existing supply chain	Dynamic based on global supply chain
Simulation	Low	High
Planning visibility	Local	Local and global
Manufacturing lead time	Fixed	Flexible
Re-planning speed	Low	High
Opportunity cost assessment	Unable	Able, based on existing commitments
Planning goal	First-cut requirements estimate (infinite capacity)	Feasible, optimal plans (finite capacity)

Table 2.1   Key Difference between APS and ERP

As we mentioned, the characteristics and concepts of APS are supported by SAP Advanced Planning & Optimization (SAP APO), the core component within SAP Supply Chain Management (SAP SCM). SAP APO provides many capabilities and functions that exist within APS, which we'll explain in the next section.

2.2 Introduction to SAP Advanced Planning & Optimization

SAP APO is used for planning, optimizing, and scheduling supply chain processes across the entire supply network. The supply chain network consists of internal locations (e.g., manufacturing plants and distribution centers), external sourcing locations (e.g., vendors and subcontractors), and external delivery locations (e.g., VMI customers).

SAP APO integrates with the SAP ERP execution system where the planning results are executed. SAP provides standard real-time Core Interface (CIF) for seamless integration between the SAP APO (planning) and SAP ERP (execution) components. Figure 2.4 depicts how the supply chain processes are supported by SAP APO modules for planning and SAP ERP for execution.

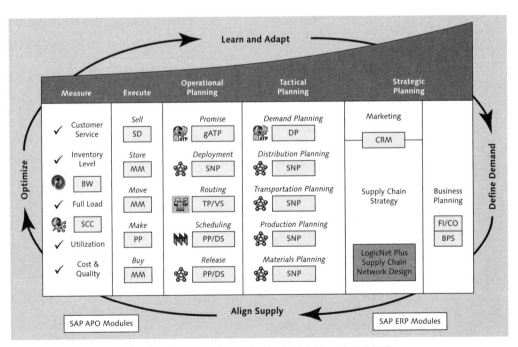

Figure 2.4 Supply Chain Processes Supported by SAP APO and SAP ERP

> **Note**
>
> You can find more detailed information on CIF in Chapter 15.

Next we'll explain the various planning modules available in SAP APO and then define the task structure in APO for demand and supply planning. We'll also provide a brief overview of the use of SAP APO.

2.2.1 Core Planning Modules

SAP APO provides five core modules that focus on planning and execution. Based on the business initiative and requirements of a company, you can implement all the modules in a phased approach or select only a module or two that deliver the highest value to the business. These core planning modules within SAP APO are the following:

- **Demand Planning (APO-DP)**
  Provides advanced forecasting and demand planning tools that enable companies to capture changes in demand signals and patterns as early as possible.

- **Supply Network Planning (APO-SNP)**
  Provides tactical supply planning capabilities with integration to purchasing, manufacturing, distribution, and transportation and creates feasible plans for these areas in a global supply network environment. Different optimization engines are available, which run on hard- and soft-constraint supply chain models. Balances supply chain costs with service levels.

- **Production Planning and Detailed Scheduling (PP/DS)**
  Provides manufacturing planning capabilities to plan materials and critical resources concurrently. Provides optimization solvers for sequencing and scheduling factory short-term plans.

- **Global available-to-promise (global ATP)**
  Provides not only basic available-to-promise checks, but also enhanced and extended decision support features to model different supply chain order fulfillment business scenarios. Integrates with production planning and detailed scheduling and SAP ERP seamlessly to provide real-time ATP dates. The aim of global available-to-promise is to determine whether an incoming order can be promised for a specified customer request date. Global ATP enhances the response time for order promising and the reliability of order fulfillment. It directly links

available resources, including both material and capacity, to customer orders and enhances the supply chain performance. The process helps with improving on-time delivery performance, sufficiently increasing stock to buffer inventories, and planning system integration.

▶ **Transportation Planning and Vehicle Scheduling (TP/VS)**
Provides transportation planners to optimally plan the capacity of transportation modes (e.g., trucks) and schedules the routes for lower transportation costs. Provides functionality of shipment consolidation, route determination, carrier selection, multi-pick, and multi-drop.

> **Example**
>
> ABC Technology plans to implement APO-DP, APO-SNP, and PP/DS to support its manufacturing and distribution planning process, for balancing its demand and supply. Also built within SAP APO is the Supply Chain Cockpit (SCC), which will provide ABC Technology business users a with a GUI to manage the supply chain network, with the exception of management (alerts) and key performance indicators (KPIs) interfaced with SAP NetWeaver Business Warehouse (SAP NetWeaver BW). Via SCC, the business users can navigate to different SAP APO applications to resolve supply chain situations.

2.2.2 Task Structure

To support a monthly sales and operations planning process within the company, a structure of planning tasks needs to be organized to be performed by demand and supply planners. This allows the company to transition the tactical plan to an operational plan, effectively causing fewer supply chain disruptions situations (for example, inventory stock outs). A business example of the supply chain planning tasks structure for a consumer goods company is shown in Figure 2.5.

The demand planners use the APO Demand Planning module for the consensus demand planning process. The supply planner models the supply chain in the APO-SNP module. APO-SNP calculates the distribution, deployment/load plan, and rough-cut capacity plan to check the feasibility of the demand and supply balance. The PP/DS module creates short- and medium-term manufacturing plans, taking input from the supply plan. SAP APO and SAP ERP integrate seamlessly on the master and transactional data flows between the two systems. Aligned within the planning tasks is the SAP APO planning horizon and granularity, as seen in Figure 2.6.

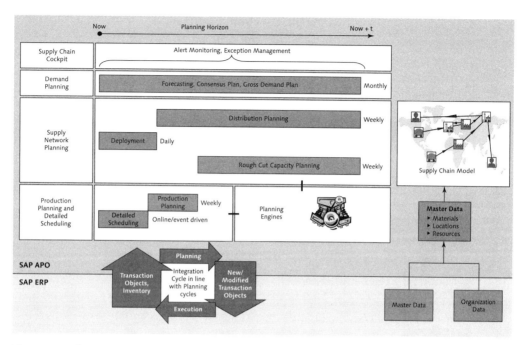

Figure 2.5 Planning Task Structure Using SAP APO

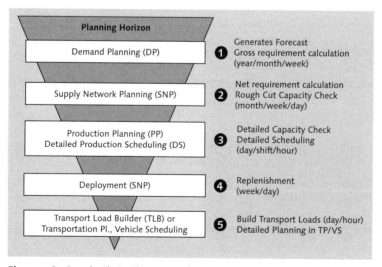

Figure 2.6 Supply Chain Planning Tasks: Horizon and Granularity

Companies usually structure their planning tasks on a weekly cycle. Planning repetitively on a weekly basis allows the companies to react more closely to the current inventory and order fulfillment situations. See the following chronological list of the weekly activities primarily performed on background batch jobs with user interaction as checkpoints to the overall process.

❶ **Generate forecast**
This process is performed in the APO-DP module with the planning horizon on monthly, weekly, or daily buckets. Daily buckets will be applicable for a supply chain with fast turnaround of products or when the product shelf life is critical.

❷ **Net requirement calculations and rough-cut capacity check**
This process is performed in the APO-SNP module with the planning horizon on monthly, weekly, or daily buckets. The process creates feasible plans for procurement, replenishment, distribution, and production.

❸ **Manufacturing detailed capacity check**
This process is performed in PP/DS module with the planning horizon on daily or hourly buckets. The process creates a shop floor execution plan.

❹ **Replenishment**
This process is performed in the APO-SNP module with the planning horizon on weekly or daily buckets. The plan provides visibility of the stock covers at distribution centers and gives alerts of stock out situations.

❺ **Build transport loads**
This process can be performed by either the APO-SNP Transport Load Builder (TLB) or TP/VS module with the planning horizon on daily or hourly buckets. The process creates transport loads for shipping to customers or transferring to internal distribution centers.

Example

ABC Technology focuses on creating a feasible master production schedule plan, which will roll into the operational distribution of goods. On the other hand, the retail distribution focuses on the vendor procurement and replenishment processes with the exception of the stock balancing process to keep the inventory flowing in the supply chain.

2.2.3 Business Benefits of Using SAP APO

The benefits of improved demand and supply planning using SAP APO can include enhanced revenue, reduction in costs, and improvement in asset management (see Figure 2.7). These benefits are achieved with better forecast accuracy, inventory availability for orders, and proper utilization of the company's supply chain resources (e.g., manufacturing and transportation).

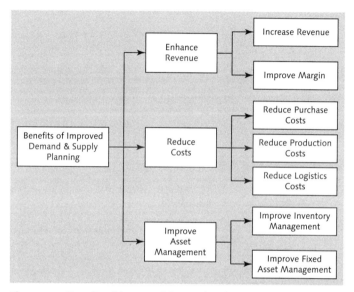

Figure 2.7 Benefits of Improved Demand and Supply Planning Using SAP APO

These three areas can be further broken into supply chain improvement areas, as explained in the following list:

- **Increase revenue**
    - Improve time to market and effectiveness of new product launches
    - Improve in forecast accuracy with proper consensus demand plan process
    - Improve customer fill rates by having the right product in the right place at the right time
    - Improve forward-looking visibility to in-market sales demand to understand supply requirements

- Improve scalability of planning processes, systems, and organization (e.g., support acquisitions and organic growth)

- **Improve margin**
  - Differentiate service based on customer and/or product
  - Improve allocation of inventory during periods of scarce supply
  - Leverage excellent service in price negotiations

- **Reduce purchasing costs**
  - Enable low-cost country sourcing through improved visibility and stability of supply needs
  - Improve supplier collaboration (i.e., longer term visibility to supply needs) and managing of supplier capacity to improve service and reduce costs
  - Improve make-versus-buy decisions based on better visibility to supply requirements and internal and external constraints

- **Reduce production costs**
  - Better use of company's global production capacity, enabling the operations strategy, through optimal sourcing
  - Improve overall supply reliability to master plan and integration with lean, pull-based production processes
  - Improve visibility of supply requirements for better long-term capacity planning
  - Improve use of contract manufacturers via improved visibility of supply–demand imbalances and outsource requirements

- **Reduce logistics costs**
  - Reduce out-of-territory shipments and premium freight charges
  - Improve visibility of total network inventory to serve the customer (i.e., reduce overall cost to serve)
  - Enable a more efficient consumption, pull-based inventory replenishment process

- **Improved inventory management**
  - Reduce total finished goods inventory required; achieve service levels through improved demand and supply planning

- ▶ Reduce excess and obsolete provisions/costs through improved product-launch and phase-out planning (linked to use-up strategies)

- ▶ Improve product portfolio management to manage complexity

- ▶ Optimize deployment of inventory across the distribution network

- ▶ Optimize customer consignment inventory through improved visibility of demand and improved replenishment process

▶ **Improve fixed asset management**

- ▶ Improve inputs to sales and operations planning process to longer-term capacity planning

- ▶ Improve make versus buy decisions based on improved visibility of demand and understanding of supply constraints and alternatives

- ▶ Improved transportation planning to improve asset productivity

SAP ERP also offers planning functions that can be compared with SAP APO functions (see Figure 2.8). Table 2.2 illustrates a further difference. This comparison is helpful to the clients who have implemented planning functions in SAP ERP and are looking to implement SAP APO in the near future. The comparison helps the project team member relate the current business process with the new SAP APO business processes.

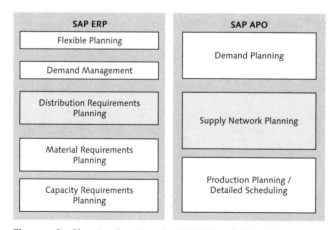

Figure 2.8 Planning Functions in SAP ERP and SAP APO

Functions	SAP ERP (MRP II/DRP)	SAP APO
Demand Planning	Flexible Planning module: ▶ Creates sales forecast at the user-defined level (e.g., product and customer) ▶ Several time buckets through batch conversion ▶ Data manipulation rules via ABAP development ▶ Limited model size ▶ Provides basic statistical forecast models ▶ Limited data storage	APO-DP module: ▶ Creates sales forecasts at any product- or customer-hierarchy level ▶ Different time buckets can be used simultaneously with data views. ▶ Easy manipulation of data via macros ▶ Unlimited model size possibility ▶ Multiple statistical forecasting models available ▶ Data storage technique different via liveCache ▶ Better interactive planning for business planners ▶ Exception management via alerts ▶ Simulations possibility
Supply Planning	Distribution Requirement Planning module: ▶ Infinite planning output ▶ Planning done per plant ▶ Planning results in table format with fewer layout customization possibilities ▶ Predefined exception messages that can be switched on or off ▶ Planning with minute precision	APO-SNP module: ▶ Various optimization possibilities with planning tools—heuristics (infinite), capable-to-match (infinite, rules-based), and optimizer (finite, cost-based) ▶ Interactive planning in a spreadsheet-type user interface that can be customized to user needs ▶ Planning performed and displayed in various time buckets (e.g., daily, weekly, monthly) ▶ Basic and advanced safety stock calculations ▶ Plans procurement, production, and distributions; feasible plans based on soft and hard supply chain constraints ▶ Aggregated planning possibility across the network ▶ Vendor Managed Inventory and collaborative supply management can also be modeled ▶ Performs production rough-cut capacity check

Table 2.2 Difference between SAP ERP and SAP APO Planning Functions

Functions	SAP ERP (MRP II/DRP)	SAP APO
Manufacturing Planning	Production Planning module: ▶ Unconstrained planning (infinite) with capacity planning as secondary step ▶ Single production plan approach ▶ Planning for internal work center resources ▶ Production orders are dispatched to create loads on work centers ▶ Performs materials resource planning run for MPS (master production schedule) materials first and then for raw materials	PP/DS module: ▶ Material and capacity planning possible ▶ Easy-to-use planning views, allowing planners to view material quantity and capacity simultaneously ▶ Unconstrained (infinite) or constrained (finite) planning can be modeled for manufacturing resources ▶ Multi-plant production can be modeled based on product availability and priorities ▶ External locations (e.g., subcontractors and vendors) can also be modeled ▶ Optimizer available for scheduling and sequencing of production plans with the objective of lower manufacturing costs ▶ Various planning algorithms and scheduling techniques available ▶ Scheduling board tool for planners to manage daily production schedule

Table 2.2 Difference between SAP ERP and SAP APO Planning Functions (Cont.)

After this overview of SAP APO, we'll look at the planning capabilities of SAP APO in the next section.

2.3 SAP APO Planning Functions

Before we look at the planning functions within SAP APO, it is good to study the four categories of input data SAP APO uses to operate and its logic toward processing. This input data feeds the mathematical model in APO, and the data accuracy results in better SAP APO planning output. As shown in Figure 2.9, the four categories are:

▶ **Supply chain context**
This data defines the physical scope of the supply chain with locations, bills of materials, routing, and the lead times across the supply chain network.

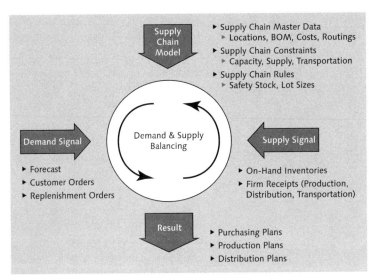

Figure 2.9 Input Categories to SAP APO Planning Logic

▶ **Supply chain constraints and business rules**
This includes the hard and soft constraints in the supply chain. The hard constraint may be the maximum capacity for resources or transportation, while the soft constraint may be a delivery date violation. The model may also input business rules in the form of customer priorities or fulfillment priorities (for example, customer sales orders vs. stock transport orders for internal transfers).

▶ **Demand signal**
This includes all the demand elements that include sales orders, customer orders, and replenishment orders.

▶ **Supply signal**
This includes all the supply elements that include inventories, production orders, and purchase orders.

Using these four categories as input, SAP APO performs a mathematical calculation to balance demand and supply in the constraint supply chain environment. During the calculation, the overall supply network is taken into consideration. The output of the process is the creation of tactical purchasing, production, and distribution plans across the network.

The supply plan proposal is next reviewed by business planners for exceptions and adjustments. Once these plans are accepted by the business, the plans are published to SAP ERP for execution. The automation of the supply planning to plan the complete network and present the result to the planner is an added value of SAP APO. The result already takes into account the supply chain resource constraint environment and provides a feasible, optimized plan the company can execute in an operational environment. Any imbalance (for example, stock out situations or capacity overload) is reported via alerts to the business for any further actions. The alerts can be material related, capacity related, or demand related.

During the operational period, SAP APO also provides the capability of re-planning the supply chain effectively. For example, in the case of a breakdown in the manufacturing process resulting in less supply than anticipated, business planners can immediately run SAP APO to identify the next feasible plans to visualize all the possibilities for resolving the supply issues.

Having looked at the basic logic and the key enablers for SAP APO, the functions are best visualized in the SAP SCM solution map, as seen in Figure 2.10.

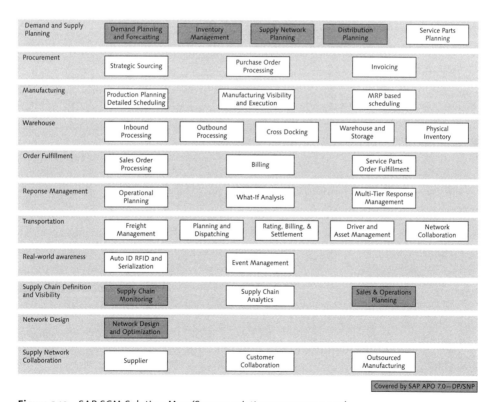

Figure 2.10   SAP SCM Solution Map (Source: *solutioncomposer.sap.com*)

Now let's go over the different related processes and functions within APO-DP and APO-SNP modules.

2.3.1 Demand Planning and Forecasting

Demand planning is defined as a process that derives the forecast based on historical sales patterns on the finished-product level. The SAP APO Demand Planning functions consist of statistical forecasting techniques, lifecycle management, promotion planning, data analysis, and calculation tools, and gives visibility at all levels of detail.

2.3.2 Inventory Management

SAP APO provides functions to calculate basic and advanced safety stock methods using demand, supply variability, and service levels. The inventory can be further decomposed into physical inventory, safety stock, build-up inventory, pipeline inventory.

2.3.3 Supply Network Planning

APO-SNP integrates purchasing, production, distribution (of demands), and transportation, creating mid- to long-term tactical, feasible planning. With version management, the sourcing decisions can be simulated and performed on the basis of a single, globally consistent supply network model.

2.3.4 Distribution Planning

The distribution planning process provides a constraint supply plan back from the source to the target location, indicating which demands can be fulfilled by the existing supply elements. The deployment run generates deployment stock transfers based on the APO-SNP stock transfers that were created during the APO-SNP run. The Transport Load Builder (TLB) then uses these deployment stock transfers to create transport loads based on predefined constraints on the means of transports.

2.3.5 Supply Chain Monitoring

Strategic supply chain design includes the definition of all demand and supply elements (e.g., inventory, forecast, and production) of the supply chain and the corresponding monitoring. This is supported by flexible alert monitoring of demand and supply situations (for example, stock outs and capacity).

2.3.6 Sales and Operations Planning

This process provides reports for business to conduct effective meetings. During the meetings, the business planners can discuss the planning currently performed. This process now needs to integrate both demand and supply, based on cost optimization.

2.3.7 Network Design and Optimization

Network design and optimization is the process of modeling the end-to-end supply chain, including all major cost elements and decision variables, and then running powerful analysis solvers to identify new strategies that will reduce cost, improve service, or mitigate risk. Using the network design and optimization approach, companies can better understand their existing supply chain structures, identify a new optimal structure, and continuously evaluate new "what-if" scenarios prior to implementing them in the real world, leading to major cost reductions and avoiding unnecessary risk.

The solution map shown previously in Figure 2.9 provides a broad view of the features available within each supply chain planning business process. The primary focus of the solution map is using demand and supply planning to support the sales and operations planning meeting.

In the next couple of sections, we'll explain APO-DP and APO-SNP in more depth.

2.4 SAP APO Demand Planning Overview

APO-DP provides a future estimate of company sales, taking into account the historical sales pattern and future planned sales and marketing promotions.

> **Note**
>
> We'll discuss the many features in further detail in the upcoming chapters; the purpose of this section is to provide a high-level overview of available features in SAP APO Demand Planning.

The basic demand planning process can be summarized in Figure 2.11. The historical data is collected from the source and based on a forecast model, and a future forecast is generated. The future forecast is further enriched by promotion planning (i.e., events) and collaborative planning. The planning data can be sliced and diced at any hierarchy of product and customer. Also, the data can be aggregated and disaggregated at any planning levels with the business ability to change the system-calculated proportions.

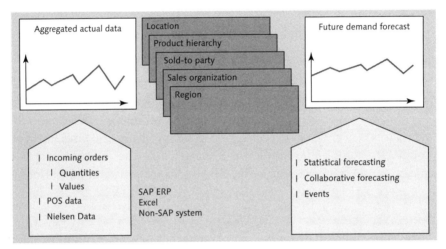

Figure 2.11 SAP APO Demand Planning Process Flow

The following sections will describe these demand planning processes in detail.

2.4.1 Statistical Forecasting

The process of statistical forecasting uses historical data points to calculate future estimates. SAP APO identifies the best-fit model based on the model that gives the lowest forecast error. The key assumption is that the history pattern will follow a similar pattern for the coming months. The method uses time series data to calculate the forecast. The main classification of forecast pattern is:

▶ **Constant**
Demand varies very little from a stable mean value.

▶ **Trend**
Demand falls or rises constantly over a long period of time, with only occasional deviations.

▶ **Seasonal**

Demand shows periodically recurring peaks that differ significantly from a stable mean value.

▶ **Seasonal trend**

Demand shows periodically recurring peaks, but with a continual increase or decrease in the mean value.

▶ **Intermittent**

Demand occurs only in some periods.

Besides various forecasting models, SAP APO also provides an automatic forecasting method, which takes the lowest forecast error (i.e., MAPE or MAD) to determine the best-fit model.

Example

The consumer goods industry will have both seasonal (for example, hats and gloves) and non-seasonal (for example, television) models identified. The computer hardware and retail distribution industries, for which the product lifecycles are short and sometimes sporadic, may require forecasting at the product group level.

2.4.2 Casual Forecasting

The process of casual forecasting includes the external market effect on the forecasting process. The business can define different casual variables to identify the correlation between the forecast and the casuals. The multiple linear regression (MLR) forecast method enables you to include external casual factors (for example, price, climatic conditions, and advertising) in the forecasting process. MLR investigates the historical influence of all these variables on demand to produce a future forecast. Different scenarios can be set up to identify the best forecast result.

Example

This forecasting method is seen in the consumer goods and retail distribution industries, for which the external environment influences (for example, competitor prices, promotions, and weather conditions) that affect the sales volume are identified. An example of this forecasting method would be increased sales of household batteries during the hurricane seasons.

2.4.3   Composite Forecasting

The process of composite forecasting allows you to combine various forecasting methods with a weighting factor (or percentage of different forecasting models) on the overall result influence. For example, a company can define a composite model of 50% exponential smoothing, 25% seasonal, and 25% trend models.

During forecast modeling, the demand planner may not be able to completely identify a specific forecasting model that fulfills the pattern. The composite allows not only the demand planner to combine the statistical methods, but also the casuals to come up with the combined forecast method. Either different statistical forecast methods can be combined, or statistical and casual forecasts can be used in composite.

2.4.4   Promotion Planning

APO-DP provides promotion planning functionality to plan sales and marketing promotions. The sales promotions are based more on product distribution channels, while the marketing is more consumer based. Examples of promotions are trade discounts, dealer allowances, product displays, coupons, contests, and free-standing inserts.

2.4.5   Collaborative Demand Planning

All demand planning data can be made available on the web for both internal and external business partners to agree on the planned quantities. APO-DP also offers customer forecast management functionality. This functionality allows for the receiving and analysis of the incoming customer forecast data. The information can be used in demand planning for the downstream planning to manage the market fluctuations. The process serves as a precursor for company to plan replenishment and procurement to prevent stock outs and overstock situations.

2.4.6   Data Management

The historical data in APO-DP is primarily stored in the SAP APO's internal SAP NetWeaver Business Warehouse component that provides data staging to SAP live-Cache. *SAP liveCache* is a database management system that has the ability to build a large memory cache and perform specially tailored functions (i.e., mathematical algorithms) against memory data structures. We'll provide more details on SAP liveCache in Section 2.7. The data is stored in characteristics combinations to be planned on. For aggregated planning, the planning results need to be disaggregated to the lowest level of details. This is achieved by using proportional factors of historical data at all levels. The planning result can also be interfaced back to SAP NetWeaver Business Warehouse for any reporting, archiving, or integrating with other legacy systems.

The planning data is displayed in the planning books, which have built-in macros. Macros are used in APO-DP not only for mathematical calculation purposes, but also for alerts based on business logic. More sophisticated macros can also be designed per business requirements to support the process.

2.4.7 Bill of Material (BOM) Forecasting

This feature allows for forecasting-dependent demand products at different planning levels by exploding the bill of materials. For example, planning of a kitting product can have a bundle of individual products, which are sold as single products as well. Planning for kits generates a dependent demand for the child products, which can be planned for supply, production, and procurement.

2.4.8 Characteristics-Based Forecasting

In APO-DP, we can create a forecast based on the characteristics of configurable end products. This concept is similar to the variant configuration in SAP ERP. The functionality allows you to forecast many different variants of the same product with a combination of several characteristics.

2.4.9 Lifecycle Management

SAP APO offers lifecycle planning (Figure 2.12) via maintenance of phase-in and phase-out profiles. A phase-in profile shows the upward forecast curve for new products we expect to display in the launch and growth phases. The phase-out profile shows the downward curve for the new products we expect to display during the discontinuation phase. A concept of like modeling is used for the new product because it can use historical data of corresponding products as the basis for a forecast.

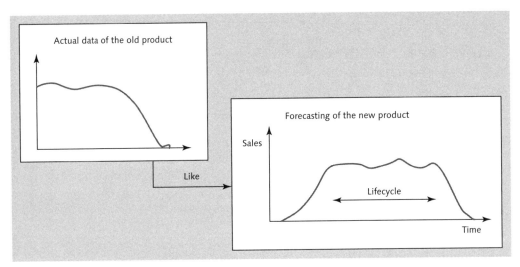

Figure 2.12 Lifecycle Planning in SAP APO

2.4.10 Transfer of Demand Plan

As a part of the sales and operations planning process, the process of analyzing and updating the demand plan provides the most accurate projection of sales. Demand planning books can be used by demand management, sales, marketing, and finance to agree on the demand plan.

Once the final demand plan is available, it can be transferred to the supply planning process and SAP NetWeaver Business Warehouse. The supply planning process can be in SAP APO, SAP ERP, or a legacy system. The transfer to SAP NetWeaver Business Warehouse is for reporting and archiving purposes.

> **Example**
>
> Demand planning helps us to build the unconstrained demand for the three business case companies: consumer goods, computer hardware, and retail distribution. This unconstrained demand now needs to be checked for material availability and capacity for supply chain resources. For consumer goods and computer hardware, the check is primarily performed with manufacturing plant, while for retail distribution, the check includes the current global inventory analysis.

The balancing of demand with supply is done in APO Supply Network Planning, which we'll discuss next.

2.5 SAP APO Supply Network Planning Overview

The SAP APO Supply Network Planning (APO-SNP) module integrates purchasing, manufacturing, distribution, and transportation in order to provide one global, consistent model of the supply. On the basis of this global model, tactical planning and sourcing decisions can be simulated and implemented. APO-SNP integrates planning and execution plans, and allows us to model different business scenarios using different solvers and master data models.

The objective of this section is to give a high-level overview of the different features in APO-SNP. These topics are further explained in detail in later chapters.

2.5.1 Supply Chain Definition

The overall supply chain network is modeled in SAP APO using the Supply Chain Engineer (SCE). SCE allows us to place locations (e.g., vendors, plants, distribution centers, and customers) on the global map and link them with transportation lanes for material flow. We also define the products and resources applicable to each location accordingly. For consistency between execution (SAP ERP) and planning (SAP APO) systems, the master data is transferred from SAP ERP using Core Interface (CIF) technology.

2.5.2 Safety Stock Planning

APO Supply Network Planning offers basic and advanced safety stock planning. With the basic safety stock method, safety stock, or safety days of supply, is maintained in a static or time-dependent way. The safety stock is calculated during the planning run. The advanced safety stock method, in the meantime, takes the demand variability (forecast), supply variability (replenishment lead time), and service level into account. The system supports both reorder cycle (i.e., reorder based on a specific time period) and reorder point (i.e., reorder placed when stock falls below a minimum level) strategies.

There is another feature available for SAP Enterprise Inventory Optimization by SmartOps. The solution provides a comprehensive, enterprise-scale process for optimizing, managing, and monitoring inventory stocking levels for every finished product and raw material component at every stocking location in a multi-tier distribution or manufacturing supply chain.

2.5.3 APO-SNP Solvers

APO-SNP offers different solvers to solve business model requirements. The three solvers are heuristics, cost optimizer, and Capable-to-Match. Let's look at the functionalities of these three solvers.

Heuristics

Based on the transportation lane, lead time, and lot sizing, this solver calculates the network sequentially and determines the sourcing requirement. This solver suits our consumer goods company, which needs the distribution center requirements to be propagated to the manufacturing locations. All the requirements are aggregated for a given material in the location for the period. A quota arrangement can also be defined for supply allocation. This solver is primarily suited for a large network with business rules for distribution and fewer bottleneck resources. Heuristics also has a feature called capacity leveling, which allows for smoothing of the production schedule either manually or using a method-based approach (i.e., heuristics-based, optimization-based, or customer-specific scheduling logic). The capacity leveling gives the capacity outlook (overload or underuse) to the planner. The business planner can modify the production or transportation resource by leveling the capacity for active resources or by using alternative resources, as shown in Figure 2.13.

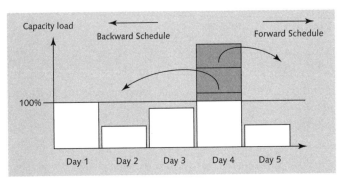

Figure 2.13 Capacity Leveling with Backward and Forward Scheduling

Optimization

This is a cost-based solver available in SAP APO. The solver searches for all feasible plans based on the most cost-effective option. A typical use of the optimizer is seen in industries for which there are high inventory holding costs with warehouse storage constraints. Consider a business such as an oil and gas company, for which the capacity for resources is constrained. The total supply chain costs consist of production, procurement, storage, and transportation costs. Additional penalty costs are factored in for increasing the production capacity, storage capacity, transportation capacity, and handling capacity. Additionally, costs for falling below the safety stock level, costs for delayed delivery, and stock out (or shortfall quantity) costs are important for modeling.

The optimizer primarily suits capital-intensive, capacity-constrained industries that have high production and storage costs. Based on the hard and soft constraints defined in the SNP optimizer profile, the most cost-efficient plan is proposed. This solver is effective when the network is complex enough to develop a sourcing plan for some of the following business decisions.

Optimization helps us to resolve which products are to be produced, transported, procured, stored, and delivered (i.e., the product mix) and their quantities. The calculation also determines which resources and which production process models (PPMs) or production data structures (PDS) are to be used (i.e., the technology mix). The end result is the dates on which products are to be produced, transported, procured, stored, and delivered, as well as the locations at which or to which products are to be produced, transported, procured, stored, and delivered.

> **Resolving an Optimization Problem[1]**
>
> Optimization problems require solutions for which the decisions need to be made in a constrained or limited resource environment. Most supply chain optimization problems require matching demand and supply when one, the other, or both may be limited. The lead time plays a critical role, as it takes time to procure, make, or deliver the goods. Since the rate of procurement, production, distribution, and transportation of resources is limited, demand cannot be immediately satisfied. Other examples of constraints are warehouse storage space and truck capacity. An optimization problem consists of four major components:
>
> ▶ **Decision variables** are within the planner's control.
>
>   ▶ When and how much of a raw material to order from the supplier
>
>   ▶ When to manufacture an order
>
>   ▶ When and how much of the products to ship to the customer or distribution center

---

1   Source: Larry Lapide, *Supply Chain Planning Optimization Report*, (AMR, 1998).

▶ **Constraints** are limitations placed upon the supply plan.

  ▶ A supplier's capacity to produce raw materials

  ▶ A production line that can only run specific hours in a day

  ▶ Warehouse space capacity to store products

  Constraints in an optimization problem are either hard or soft. Hard constraints are things like truck capacity for load build, while soft constraints are things like customer due dates. Most optimization problems designate cost penalties if a soft constraint is not met.

▶ **Objectives** maximize, minimize, or satisfy items such as following:

  ▶ Profits or margins

  ▶ Supply chain costs

  ▶ Production throughput

  ▶ Customer service

▶ **Models** describe the relationship among decisions, constraints, and objectives. These are often expressed in the form of mathematical equations. The model captures the essence of the problem and must represent important aspects of the supply chain in order to provide useful solutions.

Once an optimization problem is formulated, a solver determines the best course of action. A solver comprises a set of logical steps or algorithms embedded in a planning system to search for a solution that achieves the objective. A solver can determine three types of solutions:

▶ **Feasible solution**
Satisfies all the constraints of the problem.

▶ **Optimal solution**
The best feasible solution that achieves the objective of the optimization problem. Although some problems may yield more than one feasible solution, there is usually only one optimal solution.

▶ **Optimized solution**
A solution that partially achieves the objective of the optimization problem. It is not optimal, but it is a satisfying or reasonable one. This is usually one of the best feasible solutions.

Capable-to-Match

The third SNP solver is Capable-to-Match (CTM), which uses constraint-based heuristics to look at multiple locations for a demand and supply match. CTM is rules-based, which means it aims for fulfilling demand elements with supply elements by taking into account production and transportation capacities. The planner can put priorities on demand and supply elements. This solver is primarily suited for industries having many products and resource bottlenecks and that wants to prioritize demand and supply per allocation rules.

2.5.4   APO-SNP Subcontracting

Subcontracting is business scenario in which the company contracts with external business partners to perform specific value-added activities to reduce the overall manufacturing costs of the finished product. The subcontractor can be treated either as an external vendor or plant in the SAP environment.

The process of outsourcing can also be modeled in APO-SNP, when the manufacturer provides the subcontractor with separate materials or components, and the subcontractor uses these components and supplies the finished product to the manufacturer.

2.5.5   APO-SNP Scheduling Agreement

For vendor procurement we can define a *scheduling agreement*.

The process defines a contract quantity to be delivered by the supplier to the manufacturer over a period of time. APO-SNP plans the schedule lines using the SAP ERP master data, and the plans can be confirmed by the supplier (via web collaboration) before they are released to SAP ERP for execution.

2.5.6   APO-SNP Hierarchical Planning

Hierarchical planning (a.k.a. Aggregated Supply Network Planning) allows the business to perform planning at the aggregated level (i.e., product family) across the supply network. The hierarchical planning is primarily done at a medium- to long-term horizon and then disaggregated to a lower hierarchy (i.e., product level) at short-term horizon.

This feature provides the concept of hierarchical planning to reduce planning complexity and improve system performance. The planner can plan aggregated data either at the product or location levels (for example, the product group or family level). Once planned at the aggregated level, the plan can be disaggregated at lower item levels to maintain consistency. A business scenario from our case study might be applicable: consumer goods for which, in the long term, the product group hierarchy is performed and net requirements proposed to the manufacturing plan. Once planned at the manufacturing location, the plan is disaggregated to the product for planning at the product location level. Another business scenario would be for retail distribution, for which location hierarchy is performed, and inventory and demand are netted before raising procurement proposals to the vendor.

2.5.7 APO-SNP Distribution Planning

This process generates the deployment stock transfers and purchase requisitions for the short-term horizon, allowing the business to view the constraint supply plan from the source location. This visibility allows the business to plan proactively for situations when they foresee supply shortages. Both deployment heuristics and the optimizer are available for creating deployment orders. The TLB takes input from deployment to create transport loads based on the pre-defined constraint on the means of transports defined in the transportation lanes. Fair-share logic is applied during the situation when the supply is constrained within the network.

Another area of importance when it comes to collaboration is *Vendor Managed Inventory* (VMI). This process integrates key customers into the planning process. The customer sends the inventory and sales data, and based on this information, the vendor develops the replenishment requirements for the customer. This process improves customer service, lowers transportation costs, and minimizes inventory holding costs.

2.5.8 Supply Chain Monitoring

APO-SNP offers the Supply Chain Cockpit (SCC), which allows a business to define work areas based on their planning scope. Based on this work area, the planner can drill down on both demand and supply situations at the location levels for supply chain monitoring. SAP NetWeaver BW can also be integrated within the SCC to measure supply chain performance with KPIs.

An alert monitor integrates all the applications in SAP APO to monitor planning situations. The alerts for demand and supply planning are created primarily based on macros. There are standard alerts available, but custom alerts macros can also be written for the alert monitor to display. The alerts can display any demand, material, or capacity issues to planners, who can then take proactive actions to align the demand and supply plans.

SAP APO requires a large amount of data processing and robust technical architecture to support these functions, which we'll discuss in the next section.

2.6   SAP APO Technical Architecture

Understanding the SAP APO technical architecture is important due to its different component functions. Unlike with the SAP ERP system, the IT support group needs to understand how the optimizer and SAP liveCache function, as well as the concept of time series data storage for supporting the solution for future technical enhancements and upgrades. An SAP APO system is composed of different software components:

▶ The SAP APO database: a relational database management system (RDBMS) as in any ERP system; a database system in which data and the relationships among the data are stored in tables

▶ An SAP basis layer

▶ An SAP APO application layer

▶ An external, object-oriented SAP DB database called SAP liveCache

▶ Optimizers: a group of programs that execute optimization algorithms

▶ Internet communication manager (ICM) for communication between the SAP NetWeaver Application Server and the external world

A typical technical landscape is shown in Figure 2.14.

The SAP APO component is similar to an SAP ERP-type architecture with a DB server and *n* application servers. As with the DB server, an SAP APO system can have only one liveCache server. From the view of the application servers, this appears as a second database connection. SAP liveCache provides a native SQL interface, which also allows the application servers to trigger object-oriented functions at the database level. These functions are provided by means of C++ code, running on the liveCache server with access to the objects in the SAP liveCache memory. This is the functionality, which allows processing loads to be passed from the application server to the SAP liveCache server, rather than just accessing database data. The optimizers installed in the optimization server are called using the remote function call (RFC). The web dispatcher is connected with the database via HTTPS protocol and via Secure Sockets Layer (SSL) to the external world.

Most of the mathematical calculation is performed in SAP liveCache. The next section explains the technical functioning of SAP liveCache.

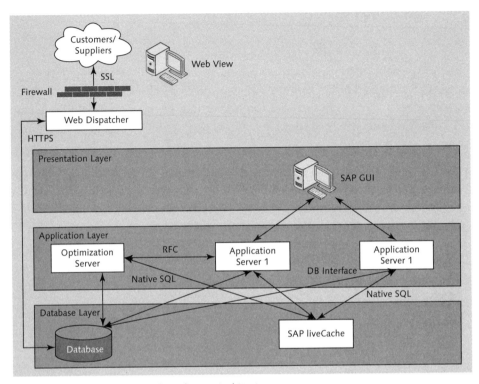

Figure 2.14 SAP APO Technical Landscape Architecture

2.7 SAP liveCache Technology

During SAP APO implementation, SAP liveCache needs to be installed after the initial installation. SAP liveCache is a database management system with the ability to build a large memory cache and perform specially tailored functions (e.g., mathematical algorithms) against memory data structures. If there are multiple clients for the same application server, we can specify a client independent of SAP liveCache. SAP liveCache is an object-oriented database management system developed by SAP that resides in a very large memory. Optimized C++ programs (COM routines) run on the SAP liveCache server and have access to liveCache data. The main objective is to optimize performance via two methods:

▸ SAP liveCache resides in main memory and therefore avoids disk input/output.

▸ Object orientation enables efficient programming technique.

SAP liveCache has a large memory and behaves like both an object-oriented and relational database. SAP liveCache can store time series and order liveCache data in structures and allows concurrent data access by several applications. A time series represents requirements and receipts elements for product and location in the aggregation form.

The key technical points related to SAP liveCache architecture are shown in Figure 2.15, allowing for large processing of planning data. SAP liveCache is a tool for high performance management of objects used by SAP APO application programs (i.e., COM routines). These objects, called OMS objects, contain application data, whose meaning is unknown to SAP liveCache. If possible, all objects are located in the main memory—in the global data cache—of SAP liveCache, but in case of a memory shortage they may be swapped out to disk. The COM routine contains SAP APO applications logic and is written in C++. APO COM routines are located in DLLs (NT) or shared libraries (UNIX). When SAP APO works with SAP liveCache, it calls COM routines by calling database-stored procedures in native SQL within ABAP code. In the C code of the database interface (DBSL), this appears as EXEC SQL CALL.

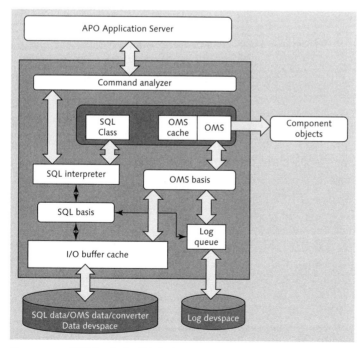

Figure 2.15 SAP liveCache 7.4 Architecture

> **More Information**
>
> For more technical details regarding SAP liveCache technology, please refer to *www.sdn.sap.com*.

SAP liveCache provides classes and class methods in the COM routines to administer their objects. The COM routine uses the SAP liveCache API to communicate with the object memory system (OMS) of SAP liveCache and to read, store, create, or delete OMS objects.

The SAP APO application uses a complex, object-orientated application model. This model is easier to implement via object-oriented programming than with the structures of a relational database. Therefore, SAP liveCache supports object-oriented programming through providing adequate C++ methods/functions. Because COM routines run in the address space of SAP liveCache, they have direct access to OMS objects, and navigation over networks of OMS objects is very fast. Typical access time is less than ten microseconds per object.

2.8 Summary

SAP APO inherits primarily all the key characteristics of an advanced planning and scheduling system. These characteristics are distinct from MRP II/DRP concepts, as seen earlier in SAP ERP systems.

SAP APO resolves the issue of demand and supply balancing with the structured approach of planning tasks. APO-DP is more strategic, while the supply components in APO-SNP in the form of replenishment, procurement, production, and distribution are more tactical and operational in nature. The primary benefits of companies implementing SAP APO are enhanced revenue with better forecasting process, reduction in costs with better inventory control, and improvement in asset management.

This chapter also depicted the SAP APO planning framework and the key functions and features embedded within the APO-DP and APO-SNP modules. The chapter closed with the high-level technical architecture of SAP APO.

The next chapter focuses on the SAP APO implementation methodology. Unlike ERP implementation, advanced planning and scheduling (APS) requires additional change management and user involvement from the beginning to the end phase of the project.

Implementing SAP APO offers different challenges, unlike traditional ERP project implementation. Understanding the SAP APO implementation methodology is important; this chapter also highlights the importance of change management and business benefits drivers in steering a successful SAP APO implementation.

3 SAP APO Implementation Guidelines

The goal of supply chain planning is to ensure the availability of the right products, in the right place, at the right time, and at the right cost. To become a best-in-class organization, the company needs to start thinking outside the box and have the willingness to shift to a new way of working for its business processes. SAP APO, in the form of technology, is critical to the success of this change for clients who have SAP ERP or other legacy applications as an execution system. However, implementing SAP APO brings along a lot of challenges in the form of supply chain transformation, since it's a decision support tool that requires strong support from the business user community. Therefore, the business and application transformations call for change management within the organization.

To meet these specific needs, in this chapter (see Figure 3.1 for a graphical representation) we'll provide the framework for developing a strategy for a supply chain transformation program. The outcome of this strategy/assessment is a list of quick-win initiatives that will not only accelerate a company's business performance, but also provide a footprint for SAP APO implementation. More specifically, we'll explain how supply chain planning projects in SAP APO are initiated and implemented. Besides providing an SAP APO implementation plan, we'll go over the global template approach and business benefits calculation, as well as a business case study to outline some of the guiding principles in an SAP APO implementation.

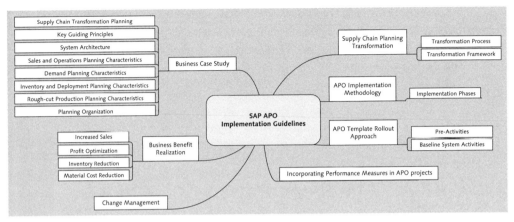

Figure 3.1 Learning Points for the Chapter (Mind Map)

3.1 Supply Chain Planning Transformation Initiatives and Prerequisites

Companies are embarking on supply chain transformation projects primarily to improve their current way of working to meet global economic challenges and market competitions. The supply chain transformation projects aim to not only improve internal business processes, but also look at opportunities to rationalize their product portfolios. Supply chain planning plays a vital role in ensuring the integration of tactical and operational plans for customer satisfaction.

A successful supply chain planning transformation always begins with defining the business case. It is important to understand that the transformation is not about installing and implementing new advanced planning and scheduling functionality in the form of an SAP SCM system, but means to transform the current way of working in business processes with the core objective of delivering concrete business benefits at the end.

> **Example**
>
> ABC Technology has recently acquired companies that are not in the SAP landscape and are using different planning systems. The company is embarking on a project to harmonize business processes, data, systems, and people roles among all the acquired companies. The project charter clearly articulates the business case for ABC Technology to pursue this project. The business case highlights the current and future business process, organizational impact, and business benefits (quantitative and qualitative).

In the following section, we'll go over the different activities that enable a successful transformation.

3.1.1   Transformation Process

A supply chain planning transformation project starts with an "end in mind" approach, with the development of a business case prior to the beginning of the program. The business case should address the questions, "why are we embarking on this transformation," and "what benefits will we derive?" The organization needs to clearly define the qualitative and quantitative success metrics. A supply chain transformation methodology[1] lists five activities required during the transformation process:

1. **Define the scope of the supply chain**
   Working with the business process owner, the transformation team identifies the process improvement initiatives. The corporate supply chain strategy should be aligned with these initiatives to determine long-term goals and a strategy to reach them.

> **Example**
>
> ABC Technology wants to implement SAP APO to improve its forecasting and supply planning processes. Current and then future state maps should be developed to come up with a world-class supply chain after identifying best-in-industry and world-class practices and comparing these to the business's existing practices. A future roadmap needs to be defined to meet corporate objectives.

2. **Change management via culture change**
   Change management plays an important role in implementing the "future state" supply chain process, structures, and business practices. The changes might require collaborative planning among internal and external business partners.

> **Example**
>
> ABC Technology wants to work with its supplier in a collaborative manner. The company plans to build a common platform with its suppliers using SAP APO functionalities to share planning information like forecast, inventory, and capacity.

---

1 Chidhambaram, *A Supply Chain Transformation Methodology,* Industrial Engineering Conference paper (Wichita State University, 2002).

3. **Decision-making with a customer focus**

   Any transformation needs to be taken from a customer viewpoint. The changed or new business process should add value to the customer's experience. These changes require tight integration between the SAP APO component and SAP ERP system to support the planning and order fulfillment business processes. In order to achieve maximum impact, the customers have to be segmented based on their specific needs.

   Example

   ABC Technology plans to apply a disciplined, cross-functional process to develop a menu of supply chain programs and create a segment-specific service package for functional teams. ABC Technology terms this package as S&OP Playbook, which outlines the business process and SAP APO functionality that will meet those requirements based on planning cycles.

4. **Establish a supply chain technology strategy**

   An efficient supply chain requires best-in-class technology and tools for forecasting, supply planning, manufacturing, and logistics decisions. SAP applications must adequately support the supply chain planning activities.

5. **Supply chain metrics**

   With the new business processes and technology implementation, business performance must be monitored. It is imperative to identify the metrics that will be improved with the transformation projects and provide a measure of the organization's supply chain goals.

   Example

   ABC Technology has identified the key supply chain metrics (forecast accuracy, master schedule attainment, and delivery performance) it plans to improve with the supply chain application implementation initiative.

Now that you understand the different required activities, we'll discuss the more technical transformation framework.

3.1.2 Transformation Framework

Once the business case has been established, the next milestone for the supply chain planning transformation is the supply chain assessment. Figure 3.2 shows a framework for the supply chain assessment. The objective of this assessment is to outline the process improvement opportunities and formulate an implementation action plan.

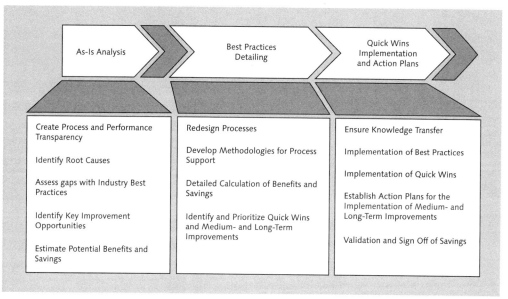

Figure 3.2 Framework for Supply Chain Assessment

Let's go over the different phases, as illustrated in the figure:

1. The as-is analysis delivers transparency on current business processes and performance. This exercise is performed by sound data gathering and analysis activity, complemented by interviews with key business users through all the process stakeholders (i.e., supply chain, as well as commercial, manufacturing, and finance). The process enables the build-up of cause-and-effect analysis trees to identify the key root causes affecting the current processes. Key opportunities are defined, and together with the business process owner, these match the necessary process improvements required to apply the industry best practices and also the underlying business benefit the company can achieve.

2. The next phase is the best practices detailing phase. This phase focuses on the redesign of the business processes in order to align with best practices and achieve necessary performance improvement by resolving the root causes.

3. The last stage is to formulate an implementation roadmap according to the complexity of the implementation versus the potential benefit of each business process initiative.

> **Example**
>
> By performing the supply chain assessment, ABC Technology has identified the key supply chain improvement areas of demand planning and inventory management.

Once the supply chain assessment is complete, the next focus on the transformation is the solution deployment. Besides the solution implementation, other small business process initiatives need to start as part of readiness for using SAP APO as a decision support tool. The readiness is performed on people, process maturity, and data quality. As a prerequisite for a successful SAP APO implementation, the project requires the following four elements:

1. **Supply chain vision**
   A clear business vision, along with business metrics, needs to be defined. Establish a baseline to measure improvements from the SAP APO implementation. The focus needs to be a specific planning problem the tool will address. Some examples are the implementation of the demand planning process or inventory reduction initiatives.

2. **Executive support**
   The project needs to receive a high level of commitment from the business leaders. A change management agent, who will educate the business users on the new process changes, needs to be identified within the organization. For example, a supply chain manager could be nominated as the business process owner to oversee the project toward completion.

3. **Resource mix balance**
   The team needs to have a good mix of business analysts and solution designers. The technical resource identifies any native functionality not supported as well as the reports, interfaces, conversions, enhancements and forms (RICEF) objects required for the project. There should also be dedicated business resources on the project with a good mix of internal and external consultant resources.

4. **Strong user involvement**
   The user community should embrace the solution design and participate in the validation process (system review/walkthrough) to ensure that it meets all

business requirements. SAP APO implementation requires users to spend a significant amount of time to learn, discover, and define ways of using the new tool.

Now that you have a better understanding of what implementing SAP APO will entail, let's move on to the next section to discover why an SAP APO implementation is so different from an SAP ERP implementation to make it to production.

3.2   SAP APO Implementation Methodology

The SAP APO implementation methodology focuses on multiple cycles of prototypes and early user involvement, which is unlike SAP ERP implementation. The business super users work closely with the project team to define various supply chain models in the form of forecasting models, inventory models, etc. Figure 3.3 shows an example of APO-DP and APO-SNP implementation project plans with different phases.

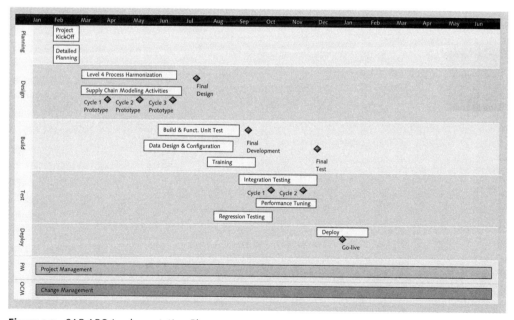

Figure 3.3   SAP APO Implementation Phases

Table 3.1 elaborates on each project phase and key activities.

Project Phase	Key Activities	Key Deliverables
Plan	▶ Define project objectives and framework ▶ Identify key value drivers	▶ Project work plan ▶ Draft initial solution architecture ▶ Key performance indicators
Analyze	▶ Develop business processes ▶ Conduct a series of workshops with business users to obtain requirements and develop processes	▶ Business scenarios ▶ Business process flow ▶ Data flow diagram ▶ Organizational impact assessment* ▶ Roles and responsibilities matrix* ▶ Training plan* ▶ Sponsorship plan* ▶ Communication plan* ▶ Site readiness*
Design	▶ Solidify detailed process design ▶ Establish guidelines for creating mock data for the prototype ▶ Conduct prototype workshops with users ▶ Define management actions required to achieve planned business case benefit levels ▶ Develop sponsorship support materials and begin to deliver	▶ Solution design ▶ Detailed process design ▶ Prototype model ▶ Test plan ▶ Identify site readiness team* ▶ Develop skills assessment* ▶ Deliver skills assessment* ▶ Develop training program* ▶ Begin organizational design*

Table 3.1 SAP APO Project Phase Activities (* Change Management)

Project Phase	Key Activities	Key Deliverables
Build	▶ Develop and test independently functioning applications, reports, and interfaces ▶ Conduct system configuration ▶ Test components and models in a stand-alone environment ▶ Complete development of interfaces	▶ Detailed business scenarios (with expected data results) ▶ Test plans and approaches ▶ Data conversion plan ▶ Developed and tested interfaces ▶ Quality assurance environment build ▶ Training environment build ▶ Training agenda* ▶ Training delivered to test participants*
Test	▶ Conduct integrated testing between SAP APO module and interfaces ▶ Conduct user acceptance testing (USAT) ▶ Conduct stress testing ▶ Conduct integration testing ▶ Conduct final stakeholder approval session	▶ User acceptance test scripts signoff by users ▶ Plan post-production support ▶ Resolve all USAT defects ▶ Production environment build ▶ Site readiness toolkit* ▶ Go-live support materials*
Deploy	▶ Track business case benefit attainment ▶ Conduct final transition to client	▶ Execute post-production support plan ▶ Execute site-specific readiness plan*
Hyper care and post-implementation	▶ Monitor system performance ▶ Identify any user knowledge gaps to be filled with on-the-job training	Checklist on planning result validation by users

Table 3.1 SAP APO Project Phase Activities (* Change Management) (Cont.)

The post-implementation phase is important for the success of an SAP APO implementation. It's important to track key metrics and fine-tune the planning models based on the business changes. The business users need to gain confidence in using the system and trust in generated planning outputs. There should be a continuous need to coach business users, after implementation, to use the solution and exploit additional features. During the project phase, some power users (key users) are part of the project team, but end users are usually not. However, the knowledge transfer to end users and their education and acceptance are especially important during and after an implementation. This is mostly provided by (internal) consultants, project team members, and key/power users.

> **Example**
>
> ABC Technology plans to conduct a routine user group and community among different planning teams to collaborate effectively. In this business user experience sharing forum, the users will be given the opportunity to demonstrate their utilization of the system and highlight any critical system issues.

Additional business requirements need to be captured and modifications made to the system in the form of new functionality introduction to better aid the planning processes.

With globalization, the companies are operating in many countries and regions. A business application template approach helps to leverage the implementation effort in new markets. This approach is explained further in the next section.

3.3   SAP APO Template Rollout Approach

Many global companies are adopting a *template* approach to harmonizing business processes, data standards, common systems, and organizational structures across different markets or regions. Implementing commonality on people, processes, data, and systems, the companies are gaining synergies in their ways of working. The template approach encompasses an end-to-end business process (for example, forecast to stock, order-to-cash, or month-end closing) and may consist of multiple system integrations.

SAP APO supports many end-to-end business scenarios as the planning input to business processes. Figure 3.4 shows a global template composition. The kernel defines the global systems (for example, SAP NetWeaver Master Data Management, which further needs to be integrated with SAP ERP for transferring the master data to SAP APO) and regional systems in the landscape. Built within the global system are business process clusters based on market business requirements. The objective during the template rollout is to make the market business requirements fit as closely as possible to the global template. A reference system provides the preconfigured global systems with prototypes demand and supply planning scenarios. During the fit/gap analysis, the market variations and unique business scenarios (for example, toll manufacturing) are identified for further template enhancements.

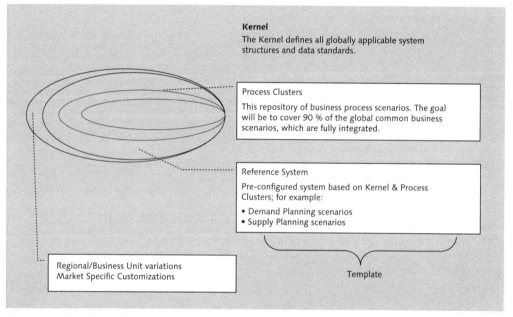

Figure 3.4 Global Template Composition

Let's go over a few of the required activities prior to rolling out the global template.

3.3.1 Pre-Activities

As part of the SAP APO template rollout preparation, the market or region performs some pre-activities. Some of the tasks relevant to planning are demand planning historical data cleansing from legacy. Based on the business rules and definitions that have already been established, the business can perform data cleansing at the source system before the transformation.

The business may also map material flow in the network. This helps to identify the physical goods flow in the network, along with constraints and lead times. A baseline configuration is performed before the fit/gap analysis to identify the variations from the global template.

For the SAP APO global template, we've provided some accelerators in the global reference systems:

- Preconfigured demand planning (APO-DP) books, per standard business scenarios
- Preconfigured Supply Network Planning (APO-SNP) books, per standard business scenarios
- Pre-built data conversions objects (for example, LSMW) to load the legacy data into SAP APO
- Globally defined roles, which can be further localized
- APO-DP forecasting modeling template (univariate time series)
- Inventory modeling template (safety stock planning)
- Factory modeling template (PP/DS heuristics)
- Legacy data collection accelerators for extract, transform, and load (ETL) tools.
- Training documentations based on the global reference system
- SAP NetWeaver BW extraction process for reporting
- Global configuration settings

Example

ABC Technology, having piloted the template for its North America region, now plans to deploy to its European and Asia Pacific regions. Since all these markets would be using the single global SAP APO instance connected with regional SAP ERP systems, the basic configurations are already in place. The primary activities for the new markets implementing SAP APO would be modeling their supply chain business processes (i.e., forecasting models, inventory models, factory models) in the application.

3.3.2 Baseline System Activities

One of the important phases in the global template rollout is the baseline system. The objective of the baseline system is to perform a fit/gap analysis with the global template and identify the impacts of the change on business processes, data, and organization structure.

Figure 3.5 shows the baseline system activities where the organization structure, customer, and product hierarchy, along with material flow mapping, are designed. This helps the market or region to identify different business scenarios and reference models for performing gap analysis with the global template. Besides loading the basic master data, the baseline system is also configured for initial baseline system testing. This provides the opportunity for the business users to visualize the system steps during the gap analysis workshop.

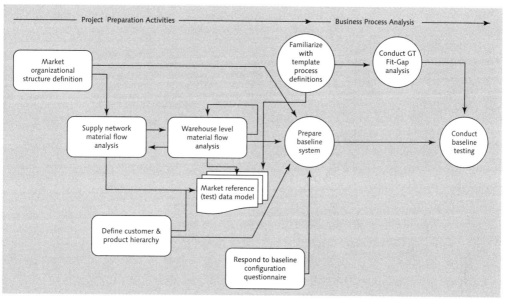

Figure 3.5 Baseline System Activities

Next, we'll discuss change management during SAP APO implementation, which plays an important role in any supply chain transformation project.

3.4 Change Management

As a decision support tool, SAP APO needs strong change management principles applied during the project lifecycle. Table 3.1 illustrated the various change management activities that need to be performed at different project phases. The key tasks for the change management are to communicate on the organizational change impacts (data, process, and system) and prepare business users for a new way of working. The readiness may come in the form of training programs for the business users, for example. Business benefits can only be realized if technology applications are implemented hand in hand with an effective change management initiative. Such an initiative will help the project team stay focused and deliver results.

Many supply chain planning projects have reported failures for the primary reason of the "J-curve" effect (see Figure 3.6) due to a large gap between the business process owners' expectation and the reality as it occurs. There are many change management models, but the underlying principles of these models echo similar messages.

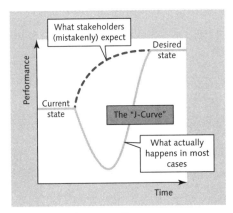

Figure 3.6 The J-Curve[2]

Supply Chain Digest[3] provides a basic change management outline:

- **Identifying the need and urgency for change (the why)**
  Perform SWOT (strength, weakness, opportunities, threat) analysis to understand the internal and external factor which will lead to change in current way of working.

- **Creating the Vision (the what)**
  Detailing the "future state."

- **Communicating (20% on what, 80% on why)**
  Communication on why we performing the change is key for business users to

---

2 Bremmer, Ian. *The J Curve: A New Way to Understand Why Nations Rise and Fall* (Simon and Schuster: 2006)

3 *www.scdigest.com*, 2008

absorb the message. A communication plan needs to be used throughout the project to highlight the changes and benefits.

▶ **Assembling the team (who will do the work)**
A right mix of skilled resources is required to steer the project. There should be good balance of technical and business resources in the project.

▶ **Empowering for success (eliminating obstacles, aligning accountability)**
Business sponsorship is important not only for project funding, but also to ensure that the project is on track by conducting routine steering committee meetings. The project uses a town hall meeting style to communicate progress to wider audience.

▶ **Mobilizing commitment (assessment, analysis, readiness, capability, training)**
Commitment needs to be seen in both the project team and business team to make the project live on time.

▶ **Architecting, designing, and measuring (the how and metrics)**
A good measure whether the changes is being adapted is to perform survey for business users to express their concerns or fear. Training plays an important role to bridge the gap for business users to understand more on the change impact. The change impact should address people, process, data, and system changes.

▶ **Celebrating short-term wins**
The project need to celebrate milestones as they progress in the journey.

SAP APO implementation transforms the current business processes, and the early participation of the supply chain manager and key business users is vital for the solution design and development. The project subject matter expert should be able to educate the business users on how to perform supply chain modeling in the system. While the focus of SAP APO is on the planning solution, the overall end-to-end business process impact should not be overlooked.

> **Important!**
>
> The solution design should integrate both the planning and execution systems well. SAP APO offers many functionalities, and implementing all of them might be overwhelming. A good balance is required to implement basic and advanced features per the business requirements.

The success rate of SAP APO implementation increases once we have the performance measure included as a business goal of the project. This topic is discussed in the next section.

3.5 Incorporating Performance Measures in SAP APO Projects

SAP APO projects should always start with aligning the vision with the company's strategy. Companies need to outline the business goals they are targeting with SAP APO implementation.

> **Example**
>
> ABC Technology has outlined the following project vision:
> Deliver superior customer service through an integrated, demand-driven supply chain by:
> ▸ Providing total supply chain visibility from suppliers to customers
> ▸ Reducing planning lead times
> ▸ Improving the new product introduction process
> ▸ Managing constraints effectively
> ▸ Developing realistic plans based on known constraints

Once the vision is aligned with the strategy, a linkage needs to be established between the functional goals and the objectives translated into SAP APO functionalities. Figure 3.7 shows how the company's strategy for supply chain planning is translated into functional objectives. These functional objectives are then further broken down into two or three objectives.

> **Example**
>
> As you can see in Figure 3.7, ABC Technology has outlined its functional objectives in the form of demand planning accuracy, inventory reduction with the overall goal of harmonizing the supply chain planning process, and improving customer delivery performance. The functional objectives are further translated into SAP APO system objectives.

Communication is key to any SAP APO project. The transformational goals need to be aligned from the beginning of the project along with clear communication on estimated business benefits that will be yielded from the project. Figure 3.8 shows an example in which the goal is to reduce the overall inventory in the company.

This program goal is then assigned to the business sponsor, who would be funding the project. The business sponsor, in turn, assigns the different objectives to the business process owner. Finally, the business process owner works with the functional units to ensure that the goal objective is met. With this approach, implementing SAP ERP and SAP APO is seen as an enabler to improve the business performance and as technology for automating some of the business activities.

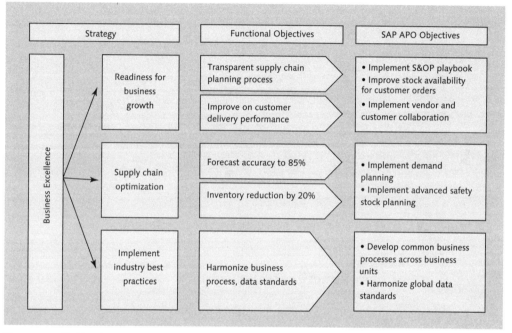

Figure 3.7 Linking Business Process Objectives to APO Functionalities

The supply chain transformation program level goals need to be cascaded down into operational measures (and targets) that can be influenced/affected by lower-level functional units involved in the change program. Ideally, employees' performance scorecards should be modified to assure alignment of employees' incentives with overall program goals and objectives.

As a part of the SAP APO business case, one of the sections is the business benefit realization, which needs to be outlined. We'll explain how to quantify and calculate the business benefits in the next section.

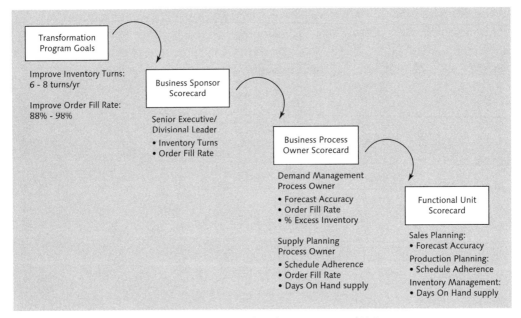

Figure 3.8 Cascading the Transformational Goals into Functional Units

3.6 Business Benefits Realization

Implementing SAP APO requires a cost-benefit analysis before the project starts. Like with SAP ERP projects, the business needs to determine and calculate their financial benefits that can be realized by implementing SAP APO. This financial calculation helps in quantifying the company's savings with the use of the SAP APO application. This is an important part of steering a successful SAP APO implementation.

One of the components for this exercise is understanding which business benefits will be realized based on the SAP APO functionalities that the business has decided to implement. Table 3.2 provides a list of some of the business benefits that companies commonly report as being realistically achievable.

Functional Area	Benefits
Forecast accuracy	Up by 15%
Safety stock	Down by 15–50%

Table 3.2 Industry Benchmarks on APS Implementation Benefits

Functional Area	Benefits
Average inventory	Down by 10–25%
Stable plan/schedule	More than 5 days
Changeover times	Down by 20%
Plant output	Up by 15–20%
Material shortages	Down by 80%

Table 3.2 Industry Benchmarks on APS Implementation Benefits (Cont.)

These benefits will manifest themselves via the operational improvements with improved customer service and on-time delivery. The benefits are also seen to achieve cost savings and a reduction in expediting customer orders and factory overtime. With better fluidity in the supply chain, the biggest benefit is seen in the reduction of the finished goods inventories and manufacturing lead times with better-quality planning data. The option of creating a simulation plan helps with the yearly budget process and provides an outlook on capacity utilization over time.

Figure 3.9 provides the tree diagram of shareholder return of value. The measurement is done on profitability and optimization use of invested capital.

The profitability of the company focuses on the increased sales revenue with better forecasting of the selling products. The cost reduction is also seen in the overall supply chain, with supply planning reliability with good utilization of supply chain resources to deliver customer orders. The capital investment is seen with lower inventory holding costs and proper assets use.

Example
ABC Technology has performed a rough, quantifiable business benefits calculation, as shown in Table 3.3 through Table 3.8, on four functional areas in which it views that the SAP APO application will improve its current business processes. The four benefit areas are increased sales, profit optimization, inventory reduction (finished goods and raw material), and material cost reduction. The calculation numbers presented are fictitious and serve only to show how the baseline calculations were performed by ABC Technology.
Table 3.3 illustrates ABC Technology's projected benefits for the next five years after the SAP APO implementation. The derivation of the benefits for each area is further explained in the coming sub-sections.

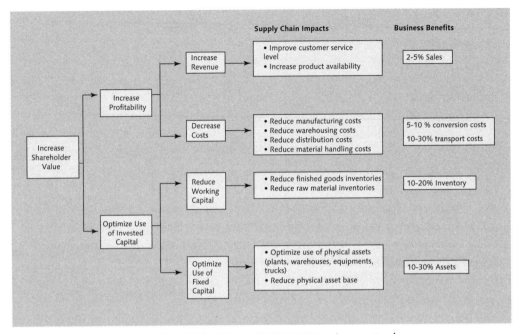

Figure 3.9 Increasing Shareholder Value with SAP APO Implementation[4]

Additional Profits Before Tax	Year 0	Year 1	Year 2	Year 3	Year 4	Year 5	5Y TOTAL
Increased sales	-	6.203	9.230	9.716	10.067	8.586	43.802
Profit optimization	-	2.545	7.032	8.636	7.954	7.326	33.494
Inventory reduction (finished goods and raw materials)	-	0.951	2.364	4.078	3.756	3.459	14.608
Material cost reduction	-	0.842	1.550	1.428	1.315	1.211	6.346
Total benefits (in millions of USD)	-	10.541	20.177	23.857	23.092	20.582	98.249

Table 3.3 Estimation Calculation for SAP APO Benefits

---

4 AMR Industry Benchmark Report (2010)

3.6.1   Increased Sales

The increase in sales is measured not only by volume of sales but also by the customer service level ABC Technology offers its customers. With the SAP APO implementation, the business can project its sales increase by ensuring the stock availability at the right location. With the right level of stock available, the customers' orders are fulfilled on time, with future repeat orders. Table 3.4 shows the additional profit with the improvement in customer service level.

Year	Year 0	Year 1	Year 2	Year 3	Year 4	Year 5
Customer service level (CSL) without SAP APO	50%	52%	54%	56%	58%	60%
CSL with SAP APO	50%	65%	75%	80%	85%	85%
Sales without SAP APO	1,523	1,545	1,569	1,592	1,616	1,640
Sales with SAP APO	1,523	1,596	1,651	1,688	1,725	1,743
Additional sales	0	50	82	96	109	103
Additional profits before tax	0	8	12	14	16	15
Time phasing factor	91%	82%	75%	68%	62%	56%
Present value of additional profits	0.0	6.2	9.2	9.7	10.1	8.6
Total present value (PV)	**43.8**					

Note: All numbers are in millions of USD

Assumed that without SAP APO target achievement is included in the sales growth rates

Achievable growth rate without SAP APO: 1.5%

1% sales increase per 4% customer service level improvement

Income from operations and recovery of fixed costs: 15%

Weighted average cost of capital (WACC): 10.2%

Year-1 sales: 1,500

Table 3.4   Sales Projection Benefit Calculation with SAP APO Implementation

ABC Technology's assets are financed by either debt or equity. *Weighted average cost of capital (WACC)* is the average of the costs of these sources of financing, each of which is weighted by its respective use in the given situation. By taking a weighted average, we can see how much interest the company has to pay for every dollar it finances.[5]

3.6.2 Profit Optimization

Margin improvement for ABC Technology will result from meeting planned new product introduction dates and improved supply allocation, enabled by full customer order visibility. Table 3.5 shows the profit optimization yielded primarily because of the collaborative planning process and better forecast accuracy results.

Year	Year 0	Year 1	Year 2	Year 3	Year 4	Year 5
Sales	1,523	1,545	1,569	1,592	1,616	1,640
Margin improvement due to SAP APO capability	0%	0.2%	0.6%	0.8%	0.8%	0.8%
Additional profits	–	3	9	13	13	13
Time phasing factor	91%	82%	75%	68%	62%	56%
Present value (PV) of additional profits	–	2.5	7.0	8.6	8.0	7.3
Total PV	**33.5**					
Note: All numbers are in Millions of USD						
Achievable growth rate without SAP APO: 1.5%						
Contribution margin: 15%						
WACC: 10.2%						
Year-1 sales: 1,500						

Table 3.5 Profit Optimization Benefit Calculation with SAP APO Implementation

3.6.3 Finished Goods Inventory Reduction

The finished goods inventory reduction is based on a better supply planning process. The process ensures the right products, at the right place, at the right time,

---

5   *www.investopedia.com*

at the right cost. The savings are primarily driven by holding fewer projected days of supply in the warehouse and ensuring that the product flow in and out of the distribution center is smooth. The supply planning process ensures that the correct level of inventory is built during the seasonal months while the year end is closed with lower inventory levels across the network. The planning process ensures that the inventory is balanced across ABC Technology's supply chain network and that there are fewer obsolescence and write-off scenarios. Table 3.6 provides a projection of the finished goods inventory reduction achieved with the more streamlined supply planning process.

Year	Year 0	Year 1	Year 2	Year 3	Year 4	Year 5
Sales	1,523	1,545	1,569	1,592	1,616	1,640
Finished goods inventory (FGI) without SAP APO (constant turns)	70	71	72	73	74	75
FGI in days of sales	11.4	11.0	10	8	8	8
FGI without SAP APO	70	68	63	51	52	52
Reduction in FGI	-	3	9	22	22	22
Additional profits before tax	0	1	2	5	5	5
Time phasing factor	91%	82%	75%	68%	62%	56%
Present value (PV) of additional profits	0.0	0.5	1.5	3.3	3.0	2.8
Total PV	**11.0**					

Note: All numbers are in millions of USD

Projected stock reduction is based on a conservative interpretation of improved stock turn figures quoted by industry benchmark (30% in 3 years).

Current FGI, in days of sales: 11.4

Material cost: 78%

WACC: 10.2%

Inventory carrying cost: 22%; includes cost of capital, price erosion, and logistics

Achievable growth rate without SAP APO: 1.5%

Table 3.6 Finished Goods Inventory Reduction Benefit Calculation with SAP APO Implementation

3.6.4 Raw Material Inventory Reduction

With better finished goods planning, the positive effect is reflected in raw material planning, as well. With better planning, the ABC Technology buyer would be procuring the raw materials based on material lead times. The improved material requirement planning process will ensure fewer shortages of raw materials and make an effective reduction in the raw material inventory possible. Table 3.7 shows the projected raw material reduction over the next five years.

Year	Year 0	Year 1	Year 2	Year 3	Year 4	Year 5
Sales	1,523	1,545	1,569	1,592	1,616	1,640
Raw material inventory without SAP APO (constant days)	28	28	28	29	29	30
Raw material inventory in days of sales	7.0	6.0	5	5	5	5
Raw material inventory with SAP APO	28	24	20	21	21	21
Reduction in raw material inventory (CF impact)	-	4	8	8	8	8
Additional profits before tax	0	1	1	1	1	1
Time phasing factor	91%	82%	75%	68%	62%	56%
Present value (PV) of additional profits	0.0	0.5	0.9	0.8	0.8	0.7
Total (PV)	**3.6**					

Note: All numbers are in millions of USD

Projected stock reduction is based on a conservative interpretation of improved stock turn figures quoted by industry benchmark (30% in 3 years)

Current raw material inventory in days of sales: 7.0

Material cost as a percentage of selling price: 65%

WACC: 10%

Inventory carrying cost: 15%; Includes cost of capital, price erosion, and logistics

Achievable growth rate without SAP APO: 1.5%

Table 3.7 Raw Material Inventory Reduction Benefit Calculation with SAP APO Implementation

3.6.5 Material Cost Reduction

With SAP APO automation and exceptions-based planning, the company can be notified if it is out of a particular product, and if there is customer demand for it, that information can be pushed to the company in real time. This leads to lower production costs, improved quality, and shorter product development cycles. Furthermore, on the demand side, customers are able to look at more than one supplier to find the best product available at the appropriate price, and also determine whether it's available in real time. All these factors contribute to the material cost reduction, as depicted in Table 3.8.

Year	Year 0	Year 1	Year 2	Year 3	Year 4	Year 5
Sales	1522.5	1545.34	1568.52	1592.05	1615.93	1640.16
Material costs	989.625	1004.47	1019.54	1034.83	1050.35	1066.11
Reduction in material costs (in percentage of costs)	0%	0.2%	0.4%	0.4%	0.4%	0.4%
Reduction in material costs without collaboration	-	1	2	2	2	2
Time phasing factor	91%	82%	75%	68%	62%	56%
Present value (PV) of additional profits without collaboration	0.0	0.8	1.6	1.4	1.3	1.2
Total PV	**6**					

Note: All numbers are in millions of USD

Baseline data

Material costs in percentage of sales: 65%

Material costs in percentage of costs: 70%

WACC: 10.2%

Assumptions

Achievable growth rate without SAP APO: 1.5%

Percentage of savings achievable without web-based collaboration with suppliers: 50%

Savings in percentage of material costs: 0.41%

Year-1 Sales: 1,500

Table 3.8 Material Cost/Benefit Calculation with SAP APO Implementation

Now that you understand the different elements in SAP APO implementation, we'll move on to explore a business case study to further drill down on the different planning characteristics involved in the implementation phases.

3.7 Business Case Study

The objective of this case study is to show how the company underwent transformation initiatives by framing key guiding principles for its supply chain planning business process. ABC Technology is operating globally and has multiple legacy systems. Planning is performed at the global and regional levels within a monthly cycle. The planning is done by business planners in the legacy system, which isn't integrated with any other systems. The company faces constant challenges with stock out situations and customer backorders.

The business planners work on a day-old snapshot data in the legacy system; once the plans are created, they are interfaced back to the execution system. A supply chain transformation program has been initiated to implement a new SAP APO system with the vision that an improvement in supply chain planning will deliver higher customer service levels, better on-time delivery of sets, and lower inventory. The project also aims to harmonize business processes and use a common system application across multiple business units. Currently, there is limited global visibility to demand, inventory, and supply requirements across the company's supply chain network.

In the following sections, we'll study how the company underwent the transformation initiative by framing key guiding principles, planning process characteristics, organizational role impacts, and system architecture.

3.7.1 Supply Chain Transformation Planning

The approach to transforming supply chain planning begins with developing a strategy and roadmap to guide the implementation program. The decided supply chain transformation plan is shown in Figure 3.10. The strategy starts with a clear definition of how the company will perform global planning and manage the global supply chain–enabling corporate strategies. The strategy requires a holistic approach in addressing both the technology and business aspects of the implementation. The approach requires a clear understanding of where and how business benefits will be achieved in order to focus the implementation and change management efforts on the areas critical to success.

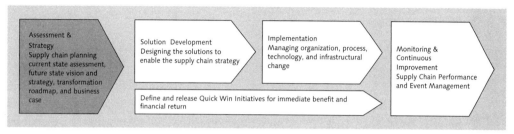

Figure 3.10 Supply Chain Transformation Approach

Following the strategy development, the company initiated a number of small quick-win projects, along with the SAP APO implementation. These small projects involved like-product portfolio rationalization, forecast modeling, and sales and operation playbook design. The "quick wins" (small projects) identified to run parallel to the implementation will help to drive change and business benefits ahead of the SAP APO implementation.

The consumer goods company is hoping for the following largest levers of benefit through improved supply chain planning:

▶ Delivering high customer service levels by better aligning product supply to marketplace demand (consumption)

▶ Reducing inventory days of supply through improved planning (reduced forecast error, differentiated service, statistically set safety stock, and improved supply reliability)

▶ Reducing inventory obsolescence through improved planning, especially in product phase-in and product phase-out planning

▶ Improving upon global asset utilization and long-term capacity planning (internal capacity and key supplier capacity) to support business growth through improved visibility to global demand, global supply capability and capacity, and constraint-based global master planning

▶ Enabling the company's sales growth through improved on-time delivery of goods and better planning and execution of new product launches

▶ Improving process integration and collaboration between functional groups through a more robust, executive-level sales and operations planning process

The company requires enhanced organizational, process, and systems capabilities to deliver this strategy.

An effective way to formulate the strategy is to create a solution roadmap. The roadmap should clearly highlight different phases on how the company plans to implement SAP APO functionalities to address its current pain points. An implementation roadmap was developed to build the necessary capabilities and implement the strategy. There are a few "quick hit" opportunities, which may be launched immediately to maintain momentum by pulling forward work/solution components that drive business benefits where SAP APO is not a prerequisite (i.e., the sales and operations planning playbook, performance metrics, and inventory policy).

3.7.2   Key Guiding Principles[6]

The supply chain transformation program that ABC Technology follows works on key guiding principles of being demand driven, aligned, and integrated. The key highlights for these three areas are as follows:

1. **Demand driven**

    ▶ Smooth flow of information and visibility, from manufacturing of goods till consumption of goods by customers

    ▶ Good understanding of customer requirements and agreement to service level targets by product class and customer class

    ▶ Use rich, demand-oriented information and demand "signals" and enable a "produce to demand" pull-based supply chain model

    ▶ Provide full, network-wide visibility to inventory and timely feedback on usage and consumption information; optimal safety stock maintained to buffer variability

    ▶ Provide different planning models approach based on product (e.g., ABC Classification, stable versus promotional, etc.), market (e.g., Americas versus Asia), and time horizon (short- versus long-term)

---

6   Harvard Business Review Publication. *HBR's 10 Must Reads on Change Management* (with featured article "Leading Change," by John P. Kotter), March 2011

2. **Aligned**

   ▸ Empower the planning organization with the authority and responsibility to make the best decision for the business

   ▸ Establish clear roles and responsibilities related to supply chain management, supported by globally consistent and aligned metrics

   ▸ Ensure tight collaboration with the business in each region to ensure inclusion of market intelligence and operational constraints into the development of a plan

   ▸ Strive for consensus on a single operating plan and understand its impact (sales and operations planning)

   ▸ Ensure tight alignment with operations functions for execution of the plan

3. **Integrated**

   ▸ Build globally integrated supply chain planning processes enabled by global visibility of demand, inventory, and production capacity

   ▸ Leverage the entire global network of the central warehouse and satellite warehouses to serve the customer in an efficient manner

   ▸ Focus on enabling a disciplined process governed by firm time fences, clear handoffs, and well-defined and understood rules of engagement

   ▸ Ensure transparency, where decision trade-offs are clearly understood by all key stakeholders

   ▸ Provide the necessary tools and technology to support a globally integrated planning organization

3.7.3   System Architecture

As part of the supply chain transformation project, the scope involves implementing demand planning, supply planning, and sales and operations planning business processes. The integrated architecture is, as shown in Figure 3.11, showing the historical sales orders and customer orders as input into the demand planning process. The supply planning is further broken down into inventory planning, deployment planning, and master schedule planning. With this architecture approach, the company's demand and supply plans are integrated with the sales and operations planning process. Various supply constraints, such as sourcing, transportation, and the factory provide key input to the supply planning process. The architecture provides a structural approach to the functional areas.

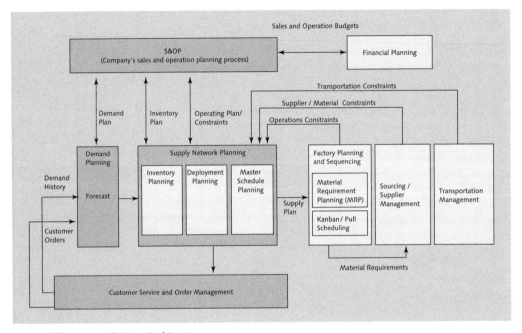

Figure 3.11 System Architecture

3.7.4 Sales and Operations Planning Characteristics

The sales and operations planning process is envisioned to be more forward looking and exceptions driven based on improved visibility to demand and supply constraints. Some of the key characteristics of current and future states related to sales and operations planning are listed in Table 3.9. These characteristics serve as business requirements during the solution phase of the project.

Category	As-Is Characteristics	To-Be Charactersitics
Process definition	▶ No formal decision-making process ▶ Metrics, reports, and escalation process not defined ▶ Not exception-based	▶ Clearly defined sales and operations planning process, including roles and responsibilities, metrics/reports, inputs/outputs, information sources, detailed calendar of events, and decisions to be made, as well as an issue resolution process by weekly planning meetings ▶ Exception driven and decision focused
Tools and technology	Legacy system does not provide simulation planning or inventory projections	▶ Simulation planning for demand, supply, and inventory projections ▶ Inventory visibility across network
Financial reconciliation	Finance is currently not involved in the sales and operations planning process.	Gaps to financial budgets assessed at the sales and operations planning demand planning meeting and at the sales and operations planning supply-balancing meeting
Sales and operations planning supply-balancing meeting	▶ Supply plan not developed for all locations ▶ No formal supply planning meeting before the sales and operations planning meeting	▶ Supply plan developed for all plants ▶ Operating plan includes forecasted demand, planned production, and resulting inventory levels by business units and locations
Sales and operations planning monthly forecast meeting	No pre-monthly forecast review meeting	Monthly forecast review meeting among supply chain, finance, sales, and marketing

Table 3.9 Charactersitcs of Sales and Operations Planning Process

Category	As-Is Characteristics	To-Be Charactersitics
Sales and operations planning meeting	Often not conducted	Formal meeting conducted with agenda
Sales and operations planning executive meeting	Limited visibility to the KPIs and business performance	Meeting is exception driven and decision focused

Table 3.9 Charactersitcs of Sales and Operations Planning Process (Cont.)

3.7.5 Demand Planning Characteristics

Using the collaborative planning approach, the company aims to improve its forecast accuracy. Some of the key characteristics of current and future states related to demand planning are listed in Table 3.10.

Category	As-Is Characteristics	To-Be Charactersitics
Differentiated planning approach	No formal differentiation in approach or focus in demand planning process	► SKU portfolio segmented by ABC Classification based on defined attributes (e.g., product velocity, strategic importance, etc.) ► Differentiated forecast approaches and targets by product group ► Planner effort focused on the most critical items
Exception-driven parameter tuning	► Unstructured approach to tuning model parameters ► Planners eyeball forecast graphs in legacy system to determine accuracy of statistical models	Alert monitors/exception reports point planners to those models in which the statistical forecast accuracy is outside predetermined tolerances

Table 3.10 Charactersitcs of Sales and Operations Planning Process

Category	As-Is Characteristics	To-Be Charactersitics
Planning hierarchies	Planners are unable to slice and dice the planning data per the planning hierarchies	Planners are able to slice and dice the planning data per different hierarchies
Bottom-up and top-down reconciliation	Planners only use top-down reconciliation functionality, making it cumbersome to enter intelligence at lower hierarchy levels	Bottom-up reconciliation enables planners to enter intelligence at more granular levels without the need for manual adjustments to higher hierarchy levels
Tighter linkage to procedures	No standard process across business units	Harmonized business process across units
New product introduction	▶ New product launch/phase-out demand plans have a high margin of error. ▶ Lack of emphasis on product phase out ▶ No defined lifecycle planning process within demand planning; ad hoc approaches used to model product lifecycles	▶ Tighter integration of new product launch process with the demand planning process ▶ Hold marketing and sales accountable for input on product launch and phase-out plans ▶ Represent product launch, growth, and discontinuation phases within planning systems to ensure better process governance
Collaboration with stakeholders	No clear consensus on the demand plan	Consensus demand plan across key stakeholders in the process

Table 3.10 Characteristics for Demand Planning Process (Cont.)

3.7.6 Inventory and Deployment Planning Characteristics

The company plans to make its inventory and deployment planning more structured (i.e., inventory policy) and pull-oriented based on inventory usage and consumption. Some of the key characteristics of current and future states related to inventory and deployment planning are listed in Table 3.11.

Category	As-Is Characteristics	To-Be Charactersitics
ABC segmentation of items	▶ ABC segmentation used by inventory planners only ▶ Service level targets by ABC not reviewed with major stakeholders (i.e., marketing, sales, or the supply chain) ▶ Desired service level is the only target segmented by ABC	▶ ABC segmentation used by all planning groups to help focus efforts ▶ Segmented service level targets to be agreed upon by key stakeholders, and impact on total expected service level to be aligned with the overall target ▶ Segment other supply chain metric targets (FA, turns, etc.)
Inventory policy and safety stock	▶ Undefined inventory policy ▶ Safety stock developed based on desired service level segmented on ABC ▶ A floor of 30 days of sales has been applied to all items, no matter their ABC segment ▶ Safety stock targets are lowered under capacity-constrained conditions	▶ Complete inventory policy, including safety stock settings, replenishment models by segment, and target cycle and safety stock levels, as well as procedures to support stock out conditions and excess inventory ▶ Define appropriate replenishment model for items that do not fit a typical statistical SS model (as opposed to setting an arbitrary inventory floor of 30 days)
Inventory projections	Time-consuming manual process performed in Excel—rarely reconciles to financials	▶ Automated process for managing locations in SAP ▶ Manual adjustments may be required for breakdown of locations not included in SAP—more granular levels
Master plan adjustment	Inventory impact of master planning changes is difficult to calculate and requires manual efforts	▶ Impact of master planning changes on inventory levels automatically calculated ▶ What-if analyses supported in a designated simulation environment

Table 3.11 Characteristics of Inventory and Deployment Planning Processes

3.7.7 Rough-Cut Production Planning Characteristics

Rough-cut production planning will be done at the global level and will be constraint-based with tighter integration with the plants to optimize the use of global production capacity. Some of the key characteristics of current and future states related to inventory and deployment planning are listed in Table 3.12.

Category	As-Is Characteristics	To-Be Charactersitics
Unconstrained, rough-cut production plan	▶ Rough-cut production plan unconstrained ▶ Capacity constraints manually evaluated in Excel or Access	▶ Unconstrained and constrained master planning views will be available in APO-SNP ▶ Constrained production plans calculated using APO-SNP capacity leveling
Level loading	▶ Performed outside SAP, and in Access or Excel	▶ Automated process through using APO-SNP
Prioritization	▶ When out of capacity, differentiating between a planned order for demand or sales, or between an item on backorder or not, is time consuming and challenging	▶ Visibility to planned orders for demand versus sales available through an SAP pegging functionality ▶ Customer segmentation is possible
Performance management	▶ Several metrics are measured differently across business units. ▶ Some metrics are manually tracked in Excel or Access	▶ Consistent metrics across business units ▶ Automated metric and report development

Table 3.12 Characteristics of Rough-Cut Production Planning Process

3.7.8 Planning Organization

Supply chain planning organizations are typically organized either by planning function/process or product group. Figure 3.12 shows the two options in which both the options report to the supply chain manager. In the first option, the organizations are divided by planning functions (i.e., demand and supply), while in the other, by product family. The company needs to evaluate its market operating model and accountability/responsibilities and judge which option works best for both internal and external business partners.

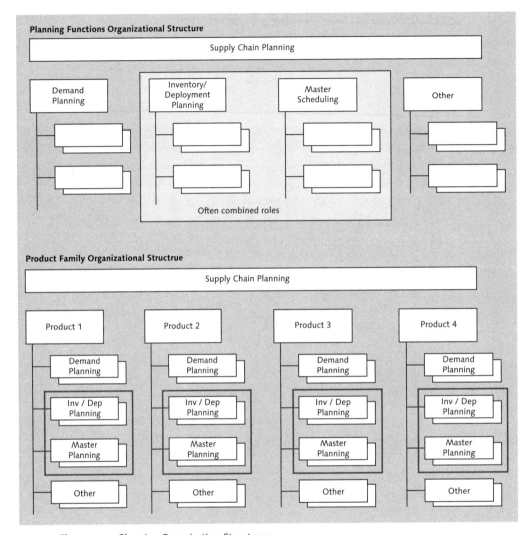

Figure 3.12 Planning Organization Structures

The consumer goods company evaluated both the options, and the advantages and disadvantages are listed in Table 3.13.

Planning Organization	Advantages	Disadvantages
Planning function: supply chain team structured by demand planning and supply planning	▸ Focus: ensures that adequate attention is devoted to each planning function and horizon. ▸ Skill set alignment: very different skill sets required across planning functions. ▸ Continuous improvement: easier to deploy process and technology improvements.	▸ Risk of sub-optimization: silo'd approach to supply chain planning. Optimizing by function may sub-optimize for the whole. ▸ Fragmented accountability: lack of end-to-end inventory and service accountability.
Product family: integrated supply chain team doing both demand and supply planning	▸ Accountability: single point of accountability for inventory and service levels by product group. ▸ Coordination: high degree of coordination across planning functions. ▸ Awareness: drives comprehensive understanding of supply chain functions and end-to-end planning process.	▸ Loss of synergies: where there are common production assets, suppliers, etc., there tends to be a loss of synergies as the total supply chain is not optimized. ▸ Loss of focus: integrated teams tend to focus disproportionate attention on the near-term horizon (fighting fires), which compromises the quality of the long-term forecast. ▸ Greater process variances: increased likelihood of non-standard processes/tools. ▸ Inhibits knowledge transfer: limits best practice sharing and slows continuous improvement.

Table 3.13 Planning Organization Options: Planning Function Versus Product Family

The business case study demonstrated how the supply chain transformation project was initiated with the key guiding principles for the company to be demand driven, aligned with its goals, and integrated.

3.8   Summary

Global supply chain planning is a critical capability to enable a company's operations strategy and to deliver exceptional customer service. The implementation of

SAP APO is initiated by supply chain transformation initiatives with business end goals/objectives in mind. This chapter presented how the global template can be deployed using the accelerator's built-in the template. The majority of the project required a solid business case to get the funding approved.

In the next chapter, we'll get you started with preparing basic SAP APO functionality in APO-DP and APO-SNP. You'll find the basic steps needed to set up these functions in your system. We use ABC Technology to highlight business requirements, current challenges in the planning cycle, and how SAP APO can help. You'll also learn about the planning framework that business planners can use to analyze demand and supply balancing via exception management.

In this chapter, you'll learn the basic planning functions that are performed in SAP APO and the basic customization and master data modeling steps to start creating your supply chain plan.

4   Preparing for Basic Planning Functionality in SAP APO

In this chapter, you'll learn the basic customization steps for APO Demand Planning (APO-DP) and the Supply Network Planning (APO-SNP) modules in SAP APO. While this task is usually performed by someone in the role of a solutions designer in the SAP APO project, this chapter also aims to help business users understand the foundation on which the SAP APO standard configurations are performed.

This chapter will help you to better understand the mathematical calculations the SAP APO system performs during the planning run. We'll also explain the APO-DP forecasting models and APO-SNP modeling objects that prepare the system for the basic planning task structure performed during the weekly planning cycle. Understanding the basic foundation will also enable you to help enhance a company's SAP APO functionality for any change in future business models.

As shown in the mind map for this chapter (see Figure 4.1) we will be discussing how we set up basic planning functionality in SAP APO. Besides highlighting the customization steps in APO-DP and APO-SNP, we'll also discuss how to set up forecasting models and a supply chain model as part of SAP APO functionality.

In this chapter, we'll delve further into using our business case study, ABC Technology, as an example. While ABC Technology is focused on both manufacturing and distribution, the company's primary focus is on inventory control and goods distribution. We'll first get started with understanding the basic planning tasks that a supply chain planner must go through with SAP APO, and see how these tasks fit into ABC Technology's methods.

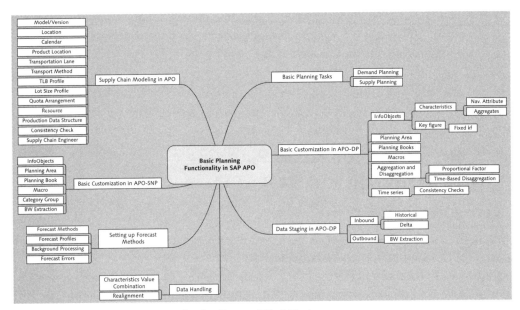

Figure 4.1 Learning Points for the Chapter (Mind Map)

4.1 Basic Planning Tasks

The goal of the supply chain planner role is to balance the demand and supply plan for their group of products. The planner performs these planning tasks on a weekly or monthly cycle.

Supply chain planning is an iterative process that consists of creating an unconstraint demand plan using the forecasting process and then optimizing various supply plans in the form of procurement, production, replenishment, and distribution plans. SAP APO is the best tool to help with these tasks, as it's a decision-support tool that outputs planning results for the supply chain planner to evaluate analysis and make any necessary changes.

> **Example**
>
> ABC Technology wants to use SAP APO to plan its laptop, desktop, and monitor products. Since it manufactures and distributes the products in North America, the company plans to use SAP APO Demand Planning for forecasting, and Supply Network Planning for replenishment and distribution supply plans. The company is challenged with providing custom products to its customer base on the shortest possible lead time in order to keep its next-day delivery value proposition.

In the following sections, we'll review the planning tasks performed by the demand planner and supply planner in the SAP APO landscape and identify the business planner's interactions with SAP APO. Understanding the planner's routine business activities is important for the SAP solution designer when it comes to designing the system per business requirements.

4.1.1 Demand Planning

The planning tasks in SAP APO are always based on algorithm programs, which the business planner can validate and adjust, if necessary. Figure 4.2 shows the schematic activity flow for Demand Planning in SAP APO.

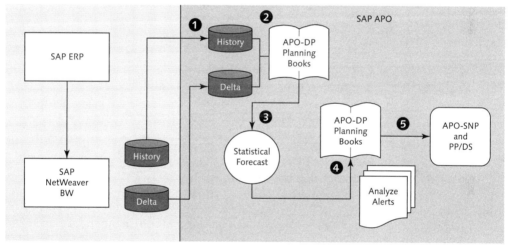

Figure 4.2 Demand Planning Tasks

Historical sales orders are required for the statistical forecasting process (❶). The history is primarily staged from SAP NetWeaver Business Warehouse (BW). SAP NetWeaver BW extracts the sales orders from SAP ERP using Logistics Information System (LIS) structures in SAP ERP. As shown in the architecture in the figure, there will be two data loads: the initial historical data for the last two or three years, and the post–go-live weekly delta loads on actual sales orders recorded in the past week. Some companies might include a custom filter in SAP NetWeaver BW to segregate sales orders based on order types for business reasons. This task is primarily performed by the company IT group; no user involvement takes place.

SAP APO has a small, built-in SAP NetWeaver BW component that can be used to stage the data coming from SAP NetWeaver BW. The data flows from SAP APO's SAP NetWeaver BW component to the SAP liveCache time series planning books (❷). The planner validates the historical data and might perform manual adjustments to the history. Once the history is adjusted, it becomes the baseline for statistical forecast calculation (❸).

Next, the baseline history serves as input for the forecasting run, which can either be set to run a model automatically or based on user definitions. In the case of the automatic forecasting model, the system selects the model that gives the lowest forecast error (for example, MAPE). Alternatively, the user may select defined forecast models for his or her product or product groups based on pre-analysis. The result of the forecasting run is analyzed by a demand planner in the APO-DP planning book (❹).

The demand planner can analyze the forecasting run by looking at the forecast errors, which are identified by the forecast model that's selected by a system or business user. Also, an alert can be set up to compare the forecast with the average sales from the last three months and provide an alert if the proposed forecast is more than, say, 25% of that value. The planner again has the ability to override the system's proposal with some judgmental adjustments. Also in this activity, the sales and marketing team enters the promotions to close the gap on the demand plan and yearly operational plan (i.e., budget).

The final demand plan then undergoes discussion in the monthly forecast review meetings before the monthly sales and operations plan. Once the supply chain and sales, marketing, and finance teams reach a consensus on the final demand plan during the business meeting, a BW snapshot is taken of the plan and released to supply planning to check on supply feasibility (❺). The release of the demand plan to supply planning can be either to one of the SAP APO functionalities (APO-SNP or PP/DS) or the SAP ERP-MRP system directly, based on procurement planning design selection.

> **Example**
>
> ABC Technology distributes its products from three distribution centers where customer orders are captured. SAP APO will perform forecasting at the location product level for the next twelve months, in monthly buckets. ABC Technology uses the combination of defined forecasting (exponential, seasonal, and linear) and automatic forecasting models, the latter being used for products for which the individual forecasting is difficult to identify.

ABC Technology's demand planner reviews the forecast and makes any adjustments in SAP APO planning books for the short horizon to better reflect market demand situations.

4.1.2 Supply Network Planning

Once the final demand plan is released to supply planning (SAP APO Supply Network Planning, in our business case), the supply planner starts his or her planning activities. The role of the supply planner is not only to check the supply feasibility of the unconstraint demand plan, but also to formulate a feasible procurement, distribution, and production plan. The supply planner communicates with sourcing units (e.g., factories and vendors) to check the feasibility of proposed plans. The supply plan is further discussed in the monthly sales and operations meeting. The supply planner needs to check both the material availability and capacity to supply the demand.

Figure 4.3 shows the schematic activity flow for SNP in SAP APO. The major activity for the business in these processes would be analyzing the SAP APO result and fine tuning the master data for any parameter corrections. The figure illustrates the following system flow:

❶ The supply chain activities require supply chain modeling before planning begins. Using transportation lanes and other SAP APO master data elements, the business user models their supply chain in SAP APO. The modeling process includes setting up the supply network and relevant master data settings for the SAP APO solvers to calculate an accurate supply plan. The core master data is transferred from SAP ERP using SAP APO Core Interface (CIF) technology. The supply chain data objects are further discussed in Section 4.7. Also defined within the supply chain model is the target inventory for each location in the supply network.

❷ Besides the master data, transaction code data is also activated via CIF between SAP ERP and SAP APO. All the SAP APO-relevant receipts, demands, and stocks are exchanged between the two systems in real time. There is a standard CIF Compare/Reconcile consistency report the IT support group needs to run periodically to ensure that all the transactional data is consistent between the SAP ERP and SAP APO systems.

153

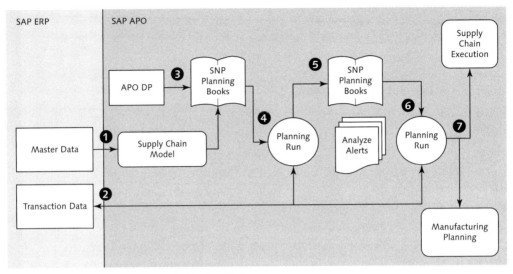

Figure 4.3 Supply Network Planning Tasks

❸ The unconstrained demand plan is released from APO-DP at the location product level. The planner analyzes the supply situation before the nightly run and makes any required adjustments (for example, increasing capacity).

❹ The nightly planning run touches the complete supply network and plans the safety stock, replenishment, distribution, and production plans. Depending on the business requirements, the first planning run can consider infinite or finite capacities.

❺ The supply planner analyzes the supply situation again and reacts based on supply alerts (for example, stock outs) to focus on items that need critical action. The planner may accept the system proposals or override with his or her own feasible plan for the sales and operations planning meeting.

❻ A second planning run is performed to re-balance the demand and supply across the network. Any excess inventory will trigger alerts for stock balancing. This planning run may run on finite capacity and constraint environment. A monthly snapshot may be taken at this stage by SAP NetWeaver BW.

❼ The final supply plan is published to the manufacturing, distribution, and procurement teams for supply chain execution. The planner may use the Transport

Load Builder (TLB) in APO-SNP to ensure that the proposed stock transport order and purchase order meet the load capacity and vendor minimums.

Example

ABC Technology's network consists of manufacturing and distribution facilities. The supply planner uses the APO-SNP planning book to review the demand and supply situations across the network following the nightly planning run. Though the supply planning is done at the weekly bucket level, the planner closely monitors the inventory levels across the network to ensure that customer orders are being fulfilled and products are produced and replenished on time.

Having studied the planner's basic tasks, we'll now move on to discuss the steps you need to follow to configure the SAP APO functionality for both APO-DP and APO-SNP.

4.2   Basic Customization in SAP APO Demand Planning

This section explains the basic customization steps for SAP APO Demand Planning (APO-DP), as well as the background information and basic definitions you need to get started. The customization steps consist of setting up a planning object structure for planning based on the product, customer, and time characteristics; identifying the key figures (for example, forecast, sales orders, promotions); and setting up the planning book and macro (used for mathematical calculation) for both background and interactive planning.

Example

ABC Technology would like to design an SAP APO planning book with different product, customer, and time characteristics. Some examples of these characteristics are product, product family, brand, customer, customer group, and calendar month. The key figures display the planning data for the identified characteristics. Some examples of the key figures are historical sales orders, forecast, and sales and marketing promotions.

The customization of APO-DP starts with a data modeling exercise in identifying InfoObjects (characteristics and key figures), which is explained in next sub-sections. The solution designer performs the customization, taking into account business requirements from demand planner business users.

4.2.1 InfoObjects

InfoObjects represent the smallest selling unit in SAP NetWeaver Business Warehouse. They define the business process and information we are seeking. An example of an InfoObject is customer, product, or historical sales order quantity. Before we start customizing InfoObjects, you need to understand some background information about them. First of all, there are five different types of InfoObjects:

► **Characteristics**
Some examples of characteristics are customer, product, material group, customer group, and location. These represent the planning levels and consist of customer and product attributes. One or more characteristics make up the key to the data record for demand planning. Characteristics are definitions for describing the business object, not the data.

► **Key figures**
Key figures represent the numeric information for the business object. There are different types of key figures: quantity, amount, date, time, number, and integer. Some examples of key figures are selling price and actual sales order quantity.

► **Time characteristics**
Time characteristics describe time reference for the business event. Some of the standard SAP time characteristics are calendar day (0CALDAY), calendar week (0CALWEEK), calendar month (0CALMONTH), calendar quarter (0CALQUARTER), calendar year (0CALYEAR), fiscal year (0FISCYEAR), and fiscal period (0FISCPER).

► **Unit characteristics**
Unit characteristics are used for providing a unit of measure for the defined key figure.

► **Technical characteristics**
Technical characteristics are used for technical purposes. An example is a request ID for storing the data load information.

These InfoObjects are translated with the data modeling, which identifies the product, customer hierarchy, and time dimensions to be used in the SAP APO planning object structure. You should always understand the dimensions of the characteristics to be used in the SAP APO database model for which you'd like to perform demand planning before you start customizing, so we'll start with a data modeling exercise.

Data Modeling Exercise

The data model defines the customer, product, or time characteristics on which we want to divide the planning data in the SAP APO planning book. As Figure 4.4 shows, we start by drawing a three-dimensional axis with product, customer, and time dimensions.

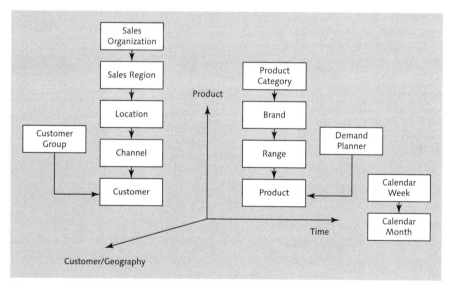

Figure 4.4 InfoObject Data Modeling

Figure 4.4 shows how an ABC Technology business planner would separate his or her data for planning and reporting purposes in SAP APO. Examples of product characteristics are product category, brand, range, and product, while customer characteristics are sales organization, sales region, location, channel, and customer. The time dimensions are calendar week and month. The planner can also identify characteristics to be used for selection and navigation but not for planning. This type of characteristic is called a *navigational attribute*. An example of a navigational attribute is the demand planner code as part of product characteristics, and the customer group for customer characteristics.

Customization Steps

Now you're ready to start creating InfoObjects.

First, create the InfoObject in the Administrator Workbench in SAP APO via the menu path SPRO • SAP REFERENCE IMG • ADVANCED PLANNING AND OPTIMIZATION • SUPPLY CHAIN PLANNING • DEMAND PLANNING • BASIC SETTINGS • DATA WAREHOUSING WORKBENCH.

In the left part of the screen of the DATA WAREHOUSING WORKBENCH, in the MODELING section, click on INFOOBJECTS. Right-click the node INFOOBJECTS and choose CREATE INFOAREA. An *InfoArea* is used for storing the characteristics and key figure catalogs relevant to the data model.

Tips & Tricks

The BW Administrator Workbench can also be accessed via Transaction RSA1.

Once you've created the InfoArea, right-click on the INFOAREA node to CREATE INFOOBJECT CATALOG. The InfoObject Catalog is used to catalog the InfoObjects, which have been created as characteristics, time characteristics, or key figures. As Figure 4.5 shows, create two separate catalogs for characteristics and key figures. The catalog is used for storing project-specific Demand Planning InfoObjects for both characteristics and key figures. Per our business case study, you need to input the product, customer, and time characteristics into the characteristics catalog, and the key figures into a separate catalog. You can maintain SAP standard characteristics and key figures starting with 9A prefix in the catalogs by directly inputting the technical field. The standard 9A prefix denotes characteristics (for example, 9AMATNR and 9ALOCNO) and key figures (for example, 9ADFCST) that are provided by SAP.

Create new InfoObjects for the required characteristics and key figures by right-clicking the catalog, selecting the option CREATE INFO OBJECT, and maintaining a technical name and description. Always select BW InfoObject to be used for data staging and extraction process. Some business examples of characteristics are product group, customer group, product, customer, sales organization, location, and material group, which all help to separate planning data into different dimensions. As

Figure 4.5 shows, we can either directly input the InfoObject or create a new one. You can access the InfoObjects via Transaction RSD1 for any further maintenance.

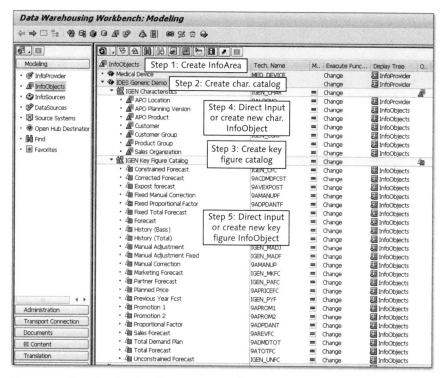

Figure 4.5 Steps for Creating Characteristics and Key Figures InfoObjects

APO-DP offers functionality in the form of a *navigational attribute,* which can be used as a characteristic in the planning book for navigation, analysis, and reporting purposes. The ABC Technology business planner can use the characteristic *Demand Planner* to segregate products for planning and the customer group, as another characteristic, for the purpose of customer segmentation. You will need to set up the navigational attribute, which helps define the selection and navigation criteria without defining them as characteristics in the demand planning structure. The first three steps (see Figure 4.6) are:

1. Assign an attribute to the characteristics. The characteristics can be accessed via Transaction RSD1 or in the BW Administrator workbench (Transaction RSA1) InfoObject folder. Double-click on the characteristics name to display the details for maintenance.

2. Next, input the characteristic that needs to serve as the navigational attribute. As shown in the figure, the navigational attribute for the customer is the customer group. Once maintained, click the NAVIGATIONAL ATTRIBUTE icon to switch on the navigational attribute.

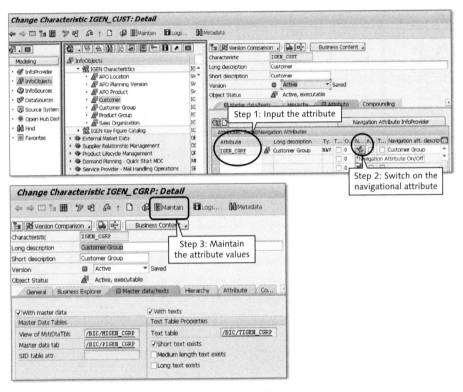

Figure 4.6 Setting up a Navigational Attribute to the Characteristics

3. The last step is to maintain the master data of the valid combination value in the table, as Figure 4.7 shows.

> **Note**
>
> You can refer to SAP OSS Note 413526 for the list of comparisons between navigational attributes and characteristics.

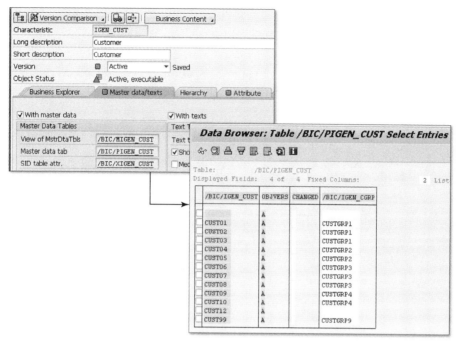

Figure 4.7 Navigational Master Data Maintenance with Valid Combinations

4.2.2 Planning Object Structure

Now that we have created the InfoObjects in APO-DP, your next step is to create the planning object structure, which will define the characteristics we want to model in the planning books. The planning object structure contains the characteristics required for planning and stored in SAP liveCache. The characteristics determine the planning level and how the data can be stored. In our business case study, ABC Technology has elected to use the most commonly used characteristics from the product and customer hierarchies.

The key here is to select all the characteristics that will be used for planning purposes. The activation of a planning object structure results in the creation of an internally generated InfoCube in which the characteristic combinations for the planning object structure are stored. Follow these steps to create the structure:

1. Create a planning object structure via SPRO • SAP REFERENCE IMG • ADVANCED PLANNING AND OPTIMIZATION • SUPPLY CHAIN PLANNING • DEMAND PLANNING • BASIC SETTINGS • S&DP ADMINISTRATION.

2. Click the PLANNING AREAS tree structure, and then choose PLNG OBJECT STRUC-
   TURES to change the path from PLANNING AREA to PLANNING OBJECT STRUCTURE.

3. Transfer all the relevant characteristics defined earlier in InfoObject from the
   right side to the left, as shown in Figure 4.8. Clicking NAVIGATION ATTRIBUTES
   displays all the attributes associated with the planning characteristics.

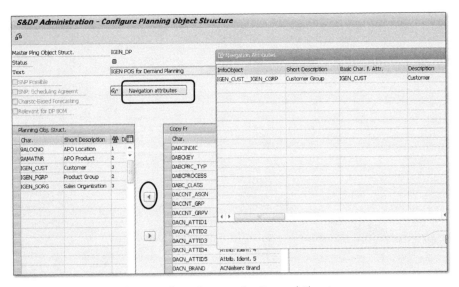

Figure 4.8 Setting up Planning Object Structure for Demand Planning

Create Aggregates

Within the Planning Object Structure, we can also define *aggregates*. The primary
purpose of the aggregate is to improve system performance while accessing the
planning data. This configuration will help the business planner access data faster
in the planning books with large selection.

Example

ABC Technology will want to define aggregates, so the demand planner has to access a
number of stock-keeping units (SKUs) for planning. The use of aggregates serves as an
indexing of the demand planning data.

The planning data is stored, in addition to the detailed level, in the aggregate levels as well. Although the use of aggregates consumes little more SAP liveCache space in memory, the planning data load access is faster with the aggregate mechanism. This is because there is no aggregation happening after you load your selection. The system knows an aggregate exists and hence loads it directly.

To create an aggregate, right-click the planning object structure and select CREATE AGGREGATE. Figure 4.9 shows an example of an activated aggregate. With this functionality, the ABC Technology planner can now use the aggregate characteristics as a selection profile when accessing large volumes of data in the SAP APO planning book.

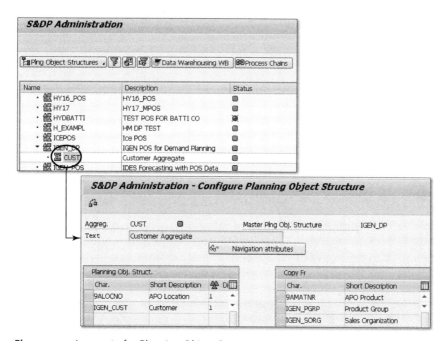

Figure 4.9 Aggregate for Planning Object Structure

> **Note**
>
> Refer to SAP OSS Note 503363 for more information on the use of aggregates in planning object structures.

4.2.3 Planning Area

A planning area is the central data structure in APO-DP. It lists all the characteristics (i.e., the planning object structure) and contains a collection of key figures to be used in the planning process. You can connect the planning area with an SAP NetWeaver BW data mart to send the historical data to APO-DP. Key figures for planning and their disaggregation types are defined for a planning area.

Before commencing the configuration of the planning area, we need to define the fiscal year variant and the storage bucket profile, which will later be assigned to the planning area. Once the business users start using the SAP APO system, more characteristics and key figures might be needed in the planning area to offer more flexibility in the planning process. These additions require deactivation of the current planning area and possible loss of planning data. For this reason, a backup of demand planning is kept either in SAP APO's internal SAP NetWeaver BW system or the SAP NetWeaver BW system to retrieve the original planning data. This contingency is also built during the system upgrade when the planning areas are deactivated and the SAP liveCache system is brought down. As a best practice, the planning data backup is routinely scheduled every month.

Define the Fiscal Year Variant

Many companies use the fiscal year variant for financial reporting purposes. To align the finance estimates with the planning volume, it would be ideal to use the fiscal year variant for the calculation. The fiscal year variant is used to determine the fiscal year, how many posting periods are available in a year, and which dates constitute the end of each period. It is recommended that the fiscal year be defined for a longer period of time than the horizon defined in the planning books.

> **Example**
>
> ABC Technology would like to plan for the next rolling twenty-four months using the last two years' historical data. For this reason, if planning is done one year back and one year ahead in the planning book, it is recommended that the fiscal variant be defined two years in the past and two years into the future.

The fiscal year variant has to be updated annually at the end of each fiscal year to reflect the periods of the succeeding years. To do this, follow the menu path SPRO • SAP REFERENCE IMG • ADVANCED PLANNING AND OPTIMIZATION • SUPPLY CHAIN PLANNING • DEMAND PLANNING • BASIC SETTINGS • MAINTAIN FISCAL YEAR VARIANT.

Next, create a storage bucket profile, which defines how the system stores the data created by APO-DP or APO-SNP. You define the storage bucket profile for a specific number of periods; thus, it is recommended that the periods be updated periodically. The fiscal variant is attached within the storage bucket profile. The customization path is SPRO • SAP REFERENCE IMG • ADVANCED PLANNING AND OPTIMIZATION • SUPPLY CHAIN PLANNING • DEMAND PLANNING • BASIC SETTINGS • DEFINE STORAGE BUCKET PROFILE. Figure 4.10 shows an example of a storage bucket profile.

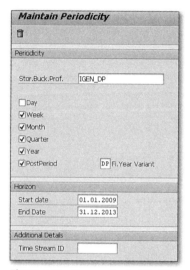

Figure 4.10 Storage Bucket Profile

Once we have defined the fiscal year variant and the storage bucket profile, we can input them into the planning area, as described in the next subsection.

Configure the Planning Area

The planning area combines the characteristics (from the planning object structure) and various key figures to further configure the planning. The planning book is where the business users perform planning analysis and adjustments to formulate a demand plan. To set up the planning area, follow these steps:

1. To customize the planning area, follow the menu path SPRO • SAP REFERENCE IMG • ADVANCED PLANNING AND OPTIMIZATION • SUPPLY CHAIN PLANNING • DEMAND PLANNING • BASIC SETTINGS • S&DP ADMINISTRATION.

2. Right-click the planning area node and select CREATE PLANNING AREA. In the planning area, specify the following in various tabs:

   ▸ The list of the key figures (created earlier as InfoObjects) to be used for planning, as seen in Figure 4.11 (KEY FIGURE tab)

   ▸ Currency to be used for planning (INFO tab)

   ▸ Unit of measure for planning (INFO tab)

   ▸ Aggregate level on which to data can be stored beside the lowest level to improve performance (AGGREGATE tab)

   ▸ Aggregation and disaggregation rules for the key figures (KEY FIGURE AGGREGATION tab)

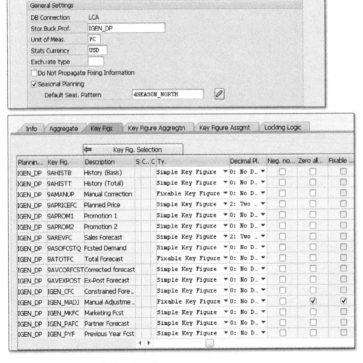

Figure 4.11 Demand Planning Area

In the PLANNING AREA • KEY FIGURE AGGREGATION tab, we can define the aggregation and disaggregation of each key figure by its calculation type and its time-based disaggregation type. In the CALCULATION TYPE field, we can mention if the key figures needs to be marked pro-rata (type S), average (type A), or a reference to a different key figure (type P).

Proportional Factors

As Figure 4.12 shows, while the majority of key figures are marked with calculation type S, the average price key figure is average A, and the manual adjustment is marked P to be based on historical key figure pro rata. Similarly to the calculation type, we maintain time-based disaggregation for defining rules for planning data disaggregation. Some examples of time-based disaggregation are either proportional allocation (type P) or no time-based disaggregation (type N). The time-based disaggregation is of particular interest in business scenarios when the majority of the sales occur during the last week or days of the month. Figure 4.12 shows different calculation and time-based disaggregation types. The main concept here is *proportional factors*. SAP APO uses proportional factors to enable the disaggregation of data down to the lowest level.

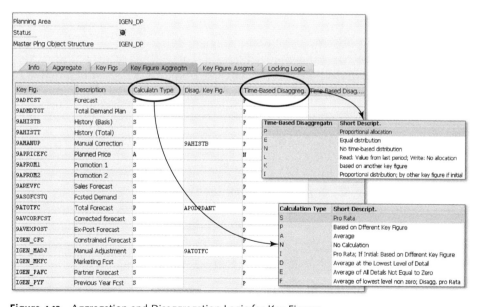

Figure 4.12 Aggregation and Disaggregation Logic for Key Figures

ABC Technology plans to calculate the proportional factors and use the calculation as a reference for the statistical forecast key figure. This will ensure that the forecast is placed at the correct location based on the historical pattern. ABC Technology has two locations where the historical sales were split at 40% and 60% for a specific month of the year. When the forecast is calculated for the same future month, the system takes the same percentage and disaggregates the forecast figures based on those values.

For some of the other product groups, the ABC Technology planner would like to have the ability to override the system-generated proportional factors and just use the time-based disaggregation to reflect the stocking policy across various tree locations in SAP APO. In this business scenario, the business planner would maintain the location-proportional factors offline and manually upload them to the planning book. The proportional factors can be generated based on actual sales history as well as manually adjusted by the demand planner.

It is recommended that the automatic generation of proportional factors be done every book month to take into account any changes in the proportional factors based on the previous book month's actual sales.

APO-DP's method of aggregation and disaggregation is called a "consistent" planning model (Figure 4.13). Using the lowest level of actual data (usually the product-location level), it generates proportional values throughout its planning network (characteristic value combinations).

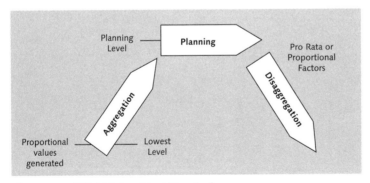

Figure 4.13 SAP APO Consistent Planning[1]

---

1   Demand Planning functionalities, *help.sap.com*

The system uses proportional factors to distribute its products nationally. The proportional factor can be overridden by the demand planner based on their experience with the product. ABC Technology would want to change its proportional factors based on the distribution centers (DC) stocking policy. These changes might be initiated due to strategic reasons or slow-moving inventory in one part of the supply network. Changing a key figure value anywhere within this planning network automatically triggers a proportional re-propagation throughout the network, which was calculated earlier. You can drill down or drill up through one or more levels. There are two main calculation types here for proportional factor calculation:

▸ **Pro rata of planning data**
The data is disaggregated according to the distribution ratio that the system derives dynamically from the existing planned data. The proportional factors are not used with this disaggregation type.

▸ **Proportional factors**
The proportional factors are percentage based and held in the key figure APOD-PDANT. Figure 4.12 shows an example for forecasting a key figure, which uses the APODPDANT key figure to disaggregate. ABC Technology would like to use the most recent year's historical proportional factor for the same bucket as this year's forecast key figure.

Time-Based Disaggregation
Besides the calculation type, we also maintain time-based disaggregation. A scenario for time-based disaggregation may occur when ABC Technology has products that always peak at month-end sales during the last week of the month. In this situation, we can define the time-based disaggregation key figure (Type K) in the planning area configuration, as shown previously in Figure 4.12, in the KEY FIGURE AGGREGATION tab, which defines the percentage split of the monthly forecast into weekly buckets. The business planner maintains the percentage, and the system uses this key figure percentage during the disaggregation of the forecast from monthly to weekly buckets. The ABC Technology planner can maintain the proportional factors and time-based disaggregation factor offline in Microsoft Excel and use the "upload" function to load it into the demand planning book.

> **Planning Area Key Figure Settings**
>
> In a production environment, it might be necessary to change the key figure settings to support new business requirements. An example would be if ABC Technology would like to integrate new proportional factor logic with the planning solution. A new feature (as of SAP SCM 7.0 onwards) in the planning area offers the flexibility to change the key figure setting without de-initializing the planning area using report /SAPAPO/ TS_LCM_PAREA_CHANGE2. However, note that de-initializing the planning area leads to a potential loss of all time series data for the planning area.

Once the planning area is configured, we next need to design a *planning book*. The planning book is where most of the calculation occurs and provides information to business users. There are usually two sets of planning books—one for business planners and the other for performing background calculations.

4.2.4 Planning Book

Your next step is to customize the planning book for your business requirements in order to define the planning information content and layout of the interactive planning screen. The planning book serves as the frontend interface to the ABC Technology demand planner users. The business planners would use the planning book for different purposes. While the primary goal would be analyzing the forecast result based on history, the planner can also remove historical outliers and perform interactive forecasting directly in the planning book. The key figure in the planning book may also provide demand planning accuracy calculations for the planner to analyze.

Planning books are highly customizable, and the screen can be designed to suit individual planning tasks. Besides having different time bucket views, the planning book can be designed to have multiple data views based on the information requirements. Each planning book can have multiple data views, giving the user flexibility to view and analyze planning information in different angles. Some examples of data views are views for historical data, key figures, and forecasting-related key figures. A typical planning book looks like what is shown in Figure 4.14, with the selection variant on the left section and the planning view section in middle. There are additional setting toolbars for downloading and uploading planning books, pivot sorting, and more.

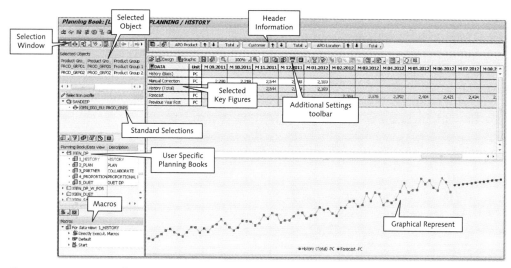

Figure 4.14 SAP APO Planning Book View

Create the Time Bucket Profile

Before creating a planning book, you need to create the *time bucket profile* to be used for the planning book. A time bucket profiles defines the historical or future time horizon for APO-DP and helps businesses to visualize their planning data in the planning book. With this step, you define which time buckets can be used for planning, how many periods of each time bucket are used, and the sequence in which the time buckets appear in the planning table.

> **Example**
>
> Since the ABC Technology planner would like to visualize planning data monthly, quarterly, and yearly, we can define time bucket profiles and switch them accordingly in the planning book. As the default for the planning book, we will assign twenty-four months of time bucket profiles in monthly buckets.

The first and second planning bucket profiles determine how the data (history and future) is viewed. Using the time bucket profile, the business can determine the historical period it would like to view and the future period for viewing forecasts. It is not determining the forecast horizon. The third planning bucket's profile is used to determine the number of forecast value periods released from APO-DP to APO-SNP. To customize the time bucket profile, follow the path SPRO • SAP

REFERENCE IMG • ADVANCED PLANNING AND OPTIMIZATION • SUPPLY CHAIN PLAN-
NING • DEMAND PLANNING • BASIC SETTINGS • DEFINE PLANNING BUCKET PROFILE,
or use Transaction /SAPAPO/TR30.

An example of a planning time bucket profile is shown in Figure 4.15, in which
the planning bucket is split between weekly and monthly buckets. This allows
the business users to view some portion of the data on the weekly buckets for
operational planning and the rest of the data on monthly buckets for tactical and
operational planning.

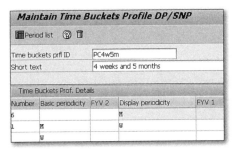

Figure 4.15 Planning Time Bucket Profile

Custom Planning Books

The interactive Planning Book Wizard (Transaction /SAPAPO/SDP8B) is available if
you need to create custom planning books. We'll walk through the planning book
creation process in the following steps:

1. Type in the new planning book name and click CREATE.

2. Input a text description of the planning book, assign a planning area, and select
   the forecasting method and proportional maintenance (Figure 4.16—❶). Click
   CONTINUE to move to the next tab.

3. Select the key figures required in the planning book for both viewing and calculations purposes. Drag and drop from the PLANNING AREA section to the
   PLANNING BOOK section (Figure 4.16—❷). Click CONTINUE to move to the next
   tab.

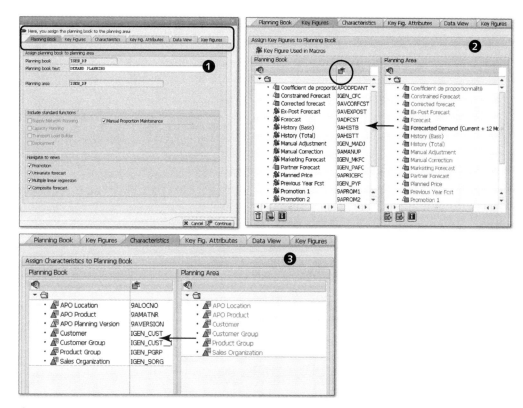

Figure 4.16 Demand Planning Book Wizard (1/2)

4. Select the planning book characteristics (used for slice and dice) required in the planning book by dragging and dropping them from the right section to the left section (see Figure 4.16 — ❸). Click CONTINUE to move to the next tab.

5. Change the key figure description to make it more easily understandable for business users. Create auxiliary key figures directly, if required for calculations (see Figure 4.17). Click CONTINUE to move to the next tab.

6. Input the time bucket profile(s) for both the past and future horizon visibility in the planning book. Select TABLE 2 if you need to design a two-tabular section in the planning book for business users (for example, if they need to view two sections to compare the volume and dollar values; see Figure 4.17 — ❹/❺). Click CONTINUE to move to the next tab. In this case, the planner can have two split planning book tables. While the top table shows the planning data in volume, the bottom table might give the planning data in dollar values.

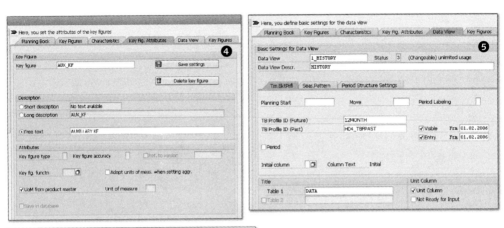

Figure 4.17 Demand Planning Book Wizard (2/2)

7. In the final step, arrange the key figure sequence you want the business users to visualize in the planning book (see Figure 4.17—❻). In this step, the solution designer needs to consult with business users to identify the layout of the key figures in the planning book. Click COMPLETE to finalize the planning book creation.

Our next step is to look at macros, which are embedded in the planning book for either mathematical calculation or alert generations.

4.2.5 Macros

A *macro* is an important component for facilitating planning tasks in a planning book. Both simple and complex macros can be designed. Some examples of simple macros are a calculation based on key figures, changing the cell color in a planning book, and copying a key figure value from one row to the next. An example of a complex macro is the generation of alerts or pop-up messages when a cell falls below a certain threshold. The macros can be triggered either interactively (i.e., manually in a planning book) or via background batch processing.

SAP APO provides a tool called the Macro Builder, which allows you to create your own custom macros to perform a variety of functions, such as mathematical, statistical, logical, and planning calculations. Macros are a prerequisite to perform some of the simple and complex mathematical calculation in APO-DP. There are no standard APO-DP macros that you can use out of the box, as the majority of planning books are custom. SAP provides some examples of macro functions, which can be used as templates for building macros.

To access the Macro Builder, follow the menu path SPRO • SAP REFERENCE IMG • ADVANCED PLANNING AND OPTIMIZATION • SUPPLY CHAIN PLANNING • DEMAND PLANNING • BASIC SETTINGS • DEFINE MACROS, or use Transaction /SAPAPO/ADVM. As seen in Figure 4.18, the Macro Builder has different screen areas, which we'll discuss in the following subsections.

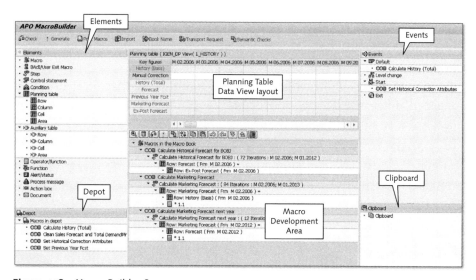

Figure 4.18 Macro Builder Screen

Elements

ELEMENTS are the building blocks of macros. You can use the following element options when building your own custom macro:

- MACRO

  Used for macro description and determining the period to be analyzed and whether interactive or mass processing is mentioned. If selected interactively, it allows business users to execute macros from the planning book.

- USER EXIT MACRO

  Used for implementing custom macros in routine code and for building complex logic in ABAP language.

- STEP

  Consists of one or more macro calculations with the number of iterations for each step. The steps need to be structured enough to follow the logic in sequence. Various business calculations can be created in logical sequence with the use of steps.

- CONTROL STATEMENT

  Used with a condition statement to define macro steps and calculations. Conditional statements like `IF` and `ENDIF` are embedded in the macro to draw the business decision tree.

- CONDITION

  Defines logical conditions together with control statements to be used in macro steps and calculations. Used in macros in conjunction with control statements to draw the business decision tree.

- PLANNING TABLE

  Consists of many sub-items for which the result of the macro calculation is assigned either in cells, rows, or columns. Used in macros to assign the calculated value to a particular cell in the planning book.

- OPERATOR/FUNCTIONS

  Arithmetic, statistical, or mathematical calculation to be performed for a specific row. Macros include operators and/or functions to calculate a specific key figure. An example would be using the `COVER_CALC` to calculate the projected days' supply for demand based on the receipt elements.

- ALERT/STATUS

  Writes alerts in the alert monitor and displays the status after the execution of a macro. The macro can execute dynamic and database alerts and write the result in the alert monitor.

▶ PROCESS MESSAGE
Defines the message text and has the system issue a message in response to the alert situation.

▶ ACTION BOX
Allows you to trigger an action that contains a function.

▶ DOCUMENTS
Can be used to trigger email notifications to the user.

Macro Development Area

The MACRO DEVELOPMENT AREA serves as a work area for the solution designer to create macros. Figure 4.19 shows an example of two macros created in the work area by dragging and dropping various elements.

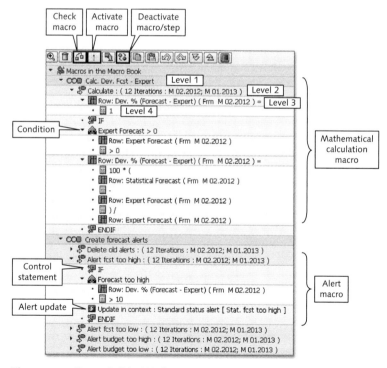

Figure 4.19 Macro Builder Work Area

The first macro creates forecast bias by subtracting the forecast from the actual, while the second macro creates alerts for the deviation based on a percentage factor. Macros are highly customizable and can easily represent some of the business exception rules. As seen in the first macro example, there are four levels defined within a macro:

▶ Level 1 is the macro description.

▶ Level 2 is a step mentioning the time horizon the macro needs to iterate.

▶ Level 3 is a result of the specific key figure from the planning table.

▶ Level 4 is the argument that is often a function or logic for the macro.

Also seen in the example are the use of the control statement, condition statement, alert update, and simple mathematical calculations. Besides the ACTIVATE MACRO icon, the other two icons (CHECK and DEACTIVATE) are helpful to troubleshoot the macro syntax errors during macro writing.

User Exit Macros

User exit macros can be used to code complex business requirements not supported by standard macro functions. Use function module EXIT_/SAPAPO/SAPMMCP6_005, which includes program ZXMUSERU0 where the user exit routine can be written.

Depot

The macros get parked in the DEPOT. Once the macros are activated and saved, they can be parked in the depot by simple drag and drop. Different statuses can be identified with macro status colors:

▶ **Green**
Indicates that the macro has no syntax or logic errors and that the macro is compiled and activated.

▶ **Yellow**
Indicates that the macro has been checked and does not have error but is not activated.

▶ **Red**
The macro is not complete.

Events

Once the macro is developed, it can be executed interactively or in a batch job. Alternatively, the macro can be triggered automatically if assigned as EVENTS in one of four types:

▶ **Default**
Macros are executed when the planner opens the planning book and selects his or her products. The macro is also regenerated once the planner performs some action and saves the result interactively.

▶ **Level change**
Macros are executed when the planner drills up and down in the interactive planning book.

▶ **Start**
Macros are executed when the planner opens the planning book and selects his selection ID.

▶ **Exit**
Macros are executed when the planner saves the plan and exits the planning book.

Process Steps for Creating a Simple APO Macro

The following list provides some simple steps for creating a macro in the Macro Workbench, which is accessed via Transaction /SAPAPO/ADVM.

1. Navigate to the macro development area. Right-click MACROS IN THE MACRO BOOK and then click CREATE NEW MACRO • ADD MACRO.

2. Give a text description of the macro. If the macro can be interactively executed in the planning book, choose any appropriate icon design in the ASSIGNED PUSHBUTTON. Click CONTINUE once done.

3. Right-click the macro name and then choose ADD MACRO ELEMENT • STEP. Give some description of the step. Click CONTINUE once done.

4. Now drag and drop ROW from the PLANNING TABLE in the ELEMENT section to the macro development area. Identify the key figure to be used for the calculation. Click ADOPT once done. If any more key figures are dragged and dropped for calculation (let's say A = B + C), select CREATE IN NEXT LEVEL for key figures B and C.

5. Drag and drop the OPERATOR/FUNCTION to the key figure calculation. Choose INSERT when inserting the mathematical operation + between two key figures B and C. Click CONTINUE once done

6. Click the CONSISTENCY CHECK before activating the macro. Any syntax errors will be identified in this step. If there are no errors, the macro name icon will turn yellow, and we can activate the macro.

7. If the macro needs to be executed every time we open the planning book or exit or change the planning level, drag and drop the macro under the DEFAULT, LEVEL CHANGE, START, EXIT options on the EVENTS section on the Macro Builder.

8. Save the macro by clicking the SAVE icon.

4.2.6 Locking Key Figures

Sometimes a business may need to lock a key figure after planning. There can be various business reasons for locking a key figure to avoid any system calculation override. For example, the ABC Technology demand planner locks the current month plan after it is released in sales and operations. This snapshot helps the company to calculate the forecast accuracy based on the snapshot.

Another business scenario when the locking function can be used is in allocation. This is often used when remaining material quantities need to be redistributed to other products (for example, promotional items) in a product group after the base product volume is fixed. The fixed value should not change if you change other values of key figures at different planning levels. To customize fixing within a key figure, follow these steps (see Figure 4.20):

1. Access the BW Administrator Workbench in SAP APO using Transaction RSA1. Define two key figures—one for the value of the key figure and the other to store the fixing information.

> **Note**
>
> Note that the second key figure type needs to be an SAP APO key figure (not BW). During the key figure creation, we get two options: an APO key figure or BW key figure type. The BW key figure type is used primarily for data staging and extraction process, while the APO key figure type is used only for planning purposes.

2. During the key figure definition, assign the second fixing key figure information on the first key figure info object within the FIXED KEY FIGURE field.

3. Access the planning area administration using Transaction /SAPAPO/MSDP_
ADMIN. In the planning area, the first key figure will have *fixed key figure* type.
This is just a validation step to ensure correct assignment of the key figure.

As a result of these steps, when a user is in the planning book and right-clicks the
Fix Cell option, a padlock icon and a pink font indicate that this value is now
fixed. If you want to automate the functionality, you can fix the key figure with a
macro by making a change in the key figure scope of the change to level fixing in
the Macro Workbench, as shown in Figure 4.20.

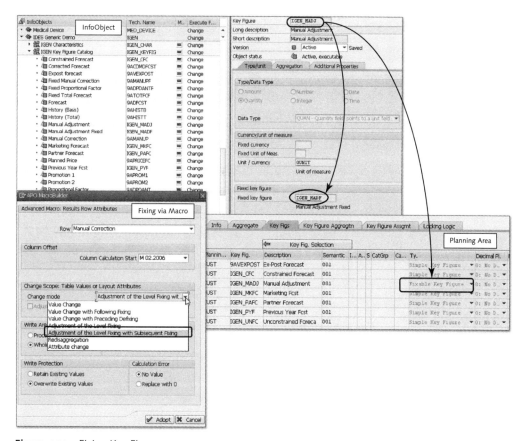

Figure 4.20 Fixing Key Figures

> **Note**
>
> Refer to SAP Notes 643517 and 687074 for more information on how to fix key figures with macros.

4.2.7 Time Series Consistency Checks

Once any new master data is maintained in SAP APO Demand Planning, we need to execute the consistency check and delta sync programs routinely. For data consistency, it is highly recommend that you check the SAP liveCache consistency on a regular basis. Table 4.1 lists all transaction codes you can use to check the time series consistency check in APO-DP.

Transaction	Description
/SAPAPO/TS_LCM_CONS_CHECK	Time series consistency check
/SAPAPO/TS_PSTRU_CONS_CHECK	Planning object structure consistency check
/SAPAPO/TS_LCM_PLOB_DELTA_SYNC	Adjust time series object in planning object structure
/SAPAPO/TS_LCM_REORG	Delete time series and time bucket profiles having no SAP liveCache anchors
/SAPAPO/OM17	Consistency check between SAP liveCache and time series
/SAPAPO/TS_PAREA_INITIALIZE	Initialize time series in planning area

Table 4.1 SAP liveCache Consistency Check Transaction Codes

Once you've performed the basic configuration, it's time to load the historical data via data staging. We'll discuss this in the following section.

4.3 Data Staging for SAP APO Demand Planning

Data staging in SAP APO Demand Planning involves both inbound and outbound flows to SAP APO. The inbound flow is the historical sales order data, which is interfaced from SAP ERP via SAP NetWeaver Business Warehouse. The outbound flow is the data extraction of demand planning data for reporting purposes. The core activities performed during the inbound and outbound staging are as follows:

► **Inbound staging**
Involved in loading the historical sales orders data and delta sales orders after system cutover.

► **Outbound staging**
Involved in the extraction of planning data from SAP liveCache for reporting and archiving purposes in SAP NetWeaver BW.

Figure 4.21 shows the schematic flow diagram for the inbound and outbound flows in SAP APO. The inbound flow starts from SAP ERP Logistics Information System (LIS) extractors for sales orders and deliveries that will load the actual sales orders into the historical InfoCube in SAP NetWeaver BW.

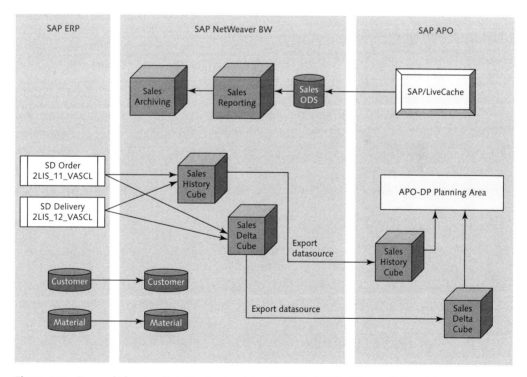

Figure 4.21 Demand Planning Data Staging Involving SAP ERP, SAP NetWeaver BW, and SAP APO

There are two InfoCubes: one for historical sales orders and the other for the delta load after the system has gone live. The material and customer master data are also interfaced with SAP NetWeaver BW to be enriched with additional material and customer attributes (for example, MRP controller or transportation zone), which are used for demand planning. The historical load usually consists of two to three years of sales order history, while the delta load consists of the last week's sales orders. Once the data is available in SAP APO-DP's internal SAP NetWeaver Business Warehouse, it can be transferred to the APO-DP area. The subsequent process creates forecasting for the materials.

The outbound data staging begins once the planning is finalized and can be published to SAP NetWeaver BW for the reporting and archiving processes. The data is extracted from time series SAP liveCache and passed into SAP NetWeaver BW objects. The main reasons to route the data staging via SAP NetWeaver BW are scalability, archiving, and reporting capabilities. The business uses the report for its monthly forecast review meeting and also for sales and operations planning meetings.

Let's see the customization steps for modeling the SAP APO inbound process of loading historical data into SAP APO InfoCube. All the customization steps are done in the BW Administrator Workbench (Transaction RSA1).

1. **Create a source system.**
   A source system indicates the system from which the transactional data and master data originated. Besides the flat file system, there are multiple other source systems available to connect with SAP NetWeaver BW in SAP APO. Examples are SAP NetWeaver BW, DBConnect, and web services. ABC Technology would like to upload the historical sales orders from both the flat file and the SAP NetWeaver BW system. To create a source system, right-click the source system type (file, BW) and select CREATE. Figure 4.22 shows the source system created from the BW Administrator Workbench.

2. **Create a DataSource.**
   After the source system, we create a DataSource. Here we specify the format of the file, which will be uploaded into the InfoCube, so this needs to be in accordance with the file format that has been decided for data upload. The ABC Technology planner has decided to load the historical sales from the flat file. Select the DATASOURCE option from the MODELING section and right-click the unassigned node to select the CREATE DATASOURCE option. Provide the source system name to be linked with the DataSource. Figure 4.22 shows DataSource creation for transactional data (historical sales).

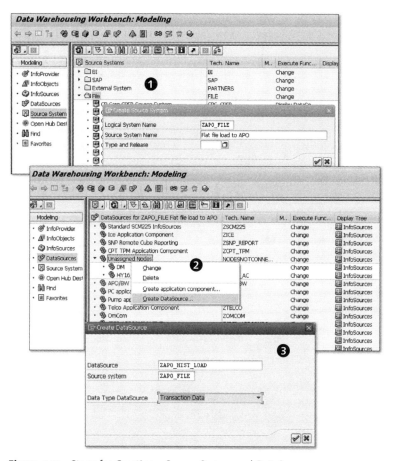

Figure 4.22 Steps for Creating a Source System and DataSource

---

Custom DataSource

Companies often build custom tables in their systems to support business requirements. Use Transaction SBIW (Generic DatasSource - Maintain Generic DataSource) for custom table extraction. Input the transactional data table name in the TRANSACTION DATA field to create the DataSource.

---

3. **Create InfoCube**.

The InfoCube serves as a data container for the planning data wherein we assign the characteristics and key figures. The InfoCube can receive data from multiple InfoSources. Follow these steps (see Figure 4.23):

▶ Access Transaction RSA1. Right-click INFOPROVIDER in the MODELING area to first create an InfoArea (step ❶).

▶ Once the InfoArea is created, right-click the created InfoArea again to create your InfoCube by choosing option CREATE INFOCUBE (step ❷).

▶ Nominate the InfoCube to be BW type in the CHOICE OF BW APPLICATION pop-up screen (step ❸/❹).

▶ In the InfoCube, directly input the dimensions (characteristics) and key figures by clicking on DIMENSIONS • CREATE NEW DIMENSIONS.

> **Note**
>
> If you have any navigational attributes attached with the characteristics, they will populate automatically in the InfoCube (step ❺).

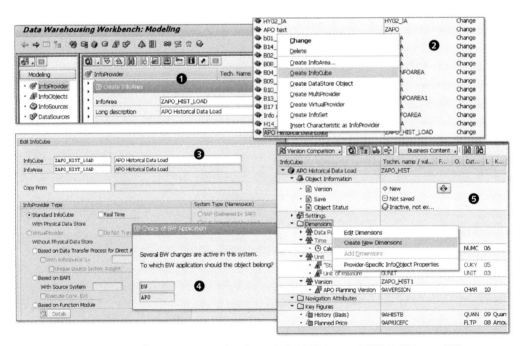

Figure 4.23 Steps for Creating an InfoCube in SAP APO's Internal SAP NetWeaver BW Component

The final InfoCube, once activated, will look like what's shown in Figure 4.24. The InfoCube will store the data to be transferred to the planning area as time series objects in SAP liveCache for demand planning.

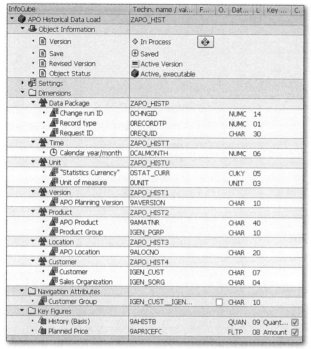

InfoCube	Techn. name / val...	F...	O.	Dat...	L	Key ...	C.
▼ 🌐 APO Historical Data Load	ZAPO_HIST						
▼ 🜨 Object Information							
• 📄 Version	◇ In Process	🔧					
• 📄 Save	⊕ Saved						
• 📄 Revised Version	═ Active Version						
• 📄 Object Status	🌐 Active, executable						
▶ ⚙ Settings							
▼ ☐ Dimensions							
▼ 🔶 Data Package	ZAPO_HISTP						
• 🔷 Change run ID	0CHNGID			NUMC	14		
• 🔷 Record type	0RECORDTP			NUMC	01		
• 🔷 Request ID	0REQUID			CHAR	30		
▼ 🔶 Time	ZAPO_HISTT						
• 🕐 Calendar year/month	0CALMONTH			NUMC	06		
▼ 🔶 Unit	ZAPO_HISTU						
• 🔷 "Statistics Currency"	0STAT_CURR			CUKY	05		
• 🔷 Unit of measure	0UNIT			UNIT	03		
▼ 🔶 Version	ZAPO_HIST1						
• 🔷 APO Planning Version	9AVERSION			CHAR	10		
▼ 🔶 Product	ZAPO_HIST2						
• 🔷 APO Product	9AMATNR			CHAR	40		
• 🔷 Product Group	IGEN_PGRP			CHAR	10		
▼ 🔶 Location	ZAPO_HIST3						
• 🔷 APO Location	9ALOCNO			CHAR	20		
▼ 🔶 Customer	ZAPO_HIST4						
• 🔷 Customer	IGEN_CUST			CHAR	07		
• 🔷 Sales Organization	IGEN_SORG			CHAR	04		
▼ ☐ Navigation Attributes							
• 🔷 Customer Group	IGEN_CUST__IGEN...		☐	CHAR	10		
▼ ☐ Key Figures							
• 🔢 History (Basis)	9AHISTB			QUAN	09	Quant...	☑
• 🔢 Planned Price	9APRICEFC			FLTP	08	Amount	☑

Figure 4.24 InfoCube with Various Dimensions (Characteristics) and Key Figures

4. **Create transformation.**

   Once the InfoCube is created, we need to define the transformation and data transfer process (DTP) for mapping the source (file) with the destination (Info-Cube). Follow these steps:

   ▸ Access Transaction RSA1 (Figure 4.25), right-click your InfoCube name, and select CREATE TRANSFORMATION (step ❶).

   ▸ In the CREATE TRANSFORMATION screen, input the DataSource to be connected with the InfoProvider (InfoCube) (step ❷/❸).

   ▸ An automatic proposal of the field mapping between the DataSource and InfoCube will be shown in the next screen. Take note of the rule type by which we can define the data transformation method (step ❹). The rule type is used for any transformation (for example, changing the unit of measure from an alternative to a base unit of measure). In the rule type, we define whether any data conversion is required from the DataSource file before loading historical data into the InfoCube.

▶ Assign a constant value to a characteristic, change the calendar day to calendar month or input routine to change the unit of measure.

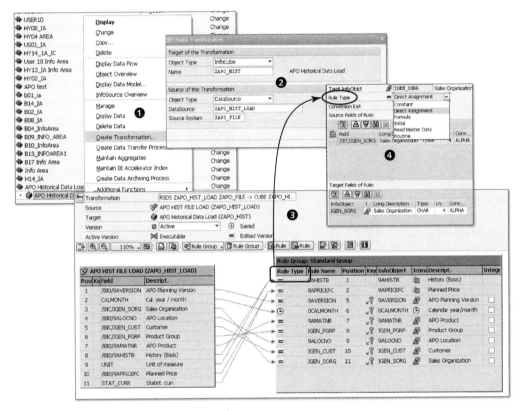

Figure 4.25 Steps for Creating Transformation

5. **Create data transfer process (DTP).**

   This process will be used to upload the file into SAP APO and schedule it as a process chain job.

   ▶ In Transaction RSA1, locate your InfoCube under the INFOPROVIDER. Under the InfoCube structure, click the DTP to input the file loading path, per the example in Figure 4.26. The DTP can be either scheduled in a process chain (Transaction RSPC or run directly via Transaction RSA1.

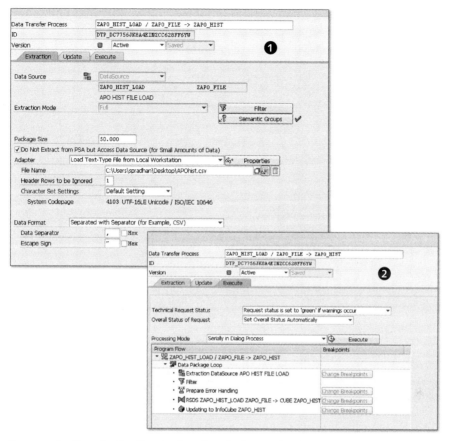

Figure 4.26 Steps for Creating the Data Transfer Process (DTP)

▷ Once the DTP process runs successfully, view the data content of the request by right-clicking the InfoCube (see Figure 4.27) and selecting MANAGE (step ❶). Highlight the InfoCube and select the icon on top, CONTENTS. This will display the InfoCube contents. Figure 4.27 also shows the data model for the InfoCube (step ❷). We can also view the data model by clicking the DISPLAY DATA MODEL option (step ❸). A graphical tree structure shows how the data from the source system (flat file) moves to DataSource, and then via DTP to the InfoCube.

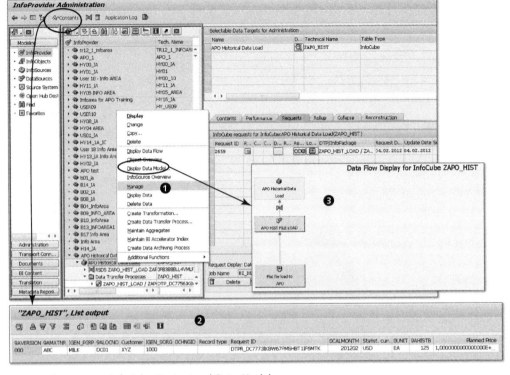

Figure 4.27 InfoCube Content and Data Model

ABC Technology uses the InfoCube not only for loading the historical files, for online reporting purposes via a virtual InfoCube with SAP APO's internal SAP NetWeaver BW component.

4.4 Data Management in SAP APO Demand Planning

APO-DP needs characteristic value combinations (CVC) to exist for every possible combination that needs to be planned. This means that every time a new product is launched or a customer/customer group starts buying a product they did not buy in the past, a new characteristic combination needs to be created in APO-DP. In the following sections, we'll show you how to create a CVC and how to work with it.

4.4.1 Creating New Characteristic Value Combinations

For new products, the new characteristic combinations will have to be created manually since the planning needs to forecast before the first actual sales occur. In our business case example, ABC Technology has implemented a new product introduction (NPI) workflow, which tracks the completion of all the master data maintenance activities in a timely manner. For situations when a customer buys an existing product for the first time, the new characteristic combinations can be generated automatically using the history of these sales. The CVC can be created either manually or automatically via Transaction /SAPAPO/MC62. For manual creation, the demand planner clicks CREATE SINGLE CHARACTERISTICS COMBINATION for the specific master planning object structure. In the next screen, the demand planner maintains all the required characteristics and presses EXECUTE ([F8]).

> **Note**
>
> You can find additional information on how to maintain characteristic value combinations in Chapter 5, Section 5.2.2.

4.4.2 Capturing History

The sales order history is captured in SAP APO's internal BW InfoProvider (Info-Cube), where we can generate the characteristics combinations automatically. This process can also be scheduled as a background batch job. To enable this process, the user needs to validate that the sales order history is available in the InfoCube using Transaction LISTCUBE, and access Transaction /SAPAPO/MC62, which is used for CVC generation using the InfoCube (see Figure 4.28). For large-volume CVC creation, it is always recommended to split the job to avoid any performance issues. You should run the time series consistency programs (see Section 4.2.7) after the CVC creation to avoid any SAP liveCache inconsistency anchor issues.

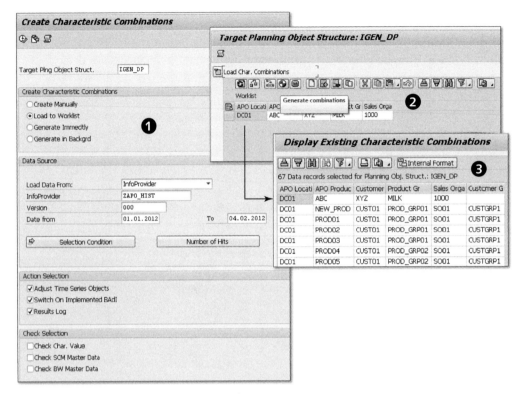

Figure 4.28 Characteristics Value Combination Creation

4.4.3 Transfer Planning Data

Once the CVC is created as SAP APO Demand Planning master data, we can transfer the planning data from SAP APO's internal SAP NetWeaver BW InfoCube to the APO-DP planning area. To do this, access Transaction /SAPAPO/TSCUBE (see Figure 4.29). Enter the InfoCube (source) and APO-DP planning area (destination) in their respective fields, as well as the planning version (active version 000).

Map the InfoObject of the InfoCube with the key figure in the planning area. The transfer of the planning data can be validated in the planning book (Transaction /SAPAPO/SDP94). During the transfer, the business planner needs to exit the planning book to avoid any data locking issues.

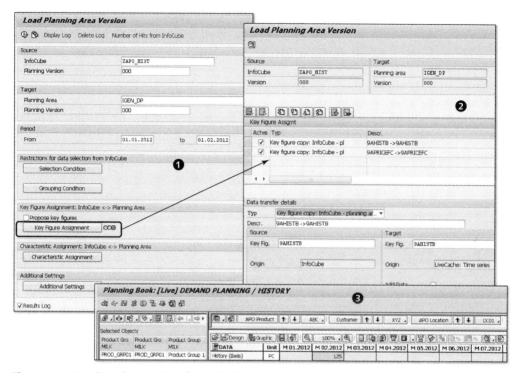

Figure 4.29 Loading Planning Data from InfoCube to Planning Area/Book

Once the history is loaded in the planning book, the planner needs to identify the best forecast model to run the product for determining future forecasts. Setting up the forecast method is discussed in the next section.

4.5 Setting up Forecast Methods

Before performing the forecast modeling in the system, the business planner needs to make some of the following decisions to start the process.

Example

ABC Technology needs to decide on the level of the product hierarchy at which to run the statistical forecast. It also needs to decide on the time bucket used for statistical forecasting, the length of history and future horizons, forecasting method, parameters within the method, and frequency of update for the forecasts.

There are two different methods of forecasting available in APO-DP: *univariate forecasting* and *casual forecasting*. The former purely studies the historical pattern and proposes the best fit model based on the lowest forecast error. The latter combines the external market factors (economic condition, price, weather, etc.) while determining the forecast.

Next, we will look at both univariate and casual forecasting methods. First, let us look at the univariate forecast methods. In our business case example, depending on product family, ABC Technology can use either of the forecasting models. While the univariate is easy to formulate, the casual requires more effort on the collection of external environment data.

4.5.1 Univariate Forecasting

This section presents the overview on forecasting model framework using univariate forecasting as example. Further explanation on the univariate forecasting is provided in Section 4.5.3.

Within the univariate forecasting method, there are more than 20 different statistical models available in SAP APO, but we can broadly classify them into two: *exponential smoothing* and *linear regression*. Exponential smoothing uses inherent properties of time series, while linear regression extrapolates a model fitted to the data. Table 4.2 provides the list of six commonly used forecast methods across the exponential and linear regression.

Forecast Method	Profile	Interactive
Single Exponential Smoothing	M11	Constant Models
Holt's Method	M21	Trend Models
Seasonal, No Trend	M31	Seasonal Models
Holt-Winters' Method	M41	Seasonal Trend Models
Linear Regression	M94	Linear Regression
Seasonal Linear Regression	M35	Seasonal and Linear Regression

Table 4.2 Commonly Used Forecast Methods in SAP APO

Figure 4.30 illustrates the forecasting model framework with steps toward identifying the best fit forecasting model:

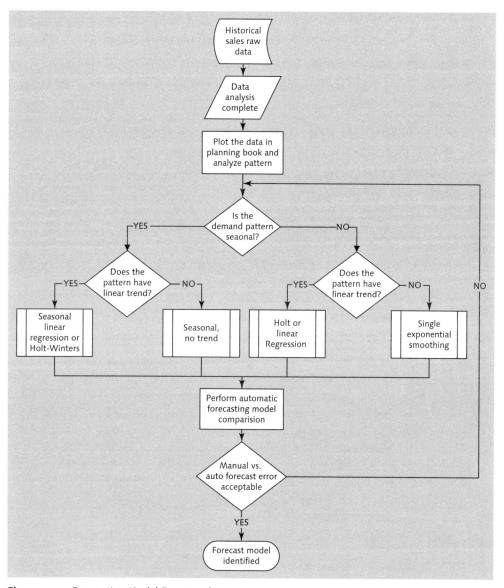

Figure 4.30 Forecasting Model Framework

1. Collect the raw historical sales data from the source system.

2. Analyze the data and perform possible manual outlier corrections on known events.

3. Load the planning data into SAP APO to study the historical pattern.

4. Perform the decision tree on demand pattern seasonality and linear trends.

5. Select the decision tree model and run an interactive forecast.

6. Run the automatic forecast selection model.

7. Compare the manually selected and automatic forecast model with forecast error analysis.

8. Reiterate the result with a similar forecast model by fine-tuning a, b, and g parameter values.

9. Alternatively, identify new forecast models until the result is satisfactory, per business requirements.

4.5.2 Forecast Definitions

Before we look at various forecast methods in more detail (later on in this section), let's look at some common definitions used in the forecasting process.

Model Parameters

The model parameters—alpha, beta, and gamma—control the weighting of each historical value. Alpha is used in basic value calculation, beta in trend value calculation, and gamma in the seasonal index calculation. Values for the parameters range from 0 to 1. Values closer to 0 will use the whole history, while values closer to 1 use only the more recent historical data. The parameters also control how reactive the forecast is to changes in the historical pattern.

Figure 4.31 graphically depicts the three parameters. ABC Technology presents the lowest value of 0.1 across all three parameters in the auto-model and lets the system perform in increments until it finds the lowest forecast error.

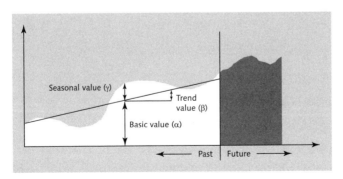

Figure 4.31 Forecasting Model Parameters

Ex-Post Forecast

An *ex-post forecast* is a forecast run in the past against historical values. The ex-post forecast is used to measure model fit. Figure 4.32 shows the ex-post forecast calculated during the forecast run. The comparison of the ex-post forecast and history gives the forecast error used for identifying best-fit model. Some of the forecast models (i.e., moving average, weighted moving average, history adopted, and manual forecast) do not generate the ex-post forecast. This analysis allows the ABC Technology demand planner to look at the outliers identified during the ex-post moving average calculation.

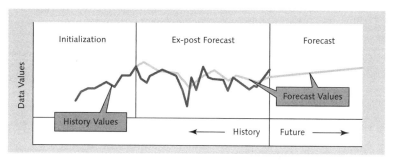

Figure 4.32 Ex-Post Forecast and Initialization during the Forecast Run

Model Initialization

As most of the model uses the recursive method to look at the history pattern, depending on the model, one or more period is required for initialization. Table 4.3 gives the list of minimum periods required by the system and ideal history for proper statistical calculation.

Forecast Method	System	Statistical
Single exponential smoothing	3	6
Holt's method	4	6
Seasonal, no trend	12	24
Holt-Winters' method	15	24
Linear regression	1	6
Seasonal linear regression	12	24

Table 4.3 Minimum Number of Periods Required by the System

Forecast Error

A *forecast error* is defined as deviation between the actual history and the calculated ex-post forecast. The lower deviation (forecast error) means the forecast has used more of the historical pattern while estimating the future forecast. The demand planner needs to closely monitor the forecast error while picking the best fit forecasting model for their products. SAP APO provides alerts in form of *diagnosis group* where the % forecast error tolerances can be defined for monitoring the forecasting result. Table 4.4 lists all the forecast errors. Industry best practice recommends using forecast errors MAPE and MAD for forecasting model identification.

Forecast Error Name	Definition	Comment
Mean absolute deviation (MAD)	The mean absolute deviation is calculated by the absolute difference between the ex-post forecast and the actual value.	The mean absolute deviation is the error calculation used to determine the best fit in the Auto Model 2 Forecasting Model. MAD is an example of absolute error.
Error total (ET)	The error total is the sum of the difference between the actual and the ex-post forecast.	
Mean absolute percentage error (MAPE)	The mean square error is the average of the sum of the square of each difference between the ex-post forecast and the actual value.	The mean absolute percentage error is the most commonly used in the industry, along with MAD. MAPE is an example of relative error.
Mean square error (MSE)	The mean square error is the average of the sum of the square of each difference between the ex-post forecast and the actual value.	

Table 4.4 Forecast Error Used for Analysis

Forecast Error Name	Definition	Comment
Square root of mean square error (RMSE)	The root mean square error is the square root of the average of the sum of the squared difference between the actual and ex-post forecast value.	
Mean percentage error (MPE)	The mean percentage error is the average percentage error of the difference between the ex-post forecast and the actual values.	Mean percentage error is the simplest of all the errors, with high chances of being skewed due to outlier record.

Table 4.4 Forecast Error Used for Analysis (Cont.)

Forecast Profile

In SAP APO Demand Planning, the logic of how a forecast is carried out is stored in the forecast profile. Since different models can be used for different products, various forecast profiles can be set up in the system. The forecast model to forecast seasonal products may be different than stable products.

The maintenance of the forecast profile is done primarily by the business users. The ABC Technology demand planner uses his or her product experience to set some of the products on the auto-forecasting model and separate others to run on a pre-defined forecasting model.

Best Practice

As an industry best practice, the forecasting model is reviewed by the business once every quarter by analyzing the forecast accuracy performance. The same forecast profile can be used for both interactive and background batch jobs.

A forecast profile is created in Transaction /SAPAPO/MC96B, as shown in Figure 4.33. Besides defining the forecast and history key figures, we also define the horizons and the forecasting model.

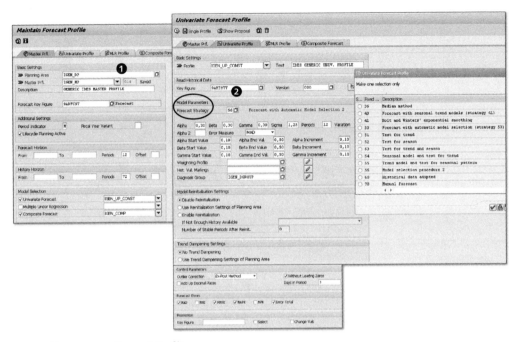

Figure 4.33 Forecast Profile

Assignment of Forecast Key Figures

Key figures can be assigned to store the calculations of forecast, corrected history, corrected forecast, ex-post forecast, and ex-post forecast MLR. This assignment is done in Transaction /SAPAPO/MSDP_ADMIN with path EXTRAS • FORECAST SETTINGS. Figure 4.34 shows the forecast key figure assignment.

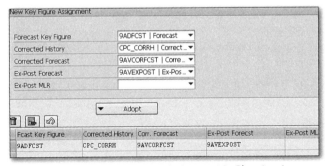

Figure 4.34 Forecast Key Figure Assignment in Planning Area

Corrected History

The outlier from the history can be corrected either manually or automatically by defining in the forecast profile—outlier correction, as shown in Figure 4.33. The correction is done for the outlier lying outside the tolerance level calculated with reference to standard deviation. The ABC Technology demand planner reviews the automatic cleansing of the outliers to ensure that the historical pattern is not touched during the correction.

Corrected Forecast

The corrected forecast takes into account the workday correction for the respective bucket. This can be achieved by maintaining the field DAYS IN PERIOD in the univariate forecast profile (Figure 4.33). An alternative would be to use a macro based on the time stream planning calendar defined in the location master.

4.5.3 Univariate Forecasting Methods

Let's study some of the commonly used univariate (statistical) models in this section.

Single Exponential Smoothing (Method 11)

This method is best suited for products with a historical pattern that does not include any seasonality or trend. Some of the ABC Technology products, such as desktops, have stable sales and will use the single exponential smoothing method. This method forecasts the next period (monthly bucket), and this value is repeated for next 12-18 months. The forecast method yields a flat line. The forecast is a weighted average of the baseline history, and the recent history is weighted more than the past periods.

A parameter value of α closer to 0 will result in a slower decline, while one closer to 1 will result in a fast decline. A recommended parameter value α is between 0.2 and 0.5. An example of a single exponential smoothing model from ABC Technology is shown in Figure 4.35.

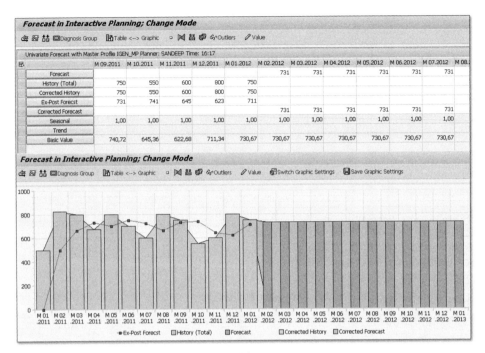

Figure 4.35 Single Exponential Smoothing Model

Holt's Method (Method 21)

ABC Technology markets some products that have specific lifecycles (for example, laptops) and need to model the upward/downward trend pattern to ensure that they do not have excess inventory when the product is being replaced with another product line. Holt's method is suitable for products with a historical pattern that does not include any seasonality but does have a consistent linear trend, upward or downward.

The forecast is a straight line, with a positive or negative slope. Two parameters are needed to estimate the forecast: α and β. As for single exponential smoothing, α controls how much weight is given to the most recent periods and β controls how strongly the trend is smoothed. A trend dampening profile can be defined in the forecast profile to smooth out the trend. A recommended parameter value for α and β is between 0.3 and 0.5. Higher values favor more recent data. An example of the Holt's method modeled from ABC Technology is shown in Figure 4.36.

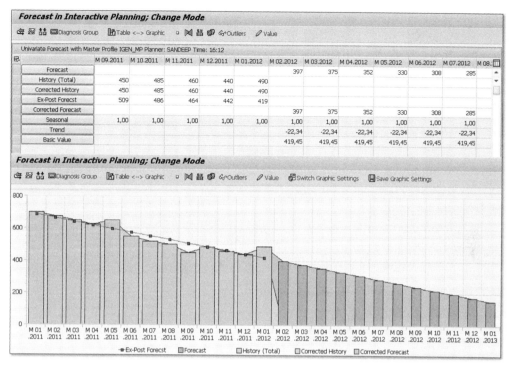

Figure 4.36 Holt's Trend Model

Seasonal, No Trend Model (Method 31)

ABC Technology also markets some products (monitors) that demonstrate some seasonal patterns during school holiday and holiday seasons. For these groups of products, the company plans to model the seasonal forecasting model. This method is suitable for products with a historical pattern that includes seasonality but no consistent trend. The forecast will copy the seasonal pattern into the future, but there will be no trend adjustment.

Two parameters are needed to estimate the forecast: α and γ. As for single exponential smoothing, a controls how much weight is given to the recent periods, while parameter γ controls the seasonal pattern used to forecast. A recommended parameter value α is between 0.3 and 0.5, and for γ, between 0.1 and 0.3. The lower value of γ favors two seasonal patterns. An example of a seasonal model from ABC Technology is shown in Figure 4.37.

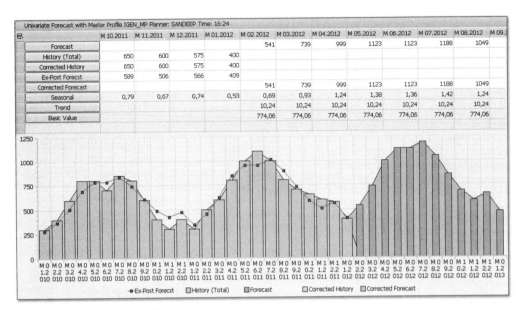

Univariate Forecast with Master Profile IGEN_MP Planner: SANDEEP Time: 16:24											
	M 10.2011	M 11.2011	M 12.2011	M 01.2012	M 02.2012	M 03.2012	M 04.2012	M 05.2012	M 06.2012	M 07.2012	M 08.2012	M 09.
Forecast					541	739	999	1123	1123	1188	1049
History (Total)	650	600	575	400							
Corrected History	650	600	575	400							
Ex-Post Forecst	589	506	566	409							
Corrected Forecast					541	739	999	1123	1123	1188	1049
Seasonal	0,79	0,67	0,74	0,53	0,69	0,93	1,24	1,38	1,36	1,42	1,24
Trend					10,24	10,24	10,24	10,24	10,24	10,24	10,24
Basic Value					774,06	774,06	774,06	774,06	774,06	774,06	774,06

Figure 4.37 Seasonal Model

Holt's Winter Model (Method 41)

This method is suitable for ABC Technology products with a historical pattern that includes seasonality and a linear trend. (For example, the company is selling some computer accessories, but they're outdated and sell worse from year to year.) The forecast will copy the seasonal pattern into the future and adjust a linear trend, upwards or downwards. Three parameters are needed for this method be set: α, β, and γ. These three parameters need to be fine-tuned with the iterative forecasting process to achieve a low forecast error values (MAD and MAPE).

Linear Regression (Method 94)

This method is an alternative to Method 21, but based on a different approach. No parameters need to be set. This method uses a classic linear regression based on the least-squares principle. This regression is extrapolated. It is the same method as the linear trend line option in Excel.

Seasonal Linear Regression (Method 35)

This method is an alternative to method 41, but based on a different approach. No parameters need to be set. This method first estimates seasonal indexes, which are used to de-seasonalize the baseline history. Then, a linear regression is applied. This regression is extrapolated, and the forecast is seasonalized back. This method weights the values in the past equally. Note also that the trend component cannot be eliminated within this method.

Croston Model (Method 80)

The Croston Model (80) is used when demand is sporadic or intermittent. The return is a constant model to meet the possible sporadic demand. This model is used by ABC Technology for some of its product line that doesn't have a stable history.

Automatic Forecasting Models

SAP APO also offers an automatic forecasting model that the business can opt to use for initial forecasting model identification or comparison purposes. The most commonly used is Auto Model Selection Procedure (Method 56). This method tests for constant, seasonal, and/or trend models while attempting to minimize error by adjusting α, β, and γ parameters. This model adjusts α, β, and γ between the values of 0.1 and 0.5 in increments of 0.1, while calculating the MAD for each iteration. The iteration with the lowest MAD is the model chosen, with the appropriate smoothing factors. Setting up the auto model allows the ABC Technology demand planner to review the system-proposed model and makes any changes as required.

> **Forecast Error Result Analysis**
>
> Implement BAdI /SAPAPO/SDP_FCST4 to record the background processing results of forecasting models in tables /SAPAPO/FCSTHEAD and /SAPAPO/FCSTACCU. Set the EV_FLAG_ACTIVE = 'X.

Mathematical Formulas[2]

Let's see some of the standard formulas used in the forecasting calculation. Table 4.5 outlines the constant, trend, and seasonal trend models and the basic formulas.

---

2   *help.sap.com*

Model	Model Parameters
Constant model	Basic value = Hist(1) where Hist(i) is the ith historical value Trend value = 0 Seasonal indices = 1 Mean absolute deviation (MAD) = 0
Trend models	Trend value = $\dfrac{\text{Hist(3)} - \text{Hist (1)}}{2}$ Basic value = $\dfrac{\text{Hist(3)} + \text{Hist (2)} + \text{Hist (1)}}{3}$ + Trend Seasonal indices = 1 Mean absolute deviation (MAD) = $\dfrac{\sum\limits_{i=1}^{3} \lvert \text{Basic value} - \text{Hist(i)} \rvert}{3}$
Seasonal models	Basic value = Mean of the historical values of the first historical season Trend value = 0 Seasonal index for a period = Historical value for that period divided by the basic value Mean absolute deviation (MAD) = 0
Seasonal trend models	Trend value = $\dfrac{\text{Hist(1+SL)} + \text{Hist(2+SL)} + \text{Hist (3+SL)} - \text{Hist(1)} - \text{Hist(2)} - \text{Hist (3)}}{(3 * SL)}$ where Hist(i) is the ith historical value and SL is the length of a season. Basic value = $\dfrac{\sum\limits_{i=4}^{SL+3} \text{Hist(i)}}{SL} + \dfrac{\text{Trend} * (SL - i)}{2}$

Table 4.5 Constant, Trend, and Seasonal Trend Model Formulas

Model	Model Parameters
	Seasonal index for a period =
	$$S(i+3) = \frac{\text{Hist }(i+3)}{\text{Basic value} - \text{Trend* (SL-i)}}$$
	Where S(i) is the ith seasonal index.
	Mean absolute deviation (MAD) =
	$$\frac{\sum\limits_{i=1}^{SL} |[\text{Basic value} - (\text{SL-i}) * \text{Trend}] * S(i) - \text{Hist}(i+3)|}{SL}$$

Table 4.5 Constant, Trend, and Seasonal Trend Model Formulas (Cont.)

Table 4.6 outlines the seasonal and trend basic formulas.

Model	Model Parameters
Seasonal and trend models	Forecast value for the period (t+i)
	P(t+i) = [G(t)+i * T(t)] * S(t-L+i)
	Where:
	Basic value: $G(t) = G(t-1) + T(t-1) + \alpha \left[\dfrac{V(t)}{S(t-L)} - G(t-1) - T(t-1) \right]$
	Trend value: $T(t) = T(t-1) + \beta \, [G(t) - [G(t-1) + T(t-1)]]$
	Seasonal Index: $S(t) = S(t-L) + \gamma \left[\dfrac{V(t)}{G(t)} - S(t-L) \right]$
	For the constant model
	T(t) = 0, b = 0, S(t) = 1.0, g = Gamma = 0
	For the trend model
	S(t) = 1.0, g = Gamma = 0

Table 4.6 Seasonal and Trend Model Formulas

Model	Model Parameters
	For the seasonal model $\quad$ T(t) = 0, b = 0 $\quad$ P(t+i) = The forecast calculated for the period (t+i) in the current period (t) $\qquad$ i = Forecasted horizon $\quad$ G(t) = The current basic value for the current period (t) $\quad$ G(t-1) = The previous basic value from the previous period $\qquad$ L = Period length (often 12) $\quad$ V(t) = Actual demand (history) for the current period (t) $\quad$ T(t) = The current trend value calculated for the current period $\quad$ T(t-1) = The previous trend value from the previous period $\quad$ S(t) = The seasonal index for the period(t) $\quad$ S(t-L) = The previous seasonal index for the period (t) $\qquad \alpha$ = Smoothing factor for the basic value 'G', $0 < a < 1$ $\qquad \beta$ = Smoothing factor for the trend value 'T', $0 < b < 1$ $\qquad \gamma$ = Smoothing factor for the seasonal indices 'S', $0 < g < 1$

Table 4.6 Seasonal and Trend Model Formulas (Cont.)

4.5.4 Casual Forecasting Methods

Casual forecasting is based on the relationship between the variable to be forecasted and an independent variable. The SAP APO casual forecasting method is based on multiple linear regression (MLR) using the ordinary least squares method. The equation for the method is simple: $y = a + bx$. This is a simple algebraic formula. It simply defines the shape of a line.

When used with regression analysis, the *y*, or dependent variable, represents the demand. This is the number we are trying to forecast. The *x*, or independent variable, represents the item that directly influences the shape of the line. *a* is the intercept, while *b* is the slope of the line. Correlation measures the strength of the relationship between the dependent and independent variables.

For example, ABC Technology uses the price as one of the casual variables in the calculation, while the other business scenario uses weather as one of the drivers for the MLR calculation.

Now that we've completed the basic customization of APO-DP, we'll move on to customizing the other important SAP APO module: Supply Network Planning.

4.6   Basic Customization in SAP APO Supply Network Planning

This section focuses on explaining the basic customization steps for SAP APO Supply Network Planning (which we'll refer to as APO-SNP). Unlike what you saw with APO-DP, where we had to create many different elements, APO-SNP uses the majority of the standard InfoObjects, characteristics, key figures, and planning books from SAP. There are multiple standard APO-SNP planning books that ABC Technology can use as a template to design its supply planning books. The flexibility of macros on these planning books allows the company to change some of the demand and supply calculations.

In the following sections, we'll show you where to find APO-SNP InfoObjects and planning materials, and how to use them.

4.6.1   InfoObjects

Standard characteristics and key figures are used in SAP-provided planning areas and planning books. The planning data in APO-SNP can be stored either in time-series based SAP liveCache or order-based SAP liveCache. The key figure information to be stored as order or time series SAP liveCache is defined in the planning area configuration. The order SAP liveCache key figures are the ones that are interfaced with CIF to SAP ERP.

The standard characteristics provided are listed in the master planning object structure 9ASNPBAS, while the key figures are displayed in standard planning areas 9ASNP01, 9ASNP02, 9ASNP03, 9ASNP04, and 9ASNP05. The master planning object structure and planning area can be accessed using Transaction /SAPAPO/

MSDP_ADMIN. If you don't see the characteristics and key figures, run report /SAPAPO/TS_D_OBJECTS_COPY from Transaction SE38 (ABAP Editor).

Additional key figures can be created to support business requirements either by navigating to the Administrator Workbench for SAP NetWeaver BW (Transaction RSA1) and following the path RSA1• EDIT • OBJECTS • INFOOBJECT, or by directly typing Transaction RSD1. Here, maintain the SAP APO key figure of quantity (QUAN) and base unit of measure 0BASE_UOM.

4.6.2 Category Group

Every key figure in APO-SNP is linked with categories. The categories are descriptions of different stock types, receipt types, or requirement types in SAP APO. A group of categories (also known as ATP elements) can be classed as a category group representing various elements. This way, the aggregation of all the categories is shown in the key figure for the specific bucket. Another important use of the category group is the ability to specify the quantity type for each of the defined categories. With this functionality, different key figures can be configured to specify the requested sales orders, confirmed sales orders, or backorders in the planning book. The flexibility of defining the category per key figure provides flexibility to businesses to distinguish the use of each demand and supply planning key figure for calculation.

> **Example**
>
> An example from ABC Technology is the inventory type taken into account for the demand and supply calculation. The company wants to take only unrestricted inventory into account and not count blocked or restricted inventory into stock calculations. Another use is separating two key figures for sales orders and deliveries.

To customize a category (see Figure 4.38), follow menu path SPRO • SAP REFERENCE IMG • ADVANCED PLANNING AND OPTIMIZATION • GLOBAL AVAILABLE TO PROMISE • MAINTAIN CATEGORY. Here you'll see all the available categories in SAP APO; these can be transferred from SAP ERP by the CIF integration model for the ATP customizing object. The activity can be performed in SAP ERP via generating and activating the CIF integration model using Transactions CFM1 and CFM2.

Similarly, you customize a category group via menu path SPRO • SAP REFERENCE IMG • ADVANCED PLANNING AND OPTIMIZATION • SUPPLY CHAIN PLANNING • SUPPLY

NETWORK PLANNING • BASIC SETTINGS • MAINTAIN CATEGORY GROUPS. As Figure 4.38 shows, the quantity type can capture the requested, original, and confirmed quantity. From the defined list of the categories, we define a new category group. Under this new category group, we input all the categories we want to display in the key figure. For some specific key figure, we can define whether the category quantity type is requested, original, or confirmed.

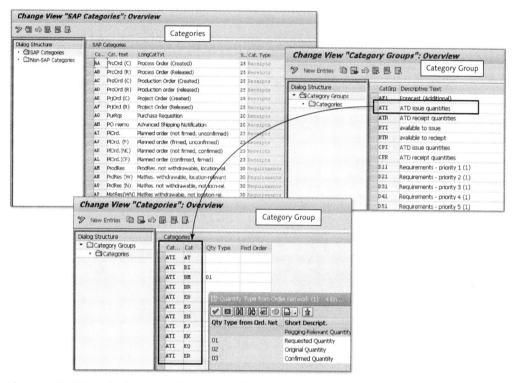

Figure 4.38 Categories Assignment to Category Group

The category and category group can be maintained in either of the following four function areas in both configurations and also during the planning data release from APO-DP to APO-SNP:

▶ **Planning area**

   Assignment of category and category group to individual key figures in Transaction /SAPAPO/MSDP_ADMIN, as shown in Figure 4.39

▸ **Demand Planning release to Supply Network Planning**
Assignment of category when releasing the demand plan from time series to order SAP liveCache. Figure 4.39 shows the Transaction /SAPAPO/MC90 demand plan release to supply planning. As shown in the figure, we maintain the TIME SERIES LIVECACHE for APO-DP to be released as ORDER LIVECACHE in APO-SNP. The forecast order category is maintained as FA.

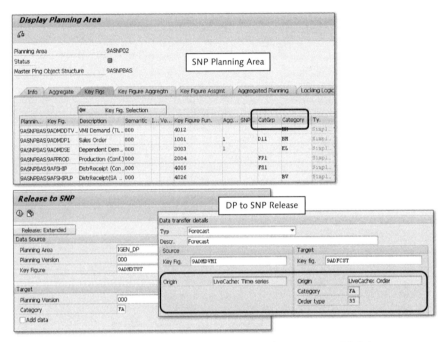

Figure 4.39 Category Group Assignment in APO-SNP Planning Area, DP Release

▸ **Location master**
Default stock category, available to deploy and available to issue fields specific to location can also be specified in location master data (Transaction /SAPAPO/ LOC3), as shown in Figure 4.40.

▸ **Location product master**
In situations when the business would like to prioritize the local forecast over internal replenishment transfers request, you need to maintain the location product master, as shown in Figure 4.40. In the SNP2 tab, maintain the category group in fields ATD/ATI to be taken into account for the APO-SNP distribution

planning process. The values maintained in the location product take precedence over the location master data category group. This allows the business to define the parameters per location product combination.

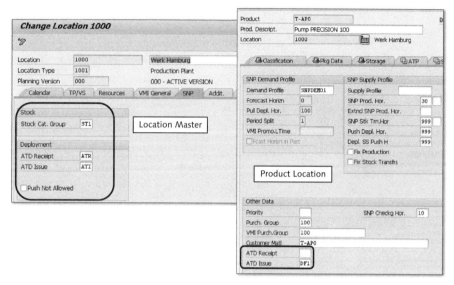

Figure 4.40 Master Data Maintenance of Category Groups

4.6.3 Planning Area

As with the demand planning area, we need to maintain planning areas for the APO-SNP business process. The planning area is where we maintain the base planning unit of measure, time bucket, and key figures. APO-SNP comes with two pre-delivered planning objects: structure 9ASNPBAS (supply planning) and 9ASNPSA (scheduling agreement). It is recommended that we use these two planning object structures during the APO-SNP planning area creation. The APO-SNP PLANNING indicator in the planning object structure automatically assigns all the APO-SNP characteristics.

Similarly to what we discussed in Section 4.2.3 regarding APO-DP, we need to create a storage bucket profile. A storage bucket profile defines how the system stores the data created in SAP liveCache and used for calculation purposes. Use Transaction /SAPAPO/TR32 to create the storage bucket profile. Unlike with APO-DP, SAP offers pre-defined APO-SNP planning areas that are recommended to be copied and used per business requirements (see Table 4.7).

APO-SNP Planning Area(s)	Description
9ASNP01	▸ Time series based. ▸ Used for supply and demand propagation for simulating changes caused by supply chain constraints to fulfill market demands. ▸ All results stored as time series for quantity and time restrictions.
9ASNP02	▸ Order based. ▸ Central planning area used for supply planning. ▸ Encompasses many basic (replenishment, distribution, and capacity) and advanced (aggregated, subcontracting, shelf life, and product substitution) functionalities in supply planning.
9ASNP03	▸ Scheduling agreement processing using SNP heuristics planning.
9ASNP04	▸ Optimization-based planning with time-dependent restrictions. ▸ APO-SNP optimizer profile lists all the constraints to be factored during the optimization run. However, there may be situations when the constraints need to be defined that are time-based. ▸ Upper limits of production, supplier capacity, transportation, or stock on hand can be defined as constraints.
9ASNP05	▸ Safety stock planning. ▸ Both basic and advanced safety stock planning can be performed in this planning area.
9AVMI03	▸ Used for deployment heuristics with consideration for demands in the source location. ▸ Used primarily for VMI scenario.

Table 4.7 List of Standard APO-SNP Planning Areas

To create your own APO-SNP planning area, copy from planning areas listed in Table 4.7 by going to Transaction /SAPAPO/MSDP_ADMIN, selecting the planning area, and right-clicking COPY. Additional custom key figures can be added if required to support the business process. Other parameters, such as defining the storage bucket profile or unit of measure, can be done in the planning area. Since the ABC Technology planner uses a different unit of measure for planning, we can specify a common planning unit of measure in the planning area.

You need to initialize the planning area by right-clicking INITIALIZE PLANNING VERSION for usage.

4.6.4 Planning Book

As explained in Section 4.2.4, the planning book serves as both the frontend user interface for the business users to plan and for batch background processing for planning cycles and alert generations. The ABC Technology business users plan to use the supply planning book to visualize the demand, supply, and inventory information on a real-time basis to make key decisions. SAP delivers standard APO-SNP planning books and recommends its customers to use these planning books as templates while building their own custom planning books (see Table 4.8).

APO-SNP Planning Book(s)	Description
9ASNP94	Interactive planning book for executing supply planning and Transport Load Builder (TLB) features. Using this planning book, the planner can create external procurement, replenishment, production, distribution, and load plans.
	There are two data views in 9ASNP94. The first data view, SNP94(1), is for supply planning, while the second data view SNP94(2) is for capacity planning. The TLB screen is accessed by using the ⛴TLB View icon.
9ASOP	This planning book is used to run the APO-SNP planning method based on supply and demand propagation.
	There are four data views in 9ASOP: Location product, transportation, PPM, and resource.
9ADRP	This planning book is similar to the 9ASNP94, with the difference being the addition of the table view, showing the distribution receipts and issues. There is only one data view on this planning book.

Table 4.8 List of Standard APO-SNP Planning Books Delivered by SAP

APO-SNP Planning Book(s)	Description
9AVMI	This planning book is for the Vendor Managed Inventory (VMI) scenario. In addition to APO-SNP data, we can display VMI receipts and demand key figures in this planning book. There are two data views for this planning: one for planning and the other for capturing external partner forecast.
9ASA	This planning book is used for the APO-SNP scheduling agreement process. There is only one data view for this planning book.
9ASNPAGGR	This planning book supports APO-SNP hierarchical planning. The book has two data views to perform aggregated planning and planning with aggregated resources.
9ASNP_PS	This planning book is used for product interchangeability when planning. The book has one data view, with additional key figures to support the product substitution features.
9ATSOPT	This planning book is used to maintain the time-based constraints for the APO-SNP optimizer. The planning book has two data views.
9ASNP_SSP	This planning book is used for basic and advanced safety stock calculations.
9ADRP_FSS	This planning book is used for the deployment heuristics to also consider the customer demand in the source location and not deploy the entire inventory for internal replenishment transfers.
9ASNP_SHLF	This planning book is used for shelf life planning. There are four additional key figures with shelf life functions to support the planning process.
9ASNP94_INTERACT	This planning book is for displaying aggregated supply planning and aggregated resource planning information.
9ASNP94_BATCH	This planning book is for running the supply planning processes in the background.

Table 4.8 List of Standard APO-SNP Planning Books Delivered by SAP (Cont.)

The custom planning book can be easily created using one of the SAP standard planning books from the table as a template. The planning book can be created in Transaction /SAPAPO/SDP8B in four steps, as shown in Figure 4.41:

❶ Define your new planning book and data view using a reference with standard data view. In our scenario, we are copying the standard 9ASNP94(1) planning book. Once you click the CREATE icon, a message will pop up mentioning that "macros were copied and are inactive".

❷ Assign your own planning area to the planning book from transaction menu path EDIT • ASSIGN PLANNING AREA.

❸ Select your planning area and click CONTINUE. An application log will be generated mentioning that the new planning area is assigned. While exiting, if this message appears again for resetting the original value, select No.

❹ Generate all the macros for the planning book in Transaction /SAPAPO/ADVM.

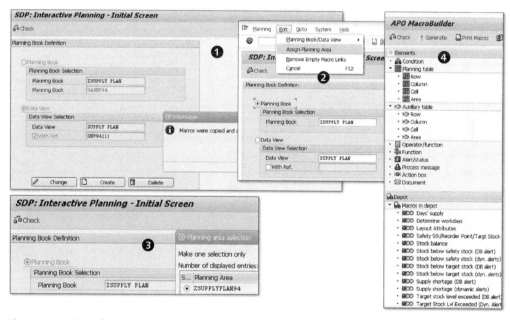

Figure 4.41 Steps for Creating a Custom APO-SNP Planning Book

4.6.5   Key Figures and Macros

The standard APO-SNP planning book provides all the vital information required for supply chain planning. Per business definitions, we can change the naming abbreviation of the key figure to make it easier for the business to understand. For example, for the SNP DISTRIBUTION DEMAND key figure, we can change the name to PURCHASE ORDERS key figure.

Let's look at the definition of standard key figures and macro calculations provided in the standard planning book 9ASNP94. As you can see in Figure 4.42, the key figures are grouped into three categories: demand, supply, and inventory.

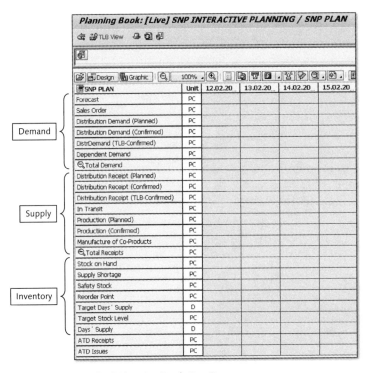

Figure 4.42   Standard Planning Book Key Figures

The business needs to clearly understand the definition of the standard key figures, as some are transactional while others are macro function calculated. Let's look at the standard APO-SNP key figure definitions in tabular form in Table 4.9.

Key Figure	Definition	Macro Calculation	Category
Forecast	This key figure initially represents the gross forecast, but once the sales orders come, it represents the net forecast (unconsumed forecast).	A consumption (forecast/sales orders) based on the requirement strategy of the product performs the forecast consumption function.	FC req: Forecast requirement
Sales order	Requested sales orders and open deliveries. Additional custom key figures can be defined to identify the confirmed sales orders based on quantity type maintenance in the category group.		
Distribution demand (planned)	This key figure represents the stock transfer requisitions from the supply network. This replenishment will include unconstraint requirements to fulfill both possible customer backorders and additional stock build in other distribution centers.		BC: Stock transfer reservation BH: Stock transport requisition BJ: Supplier scheduling agreement requirement EB: SNP release for stock transport requisition ED: SNP VMI sales order HJ: SNP suppliers schedule agreement release

Table 4.9 Standard APO-SNP Key Figure and Macro Definitions[3]

---

3 *help.sap.com*

Key Figure	Definition	Macro Calculation	Category
Distribution demand (confirmed)	This key figure represents the outgoing constraint supply plan after the SNP deployment run.		EG: Deployment: Purchase requisition EH: Deployment VMI sales order
Distribution demand (TLB confirmed)	This key figure represents the stock transport order (outgoing load plan) build after the SNP TLB interactive or batch run.		BI: Stock transport order
Dependent demand	This key figure represents demand in the form of a BOM explosion.		AY: Dependent demand EL: SNP dependent demand AU: Order reservation without withdrawal AV: Order reservation with withdrawal
Total demand	This key figure adds all the demand elements highlighted in the above rows.	Sub-macro of stock balance. Adds all the demand elements. `Forecast + Sales Order + Distribution Demand (Planned) + Distribution Demand (Confirmed) + Distribution Demand (TLB Confirmed)+ Dependent Demand`	

Table 4.9 Standard APO-SNP Key Figure and Macro Definitions (Cont.)

Key Figure	Definition	Macro Calculation	Category
Distribution receipt (planned)	This key figure represents the proposed purchase requisitions to the source location.		AG: Purchase requisition BD: Stock transfer reservation BE: Scheduling agreement schedule line EA: SNP purchase requisition HG: SNP scheduling agreement schedule line
Distribution receipt (confirmed)	This key figure represents the confirmed purchase requisitions to the source location.		EF: Deployment purchase requisition
Distribution receipt (TLB confirmed)	This key figure represents the purchase order to the source location.		BF: Purchase order item schedule line
In transit	This key figure represents the goods in transit to the destination location.		AH: Advanced shipment notification EI: In transit
Production (planned)	This key figure represents the SNP planned production.		EE: SNP planned order
Production (confirmed)	This key figure represents the production plan created by the manufacturing module.		AC: Production order (created) AD: Production order (released) AI: Planned order (firmed, unconfirmed) BU: Inspection lot

Table 4.9 Standard APO-SNP Key Figure and Macro Definitions (Cont.)

Key Figure	Definition	Macro Calculation	Category
			AJ: Planned order (not firmed, confirmed)
Manufacture of co-products	This key figure represents the receipt elements for the co-product.		EM: Receipt from manufacture of co-products
Total receipts	This key figure adds all the supply elements highlighted in the above rows.	Sub-macro of stock balance. Adds all the supply elements. `Distribution Receipt (Planned) + Distribution Receipt (Confirmed) + Distribution Receipt (TLB Confirmed) + In Transit + Production (Planned) + Production (Confirmed) + Manufacture of co-products`	
Stock on hand	This key figure represents stock on hand at different periods	Sub-macro of stock balance. Calculated as: `Unrestricted inventory + receipts - demand or projected stock on hand + incoming receipts - outgoing demand`	

Table 4.9 Standard APO-SNP Key Figure and Macro Definitions (Cont.)

Key Figure	Definition	Macro Calculation	Category

Supply shortage	This key figure represents how short on inventory the company is versus demand.	The supply shortage value is dependent upon the stock on hand projected key figure. The macro equations reads as follows:
		
		`IF the Stock on Hand Projected Key Figure > = 0,`
		
		`THEN`
		
		`Stock on Hand Initial = Stock on Hand Projected`
		
		`AND Supply Shortage = 0`
		
		`ELSE IF`
		
		`Stock on Hand = 0`
		
		`THEN Absolute Value (Stock on Hand Projected)`
		
		`END`	

Safety stock	This key figure is used for safety stock calculation by function `SAFETY_CALC`. The advanced safety stock method takes into account demand, supply variability, and service level.	Calculated by a sub-macro to the `Safety Stk/Reorder Point/Targt Stock Lvl` macro	

Table 4.9 Standard APO-SNP Key Figure and Macro Definitions (Cont.)

Key Figure	Definition	Macro Calculation	Category
Days' supply	This key figure represents the days of supply the company is holding inventory against future demand.	Macro calculation (`Stock on Hand / Total Demand) * Days in the Period`. The number of days in the period is another macro: workdays.	
Reorder point	This key figure represents the reorder point and returns the function `REORDER_CALC`.	The standard macro adds the safety stock during the reorder point calculation.	
Target days of supply	This key figure is calculated through use of the `TARGET_DAYS` function.		
Target stock level	This key figure is calculated through use of the `TARGET_CALC` function.	The standard macro adds the safety stock during the target stock level calculation.	
ATD receipts	This key figure is used in the deployment planning and calculates the available-to-deploy quantity from the source location.		Populates per the location or location product master data maintenance.
ATD issue	This key figure is used in the deployment planning and calculates the available-to-issue quantity from the source location.		Populates per the location or location product master data maintenance.

Table 4.9 Standard APO-SNP Key Figure and Macro Definitions (Cont.)

4.7   Supply Chain Modeling for SAP APO Supply Network Planning

The APO-SNP process starts with the business deciding how it wants to model its supply chain in the SAP APO system. The modeling not only reflects mapping the distribution network in SAP APO, but also defines parameters based on supply chain constraints. Supply chain modeling is one of the key activities that require business involvement and validation. In the modeling, ABC Technology defines not only the network structure for its distribution, but also master data parameters to reflect the business requirements. While the ABC Technology desktop and monitor businesses may have structured network models, the laptop business distribution might look more like a web network.

In this section, we'll highlight the data elements that make up the supply chain model in APO-SNP. These elements are primarily master data settings needed to support APO-SNP planning business processes. Before we get started, however, a clear understanding of master data modeling is required before we begin the planning process in APO-SNP.

4.7.1   Model and Planning Versions

The model in SAP APO stores all the master data (i.e., location, product, transportation lanes, and production data structures) and can have multiple linked versions. The version primarily stores the transaction data for the model master data definitions. All the data versions are stored in SAP liveCache for the business to access and analyze the planning data. However, there will be only one active version 000, which synchronizes the transactions between SAP ERP and SAP APO. The other simulation versions created will be snapshots of the active version and can be used for what-if analysis.

The model and version are created via menu path ADVANCED PLANNING AND OPTIMIZATION • MASTER DATA • PLANNING VERSION MANAGEMENT • MODEL AND VERSION MANAGEMENT (TRANSACTION /SAPAPO/MVM). Figure 4.43 shows the model and version creation with some version options for APO-SNP:

▶ CHANGE PLANNING ACTIVE
   Used by APO-SNP heuristics for net change planning.

▶ NO PLANNED ORDER WITHOUT SUPPLY SOURCE
   APO-SNP optimizer looks for valid production data structure (PDS) or

production process model (PPM) and if checked, will not create planned orders unless referenced to PDS or PPM.

▶ CONSIDER STOCK TRANSFER HORIZON OF SOURCE LOCATION
Affects the APO-SNP heuristics and CTM planning process by defining a time fence for the distribution receipt where the new requirements can only be fulfilled after the stock transfer horizon.

▶ LOCAL TIME ZONE
Enter a check mark to consider a local time zone instead of UTC.

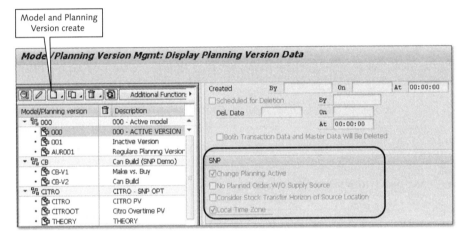

Figure 4.43 Model and Planning Version Management in SAP APO

4.7.2 Location

Locations in SAP APO represent both internal and external physical entities in the supply chain model. The physical entity can also represent external business partners, such as vendors and customers. Only locations that the business wants to include in the supply chain model need to be transferred to SAP APO. The location master is transferred from SAP ERP via CIF.

Maintain Location Master Data

The menu path for the location master data maintenance is ADVANCED PLANNING AND OPTIMIZATION • MASTER DATA • LOCATION • MAINTAIN LOCATION (TRANSACTION /SAPAPO/LOC3). The LOCATION tabs that are relevant for APO-SNP are CALENDARS, RESOURCES, SNP, and EXTRA ATTRIBUTES.

▶ In the CALENDAR tab, we maintain the shipping, receiving, and production calendars (time stream). The time stream calendar is maintained via Transaction /SAPAPO/CALENDAR. This offers the business the flexibility to specify the calendar per location. The shipping calendar refers to the weekdays when the goods can be outbound from the warehouse, and similarly, the receiving calendar specifies the weekdays the goods can be received inbound to the warehouse. The production calendar specifies the manufacturing plant calendar for production schedule.

▶ In the RESOURCE tab, we can maintain storage and handling resources. While the storage calendar can be used for measuring the warehouse capacity for the specific location, the handling resource can be used to take into account the goods receipt processing time in SAP APO in the business scenario in which the production needs additional time for quality.

▶ In the SNP tab, we represent the stock, available to deploy, and available to issue category groups for APO-SNP calculations. The business can model which receipts it wants to distribute per its business rule.

▶ In the ADDT. tab, we can maintain five additional, freely definable attributes for the location used for selection, planning, or reporting purposes. The attributes can be defined in the configuration path SPRO • SAP REFERENCE IMG • ADVANCED PLANNING AND OPTIMIZATION • MASTER DATA • MAINTAIN FREELY DEFINABLE ATTRIBUTES. The attributes are stored in table /SAPAPO/LOC.

Figure 4.44 shows the various location master tabs and the calendar maintenance.

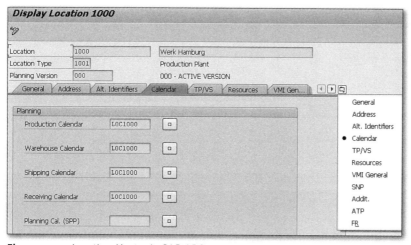

Figure 4.44 Location Master in SAP APO

4.7.3   Location Product

The *location product* represents the material master from the SAP ERP system. The SAP APO location product is transferred via CIF from SAP ERP. The product master has global and location-specific properties maintained similarly to the SAP ERP material master. SAP APO uses SAP ERP as the source system for the master data creation. The business can identify whether it would like the real-time changes to reflect from SAP ERP to SAP APO or in batches.

Maintain Location Product Master Data

These settings of master data transfer in SAP ERP are maintained in Transaction CFC9. The menu path for the location product master data maintenance is ADVANCED PLANNING AND OPTIMIZATION • MASTER DATA • PRODUCT • MAINTAIN PRODUCT (Transaction /SAPAPO/MAT1). Let's look at various product master fields relevant to the APO-SNP planning process in Table 4.10. The SAP APO master data fields in the table are maintained in different ways. For example, while the majority of the master data is transferred via CIF from SAP ERP, some of the master data is directly maintained in SAP APO. The maintenance in SAP APO can be done either with mass maintenance Transaction MASSD or other data maintenance (e.g., LSMW) techniques. Let's look at the fields that are transferred via CIF or SAP APO-specific techniques in Table 4.10.

Tab (Global: common to all locations, location: specific to the single location)	Master Data Field (CIF/APO)	Definition
Administration (location)	SNP planner (CIF)	Planner code assigned for planning book, background processing, and alerts selections
Properties (global)	Material group (CIF)	Used planning book, background processing, and alerts selections
	Product hierarchy (CIF)	Used for planning books, background processing, and alerts selections
	Transportation group (CIF)	Grouping of products while building transport loads

Table 4.10   SAP APO Location Product Master Data Fields

Tab (Global: common to all locations, location: specific to the single location)	Master Data Field (CIF/APO)	Definition
	SDP relevance (APO-specific)	Indicator for excluding products planning in APO-DP and APO-SNP
	Weight (CIF)	Product attribute used in SNP TLB
	Volume (CIF)	Product attribute used in the SNP TLB
	Stacking factor (CIF)	Product attribute used in SNP TLB, which indicates how many pallets can be stacked over each other
	Shelf life (CIF)	Indicates how many shelf life days the product has before expiring and includes maturation time
	Planning with shelf life (CIF)	Indicator for considering shelf life for APO-SNP planning processes
	Maturity time (CIF)	The incubation period after the production receipt before the product can be shipped to customers for sales
	Required minimum shelf life (CIF)	Used in shelf life planning and indicates the minimum shelf life required on batches for sales
	Required maximum shelf life (CIF)	Used in shelf life planning and indicates the maximum shelf life required on batches for sales
	Additional data (APO-specific)	Additional attributes specific to the product to be used in the planning process (for example, price). Up to three freely definable attributes can be defined specific to the location product to support the planning process.

Table 4.10   SAP APO Location Product Master Data Fields (Cont.)

Tab (Global: common to all locations, location: specific to the single location)	Master Data Field (CIF/APO)	Definition
		The attributes can be defined in configuration path SPRO • SAP REFERENCE IMG • ADVANCED PLANNING AND OPTIMIZATION • MASTER DATA • MAINTAIN FREELY DEFINABLE ATTRIBUTES. The attributes are stored in table /SAPAPO/ MATKEY.
Unit of measure (global)	Unit of measure (CIF)	Defines all the available alternative units of measure for planning. A scenario may consist of different products being planned in different purchasing units of measure. To get planning consistency, a common planning unit of measure may be defined for the SAP APO planning book.
SNP1 (location)	Penalty costs (APO-specific)	Location-dependent penalty cost to be used by the APO-SNP optimizer can be defined here. Penalty costs can be defined for no delivery, delay, and maximum delay across various demand types (e.g., forecast, customers, and sales orders).
SNP2 (location)	Demand profile (APO-specific)	The profile helps to determine how demand is calculated during the SNP heuristics and deployment planning runs. We can define the FORECAST HORIZON field, where the forecast is not taken into account; PULL DEPLOYMENT HORIZON, where planned distribution demands are considered for deployment; and PERIOD SPLIT for disaggregating the demand release to supply plan.

Table 4.10 SAP APO Location Product Master Data Fields (Cont.)

Tab (Global: common to all locations, location: specific to the single location)	Master Data Field (CIF/APO)	Definition
	Supply profile (APO-specific)	The profile helps to determine how supply is calculated in the SNP heuristics and deployment planning runs. We can define in APO-*SNP production horizon*, where SNP production plans are not created, and similarly in *SNP Stock Transfer Horizon*, where stock transfers are not created. We can also define the *push deployment horizon*, where planned distribution receipts are considered for deployment. If the indicators for FIX PRODUCTION and FIX STOCK TRANSFERS are checked, the earlier planning results are fixed for the APO-SNP production horizon and SNP stock transfer horizon during the SNP heuristics and optimizer runs.
	Deployment profile (APO-specific)	The profile helps to determine the distribution rules for deployment heuristics during the planning run. *Push distribution* covers various scenarios when the available-to-deploy (ATD) is enough to cover the demand. The *fair share rule* is defined for scenarios when demand is greater than supply (see Chapter 5).
	Demand at source location (APO-specific)	The two fields—CONSIDER SALES ORDERS and CONSIDER FORECAST—can be checked if we want deployment heuristics to take into account the source location sales orders and forecast during the real-time deployment run.

Table 4.10 SAP APO Location Product Master Data Fields (Cont.)

Tab (Global: common to all locations, location: specific to the single location)	Master Data Field (CIF/APO)	Definition
	SNP interactive order creation (APO-specific)	THE NO FIXING indicator can be checked to undo any fixing for any APO-SNP orders created by the planner in the planning book.
	CTM settings (APO-specific)	TIME BASED PRIORITY and DEMAND SELECT HORIZON can be defined for product-location specific during the CTM planning run.
	Other data (CIF- and APO-specific)	Defines the *product priority, ATD receipts, and ATD issues* for the location product. The product priority is used in CTM and APO-SNP optimizer runs. The ATD defined in the location product is taken into account in the APO-SNP deployment and TLB runs.
Demand (location)	Proposed strategy (CIF)	Primarily transferred from SAP ERP material master strategy group. The *proposed strategy* helps in determining how the forecasted demand is produced and consumed with sales orders. The CONSUMPTION MODE directs on the forward or backward consumption direction, as well.
	Pegging (APO-specific)	Considers fixed or dynamic pegging strategy
	Available stock (APO-specific)	Settings for additional stock category to be considered in the APO-SNP CTM run
Lot size (location)	Procedure (CIF)	Define various lot size procedures to be used during the APO-SNP planning run. The lot size procedures available are LOT-TO-LOT, PERIODIC, FIXED, and REORDER POINT.

Table 4.10 SAP APO Location Product Master Data Fields (Cont.)

Tab (Global: common to all locations, location: specific to the single location)	Master Data Field (CIF/APO)	Definition
	Quantity determination (CIF)	Defines the MAXIMUM LOT SIZE, MINIMUM LOT SIZE, ROUNDING VALUE, TARGET STOCK LEVEL METHOD, and TARGET DAYS OF SUPPLY. The lot size parameters and target stock level methods are used during the APO-SNP planning run.
	Scheduling (APO-specific)	Define the *safety days of supply* and *period factor*. The safety days' supply used in APO-SNP and CTM (safety time) identifies the number of workdays over which the system has to take into account future demand when calculating safety stock. The period factor signifies when the availability date/time needs to be scheduled in the bucket, on the range of 0 to 1. The value of 1 signifies a date toward the end of the bucket And is only used if the period factor is not defined in the transportation lane.
	Stock data (APO-specific)	Defines the safety stock, reorder point, and max stock level. Also defines the basic and advanced safety stock method to be used. For the advanced safety stock method, additional fields like SERVICE LEVEL, DEMAND FORECAST ERROR %, and REPLENISHMENT LEAD TIME FORECAST ERROR % are maintained.

Table 4.10 SAP APO Location Product Master Data Fields (Cont.)

Tab (Global: common to all locations, location: specific to the single location)	Master Data Field (CIF/APO)	Definition
Procurement (location)	Procurement type (CIF)	This field defines whether the product is produced in house, externally procured, or a combination of both.
	Procurement costs (APO-specific)	Used in APO-SNP optimizer for cost calculations.
	Stock cost (APO-specific)	*Production storage cost* and *safety stock cost* are used for APO-SNP optimizer calculation.
	ABC indicator (CIF)	Defines whether the product is fast moving or slow moving based on the ABC indicator.
GR/GI (location)	Processing times, in days (CIF)	Defines the *goods receipt processing time* and *goods issue processing time* to take into account additional time for handling and quality checks. Added on top of transportation lead times during the availability date calculation.
	Capacity consumption (APO-specific)	The field STORAGE CONSUMPTION PER BASE UOM can be used for the storage capacity. Handling resource capacity consumption can also be defined.
	Shipping (CIF)	Loading group can be used for SNP TLB during the load building.

Table 4.10 SAP APO Location Product Master Data Fields (Cont.)

Tab (Global: common to all locations, location: specific to the single location)	Master Data Field (CIF/APO)	Definition
Extra (location)	Freely definable attributes (APO-specific)	Up to five freely definable attributes can be defined specifically to the location product to support the planning process. The attributes can be defined in configuration path SPRO • SAP REFERENCE IMG • ADVANCED PLANNING AND OPTIMIZATION • MASTER DATA • MAINTAIN FREELY DEFINABLE ATTRIBUTES. The attributes are stored in table /SAPAPO/MATLOC.

Table 4.10 SAP APO Location Product Master Data Fields (Cont.)

Example

ABC Technology would like to change some of the parameter values during the standard transfer using CIF. These changes are done via CIF user exit enhancement, which will be explained in detail in Chapter 15.

4.7.4 Resources

Resources in the form of production, transportation, and storage represent a pool of capacity for checking supply plan feasibility. As APO-SNP uses bucket-oriented planning, the planning time buckets are represented by day denominations. The resource to be used for APO-SNP production plan creation is either a bucket, single-mixed, or multi-mixed resource. The bucket resource shows the capacity consumption once the production orders are planned. The single-mixed and multi-mixed resources can be used for the APO-SNP and PP/DS planning processes. While the single-mixed resource has a single capacity (100%) the multi-mixed may have more than a single capacity (> 100%).

> **Example**
>
> Depending on the solvers used by ABC Technology, different resources might be used. For product families using the APO-SNP heuristics as a planning engine, we only need a production resource for manufacturing and a handling resource for modeling goods receipt lead time. For another set of product families, various resources in the form of production and transportation can be used for cost optimization.

The SAP APO resource master data is primarily maintained in SAP ERP. The business user maintains the SAP ERP master data using Transaction CR02. The SAP APO resource master is transferred from the SAP ERP work center and capacity master data. As shown in Figure 4.45, within the capacity maintenance, we can maintain the parameters for the SAP APO resource. Also via Transaction CFC9 in SAP ERP, we can direct the CIF to create a single-mixed or multi-mixed resource in SAP APO.

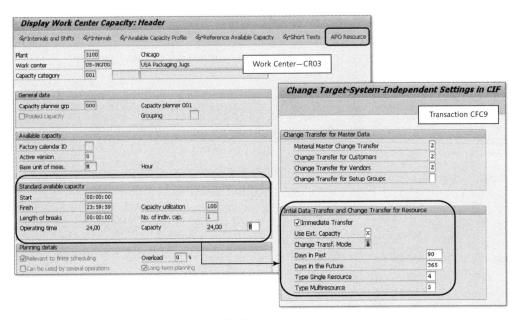

Figure 4.45 Resource Settings in SAP ERP

Once transferred from SAP ERP (see Figure 4.46), various planning parameters can be maintained in SAP APO. The menu path for the resource master data maintenance is ADVANCED PLANNING AND OPTIMIZATION • MASTER DATA • RESOURCE • MAINTAIN

RESOURCE (Transaction /SAPAPO/RES01). One such important parameter is the definition of APO-SNP bucket capacity for us to analyze the bucket consumption. The purpose of the resource in APO-SNP is to provide a rough-cut capacity plan, which is managed by capacity variant settings. Here, we can define the normal, maximum, and minimum capacities (defined by quantity/rates). Follow these steps (see Figure 4.46):

1. Create a definition of the quantity/rate per bucket. Define the bucket capacity for normal, minimum, and maximum for the period type (single day).

2. Create capacity variants. Assign the three capacity definitions to three capacity variants in the SAP APO resource master data.

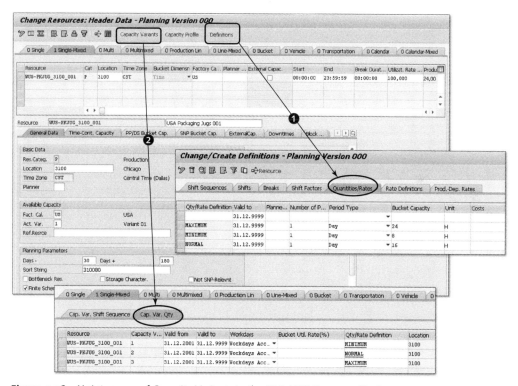

Figure 4.46 Maintenance of Capacity Variants in the SAP APO Resource Master

3. Once the variants are maintained, we can see all three capacities in the APO-SNP planning book. The business planner gets the visibility of the maximum, minimum, and normal capacities for the modeled resource (see Figure 4.47).

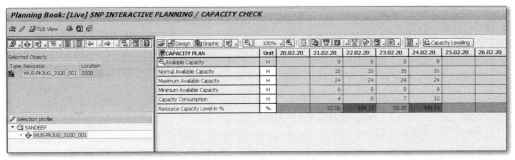

Figure 4.47 APO-SNP Capacity Planning Book

> **Resource in SAP liveCache**
>
> Run report /SAPAPO/CRES_CREATE_LC_RES periodically to correct any inconsistencies in the resource master creation in SAP liveCache.

4.7.5 Production Data Structure (PDS)

The PDS/PPM functionality represents the combination of the work center and BOM in SAP APO. The master data is transferred via CIF from production version. The SAP ERP production version combines both routing and BOM master data. The APO-SNP PDS is generated directly from SAP ERP, while the APO-SNP PPM is converted from PP/DS PPM in SAP APO via a generation report.

The PDS is used to calculate production time, production cost, material flow, and resource loads in the plant. The menu path for the PDS master data maintenance is ADVANCED PLANNING AND OPTIMIZATION • MASTER DATA • PRODUCTION DATA STRUCTURE • DISPLAY PRODUCTION DATA STRUCTURE (TRANSACTION /SAPAPO/ CURTO_SIMU). The PDS (see Figure 4.48) has an operation category to define the production activities. For each activity, there can be modes (resources) and components (product) assigned. The mode contains the throughput rate to produce the base quantity. The components represent the input and output components of the operation.

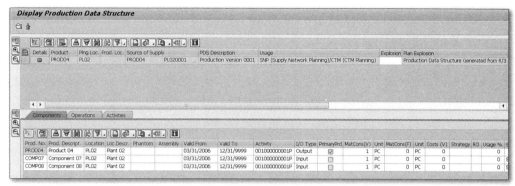

Figure 4.48 Production Data Structure in SAP APO

The following information summarizes the PDS shown in the figure:

▶ Each PDS includes one or more operations, which are steps in the production process.

▶ Each operation includes one or more activities, the components consumed by the activity, and their sequence within the operation.

▶ The PDS has validity parameters by lot size and time intervals.

▶ The variable costs defined for a PDS include the costs of input material as well as the cost of production.

Since PDS is bucket oriented, the production lead time is calculated based on the critical path operations, in days, and with the use of the resource factory calendar (Figure 4.49).

APO-SNP PDS

The APO-SNP PDS generated from SAP ERP can be influenced by using one of the following BAdIs:

▶ **/SAPAPO/CURTO_SNP**
Calculate bucket consumption of resources with the CALC_BUCKET_CONSUMPTION method of this BAdI. This method, which executes standard calculation of bucket consumption, is active automatically. However, you can change the calculation.

▶ **/SAPAPO/CULLRTOSNP**
Carry out optimization-based APO-SNP planning. You can use the FILL_COST_FIELDS method of this BAdI to fill the SNP PDS cost fields.

Per SAP SCM 7.0 Enhancement Pack 2, SAP provides new Transaction /SAPAPO/CURTO_EDIT to change the SNP PDS header data in SAP APO locally.

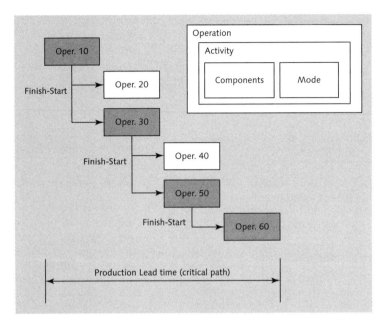

Figure 4.49 Production Lead Time Calculation in APO-SNP PDS

4.7.6 Transportation Lanes

Transportation lanes represent the material flow between two physical locations in SAP APO. A means of transport is also defined within the transportation lane with appropriate truck capacity and transportation duration, as shown in Figure 4.50.

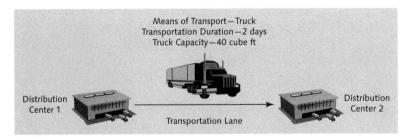

Figure 4.50 Transportation Lane in SAP APO

The menu path for the transportation lane master data maintenance is ADVANCED PLANNING AND OPTIMIZATION • MASTER DATA • TRANSPORTATION LANE • MAINTAIN TRANSPORTATION LANE (TRANSACTION /SAPAPO/SCC_TL1). The transportation lane has three views: PRODUCT, MEANS OF TRANSPORT, and PRODUCT SPECIFIC MEANS OF TRANSPORT, as shown in Figure 4.51.

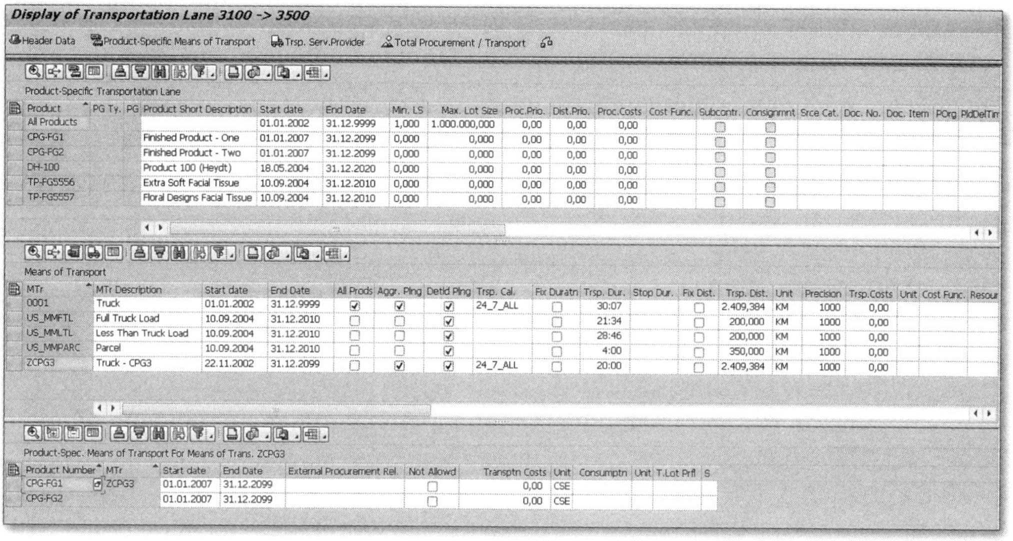

Figure 4.51 SAP APO Transportation Lane: Three Views

In the PRODUCT view, the product validity date, minimum/maximum lot size, cost function, block indicator, and form of procurement (e.g., subcontracting, consignment, and standard) are maintained.

In the MEANS OF TRANSPORT view, one or more mean of transport is assigned to the transportation lane, transportation duration, transport calendar, and cost of transport method. Also defined is the TLB with the loading method (i.e., straight loading or load balancing). If the straight loading method is used, the deployment orders are sorted per the product loading group, while the load balancing attempts to distribute multiple products in the same truck.

In the PRODUCT-SPECIFIC MEANS OF TRANSPORT, we define the transport resource capacity consumption, lot size profile, and specific costs.

The TLB profile is maintained via Transaction /SAPAPO/TLBPRF and defines the capacity constraints to meet vendor minimums while cutting purchase orders to truck loads and building stock transport orders for internal replenishments. The TLB constraint parameters are defined in Transaction /SAPAPO/TLBPARAM

4.7.7 Quota Arrangement

For multi-sourcing business scenarios, we can set up quota arrangement so that the demands are based on pre-defined quota. For example, two manufacturing locations are sourcing the same product to the distribution center. We can define the percentage each sourcing should receive of the net requirements from the distribution centers. The menu path for the quota arrangement master data maintenance is Advanced Planning and Optimization • Master Data • Quota Arrangement • Maintain Quota Arrangement (Transaction /SAPAPO/SCC_TQ1).

Figure 4.52 shows a business example in which ABC Technology has two suppliers sourcing raw materials to the manufacturing facility. Once the goods are produced, they are distributed to three distribution centers based on quota allocation. We have maintained quota arrangement for both inbound and outbound material flow to the manufacturing plant.

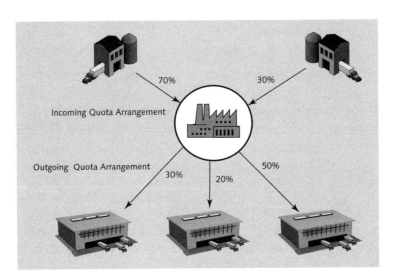

Figure 4.52 Quota Arrangement in APO-SNP

4.7.8 Supply Chain Engineer

Supply Chain Engineer is an SAP APO functionality that can be used to create and maintain supply chain models in pictorial form. There is no configuration required; you just need to have master data maintained on the supply network. The supply chain model consists of the specific planner work area in scope and all SAP APO data objects to be planned.

Supply Chain Engineer is also used for mass maintenance of master data. The model consists of a node and links among the physical locations, with material flow direction represented by transportation lanes. The menu path for the supply chain engineer master data maintenance is ADVANCED PLANNING AND OPTIMIZATION • MASTER DATA • SUPPLY CHAIN ENGINEER • MAINTAIN MODEL (TRANSACTION /SAPAPO/SCC07). Figure 4.53 shows the supply chain engineer with a graphical representation of the model on the top of the screen and master data elements (work area) on the bottom. Add objects to the supply chain engineer by right-clicking and selecting the ADD OBJECTS TO WORK AREA option. The users input their respective master data objects (i.e., location, location products, and PDS). Based on the location product combination, the transportation lanes are automatically generated in Supply Chain Engineer.

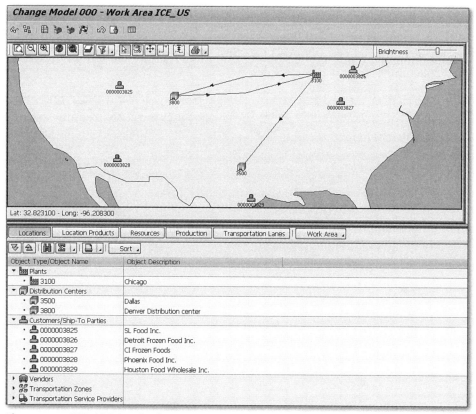

Figure 4.53 SAP APO Supply Chain Engineer

Another important use of the Supply Chain Engineer is for master data model consistency check. The model consistency checks not only for all the master data consistency, but also how the model will behave when running various APO-SNP engines. Business users can routinely run the consistency check by using Transaction /SAPAPO/CONSCHK.

4.8 Summary

In this chapter we explained the basic configuration tasks for APO-DP and APO-SNP. While the configuration for APO-DP is flexible, the configuration for APO-SNP is more structured and standard. The main reason for the latter is its integration with SAP ERP.

The chapter also explained how to set up the forecast model in APO-DP and framework for identifying the best forecast method. The chapter ends by explaining the supply chain modeling using APO-SNP and prepares the planner for performing basic planning.

The next chapter introduces the basic navigations and demand and supply plans that can be formulated in SAP APO. The chapter uses a weekly planning cycle to explain different functions within SAP APO Demand Planning and Supply Network Planning.

This chapter teaches the demand and supply planner who will be using the system how to navigate in SAP APO and perform interactive planning. The planner will understand the building blocks for demand and supply planning based on a weekly cycle.

5 Basic Interactive Planning in SAP APO

Understanding the basic navigation and functionality of SAP APO can be challenging to new business users who are using this component for the first time. Because SAP APO is a decision support tool, any business users who experience the application for the first time will not only need to learn the basic navigation but also be able to translate the business process activities that have been defined by the company into the SAP APO system.

In this chapter we will learn six distinct topics related to basic interactive planning in SAP APO (see Figure 5.1). You'll find an overview of interactive demand and supply planning and a discussion that highlights the core interactive functions for business users. We'll also cover alerts and simulation planning.

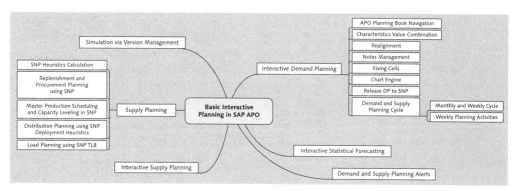

Figure 5.1 Learning Points for the Chapter (Mind Map)

More specifically, we'll teach you the basic navigation process and provide SAP APO building blocks with SAP APO transactions for creating demand and supply plans in the tool. Besides navigating through the transactions, you'll also find some steps for the initial setup of the interactive planning activities.

The chapter will first highlight the planning cycle and then explain the interactive demand planning and supply planning activities in SAP APO. The chapter follows the business case study of ABC Technology from earlier chapters to explain the techniques. Note that this focuses more on the weekly activities that ABC Technology planners would be performing interactively in SAP APO.

5.1   Demand and Supply Planning Cycle

As a part of the larger sales and operations planning process, every company tries to balance market demand with supply based on a planning cycle. Both the demand and supply planners are actively engaged in this overall process both from an operational and medium- to long-term perspective. The business planner monitors and adjusts the plan interactively in SAP APO based on current supply chain situations and constraints. These constraints can happen due to delays in materials from suppliers, product breakdown, or quality issues with products. The demand and supply planning process is divided into one monthly and iterative weekly planning cycle.

> **Example**
>
> As part of a supply chain transformation initiative, a new supply chain planning business processes is being introduced as part of the new implementation of SAP APO at ABC Technology. The introduction of new business processes aims to streamline the company's current planning activities. While the monthly planning cycle follows the sales and operations planning process, the weekly planning cycle aims for a systematic and continuous monitoring of both the short- and medium-term demand and supply plans. The weekly cycle is also a more exception based approach, with a focus on more critical operational issues (such as product stock outs and production shutdowns).

Figure 5.2 shows that the planning starts with monthly buckets in the sales and operations process. The demand and supply planning process is done on a 24-month planning horizon, and the primary focus is on monitoring business targets and company performance. The monthly plan is then broken down into weekly plans for shorter horizons as it enters the operational execution stage of a one- to two-month horizon. The primary focus of the plan here is the management of short exceptions between demand and supply plans.

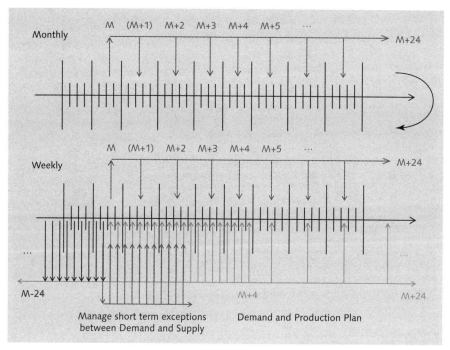

Figure 5.2 Monthly and Weekly Planning Cycles

ABC Technology has two planning groups: consumer and commercial. For the consumer division, the company has two planners—a demand planner and a supply planner—performing the weekly activities, while for the commercial division, the single supply chain planner manages both the demand and supply activities. Figure 5.3 shows a breakdown of weekly activities the demand planner and supply planner performed. Both planning groups follow the weekly planning cycle to keep track of demand and supply plans. The weekly cycle is an iterative planning process with assumptions that as we plan closer to the execution horizon the more accurate the projected demand and supply plan will be.

Since the planning activities for both the demand and supply planners varies for each day of the week, each planner has to analyze the plan interactively in SAP APO, make adjustments if required, and communicate the plan to the customer service and logistics teams. The challenge for new business planners is to first understand the input and output activities and the use of SAP APO to formulate the plan, which can be translated into an execution plan. Let's now review these activities in more detail:

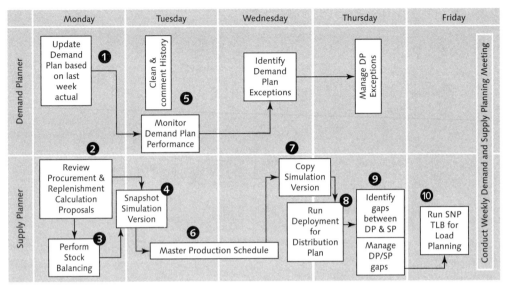

Figure 5.3 Weekly Planning Activities for Demand and Supply Planners

1. The demand planner adjusts the short-term forecast (for example, *wk+2* horizon) based on the past week's actual sales orders. The planner also cleans any known event outliers, which he doesn't want to include in the historical sales pattern for the future forecast. The new demand plan changes are then released interactively to APO-SNP.

2. The supply planner reviews the APO-SNP nightly planning run result, which includes an external procurement plan and internal stock replenishment plan. The planner analyzes the supply situations across the network and confirms the plan.

3. While analyzing the planning result, the planner is also given an alert for the stock balancing situation. This scenario may occur when the distribution center holds excess inventory (25–40% more than its planned forecast), and the goods are shipped to other distribution warehouses where customer sales are still fluid.

4. The master production scheduler may opt to perform a simulation version of the planning. This allows the planner to work on a static snapshot of inventory and a day's supply/stock covers at the distribution centers and manufacturing locations.

5. The demand planner monitors the weekly actual sales orders against the forecast for any exceptions. He also monitors the promotions activities and cleanses the actual historical sales orders to be used for the forecasting process.

6. Using capacity leveling and other available techniques (such as alternative resource balancing and aggregated resource planning), the planner formulates the master production schedule (MPS) plan. The planner only focuses on making the rough-cut capacity plan for the bottleneck resources and reaches a consensus with the manufacturing sourcing for the *wk+ 2* horizon on the production plan.

7. Once the constraint production plan is created in the simulation version, it's copied back to the active version.

8. A distribution plan is created based on the MPS plan to provide the projected stock cover at various distribution centers. The planner may overwrite the system-proposed deployment plan based on his or her judgment of the product portfolio.

9. Based on the constraint supply plan, demand and supply balancing is performed to see if there are any supply constraints that need to be addressed.

10. As the last business process in the weekly chain, the SNP Transport Load Builder is run once the deployment plan is validated. The loads are built based on the vendor minimum (minimum order quantity) for procurement or stock transport orders based on truck configuration (pallets, volume, or weight), or any other business priorities (for example, vendor freight minimums).

ABC Technology closes the week with a weekly operational meeting between the demand and supply planning functions in which corrective actions are agreed upon for the demand and supply gaps that cannot be immediately resolved. This new business process introduced at ABC Technology is being supported by SAP APO.

In the next few sections, we'll study how these tasks are performed in the component.

5.2   Interactive Demand Planning

Interactive demand planning is a process that focuses on creating an unconstrained demand plan (without considering supply constraints) to be released to supply planning. The interactive demand planning tasks consist of analyzing the system-generated forecast, making any changes to the forecast by running interactive forecasting, and acting on any demand plan alerts. The interactive planning also consists of formatting the layout of the SAP APO planning books for business planner usability.

This section guides ABC Technology business planners in SAP APO Demand Planning basic navigation, maintenance of master data, and creation of interactive demand plans. While the primary focus for the business planner is to navigate within the SAP APO component, the ability of the planners to create interactive forecasting is also an important exercise in interactive planning. The demand planner ensures that the plan is consistent in SAP APO and reflects any recent adjustments or changes.

5.2.1 SAP APO Planning Book Navigation

The ABC Technology demand planner performs the majority of planning tasks in the SAP APO planning book. The planning tasks may consist of reviewing the forecast per product family (laptop, desktop, and monitor). The planner views the planning data in the SAP APO planning book and may change the layout of the planning book for business user usability for analyzing and adjusting the plans. The planner also views the alerts directly in the planning book.

The planning book can be accessed via Transaction /SAPAPO/SDP94. Figure 5.4 shows the various sections in the planning book. While the planner would be working primarily in the data area, the other areas serve as basic toolbars for the planner.

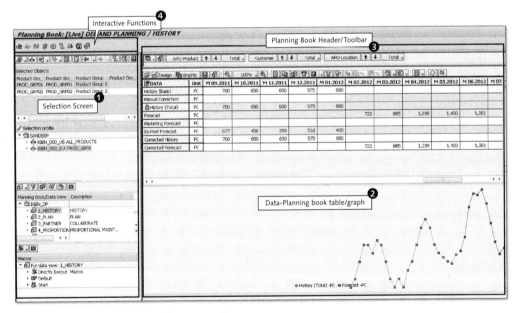

Figure 5.4 Interactive Planning Book

In the following subsections, we'll explain how to navigate the different areas and functions of the planning book.

Selection Profile

Upon initially entering the planning book, the planner defines the selection profile as the first task. Here, the planner will identify which characteristics he wants to plan and at which aggregation level. At ABC Technology, the planner wants to see his product groups drilled further down at the product and location levels.

The business planner starts by defining the selection profile in the planning book. The selection profile, if saved, allows the planner to save a variant selection for future use. Selection profiles allow business planners the ability to save searches that are to be used again. These are similar to saving variants, and the system will automatically load the data selection into the selection window. To create a selection profile, click the SELECTION WINDOW button (⚙). On the resulting screen, enter characteristics you'd like to plan with, as shown in Figure 5.5. As you can see, the business planner enters the characteristics level in which he wants to perform planning (step ❶). Once saved, the selection profile can be made a favorite. To do this click, the pencil icon to transfer the newly created selection profile to a user folder (step ❷).

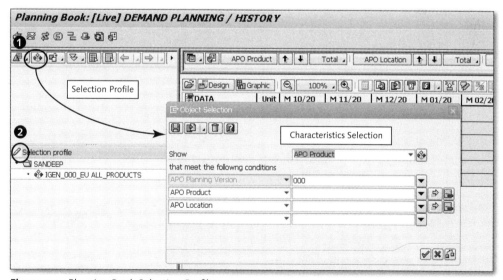

Figure 5.5 Planning Book Selection Profile

To save the selection, click SAVE.

Once the selection profile is saved, it needs to be transferred to the end user's personal folder. Click the pencil icon next to SELECTION PROFILE, as shown in Figure 5.5.

In the resulting screen (see Figure 5.6), the user can create sub-folders, delete items, and move selections across to their personal folder.

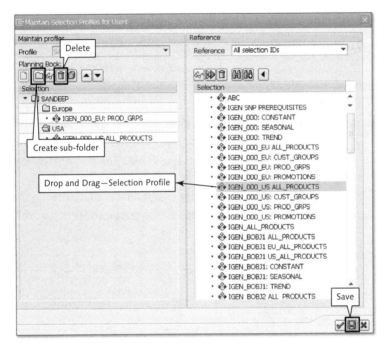

Figure 5.6 Selection Profile Management

Planning Book Toolbar

The planning book top toolbar has the following buttons, as shown in Table 5.1. This toolbar helps business to edit on the plans and slice/dice the planning data.

Button	Description
	SWITCH SHUFFLER ON/OFF Switches the left-hand sort and select area on or off, allowing a larger view of the demand data

Table 5.1 Planning Book Toolbar

Button	Description
or	DISPLAY/CHANGE Enables the switching between display and change mode Note: This button only displays when demand data is loaded in the right-hand side of the screen
	HEADER ON/OFF Displays or hides header toolbar

Table 5.1 Planning Book Toolbar (Cont.)

InfoObject Toolbar

The InfoObject toolbar is located in the selection area and has various functions. This toolbar helps the planner to properly select the objects for display (see Table 5.2).

Button	Description
	VIEW SELECTION Allows the inclusion or exclusion of three of the four selection windows, or displays the selection windows if they have been hidden
	SELECTION WINDOW Use to create a new selection, or load a saved selection
	DISPLAY DEPENDENT OBJECTS Displays objects that depend on the current selection
	DRILL DOWN Use to drill down data that depends on the current selection
	SELECT ALL Use to select all entries in the list
	DESELECT ALL Use to deselect all entries in the list

Table 5.2 SAP APO Planning Book InfoObject Toolbar

Button	Description
	PREVIOUS SELECTION Use to navigate to the previous selection
	NEXT SELECTION Use to navigate to the next selection
	CHOOSE SELECTION FIELDS Use to select which fields to display in the data selection window
	DISPLAY CURRENT SELECTION Displays the selection profile characteristics values
	SELECTOR HELP Displays help for using the InfoObject toolbar

Table 5.2 SAP APO Planning Book InfoObject Toolbar (Cont.)

Loading Data into the Planning Book

You have the following options to load the data from the selection screen into the planning book data area, as explained in Table 5.3.

To load...	Then...
A single record	Double-click the record.
More than one record at once	► Click the first record. ► Hold the Ctrl key. ► Click the other records to load. ► Click the LOAD DATA button.
All records at once	► Click the SELECT ALL button. ► Click the LOAD DATA button.

Table 5.3 Planning Book Loading Data

Planning Book Header

Planning book headers are used to drill the aggregated planning data to different levels or lower levels for further analysis (see Figure 5.7).

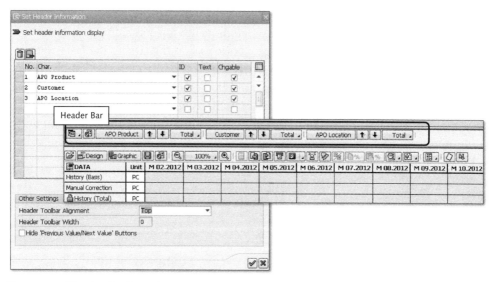

Figure 5.7 Planning Book Header

To set up the headers, click the HEADER ON/OFF button (⬛) on the PLANNING BOOK toolbar. Click the HEADER INFORMATION SETTINGS button (⬛). This will display a dialogue window in which you can specify the number of characteristics to drill down. Once maintained, the header will appear on the top of the planning data area. Once the header appears, use the functions in Table 5.4 to drill up and down.

Function	Use To:
Scroll Click either of these buttons: ⬆ ⬇	Scroll up or down through the individual items under a header; for example, by product.
Total Total ⬛ Select Total	Display an aggregated total for all the selected CVCs.
Details (all) Details (all) ⬛ Select Details (all)	Display line-item details for that header (characteristic attribute).

Table 5.4 Planning Book Header Settings

There are two more toolbars (see Figure 5.8) that assist the planner during interactive planning. The first toolbar is located on the top-left side; we can use it to execute interactive forecasting and promotion planning. Using the USER-SPECIFIC settings, the planner can define the characteristics he or she would like to view in the header settings. The second toolbar, located on top of the planning area, assists with analyzing the data with some basic functions in the form of setting calculation rules, displaying table/graphical planning book, and triggering and displaying alerts.

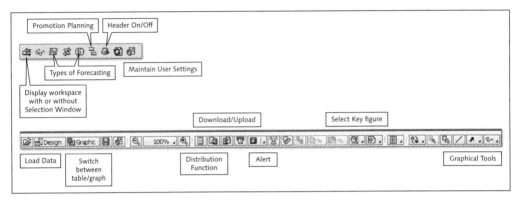

Figure 5.8   Interactive Function and Planning Book Toolbars

User Settings

In many instances, the ABC Technology planner would like to preset their navigation path and key figure layout when they open the SAP APO planning book. The *user settings* functionality provides that flexibility to be stored for each selection profile/username combination. We can define some preset configuration that allows the business planners to directly access the saved layout configuration. User settings allow the ABC Technology planners to set some of their defaults for opening the planning book: data view and selection profile combinations. The following settings are available:

▶ KEY FIGURE (HIDE)
Select key figures you do not want to display in the planning book.

▶ UNIT CONVERSION
Loads the planning data based on the unit of measure maintained. The SAP APO product master (Transaction /SAPAPO/MAT1) will have both base unit of measure and alternative unit of measure maintained.

▶ NAVIGATION PATH (DRILLDOWN)
Define the drilldown path by selecting the required characteristics in order.

▶ HIDE TOOLBAR FUNCTIONS
Select the icons that appear on top of planning data area (header).

▶ PIVOT SORTING
Defines the order in which characteristics appear in interactive planning for the selected planning data. This function is only triggered during the drill down.

▶ OTHER
A variety of user specific functions can be defined here; for example, pivot sorting, loading selection data, switching columns, and rows.

5.2.2 Characteristic Value Combination (CVC) Maintenance

A characteristic value combination (CVC) is a form of master data required for demand planning that consists of a combination of characteristics with which we can perform demand planning. A CVC acts as a prerequisite for displaying any planning data in the SAP APO planning book.

Example

ABC Technology will need a CVC for all three product lines of laptop, desktop, and monitor. Each CVC is a unique record with characteristics from the product hierarchy (product group, brand, etc.) and customer hierarchy (customer group, customer, channel, etc.). For example, a CVC for a single monitor group would have the product number, product group, customer, customer, and location records. Like any other master data, the business planner would need to create, change, or delete CVCs per the business requirements.

The planning data gets stored in the SAP liveCache time series based on the CVC. The management of the CVC is done via menu path ADVANCED PLANNING AND OPTIMIZATION • MASTER DATA • APPLICATION SPECIFIC MASTER DATA • DEMAND PLANNING • MAINTAIN CHARACTERISTICS VALUES, or via Transaction /SAPAPO/MC62. All the CVC maintenance (create, change, and delete) is done via the CVC workbench.

While the CVC is primarily created automatically based on historical sales data in the SAP NetWeaver BW InfoProvider, it may occasionally need manual maintenance. The maintenance might be initiated when the product has been phased out and is not selling anymore or if there has been some structural change in the supply chain network that requires re-mapping of the history to new CVC master data. While the CVCs are primarily created using the actual sales orders, the business planner may need to create new CVCs for new products for which there is no historical sales data.

Figure 5.9 shows the CVC management transaction from which single or mass CVCs can be created or deleted. The figure shows different data sources for the mass creation of CVCs in the form of an external file, InfoProvider, planning object structure, or BAdI. Also seen in the figure is an additional option where the business planner can directly maintain the new CVC in Excel or a flat file and load it into SAP APO for CVC creation. Once the flat file record is loaded, you'll need to generate them in next selection screen to create the records.

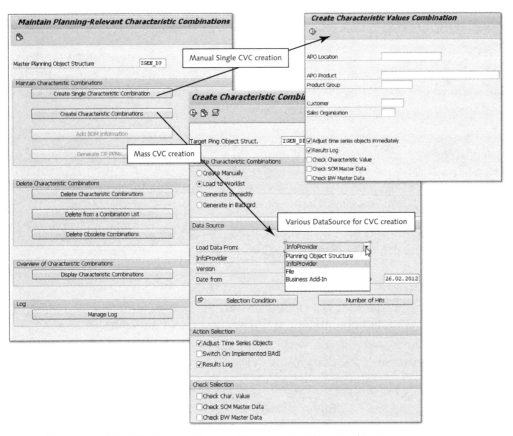

Figure 5.9 SAP APO Demand Planning Characteristics Value Combinations

Once the new CVC is created, it's also recommended that you run the following consistency reports:

▶ Report /SAPAPO/TS_LCM_CONS_CHECK for the specific APO-DP planning

▶ Report/SAPAPO/TS_LCM_PLOB_DELTA_SYNC for the planning object structure to establish data consistency in SAP liveCache

Another given option is the maintenance of single CVC also directly by manually maintaining the characteristics value as shown in the figure. Always checkmark the ADJUST TIME SERIES OBJECTS IMMEDIATELY field to have the record created in SAP liveCache.

5.2.3 Realignment

In SAP APO, APO-DP offers the functionality of *realignment* to perform any major restructuring of APO-DP planning data based on recent company organizational decisions (for example, the closure or acquisition of a new warehouse).

Example
ABC Technology is closing one of its warehouses and opening a new one. Because there are structural changes in the supply chain, the company will need to move the history of all products in the old warehouse to all the same products in the new warehouse.

To perform realignment, follow menu path ADVANCED PLANNING AND OPTIMIZA-TION • DEMAND PLANNING • ENVIRONMENT • DATA ADMINISTRATION • DATA REALIGN-MENT, or access Transaction /SAPAPO/RLGCOPY. As shown in Figure 5.10, the realignment can be performed either at the planning area level or at InfoCube level (before transferring to the planning area). In both scenarios, the first step (❶) is to create a realignment table with the desired characteristics, and the second step (❷) is to maintain the realignment table with the characteristics values. The figure shows the two options of performing the realignment at either the planning area level or the InfoCube level.

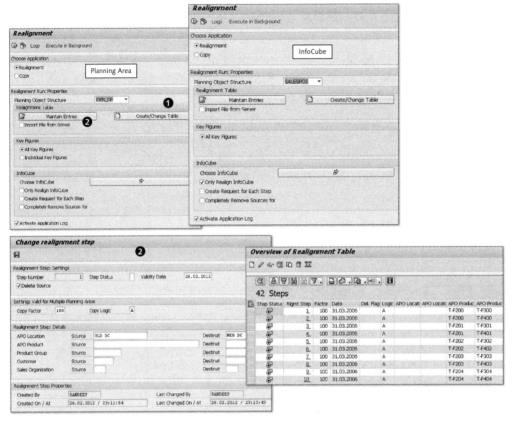

Figure 5.10 Realignment: Planning Area and InfoCube

5.2.4 Notes Management

During planning analysis, the business planner sometimes needs to write notes on any changes performed in the planning book. This helps the business planner to capture the specific reason the changes were made to the demand plan. This can also form part of a forecast meeting recording in which a consensus is reached on the demand plan. In other instances the notes reference can be as simple as removing the outliers, which result from sales and marketing promotions, from the actual sales orders.

The notes management functionality is available in the planning book. To access it, right-click a particular cell and click DISPLAY NOTE (see Figure 5.11) for both writing and displaying the note box in the bottom of the APO planning book. The notes can later be downloaded via report /SAPAPO/TS_NOTES_DOWNLOAD.

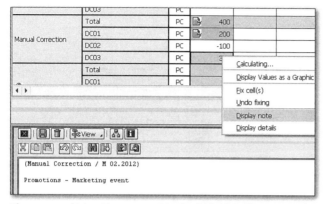

Figure 5.11 Notes Management in the SAP APO Planning Book

5.2.5 Fixing Cell

Once the planning is complete, the user may opt to lock the figures so that key figure values can't be changed either by the system planning run or other circumstances. ABC Technology planners use this technique during their weekly meeting, in which the consensus is reached on the plan quantities for execution. Following the meeting, the planner will fix the cell or lock the quantities in the planning book to ensure they are not changed or overwritten by an SAP APO background planning run. For any alterations, the planner would unfix the cell and change the quantity in the SAP APO planning book.

In this situation, highlight the cell, right-click, and choose FIX CELL(S) to lock the cell from any changes (❶). Figure 5.12 shows a business scenario in which the value is fixed for a particular distribution center. Upon releasing a different value at the aggregated level, the original value remains unchanged for the fixed cells and the new quantity is redistributed or reallocated among other warehouses (❷). This ensures that the earlier allocation is intact and any changes affect the reallocation on the other distribution centers only.

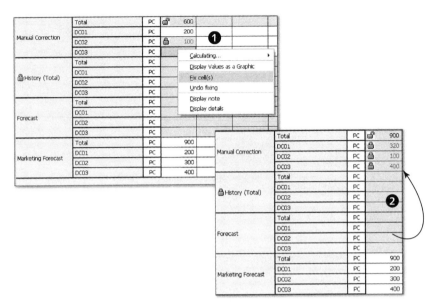

Figure 5.12 Fixed Cell Business Scenario

5.2.6 Chart Engine

Much of the business analysis is done in the form of analytics. The interactive planning book offers functionality in the form of the chart engine, which can be integrated with the SAP APO interactive planning desktop to present a graphical view of the planning data.

Within the planning book in the design mode, select the SWITCH GRAPHIC SETTINGS button (⊞) to bring up the chart designer. As shown in Figure 5.13, the chart designer has three distinct areas:

▶ **Chart preview**
Displays what your chart looks like with the properties you set.

▶ **Chart elements**
Contains all the elements of the chart.

▶ **Property area**
Displays properties of each individual chart element.

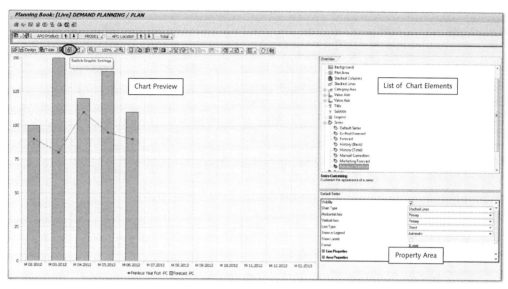

Figure 5.13 Chart Engine in the Interactive Desktop

The chart element properties are explained in Table 5.5.

Chart Element	Properties
GLOBAL SETTINGS	Chart type and dimensions, color settings for transparency, screen and data series, font, and data gaps
LAYOUT	Position of chart in the plot area and position of title, subtitle, and legend
BACKGROUND	Color and pattern of background and border (that is, all the chart except the plot area)

Table 5.5 Chart Element Properties[1]

---

1 Source: *help.sap.com*

Chart Element	Properties
PLOT AREA	Color and pattern of the plot area, the area on which the chart is drawn (without the axis label), and the frame around the plot area
BAR, COLUMNS (DEPENDS ON CHART TYPE)	Position and layout of the chart type–specific properties
CATEGORY AXIS	Scaling, labeling, and layout of the category axis (only for charts with a category axis)
VALUE AXES 1 AND 2	Scaling, labeling, and layout of the value axis (only for charts with relevant axes)
TITLE AND SUBTITLE	Text, position, and appearance of the title and subtitle of a chart
LEGEND	Position and appearance of the legend
SERIES	Layout settings for a data series. For charts with multiple data series, different chart types can be assigned to the various data series here
POINTS	Layout settings for individual data points
TEXTURES	Selection of texture images for formatting areas
DATA SERIES AND CATEGORIES	For changes to label texts and creating trend lines

Table 5.5 Chart Element Properties (Cont.)

SAP Chart Engine

SAP Note 1435310, Documentation for Chart Functionality in Interactive Planning, gives a more detailed explanation of the chart engine. SAP Note 1270012, Chart: Copy Chart Settings to Other Users, is also helpful.

5.2.7   Releasing the Demand Plan from APO-DP to Supply Planning

In SAP APO, the demand and supply planning is performed in two distinct planning areas. While the demand is created unconstrained, the supply is always constrained. Based on the monthly or weekly planning cycle, once the demand planning is created in APO-DP, the plan needs to be released to supply planning (either in SAP

ERP or APO-SNP). The supply planning looks at this unconstraint demand plan and tries to balance it with available supply (inventory and production).

The demand planner may also occasionally change the demand plan to better reflect market situations and may like to release the adjusted demand plan immediately instead of waiting for the weekly background job. The demand planner can release the demand plan into APO-SNP interactively using Transaction /SAPAPO/MC90. For a mass release, the background processing job uses the release profile defined in Transaction /SAPAPO/MC8S. As Figure 5.14 shows, the demand plan release from APO-DP to APO-SNP that creates a category order SAP liveCache.

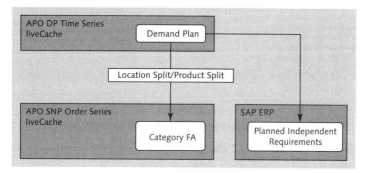

Figure 5.14 SAP APO Demand Plan Release to APO-SNP and SAP ERP

Optionally, the demand plan can also be released to SAP ERP in the form of planned independent requirements as shown in the figure. Both SAP ERP and APO-SNP require the demand to be published in a product location combination. In some occasions, the demand plan won't have location characteristics, which is why SAP has provided the location split functionality, which is explained next.

Location Split

Supply planning is always performed at the location product level. In a business scenario in which the location is not mapped as planning characteristics in a demand planning CVC, we need to define an interim location split table to provide a mapping table to transform the demand plan to a location-specific plan when released to APO-SNP. This scenario can arise when the demand planning is done at the country level and not at the plant level.

If the location is not defined as one of the planning characteristics in APO-DP, you can define the location split table using Transaction /SAPAPO/MC7A. Location proportions (percentages) can be maintained in the location split. Also, the product split can be maintained during the release using Transaction /SAPAPO/MC7B to transform the material number in APO-DP to another material number in supply planning.

Bucket Consistency

The demand plan is primarily performed on a monthly bucket, while the supply plan is performed on a weekly bucket. Access Transaction /SAPAPO/MC90 and select the pre-defined APO-DP bucket profile and daily planning bucket profile. You can define the buckets in Transaction /SAPAPO/TR30 by choosing the planning horizon in days, weeks, or months.

As Figure 5.15 shows, there can be two scenarios for the release. If only the APO-DP planning bucket profile is defined, the monthly bucket is released to the first weekly bucket in APO-SNP. If both the planning bucket and daily bucket profiles are defined, the monthly bucket is disaggregated to the weekly buckets based on the *period split* factor defined in the LOCATION PRODUCT • SNP2 tab (Transaction /SAPAPO/MAT1) or directly in Transaction /SAPAPO/MC90.

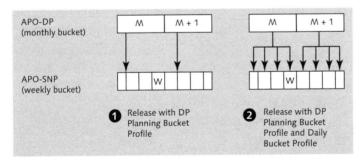

Figure 5.15 Disaggregation of a DP Monthly Bucket into SNP Weekly Buckets Using the DP Planning Bucket Profile and Daily Bucket Profile

Having looked at some basic navigation and settings, let's now look at the interactive forecasting process in APO-DP.

5.3 Interactive Statistical Forecasting

Statistical forecasting is primarily performed in the background using historical sales orders and forecasting models as input. In many situations, the mathematical calculations may not reflect the business equations, or the forecast errors coming from the forecasting run may be too high. In this scenario, the plan interactively runs statistical forecasting models from the demand planning book to identify the best-fit forecasting model. The planner identifies the forecasting model he is comfortable with and then assigns the forecast model to the product to be taken care of in next background forecasting job. The instance of the planner identifying the forecasting model and assigning the new forecast model to the product encompasses the interactive statistical forecasting process.

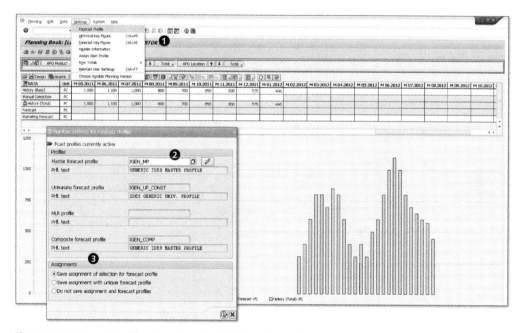

Figure 5.16 Interactive Planning: Preparing to Run a Forecast

Based on the planning framework outlined in Chapter 4, Section 4.5, the planner can perform the statistical forecasting interactively as well. As Figure 5.16 shows, the planner begins by selecting the FORECAST PROFILE from the menu bar (step ❶) and may wish to save his or her forecast profile following interactive planning. In the forecast profile, the planner identifies the forecasting model (step ❷) that he wants to run the forecast on. The last setting on the forecast profile is whether the planner wants to save the product selection on the forecast profile (step ❸). This way the product will inherit this forecast model for future forecast runs. When you click the STATISTICAL FORECASTING icon (⊠), you'll see a screen where the forecast result and parameters are displayed.

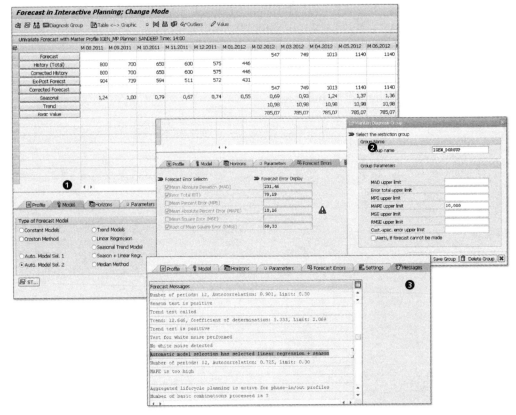

Figure 5.17 APO-Proposed Forecasting Model Based on Lowest Forecast Error

As Figure 5.17 shows, the planner reviews the forecasting parameters, forecast errors (with alert definitions in the diagnosis group), and the forecasting model proposed by SAP APO. The ex-post forecast and the corrected history calculations are also seen in this interactive screen. You can opt to switch to a graphical display for better analysis by clicking the TABLE <--> GRAPH option in the interactive screen. As seen in Figure 5.17, the planner can interactively select a different forecasting model (❶) and then run interactive statistical forecasting by executing the STATISTICAL FORECASTING icon. The forecast error (❷) is viewed in the FORECAST ERROR tab, where the business user looks at MAD and MAPE forecast errors. The overall goal is to identify the model with the lowest error. The lower the error, the more closely the forecast is following the historical sales pattern. The diagnosis group can define the upper and lower limits for alert generation. The MESSAGES (❸) tab shows which forecast model the system has identified when running an automatic forecast model.

For further analysis, the demand planner may look at removing historical outliers either by manually adjusting the history key figure in the planning book or defining the system in the forecast profile to perform corrections based on the ex-post method. As Figure 5.18 shows, the planner can choose the outlier correction, and the result can be immediately seen through corrections in the history. You can see the corrections by clicking the OUTLIERS icon.

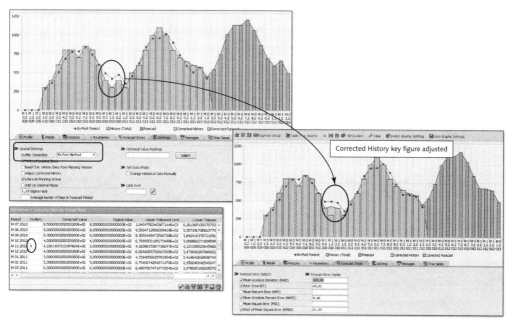

Figure 5.18 Outlier Correction by SAP APO and Seen in the Corrected History Key Figure

As Figure 5.19 shows, the planner can compare different forecasting models by clicking the FORECAST COMPARISON (⚏) icon. The user saves the forecast profiles for different products, and the profiles are stored in Table /SAPAPO/DP_FCST2, which can be extracted at later stage for analysis.

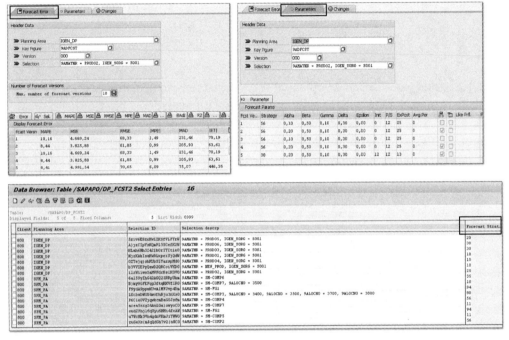

Figure 5.19   Forecast Comparison and Forecast Strategy Table

---

SAP APO Forecasting

You can find more information about SAP APO forecasting in SAP Note 388260: APO Consulting Forecast: Automatic Model Selection and Note 394076: Consulting: User-Exits and BAdIs in the Forecast Environment.

Once the demand plan is developed, the supply planner starts working on the supply planning side. In next few sections we'll see how the ABC Technology supply planner performs interactive supply planning using SAP APO.

5.4   Interactive Supply Planning

Interactive supply planning consists of balancing unconstrained demand with the supply plan, taking into account supply chain constraints.

Figure 5.20 shows the supply planning workflow in which the ABC Technology planner begins by analyzing the demand and supply situation in the network by (❶) creating procurement and replenishment plans and then moves to (❷) performing the master production schedule with rough-cut capacity planning for critical resources. The supply plans become a handover to supply chain execution with the creation of feasible load plans (❸) based on vendor minimums or truck load capacity.

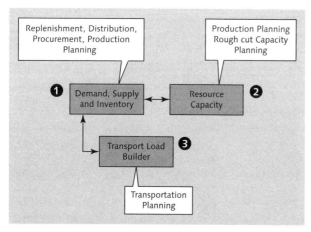

Figure 5.20 Supply Planning Workflow

Supply planning is always performed at the *product/location* combination. The planning toolbar (see Figure 5.21) consists of basic navigation similar to APO Demand Planning. An additional toolbar is provided to perform an interactive planning run using SNP heuristics and the optimizer.

Note

In this chapter, we're only focusing on the use of SNP heuristics solvers, while the other solvers (CTM and optimizer) will be discussed individually in Chapters 10 and 11.

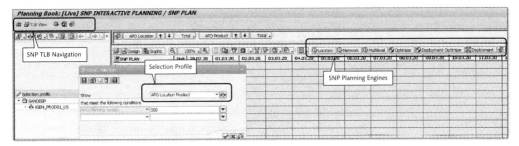

Figure 5.21 SNP Interactive Planning Book Toolbars

Using one of the SNP algorithms (heuristics, CTM, or optimizer), ABC Technology calculates replenishment, production, and distribution plans. Based on a weekly planning cycle, the SNP algorithm calculates different planning outputs considering supply constraints (example capacity) during different days of a week. An example can be replenishment calculation on Monday, a master production schedule on Tuesday/Wednesday, and distribution and load planning on Thursday/Friday.

The business planner reviews and validates the different set of supply plans. Using SNP solvers, the planner formulates medium- to long-term distribution and production plans. The goal of the planner is to design a supply chain model in the system that synchronizes the activities of purchase, production, and distribution departments. Also, safety stock planning is performed to ensure that there is additional buffer in the supply chain for any market fluctuations and to ensure the timely delivery of products to customers.

Table 5.6 lists the supply planning tasks and outputs that the planner performs using APO SNP.

Planning Tasks	Output
▶ Identify sources for finished products in network ▶ Plan and consider safety levels in network locations ▶ Distribute net requirements to plants for production planning ▶ Identify production resources in plants ▶ Explode bill of materials in plants ▶ Identify sources for supply of raw materials and components	▶ Purchase requisitions ▶ Stock transport purchase requisition ▶ SNP-planned orders

Table 5.6 APO-SNP Planning Tasks and Output

The calculation engine for the entire supply plan is SNP heuristics. The key to APO-SNP is the solver calculations, which we'll explain in the next section. Let's now see how heuristics works in the background to create feasible network plans.

5.5 SNP Heuristics

APO-SNP provides programming algorithms to solve supply planning situations. There are three solvers (algorithms) available in APO-SNP in the form of *heuristics*, *optimizer,* and *Capable-to-Match* (CTM). The heuristics algorithm is intended to solve certain planning problems in an analytic and reproducible way without necessarily finding the optimal solution. The optimizer focuses on cost-based optimizations, while CTM works on demand and supply priorities.

For the interactive planning process, SNP heuristics is simplest to understand and widely used for the rough-cut planning process. During the interactive planning process, the business planner can trigger SNP heuristics directly from the SAP APO planning book and view the planning result. The supply planner can run heuristics interactively from the SAP APO planning book using any of these three different methods:

- ▶ **Location heuristics**
  The system plans the specified products at the specified location. Location heuristics features include:

  - ▶ The planning is performed at a single specified location only.

  - ▶ The system explodes dependent demand for one BOM level at the production location in the planning direction. The planning direction refers to the time axis.

  - ▶ However, dependent demand is neither fulfilled nor further propagated throughout the supply chain.

  - ▶ The system uses this information only to generate stock transport requisitions, planned orders, and purchase requisitions.

- ▶ **Network heuristics**
  The system plans the specified products at all specified locations in the network to which the selected product is assigned. Network heuristics features include:

  - ▶ The planning is performed for complete network locations.

▶ The system explodes dependent demand for one BOM level at the first production location encountered in the planning direction.

▶ However, dependent demand is neither fulfilled nor further propagated through the supply chain.

▶ The system uses this information only to generate stock transport requisitions, planned orders, and purchase requisitions.

▶ **Multi-level heuristics**
The system plans all products specified at all locations, whether they are finished, intermediary, or purchased goods from the highest level down to the lowest BOM level. Multi-level heuristics features include:

▶ The planning is performed for complete network locations. In other words, the system plans all products specified, including all dependent demand.

▶ The multi-level heuristic is performed across all locations to which the selected products are assigned, as well as across all locations to which dependent products are assigned.

▶ The system uses this information only to generate stock transport requisitions, planned orders, and purchase requisitions.

> **Example**
>
> ABC Technology has a large network of distribution centers and has decided to use a heuristics engine for its supply planning calculations. The company selected the heuristics method because it was easy for business planners to derive the planning result and work on exceptions. ABC Technology was also looking for planning solvers that take the basic lot sizing and lead time calculation during the calculation. The heuristics is quantity-based and plans the complete supply network during a single run. The company plans to use the multi-level heuristics for creating stock transport requisitions across location, planned orders at production plants, and purchase requisitions toward suppliers for material procurement. Using multi-level heuristics, the bill of material components will also be planned at the manufacturing location.

Figure 5.22 shows an example in which the distribution center net requirements (demand minus supply) flow down to the factory as a replenishment plan. The master production schedule is created in the factory location with a BOM explosion. The procurement plan is proposed to the vendor for the supply of raw materials. Once manufactured, the finished goods are distributed (deployed) back to the distribution center for a better understanding of stock projections with a constrained material plan.

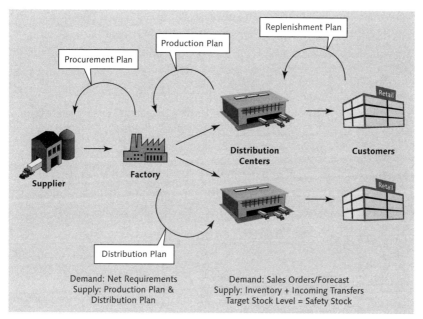

Procurement Plan

Production Plan

Replenishment Plan

Distribution Plan

Supplier

Factory

Distribution Centers

Customers

Demand: Net Requirements
Supply: Production Plan &
Distribution Plan

Demand: Sales Orders/Forecast
Supply: Inventory + Incoming Transfers
Target Stock Level = Safety Stock

Figure 5.22 SNP Heuristics Network Calculation

5.5.1 Heuristic Engine Run Process

Now, let's look at how heuristics performs in the backend once either triggered interactively from the planning book or scheduled as a background processing job. The only primary requirement from the user perspective to use this solver is the proper master data setup reflecting the supply chain model. The processing logic of heuristics algorithm was simple for ABC Technology planners to understand. The heuristics can be performed interactively by business user using the LOCATION, NETWORK, and MULTILEVEL icons in the SAP APO planning book.

The logical sequence with which the heuristics engine runs is as follows:

1. Planning data is read from SAP liveCache.

2. Prior to running SNP heuristics, we need to calculate the sequence of locations for running the algorithm. This is defined as "low-level coding" in SAP APO, which means that each location is assigned a number (0, 1, 2, 3, and so on). SNP

heuristics uses the low level code to sequence the location for propagating the demand from one destination location to the next level of source location. A low-level coding is run to identify the location sequence with which the heuristics needs to run to identify the source location. The transportation lane sequence defines this network sequence. The low-level coding is calculated using Transaction /SAPAPO/LLC for a specific planning version (for example, 000).

3. The demand is calculated based on the planning strategy that controls the consumption of forecasts and sales orders. If the forecast horizon is maintained in the SNP2 tab of the location product master data, the forecast is not considered for that specific horizon.

4. The projected stock is calculated as total demand less total receipts. This calculation is performed in the stock balance macro in the planning book. You can manipulate the heuristics result by making changes to this macro.

5. The target stock is calculated based on target days of supply requirements and safety stock.

6. The net requirement calculation becomes target stock less projected stock.

7. Lot sizing rules (lot-for-lot, fixed, period, and target days of supply) and parameters (minimum, maximum, and rounding) are applied to the net requirement proposal.

8. The procurement type is identified next, whether in-house production (value = E) or external procurement (value = F). If quota arrangement master data is maintained, it will overrule the procurement type. Quota arrangement is used for the multi-sourcing scenario in which the distribution center can receive products from multiple sources.

9. For manufacturing plants, the production data structure (PDS) or production process model (PPM) is identified and the bill of materials is exploded with routing definitions. The receipt elements are created accordingly, which consumes the resources to identify capacity.

10. With the receipt elements, the resource capacity of bottleneck resources can be evaluated.

11. The entire above process is repeated through each level in the network per the low-level coding. Each location creates stock transfers and production and

purchase requirements. The process also generates dependent demand and a procurement plan for raw materials.

These steps are performed in the background by the heuristics engine. The planning output is displayed in the SNP interactive planning book. Let's see next how the results are displayed in the planning books under which key figures.

5.5.2 Replenishment and Procurement Using SNP Heuristics

The initial situation at the ABC Technology distribution center (see Figure 5.23) depicts a scenario in which there are physical inventory and demand elements with planned shortages in coming weeks. The day's supply key figure shows how far the existing inventory can fulfill the future forecast. This process allows ABC Technology to replenish its warehouses with stock based on the projected forecast. At the same time, the system proposes the procurement of critical-component raw materials. The *critical components* are materials for which sourcing needs to planned well in advance because of longer lead times, sourcing from unreliable vendors, high material value, allocation from suppliers, or other factors.

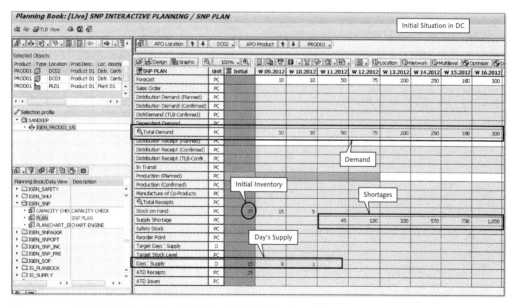

Figure 5.23 Initial Situation in the DC Before the SNP Heuristics Run

Here are the process steps to set up replenishment and procurement in SAP APO:

1. The supply planner runs the multi-level heuristics interactively to plan the complete network related to this product. The shortage serves as a net requirement and becomes planned receipts after the planning run (see Figure 5.24).

2. The factory receives these requirements in the key figure distribution demand (planned) and plans production with bucket capacity.

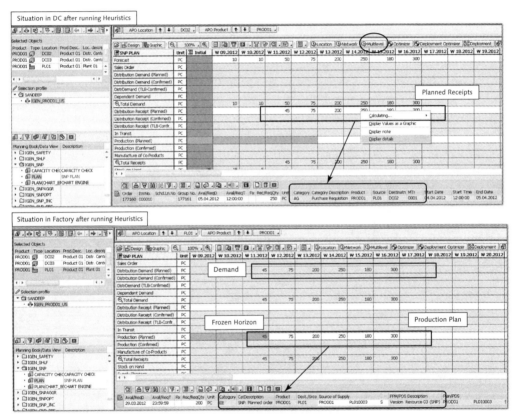

Figure 5.24 Situation in the DC and Factory after the SNP Planning Run

3. The SNP-planned orders use the PDS and explodes the component and raw materials required for finished goods manufacturing. The SNP-planned orders also consume the resource capacity.

4. The procurement plan (see Figure 5.25) is created for raw materials from the supplier with proper lead-time scheduling.

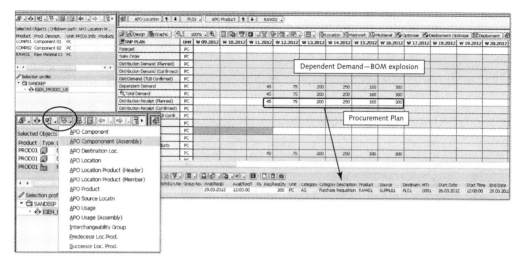

Figure 5.25 Procurement Proposals to the Suppliers for Raw Materials

5.5.3 Master Production Schedule and Capacity Leveling Using SNP Heuristics

The ABC Technology supply planner next evaluates the production feasibility as the initial plan proposed by SNP heuristics with infinite resource and material capacity. As Figure 5.26 shows, the planner accesses the capacity data view with the selection profile of APO RESOURCE. The planner inputs the critical resource he wants to evaluate. The supply planner is interested in evaluating the critical or bottleneck production resources for medium- to long-term planning. Once the capacity information is displayed, the planner can perform capacity leveling to balance the resource utilization. He achieves this by clicking the CAPACITY LEVELING icon and inputting the parameters, such as maximum percentage of utilization or backward/forward utilization. This process allows ABC Technology to create a rough-cut production plan and evaluate the resource capacity.

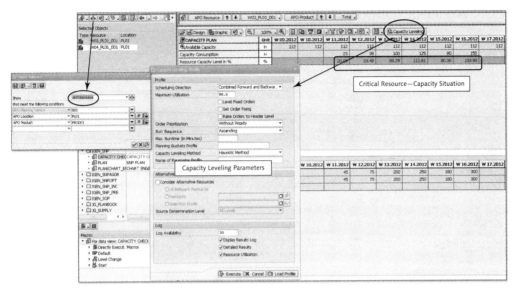

Figure 5.26 Master Production Scheduling with Capacity Leveling

The planner views the future capacity projection and finds some capacity overloads. To resolve this situation, the planner can take various options, as illustrated in Table 5.7.

Capacity Management	Perform Activity in APO SNP
Capacity leveling for the bottleneck resource to move the SNP-planned orders between buckets. Perform backward and/ or forward scheduling.	Use SNP heuristics capacity leveling. As Figure 5.26 shows, the planner runs the capacity leveling either interactively or via background Transaction /SAPAPO/ SNP05. Running interactively offers the opportunity to analyze before saving the result for publication. The capacity profile can either be changed or created as master data. Figure 5.27 shows the result after running the capacity leveling. The result is published back to the SNP interactive planning book in the *production plan* key figure.

Table 5.7 Capacity Management Using APO-SNP

Capacity Management	Perform Activity in APO SNP
Plan for additional shifts for overload buckets.	Change the SAP APO resource master (Transaction /SAPAPO/RES01) to add more capacity to the resource. This is achieved by defining an active variant in the resource with different capacities (shifts).
Plan on alternative if available.	Another option in the capacity leveling is to balance the two resources evenly. As Figure 5.28 shows, the parameter can be set and the heuristics run to even the planned orders using the two resources. If we only want the overload to move to the alternative resource, this will require a BAdI modification (/SAPAPO/ SNP_CAP).

Table 5.7 Capacity Management Using APO-SNP (Cont.)

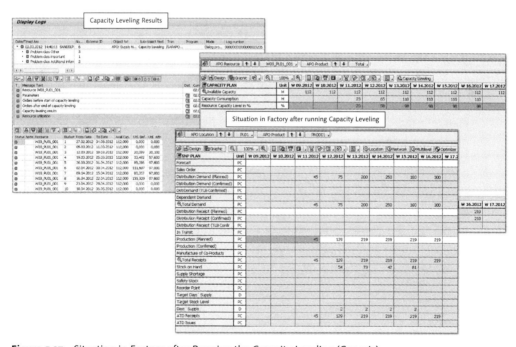

Figure 5.27 Situation in Factory after Running the Capacity Leveling (Generic)

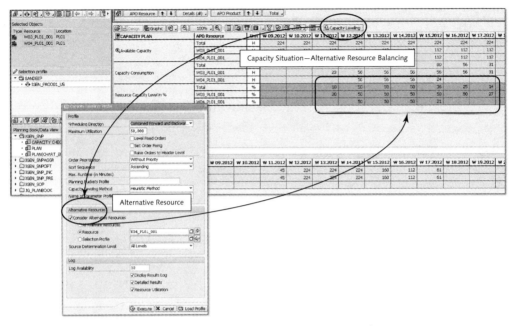

Figure 5.28 Alternative Resource Balancing with SNP Capacity Leveling

5.5.4 Distribution Planning Using SNP Deployment Heuristics

Once the manufacturing location has completed creating the feasible production plan, this plan needs to be translated into a distribution plan. The distribution plan tells the distribution center what quantities it can expect for specific buckets (weekly). The distribution or deployment plan is the constrained supply plan from the source location to the destination location as an indication of what is planned to be shipped against the original requirements from the destination location. With the distribution plan, the stock cover projection can be properly visualized at different warehouse locations, and supply chain actions can be taken proactively to balance demand and supply. This process allows ABC Technology to distribute its products across a network based on its business priorities and stocking policies.

The calculation of deployment takes into account available-to-deploy (ATD) receipts and issue elements. ATD indicates what requirement and supply categories can be accounted for in the calculation. For example, if for inventory to be deployed we only want to account for unrestricted and quality stock types and not restricted or blocked stock types, we mention those in the ATD categories.

Example

ABC Technology plans to use this deployment plan in the available-to-promise (ATP) process as well. For customer orders, it can use the incoming deployment plan as ATP quantities for the customer order confirmation process. Depending on the business scenario, different receipts and issue categories can be included in the ATD category.

5.5.5 Master Data Maintenance

APO-SNP deployment requires master data setup for the distribution planning process to work. Depending on the different distribution strategies, different master data settings need to be defined. The majority of the master data is maintained in the location product (Transaction /SAPAPO/MAT1) in the SNP2 tab. Some of the mandatory master data are as follows:

▶ The PULL DEPLOYMENT HORIZON defines the time period for the ATD issue calculation, while the PUSH DEPLOYMENT HORIZON defines the time period for the ATD receipts calculation.

▶ Also maintained in the master data are the various deployment strategies—*pull, pull/push, quota arrangement,* and *push*—taking the safety stock horizon into account.

▶ The *fair share* rule defines the allocation of constraint supply to the demand with options of percentage distribution by demand, percentage fulfillment by target, percentage by quota arrangement, and division by priorities.

Figure 5.29 gives an example for a business scenario using different deployment strategies. The figure shows three primary deployment scenarios: pull, pull/push, and push. In the pull scenario, only the required demand quantities are pulled by the destination (distribution center), and the remaining production quantities are left behind at the source (manufacturing facility). In the pull/push scenario, similarly to the pull scenario, the destination pulls all the required demand but within the defined push horizon. In the push scenario, all the quantities from the source location are pushed to the destination location within the push horizon.

	W1	W2	W3	W4	W5	W6	W7
Initial situation:							
Demand at DC	200	200	200	200	200	200	200
Supply at Plant	200	1000	500				
After Pull Scenario:							
Quantity moved to DC	200	200	200	200	0	0	0
Stock remaining in plant	0	800	1100	900	900	900	900
or							
After Pull-push Scenario:							
Quantity moved to DC	200	600					
Stock remaining in plant	0	400	900	900	900	900	900
or							
After Push Scenario:							
Quantity moved to DC	200	1000					
Stock remaining in plant	0	0	500	500	500	500	500

(Push horizon spans W1–W2; Pull horizon spans W3–W4)

Figure 5.29 Different Available Deployment Strategies

Deployment Strategies

ABC Technology uses different deployment strategies to distribute its products in the network. Based on different product strategies for laptops, desktops, and monitors, ABC Technology wants to use pull/push distribution to ensure stock availability in the distribution center and avoid keeping any finished goods inventory in the manufacturing facility. The four deployment strategies available in APO-SNP are as follows:

▶ *Pull/push* distribution setting (enter P - PUSH DISTRIBUTION in the field)

  ▶ All supply is distributed immediately to demand locations to meet all demand within the pull deployment horizon.

  ▶ Requirement dates specified by demand locations are not taken into account.

  ▶ Stock is pushed as soon as it becomes available at the source location.

  ▶ As with pull distribution, normally demands outside the pull horizon are not considered as relevant for supply planning.

▶ *Push by demands* setting (enter X - PUSH DISTRIBUTION in the field)

  ▶ All supply is distributed immediately to demand locations for the entire planning horizon.

  ▶ Meets all requirements irrespective of any time horizon in the future.

  ▶ Pull deployment horizon is not taken into account in this instance.

► *Pull* distribution setting (leave PUSH DISTRIBUTION field blank)

  ► All demand within pull deployment horizon is considered by deployment planning.

  ► Distribution is made on due dates specified for each demand at each demand location.

  ► No supply is distributed to any demand source in advance of requirement date (nothing is pushed out early).

► *Pull* distribution setting (enter Q - PUSH DISTRIBUTION in the field)

  ► Push based on quota arrangement master data where the percentage of supply allocation to locations is defined.

  ► All supply is distributed immediately according to quota arrangements specified for demand locations.

  ► Requirements situation at target locations is not taken into account.

Fair Share Rule

During some seasonal periods, ABC Technology finds that demand exceeds supply, and in this case the deployment needs to apply the fair share rule for distributing the supply plan based on current ATD quantity. *Fair share* means allocation of supply redistribution for scenarios when the supply is less than demand. This allocation can be defined by different rules.

Example

ABC Technology uses the fair share rule based on demand to distribute prorated supply based on initial demand requested.

There are four fair share rules existing in APO-SNP for alternative methods of allocating restricted supply of product to demand:

► **Fair share rule A**
  The objective of fair share rule A is to distribute limited supply to all demand locations in proportion to requested demand quantities. As Figure 5.30 shows, the demand from each distribution center (DC) is taken as a proportion to identify the deployment quantity.

Fair share Rule A (% split by demand)	16-Feb-09	17-Feb-09	18-Feb-09
Available to Deploy (ATD)	1000	900	400
Demand DC1	100		200
Demand DC2		500	600
Quantity deployed to DC1	100		100
Quantity deployed to DC2		500	300

Figure 5.30 Fair Share Rule A

▶ **Fair share rule B**

The objective of fair share rule B is to raise stock levels at all demand locations to approximately same percentage of the target stock level. As Figure 5.31 shows, the deployment results use the target stock level as a proportion to distribute the stock.

Available to Deploy (ATD) from source:		300	
Fair share rule B (% of target stock)	DC1	DC2	DC3
Projected stock	50	500	0
Target stock level (based on min safety days)	500	700	200
% of Target stock level before deploy	10%	71.40%	0%
Deploy result	200	0	100
% Target stock level result	50%	71.40%	50%

Result: SNP attempts to get DC1 and DC3 as close as possible to DC2 and to each other. If starting with negative projected stock level, system first attempts to raise stock level up to zero, before attempting to raise all levels to same percentage of target. Uses additional CPU usage for processing.

Figure 5.31 Fair Share Rule B

▶ **Fair share rule C**

The objective of fair share rule C is to distribute stock according to demand priorities and/or quota arrangement at demand locations. As Figure 5.32 shows, the deployment orders are based on the outbound quota arrangement proportions maintained.

Outbound quota arrangement:		DC1=30%, DC2=70%	
Fair share Rule C (split by outbound quota)	16-Feb-09	17-Feb-09	18-Feb-09
Available to Deploy (ATD)	1000	900	400
Demand DC1	100		200
Demand DC2		500	600
Quantity deployed to DC1	100		120
Quantity deployed to DC2		500	280

Figure 5.32 Fair Share Rule C

▶ **Fair share rule D**

The objective of fair share rule D is to distribute stock according to distribution priorities of transportation lanes. Figure 5.33 shows an example of fair share priorities for one of the DCs based on the priority set in the transportation lane.

Priority of outbound transport lane: DC2=1, DC1=2			
Fair share Rule D (split by lane priority)	16-Feb-09	17-Feb-09	18-Feb-09
Available to Deploy (ATD)	1000	900	400
Demand DC1	100		200
Demand DC2		500	600
Quantity deployed to DC1	100		0
Quantity deployed to DC2		500	400

Figure 5.33 Fair Share Rule D

5.5.6 Interactive SNP Deployment Planning

Now that we understand the master data settings requirement for SNP deployment, we can perform an interactive deployment planning run from the SNP planning book. The planner performs the interactive deployment heuristics run from the SNP planning book by first maintaining the deployment user settings. In the settings (click 🔲) the planner can opt to run based on the most recent SNP heuristics result or real-time results, which simulates the SNP deployment run again. The requirement of running real-time deployment arises if there has been any change in the demand or supply situation since the last planning run or if the planner has made some changes and wants to see how the changes reflect in the current situation.

Once the user settings are saved, perform the deployment heuristics by clicking the DEPLOYMENT icon at the source location. The deployment quantity is seen distributed from the source location to target locations based on the ATD quantity. Figure 5.34 shows the deployment result at the plant and distribution centers.

The results are seen in the key figures DISTRIBUTION DEMAND (CONFIRMED) at the source location and DISTRIBUTION RECEIPTS (CONFIRMED) at the target location. With the deployment result output, the planner can analyze the stock projection. In a constraint supply planning scenario, the business planner is now able to see if there are any products out of stock or any other supply chain situations (for example, delays or excess supply). The business planner monitors the plan by looking at the DAYS SUPPLY key figure and the SUPPLY SHORTAGE key figures.

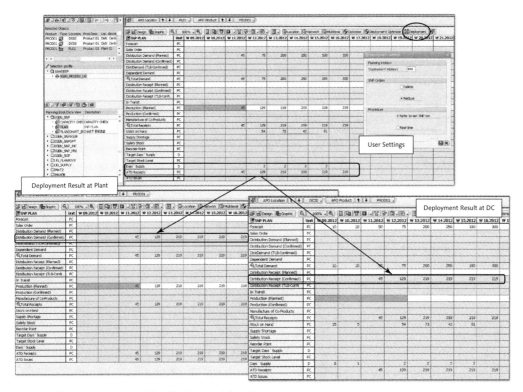

Figure 5.34 Interactive Deployment Result

5.6 Load Planning Using the SNP Transport Load Builder

The distribution plan created in Section 5.5.4 now needs to be translated into execution steps. In the execution steps, the distribution plan needs to be translated into truck loads for shipments to make the transportation cost economical. The creation of this load plan can be performed using SNP Transport Load Builder (TLB) functionality, either interactively from the SAP APO planning book or as part of a background processing job. The load plan primarily creates a stock transport order or purchase order for execution. After deployment planning, the next step is for the supply planner to perform load planning for execution. Usually, the load building is done for the following week's shipments.

The TLB uses the deployment result as input to build truck loads or other transport units based on capacity constraints. The constraints can be modeled in the form of either vendor minimums or transport truck loads (weight, volume, or pallets) for transfers.

The TLB profile is maintained in Transaction /SAPAPO/TLBPRF. Here we define the parameter (weight, volume, and pallets) constraints to limit the truck load build, as well as the minimum and maximum limits for each parameter and Boolean criteria (AND, OR, etc). The TLB profile is assigned to each transportation lane and transportation method combination. The profile defines constraints in the following terms:

▶ Number of pallet positions (min/max), where X pallets stacked = 1 pallet position

▶ Volume (min/max)

▶ Weight (min/max)

▶ Defines pull-in horizon

    ▶ Specified in days from today's date to cumulate all the deployment purchase requisitions to form a load plan.

    ▶ When calculation ends with incomplete loads in one bucket, TLB uses future deployed stock transfers (within this pull-in horizon) to make a complete load.

Figure 5.35 shows various fields used in the TLB planning, which we explain here:

▶ PULL-IN HORIZON
Used to identify the deployment orders that can be pulled forward for load consolidation. ABC Technology consolidates the deployment orders for one whole week, maintaining seven days as PULL-IN HORIZON.

▶ LOADING METHOD
Defines the distribution of product during the load building process. The two options are:

    ▶ LOAD BALANCING: Equal percentage distribution of all products in all shipments

▶ STRAIGHT LOADING: Consolidates similar products from same loading group class. The loading group is maintained in the product master in the GR/GI tab.

ABC Technology maintains load balancing since they have single sourcing for each product category.

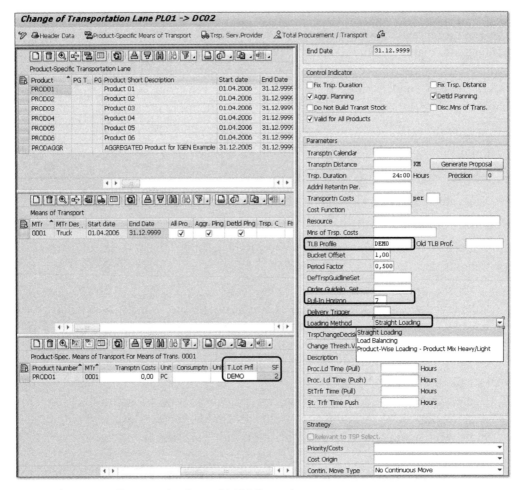

Figure 5.35 Transportation Lane with TLB Parameters

▶ LOT SIZE PROFILE
Both TLB and Deployment use lane-dependent lot size profiles to determine how to build transport loads (rounding values). Lot size profiles define typical,

frequently used min/max lot sizes and rounding multiples. Lot size profiles are entered on the product-specific level of the transportation lane.

▶ STACKING FACTOR

Defines how many times pallets of specific product can be stacked on top of each other. Is used during a TLB run to calculate the number of pallet positions used in a means of transport. Parameters can be entered at three different levels in SAP APO:

- ▶ Product: in GENERAL DATA tab of the product master
- ▶ Product at location
- ▶ Transportation lanes: at the level of product-specific means of transport. If maintained, the transportation lane value takes precedence over the product level value. The load planner performs load planning either interactively from the SNP planning book by clicking the TLB VIEW icon or via Transaction /SAPAPO/SNPTLB. The process can also be executed by running the TLB in the background via Transaction /SAPAPO/SNP04.

The selection profile for the TLB is always TRANSPORTATION LANE, where either one of a combination of destination locations, source locations, or SAP APO locations needs to be entered. In the interactive screen, the planner has two options for creating the load planning: either by running the TLB heuristics or manually creating the load plans.

ABC Technology runs TLB every week for the following week's truck loads. The SNP-TLB algorithm consolidates the distribution plan for the following week and creates multiple truck loads. The TLB is performed in a background job. The business planner only creates manual truck loads in TLB for exception scenarios.

Before starting his tasks, the user checks the TLB PARAMETERS button (⊞) for the selected horizon and determines whether the TLB profile is correctly assigned.

To create interactive planning, follow these steps, as shown in Figure 5.36:

1. Right-click one of the deployment orders and select FOR TLB SHIPMENTS (PARTIAL/ ENTIRE QUANTITY).

2. Drag and drop the subsequent deployment to consolidate similar shipments.

3. If the min/max capacity range is violated, the OVERLOAD TLB screen is highlighted in red. By clicking the TLB orders, you can bring up the products, quantities, and capacity they are occupying on the means of transport in the lower screens.

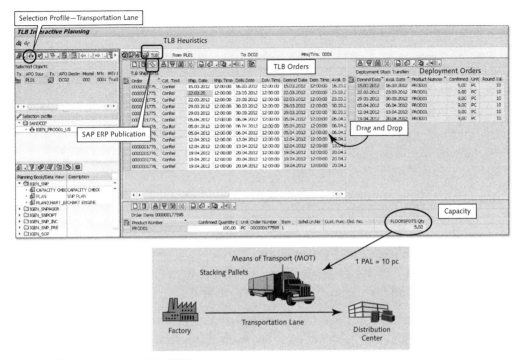

Figure 5.36 Interactive TLB Screen

Figure 5.36 shows the TLB interactive planning screen subsequent to running the TLB heuristics. The heuristics, using the stacking factor for the pallet floor spots, has proposed multiple truck loads. The unconverted deployment balance remains as deployment orders. Once you've reviewed the TLB orders, you can publish them to the SAP ERP system by clicking the TRANSFER TO OLTP icon (⊞). The planner can define settings to publish the orders automatically and immediately, or wait for change pointers to be published periodically at a later stage using Transaction /SAPAPO/C5. The transfers of APO-SNP orders (automatic, periodically, or no transfer) are maintained in Transaction /SAPAPO/SDP110.

TLB

Please refer to the following SAP Notes for information regarding the TLB in APO-SNP:

▶ SAP Note 514947: Steps for using TLB without deployment and directly from SNP transfers.

▶ SAP Note 710198: Steps to model additional parameters then standard SAP provided parameters.

> ▶ SAP Note 1358057: Refers to BAdI for changing the input and output values during the TLB run. Example: BAdI method CONVERT_TLBDEMAND_TO_RECOMM—we can modify the shipments generated by the TLB engine to customer needs.

5.7   Demand and Supply Planning Alerts

Alerts are mechanisms that a business can use in the SAP system to identify any exception that requires a specific action. SAP APO alerts support the exception management process, allowing business users to analyze and correct planning situations. The user can view the alerts in either the alert monitor or directly in the SAP APO planning book. Both demand and supply planners can view their alerts in these respective areas.

There are both standard and custom alerts available in SAP APO, which comprise *exception management*. Exception management is defined as when the planning situation is outside the defined tolerance range and there is a subsequent demand and supply imbalance. *Standard alerts* are pre-configured alerts provided by SAP based on industry best practices. The *custom alerts* are additional alerts that need to be configured to meet business requirements for exception management.

The majority of alerts are configured using SAP APO macros. The business planner can select the alerts (standard and custom) they are interested in monitoring while defining their alert profile. Custom alerts (Transaction /SAPAPO/ATYPES_SDP) are written as macros in the planning book to identify company-specific critical information.

Example

The exception management process allows ABC Technology to control its supply chain situations. The business planners plan to set up both demand alerts and supply alerts. For demand alerts, the business planner would like to monitor the forecast error coming as a result of the forecasting run. Any sign of high forecast error gives a signal to the demand planner to review their forecasting model. Additionally, the demand planner monitors the forecast and sales order on weekly basis to ensure stock availability.

On the supply side, the supply planner monitors the shortages for critical products to plan replenishment on time. The supply planner also monitors the inventory levels of his products that are within the minimum and maximum stock covers to avoid any excess or shortage situations.

In the following sections, we'll explain the different types of alerts that are available, and then teach you how to work with these alerts to better manage your business processes.

5.7.1 Types of Alerts

There are two types of alerts available in SAP APO: dynamic and database. *Dynamic* alerts are generated in real time based on the current planning situation, while *database* alerts are written in the system database for a planning situation at a specific point in time.

Let's assume we had a supply shortage yesterday before the alert macro background job, so the database alert will be written in the system highlighting the shortage. In the same example, if today there were some goods receipts in inventory, the dynamic alert will capture the current situation and report if any shortages still exist. The main difference is that dynamic alerts are not stored in tables, while the database alerts are stored in tables. The database alert is calculated via a planning job, while the dynamic alert is triggered when the alert profile is called.

5.7.2 Visualizing Alerts with the Alert Monitor

The Alert Monitor is a central working tool for business planners to view, prioritize, and analyze their list of alerts. The Alert Monitor is used for both the evaluation and processing of alerts. The alerts can be visualized in many ways in SAP APO. They can be displayed as standalone in the Alert Monitor (Transaction /SAPAPO/AMON1), in the SAP APO interactive planning books, or in the Supply Chain Cockpit (Transaction /SAPAPO/SCC02). The most preferred option is the Alert Monitor for easier access and flexibility in grouping alerts of high importance. The business planner can work through the alert list and directly access the SAP APO planning book for a particular location product selection from the Alert Monitor. You can set up alerts by following these steps:

1. Access Transaction /SAPAPO/AMON_SETTING and create an application-specific alert profile by right-clicking and selecting CREATE (step ❶) (see Figure 5.37).

2. Provide the PROFILE ID with a description and select SUPPLY AND DEMAND PLANNING in the alert monitor (AMO) application (step ❷).

3. Identify the alert type, planning book, and data view to run the alerts (step ❸). Also, select the alert you are interested in displaying.

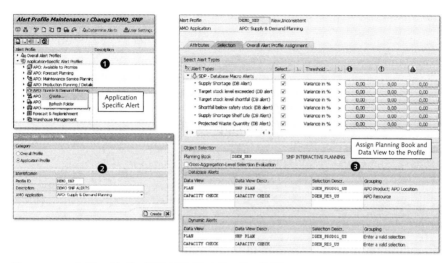

Figure 5.37 Setting Up the SAP APO Alert Monitor (1/2)

4. Assign the application-specific profile to the overall alert settings and specify the horizon for which alerts are generated (step ❹) (Figure 5.38).

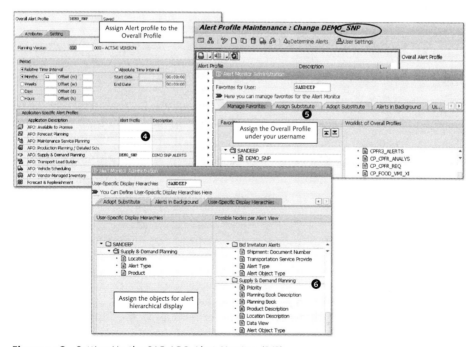

Figure 5.38 Setting Up the SAP APO Alert Monitor (2/2)

5. Assign the overall profile settings to the user name (step ❺).

6. Define the display hierarchical form in which the alerts need to be grouped while displaying in the Alert Monitor (step ❻). In our example, the planner will view all the alerts for location first, and then the alert type (demand or supply alert) will be displayed, followed by a list of products that have generated alerts.

You can also visualize the alert in the interactive planning book (Transaction /SAPAPO/SDP94) by assigning the alert profile by clicking SETTINGS on the top menu path. Table 5.8 illustrates commonly used demand and supply alerts.

Alert Type	Purpose
First Backlog	Indicates the week of the first backlog situation
ATS Backlog	Indicates an issue with the short-term stock available to sell
Safety Stock Violation	Indicates a violation of safety stock figures
Exceeding Days Supply	Indicates an overstocked situation
No Forecast	Indicates missing forecasts on an FG product level

Table 5.8 Demand and Supply Planning Alerts

5.7.3 Methodology: The Decision Tree

There are different methods and techniques you can use to react to alerts that are generated in SAP APO. For example, some of these methods are reports, decision trees, or workflows. The decision tree technique describes the structured thinking process a planner has to follow when managing alerts. The decision tree serves as a better logical process to apply human analysis than a report or workflow mechanism. They cover the necessary steps, starting with the identification of an alert and ending with the execution of the corrective action to resolve the exception.

A decision tree needs to be created to formalize the management of each individual alert type defined in SAP APO. Decision trees are primarily created by a business cross-functional team and indentify the business activities that mitigate the risk of any exception supply chain scenario. It also serves as a means of communication for highlighting any operational or medium-term issues in the supply chain.

Figure 5.39 shows an example of the supply planning alert for a stock out situation within ABC Technology and how the business process issue is resolved with proactive action. The figure shows that once the alert is detected, a signal is sent to the planner to look at the possibility of resupply from other locations. If resupply is not possible, the manufacturing plant is approached to consider the possibility of a capacity increase. With this overall process, the stocking policy is also reviewed for the product.

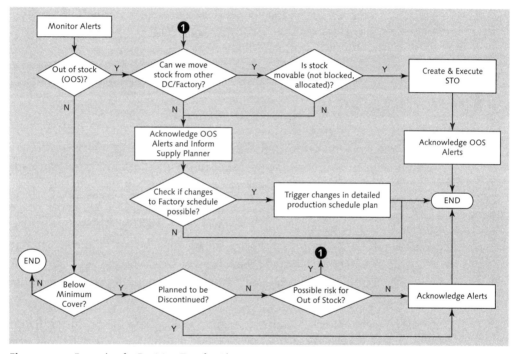

Figure 5.39 Example of a Decision Tree for Alert Management

5.8   Simulation via Version Management

SAP APO version management offers the capability for the planner to plan in simulation mode without affecting the normal operational planning process. An example of version management can be seen in the ABC Technology weekly planning process, as highlighted in Section 5.1, for which the supply planner performs the master production schedule in a simulation version. This allows the planner to look at various sourcing alternatives before finalizing the feasible constrained production plan. Another example of a business scenario would be when a business wants to simulate whether they should manufacture in-house versus procure the products from external suppliers. The planner would look at the resource capacity constraint based on the projected forecast and inventory to perform the analysis.

> **Note**
>
> SAP APO planning data (master and transaction) is stored in the active planning version. We explained earlier in Chapter 4, Section 4.7.1, how to create models and versions. There can be multiple versions created for a specific supply chain model. Only one version (active 000) integrates with the SAP ERP system, and the rest of the versions can be treated as simulation versions.

Figure 5.40 shows the version management process in APO, with the following three simple steps:

1. The first step is to copy all master and transaction data from the active version to a simulation version using Transaction /SAPAPO/VERCOP. Once copied, the simulation version will have the snapshot of the master and transaction data. ABC Technology plans to keep a weekly snapshot for any planning deviation comparisons.

2. The business supply planner can make any changes to his or her planning scope (product family in the supply network). The planner, for instance, may want to increase the production capacity in the future to balance the demand during the peak season. In this step, the planner may change both master and transactional data.

3. Once the changes are made in the simulation version and the planner is happy with the result, he can opt to immediately merge his planning results back into the active planning version (000) separately using Transaction /SAPAPO/VERMER. We can use this function to copy four SNP key figures from a planning version back into the active version. PP/DS order data cannot be copied. The following is a list of the SNP key figures:

   ▸ Planned production (key figure 9APPROD, key figure function 2001)

   ▸ SNP distribution receipt (key figure 9APSHIP, key figure function 4001)

   ▸ Deployment distribution receipt (key figure 9AFSHIP, key figure function 4005)

   ▸ Safety stock (key figure function 3003)

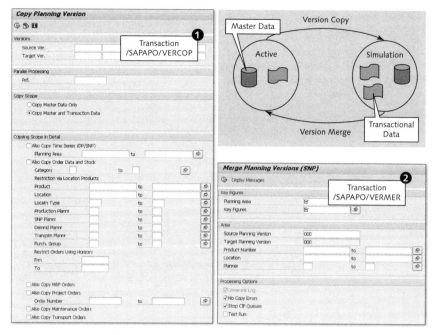

Figure 5.40 Version Management in SAP APO

5.9 Summary

We've now explored the basic planning functionalities in SAP APO. In this chapter, you learned that APO-DP and SNP both support the weekly planning basic activities to be performed by the planner. The chapter teaches the basic navigation in the interactive planning book, where both the demand and supply planner spends majority of time planning.

This chapter also looked at how statistical forecasting can be performed interactively and fine-tuned for more accurate forecast results. Using SNP heuristics as a supply planning solver, this chapter demonstrated the different business processes of procurement, production, and distribution being supported by APO-SNP. Toward the end, the chapter touched on the alerts and version management functionality in SAP APO.

The next two chapters will focus on modeling complex business scenarios and variants in the SAP APO environment.

This chapter explains the advanced functionalities available within SAP APO in the form of demand planning. We'll go over the most important and commonly used features that relate to demand planning business processes and help you understand and use each functionality.

6   Advanced Demand Planning Concepts in SAP APO

As we've already established, APO-DP is the key input to a company's sales and operations planning process. During the demand planning process, the planner has to incorporate various business rules to make the plan more feasible and realistic for execution.

As shown in the mind map for this chapter (see Figure 6.1), we will cover the advanced topics in APO-DP. These topics will include configuration, master data set up, and business scenario testing process. More specifically, the advanced concepts in this chapter cover the management of commonly used business processes in the area of new product introductions, sales and marketing promotion planning, seasonal planning, and bill of materials (BOM) forecasting.

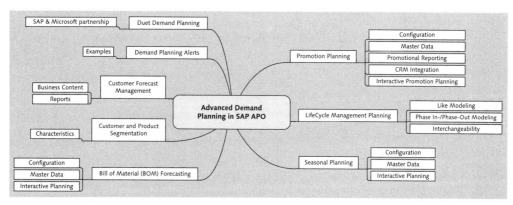

Figure 6.1   Learning Points for the Chapter (Mind Map)

In the following sections, we'll discuss promotion planning, lifecycle planning, seasonal planning, and customer and product segmentations, along with Customer Forecast Management (CFM). We'll explain how these features are important to the functionality of APO-DP and show you how to get started using them.

6.1 Promotion Planning

The total demand plan formulated in SAP APO consists of a statistical forecast (baseline) and a promotions volume. Examples of promotions may include campaign activities, trade activities, sampling activities, or cannibalizations. SAP provides the SAP CRM (Customer Relationship Management) suite, which can plan promotions and interface with SAP APO for planning. It also provides the option of entering promotions planning directly into SAP APO.

> **Example**
>
> ABC Technology uses a combination of the method of interfacing promotional events from the SAP CRM system and manual maintenance of promotions directly in SAP APO. ABC Technology sales and marketing group for the laptop division uses the SAP CRM system for planning trade promotions, while the monitor group maintains the promotions in the SAP APO-CRM planning book directly.
>
> Since the promotions volume is greater for the laptop group, the use of the SAP CRM system provides easier maintenance; because the monitor divisions has only a few promotions, they prefer to maintain this information directly in SAP APO. With both techniques, the promotions are captured and calculated along with a baseline forecast to derive a final demand plan in SAP APO.

Performing promotion planning directly in SAP APO allows the demand planner and trade promotion planner to view the result in a consolidated form. The trade promotion planner plans at a similar characteristics level as the demand planner. Integrating SAP CRM promotions from an external system requires interfacing and additional mapping to match the SAP APO characteristics levels. Let's look at both of these methods in the following sections.

6.1.1 Promotion Planning with SAP APO

Promotions in SAP APO are entered into a specific planning book via key figures. Depending on the business requirements, you might want to have separate key figures for sales and marketing.

> **Example**
>
> The ABC Technology sales and marketing division runs the promotions and campaigns on different characteristics levels. While the marketing team is more focused on the product, the sales team focuses on the customer channel for launching the promotions. For this reason, the promotions level for ABC Technology's sales campaign runs will be separate from trade marketing promotions. This also allows for tracking the sales and marketing promotions' success for post-evaluation.

An important concept to keep in mind when working in APO-DP is the *promotion base*, which allows promotions to be entered at different characteristics levels. For example, we can create one promotion base at the product level for marketing events and a separate promotion base at the customer and product levels for sales campaigns. Promotion bases offer this flexibility and can also be time based, which is ideal because each sales and marketing promotion may run events at different product and/or customer aggregation (hierarchy) levels.

The steps for setting up promotion planning in SAP APO are as follows:

1. Maintain promotion attribute types (Transaction /SAPAPO/MP31). Here, we maintain different attributes, which can be entered during promotion creation and also used for post-promotion reporting. The user enters the attribute name (for example, summer sales, Thanksgiving, winter sales, discount) and saves the result.

2. Maintain promotion key figures (Transaction /SAPAPO/MP33). Assign the promotion key figure to the planning area. In this transaction, we enter the promotion key figure and one promotion characteristic for a specific planning area.

3. Maintain promotion base (Transaction /SAPAPO/MP40). Define the promotion name, time period for the promotion, and the characteristic levels on which the promotion will be running. Figure 6.2 shows an example of promotion base creation at the product level.

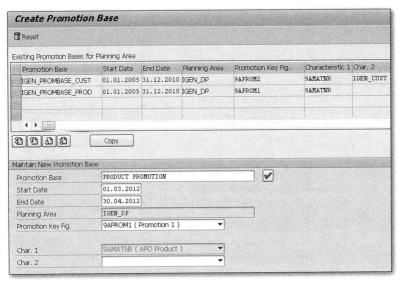

Figure 6.2 Setting up a Promotion Base in APO Demand Planning

4. Now, create an interactive promotion in the SAP APO planning book by clicking the PROMOTION PLANNING (⇄) icon.

5. Next, click the CREATE PROMOTION (◻) icon to enter the promotion details. Figure 6.3 shows an example: ABC Technology wants to offer a 25% promotional discount on its product for a specific promotion period. The key information entered is of the promotion type, which defines whether the promotion is in absolute numbers (units) or a percentage of the baseline figure. If the promotions will lead to cannibalization of other related products, we maintain a group for that here, which defines the cannibalization factors. The cannibalization groups together products whose sales are impacted, positively, negatively, or both, by the same promotion. The group is maintained in Transaction /SAPAPO/MP32 and then maintained by collaboration between the demand and trade planner while the planner creates the promotion in the APO-DP planning book. Once all the details are entered, click SAVE.

6. Select the SHUFFLER icon (🎲) and define the promotion characteristics level (for our example, product characteristics) for which you would like to create promotions. Input the product and/or customer characteristics value for which the promotion needs to be created. Highlight the characteristics (❶) and click ASSIGN OBJECTS (❷), as shown in Figure 6.4.

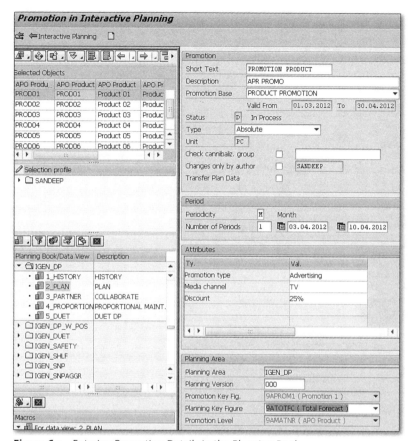

Figure 6.3 Entering Promotion Details in the Planning Book

Figure 6.4 Inputting Planned Promotional Volumes in the Planning Book

7. Once the promotions are ready for the publication, the marketing planner will need to change the promotion status by using the STATUS (⊙▣) icon. The initial status is always DRAFT. OFFERED TO CUSTOMER and CONFIRMED BY CUSTOMER

are for informing the planner that the promotion is planned for an upcoming event or campaign. All three statuses have a yellow traffic light in the selector for promotions. There are two additional promotion statuses: IN PROCESS and EXPIRED, IN THE PAST. The former status still shows the promotion as a draft and a yellow status, while the latter does not allow for any changes on the promotion since the date is in the past. The statuses PLANNED, IN THE FUTURE AND ACTIVE (Figure 6.5) take interactive planning into account to make the promotion complete. Setting this status publishes the promotion to the planning book key figure, and the selector changes to a green traffic light.

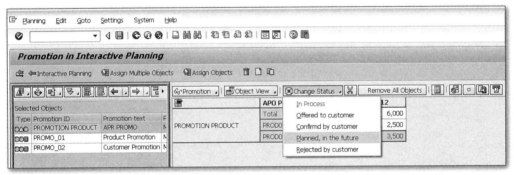

Figure 6.5 Setting up a Promotion Status

Interactive Promotion Planning Book

The interactive promotion planning book, accessed via the APO-DP planning book Transaction /SAPAPO/SDP94, offers multiple views for analysis. Figure 6.6 shows the three views that can be triggered by clicking the OBJECT VIEW icon in the promotion planning book display:

❶ PROMOTION DATA
Shows the promotion data for the selected characteristics. In our example, the promotion is done at the product level.

❷ PLANNING DATA
Shows the promotion with the baseline forecast for the comparison and percentage difference between the two key figures. This helps to visualize the planned uplift percentage.

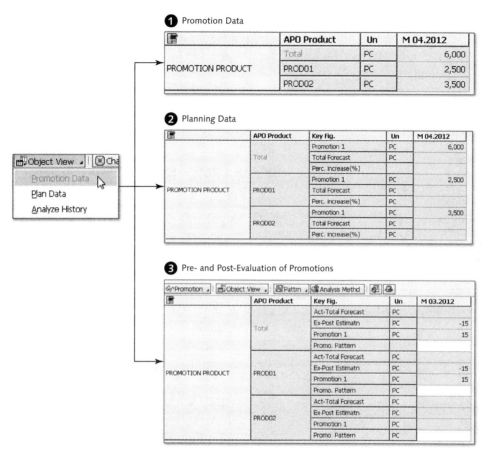

Figure 6.6 Promotional Planning Views

❸ PRE- AND POST-PROMOTION EVALUATION

Available only in the promotion view, we can store the promotion price, baseline price, and cost of the promotions for evaluation.

▸ POST-EVALUATION: Evaluation of actual data in relation to the promotional effect on actual sales. Important analysis to measure the promotional success.

▸ ANALYZE HISTORY: Derives the promotions pattern from historical data.

Promotional Reports

There are a couple of standard promotion reporting options available in APO-DP. These reports provide basic information on the promotions and forecast key figures at the promotion base (i.e., promotion characteristics level) for a given period of time. Using these reports, the business user can analyze the uplift on the baseline forecast and coordinate with the supply planner for supplies. The reports also provide the promotion attribute type dimensions. These reports can be accessed via Transaction /SAPAPO/MP41B or /SAPAPO/MP39. For the first report, settings need to be defined in Transaction /SAPAPO/MP41A. The setting identifies the planning area and planning book from which the information needs to be displayed.

6.1.2   Promotion Planning with SAP CRM: Integrating SAP APO and SAP CRM

For a specific product category (laptop), ABC Technology uses SAP Customer Relationship Management (CRM) for sales and marketing planning activities. For this product line, the forecast baseline is calculated in SAP APO and then flowed from SAP APO to SAP CRM. Now the trade planner sees the baseline forecast in SAP CRM and is able to plan the uplifts against this volume. The ABC Technology trade planner plans 3-5% uplift over the baseline forecast for the promotional activities. The trade marketing planner plans the promotions and provides the event's data back to SAP APO to consolidate the demand plan. For other product lines (monitors and desktops) for which the volume is less significant, the promotion planning is performed directly in APO-DP.

The planning dimensions for SAP CRM and SAP APO differ as each of the sales, marketing, and supply chain functions look at different characteristics during planning. For example, while APO-DP plans at the product level, marketing may plan at the product brand or planning customer level. Another difference is that SAP CRM doesn't have location details, while SAP APO needs the location details for sourcing and distributing the promotion volumes planned in SAP CRM. Figure 6.7 shows the schematic flow diagram among the various SAP systems for promotion planning.

The SAP APO-CRM integration flow requires activation of the BAdI interface and uses BAPI technology to post the promotions to the SAP APO planning system and to accept promotions from the SAP CRM system. We also need to make the planning book applicable for promotional planning during the planning book creation process (Transaction /SAPAPO/SDP8B). The key steps to integrate SAP APO with SAP CRM at a high level are as follows:

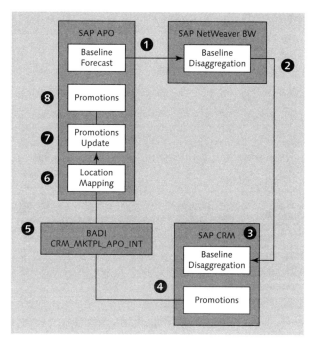

Figure 6.7 CRM Integration with APO-DP for Promotion Planning

❶ APO-DP plans the baseline forecast based on historical sales data. The planning might not have all the customer hierarchy levels in SAP APO.

❷ The baseline forecast is passed to SAP NetWeaver Business Warehouse for further disaggregation to all levels of the customer hierarchy. SAP NetWeaver BW has all the attributes of the product and customer hierarchy.

❸ The baseline forecast at the all-customer hierarchy level is then passed to SAP CRM planning folders.

❹ Based on the baseline forecast input and the sales and marketing calendar, the marketing or sales planner inputs the promotions activities in SAP CRM.

❺ The planned promotions are then interfaced via a middleware layer in the form of a B-DOC (business document) to SAP APO via BAdI CRM_MKTPL_APO_INT, which publishes the promotions events into SAP APO. Usually this interface works well in batch processing during night, with the queues processing from SAP CRM. In SAP APO, the promotions details are written by BAPI_PRMSRVAPS_SAVE-MULTI.

❻ The promotions are created in SAP APO based on the maintained combinations of defined product and customer characteristics. If SAP CRM does not send the location detail, a mapping table will need to be maintained to map the promotions to the locations.

❼ The promotion update program /SAPAPO/PROMOTION_UPDATE, along with standard macros, change the promotion status and publish the promotions details to the interactive planning book.

❽ The business user views the promotions and may opt to make final changes while completing their total demand plan calculation.

> **Example**
>
> To support the promotion activities in the company, ABC Technology launches a new product line for its laptop business every four months. This calls for a robust planning process in the new product introduction (NPI) to ensure that the old product phases out smoothly before the new product is launched onto the market.

The NPI process is supported by the APO-DP lifecycle management process, which we'll discuss in the next section.

6.2 Lifecycle Planning

SAP APO supports the business process of new product introduction (NPI) via the lifecycle planning functionality. APO-DP offers this functionality in the form of two functions: *like modeling* and *phase-in/phase-out modeling*. The following list provides the definitions of these two features:

▸ **Like modeling**
When a new product characteristic with no history needs to be forecasted, we can use the like modeling feature. This feature allows a business to map the historical data of a similar product for forecasting purposes. Another option is to use the realignment feature of copying the history of the old product to the new product, but this increases the data volume in the system. The process of realignment was explained in Chapter 5, Section 5.2.3.

▸ **Phase-in/phase-out modeling**
The feature of phase-in and phase-out modeling helps to determine the growth and discontinuation pattern for the product. We can define a percentage factor

to show the growth of the new product towards maturity and then gradual discontinuation.

Example

In recent years, ABC Technology has written off a lot of inventory because of product obsolescence due to lack of proper planning. The inventory write-off was not only for its finished goods, but also for its raw material inventory. New products were being launched before ABC Technology evaluated the old product inventory and sales, resulting in huge inventory piling of finished goods and raw materials for old products.

ABC Technology plans to streamline this process and mitigate product waste using the lifecycle planning functionality in SAP APO. They will now be able to phase out the old products properly, before bringing in any new products. Also using this functionality, ABC Technology will be able to forecast new products (with no sales history) using the like modeling concept of mapping similar-product histories to generate a forecast. Using this functionality, ABC Technology will get better forecast estimates and reduce its product obsolescence.

In the following sections, we'll use the example of ABC Technology to show you how to model lifecycle planning in APO-DP, as well as how to use an alternative called product interchangeability.

6.2.1 Phase-In/Phase-Out Modeling

ABC Technology has a new product that will be replacing an old product, and needs to map the historical sales of the old product to determine how the new product may do on the market. This will help ABC Technology plan how much material, manpower, and storage space it will need. In this situation, a phase-in and phase-out strategy is defined for the new and old product. To use phase-in/phase-out modeling, follow these steps:

▶ Access Transaction /SAPAPO/MSDP_FCST1 (see Figure 6.8). The business user maintains the master data for specific planning area. The like profile highlights the new product from which the historical sales need to be mapped (step ❶). Maintain the old product number for the characteristics 9AMATNR.

▶ The phase-in profile highlights the percentage factor for new product growth to maturity (step ❷). Maintain the percentage of the forecast for the new product for specific time horizon. The example in the figure shows a gradual increase in the forecast from month 1 to month 4.

311

▶ The phase-out profile highlights the percentage factor for the old product to discontinuation (step ❷). Similar to the phase-in profile, maintain the phase out profile on how the old product will diminish over the upcoming months.

▶ Assign the phase-in and phase-out profiles to the new product along with the like profile (step ❸). Finally, the planning area assignment is done for the new product and location combination with the like profile, phase-in profile, and phase-out profile.

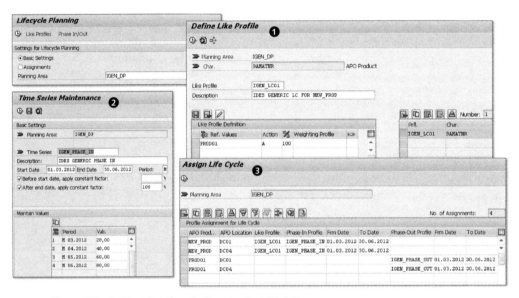

Figure 6.8 Setting Up Lifecycle Planning in APO-DP

You also need to activate lifecycle planning in the forecast profile. To do this, access Transaction /SAPAPO/MC96B, as shown in Figure 6.9, and activate the setting by selecting the LIFECYCLE PLANNING ACTIVE field. This ensures that the forecasting planning will take the lifecycle planning master data into account.

Once you've selected these settings, you can start directly performing the interactive forecasting in the SAP APO planning book. When you run the forecasting for the old product, you'll observe (as shown in Figure 6.10) a gradual decrease in volume, as highlighted earlier by the phase-out profile. This decrease in the forecast volume is based on the phase-out percentage defined in the earlier step and ensures that the product will phase out smoothly before the launch of the new product and the entire inventory will be consumed.

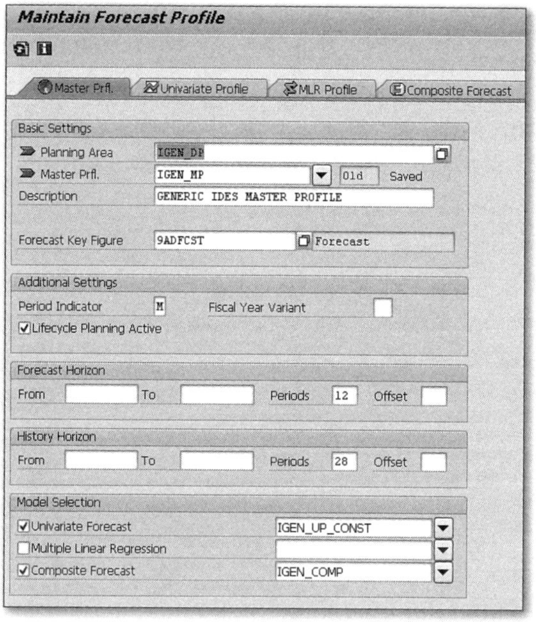

Figure 6.9 Activating Lifecycle Planning in the Forecast Profile

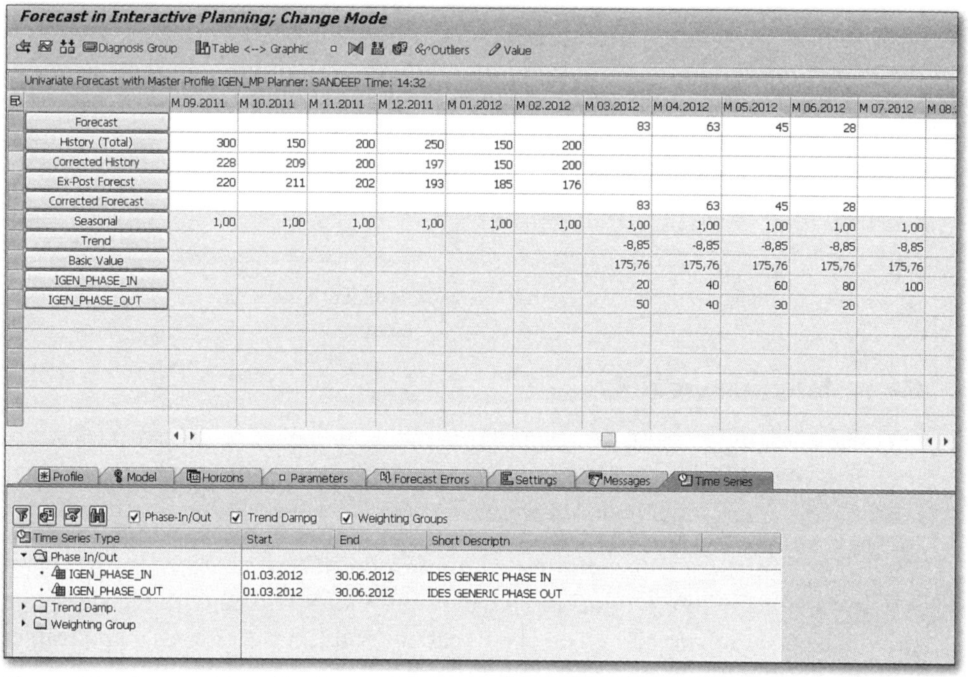

Figure 6.10 Running Interactive Forecasting for an Old Product (Phasing Out)

Next, the business planner interactively runs the forecast for the new product from the SAP APO planning book by accessing Transaction /SAPAPO/SDP94 (see Figure 6.11). The planner identifies the aggregation level at which he or she wants to execute the forecast, and then runs the forecast. Running the forecast for the new product (with no history) results in mapping of historical data (like modeling) and the use of the phase-in profile to gradually increase the forecast volume from growth to maturity.

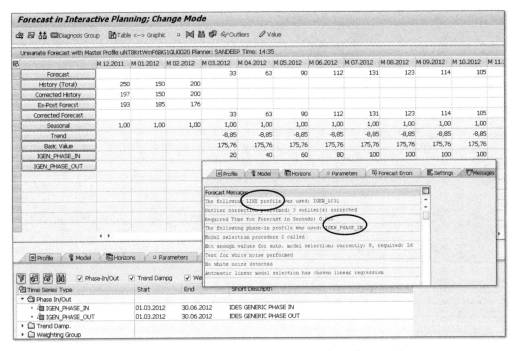

Figure 6.11 Running Interactive Forecasting for a New Product (Phasing In)

6.2.2 Interchangeability

Lifecycle planning can also be activated via the interchangeability group (Transaction /INCMD/UI), whereby the product-to-product relationship can be maintained for the DP settings, as shown in Figure 6.12.

The business planner can perform this transaction in few simple steps. The first activity is to define the product interchangeability master data with the successor and predecessor relationship. The planner assigns multiple locations, if applicable.

Next, click the DP SETTINGS icon to view the master data related to lifecycle planning. The bottom of the screen also shows the same screen as lifecycle planning Transaction /SAPAPO/MSDP_FCST1.

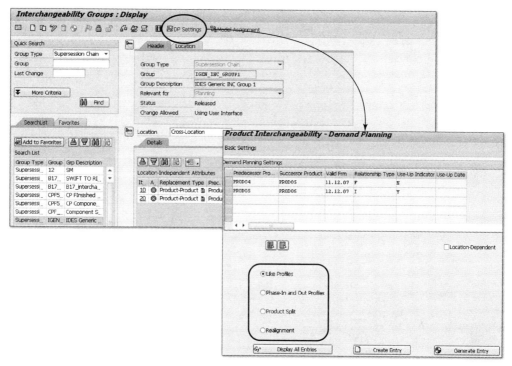

Figure 6.12 Interchangeability Group Supporting Lifecycle Planning

6.3 Seasonal Planning

APO-DP offers a seasonal planning functionality for which the business environment demonstrates a seasonal working pattern in planning activities. The APO-DP seasonal functionality offers flexible, time-based aggregation of planning for a specific seasonal year. We can define different seasonal year based on product family selling pattern.

We can model freely definable seasons and planning years, which are assigned to the characteristics combinations. This functionality allows ABC Technology to define different seasonal patterns for its products and offers flexibility in separately modeling different product groups. With this approach, ABC Technology can define separate seasonal years for each product family. To this benefit, the production capacity can be fully aligned with the definable seasoned products by geography (for example, region).

Industry Application

This functionality is most commonly used in the Apparel and Footwear (AFS) industry, which is a highly seasonal business based on weather conditions of specific regions. This seasonality calls for tight control over product sales and inventory availability. SAP's AFS industry solution features a seasonal function to define and control seasonal delivery periods and handle specific order periods honoring season-related deadlines. This allows the company to have full control over customer orders, articles, and time frames within order processing.

Let's walk through the steps to set up seasonal planning.

1. Access Transaction /SAPAPO/SDP_SEASON. As shown in Figure 6.13, create a season, and then maintain the seasonal pattern by clicking the SEASON MAINT. button (❶) and entering the respective season names.

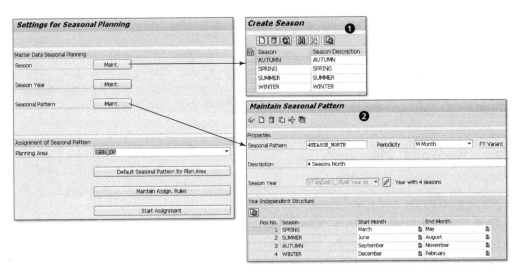

Figure 6.13 Setting up Seasons in APO Demand Planning

2. By clicking the SEASONAL PATTERN MAINT. button (❷), we maintain the respective time periods for the seasons defined in step ❶. The seasonal pattern defines the

range of months to which that season applies. In our example, we've defined a seasonal pattern for a northern region. The season pattern has four seasons (SPRING, SUMMER, AUTUMN, WINTER) with the validity months.

3. Next we need to assign the seasonal pattern in the planning area (see Figure 6.14). This is done either by changing the planning area from planning area administration Transaction /SAPAPO/MSDP_ADMIN or using the same seasonal Transaction /SAPAPO/SDP_SEASON. In the latter transaction, you can access the planning area by clicking DEFAULT SEASONAL PATTERN FOR PLAN. AREA button (❶) for assigned planning area. Then, select the SEASONAL PLANNING field and assign one default seasonal pattern to the planning area, as shown in Figure 6.14. Assigning the seasonal pattern to the planning area makes it available to all the planning books subsequently created.

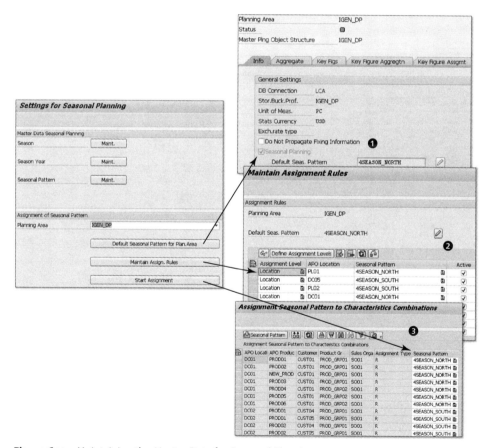

Figure 6.14 Maintaining the Master Data for Seasonal Planning

4. Once completed, as a part of master data maintenance for seasonal planning, maintain all the locations where the seasonal pattern will apply by clicking the MAINTAIN ASSIGN. RULE button (❷) and maintaining all the relevant locations where the seasonal pattern is active.

5. The last step is to assign the seasonal pattern to the applicable CVC. This is done by clicking the START ASSIGNMENT button (❸) and maintaining seasonal pattern for each CVC.

The seasonal planning settings are now available in the interactive DP planning book. As shown in Figure 6.15, click the USER SETTINGS dropdown icon to display the seasonal bucket in the planning book. You can also view the seasonal year consolidation by selecting the STANDARD YEAR option, as shown in the figure. Instead of a monthly time buckets display in the planning book, now the planning data will be displayed with different time buckets in the form of a seasons/year bucket.

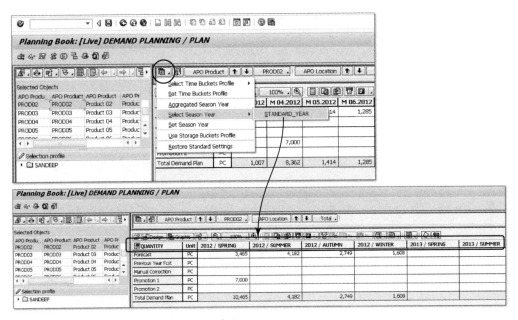

Figure 6.15   Interactive Planning with Seasons

6.4 SAP APO Demand Planning Bill of Material Functionality

APO-DP provides functionality via a bill of material (BOM) that allows you to define relationships between products and provides flexibility to define dependent and independent requirements for planning. For instance, there are many business situations when products are bundled and sold in the form of a kit, either for promotional reasons or complex shipping customization. A typical scenario would be that all the materials have their individual forecasts, and the dependent demands need to be added on top to reflect the correct volume for supply planning. A BOM bundles these components, where we define the unit of measure conversion factors and the parent-child relationships.

Example

This functionality gives ABC Technology the ability to forecast its component items properly. For promotional reasons, ABC Technology offers many of its products in bundles, in which two or more finished goods (which can also be sold individually) are packaged to form a new promotional product. Depending on the sales, this configuration keeps changing every two to three months, allowing them to keep the customer engaged. In this situation, ABC Technology would like to forecast for bundled products separately from the individual products. APO-DP BOM functionality offers them the functionality to consolidate the demand for both dependent demand and individual forecasts for supply planning.

In the following sections, we'll take a look at the configuration and master data objects to model this business scenario in the APO-DP BOM functionality.

6.4.1 Creating a New Planning Object Structure

In the APO-DP BOM functionality, you need to assign a characteristics combination in the planning object structure. The characteristics are the objects taken from the product and customer hierarchy, which businesses uses for planning purposes. For example, ABC Technology uses location and product as two main characteristics for displaying and planning data related to bill of material. Now let's see how the configuration is done for this functionality:

1. Using Transaction /SAPAPO/MSDP_ADMIN, create a planning object structure named BOM to which to assign the required characteristics for the business scenario.

2. Assign the BOM characteristics combination ID, BOM production type, location, product, and APO PPM/PDS name to the master planning object structure by transferring the relevant characteristics from the right column to the left column, as shown in Figure 6.16, step ❶. Make sure to also check the RELEVANT FOR DP BOM indicator in the header section. The next step (❷) for the planning area is explained in the next section.

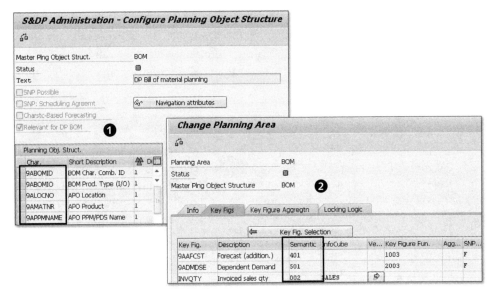

Figure 6.16 Setting up a Planning Object Structure and Planning Area

6.4.2 Creating a New Planning Area

Next, you need to create the APO-DP planning area, which defines the basic planning parameters used by the business. For ABC Technology, the basic parameters can be the planning base unit of measure (for example, each) used for planning, currency used for financial calculations, storage bucket profiles (for historical and future horizons, the planning data is stored in SAP liveCache) for historical and future data analysis, and key figures. The selected key figures can be forecast or dependent demand. The dependent demand will store the component demand once the bundled product is planned in the forecast key figure. To create the APO-DP planning area, follow these steps:

1. In the planning area, our first step is to assign the key figures to the planning area. Access Transaction /SAPAPO/MSDP_ADMIN and select your DP BOM planning area.

2. For the functionality to work, we need to nominate three key figures to the planning area. The first key figure is the forecast (technical name 9AAFCST), which will serve as independent demand for the parent item. The second key figure is the dependent demand (technical name 9ADMDSE) for the child items in BOM. The third key figure is optional for capturing actual sales orders (for example, technical name INVQTY).

3. Next we need to define the semantic to the key figure. The key figure serves as a data container, and the semantic provides the business meaning to what form of data is stored on the specific key figure. For the functionality to work, we need to assign semantics to all the key figures. Semantics provides meaningful business definitions to the key figure for storing data in SAP liveCache. SAP provides semantics ranging from 401 to 699 for DP BOM time series. As shown in Figure 6.16, we have assigned semantic 401 (independent demand) to the forecast key figure, and 501 (dependent demand) to the dependent demand key figure.

> **Note**
>
> Always run report /SAPAPO/TS_PAREA_INITIALIZE to initialize the new planning area for creating new planning time series objects. In the report selection, input information regarding the planning area and the planning time horizons.

6.4.3 Define a New Planning Book

The ABC Technology business planner uses the APO-DP planning book to perform forecasting and look at the BOM explosion for the component materials. The planning book serves as a business decision support tool for the ABC Technology business users to adjust the individual forecasts and bundled item forecast plans before the release to supply planning. Based on the current planning situation, the planner can also release the demand plan to supply planning for the parent and component individually from the planning book.

Now we need to link the planning book with the planning area we created earlier so that it inherits the characteristics and key figures. Follow these steps:

1. Access Transaction /SAPAPO/SDP8B by following the menu path EDIT • ASSIGN PLANNING AREA. The planning book can include multiple data views. The data view defines which key figures are visible to the business planners for which characteristic combinations.

2. For our ABC Technology business scenario, create two planning tables within the same data view: the first table on the top showing the independent demand for the parent material, and the second table in the bottom for component-dependent demands. This will allow the flexibility to the demand planner to view both the forecast and dependent demand for the parent and component items in a single view. As shown in Figure 6.17, we can define two planning tables (INDEPENDENT DEMAND and DEPENDENT DEMAND) in single data view.

3. In the planning book definition (Transaction /SAPAPO/SDP8B), we can define the time horizon for which the data view is applicable. ABC Technology plans for rolling 12 months, as defined in Figure 6.17.

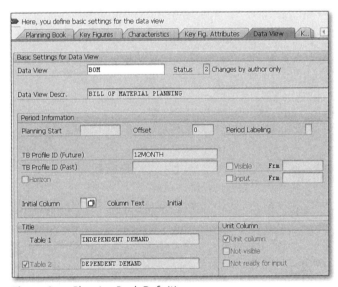

Figure 6.17 Planning Book Definition

4. You can create the DP BOM planning book using the planning book wizard by following steps in Transaction /SAPAPO/SDP8B.

6.4.4 Maintaining the Production Process Model (PPM) or Production Data Structure (PDS)

PPM/PDS is the master data used in SAP APO, primarily for capacity and material consumption calculation although it can also be used in APO-DP for BOM forecasting purposes. PPM/PDS is created in SAP APO via the Core Interface (CIF) from the SAP ERP system. The routing and BOM information is combined during the transfer to create unique SAP APO PPM/PDS plans.

> **Example**
>
> ABC Technology needs to select one master data area (PDS or PPM) to define its process. In the ABC Technology scenario, we just need to define the bill of material (bundled product and component products) for the planning purpose. When we plan the bundled product the component items should immediately be exploded based on PDS or PPM structure. For DP BOM functionality, we need to create DP PDS or PPM to make it available in the APO-DP planning area for planning.

In the next section, we'll explain how to create a PPM/PDS in APO-DP.

DP PDS Generation via APO-SNP or PP/DS PDS

Using CIF, we can transfer both the PP/DS and Supply Network Planning (SNP) PDS structures into SAP APO. You can generate the DP PDS from Transaction /SAPAPO/CURTO_GEN_DP by selecting either the SNP or Production Planning and Detailed Scheduling (PP/DS) PDS option.

APO-DP PPM Generation via APO-SNP or PP/DS PPM

The CIF only transfers PP/DS PPM to SAP APO. For the transfer option, the CIF generates SNP PPM/PDS from where the DP PPM/PDS can be generated. The SNP PPM is then generated within SAP APO using Transaction /SAPAPO/PPM_CONV. The DP PPM needs to be generated from Transaction /SAPAPO/MC62 (shown as step ❷ in Figure 6.18 in the next section). Various SNP PPM plans are shown as options that can be selected and then generated via GENERATE icon (⊕). After generation, the DP PPM needs to be assigned to the model via MODEL ASSIGNMENT icon (🛠).

Another option is to manually create PPM in SAP APO directly with BOM definitions using Transaction /SAPAPO/SCC03.

Upon completion of the either PPM or PDS generation, they are then assigned to the CVC master data, which contains all the valid characteristics combinations for planning.

The maintenance of CVC is explained in the next section.

6.4.5 Maintenance of Characteristic Value Combinations (CVC)

CVC defines the combination of characteristics for which you want to perform demand planning. ABC Technology needs to define individual CVCs for both its bundled products and component products. Also, within the CVC we define whether the product is an input or output item in the bill of material with reference to the production data structure (PDS) master data. CVCs are created and deleted using Transaction /SAPAPO/MC62. The maintenance of CVC is done in three steps, as shown in Figure 6.18. The prerequisite for step ❷ is the creation of the production data structure (PDS) or production process model (PPM).

❶ **Create CVCs**
Create a CVC for the product/location combination without an APO PPM/PDS assignment. As shown in Figure 6.18, click CREATE CHARACTERISTICS COMBINATION to input product and location characteristics. The APO PPM/PDS will be displayed as grayed out.

❷ **Generate DP PPMs**
This step was performed in Section 6.4.4 during the DP PPM creation process. Report /SAPAPO/DP_BOM_LIST provides the steps for DP PPM generation.

❸ **Add BOM information**
Assign PPM/PDS to the CVC. To do this, click ADD BOM INFORMATION to run the program (as shown in Figure 6.18) to automatically assign the generated DP PPM/PDS to the CVC. The program logic deletes the originally created CVC and recreates individual CVCs with input and output products for the same PPM/PDS structure.

Tips & Tricks

Always run report /SAPAPO/TS_LCM_CONS_CHECK on a daily basis as part of the background job schedule to resolve any SAP liveCache anchor inconsistency. For DP BOM, two additional checks in the form of EXTENDED DP BOM CHECK and FORCE DP BOM PROPAGATION are available for creating consistent CVC master data. In the report selection, input information regarding the planning area and the planning time horizons.

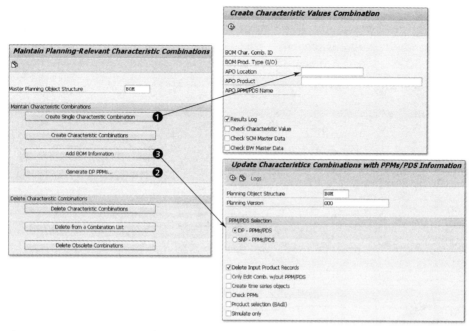

Figure 6.18 Setting up a CVC for DP BOM

A typical CVC structure is shown in Figure 6.19, which shows the two characteristics—product and location—selected earlier for the planning object structure, along with the BOM input/output ID and relevant APO PPM/PDS name.

Display Existing Characteristic Combinations

17 Data records selected for Planning Obj. Struct.: BOM

BOM I/O ID	APO Locati	APO Produc	APO PPM/PDS Name	
I	1000	102-100	P-102_2300_SNP	
I	1000	102-300	P-102_2300_SNP	
O	1000	P-102	P-102_2300_SNP	
I	1000	102-100	P-102_1000	
I	1000	102-300	P-102_1000	
O	1000	P-102	P-102_1000	
I	1000	102-110	102-10099991231235959	
O	1000	102-100	102-10099991231235959	
I	1000	102-310	102-30099991231235959	
O	1000	102-300	102-30099991231235959	
I	1000	102-310	102-30099991231235959	2
O	1000	102-300	102-30099991231235959	2
I	1000	102-100	P-103_DP	
I	1000	102-110	P-103_DP	
I	1000	102-300	P-103_DP	
I	1000	102-310	P-103_DP	
O	1000	P-103	P-103_DP	

Figure 6.19 CVC Structure for DP BOM

You can now see the end result in the APO-DP planning book by selecting all the products. The planning book (see Figure 6.20) displays the independent and dependent demand key figures separately based on the CVC and PPM/PDS definitions.

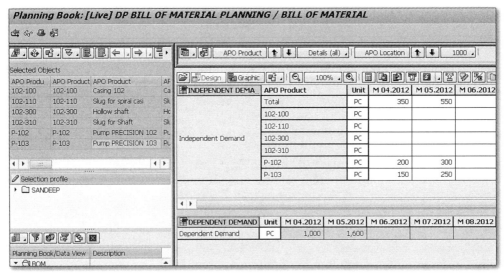

Figure 6.20 DP BOM Planning Book

6.5   Customer and Product Segmentation

In this section, we'll discuss two segments that are useful for analyzing the business performance in APO-DP. *Customer segmentation* is the process of dividing a company's customer base into customer groups of that are similar in specific ways that are relevant to marketing, such as distribution channel, pricing strategy, or promotions for a specific customer group. You can analyze the segmentation in SAP APO using the Pareto Principle of the 80/20 rule to identify the customers or customer groups with high volume sales or who are generating high sales values.

> **Example**
>
> ABC Technology separates its customers into different tiers based on sales volume and strategic partnerships. It has classified the customers into customer classes (A, B, C, and REST) and customer accounts (key account or traditional account).

Product segmentation is the process by which the company produces a single core product with relatively minor variations and then markets it to different customer groups under different brand names to increase their market share while reducing the cost of developing radically different products. The mechanics of product segmentation allow the company to distribute its high-cost product; for example, across different target groups. Instead of having one product with one market and one supply-and-demand curve (essentially putting all the manufacturer's eggs in a single basket), the manufacturer can sell sister models of the product at different prices to different market segments.

Example

ABC Technology performs product segmentation by definition of product brand by separating its product lines into multiple brands offering a range of products with different pricing. ABC Technology has segregated their laptop brands with different pricing models according to custom or built-in laptops. During planning, the business often has to analyze the volume to ensure they're selling a good product mix in the market.

Using APO-DP, ABC Technology can perform an analysis to study the market (i.e., customer and product) segmentation. This study is made easy with the use of the SAP APO CVC definition, which allows ABC Technology to slice and dice the planning data in different dimensions. The CVC contains all the attributes from the customer and product hierarchies and can easily provide the planning data based on different aggregation levels. Recent market trends for ABC Technology have shown that channeling slight variations of different products and services to different groups of its customer base helps to increase market share, improve revenues, and reduce costs. The segmentation information can also help with the sales and operations planning process.

Figure 6.21 shows the multiple hierarchical dimensions in the form of product, customer, and geography. During their planning process, the ABC Technology supply chain planner analyzes the planning data first from the geographical perspective to ensure correct inventory levels, and then looks at the product mix and customer orders to ensure correct supply allocation. The planning dimensions also help the business planner to perform forecast accuracy based on different parameters (product group, location, etc.). The aggregation level for analysis can also provide input based on which forecasting run is carried out or which promotions are run.

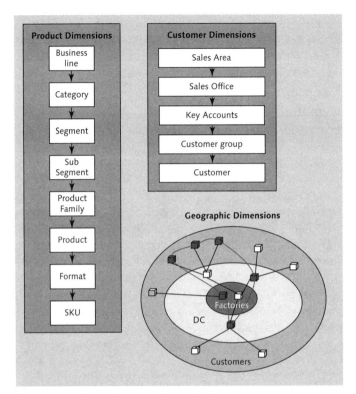

Figure 6.21 Market Segmentation Definitions

APO-DP provides the capability to the planner to perform top-down or bottom-budget calculations on different aggregation levels based on the different inputs from the sales and marketing teams. The planner can analyze the data in the APO-DP planning book based on different CVC aggregation levels. The planner can also make use of Planning Book Chart engine functionality to draw a graphical form of the planning data.

6.6   Customer Forecast Management

Customer Forecast Management (CFM) is a capability function within APO-DP that allows businesses and their customers to collaborate in the area of forecasting. Customers communicate by sending their forecast, which can be integrated with the company demand and supply planning process, as shown in Figure 6.22.

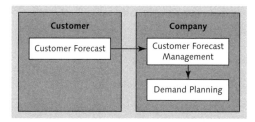

Figure 6.22 Customer Forecast Management Business Process

The integration of CFM provides the following benefits to ABC Technology:

▶ Increased visibility on what the customer is selling in the market

▶ The ability to proactively react on upstream and downstream supply chains

▶ Increased sales and fewer lost sales with the prevention of stock outs

▶ Increased customer satisfaction level with improved order fulfillment

APO-DP provides standard business content to support the CFM integration. As shown in Figure 6.23, the technical flow integration steps are as follows:

❶ The customer sends the forecast file either via IDoc or a manual flat file. The inbound processing is supported by IDoc type PROACT or DELFOR, with message variant CFM. Once the IDoc is processed, the data is available in table /SAPAPO/CFM_IDOC.

❷ The customer forecast data is loaded into the internal SAP APO Business Warehouse component via IDOC table or a provided CSV file. Standard InfoCube 9ACFM_C and MultiProvider 9ACFM_MP are provided as standard business content with a process chain to upload the forecast data.

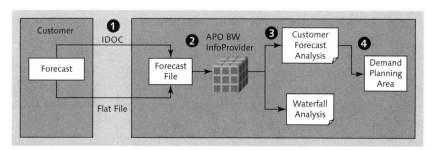

Figure 6.23 Technical Data Flow for Customer Forecast Management

❸ Two Web Dynpro reports in the form of Customer Forecast Analysis and Waterfall Analysis are available for analysis. The services need to be activated in Transaction SICF in the WEBDYNPRO • SAPAPO FOLDER for running these two analysis reports. Perform the Forecast Analysis Run via Transaction /SAPAPO/CFM_ANALYSIS which checks for data readiness, completeness, and forecast comparisons within defined tolerances. Once the check is performed, the report can be visualized via Transaction /SAPAPO/CFM_POWL which shows various alerts and approval options. The Waterfall Report, which allows you to visualize the forecast quantities at different time horizons, can be accessed via Transaction /SAPAPO/CFM_WFALL.

❹ The last step is to release the customer forecast to the APO-DP area. This can be done via either the UI approval or automatic background processing using Transaction /SAPAPO/CFM_FC_REL.

6.7   SAP APO Demand Planning Alerts

SAP APO Demand Planning alerts (which we'll refer to as DP alerts) serve as an alert notification mechanism for exception management in the overall demand and supply planning process. SAP provides standard DP alerts, which users can view in the Alert Monitor. SAP also offers flexibility in defining custom macros (for example, monitoring forecast versus sales orders) which helps the demand planner to perform his planning activities efficiently. The list of custom alerts is primarily designed to proactively identify any exception in the demand planning process.

Exception management is the process of identifying the issues and making changes or adjustment to the operational plan. This process becomes important for ABC Technology when the customer sales orders deviate from the original forecast. A specific customer may order too much or too little, which can affect the demand and supply allocation.

Example

The ABC Technology demand planner monitors the customer orders and forecast pattern with the use of the alerts to proactively react on the current market situation. With this process, the ABC Technology demand planner focuses on working on the products that require the utmost attention and setting business priorities. Using the tolerance limits and alert prioritization, the ABC Technology planner works on the alerts list to resolve critical product issues first before working on the other product issues. Various alerts specific to APO-DP can be set up to identify the exceptions on the business process.

The demand planner accesses the system generated via the Alert Monitor in Transaction /SAPAPO/AMON1. The following are some example of DP alerts:

- Related to the future (created on daily basis):
  - Sales orders exceed demand plan in the future horizon
  - Promotion quantity has changed
- Related to history (created on weekly basis):
  - Actual sales order over x% tolerance to the demand plan
  - Actual sales order below x% tolerance to the demand plan
  - Obsolete characteristic combinations

Tips & Tricks

Another functionality worth mentioning is the *planner homepage* available with SAP SCM 7.0 EHP2 (Enhancement Pack 2). The planner homepage is an interactive web screen the SAP APO planner uses as a central point of entry to access favorite tasks and reports, key planning-relevant information, and an overview of the alerts that are relevant to the planner's activities. The planner can take advantage of the planner homepage functionality to integrate within their daily planning activities process. The functionality requires activation of the business function in Transaction SFW5.

Two types of alerts are available: dynamic and database (refer to Chapter 5, Section 5.7 for more details). The dynamic alert can be triggered in real time on the planning books. Once the planner reacts to the situation, the alert will disappear. The database alert is triggered via a background batch job and stored until refreshed in the next batch run.

6.8   Duet Demand Planning

Duet Demand Planning is a functionality provided for performing the demand planning business process in a Microsoft Excel spreadsheet. This allows for implementing a lite version of APO-DP in Microsoft Excel and then integrating it back into SAP APO.

Example

This product will be useful for the ABC Technology sales and marketing teams, who are primarily offsite working with customers and planning promotions. They can plan offline and then integrate with SAP APO once back on the company's network.

This Duet product is jointly provided by SAP and Microsoft. Duet uses Microsoft Excel (Figure 6.24) to create planning sheets as well as analyze and manage demand planning data from the SAP Supply Chain Management application. The product is available with Microsoft SharePoint 2010.[1]

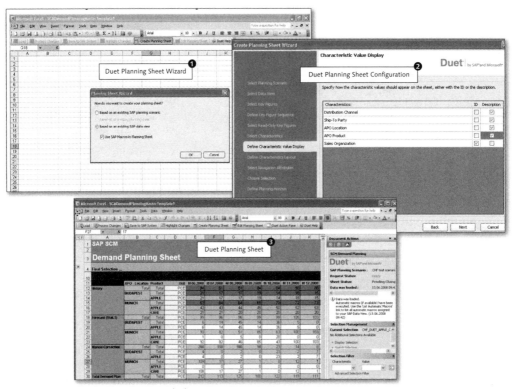

Figure 6.24 Duet Demand Planning

The demand planner can use the full Excel capabilities (side calculations, referencing other spreadsheets, sums, etc.) to analyze and prepare updated demand plans. All

---

1 Source: *www.duet.com*

the planning can be done offline—for example, when the planner is meeting with at a client or vendor. Once the demand plan is complete, Duet will synchronize the new information with the SAP SCM application, and the new plan is automatically available to be used for the next ordering and production cycle.

6.9   Summary

In this chapter, we discussed advanced demand planning concepts. We first went over some recommendations for using promotion planning in SAP APO or in SAP CRM.

Lifecycle management is an important topic for the business process of new product introduction (NPI) and is explained in detail. The chapter also touches on seasonal planning, DP BOM forecasting, and other miscellaneous topics of customer and product segmentation, alerts, and customer forecast management.

The next chapter focuses on advanced supply planning concepts. The advanced topics cover many real-life business variant and scenarios solved by SAP APO planning functionalities.

Now, delve into the advanced functionalities for supply planning available in SAP APO. These advanced features offer opportunities to explore more functionalities within APO-SNP to support complex business scenarios and variants.

7   Advanced Supply Planning Concepts in SAP APO

Before you can start constructing your supply chain, you need to also consider supply planning functionalities, which require you to model the supply chain based on your different business requirements and product characteristics. This chapter focuses on the out-of-the box functionalities offered by SAP to manage different supply planning business scenarios, such as safety stock planning, aggregated planning, shelf life, subcontracting, planning strategies, interchangeability, and many more. These advanced features (primarily in APO-SNP) try to close the gap between complex business scenarios and core business processes. For example, a weekly supply planning cycle can be supported by basic APO-SNP features, but the inclusion of shelf life, subcontracting, or interchangeability in the planning cycle opens up new exploration of advanced functionalities in APO-SNP.

As shown in the mind map for this chapter (see Figure 7.1) we will be covering the advanced supply planning topics in SAP APO. The topics will explain the configuration in APO-SNP, master data set up, and business scenario testing process to solve many complex business scenarios.

In this chapter, we'll introduce those new advanced planning functionalities that can be integrated within the traditional planning cycle process, and then explain configuration steps. The chapter continues to use ABC Technology as a case study; the company is pursuing improvements to its existing supply chain planning deficiencies and integration issues.

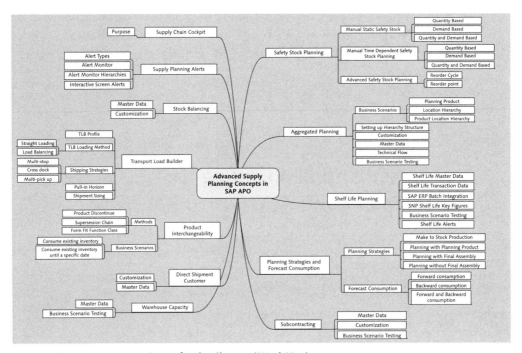

Figure 7.1 Learning Points for the Chapter (Mind Map)

7.1 Safety Stock Planning

Safety stock (also known as buffer stock) is an extra level of stock that ABC Technology intends to hold to mitigate the risk of supply shortages in the environment of demand and supply uncertainty. Holding inventory to a certain level ensures that ABC Technology business operations will run smoothly and according to plan.

The calculated safety stock should account for both demand and supply variability. The demand variability occurs primarily due to forecast accuracy, and the supply variability occurs due to the replenishment lead time accuracy. Another component that must be accounted for in the safety stock calculation is the customer service level; i.e., a higher service level accounts for higher safety stock holding.

The finished goods stock can be broken into three components, as shown in Figure 7.2:

▶ **Cycle stock**
Held in the warehouse as a function of replenishment frequencies and minimum lot size. Calculated based on replenishment plan and minimum lot size.

▶ **Pipeline stock**
Stocks still in transit to the warehouse.

▶ **Safety stock**
Buffer stocks to manage demand and supply variability.

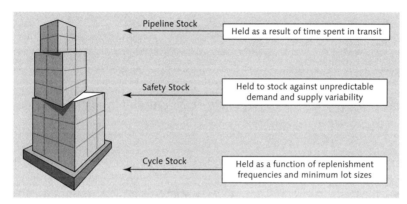

Figure 7.2 Finished Goods Stock Components

Another way we can view the stock components is to look at the cyclical chart of finished goods stock replenishment. As Figure 7.3 shows, the safety stock defines the minimum stock level that ABC Technology wants to hold. Built on top of the safety stock are the pipeline stock and the cycle stock. The *cycle stock* is traditionally calculated using the economic order quantity (EOQ) equation, which takes the lead time and replenishment as well inventory holding cost into account. Another way to calculate the cycle stock is to hold minimum stock to meet market demands before the new inventory arrives from the supplier or manufacturing location. The *pipeline stock* depends on the replenishment lead time. The cycle stock is calculated as a minimum ordering lot size. More explanation of inventory types is provided in Chapter 12.

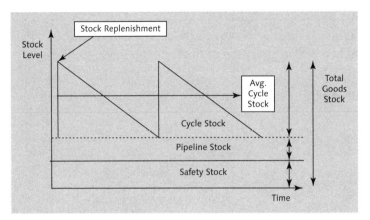

Figure 7.3 Finished Goods Stock Replenishment Cycle (Consumption-Based Planning)

APO-SNP offers three different types of safety stock calculation methods, which we'll discuss in the following sections.

7.1.1 Manual Static Safety Stock Planning

The static (i.e., constant over time) safety stock method is best to combat any demand upsurges and meet customer orders on time. The calculation proposes that the buffer (or excess inventory) be stored in the warehouse to manage any uncertainty in the supply chain (for example, customer order or supply delay). ABC Technology classifies its product portfolio into different segments and plans to use different safety stock strategies to manage any demand and supply imbalance. APO-SNP offers three calculation methods (maintained in the SAP APO product master, in the SAFETY STOCK METHOD field under the LOT SIZE tab) under this class:

▸ **SB (quantity-based)**
Safety stock from the location product master. The user defines the required safety stock in the SAP APO location product. The same safety stock level is applied to each bucket in the APO-SNP planning book.

▸ **SZ (demand-based)**
Safety days' supply from the location product master. The user defines the number of calendar days that the safety stock must be able to cover, assuming there are no incoming receipts (planned or actual). Take note that the calculation for this safety stock method is always defined and displayed in calendar days, not work days.

▶ **SM (both quantity- and demand-based)**
The maximum of either safety stock or safety days' supply defined in the location product master. The system reads the safety stock method from the product master and compares both the SB and SZ safety stock values. It then applies the greater of the two values as the final safety stock level.

The fixed quantity (SB) and safety days' supply (SZ) require a good understanding of the safety stock level the company wants to hold at the location product combination. Both of these methods expose the risk of high obsolescence and inventory holding cost as they are purely judgmental.

Setting up Static Safety Stock Planning

To set up manual static safety stock planning in the SAP system, you maintain the master data settings in the location product master by accessing Transaction /SAPAPO/MAT1. As Figure 7.4 shows, under the LOCATION PRODUCT LOT SIZE tab, we maintain the SAFETY STOCK, SAFETY DAYS SUPPLY, and SAFETY STOCK METHOD fields to calculate the safety stock.

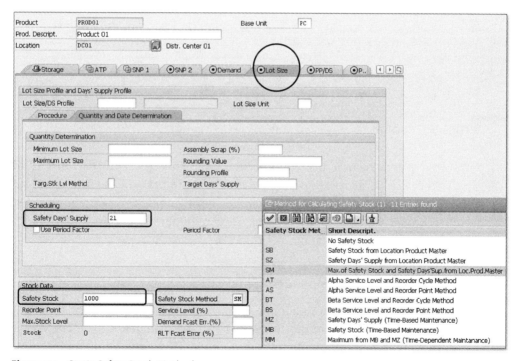

Figure 7.4 Static Safety Stock Methods

An example is shown in the APO-SNP planning book (see Figure 7.5), where ABC Technology tries to plan safety stock for its monitor products using the SZ method. Per the definition the safety stock, the key figure in the SAP APO planning book takes the maximum of the fixed safety stock quantity (1000 units) vs. safety days' supply (21 days) during the safety stock proposal. In the example, the system identifies the SZ method on the first bucket (week 15) based on safety days' supply, while the subsequent buckets (week 16–18) revert back to the SB method based on the safety stock quantity.

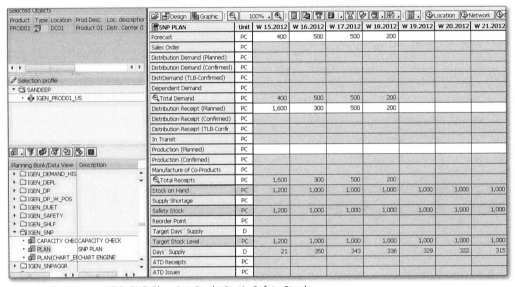

SNP PLAN	Unit	W 15.2012	W 16.2012	W 17.2012	W 18.2012	W 19.2012	W 20.2012	W 21.2012
Forecast	PC	400	500	500	200			
Sales Order	PC							
Distribution Demand (Planned)	PC							
Distribution Demand (Confirmed)	PC							
DistrDemand (TLB-Confirmed)	PC							
Dependent Demand	PC							
Total Demand	PC	400	500	500	200			
Distribution Receipt (Planned)	PC	1,600	300	500	200			
Distribution Receipt (Confirmed)	PC							
Distribution Receipt (TLB-Confir…	PC							
In Transit	PC							
Production (Planned)	PC							
Production (Confirmed)	PC							
Manufacture of Co-Products	PC							
Total Receipts	PC	1,600	300	500	200			
Stock on Hand	PC	1,200	1,000	1,000	1,000	1,000	1,000	1,000
Supply Shortage	PC							
Safety Stock	PC	1,200	1,000	1,000	1,000	1,000	1,000	1,000
Reorder Point	PC							
Target Days' Supply	D							
Target Stock Level	PC	1,200	1,000	1,000	1,000	1,000	1,000	1,000
Days' Supply	D	21	350	343	336	329	322	315
ATD Receipts	PC							
ATD Issues	PC							

Figure 7.5 APO-SNP Planning Book: Static Safety Stock

Also, the planner will notice that after the SNP heuristics calculation that eliminated the supply shortage, the target stock level and stock on hand (projected) key figures both match the safety stock planning key figure. This method ensures that ABC Technology will hold safety stock as its minimum target stock level during the supply planning calculation.

7.1.2 Manual Time-Dependent Safety Stock Planning

Unlike the static safety stock planning, the *manual time-dependent safety stock* offers the flexibility to freely define the inventory target based on time-dependent forecast estimates. Instead of the number of same safety days' supply throughout the year, the planner can adjust his plan to increase the safety days' supply during the peak season and then reduce the safety days' supply inventory as the year end approaches in order to report less inventory coverage for year-end reporting purposes.

APO-SNP has three time-dependent safety stock methods (maintained in the SAP APO product master, in the SAFETY STOCK METHOD field under the LOT SIZE tab) that can be used for this purpose:

▶ **MB (quantity-based)**
Safety stock (time-dependent maintenance). The user defines the required safety stock in the APO-SNP planning book under key figure SAFETY STOCK (PLANNED) for each planning bucket. The distribution function in the planning book can be used for manual maintenance.

▶ **MZ (demand-based)**
Safety days' supply (time-dependent maintenance). Similar to the earlier method, the user can define the SAFETY DAYS' SUPPLY key figure in the APO SNP planning book per planning bucket.

▶ **MM (both quantity- and demand-based)**
A maximum of either safety stock or safety days' supply defined in time-dependent buckets in the APO-SNP planning book. The system reads the safety stock method in the product master and compares both the MB and MZ safety stock values. It then applies the greater of the two values as the final safety stock level.

Setting up Time-Dependent Safety Stock Planning

Standard key figures are available in planning book 9ASNP_SSP in planning area 9ASNP05 for manual maintenance of safety stock targets, either in SAFETY STOCK (PLANNED) or SAFETY DAYS SUPPLY key figures, as shown in Figure 7.6.

Figure 7.6 shows an example for ABC Technology's desktop products. In the example, the planner maintains the time-dependent parameters in the APO-SNP planning book (Transaction /SAPAPO/SDP94) under key figures SAFETY STOCK (PLANNED) and/or SAFETY DAYS' SUPPLY. As the example shows, the first bucket (week 15) takes the safety days' supply as safety stock, while in the second bucket (week 16) it considers the safety stock (planned). The SAFETY STOCK key figure then calculates the required buffer safety stock based on the safety stock method using APO-SNP macro SAFETY_CALC.

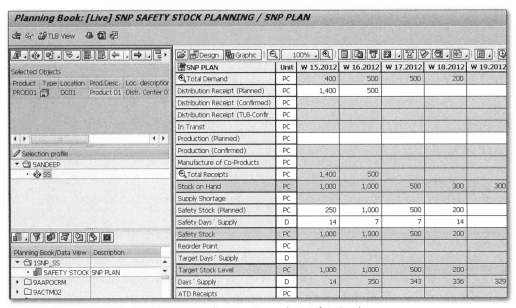

Figure 7.6 APO-SNP Planning Book: Time-Dependent Safety Stock

7.1.3 Advanced Safety Stock Planning

Advanced safety stock planning focuses on the statistical method calculation. A business may find it beneficial to use this method for products that have high demand and supply variability. Unlike the static or time-dependent safety stock methods, the statistical safety stock works on algorithm calculation. In this method, the system based on the algorithm identifies the optimal safety stock quantity for each time bucket. The calculation is based on the premise that it is mathematically possible to calculate the safety stock level to prevent any stock out situations, taking into account demand and supply variability and the target customer service level. The demand variability takes into account the forecast/sales order variation, while the supply variability is measured based on vendor lead time variations.

> **Example**
>
> ABC Technology plans to use this method for its laptop products, for which the calculation takes into account both the demand variability in the form of forecast accuracy and supply variability in the form of supplier lead time accuracy.

There are four different methods available under the advanced safety stock planning:

- **AT**: α- service level and reorder cycle method
- **AS**: α- service level and reorder point method
- **BT**: β- service level and reorder cycle method
- **BS**: β- service level and reorder point method

The advanced safety stock depends on the service level targeted by the company. Depending on the product, ABC Technology's classification of consumption, and the distribution network (regional, branch), the company can strategize its service level offering accordingly with the following methods:

- **Alpha service level settings AS and AT (event-driven)**
  Use this method when the company has a complete deliveries policy.
- **Beta service level settings BS and BT MZ (demand-based)**
  Use this method when the company has a partial deliveries policy.

The formula for safety stock calculation is:

Safety Stock = K× Square Root of { Average lead time × Square of demand variation(standard deviation) + Average demand × Square of lead-time variation (standard deviation)}

K is defined as the service factor that is used as a multiplier with the standard deviation to calculate a specific quantity to meet the specified service level.

Note on Service Factors

A *service factor* is calculated by using the inverse of the standard normal cumulative distribution with a mean of zero and standard deviation of one. Too confusing? Just use the NORMSINV function in Excel. If your desired service levels is 92%, take NORMSINV (92%) = 1.41.

Setting up Advanced Safety Stock Planning

Setting up advanced safety stock requires master data maintenance and execution of the standard SAP safety stock program. The end result is the SAFETY STOCK key figure being calculated in the APO-SNP planning book. Maintain the following master data elements (as shown in Figure 7.7) in the SAP APO location product (Transaction /SAPAPO/MAT1):

▶ SAFETY STOCK METHOD
Specifies the safety stock method you want to implement at the location product level.

▶ SERVICE LEVEL %
Percentage specifying the proportion of customers requirement for which you want to fulfill on time and need projected warehouse inventory.

▶ DEMAND FORECAST ERROR %
Percentage specifying the forecast accuracy of planned forecast vs. actual sales orders. The lower the percentage, the more accurate the demand forecast. This value can be maintained directly in the product master or referenced in the APO-DP planning book with the historical forecasts and sales orders.

▶ REPLENISHMENT LEAD TIME (RLT)
Number of calendar days to produce or procure the product.

▶ RLT FORECAST ERROR %
Percentage specifying the lead time accuracy of planned RLT vs. actual RLT. The lower the percentage, the smaller the deviation between the forecasted RLT and actual RLT. This value can be maintained directly in product master or referenced in the APO-DP planning book with the historical forecasted RLT and actual RLT.

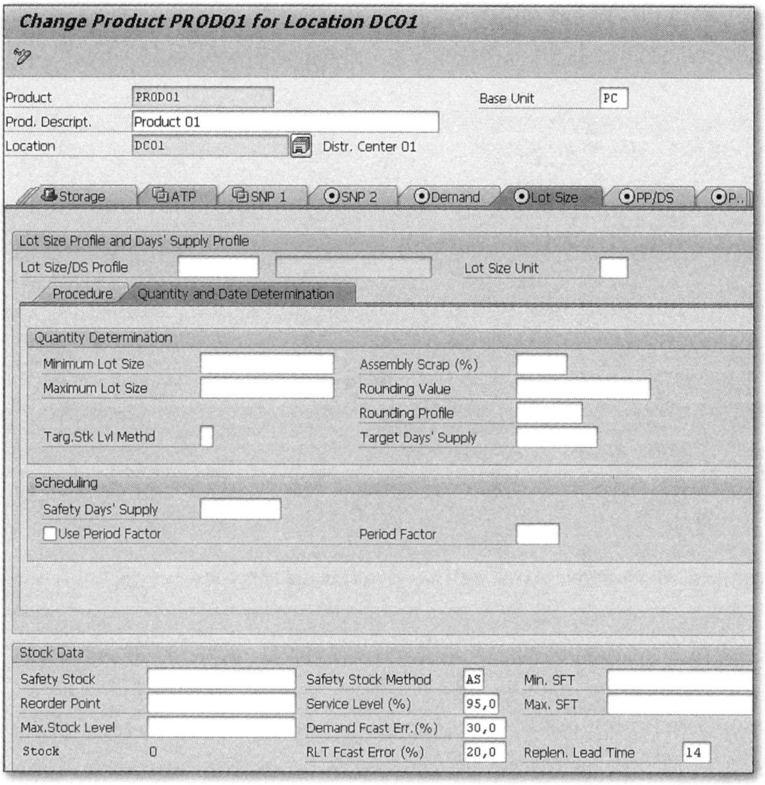

Figure 7.7 Advanced Safety Stock Planning Master Data

Within the advanced safety stock, there are two types of calculation methods, as shown in Figure 7.8:

- **Reorder cycle policy (periodic lot size procedure)**
  Replenishment orders (order quantity: q) can only be placed in certain periods; i.e., each t period, an order can be triggered.

- **Reorder point policy (periodic review)**
  Replenishment orders (order quantity: q) are placed based on the current inventory level; i.e., if a certain stock level (reorder point s) is reached, then an order is triggered.

The advanced safety stock either is calculated in a background batch job or can be executed interactively by the user. If running interactively, the business user identifies the products to run by defining the planning book selection profile in the safety stock calculation program. The program to calculate the safety stock is /SAPAPO/ RSDP_CALC_SAFETY_STOCK (also accessed via Transaction /SAPAPO/MSDP_SB).

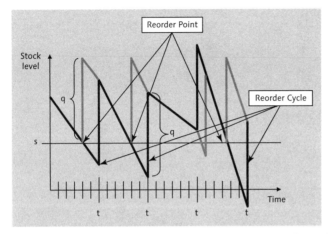

Figure 7.8 Reorder Point and Reorder Cycle in APO-SNP Advanced Methods

As Figure 7.9 shows, we select the SAFETY STOCK (PLANNED) key figure where the calculation should reside after running the program. The planning output is seen in the SAP APO supply planning book under the SAFETY STOCK (PLANNED) key figure.

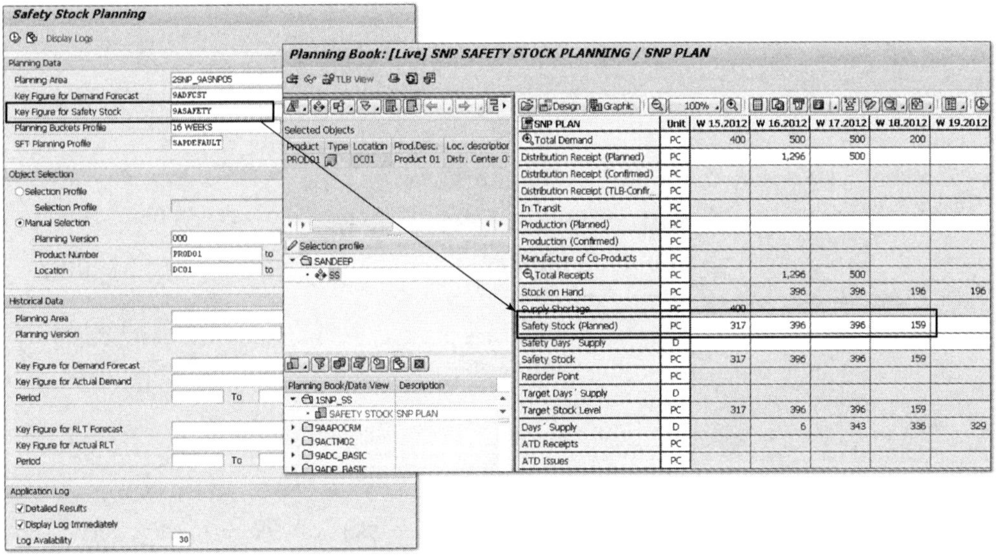

Figure 7.9 APO-SNP Safety Stock Program

7.2   Aggregated Planning

Aggregated planning in APO-SNP (also known as *hierarchical planning*) offers a scalable and flexible functionality, which can be modeled to suit unique business requirements (also referenced in Chapter 2, Section 2.5.6). This functionality benefits businesses that have high supply chain model performance, and planning at a higher level reduces the complexity. By this, we mean that a company can plan at a higher aggregation planning level, rather than planning at a lower level, such as at individual SKUs.

Example

Aggregated planning in APO-SNP allows ABC Technology to plan groups of products, like product families, instead of planning at the level of individual SKUs at each plant or warehouse. In this scenario, every product will be assigned to one product family (for example, laptop, desktop, or monitor), and each location will be assigned to one virtual location. The end result is that ABC Technology would be planning at the aggregated product family level. This planning at the aggregated level will be performed in the virtual location. The virtual location (aggregated) in turn will contain a list of locations for planning.

A similar business scenario holds true for location hierarchy as well. Various APO-SNP planning algorithms (heuristics, optimizer, and capacity leveling) can be performed on the product or location group levels.

After the APO-SNP aggregated planning run, the new replenishment elements on the group level is disaggregated to the item level by using a fair share rule to ensure that the plans are consistent at all levels of aggregation. The resource capacity check and capacity leveling can be performed at the aggregation level as well. The key business benefits seen by ABC Technology to implementing aggregated planning are:

▶ Improved medium- to long-range inventory and capacity planning

▶ Reduced workload for the planner as planning is performed at a higher aggregation level

▶ Possibility of defining more constraints at the group level while performing capacity planning and capacity leveling

▶ Consistent bottom-up and top-down planning

In the following sections, we'll take a look at different aggregated planning scenarios and the master data and customization steps you need to set up these business scenarios.

7.2.1 Hierarchical Planning Scenarios

Hierarchical planning forms a planning framework for solving multiple planning scenarios. A *hierarchy* can be formed for product, location, resource, and production process models. These hierarchies can be defined not only for reporting, but also for planning purposes. Let's look at typical scenarios (shown in Figure 7.10) in which hierarchy planning can support the business requirements.

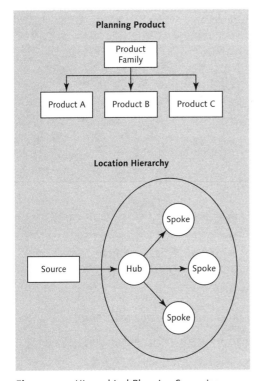

Figure 7.10 Hierarchical Planning Scenarios

Scenario 1

The first business scenario centers on the *planning product*. In this business scenario, the ABC Technology planner would group the portfolio of the laptop, monitor, or desktop group into a consolidated product or product family level. The ABC Technology planner would see all his or her laptop products grouped into a single laptop aggregated product or product family. So instead of planning at each product at every location, the planner would just plan at a single product or product family level. This process of aggregated planning makes his work manageable. Though planning at a product family, the plan still needs to be disaggregated as the packaging/labeling unit of measure is different across products.

Scenario 2

The second business scenario revolves around the *location hierarchy*. The ABC Technology planner works on a hub-spoke model in his supply chain distribution network. So instead of planning at every distribution center and branch, the planner plans at the consolidated location. He would like to consolidate all his satellite distribution center inventory and forecast requirements, or spokes, at a hub for regional planning. This will ensure that he is optimizing the inventory and not procuring any additional units from the supplier.

Scenario 3

The third scenario is a combination of both product and location. The ABC Technology planner would still like to plan at the product family level but also needs to define the primary location. The entire location product's forecast and inventory would be aggregated at this primary location for planning purposes. The supplier ships the goods to the primary location, and they are then further distributed to other warehouses in the supply network.

A business scenario exists in which the ABC Technology warehouse has a storage capacity constraint. So, the planning is done at the primary location product level, and once the goods are supplied from the supplier to the primary location, then the redistribution of inventory to other warehouses occurs. Upon redistribution of the inventory, the individual warehouses are able to visualize their warehouse capacity constraint.

We'll go over the details of how to set up the hierarchy structure in the following section.

7.2.2 Setting up the Hierarchy Structure

Here we'll use the hierarchy structure based on our last business scenario in which the location product business requirement needs to be set up on the configuration. Follow the customization path SPRO • ADVANCED PLANNING AND OPTIMIZATION • MASTER DATA • HIERARCHY • DEFINE HIERARCHY STRUCTURE.

Now you define the individual and generated hierarchies. Per our scenario, we maintain the product group (for example, laptop) and assign all the laptop SKUs to the product group. Similarly, we maintain the location group (aggregated) and assign the location(s). During the master data creation, we only need to define the individual hierarchy, and once maintained, the generated hierarchy can be automatically published for planning purposes.

You can now automatically generate the location product hierarchy by pressing the PROPAGATION icon (⊞) from the two hierarchies maintained (product group and location group). As Figure 7.11 shows, the individual hierarchies are location and product. In the location, we define the location group as Level 1 and the individual location as Level 2. Similarly, for the product, we define the product group as Level 1 and the individual product as Level 2. These two individual hierarchies can then be joined to make a generated hierarchy based on the configuration definition (shown in Figure 7.11). The generated hierarchy can have location as Level 1 and product as Level 2 during the generation.

For our second business scenario, we do not need the product group node as Level 1 in the individual hierarchy; only mentioning the location as Level 1 will meet our business requirements.

7.2.3 APO-SNP Customization

SAP provides standard planning area 9ASNP02 and planning books 9ASNPAGGR to support the aggregated planning functionality. In the planning area, the KEY FIGURES and the AGGREGATED PLANNING tabs are the two most important settings we need for the aggregated planning.

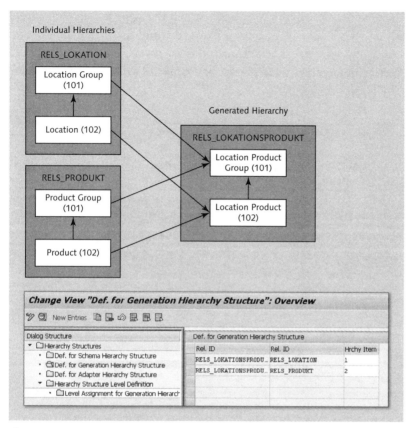

Figure 7.11 Setting up a Hierarchy Structure

For planning area administration, follow the interactive menu path ADVANCED PLANNING AND OPTIMIZATION • SUPPLY NETWORK PLANNING • ENVIRONMENT • CURRENT SETTINGS • ADMINISTRATION OF DEMAND PLANNING AND SUPPLY NETWORK PLANNING, or access Transaction /SAPAPO/MSDP_ADMIN.

As Figure 7.12 shows, the AGGREGATION indicator signifies whether we are aggregating the specific key figure at the group level. In the planning area, we need to perform couple of settings. The first is under the KEY FIGURE tab, where we need to maintain the aggregation definition for the FORECAST and STOCK key figure. Since we want the forecast and inventory to aggregate for netting calculation reasons, we need these settings. In the figure, we see the FORECAST key figure as a value of one, which signifies the aggregation at the group level.

Similarly to the FORECAST key figure, we also maintain the aggregation at the group level (value 1) for sales orders, distribution demand (confirmed), and stocks. The next setting is under the AGGREGATION PLANNING tab. Here we need to maintain the aggregation hierarchies *location product, PPM,* and *resource hierarchy,* created earlier, in the hierarchy master data.

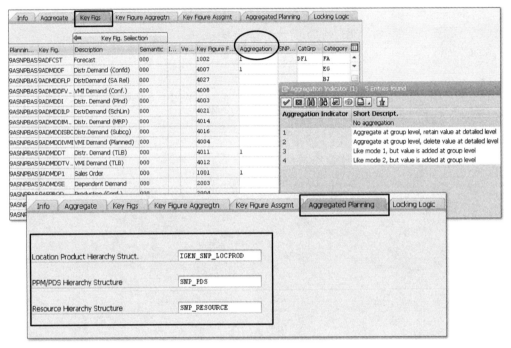

Figure 7.12 Aggregated Planning Settings in the APO-SNP Planning Area

You finish customization by copying the standard planning area 9ASNP02 to a custom planning area. The planning area specifies the planning unit of measure, storage bucket profile, and the aggregation level.

Next, define your custom planning book using Transaction /SAPAPO/SDP8B. Copy the SAP-delivered planning book 9ASNPAGGR with two data views, SNPAGGR(1) and SNPAGGR(2). The first data view is for supply planning, while the second view is for capacity planning.

After copying the planning book, assign the new planning area as the custom planning book copies the original planning area 9ASNP02. In the planning book maintenance transaction (/SAPAPO/SDP8B), select the ASSIGN PLANNING AREA option in the EDIT menu and choose the appropriate planning area for the planning book.

Next, activate all the copied default macros in the macro workbench using Transaction /SAPAPO/ADVM by selecting the appropriate planning book and data view combination and clicking the GENERATE icon.

Take note: the copied planning book (9ASNPAGGR) is different than the original planning book (9ASNP02), as the former has additional key figures and macros built to support the aggregation and disaggregation functions.

Disaggregation Enhancement

SAP provides BAdI /SAPAPO/SDP_DISAGG to define your own logics for disaggregation, which is not supported by standard macros.

7.2.4   Preparing Master Data

Once the customization is completed for the hierarchy, planning area, and planning book/macro, we can maintain the hierarchy master data. Maintain the master data via interactive menu path ADVANCED PLANNING AND OPTIMIZATION • MASTER DATA • HIERARCHY • MAINTAIN HIERARCHY, or through Transaction /SAPAPO/RELHSHOW.

For our ABC Technology business scenarios, we need three hierarchies: location product, production data structure (PDS), and resource. The planner begins the master data maintenance with individual product and location hierarchies. Click the ADD OBJECT icon (🔲) to define your product group and location group, and then input your individual products and locations. Once the individual hierarchies are maintained, auto-generate the location product hierarchy by clicking the UPDATE icon.

Figure 7.13 shows the combination of two individual hierarchies into the generated hierarchy, as explained in earlier in Section 7.2.2. The name of the generated hierarchy should match the one we input into the APO-SNP planning area.

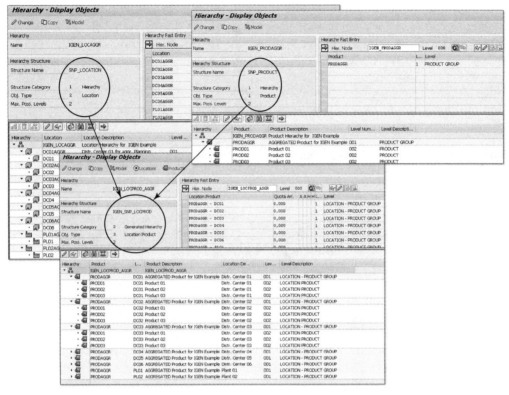

Figure 7.13 APO-SNP Location Product Hierarchies

Now that you've maintained the location product hierarchy master data, you need to maintain the APO-SNP PDS and resource master hierarchy, as Figure 7.14 shows. As with the product group hierarchy, we can maintain the APO-SNP resource hierarchy by mentioning the hierarchy name, right-clicking the hierarchy object, and choosing the ADD OBJECTS option. In this option, we input all the resources, or PDS, to be grouped as hierarchy objects. The planner will notice the hierarchy tree structure, once it is maintained, as shown in Figure 7.14. This will allow us to perform a capacity check at the resource group level.

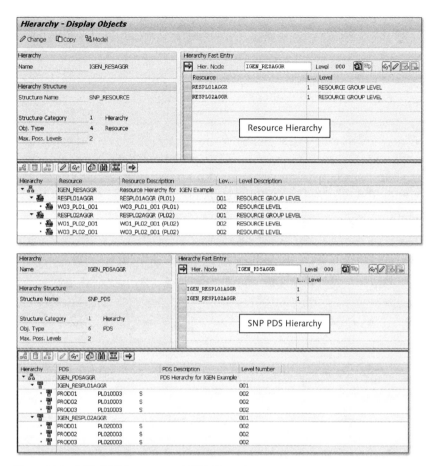

Figure 7.14 APO-SNP Resource and PDS Hierarchy

7.2.5 Technical Design Flow

After the customization and master data maintenance discussed in the earlier sections, we are now in a position to perform technical design testing. Figure 7.15 shows the overall technical design flow for the APO-SNP aggregated planning. The automated business process steps to support this technical design for the planning are as follows:

❶ The net demand for each SKU at the warehouse location(s) is aggregated at the product group level. Any distribution demand TLB confirmed in the form of stock transport orders are also aggregated.

❷ APO-SNP network heuristics is performed at the aggregated location. This planning run results in distribution demand/receipt and production plan creation at the plant location.

❸ Capacity leveling is performed at the plant for the resource hierarchy defined earlier in master data. The production plan is smooth and forms a constraint plan.

❹ APO-SNP network disaggregation, which forms the critical step in disaggregating the plan from higher levels to lower levels, is performed next. The logic of the disaggregation is embedded in the NET REQUIREMENT (DISAGGREGATION) key figure (technical name NETDM). This key figure, seen in the planning book, helps you to visualize the accumulated values for each SKU.

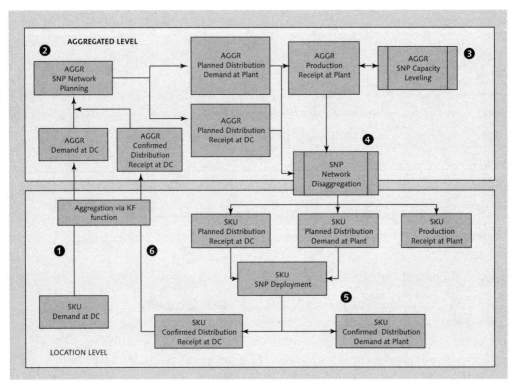

Figure 7.15 APO-SNP Aggregated Planning Technical Flow

❺ APO-SNP deployment forms the next step in passing the constraint supply plan at the SKU level. After the deployment run, the planner is available to look at the alerts to check which SKUs are encountering critical shortage issues.

❻ The aggregation key figure function aggregates the confirmed purchase orders and stock transport orders in the aggregated planning book to reconcile both the top-down and bottom-up quantities for each planning bucket.

7.2.6 Testing Business Scenario

Once the net demand is formulated in the distribution center locations, the aggregated distribution demand is seen at the product group level. In our example, as Figure 7.16 shows, the demand and inventory will be aggregated and the manufacturing location will receive the net distribution demand. The manufacturing will then plan at the infinite resource capacity and then perform capacity leveling to create a finite capacity plan. As a result, we can now view the aggregation of the DISTRIBUTION DEMAND in the APO-SNP planning book at the PRODAGGR product group level. Running the APO-SNP network heuristics (press NETWORK) results in network balancing of demand and supply at the product group level. Until now, everything seemed balanced because of the infinite resource capacity run.

The next step is to run capacity leveling to smooth the production with the CAPACITY LEVELING icon. Capacity leveling can be performed interactively or in a batch. Before running the capacity leveling, specify the scheduling parameters, alternative resource balancing, and maximum resource utilization percentage.

After the capacity leveling, we need to disaggregate the plan to the SKU level to see the impact of the capacity leveling. You can trigger the disaggregation by clicking the NETWORK DISAGGREGATION icon. Notice that the demand and supply have each dropped down one line to their respective aggregated lines (see Figure 7.17). The plan is now available in the plant to perform APO-SNP deployment at the SKU level.

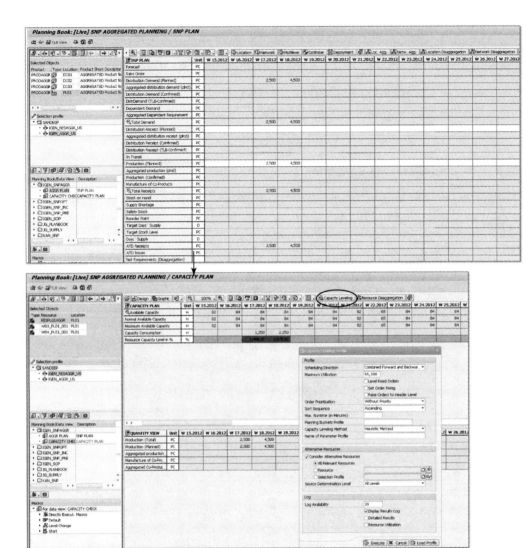

Figure 7.16 APO-SNP Aggregated Planning: Capacity Leveling

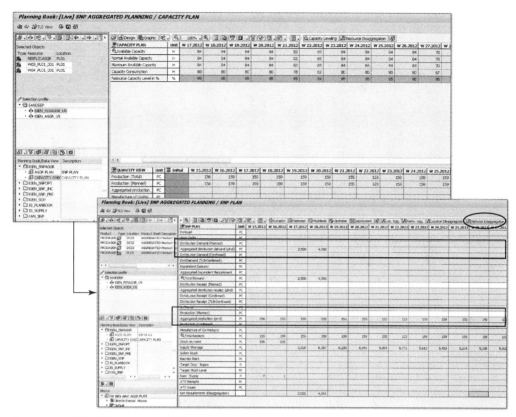

Figure 7.17 APO-SNP Aggregated Planning: Network Disaggregation

Once the APO-SNP deployment run is performed in the background or interactively, we can view the incoming distribution receipt at distribution centers (see Figure 7.18) by looking at the DISTRIBUTION RECEIPT (CONFIRMED) key figure. The planner will react to the critical shortage and the situation. A clear projection of any stock out situations is clearly seen in the APO-SNP planning book.

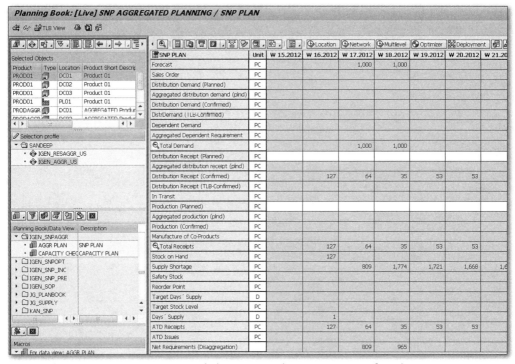

Figure 7.18 APO-SNP Aggregated Planning: Distribution Receipt Confirmed at DC

7.3 Shelf Life Planning

Shelf life is the length of time within which a specific product, such as consumer foods, beverages, pharmaceutical drugs, chemicals, and many other perishable items, needs to be consumed before it is considered unsuitable for sale, use, or consumption. In some countries, a best before, use by, or freshness date is required on packaged perishable foods. Shelf life planning functionality helps these companies prevent waste and stock out situations in their supply network. Shelf life is common not only among consumer foods and beverages, but also in pharmaceutical and other industries.

> **Note**
>
> While APO-SNP supports the shelf life feature, a close integration is required with SAP ERP physical batches to make the overall process successful.

In the following sections, we'll go over master data, transactional data integration, customization, alerts, and business scenario testing related to maintaining a proper shelf life practice.

7.3.1 Shelf Life Master Data

You need to maintain the master data for shelf life in both the SAP ERP and SAP SCM systems. Most of the material master data is maintained in SAP ERP and then transferred to SAP SCM (APO) system via the Core Interface (CIF). To maintain the master data in SAP ERP, access SAP ERP Transaction MM02 and navigate to the GENERAL PLANT DATA/STORAGE 1 view. The field definitions (as shown in Figure 7.19) in SAP ERP are as follows:

▶ MINIMUM REMAINING SHELF LIFE
Minimum number of days the product should have for selling to the consumer.

▶ TOTAL SHELF LIFE
Total shelf life of the product from production until the expiration date.

▶ PERIOD INDICATOR
Identifies time unit of measure for minimum REMAINING SHELF LIFE and TOTAL SHELF LIFE fields.

▶ ROUNDING RULE FOR SHELF LIFE
Rounding rule for placing the expiration date at the beginning or end of the period.

▶ STORAGE PERCENTAGE
Identifies the minimum shelf life the product needs to hold during shipping from one location to another.

As with SAP ERP, maintain the following fields in SAP APO via CIF (see Figure 7.19) or via Transaction /SAPAPO/MAT1 [located in the PROPERTIES view]):

▶ PLANNING WITH SHELF LIFE
Determines whether shelf life functionality is considered for this product. Set by CIF, a value is maintained in the TOTAL SHELF LIFE field in SAP ERP.

▶ SHELF LIFE
Filled via CIF from TOTAL SHELF LIFE field in SAP ERP. Value is maintained in days.

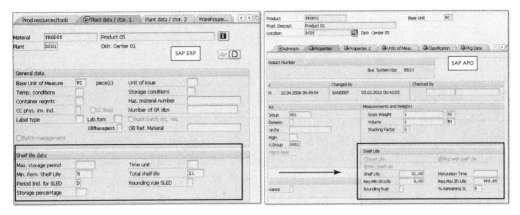

Figure 7.19 Shelf Life in Material Master (SAP ERP) and Location Product /SAPAPO/MAT1 Master Data Maintenance

▶ MATURATION TIME
Quality time period between the production of the material and its use. Currently not filled via CIF. Value is maintained in days.

▶ REQUIRED MINIMUM SHELF LIFE
Minimum shelf life a stock/receipt element must have to cover a demand. Filled via CIF from field MINIMUM REMAINING SHELF LIFE from SAP ERP. Value is maintained in days.

▶ REQUIRED MAXIMUM SHELF LIFE
Maximum shelf life a stock/receipt element must have to cover a demand. Currently not filled via CIF. Value is maintained in days.

▶ ROUNDING RULE
Filled via CIF from fields ROUNDING RULE FOR SHELF LIFE and PERIOD INDICATOR FOR SHELF LIFE in SAP ERP.

▶ PERCENTAGE REMAINING SHELF LIFE
Filled via CIF from field STORAGE PERCENTAGE from SAP ERP.

7.3.2 Shelf Life Transaction Data

The shelf life information for a physical stock is stored in a *batch*. A batch in SAP ERP contains all the characteristics information about that inventory: the date of manufacture, the shelf life expiration date, and the available from date (day after end of maturation time). These attributes can be entered manually during the goods receipt (SAP ERP Transaction MIGO) of the inventory either from the manufacturer or external supplier.

The warehouse personnel enter the date of production for the batch and system based on material master to determine the shelf life date. If the shelf life expiration date is missing, it is calculated from the date of manufacture and the total shelf life from master data.

An example of a batch is shown in Figure 7.20, with the production date and shelf life expiration date. A material needs to be activated for batch management in the material master (SAP ERP Transaction MM02) for batch creation. The batch information can be accessed either via batch SAP ERP Transaction MSC2N or via batch information cockpit (BMBC).

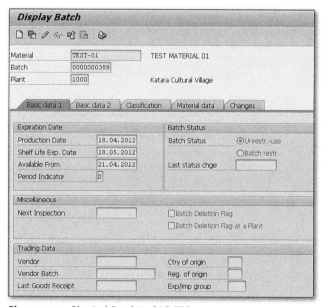

Figure 7.20 Physical Batch in SAP ERP

The batch information from SAP ERP is transferred to SAP APO via CIF; you can view it in Transaction /SAPAPO/RRP3 in the SL DATE 2 field. The SAP APO Shelf Life Expiration Date (SLED) behaves differently based on the SAP ERP batch status, stock type, and Quality Management (QM) usage decision. Table 7.1 shows the APO SLED calculation under different combinations.

Batch Status	Stock Type	Quality Usage Decision	APO Shelf Life Expiration Date (SLED)
Unrestricted	In Quality Inspection	Pending	Planned (inspection lot end date and product master total shelf life)
Unrestricted	Unrestricted	A	Actual (from batch master)
Unrestricted	Blocked	N/A	Actual
Unrestricted	Return	N/A	SAP APO doesn't consider return stock
Restricted	In Quality Inspection	None	Planned (material document posting date + product master total shelf life) – rare instance when material is put in restricted status while in quality inspection (QI)
Restricted	Restricted	None	Planned (material document posting date + product master total shelf life) – rare instance when material is moved to another location prior to usage decision
Restricted	Restricted	A	Business scenario where material is moved to another location after a Quality Management (QM) usage decision
Restricted	Blocked	N/A	Actual
Restricted	Return	N/A	SAP APO doesn't consider return stock

Table 7.1 SAP APO SLED Integration with SAP ERP Batch Management

To transfer the batch shelf life dates from SAP ERP to SAP APO, the integration model needs to have active characteristics, classes, and batches. The integration model (CIF) is created/generated and activated in SAP ERP Transactions CFM1 and CFM2.

Shelf Life Integration: Relevant SAP Notes

SAP Notes 391018 and 751392 explain integration of batches into SAP APO from SAP ERP. Other relevant notes regarding shelf life are:

▶ Note 810694: Shelf life with initial production date not transferredNote 1028924: CIF classification: Deletion of characteristic value

▶ Note 1366888: Deleting values in batch classification

▶ Note 78235: Revaluating reference characteristics in batch classification

▶ Note 979779: Deleting values in batch classifications

In addition to other business processes, ABC Technology has also activated the shelf life for its procurement process. The users can now view the shelf life information in purchase requisition and purchase orders.

The purchase requisitions and purchase orders also contain the shelf life information, which is transferred to SAP APO for planning. Figure 7.21 shows the purchase requisition and purchase order fields where the shelf life data is populated.

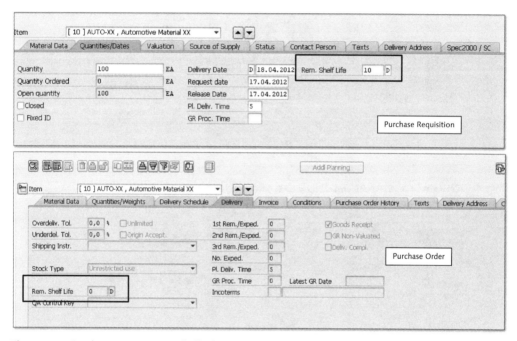

Figure 7.21 Purchasing Document Shelf Life Data

7.3.3 SAP ERP Batch Integration

Let's look at the basic configuration for batches in SAP ERP to support the batch integration with SAP APO.

Characteristics and Class

There are six characteristics of importance for batch integration:

- ▶ LOBM_APO_SL_MIN: Minimum shelf life/maturity (in seconds)

- ▶ LOBM_APO_SL_MAX: Maximum shelf life/shelf life (in seconds)

- ▶ LOBM_APO_SL_UTC: Reference time stamp of batch

- ▶ LOBM_VERAB: Availability date

- ▶ LOBM_VFDAT: Expiration date, shelf life

- ▶ LOBM_HSDAT: Date when batch was produced

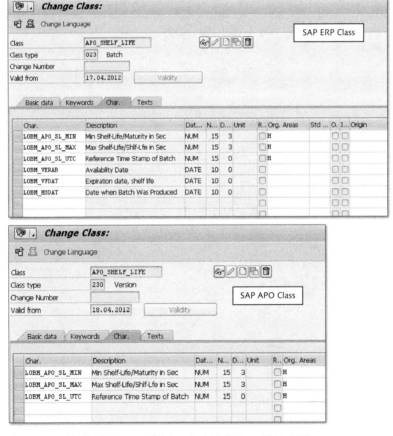

Figure 7.22   Shelf Life Class Definitions in SAP ERP and SAP APO

The characteristics need to be assigned to the class with the class type 023 (batch). Only the characteristics with organizational areas are transferred to SAP APO. As Figure 7.22 shows, the SAP APO shelf life class is shown in SAP ERP and SAP APO, whereby only the first three characteristics with organizational area are transferred. The characteristics are accessed via Transaction CT04, while the class can be accessed via Transaction CL02.

Before the class is transferred from SAP ERP to SAP APO via CIF, we need to perform class organization customization in SAP APO. Follow the SAP APO Transaction O1CL, select /SAPAPO/VERKEY (Version 000), and enter class type 230 in the ORGANIZATION AREAS class type (see Figure 7.23).

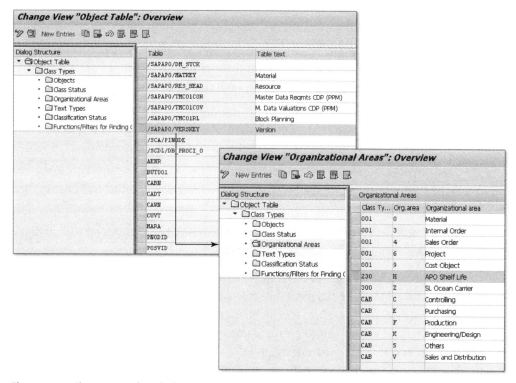

Figure 7.23 Class Type Link with the Organizational Area

7.3.4 Shelf Life Key Figures

APO-SNP provides standard planning book 9ASNP_SHLF for performing shelf life planning. The planning book provides four basic key figures for shelf life calculation but lacks in planning the projected wastage quantity during the heuristics run. However, this issue can be mitigated by adding a new key figure and macro for the PROJECTED WASTAGE QUANTITY to TOTAL DEMAND key figure. This will enable businesses to plan for a projected wastage quantity and not run into stock out situations.

Also, we can define a days of SUPPLY (SHELF LIFE) key figure to take into account stock that is not expiring. The key figures are calculated via a macro with an embedded SAP function module. The definition of the first four standard and two custom key figures are as follows:

- ▶ EXPIRY QTY displays the total quantity of the batches that will expire in a given month without regard to demand.

- ▶ PROJECTED WASTAGE QTY displays the remaining quantity of the expiring batches after considering pegged demand consumption prior to expiry.

- ▶ STOCK ON HAND (SHELF LIFE) displays the quantity of inventory remaining after considering demand consumption and the shelf life of all batches on hand (i.e., the total inventory not expiring in that month after demand has been fulfilled).

- ▶ SUPPLY SHORTAGE (SHELF LIFE) displays the shortage quantity in the case in which the stock on hand (shelf life) is not sufficient to fulfill demand.

- ▶ ADDITIONAL DEMAND (SHELF LIFE) equals the projected wastage and is the key figure used to consume the expiring material out of inventory and enable shelf life planning.

- ▶ DAYS OF SUPPLY (SHELF LIFE) calculates days of supply using stock on hand (Shelf Life), therefore considering only stock that is not expiring.

The PROJECTED WASTAGE QUANTITY key figure calculation is based on the dynamic pegging function. This function automatically links requirements for a location product with suitable stock or receipt elements. If there is any change in planning, a new dynamic relationship is created and adjusted with the new plan. Figure 7.24 shows an example of dynamic pegging with a FIFO (first in first out) relationship where the receipts elements are pegged with requirements elements as per the earliest date sequence.

Business Scenario

Let's see how the shelf life planning comes into play in interactive planning. Figure 7.25 shows a business scenario for a consumable product of which there are 200 units of receipt elements, but the demand requirements of 200 units are placed in a different bucket for consumption. One of the demand elements is placed in a bucket after the expiration date of 100 units of receipts. In a standard situation, the planner will get an alert about the wastage and will react to the situation accordingly. An alternative solution for automating the business scenario is to capture the additional demand (shelf life) and populate the total demand key figure with the use of an SAP APO macro to keep the wastage key figure to the TOTAL DEMAND key figure.

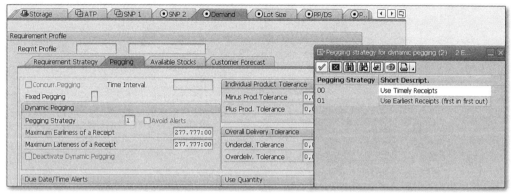

Figure 7.24 Pegging Strategy for Shelf Life Planning

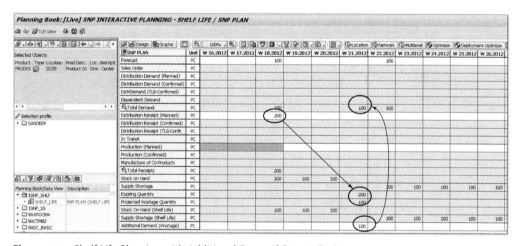

Figure 7.25 Shelf Life Planning with Additional Demand Due to Expiry

In this way, during the next APO-SNP planning run, 100 units will be proposed to make the demand and supply plan balanced. Next, the planner can run SNP heuristics interactively by executing one of the three heuristics methods by clicking the LOCATION, NETWORK, or MULTILEVEL icon in the interactive planning book.

Figure 7.26 shows the post-heuristics run in which the demand is fulfilled by a new receipt element leaving the wastage of 100 units.

Planning Book: [Live] SNP INTERACTIVE PLANNING - SHELF LIFE / SNP PLAN											
SNP PLAN	Unit	W 16.2012	W 17.2012	W 18.2012	W 19.2012	W 20.2012	W 21.2012	W 22.2012	W 23.2012	W 24.2012	W 25.2012
Forecast	PC			100				100			
Sales Order	PC										
Distribution Demand (Planned)	PC										
Distribution Demand (Confirmed)	PC										
DistrDemand (TLB-Confirmed)	PC										
Dependent Demand	PC										
Total Demand	PC			100				100	100		
Distribution Receipt (Planned)	PC			200				100			
Distribution Receipt (Confirmed)	PC										
Distribution Receipt (TLB-Confir	PC										
In Transit	PC										
Production (Planned)	PC										
Production (Confirmed)	PC										
Manufacture of Co-Products	PC										
Total Receipts	PC			200					100		
Stock on Hand	PC			100	100	100					
Supply Shortage	PC										
Expiring Quantity	PC							200			100
Projected Wastage Quantity	PC							100			
Stock On Hand (Shelf Life)	PC			100	100	100					
Supply Shortage (Shelf Life)	PC										
Additional Demand (Wastage)	PC								100		

Figure 7.26 Post-Heuristics Shelf Life Situation

7.3.5 Shelf Life Propagation

Shelf life propagation is defined as the capability to dynamically peg the requirement and receipt after the SNP planning run. The transportation and production durations are factored into the propagations. You can access this feature via Transaction /SAPAPO/SNP10 or report /SAPAPO/RSNP_SHLF_PROP. Running the shelf life propagation program will ensure that all the receipts and requirement elements are properly matched and that the wastage is calculated based on the current situation.

7.3.6 Shelf Life Alerts

Shelf life planning alerts help the planner react to supply situations due to shelf life expiration issues. SAP APO provides standard alerts in both APO-SNP and Production Planning/Detailed Scheduling (PP/DS) related to shelf life. The alerts are accessed in the Alert Monitor via Transaction /SAPAPO/AMON1.

> **Note**
>
> Refer back to Chapter 5, Section 5.7, for information on how to set up the Alert Monitor.

The alerts in APO-SNP alerts available in both dynamic and database form are:

- Supply Shortage Shelf Life
- Projected Waste Quantity

The shelf life functionality works on specific restrictions to adhere to the requirement and receipts pegging relationship. These restrictions are as follows:

- Maturation time of supply before due date of demand element
- Expiration of supply after minimum required shelf life of demand element
- Expiration of supply before maximum required shelf life of demand element

The following list provides the few PP/DS standard alerts that look at the above restrictions and alert the business planner of the supply planning situations:

- Maturation time not completed (requirement/receipt)
- Shelf life too short (requirement/receipt)
- Shelf life too long (requirement/receipt)
- Receipt without pegging relationship with expiration date

7.4 Planning Strategies and Forecast Consumption

Planning strategies play an important role in determining whether the net requirements are used for planning purposes or triggering of production or are consumed using existing customer requirements (for example, sales orders).

> **Note**
>
> A *planning strategy* in SAP ERP is known as a *requirement strategy* in SAP APO.

For every planning strategy, we define the consumption process by the combination of requirement types from Demand Management and Sales Order Management in SAP ERP. *Consumption strategies* help in determining how requirement quantities and dates are compared to actual customer requirements to perform forecast consumption. In the consumption process, the system compares planned independent requirement quantities and dates with actual customer requirements. The requirement types entered when maintaining planned independent requirements is compared with the customer requirement types specified in SAP ERP Customizing. A

371

consumption is defined as a comparison of planned independent requirement (PIR) quantities with the requirements quantities from customer requirements that can lead to a reduction in the PIR.

Example

The consumption process is important for ABC Technology to understand the difference between the gross forecast and net forecast, which needs to feed the supply planning process. The gross forecast for ABC Technology is planned in APO-DP and released to APO-SNP. Once the customer sales orders are interfaced from SAP ERP, the forecast in APO-SNP is consumed by the customer sales orders and becomes the net forecast. ABC Technology would like to differentiate between gross and net forecasts during its supply planning calculations.

Let's look at the most commonly used planning strategies.

▶ **Make-to-stock production (Identifier 10 in both SAP ERP and SAP APO)**
All planning is performed on planned independent requirements (forecast) because it's assumed that customers are buying stock from the warehouse. Some important things to note about this strategy are:

  ▶ The sales orders are not MRP-relevant; however, they are displayed.

  ▶ The sales orders are pulled from stock, the material withdrawn is a reduction in the sales order, and the planned independent requirements (forecast) are reduced at goods issue.

  ▶ Forecast consumption is not carried out, and all the old, past-due forecasts need to be deleted routinely.

▶ **Planning with final assembly (Identifier 40 in SAP ERP and 20 in SAP APO)**
All planning is performed on planned independent requirements (forecast) and sales orders. Some important things to note about this strategy are:

  ▶ Once created, the sales orders replace the planned independent requirements.

  ▶ Any additional planned independent requirements not consumed by sales orders can be set to zero using Transaction /SAPAPO/MD74. If the planned independent requirements are created in SAP ERP, we use SAP ERP Transaction MD74 for PIR reorganization.

  ▶ To avoid demand inflation, it's important to use the forecast consumption process for this business scenario. This will ensure that the supply planning is planning correct volumes at sales orders (short term) and forecast (medium and long term).

▸ **Planning without final assembly (Identifier 50 in SAP ERP and 30 in SAP APO)**
All planning is performed only on planned independent requirements for finished goods and not for component or raw materials; however, the higher material is only produced when an actual customer requirement exists. The planned order in SAP APO cannot be converted to a production order as it is only used to generate the dependent requirements for components procurement.

▸ **Planning with planning product (Identifier 60 SAP ERP and 40 in SAP APO)**
All planning is performed at planning product, which is not a true selling product but a type of product hierarchy. The forecast is performed at the planning product level. Once the sales orders are received for any lower associated product (not to be confused with components within the BOM structure), the forecast of the planning product is consumed.

To set a requirement strategy in your SAP APO system, follow menu path SPRO • ADVANCED PLANNING AND OPTIMIZATION • SUPPLY CHAIN PLANNING • DEMAND PLANNING • BASIC SETTINGS • CONSUMPTION • SPECIFY REQUIREMENT STRATEGIES. As Figure 7.27 shows, SAP APO uses planning segments to store sales orders, forecasts, and manufacturing orders.

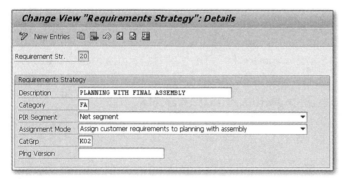

Figure 7.27 SAP APO Requirement Strategy Customization

We'll go over how to set the main screen elements in the next sections.

7.4.1 Planned Independent Requirement Segment (Requirement Planning)

Depending on how you set the PIR SEGMENT field, you can have the system perform different requirement planning. The main task of the PIR segment is to dictate whether the product is make-to-stock or make-to-order, and also to direct whether the inventory should be included with warehouse inventory or customer-specific inventory. The options available in the PIR segment are as follows:

► **Net segment**
This method, used in make-to-stock, considers both sales orders and forecasts for requirements planning. The good receipt of the inventory updates the warehouse stock quantity.

► **Planning without final assembly with individual requirement segment**
This method, used in make-to-order, considers only sales orders and no forecasts. The product forecast is created pro forma and is only used for dependent requirement planning of the components. The sales order consumes the forecast, if available. The goods receipt of inventory is either allocated to sales orders or project order (SAP ERP WBS element).

► **Planning without final assembly and without individual requirement segment**
With this method, as with the prior methods, the production is performed only when the sales order is entered into the system. The forecast is used to generate the dependent requirement for the components procurement. This is equivalent to SAP ERP strategy 52 and, as opposed to the above, there are no individual requirement segments for the sales orders. There is no requirement strategy in standard SAP that currently uses this method.

► **Characteristics-based planning without final assembly**
This method is similar to the second method in this list, but is used in the variant configuration environment.

7.4.2 Assignment Mode (Forecast Consumption)

Another field of interest in this customization is the ASSIGNMENT MODE. There are four assignment modes defined in Table 7.2, which defines how the forecast is consumed and in which segment.

Assignment Mode	Definition
Assignment of customer requirements to planning with assembly	Customer sales orders consume the product's forecast in the net segment.
Assignment of customer requirements to planning without assembly	Customer sales orders consume the product's forecast in the planning without final assembly segment.
Assignment of customer requirements to planning product	Customer sales orders consume the planning product's forecast in the planning without final assembly segment. In this case, an incoming sales order does not consume its own forecast but that of a planning product instead. This mode is used commonly in the variant configuration environment.
No assignment	No forecast consumption is carried out. The assignment method in SAP APO corresponds to the consumption/allocation indicator in the SAP ERP planning strategy.

Table 7.2 Assignment Mode Definitions in SAP APO

7.4.3 Category Group (Forecast Consumption)

In the category group (CatGrp field), define the customer requirements category to be used for forecast consumption. For assembly planning, you can use category group K02, where the dependent requirement category is included, as well. The customization path for the requirement strategy in SAP APO is SPRO • Advanced Planning and Optimization • Supply Chain Planning • Supply Network Planning • Basic Settings • Maintain Category Groups.

The consumption master data is found in the location product master Transaction /SAPAPO/MAT1 – Demand tab (see Figure 7.28). The master data maintained in SAP ERP material master gets transferred to SAP APO via CIF. The IT user can set up material master integration model (SAP ERP Transaction CFM1/CFM2) to send the master data.

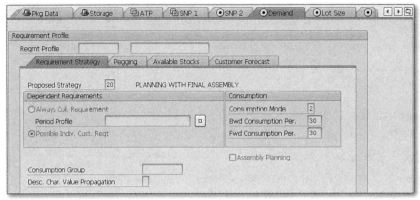

Figure 7.28 SAP APO Location Product Master Data: Requirement Strategy

There are three available modes that are used to perform consumption of a product. Figure 7.29 shows the backward and forward consumption process in APO-SNP.

▶ **Backward consumption**
   Consumes the sales order, dependent requirement, or reservation quantity from the requirement quantity requested before the requirement date.

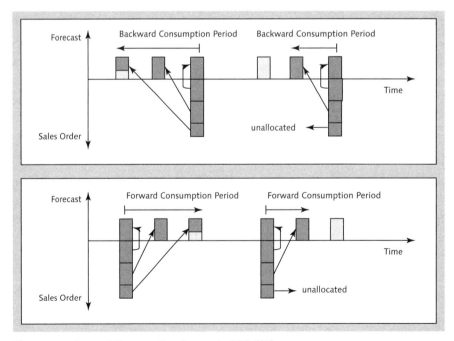

Figure 7.29 Forecast Consumption Process in APO-SNP

▸ **Forward consumption**
Consumes the sales order, dependent requirement, or reservation quantity from the requirement quantity requested after the requirement date.

▸ **Backward consumption and forward consumption**
Occurs on the sales order, dependent requirement, or reservation quantity from the requirement quantity requested before the requirement date, if the requirement is not satisfied then forward consumption begins.

7.5 Subcontracting

The subcontracting process allows a company to outsource their non-core functions as well as manage resource capacities when the demand is high. APO-SNP integrates seamlessly with SAP ERP and provides a complete planning and execution solution. The subcontracting-integrated solution supports demand management, vendor capacities, stock movements at vendor locations, and billing processes. There are three distinct business scenarios supported in the APO-SNP functionality, as shown in Figure 7.30.

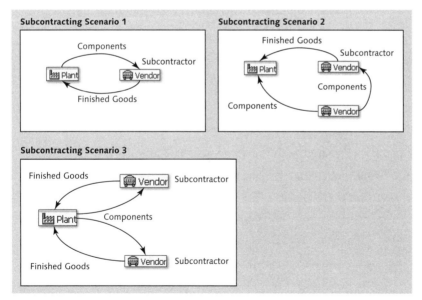

Figure 7.30 APO-SNP Subcontracting Scenarios

In the first scenario, the manufacturing location sends the components to the subcontractor. The subcontractors perform the value add and send the finished goods back to the manufacturing location.

In the second scenario, the subcontractors receive the components from an external supplier and then supply the finished goods to the manufacturing plan.

In the third scenario, the manufacturer may send the components to separate subcontractors and then receive the finished goods from both external parties.

In the following sections, we'll explore the master data and planning book information and processes needed to use these different scenarios.

7.5.1 Master Data Requirements

Before we look at the integration between SAP ERP and SAP APO, let's list all the master data sets needed in SAP ERP and SAP APO to model the subcontracting scenario.

SAP ERP Master Data

Make sure you have maintained the following master data requirements in SAP ERP:

▶ **Work center master (SAP ERP Transaction CRC1)**
The resource is created within the manufacturing location where the goods will be received from subcontracting. The resource is to be used within the routing master data and will require processing unit capacity header (08) with productive time.

▶ **Routing (SAP ERP Transaction CA01)**
A simple routing is created with the above resource and BOM definition.

▶ **Production version (SAP ERP Transaction C223)**
Create a production version by combining the resource and routing. It's better to keep the subcontracting version separate with a new number range. The production version can be transferred to SAP APO via CIF using one of the settings in Transaction CFM1, as shown in Figure 7.31.

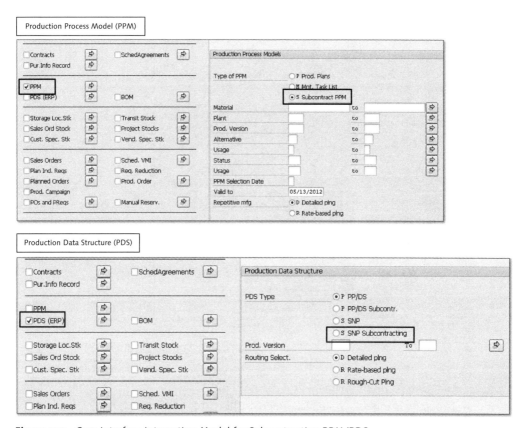

Figure 7.31 Core Interface Integration Model for Subcontracting PPM/PDS

▶ **Purchasing info record (SAP ERP Transaction ME11)**
The production version is now assigned to the subcontracting purchase info record beside other parameters. An example of a purchasing info record with a production version is shown in Figure 7.32.

SAP APO Master Data

The other set of master data required in SAP APO are:

▶ **Location master (Transaction /SAPAPO/LOC3)**
The manufacturing plant and subcontracting vendor are transferred from SAP ERP via CIF. The subcontracting is transferred with the use of the CIF integration model in SAP ERP Transactions CFM1/CFM2.

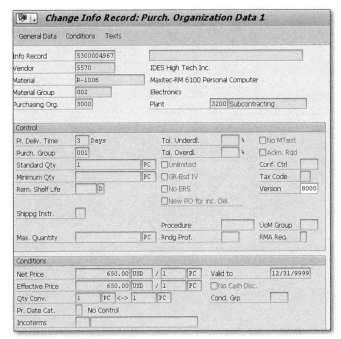

Figure 7.32 Subcontracting Purchasing Info Record with Production Version

▶ **Location product (Transaction /SAPAPO/MAT1)**
The subcontracting materials need to be extended directly in SAP APO. The master data can be created manually or extended with the use of the Legacy System Migration Workbench (LSMW).

▶ **Resource master (Transaction /SAPAPO/RES01)**
The work center created in SAP ERP is transferred to SAP APO using CIF.

▶ **Transportation lane (Transaction /SAPAPO/SCC_TL1)**
The transportation lane is created by the CIF integration model for the purchasing info record. The subcontracting purchasing document number is transferred in the transportation lane (see Figure 7.33) for the finished goods. To supply the components from manufacturing or an external vendor to the subcontractor, the reverse transportation lane needs to be created directly in SAP APO.

▶ **Production process model (Transaction /SAPAPO/SCC03)**
The PPM structure is also transferred from SAP ERP via CIF. If the subcontracting master data, in the form of resources, routing, and production versions, is

not maintained in SAP ERP, the corresponding master data are created directly in SAP APO.

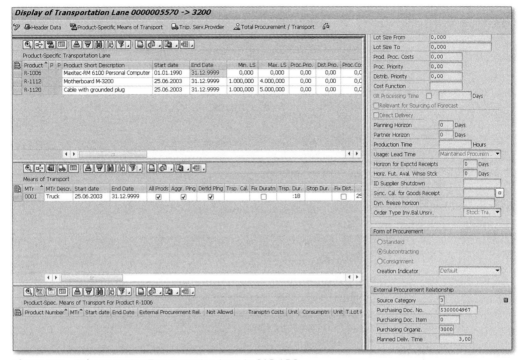

Figure 7.33 Subcontracting Transportation Lane in SAP APO

7.5.2 Planning Book

APO-SNP provides standard planning book 9ASNPSBC to support the subcontracting business scenario. The standard planning book has additional key figures for capturing the subcontracting purchase requisitions and planned orders transaction. Figure 7.34 shows the standard planning book with additional subcontracting key figures for planning at both the manufacturing and subcontractor locations. The standard subcontracting planning book 9ASNPSBC is primarily copied and activated using Transaction /SAPAPO/SDP8B (refer back to Chapter 4, Section 4.6.4 for more details).

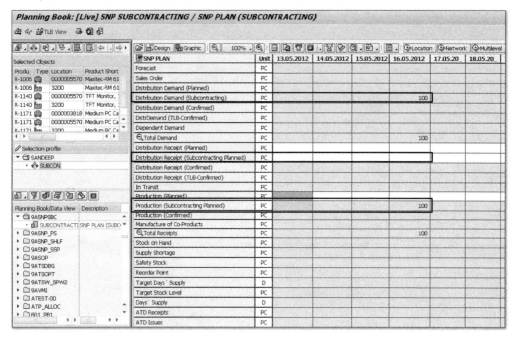

Figure 7.34 APO-SNP Subcontracting Planning Book with Additional Key Figures

The subcontracting scenario can be planned by either of the planning solvers, heuristics algorithm, or optimizer run; the system determines a subcontractor as the source of supply for a product requirement and generates a subcontracting purchase requisition (❶) to transfer the material from a source (subcontractor) location to the destination (plant) location, as shown in Figure 7.35. The system also locates the valid PPM at the subcontracting location to generate an in-house production order (❷) for the parent item in the source location. The planned order performs a bill of material (BOM) explosion that triggers the component goods movement from the factory to the subcontracting location in the form of a purchase requisition (❸). An additional purchase requisition is raised for the external vendor to supply components to the subcontractor. The materials are goods issued from the manufacturing location using SAP ERP Transaction ME2O.

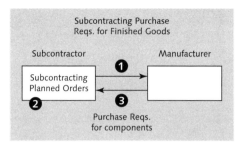

Figure 7.35 APO-SNP Subcontracting Scenario

7.6 Warehouse Capacity Overview

In many supply chain situations, warehouse capacity serves as a constraint because there isn't enough storage space. In this scenario, planning needs to consider the storage capacity and provide an outlook on warehouse consumption. There can also be a business requirement to view the planning information in the form of pallets for evaluation of the warehouse storage capacity.

> **Example**
>
> ABC Technology has recently opened new distribution centers that have storage space capacity constraints. The warehouses can only store inventory up to five days of sales. Because of the lack of space, they have been spending a lot of money moving inventory across distribution centers just to find space for it. The company would like the capability in the SAP APO system to monitor the planned receipts and make adjustments in the plan to avoid unnecessary transportation and handling costs.

APO-SNP helps in modeling the warehouse capacity overview with a couple of simple master data settings. The output of capacity is seen in the SNP planning book under capacity overview.

7.6.1 Master Data

Make sure that the following master data settings are maintained in SAP APO:

▶ **Resource master (Transaction /SAPAPO/RES01)**
A storage resource is first created with bucket definition. The resource outlines the capacity of the warehouse. An example of a storage resource with volume capacity is shown in Figure 7.36.

▶ **Location master (Transaction /SAPAPO/LOC3)**
The storage capacity is then maintained in the location master under the RESOURCE tab, in the STORAGE RESOURCE field.

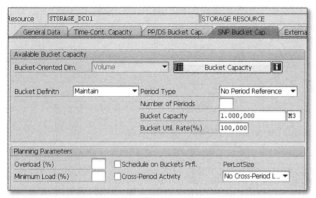

Figure 7.36 Storage Resource Definition in SAP APO

▶ **Location product master (Transaction /SAPAPO/MAT1)**
The consumption of the product toward the storage is maintained in the GR/GI tab in the STORAGE CONS. PER BUN field. An example is shown in Figure 7.37.

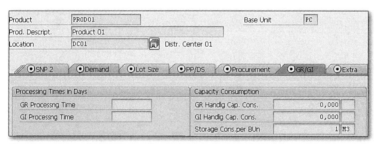

Figure 7.37 Product Storage Consumption Master Data

7.6.2 Perform the APO-SNP Planning Run

Once the master data settings are complete, we can perform an APO-SNP planning run, which generates receipt elements (refer to Chapter 5, Section 5.5 on planning run details). These receipt elements start consuming the storage resource. The capacity consumption can be visualized in SNP standard planning book 9ASNP94 (Transaction /SAPAPO/SDP94) under the CAPACITY DATA view.

Figure 7.38 shows how the capacity consumption can be seen, as well as an option for capacity leveling in the scenario of an overload. The figure shows two important indicators related to resource capacity: available capacity and capacity consumption. With these, the planner is able to judge the buckets where there is overload or under-utilization of resources. The interactive screen also provides the option of smoothing the resource capacity with the use of capacity leveling functionality or adjusting the resource capacity variant in the SAP APO resource master (refer to Chapter 5, Section 5.5.3 for more details.)

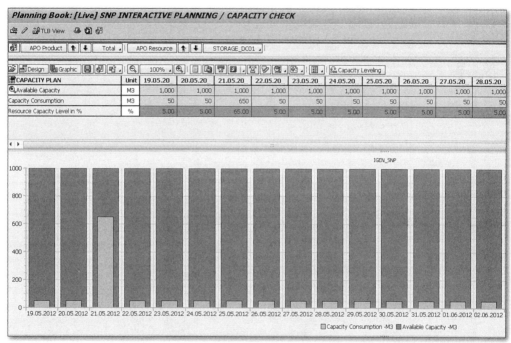

Figure 7.38 APO-SNP Planning Book: Warehouse Consumption

7.7   Direct Shipment Customers

For cost-saving reasons and improving customer satisfaction, ABC Technology wants to model its supply chain for direct delivery of goods from the either the supplier or manufacturing location to the end customers. APO-SNP supports this process with customization and master data settings. Figure 7.39 shows an example in which the goods are shipped directly from the manufacturing once there is high volume demand and transportation thresholds are met.

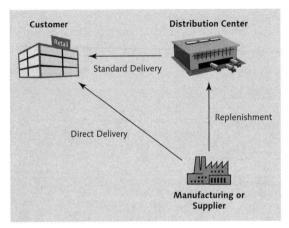

Figure 7.39 Direct Shipment Business Scenario

The direct delivery can be activated in SNP heuristics via the SAP APO menu path SPRO • ADVANCED PLANNING AND OPTIMIZATION • SUPPLY CHAIN PLANNING • SUP-PLY NETWORK PLANNING • BASIC SETTINGS • MAINTAIN GLOBAL SNP SETTINGS. In the APO-SNP global settings (see Figure 7.40), maintain the direct delivery relevancy in the HEU: DIRECT DELIVERY field.

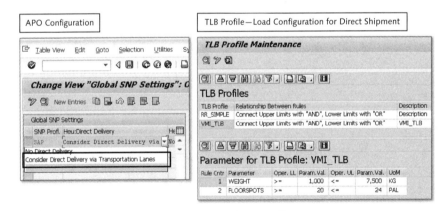

Figure 7.40 Direct Delivery Customization and TLB Profile Maintenance

The SNP Transport Load Builder (TLB) is a functionality used for creating transportation load shipments (you can find more details on TLB functionality in Section

7.9). Next, access Transaction /SAPAPO/TLBPRF and maintain the TLB profile for the direct delivery shipment and the load consolidation of products that can be applicable for direct shipment. Figure 7.40 shows an example of a TLB profile.

Access Transaction /SAPAPO/SCC_TL1 to flag the direct shipment for the normal transportation lane from manufacturing to DC (see Figure 7.41). The TLB profile created earlier needs to be input into the direct delivery transportation lane from the manufacturing location to the customer.

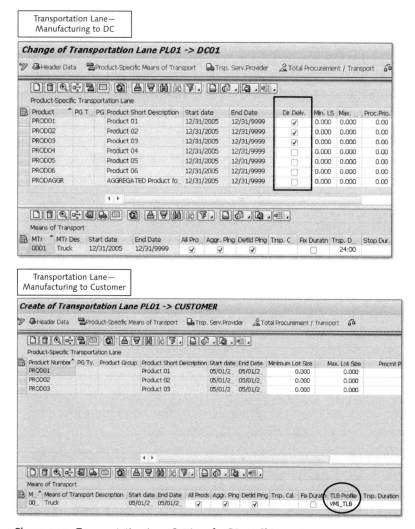

Figure 7.41 Transportation Lane Settings for Direct Shipment

The logic during SNP heuristics planning looks at the customer demand and possibility of fulfilling per the TLB threshold limits. Even though we are creating a TLB order, the SNP heuristics searches the TLB master data parameters for the direct delivery–flagged transportation lane to check on the possibility of direct shipment and make decisions on proposals. The remaining product quantities that do not pass the TLB threshold are switched back to the normal replenishment transportation lane to the distribution center. This direct shipment logic is only applicable for SNP heuristics and is not factored into the SNP deployment. The direct shipment can be modeled in the deployment run using the fair share deployment strategy.

7.8 Product Interchangeability in APO-SNP

The product interchangeability functionality in APO-SNP helps businesses to transfer demand from one product to the next. This process helps companies estimate how to align their forecasts with inventory projections.

> **Example**
>
> This functionality helps ABC Technology with product lifecycle management by keeping a check on its old product (laptop, monitor, and desktop groups) inventory before launching a new product line for the same product brand. The functionality helps ABC Technology define a time horizon for when production and shipping can begin for the new product and also the last date when the old product can be sold in the market.

This is applicable for business scenarios of product discontinuation, supersession chain, or form-fit function (FFF). There are the three methods in interchangeability that can be modeled in APO-SNP:

▶ **Product discontinuation**
  This scenario applies to new product lifecycle management when the new product is planned to replace a similar old product. The process of interchangeability is used to manage product obsolescence whereby the old product inventory is depleted until the new product receipts are introduced.

▶ **Supersession chain**
  This scenario is similar to product discontinuation: the receipt elements are searched in the chain of products. If no existing receipt elements are found, the system creates receipt element for the last product in the supersession chain.

▶ **Form fit function (FFF) class**
This scenario is used in grouping a number of products that show similar characteristics in form, fit, and function. This scenario will apply when any product demand can be replaced by receipt of child products in the group.

APO-SNP interchangeability can be activated with a couple of steps. First, activate APO-SNP interchangeability (see Figure 7.42) via menu path SPRO • ADVANCED PLANNING AND OPTIMIZATION • SUPPLY CHAIN PLANNING • SUPPLY NETWORK PLANNING • BASIC SETTINGS • MAINTAIN GLOBAL SNP SETTINGS. In the configuration setting maintain the field SNP:INTERCH. as PRODUCT INTERCHANGEABILITY ACTIVATED, as shown in the figure.

Next we need to maintain the attribute properties for the supersession chain. This is performed in menu path SPRO • SCM BASIS • MASTER DATA • PRODUCT AND LOCATION INTERCHANGEABILITY • APPLICATION SETTINGS • MAINTAIN ATTRIBUTE PROPERTIES FOR SUPERSESSION CHAINS. SAP provides standard attributes that can be flagged active, per business requirements, as Figure 7.42 shows.

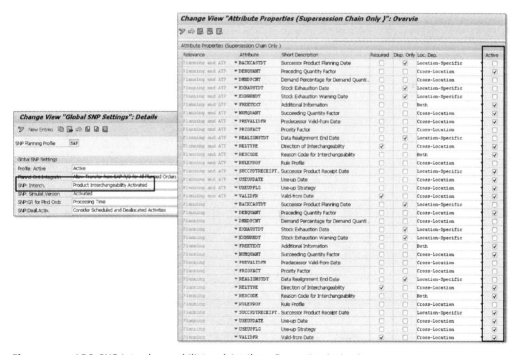

Figure 7.42 APO-SNP Interchangeability and Attribute Properties Activation

> **APO-SNP Interchangeability**
>
> SAP Note 1057389 provides tips on the maintenance of interchangeability group range, number range, and planning package number range.

SAP also provides standard planning book 9ASNP_PS with data view PROD_SUBST. This book has additional key figures: substitution demand (InfoObject 9APSUBAB) and substitution receipts (InfoObject 9APSUBZU) required for the interchangeability calculations. These objects need to be added to the new planning object structure and planning areas using Transaction /SAPAPO/MSDP_ADMIN.

We add these key figures in the planning area KEY FIGURE tab. There are also additional macros that look at the interchangeability master data parameters and perform the calculation in the data view. The new key figures are also added to the general APO-SNP planning book macros (for example, the stock balance macro). The macros can be displayed and adjusted in macro workbench Transaction /SAPAPO/ADVM.

Let's look at two different scenarios in the next sections that explain the interchangeability functionality and master data settings required in the APO-SNP environment.

7.8.1 Scenario 1: Consume Existing Inventory

In the first business scenario, ABC Technology wants to consume all of the existing inventory for the old material of 19-inch monitors for the new material demand of the updated and larger 21-inch monitor. Once all the inventory of 19-inch monitors has been depleted, the new material receipt elements for 21-inch monitors are planned.

Figure 7.43 shows an example in which the old material is Product A (19-inch monitor) and the new replacing material is Product B (21-inch monitor). A phase-in date is defined for the Product B forecast. Since the inventory for Product A still exists, it consumes the forecast for Product B until the time period when all the inventory of Product A is consumed. After the complete consumption, the demand for Product B is fulfilled by receipt elements of Product B itself.

This scenario is modeled in APO-SNP via interchangeability master data maintenance in Transaction /INCMD/UI. For new records, maintain the below field attributes per the definitions given in Table 7.3.

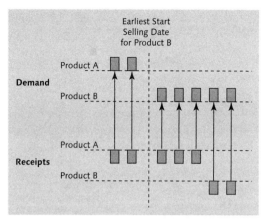

Figure 7.43 APO-SNP Product Interchangeability Complete Use-Up Scenario

Field(s)	Field Definition
GROUP ITEM NUMBER	Identifies steps in master data with multiples of 10.
REPLACEMENT TYPE	Defines the replacement type between members in interchangeability, for example, product-product or assembly-assembly types. Defined in the configuration.
PRECEDING MEMBER TYPE	Based on the replacement type, the member type is entered here (for example, product).
PRECEDING PRODUCT	The product code of the phasing-out (old) product is maintained.
PRECEDING PRODUCT DESCRIPTION	The product description is auto-populated from the product master.
PRECEDING QUANTITY FACTOR	There might be a business scenario in which there exists a proportional quantity relationship between the new and old products. For example, with packaging size, the old product could be of large size being replaced by a smaller product. The proportional quantity for the old product is maintained.
SUCCEEDING MEMBER TYPE	Based on the replacement type, the member type is entered here (for example, product).
SUCCEEDING PRODUCT	The product code of the phasing-in (new) product is maintained.

Table 7.3 APO-SNP Interchangeability Field Attributes

Field(s)	Field Definition
SUCCEEDING PRODUCT DESCRIPTION	The product description is auto-populated from the product master.
SUCCEEDING QUANTITY FACTOR	The proportional quantity relationship for the new product is maintained.
VALID FROM	Specifies the date from which the new product becomes effective (the earliest start selling date for new product).
DIRECTION	FULL or FORWARD. Full indicates that the products are interchangeable in both directions, while forward indicates only one direction of replacement.
USE UP	YES indicates that the systems should only create receipt elements for the new product once the receipts of the old product have been exhausted.
	NO indicates that the system should start planning for the new product, effective from the valid-from date onwards.
	RESTRICTED indicates the date (use up) until the old product receipts can fulfill new product demand. After this date, the old product receipts are invalid.
USE UP DATE	Reflects the date until the old product receipts are considered valid.
REASON CODE	Defined in customization for options representing reasons for maintenance of substitution.
ADDITIONAL INFORMATION	Additional text information for easy reference.

Table 7.3 APO-SNP Interchangeability Field Attributes (Cont.)

Master Data Steps

The system steps (Transaction /INCMD/UI) to maintain the master data for this business scenario are shown in Figure 7.44.

❶ Enter the old and new product details. Maintain the predecessor and successor products.

❷ Enter the validity date when the new product can commence selling. Also indicate the substitution direction and use-up strategy. The example in the figure shows the full direction in forward to consume (use up) the complete inventory before the new product receipts are planned in the system.

❸ Assign the master data to the model. When you click the MODEL ASSIGNMENT icon, a different screen will be displayed where you can drag and drop the model 000 from the right side to the left side under the Interchangeability group. Save the screen and return to the main screen.

❹ Once saved, release the master data for usage by SNP heuristics or optimizer.

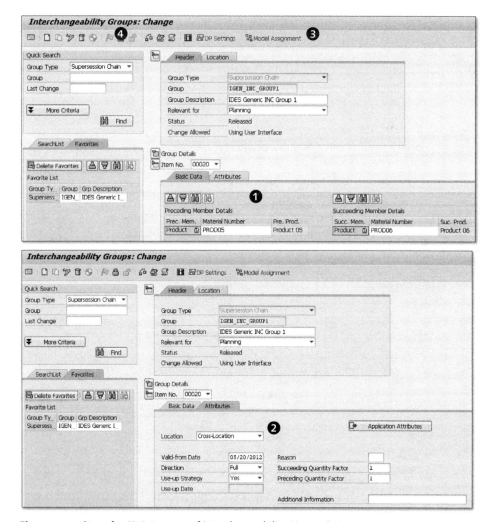

Figure 7.44 Steps for Maintenance of Interchangeability Master Data

The result of the planning run can be visualized in the SNP planning book for interchangeability. Figure 7.45 shows the four steps in the process.

❶ The forecast for the old and new products are published from APO-DP. The phase-in date for the new product in demand planning is aligned with the supply planning valid-from date in interchangeability master data.

❷ During the SNP heuristics run, the forecast of the new product is mapped with the SUBSTITUTION DEMAND (PLANNED) of the old product for consuming the existing inventory (receipts) of the old product.

❸ SNP heuristics also creates the SUBSTITUTION RECEIPTS (PLANNED) for new product until the period the old product inventory is consumed.

❹ Any additional receipts are planned on the new product once the inventory of the old product is consumed.

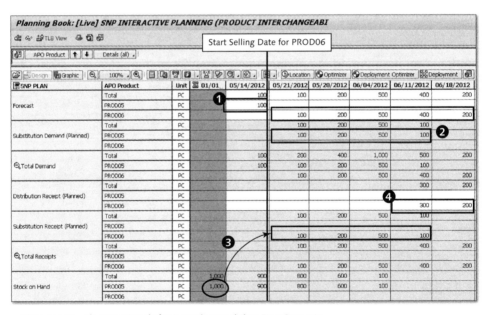

Figure 7.45 Planning Result for Interchangeability First Scenario

7.8.2 Scenario 2: Consuming Existing Inventory until a Specific Date

In the second business scenario, the business requirement calls for consuming all the existing inventory for ABC Technology 17-inch laptop (old material) until a specific date for the new 15-inch laptop material demand. After the use-up date, the receipts elements are planned for the new 15-inch laptop product even though there is stock available for the old 17-inch laptop product. Once all the inventory has been depleted, the new material receipts elements are planned. Figure 7.46 shows an example where the old material is Product A and the new replacing material is Product B.

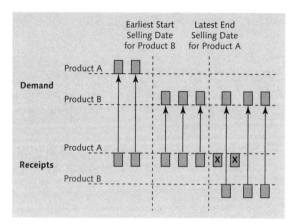

Figure 7.46 APO-SNP Product Interchangeability Complete Use-Up Date Scenario

A phase-in date is defined for the Product B forecast. Since the inventory for Product A still exists, it consumes the forecast for Product B until the specific use-up date. After the use-up date, the receipts are planned for Product B directly to match the Product B demands. This requires a small modification on the master data from the previous business scenario.

Master Data

Access the master data via Transaction /INCMD/UI to change the USE-UP STRATEGY field to "restricted." Also maintain the use-up date, which signifies the latest end-consumption date of receipts for the old product (see Figure 7.47 for an example).

When you run SNP heuristics planning, the result is receipts for the old product not getting consumed after the use-up date. The macro populates the message, "Stock invalid: can no longer be used," highlighted in yellow, in the APO-SNP planning book with (see Figure 7.48).

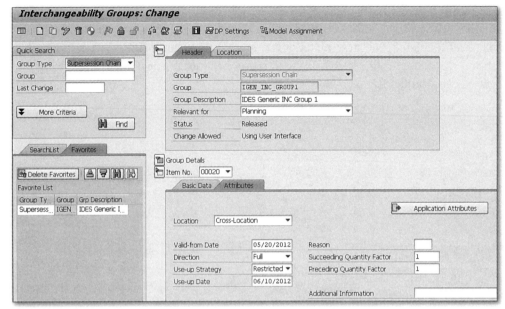

Figure 7.47 Interchangeability Use-Up Strategy and Date Maintenance

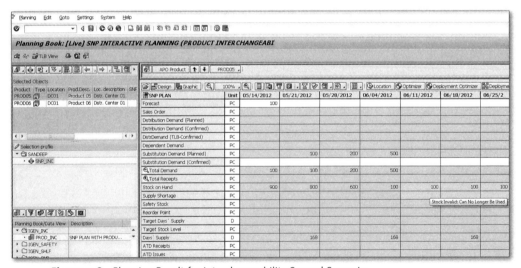

Figure 7.48 Planning Result for Interchangeability Second Scenario

7.9 Transport Load Builder

The purpose of the Transport Load Builder (TLB) is to combine the replenishment orders and create feasible transportation units based on business rules. The business rule defined by a company can be either resource capacity constraint or defined vendor minimums to create feasible stock transport orders or purchase orders. The TLB, besides building loads, also supports multiple business scenarios in the form of cross-docking, multi-stop, and upsizing/downsizing loading methods. The main objective of the TLB in the transportation business process is to do the following:

▶ Build transport loads that are within the parameter limits (weight and/or volume).

▶ Straight (single product) loading or load (multiple products) balancing for specific means of transports.

▶ Shipment loads based on pallet sizes. Cost-based shipment optimization. During upsizing and downsizing, the TLB determines the penalty costs to identify the best shipment loads.

Example

The ABC Technology network consists of shipping laptop, monitor, and desktop products from manufacturing locations to distribution centers. The transportation planner needs to perform transportation planning in advance to inform the carriers three to four days in advance of actual shipments. The goods are primarily transported in trucks between the two facilities. The transportation planner uses TLB to plan whether they will need 48- or 58-cubic-foot line haul trucks or LTL (less than truck load) for a particular bi-weekly shipment.

The overall goal of the transportation planner is to consolidate shipments to keep the transportation costs down. The planner needs to develop his stock transport orders based on truck capacity constraints and material availability for shipments.

In the following sections, we'll go over the different aspects of the TLB.

7.9.1 TLB Profile

You maintain the TLB profile in Transaction /SAPAPO/TLBPRF. The TLB profile defines the parameter limits for resource capacity in terms of volume, weight, and pallets. You can also define different rules for these parameters. During the initial TLB heuristics run, the system proposes orders to fulfill the load between maximum and minimum load limits. The parameters (weight, volume, pallets) can be combined while creating the TLB profile. Figure 7.49 shows an example displaying various rules in different units of measure for TLB load optimization.

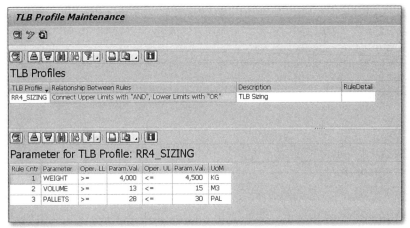

Figure 7.49 TLB Profile Example

7.9.2 TLB Loading Method

The TLB can form two types of loading methods, which are defined in SAP APO transportation lane master data (Transaction /SAPAPO/SCC_TL1) at means of transport method definition.

- ▶ **Straight loading**
  While building load shipments, the TLB tries to combine the same types of products or products defined in the same loading group. The loading group field is defined in the SAP APO location product master (GR/GI tab).

- ▶ **Load balancing**
  TLB tries to distribute all products across shipments in equal proportions.

While the straight method optimizes the transport, there are sales opportunities that can be missed if a proper batch of products is not shipped from the source. The load balancing method ensures both fast- and slow-moving goods are shipped from the source in proportions, which, again, can lead to backorders for fast-moving products.

7.9.3 Shipping Strategies

The TLB supports multiple shipping strategies, including multi-stop, cross dock, and multi-pickup. The main objective of these strategies is to reduce the number of goods movement and work on goods consolidation for delivering or picking up products during transportation. They all support transportation optimization opportunities and lead to cost initiatives within the ABC Technology supply chain.

Example

The ABC Technology transportation planner, now using SNP TLB functionality, can plan consolidated trucks to the distribution centers and directly to the direct customers' warehouse. The transportation planner has complete visibility on how many shipments will be required on a weekly basis and is able to better negotiate freight and service terms with carriers. To model the multiple shipping strategies, ABC Technology has to define the *transportation zone*, which serves as a geographical region where the same shipment can serve multiple warehouses or customers during the shipment milk-run.

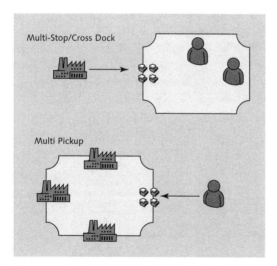

Figure 7.50 Transportation Zone in SAP APO

The transportation zone concept in SAP allows us to group logical locations under one hierarchy. Figure 7.50 shows two examples of how a transportation zone can be modeled in SAP APO. In the first business scenario of multi-stop/cross docking, a single transportation lane is created between the manufacturing source and transportation zone. Under this transportation strategy, the multiple customers (ship to) who will all have the goods delivered under the same TLB shipment are grouped. In the second business scenario, multiple multi-pickups (ship from) are grouped under one TLB shipment for delivery to customers.

Prerequisites

To model these business scenarios, there are a couple of master data configurations that are required as a prerequisite:

1. Define the hierarchy structure for the Transportation Zone (see Figure 7.51, ❶) via path SPRO • SCM BASIS • MASTER DATA • HIERARCHY • DEFINE HIERARCHY STRUCTURE. Here, define a new hierarchy structure for a multi-stop location that has the location group as Level 1 and individual location as Level 2 in the hierarchy structure.

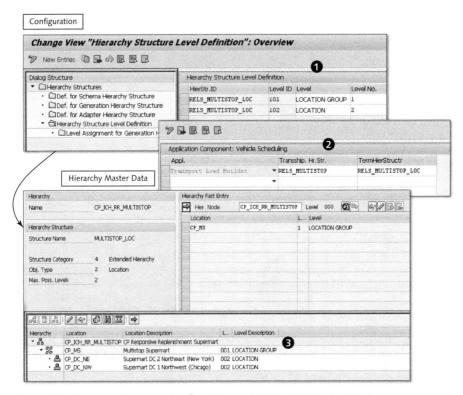

Figure 7.51 Transportation Zone Configuration and Master Data in SAP APO

2. Next, maintain the transportation-relevant hierarchy (see Figure 7.51, ❷).The customization path is SPRO • Advanced Planning and Optimization • Transportation Planning and Vehicle Scheduling • Basic Settings • Maintain Transportation Relevant Hierarchy. In this configuration, we assign the hierarchy structure created in step ❶ to the TLB application. This ensures that, during the TLB planning run, the algorithm looks at this hierarchy structure.

Master Data

Next, on the master data side, we create a Transportation Zone for location type 1005 or Stock Transfer Point of location type 1006 for cross-docking scenarios. We assign the relevant locations (customers or manufacturing locations, depending on our business scenario) to the hierarchy master data for the transportation zone. The hierarchy master data (Figure 7.51, ❸) is maintained via Transaction /SAPAPO/RELHSHOW.

Besides the hierarchy master data, we also need to maintain the transportation lane master data (Transaction /SAPAPO/SCC_TL1). Here, maintain the transportation zone as a destination location, and the manufacturing plant as the source location. Assign the products that will flow in this transportation, along with the transportation method (for example, truck). In the TLB planning book (Transaction /SAPAPO/SNPTLB), the user uses the shuffler (⬛) to find the locations for performing the TLB shipments, as shown in Figure 7.52. Similarly, maintain the transportation lane from the source directly to customers (multi-stop business scenario) and also to the transportation zone. As shown here, we select the transportation lane as the selection object in the TLB planning book. While the source location is the production plant, the destination locations can be distribution centers, customers, or transportation zone.

In the TLB interactive planning, the TLB considers the deployment stock transfer or replenishment orders for locations that are assigned to the transportation zone. After running the replenishment plan at the customer, we need to run TLB shipment on the transportation zone lane.

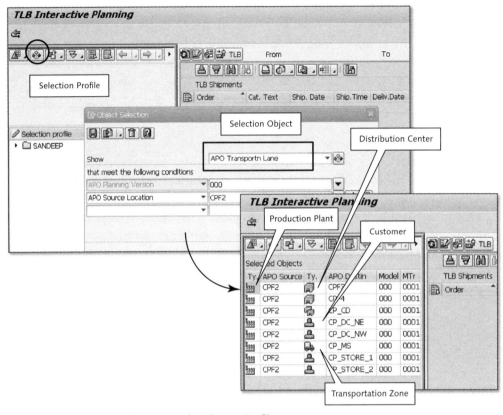

Figure 7.52 TLB Planning Book: Selection Profile

7.9.4 Pull-In Horizon

The TLB pull-in horizon specifies the number of days from the current date in which TLB can take into account the deployment or replenishment orders while constructing TLB shipments, and is defined in days in the SAP APO transportation lane master data (Transaction /SAPAPO/SCC_TL1). The pull-in horizon is maintained for each transport method, such as a truck. TLB looks at the horizon if it cannot find any deployment orders to make a TLB shipment based out of the TLB profile upper/lower limits. The pull-in horizon is also used in the shipment sizing when constructing TLB shipments.

7.9.5   Shipment Sizing

Shipment sizing is a process within TLB in which, after constructing TLB shipments, the partial remaining quantities that do not fall within the parameters limit are flexed for upsizing or downsizing opportunities to form additional shipments. In upsizing, the system adds the deployment orders in pull-in horizon to construct additional shipments, while in downsizing, the system will subtract deployment orders within the pull-in horizon for a future shipment creation process. SAP APO transportation lane master data contains two important fields related to shipment sizing:

▶ **Decision basis for shipment sizing**
Specifies the method for TLB to consider during the shipment sizing. Two methods are available for TLB shipment construction:

  ▶ **Threshold, based on remains of shipment sizing**
  The system determines the mean rounding value based on upper and lower limits. Next, the remaining quantity is divided with this mean value. The output is then compared with the threshold value to decide whether to upsize or downsize.

  ▶ **Threshold, based on shipment sizing result**
  The system determines the rounding value for both upsizing and downsizing. Next, the summation of upsizing and downsizing is divided by the downsizing rounding value. This number is then compared with the defined threshold value to decide whether to upsize or downsize.

▶ **Change threshold value**
A value between 0 and 1 is populated in this field. For values closer to 0, the TLB will decide to use the upsizing method, while for values closer to 1, the TLB selects a downsizing method.

The configuration of the shipment sizing (see Figure 7.53) is defined in the path SPRO • ADVANCED PLANNING AND OPTIMIZATION • SUPPLY CHAIN PLANNING • SUPPLY NETWORK PLANNING • BASIC SETTINGS • MAKE TLB BASIC SETTINGS.

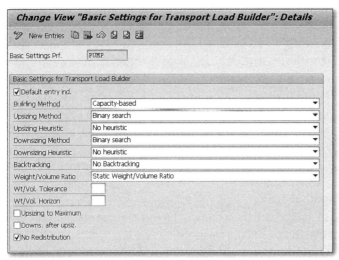

Figure 7.53 TLB Shipment Sizing Configuration

Let's look at the definition of these configuration settings for all mandatory fields:

▶ BUILDING METHOD
Specify whether the system uses product rounding or means of transport capacity value for building loads.

▶ UPSIZING METHOD
Specify how you want the TLB to react when there are remaining quantities after the TLB run. You can specify whether to upsize or downsize to create the next feasible shipment loads.

▶ UPSIZING HEURISTICS
You can mention the system to avoid large rounding values that would prevent the creation of valid loads when upsizing and downsizing.

▶ BACKTRACKING
You can determine how TLB should proceed when transport loads are not built due to large rounding values.

▶ UPSIZING TO MAXIMUM
Systems are loaded to the upper parameter limit for every possible shipment.

▶ SHIPMENT DOWNSIZING AFTER SHIPMENT UPSIZING
You can specify whether the system is to perform downsizing after the upsizing method fails during the shipment load creation.

▶ REDISTRIBUTION
Specify for the system to create all load shipments as close as possible to upper parameter limits in the TLB profile to optimize transportation resources.

7.10 Stock Balancing

In many supply chain situations, there's an imbalance of inventory across the network; it's the supply planner's job to rectify these situations by physical goods movement across the network. The stock balancing exercise is more like a stock out pull than excess inventory push business scenario. The supply planner reviews the stock out situations across the regional network and balances the inventory. By planning these receipts' inward movement, there are fewer net requirements flowing either to manufacturing to produce more or procure more from suppliers.

The important SAP APO master data required for performing the stock balancing exercise is the transportation lane. Besides the normal replenishment lane, there should be a balancing lane maintained as well. To make it easier, the balancing transportation lane can be maintained at the product group level instead of the product level.

Example

ABC Technology has recently opened multiple warehouses in the network. The supply planner needs to look at the inventory at warehouse locations before placing a new net requirement at the manufacturing location. Currently, the planner performs this exercise offline to calculate the excess inventory at each location and performs an inventory balancing exercise by creating a stock transport order between the locations before the weekly planning cycle, which places the net requirement to the manufacturing site. With APO-SNP stock balancing, the planner hopes to design an excess key figure (based on demand threshold) in the SAP APO planning book and manually deploy the inventory across by creating stock transport order in TLB.

To maintain the transportation at the product level, maintain the product group type (see Figure 7.54, ❶) customization in path SPRO • SCM BASIS • MASTER DATA • PRODUCT • PRODUCT GROUPS • DEFINE PRODUCT GROUP TYPES. Also maintain the product group definition (see Figure 7.54, ❷) in customization path SPRO • SCM BASIS • MASTER DATA • PRODUCT • PRODUCT GROUPS • DEFINE PRODUCT GROUPS.

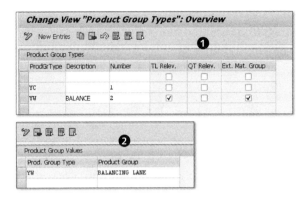

Figure 7.54 SAP APO Product Group: Setting up Transportation Lane Relevancy

We can now readily maintain the product group type master data. Start with the SAP APO location product master (Transaction /SAPAPO/MAT1) in the PROPERTIES 2 tab and transportation lane master data (Transaction/SAPPO/SCC_TL1), as shown in Figure 7.55.

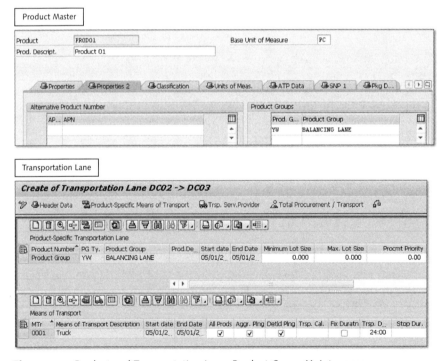

Figure 7.55 Product and Transportation Lane: Product Group Maintenance

To avoid any cyclical issues between the replenishment lane and balancing lane, we can either maintain SAP APO quota arrangement master data (/SAPAPO/SCC_TQ1) with zero quota or use the BLOCK indicator in the SAP APO transportation lane. This will ensure that the SNP heuristics or optimizer is not planning for these lanes during the normal replenishment planning cycle. Figure 7.56 shows the inbound quota arrangement maintained with zero quota arrangement.

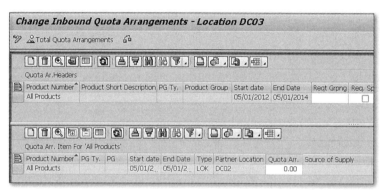

Figure 7.56 SAP APO Quota Arrangement

The stock balancing can be done either manually for simple networks or automatically for more complex supply chain networks. Figure 7.57 shows a hub and spoke model in which the balancing is performed among the distribution centers (spokes) before sending the net requirements to the hub location. In the manual exercise, the planner takes the input from the APO-SNP planning output and exceptions management process to locate alerts of critical stock out situations by looking at days of supply and uses SNP interactive TLB to create manual stock transfers. These stock transfers are then published to the SAP ERP system as stock transport orders for execution.

In the automation process, a custom logic needs to be written to identify excess across the supply chain network. The excess can simply be quantity percentage over maximum stock level for the location. Next, a balancing location sequence needs to be identified to fulfill any stock out situations. This location sequence can consider the transportation cost and whether it is economical to make the balancing move. Deployment orders are proposed by automatically unblocking/blocking transportation lanes during the process. Once the planner accepts the proposal, the TLB can be run to create load shipments.

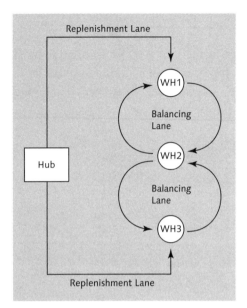

Figure 7.57 Building Balancing Transportation Lanes

7.11 Supply Planning Alerts

An *exception* (alert) is an unexpected event or problematic situation that occurs during the execution of a plan and disrupts the existing process flow of business activities. The situation may have a ripple effect on the downstream or upstream supply chain. The Alert Monitor in SAP APO is designed to help you to identify exceptions proactively and act on them before they turn into problems. The Alert Monitor allows you to identify which types of exceptions you want to be notified of and also prioritize alerts to avoid information overload. You can access the Alert Monitor via Transaction /SAPAPO/AMON1, which allows you to separate alerts in three priorities, as shown in Table 7.4.

The alerts are defined with the threshold values along with the relational operator (< or >) to define the alert priority. The user defines these thresholds and priorities in the alert profile defined within the Alert Monitor transaction.

Icon	Description
[i]	Informational alert (lowest priority)
[!]	Warning alert (medium priority)
[⚡]	Error alert (highest priority)

Table 7.4 Setting up Priorities in Alerts

Some of the common supply planning alerts are listed in Table 7.5.

Alert Type	Purpose
Critical Stock Out	In this business situation, the location is currently out of stock and needs immediate supply to replenish customer backorders.
Days of Supply Coverage: More/Less	This is the trigger for the business to react when the inventory coverage is under or over the target.
Capacity Overload/ Under Load	This alert looks at the resource capacity for resources that are overloaded or underutilized and need action for better efficiency.
Shelf Life Alerts	This group of alerts helps in alerting when the products will expire and need additional demand replenishment.
Past Due Alerts	This alert gives a signal on the all the open orders that are past due for which no action was taken and which need to be rescheduled to future dates per the current situation.

Table 7.5 Supply Planning Alerts

Let's next look at the various steps for setting up the Alert Monitor for business planners to use.

7.11.1 Managing Favorites in the Alert Monitor

You need to manage your favorites to open an alert profile in the Alert Monitor. Only the profiles that have been assigned to the favorites can be chosen in the Alert Monitor.

409

1. Follow SAP menu path ADVANCED PLANNING AND OPTIMIZATION • SUPPLY CHAIN MONITORING • ALERT MONITOR, or use Transaction /SAPAPO/AMON1.

2. Click the FAVORITE MANAGEMENT button; this opens the ADMINISTRATION OF FAVORITES table. The table on the left side of the FAVORITE SETTINGS window is the SELECTION table for your favorites. The table on the right side is the WORK LIST OF OVERALL PROFILES table. Use the drag and drop function to drop the required profiles on your username on the left side

3. Click the SAVE button and then the CONTINUE button.

To remove the favorite, drag and drop it from the left (USER folder) to the right (OVERALL PROFILES folder). Click the CONTINUE ([Enter]) button.

7.11.2 Using the Alert Monitor

The Alert Monitor can display a wide range of alerts. The planner can configure the Alert Monitor so that it only displays certain types of alerts and can also set the priority of the alert (error, warning, or information). Also, the planner is able to maintain the alert profile to change the settings when an alert is caused.

To open the Alert Monitor, double-click Transaction /SAPAPO/AMON1 (ALERT MONITOR). Choose a favorite to display the alerts contained in the profile. After you have chosen an alert profile, you can click the REDETERMINE ALERTS button to display the alerts.

In Figure 7.58, you can see the content of the Alert Monitor. First you have the profile name (favorite). All alerts for the planner work area are contained in this profile. Below the favorites, an overview of the existing alerts is displayed. With this overview, you can choose which alerts will actually be displayed in the bottom part of the screen. The planner can also create their own layout to display the alerts.

The planner can analyze the alert list, supported by different information regarding an alert. The planner could sort the alerts, for instance, by date (start date of the week in which alert is valid) and/or by product description, etc. Therefore, the planner has to click the ASCENDING button (🔒) and choose/sort the criteria that are required, as shown in Figure 7.59.

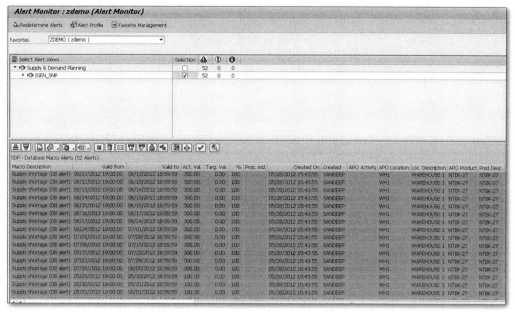

Figure 7.58 Alert Monitor in SAP APO

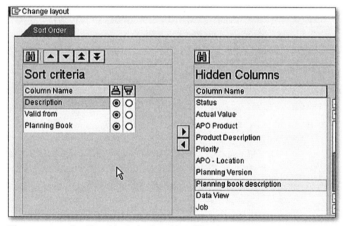

Figure 7.59 Sorting Alerts in the Alert Monitor

To analyze the details of the planning situation of a desired product, the planner has to right-click the alert row and select SUPPLY AND DEMAND PLANNING. The interactive planning book will appear, as shown in Figure 7.60.

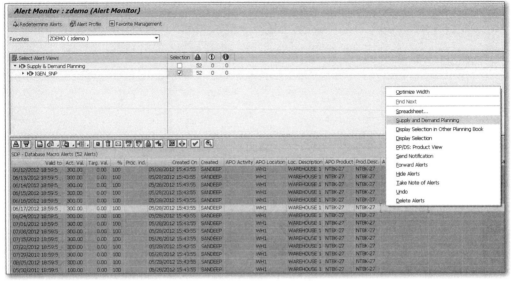

Figure 7.60 Opening the Alert Profile in the SNP Planning Book

The system will automatically load the product for a single selection, but for multiple selections, the planner will need to select the products individually in the planning book. To get back to the alert monitor, the planner has to click the BACK button.

After reviewing the planning situation, the planner has to update the alert list. If the problem could be solved, the planner can mark the row and click the DELETE button to delete the alert message. If the problem could not be solved but the planner wants to mark the message as reviewed, the planner marks the row and click the green checkmark icon. To hide an alert the planner clicks ▣.

> **Note**
>
> To include and display additional attributes in the Alert Monitor, SAP provides BAdI /SAPAPO/AM_ALERTLIST for enhancement.

7.11.3 Alert Monitor Hierarchies

We recommend that you perform some display configuration for the Alert Monitor to improve the structural display of the alert types based on what the planner wants to action first in the Alert Monitor. For example, the planner would like to view alerts based on location first, and then based on alert type, followed by products having issues. Follow the steps to set up an alert hierarchy in the Alert Monitor as shown in Figure 7.61:

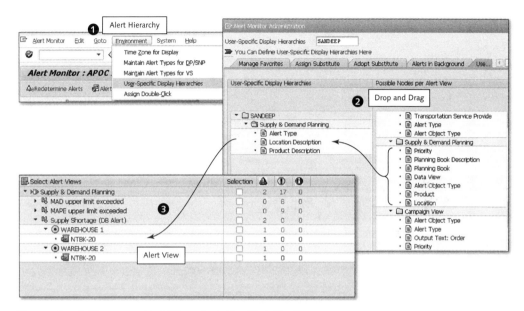

Figure 7.61 Setting up an Alert Hierarchy in the Alert Monitor

1. Inside the alert monitor (Transaction /SAPAPO/AMON1) go to the menu and choose USER-SPECIFIC DISPLAY HIERARCHIES (step ❶).

2. Drop and drag the objects from right side of screen to the SUPPLY AND DEMAND PLANNING folder in the Alert Monitor Administration screen (step ❷). To remove any object on the left side of folder, just double click the object. Save and exit (F8) the screen.

3. Now the alerts will be displayed as per the view designed in the alert hierarchy (step ❸). In the example shown in Figure 6.61 we can see the upper hierarchy is the Alert Type (level 2) which is followed by Location (level 2) and then by Product (level 3).

Using this technique, the business planner can prioritize the alerts they want to start looking at first in the Alert Monitor.

The second hierarchy groups the alerts according to location (LOCTX), and the third hierarchy groups the alerts according to material short text (MAKTX). Figure 7.62 shows how this looks.

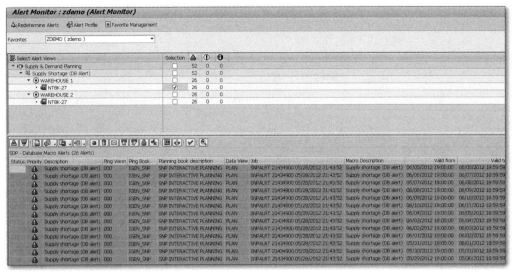

Figure 7.62 Display Alerts Using Hierarchy

Useful criteria available for creating hierarchies are:

▶ **AT_ID:** Alert name

▶ **9ALOCNO:** Location number (e.g., 1001)

▶ **LOCTX:** Location text

▶ **9AMATNR:** Material number

▶ **MAKTX:** Material short text

7.11.4 Alerts in the Interactive Planning Screen

The purpose of viewing alerts in interactive planning is access alerts quickly in real time during the planning process. The detailed steps for the planner to perform various tasks related to alerts in the SNP planning book are as follows:

1. **Open interactive planning**
   Double-click Transaction /SAPAPO/SNP94. This opens the INTERACTIVE PLANNING screen for supply planning.

2. **Show alerts**

   ▶ Select a planning book/data view.

   ▶ Make an object selection.

▶ Load data for the selection.

▶ Click the CHOOSE (⚡📋) button.

▶ Click one of the shown options. A new window appears in the right corner, down below the screen. Now all alerts according to the planning version, planning book, or product selection are displayed. If the user clicks the DIS-PLAY/REFRESH ALERTS button for the first time, a message comes up: "No alert profile was selected."

▶ Confirm this message by clicking [Enter] and repeat steps to assign the user to an alert profile.

3. **Execute alert macros manually**

▶ Go into change mode of the planning book.

▶ Right-click the alert macro for the alert, which should be updated. The alert macro is located in the MACROS window in the lower left corner. A small window appears.

▶ Click the EXECUTE MACRO window.

> **Note**
>
> The alert macros, which create the alerts, will be executed automatically every night. To have actual values, it is also possible to execute the alert macros manually.

4. **Hide alerts**
To hide the alert screen again, click the ALERT MONITOR/TEXT EDITOR OFF (🗜) button.

5. **Change status of alerts (acknowledgement of alert)**

▶ Click the alert you want to change the status for. To select more than one alert in a row, hold the [Shift] key and click the first and then the last alert in the row. To select several alerts that are not in a row at the same time, hold the [Ctrl] key while selecting the different alerts.

▶ Click the ACKNOWLEDGE ALERTS (✔) button in the ALERT window.

▶ Click the UNDO (🖌) button to change the alert to the previous status.

6. **Hide/show alerts (for better overview of alerts)**

▶ Click on the alert you want to hide.

▶ Click the HIDE ALERTS (■) button in the ALERT window.

► To show the hidden alerts again, click the SHOW ALERTS (⊙) button. A new window opens.

► Within the new window, click the alert(s) you want to unhide.

► Click on the SHOW button within the new window.

7. DELETE ALERTS

► Click the alert(s) to delete.

► Click the DELETE ALERTS button.

8. ASSIGN USER TO ALERT PROFILE

► Click SETTINGS from the top menu.

► Choose ASSIGN ALERT PROFILE.

► If no profile is assigned to the row ALERT PROFILE: SDP or to the row ALERT PROFILE: FORECAST, click the CHOOSE (⊡) button for this row, select an alert profile, and click the CONTINUE button.

► Click the COPY button.

7.12 Supply Chain Cockpit

Built within SAP APO is the Supply Chain Cockpit, which consists of a graphical instrument panel for managing and controlling the supply chain. Using the cockpit, the business planner can get a holistic view of the supply chain across multiple locations and multiple functions. The Supply Chain Cockpit integrates with the Supply Chain Engineer and Alert Monitor to provide visibility on not only the transaction data but also the supply chain model (master data) driving the transactions and the current exception situations.

Figure 7.63 displays the Supply Chain Cockpit, where the planner can define his planning work area and locate exceptions occurring in the supply chain. The Supply Chain Cockpit can be accessed using Transaction /SAPAPO/SCC02. The planner inputs the planning version/model and work area while calling the Supply Chain Cockpit. The work area is the one we had configured in Chapter 4, Section 4.7.8, by defining all the data objects in the Supply Chain Engineer.

The only setup requirement is that, once inside the cockpit, the demand and supply planning alert profiles can be added by accessing the header menu path SETTINGS •

USER PROFILE. The business user is now able to visualize the alerts for each location in graphical cockpit form, as shown in Figure 7.63.

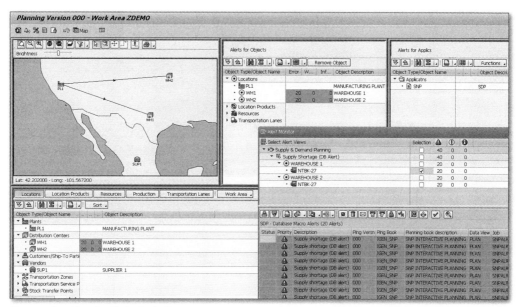

Figure 7.63 Supply Chain Cockpit

7.13 Summary

Supply planning involves many complex business scenarios that need modeling to support complex business requirements and repetitive prototypes to find the right solution to business requirements. In this chapter, we looked at various APO-SNP functionalities that support tactical and operational planning processes in the company supply chain. Functionalities like the TLB, stock balancing, and warehouse capacity are more execution related and operational. The set of functionalities like safety stock planning, interachangeability, subcontracting, direct shipment, shelf life, and aggregated planning are more tactical in nature. A good supply planner needs to understand how these different business variants can be modeled using APO-SNP.

The next chapter focuses on collaborative planning, which in recent years has been gaining traction, allowing companies to look beyond their own four walls to find opportunities for collaborating with their internal and external business partners.

Collaborative planning occurs between internal and external business partners to reach a consensus on balanced demand and supply plans.

8   Collaborative Planning with SAP APO

In recent years, there has been an increase of supply chain collaboration among companies with the primary goal of reducing operating costs and increasing customer satisfaction. Both internal and external collaboration improves a company's supply chain performance in meeting customer demands, reducing inventory, and increasing market share.

As shown in the mind map for this chapter (see Figure 8.1) we'll be covering SAP APO Collaborative Planning. The various topics covered will explain the key concepts between demand and supply collaborative planning, as well as basic settings for SAP APO Collaborative Planning. This chapter presents the supply chain collaborative principles and functionalities provided by SAP APO. We'll first start with an overview of what collaborative planning is, and then see how this works in both SAP APO-DP and SNP. We then delve into the configuration activities in SAP APO and understand how to set up Vendor Managed Inventory. We'll end with overviews on how to integrate collaborative planning with SAP Supply Network Collaboration and how global companies will benefit from global and regional planning.

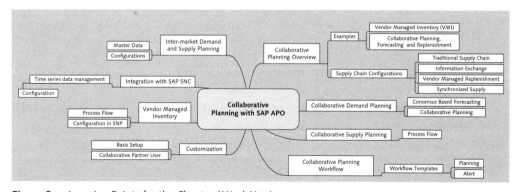

Figure 8.1   Learning Points for the Chapter (Mind Map)

8.1   Collaborative Planning Overview

In a collaborative supply chain, the business partners exchange planning information as well as inventory information to make the supply chain planning information transparent. The transparency of planning ensures that both the business partners are aligned with less disruption in the supply chain. This collaboration has led companies to implement some industry-leading concepts, such as Vendor Managed Inventory (VMI) and collaborative planning, forecasting, and replenishment (CPFR). These concepts form industry best practices for companies who have shown high supply chain maturity on high planning and inventory collaboration, as shown in Figure 8.2:

- ▶ **Vendor Managed Inventory (VMI)**
  This concept involves a business model in which an agreement is reached between the buyer and supplier, whereby the supplier takes responsibility for keeping the agreed level of inventory at the buyer's consumption location. The supplier monitors the buyer demand, closing to ensure the inventory levels are optimal for just-in-time (JIT) supply to the buyer's manufacturing location. A good example of this concept is seen in the automotive industry, where raw materials are supplied just in time for car production.

- ▶ **Collaborative planning, forecasting, and replenishment (CPFR)**
  This business model combines multiple trading partners' intelligence in planning and fulfillment of customer demand. CPFR introduces sales and marketing best practices (such as category management and point-of-sale [POS] forecasting) to overall supply chain planning by increasing stock availability to customer demands. This concept aims to reduce inventory, transportation, and logistics costs. A good example is seen in the retail distribution industry, where the retailer exchanges the POS and inventory information with the supplier for generating a replenishment plan.

The logistics research group within Helsinki University of Technology (*http://lrg. tkk.fi/logistics/*) has defined a simple framework for supply chain collaboration, as shown in Figure 8.2. Supply chain configurations can be different based on their inventory control and planning collaborations.

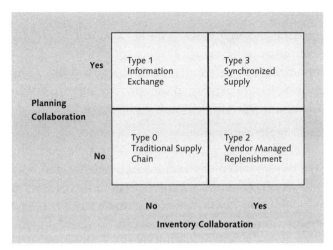

Figure 8.2 Supply Chain Configuration for Collaboration

AMR Research Industry Report, 2010, has found that based on a company's supply chain maturity, it fits into one of these configurations as part of its supply chain collaboration. Let's discuss these supply chain configurations in more detail:

▶ **Type 0: Traditional supply chain**

"Traditional" means that each level in a supply chain will issue purchase orders and replenish stock without considering the upstream and downstream tiers of the supply chain. There is no formal collaboration between the supplier and buyer. This lack of collaboration often leads to a *bullwhip effect* in the supply chain, in which a series of events leads to supplier demand variability up the supply chain. The bullwhip effect signifies that there is a large swing of inventory across the supply chain in response to the changes in demand. Trigger events include the frequency of orders, varying quantities ordered, and the combination of both events by downstream partners in a supply chain. As the orders make their way upstream, the perceived demand is amplified and produces what is known as the bullwhip effect.[1] A good business example of this configuration is a manufacturing and distribution company that places purchase orders to its supplier based on the lead time and material requirement planning (MRP) run.

---

1 H. Lee, V. Padmanabhan, and S. Whang, "The Bullwhip Effect in Supply Chains," Sloan Management Review, Spring 1997, 93-102.

▶ **Type 1: Information exchange**
Information exchange or sharing means the supplier and buyer order independently, but still exchange information on capacity and long-term planning. For example, a retail company exchanges its weekly point-of-sale and inventory levels as information to the suppliers to judge their capacity and long-term planning. The formal replenishment is still done via raising purchase orders.

▶ **Type 2: Vendor management replenishment**
In this configuration, the task of generating the replenishment is passed to the supplier, who manages the buyer's inventory and service levels for customer order fulfillment. A business example of this configuration can be taken from the fast-moving consumer goods industry, where consignment stock is placed in the retail locations for consumption by various suppliers. However, the supplier is occasionally challenged to match demand and supply because not all its customers participate in the vendor management replenishment program for planning consolidation.

▶ **Type 3: Synchronized supply**
Synchronized supply eliminates one decision point and merges the replenishment decision with the production and materials planning run performed by the supplier. The supplier takes charge of the replenishment inventory process to control its operational manufacturing process and can react immediately to any demand variations in this configuration. For example, a distribution company uses radio frequency identification (RFID) technology to capture real-time demand to make it available for the inventory controller.

Companies need to decide which supply chain configuration will work best based on their supply chain structure (geographical dispersion) and product characteristics (stability, demand pattern).

SAP APO offers an Internet technology platform for companies to collaborate their supply chain activities. SAP APO Collaborative Planning is designed to do the following:

▶ Exchange planning information seamlessly among business partners

▶ Allow business partner users to read and edit the planning data

▶ Restrict user access based on the authorization model

▶ Support exception-based management

- ▶ Support the consensus planning process

- ▶ Integrate with SAP APO planning business processes

Having looked at the four types of configurations, the leading companies are collaborating with their business partners in the areas of demand and supply. The focus of this collaboration is on both planning information and inventory information (Type 2 and Type 3). In the next couple of sections, we'll study how the SAP APO Collaborative Planning processes are integrated within internal demand and supply business processes.

8.2 Collaborative Demand Planning

Collaborative demand planning is supported by two main concepts:

- ▶ *Consensus-based forecasting* allows multiple functions in an organization to create their own plan and then come to an agreement on a consensus demand plan, which drives the supply plans.

- ▶ *Collaborative planning* links all the functions with the use of SAP APO planning books and advanced macros to formulate the business plan as a consensus demand plan.

Example

In global supply chain situations, many companies have their functions spread across different locations. With global market expansion, ABC Technology has opened offices in different global regions. ABC Technology, headquartered in Silicon Valley, California, has sales offices in different regions (North America, Europe, and Asia). The role of the global demand planner is to consolidate the forecast from each region and work with the manufacturer to ensure that the supplies are properly planned. In this scenario, the company uses collaborative demand planning effectively to ensure the demands are entered and consolidated in the monthly cycle with the correct level of communication.

The business process for consensus-based forecasting consists of the following steps (also shown in Figure 8.3):

1. A department-specific forecast is created among the sales, marketing, and logistics teams. Sales forecasts are focused more on channel distribution, promotion, and market competition and are both product and customer based. Marketing forecasts are purely on product- and price-based promotions. Logistics

forecasting focuses on product location and is purely operational in nature to ensure the inventory availability for customer order fulfillment.

2. The forecast is further shared with the customer or channel partner for any feedback based on the current market situation. The forecast is shared via the SAP APO planning book made available on the Internet.

3. Once the teams have completed the individual forecasting, the figures are consolidated for the monthly forecast review meeting. The monthly forecast review meeting consolidates the overall demand, and agreement is reached among the functions on what the company would be selling in the short-term horizon.

4. Manual adjustments are made possible via exception alerts for unexpected events in the supply chain.

5. Forecast accuracy is checked between actual and forecast data at the end of each month.

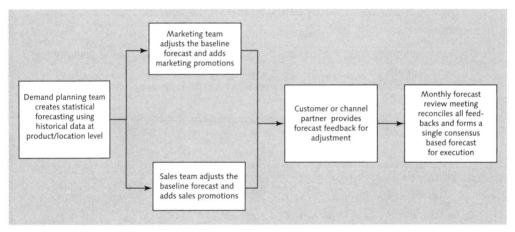

Figure 8.3 Collaborative Consensus-Based Forecasting

The CPFR is another demand planning example for the SAP APO Collaborative Planning functionality that can be implemented. The steps in the CPFR process are modeled using SAP APO planning books and advanced macros. Multiple business partners can view the SAP APO planning book, and the information restrictions can be modeled by data selection for the business partners in the planning books.

The CPFR process consists of a dynamic business-to-business workflow between the buyer and supplier. The information is shared via Internet technology. The basic seven-step process flow for CPFR[2] is as follows (also see Figure 8.4):

1. Agree on the process. Define each business partner's roles, commit to resources, and agree on an exception handling process and performance management.

2. Create a joint business plan and establish products to be jointly managed, including category roles, strategy, and tactics.

3. Develop a single forecast of consumer demand based on combined promotion calendars and analysis of point-of-sale data and casual data.

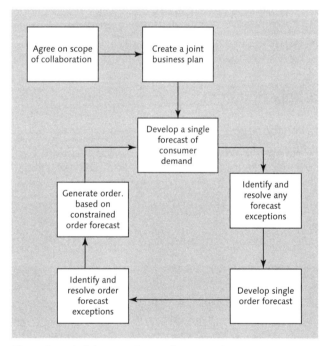

Figure 8.4 Collaborative Demand Process: CPFR

4. Identify and resolve forecast exceptions. This is achieved by comparing the current measured values, such as stock levels in each store, adjusted for changes such as promotions against the agreed-upon exception criteria (e.g., in-stock level or forecast accuracy targets).

---

2 SAP Collaborative Planning, SAP white paper 2010

5. Develop a single order forecast that time phases the sales forecast while meeting the business plan's inventory and service objectives and accommodating capacity constraints for the manufacturing and shipping process.

6. Identify and resolve exceptions to the forecast, particularly those involving a manufacturing constraint in delivering specified volumes.

7. Generate orders based on the constrained order forecast. The near-term orders are firmed, while the long-term orders are used for planning.

The use of collaborative demand planning is seen primarily in distribution-oriented companies. Manufacturing and distribution companies rely on the collaborative supply chain to make their supply chain tight.

The next section explores the collaborative supply planning opportunities to see how the collaboration can be performed in the upstream supply chain.

8.3   Collaborative Supply Planning

Similar to what you saw with collaborative demand planning, Internet technology can enhance the supply planning side as well, with extension toward supplier collaboration. In the collaborative supply planning process, the supplier is modeled in SAP APO as location, and the APO-SNP planning run includes the supplier location, giving both short- and long-term visibility. The supplier can then log on using the Internet technology to view the planning data and make any changes based on their resource capacity and material availability constraint.

> **Example**
>
> The ABC Technology manufacturer needs to collaborate with a large pool of suppliers for sourcing raw materials. Recently, they have been using several different means of communication (i.e., email, fax, letters, and phone calls) to communicate with their suppliers. Now, with the collaborative supply planning approach, the company plans to streamline its procurement business process and standardize its transactional data communication with suppliers. The company would now be communicating all its planning information via the web and plans to exchange the purchasing and accounting documents (i.e., purchase orders, advance shipping notifications, and invoices) electronically with the SAP SCM future footprints in the future.

Figure 8.5 shows the process steps for Collaborative Supply Planning in SAP APO. The business steps are as follows:

❶ The manufacturer performs the supply planning run and generates requirements for the supplier. These requirements are seen in the APO-SNP planning book by both the manufacturer and supplier based on the agreed planning cycle. The planning bucket can be daily for short-term planning and weekly for medium- to long term-planning.

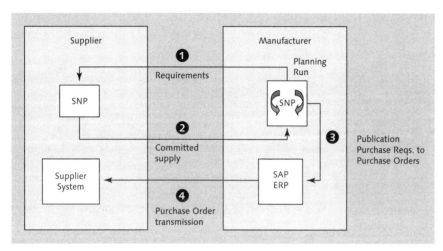

Figure 8.5 Collaborative Supply Planning Process Flow

❷ The supplier checks its internal resource capacity and material availability and confirms a committed supply plan in the APO-SNP planning book. The manufacturer re-runs the APO-SNP planning run to balance the demand and supply plan based on supplier feedback.

❸ Based on the supplier lead time, the purchase requisitions generated by the planning run and confirmed by the supplier are confirmed to the purchase orders. The purchase orders are published to the SAP ERP system.

❹ The purchase orders in the SAP ERP system are transmitted to the supplier system via electronic data exchange (EDI).

One of the key drivers for both the collaborative demand and supply planning processes is the use of the planning workflow. The workflow ensures that the planning tasks as planned are being executed as planned without any deviation. The concept of this collaborative planning workflow is explained in the next section.

8.4   Collaborative Planning Workflow

The overall goal of collaborative planning is to involve both internal and external business partners in reaching a consensus on demand and supply planning. For process steps between the collaborative partners that need to be structured, SAP provides an APO collaborative workflow template to manage the overall process. The workflow monitors the sequence of steps for business users involved in the planning process. The template can be used as an example and adapted to meet specific business requirements.

> **Example**
>
> ABC Technology would like to use the collaborative workflow planning process to inform the supplier after the APO-SNP planning run. The workflow will trigger an email alert notification to the supplier to view the supply plan. Using a web browser, the supplier will access the planning book. This automated process ensures that both ABC Technology and the suppliers are following the weekly supply planning process to ensure that the correct raw materials are shipped on time to meet customer orders. ABC Technology has seen a huge reduction in the communication gap since the deployment of this workflow process.

SAP provides two workflow templates—CLP_PLANNING and CLP_ALERTS—which can be used in the collaborative planning process (as shown in Figure 8.6). The workflow template can be accessed via workflow builder transaction SWDD. The details of these two templates are as follows:

► **CLP_PLANNING**
This template creates a work item for the supplier to access the SNP planning book. After the supplier has reviewed the supply plan and made changes, he or she can confirm by clicking the confirmation button. The work item is then assigned "Complete" status and removed from the work list.

► **CLP_ALERTS**
This template is used to alert the manufacturer planner when there is an imbalance of demand and supply in the planning situation. An email alert is sent to the planner with the work item. Once the planner clicks the work item, he has three options: progress on the alert, ignore the alert, or cancel for future progressing.

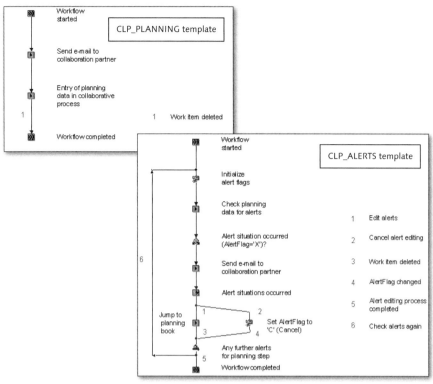

Figure 8.6 SAP APO Collaborative Workflow Templates

The use of the collaborative workflow template ensures that the entire supply chain situation is properly executed, involving both internal and external business partners.

8.5   Collaborative Planning Configuration Steps

In this section, we'll go through all the configuration steps required to set up SAP APO Collaborative Planning. The initial setup of the collaborative planning process largely depends on setting up the web application server (WAS) infrastructure. This infrastructure serves as a means of communication for exchanging information between the business partners. This setup applies to the entire SAP APO collaborative process.

> **Note**
>
> As of release 6.40 of the SAP Web Application Server, a large part of the Internet Transaction Server was integrated in the kernel of the SAP Web Application Server (under the title "SAP Integrated ITS"). Due to this change, it is no longer necessary to install or use separate Internet Transaction Servers, as of release 6.40.
>
> Internet Communication Manager (ICM) is a component within SAP Web Application Server that provides the communication layer between the SAP system (SAP Web AS) and the outside world via the protocols HTTP, HTTPS, and SMTP. In its role as a server, the ICM can process requests from the Internet that arrive as URLs with the server/port combination that the ICM can listen to. The ICM then calls the relevant local handler for the URL in question.

Let's go over the technical setup and basic configuration in the following sections.

8.5.1 Activate ICF Services

Activate the Internet communication framework (ICF) with Transaction SICF. Once the Transaction is executed, trace the default_host tree path */sap/bc/gui/sap/its/* to activate relevant services:

- ► CLPSDP (Collaborative Supply and Demand Planning)
- ► CLPBID (Collaborative Transportation Planning)
- ► CLPPROMCAL (Collaborative Promotion Planning)
- ► CLPGLOBAL (common service for Collaborative Planning)

Activate the services by right-clicking the services and test the services, as well.

8.5.2 Maintain Entries in Table TWPURLSVR

Using Transaction SM30, maintain the following entries in Table TWPURLSVR:

- ► LOGICAL SYSTEM: The name of the logical system that you are working with
- ► WEB SERVER: The name of the ITS web server with the corresponding port
- ► WEB PROTOCOL: The log to be used (HTTP or HTTPS)

> **Note**
>
> SAP Note 720121 (Collaborative Planning) and 526835 (SAP ITS Installation) provide some valuable tips for troubleshooting.

8.5.3   Maintain ICM Monitor

Using Transaction SMICM, maintain the web services per your business requirements by following the header menu path GOTO • SERVICES. Maintain the service
port and host name correctly for the HTTP service.

8.5.4   Publish Internet Services

As referenced in SAP Note 816973, follow these steps to publish the Internet services (see Figure 8.7):

1. Go to Transaction SE80, select INTERNET SERVICE in the REPOSITORY BROWSER'S
   dropdown box, and enter the name of the service. For Internet service, there
   will be four services available: CLPSDP, IAC, SYSTEM, and WEBGUI. Perform
   the next steps for each of the services individually.

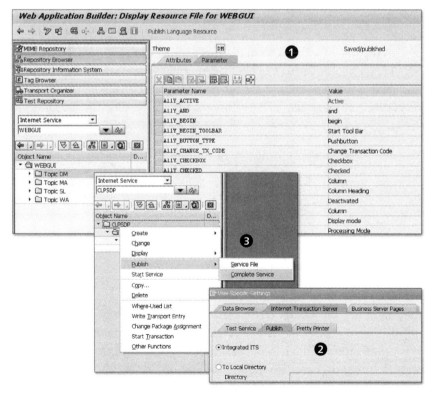

Figure 8.7   Publication of Internet Services

2. Double-click the service's name in the tree that appears below the service.

3. On the right side at the top, find the service name followed by its status (SAVED/PART-PUBLISHED, PUBLISHED, etc.). Double-click this status text to see detailed information on the date and time the service was last published to the (possibly various) ITS sites (step ❶).

4. In order to publish the service, choose UTILITIES • SETTINGS from the menu, go to tab INTERNET TRANSACTION SERVER, sub tab PUBLISH, and select INTEGRATED ITS (step ❷).

5. Close the pop-up, right-click the service name in the tree on the left side and select PUBLISH • COMPLETE SERVICE from the context menu (step ❸).

> **Warning!**
>
> Do not use the PUBLISH button in the main toolbar or the PUBLISH entry in the UTILITIES menu. Both will only publish the single file currently displayed instead of the complete service!

The services that needs to be activated are WEBGUI, CLPSDP, AMON, AMON_STATIST, CLPBID, CLPGLOBAL, CLPPROMCAL, and two special services: SYSTEM and IAC. Service SYSTEM should always be published correctly—it is required by all services that make use of SAP Integrated ITS. Service IAC needs to be published if you want to use services other than WEBGUI (= SAP GUI for HTML).

> **Tips & Tricks**
>
> SAP Notes 932917 (Collaborative Planning) and 678904 (New Storage Structure) provide some valuable tips for troubleshooting during the templates, service files, and mime objects publication.

8.5.5 Collaboration Partner User

Maintain settings per Table 8.1 for the collaboration partner user. The collaboration partner identifies the collaborative business partner with whom we will be exchanging planning information. The settings in Table 8.1 are maintained to ensure that correct authorization is given to the partner for accessing the information from the Internet. These settings are also required to ensure that the SAP APO planning book is correctly displayed in the web browser.

User Settings	Maintenance Steps
General requirements for interactive supply and demand planning (for all types of data exchange)	Maintain the following settings: ▶ Assign a planning book to the user (DEMAND PLANNING • ENVIRONMENT • CURRENT SETTINGS • ASSIGN USER TO PLANNING BOOK) ▶ Assign selection profiles to the user (DEMAND PLANNING • ENVIRONMENT • SELECTION ORGANIZATION • MAINTAIN SELECTION ASSIGNMENTS)
Settings for drill down in the Internet planning books	▶ Maintain the header information of the planning view (DEMAND PLANNING • PLANNING • INTERACTIVE DEMAND PLANNING • SETTINGS • HEADER INFORMATION). ▶ Choose the characteristics for which you wish to enable drill down and select the CHANGEABLE indicator. This setting must be made when logged on in the SAP APO function as the external user. Otherwise, the settings have no effect.
Display graphic in Internet planning books	Maintain the following data under SYSTEM • USER DEFAULTS • OWN DATA on the PARAMETERS tab page: Parameter `/sapapo/clp_webgraph`, value X. In the Internet planning book, the external partner can then show or hide a graphical representation of the data by clicking the GRAPHICAL icon (⬛). Note that it is not possible to use the graphic display in connection with the drill down function. The graphic function is not available after a drill down.
Settings for notes in Internet planning books	Maintain the following data under SYSTEM • USER DEFAULTS • OWN DATA on the PARAMETERS tab page: Parameter `/sapapo/clp_webnote`, value X.

Table 8.1 Collaboration Partner User Settings

User Settings	Maintenance Steps
	In the Internet planning book, the user can then click the NOTES icon (📝) to switch to note mode in order to enter notes on the data. To be able to enter notes, the business user must use a unique selection; that is, they must have carried out a drill down.
Settings for the export of data	Maintain the following data under SYSTEM •USER DEFAULTS • OWN DATA on the PARAMETERS tab page: Parameter /sapapo/clp_webdown, value: ▶ XLS (if you want to process the data in Microsoft Excel) ▶ CSV (if you want to process the data using other software) In the Internet planning book, the user can then export the data with the EXCEL icon (📊).
Settings for sorting the data in the case of drill down	Maintain the following data under SYSTEM • USER DEFAULTS • OWN DATA on the PARAMETERS tab page: Parameter /sapapo/clp_webpivot, value X. When the user has drilled down on a characteristic, they can then switch between the following two displays in the Internet planning book with the SORT icon (🔀): ▶ Sorting of data by key figures ▶ Sorting of data by the drill down characteristic (e.g., product)
Settings for header lines in drill down	Maintain the following data under SYSTEM • USER DEFAULTS • OWN DATA on the PARAMETERS tab page: Parameter /sapapo/clp_rephead, value X. The header line is then shown in the Internet planning book between the objects for which the user has carried out a drill down.

Table 8.1 Collaboration Partner User Settings (Cont.)

User Settings	Maintenance Steps
	You have chosen a drill down by products and maintained the value X for the parameter `/sapapo/clp_rephead`. The data on the products is then separated by the header line.
Settings for header lines	Maintain the following data under SYSTEM • USER DEFAULTS • OWN DATA on the PARAMETERS tab page: Parameter `/sapapo/clp_webbhead`, value X. The header line is then repeated as a footer line in the Internet planning book.
Settings for column width	Maintain the following data under SYSTEM • USER DEFAULTS • OWN DATA on the PARAMETERS tab page: Parameter `/sapapo/clp_row_wi`, values S, M, L, XL and ' ' (default). This user parameter enables you to adjust the width of the fixed columns (key figure and characteristic descriptions) in the event of display problems in an Internet planning book. ▸ S and M, if you want to display more columns This may result in the descriptions of the key figures and characteristics being incompletely displayed. ▸ L and XL, if you need wider columns for more text
Settings for page up/down	By setting this user parameter, you can enable a paging function. The external partner chooses: ▸ ▲ or ▼ to move up or down a line ▸ ▲ or ▼ to move up or down a page ▸ ▲ or ▼ to move to the top or bottom of the planning book. Maintain the following data under SYSTEM • USER DEFAULTS • OWN DATA on the PARAMETERS tab page: Parameter `/sapapo/clp_drilldown`, value *N*, where *N* is the number of rows that are displayed on one page.

Table 8.1 Collaboration Partner User Settings (Cont.)

435

Using Transaction /SAPAPO/CLPISDP, the collaborative user can log on to the web browser. The user selects the planning book and selection profile and clicks CHOOSE. The planning book is displayed with various user functions, as discussed in Table 8.1 (also shown in Figure 8.8). As seen in the figure, the user can select the planning book (as per authorization) and the selection profile. Beside the interactive planning book display there are various other user functions (for example, graphical display) that the user can trigger.

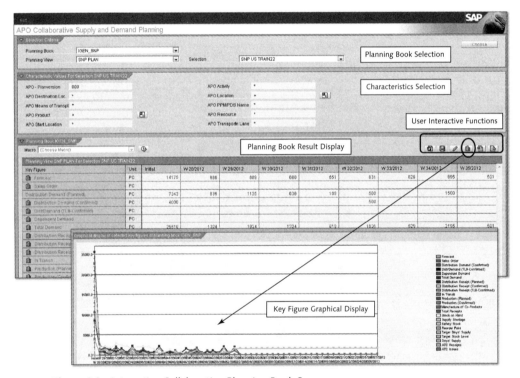

Figure 8.8 Interactive Collaborative Planning Book Screen

Now that we've seen the collaborative planning configuration steps, let's look at the specific business scenario of Vendor Managed Inventory (VMI). We'll study in the next section how the collaborative planning process fits into the VMI business scenario.

8.6   Vendor Managed Inventory

Vendor Managed Inventory (VMI) is a supply chain business model that serves as a means of optimizing supply chain performance. In this model, the manufacturer (ABC Technology) is responsible for maintaining its customers' inventory levels — the company has access to the customers' inventory data and is responsible for generating purchase orders to be sent to the customer. ABC Technology receives electronic data (usually via EDI or the Internet) that tells it the customers' sales and stock levels. The manufacturer can analyze every item that the customer carries, as well as true point-of-sale data. The manufacturer is responsible for creating and maintaining the inventory plan. Under the VMI, the ownership of inventory is not changed.

The implementation of VMI provides value-added services by the manufacturer for its customers. Both business partners have clear visibility on the inventory and consumer sales pattern, ensuring that the manufacturer is constantly adjusting its plan to better replenish and fulfill customer demands. By ensuring the stock availability, the manufacturer improves customer satisfaction. Some other VMI benefits are lower transportation costs and reduced inventory levels.

The concept of VMI has a strategic fit where the following conditions are met:

▶ Key customers make up a large percentage of the vendors' sales figures.

▶ Products are standardized and requested on a repetitive basis.

▶ There is no excessive product proliferation, so demand patterns are stable, and non-sporadic demand can be assumed.

▶ Transaction costs for order processing and production planning are high.

Example

ABC Technology wants to effectively collaborate with its key distributors (customers) to ensure that it's shipping custom products per customer demands. As soon as the customer provides the product configuration information to the distributors, the plan is sent to ABC Technology. Based on the production schedule, the configuration products are assembled within hours of order receipt and dispatched either to the warehouse or directly to the distributor. ABC Technology has complete visibility on the distributor inventory and forecast to ensure that it keeps correct inventory levels for the component items.

As Figure 8.9 shows, VMI eliminates the planning process primarily on the customer's side and eliminates redundant process steps. The implementation of the VMI process eliminates much of the purchasing process on the customer side. With the exchange of the sales and inventory information, the manufacturer plans for the replenishment of the inventory.

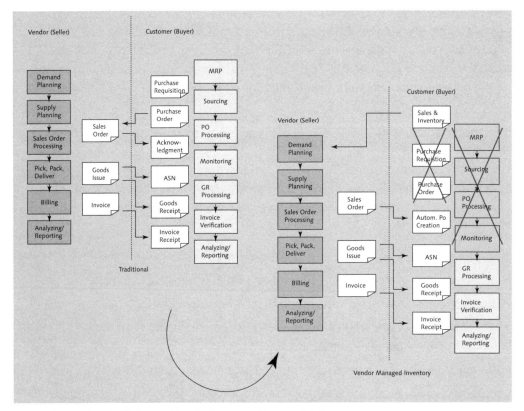

Figure 8.9 VMI Process Flow between the Buyer and Seller

The customer's ERP system automatically creates the purchase order for the replenished inventory goods receipt. The figure maps the traditional versus vendor-managed process and crosses out the processes that are eliminated with VMI implementation, leading to cost savings. All material requirements planning for the customer is done by the manufacturer. The customer sends the updated information on the sales and inventory to the manufacturer on a weekly cycle basis for planning. The purchase is also created by the manufacturer on the customer's behalf.

8.6.1 VMI Model and Technical Flow

The VMI scenario can be modeled in APO-SNP with maintenance of the following SAP APO-specific master data:

▶ Customer and vendor locations

▶ Maintenance of planning parameters for both customer and vendor locations

▶ Transportation lane between the vendor and customer with lead times

The technical flow, as Figure 8.10 shows, will have the following steps:

❶ Transmission of EDI Message 852 PROACT, which will map the actual sales, stocks, and forecast data in the APO customer locations. A statistical forecasting can be performed to calculate the baseline forecast. The baseline forecast is added with any running promotions for the customer to formulate the total demand plan.

❷ The total demand plan is then released to APO-SNP for net requirement calculations. SNP heuristics, deployment, and TLB are run as part of the planning cycle to generate VMI sales orders to the customer location. APO-SNP takes into account the lead time, re-order point, and safety stock during the proposal.

❸ The VMI sales orders are published to SAP ERP; automatic purchase orders are created in SAP ERP.

❹ The vendor sends out EDI Message 855 ORDRSP as purchase order acknowledgement with the quantity and delivery date. This allows the customer to update their ERP system.

❺ The customer can revert back with purchase order alteration using EDI Message 860 ORDCHG. The vendor then sends the advance shipping notification using EDI Message 857 DESADV. This informs the customer what exactly is being shipped by the vendor and when.

❻ After the physical receipt of the goods, the customer transmits EDI Message 861 STPOD RECEIPT ADVISE. As the last step, the invoice is sent via EDI Message 810, and payment is received from the customer via EDI Message 820.

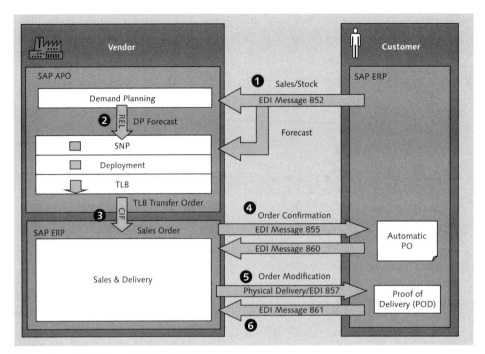

Figure 8.10 VMI Scenario Technical Flow

8.6.2 Configuring VMI Scenario in SAP SNP

The primary customization for the VMI is done in the APO-SNP functional area.

Step 1: Activate Extended Scheduling

First, activate the extended scheduling in SAP APO for the VMI sales orders. This is done by following customization path SPRO • ADVANCED PLANNING AND OPTIMIZATION • SUPPLY CHAIN PLANNING • SUPPLY NETWORK PLANNING • VENDOR MANAGED INVENTORY • ACTIVATE EXTENDED SCHEDULING.

Perform the activation by clicking the check mark on field EXTENDED VMI SCHEDLG. This shipment and transportation scheduling function is relevant if the availability check (ATP) is done in SAP APO instead of SAP ERP. All the relevant product location master data is taken into consideration for determining the material availability date, as shown in Figure 8.11.

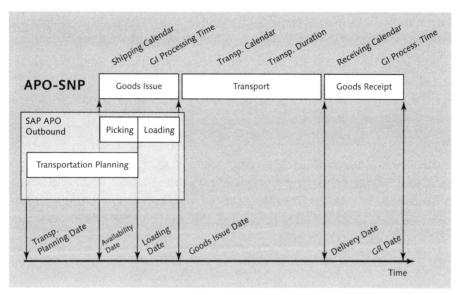

Figure 8.11 VMI Sales Order Scheduling in SAP APO

Step 2: Capture Stock in Transit

The next configuration is for capturing the stock in transit message. This message helps in processing stock in transit based on different options. For a customer location, we define whether the stock in transit is due to the delivery, purchase order quantity, or sales/stock information. The customization path is SPRO • ADVANCED PLANNING AND OPTIMIZATION • SUPPLY CHAIN PLANNING • SUPPLY NETWORK PLANNING • VENDOR MANAGED INVENTORY • MAINTAIN IDOC SETTING FOR STOCK IN TRANSIT. Stock in transit is represented by deliveries. Deliveries are transferred online using the Core Interface (CIF).

In the following situations, the deliveries are not transferred automatically by CIF:

▶ SAP ERP provides report RLOADVMI to transfer initial stock in transit to SAP APO in the VMI scenario. The report selects deliveries that were posted as goods issues. After these deliveries have been transferred to SAP APO, the stock in transit is created in the location of the VMI customer using SAP APO for the first time. The deliveries, which have been created beforehand, cannot be transferred from SAP ERP to SAP APO using CIF.

▶ Each time after the initialization of the SAP liveCache, orders with category "In Transit" cannot be transferred using CIF by activating the integration model.

To solve the problem, report RLOADVMI has been created in SAP ERP. This report selects all deliveries according to specific criteria and transfers them to SAP APO. Both a test mode and a transfer mode are available. The test mode only shows you a list of the deliveries in transit.

The PROACT XML file, which interfaces the sales and stocks information, is mapped next. The customization path is SPRO • ADVANCED PLANNING AND OPTIMIZATION • SUPPLY CHAIN PLANNING • SUPPLY NETWORK PLANNING • VENDOR MANAGED INVENTORY • MAINTAIN SETTING FOR XML MESSAGES. As Figure 8.12 shows, here we define the XML message time series key figure with the planning area InfoObject where the field values need to be posted.

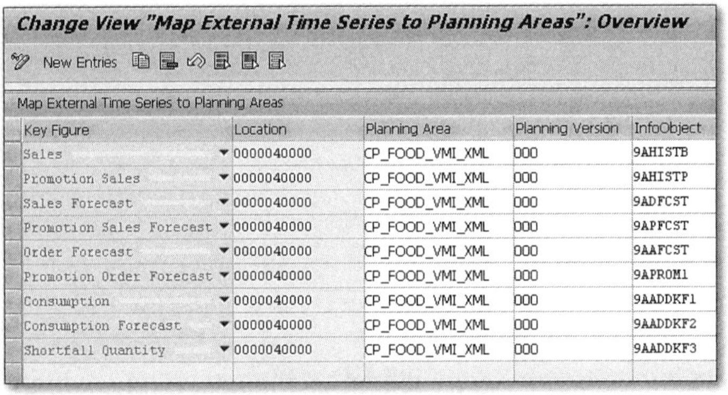

Change View "Map External Time Series to Planning Areas": Overview

🦅 New Entries 🗎 🗐 🖉 📑 📑 📑

Map External Time Series to Planning Areas

Key Figure	Location	Planning Area	Planning Version	InfoObject
Sales	▼ 0000040000	CP_FOOD_VMI_XML	000	9AHISTB
Promotion Sales	▼ 0000040000	CP_FOOD_VMI_XML	000	9AHISTP
Sales Forecast	▼ 0000040000	CP_FOOD_VMI_XML	000	9ADFCST
Promotion Sales Forecast	▼ 0000040000	CP_FOOD_VMI_XML	000	9APFCST
Order Forecast	▼ 0000040000	CP_FOOD_VMI_XML	000	9AAFCST
Promotion Order Forecast	▼ 0000040000	CP_FOOD_VMI_XML	000	9APROM1
Consumption	▼ 0000040000	CP_FOOD_VMI_XML	000	9AADDKF1
Consumption Forecast	▼ 0000040000	CP_FOOD_VMI_XML	000	9AADDKF2
Shortfall Quantity	▼ 0000040000	CP_FOOD_VMI_XML	000	9AADDKF3

Figure 8.12 XML PROACT Message Mapping

Step 3: Create Customer PO Number in SAP APO

The last SNP VMI configuration step performed is the purchase order number creation in SAP APO for the customer. An internal number range is used for assignment, and the number interval can be defined per ship-to party, sold-to party, and VMI purchasing group parameters. Figure 8.13 shows an example. The customization path is SPRO • ADVANCED PLANNING AND OPTIMIZATION • SUPPLY CHAIN PLANNING • SUPPLY NETWORK PLANNING • VENDOR MANAGED INVENTORY • MAINTAIN PURCHASE ORDER NUMBER ASSIGNMENT IN SAP APO.

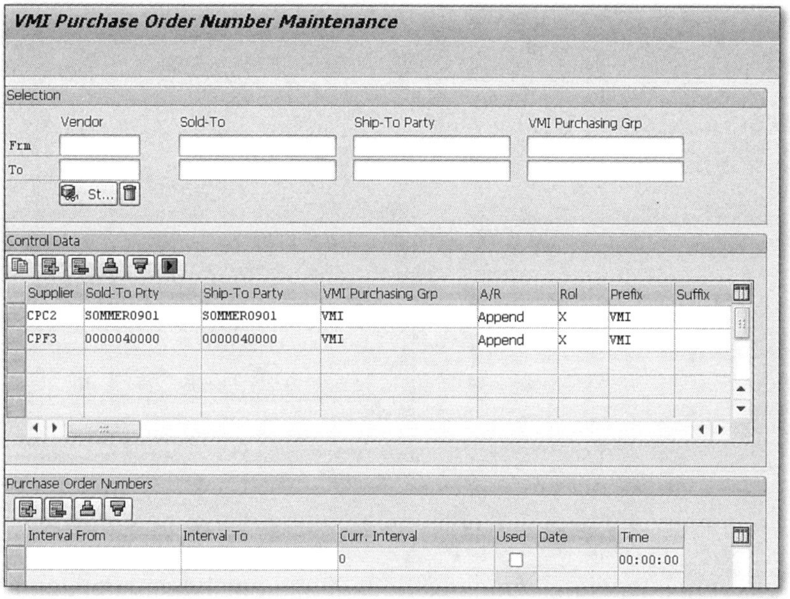

Figure 8.13 Purchase Order Number Assignment for VMI Scenario

An alternative solution for supplier collaboration is provided in the form of SAP Supply Network Collaboration (SNC), which provides a platform for exchanging procurement transactional data via the web instead of EDI. This technology is discussed in the next section.

8.7   Integrating SAP Supply Network Collaboration with SAP APO: Overview

SAP Supply Network Collaboration (SNC) is a solution in SAP SCM that provides a collaborative platform for exchanging information without high investment in EDI. The solution provides standard business scenario examples and activation of standard SAP services and can be deployed in a rapid timeframe. Using the SAP NetWeaver platform, SAP SNC can collaborate with internal and external business partners to provide extended visibility. SAP SNC enables manufacturers to collaborate closely with suppliers, customers, or outsourced partners (see Figure 8.14).

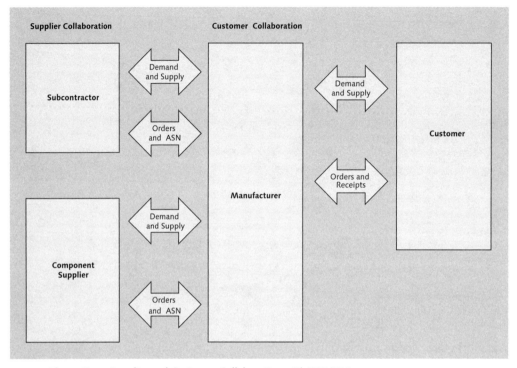

Figure 8.14 Supplier and Customer Collaboration with SAP SNC

An example of application and documents integration between SAP APO and SAP SNC is the *responsive replenishment* business process. This business process is a real-time, demand-driven, replenishment scenario between the supplier and customer including building shipment loads for the short term.

Example

ABC Technology plans to deploy SAP SNC integrated with SAP APO toward its key supplier to streamline the purchasing process. SAP SNC will provide a real-time transactional flow of purchase orders, advance shipping notification, and invoice data. The supplier will closely monitor the ABC Technology raw material inventory and replenish it frequently based on shipment loads. This will provide ABC Technology with both a faster procurement cycle and the ability to synchronize the supply with the changing demand.

Figure 8.15 shows the normal forecast collaboration process between the supplier and customer. The customer sends a routine forecast file, which is compared with the weekly forecast generated in SAP SNC. A consensus forecast is reached between the customer and supplier and released back to the supplier. The only integration with SAP APO is the optional step of sending the final forecast via XML file message ProductForecastNotification (PFN). Transaction /SCA/FCST_OUT is used to send the forecast files from SAP SNC to APO. All the integration communication in this scenario is done via the SAP process integration (PI) system.

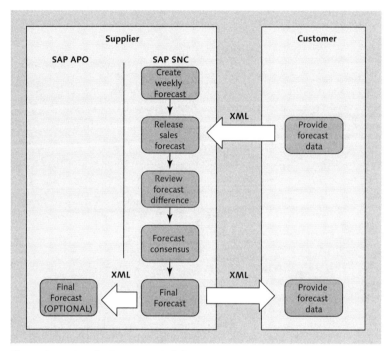

Figure 8.15 SAP SNC Forecast Collaboration

As an optional step, the communication between SAP SCM and SNC can use the time series data management (TSDM) technology concept, which is explained in the next section.

Time Series Data Management

This solution is a data management module in SAP Supply Chain Management (SAP SCM) that you can use to create and call time series data within the SAP SCM component. The time series data is stored in time bucket and cluster form. By storing the time series in cluster form, the table entries size is reduced with improved performance.

Using TSDM mapping allows the SAP APO planning key figure to be visible in the SAP SNC planning table. To achieve this integration, we need to perform a couple of customizations and BAdI implementation.

As Figure 8.16 shows, the first step is to do the parameter mapping, as shown in the step ❶. The customization path is SPRO • SCM BASIS • CONFIGURE PARAMETERS. The SAP APO InfoObject we want to map is defined with the standard SAP SNC key figures in this step.

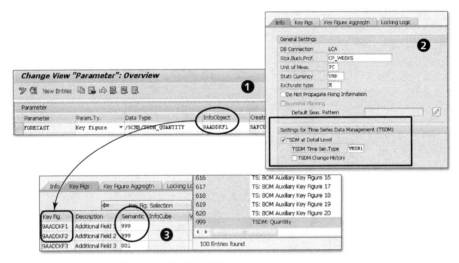

Figure 8.16 TSDM Configuration in SAP APO

The next configuration is to make the planning area TSDM compatible. We perform the second and third step using Transaction /SAPAPO/MSDP_ADMIN and making changes in the relevant SAP APO planning area (❷). We input the TSDM type in the INFO and KEY FIGURE tabs and specify the SAP APO key figure semantic to 999 (TSDM quantity), as shown in Figure 8.16. The last technical step (❸) is to implement BAdI /SAPAPO/SDP_TSDM by specifying all the relevant characteristics. SAP APO passes the planning book details at the product location characteristics combination level.

Companies with global SCM instance server use same SAP APO functionalities to plan many regions in a single application instance. This provides an advantage on global visibility of plan and inventory information. This single SCM instance possibly is integrated with multiple SAP ERP systems serving different regions. With the use of common SAP SCM instances, different regions have to adhere to business rules to work in cross-market collaboration processes. The concept of inter-market demand and supply planning in a single advanced planning and optimization instance is explained in the next section.

8.8 Inter-Market Demand and Supply Planning in the Same Advanced Planning and Optimization Application Instance

There are many situations when global companies are implementing advanced planning and optimization functionality in a single SAP APO application server. In this scenario, all the global and regional planning is done in the same SAP APO application server—this single server can be connected with different ERP systems for execution and financial reasons.

> **Example**
>
> ABC Technology has deployed a single SAP APO instance for its global planning process. Their SAP SCM system is connected with three different regional SAP ERP systems. Built within the ABC Technology supply chain model, we have scenarios in which there is an exchange of goods across different regions (e.g., United States to Europe). We call this goods movement across geographical boundaries and planning *inter-market*. This leads to situations in which one market (United States) serves as a producer, and the other market (Europe) serves as the receiver. Both regional markets maintain their separate master data and establish planning cycle principles to plan for goods movement across geographic boundaries.

By implementing inter-market demand and supply planning, companies have seen benefits in planning visibility and speed action on any supply chain situation. The metrics that have improved are in planning lead time reduction, stock cover reduction, and stock freshness supply to the customer. Figure 8.17 depicts the planning situation in which two countries or markets have defined physical boundaries but are connected by SAP APO transportation lanes in the system.

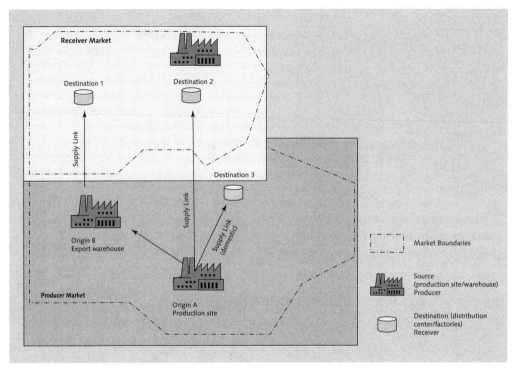

Figure 8.17 SAP APO Inter-Market Model

To maintain discipline in the system, both the producer and receiver need to agree on SAP APO master data modeling. Table 8.2 lists all the master data and configuration for initial setup to be performed in SAP APO and the SAP ERP system and who owns the specific objects.

System	Type	Data Object	Ownership
SAP SCM	APO Master	Transportation lane	Producer
SAP SCM	APO Master	Incoming quota	Receiver
SAP SCM	APO Master	Minimum and maximum stock covers	Receiver
SAP SCM	APO Master	Maturity time	Producer
SAP SCM	APO Master	Goods receipt	Producer (factory)

Table 8.2 SAP APO Inter-Market Planning Parameters Maintenance Ownership

System	Type	Data Object	Ownership
SAP SCM	APO Master	Goods receipt	Receiver (DC)
SAP SCM	APO Master	Goods issue	Producer
SAP SCM	APO Master	Transport duration in TLB profile	Producer
SAP SCM	APO Master	Stock transfer horizon	Receiver
SAP SCM	APO Master	Shipping calendars	Producer, Receiver
SAP ERP	Material Master	Salvage days before expiry date	Producer
SAP ERP	Material Master	Days before moveable: QA	Producer
SAP SCM	APO Master	Deployment profile: pull and pull/push	Producer
SAP SCM	APO Master	Deployment profile: pull/push	Producer
SAP SCM	APO Master	Deployment profile: pull	Receiver
SAP ERP	Master Data	Creation of purchasing info record at the receiver location for the supplying plant as vendor and for material	Receiver
SAP ERP	Master Data	Purchasing source list	Receiver
SAP ERP	Master Data	Creation of necessary pricing conditions required to be maintained in R/3 purchasing info record	Receiver
SAP ERP	Master Data	Condition records PI01 (IV01: intercompany pricing)	Producer
SAP ERP	Master Data	Condition records for intercompany return	Producer
SAP ERP	Master Data	Condition record for inter-company transfer pricing	Receiver

Table 8.2   SAP APO Inter-Market Planning Parameters Maintenance Ownership (Cont.)

System	Type	Data Object	Ownership
SAP SCM	Master Data	Transportation scheduling (picking and transit)	Producer
SAP ERP	Master Data	Batch search strategy	Producer
SAP ERP	Customizing	Assign plant to customer	Plant owner
SAP ERP	Customizing	Route determination	Producer
SAP ERP	Customizing	Define purchasing document type	Producer
SAP ERP	Customizing	Assign delivery type/checking	Producer
SAP ERP	Customizing	Global availability checking rules	Producer
SAP SCM	Customizing	Planner code for inter-market	Producer, Receiver
SAP ERP	Customizing	Transportation: vehicle types	Producer
SAP ERP	Customizing	Partner profiles and GLN codes	Producer, Receiver
SAP ERP	Vendor Master	Vendor master: general data	Plant and company owner
SAP ERP	Vendor Master	Vendor master: company code data (of the company the plant/company code belongs to)	Plant and company owner
SAP ERP	Vendor Master	Vendor master: company code data (extension to receiver's company code)	Receiver
SAP ERP	Vendor Master	Vendor master: purchasing organization data (of purchasing organization the plant/company code belongs to)	Plant and company owner
SAP ERP	Vendor Master	Vendor master: purchasing organization data (extension to receiver's purchasing organization)	Receiver

Table 8.2 SAP APO Inter-Market Planning Parameters Maintenance Ownership (Cont.)

System	Type	Data Object	Ownership
SAP ERP	Customer Master	Customer master: general data	Plant and company owner
SAP ERP	Customer Master	Customer master: company code data (of the company the plant/company code belongs to)	Plant and company owner
SAP ERP	Customer Master	Customer master: company code data (extension to producer's company code)	Producer
SAP ERP	Customer Master	Customer master: sales organization data (of sales org the plant/company code belongs to)	Plant and company owner
SAP ERP	Customer Master	Customer master: sales organization data (extension to producer's sales organization)	Producer
SAP ERP	Material Master	Material master: basic data	Producer
SAP ERP	Material Master	Material master: plant-related data	Plant owner
SAP ERP	Material Master	Material master: warehouse-related data	Warehouse Owner
SAP ERP	Material Master	Material master: sales-related data	Sales organization owner
SAP ERP	Material Master	Material master: minimum remaining shelf life (MARA-MHDRZ)	Bilateral
SAP ERP	Material Master	Material master: total shelf life (MARA-MHDHB)	Bilateral
SAP ERP	Material Master	Material master: transportation group (MARA-TRAGR)	Producer
SAP ERP	Material Master	Material master: rounding rule SLED (MARA-RDMHD)	Bilateral

Table 8.2 SAP APO Inter-Market Planning Parameters Maintenance Ownership (Cont.)

System	Type	Data Object	Ownership
SAP ERP	Material Master	Material master: stacking factor (MARA-STFAK)	Bilateral
SAP ERP	Material Master	Material master: order unit (MARA-BSTME)	Bilateral

Table 8.2 SAP APO Inter-Market Planning Parameters Maintenance Ownership (Cont.)

With the correct modeling of the supply chain planning process in single-instance APO, companies can gain high visibility of demand and supply planning information for making correct supply chain decisions.

8.9 Summary

Recently, globalization has prompted an increase in supply chain collaboration. This collaboration creates a common pace of information sharing, replenishment, and supply synchronization among business partners, which helps business partners. The core benefits of collaborative planning are customer satisfaction, reduced inventory costs, reduced transportation costs, reduced demand and supply variability, improved forecast accuracy, high customer order fill rate, and reduction in administration costs.

SAP APO Collaborative Planning provides a platform for companies to reduce inventory and the bullwhip effect in the supply chain. This chapter explained the collaboration framework based on a company's supply chain maturity and showed how collaborative demand and supply planning can be formed in the SAP APO landscape. The chapter also demonstrated how the VMI and CPFR concepts can be implemented and modeled in SAP APO.

The next chapter focuses on the supply chain reporting coming out of SAP APO. Reporting is becoming critical for companies not only to form supply chain scorecards on performance, but also to diagnose any root cause in their supply chain. The chapter provides insight on SAP APO integration with SAP NetWeaver Business Warehouse for staging, extracting, transformation, and reporting processes. The chapter also provides data models for demand and supply chain reporting.

You now understand how SAP APO Demand Planning and SNP work, but how can you tell if they're working the way they should? This chapter provides essential information on how to monitor business performance and supply chain improvement initiatives.

9   Demand and Supply Planning Reporting

Demand and supply planning reporting generates important information for business performance monitoring and helps companies to track their sales and operation planning decisions. Reporting plays an integral role in closing the loop between planning and execution. Supply chain reporting is done at strategic, tactical, and operational levels to better understand the market and serve the customer by keeping the supply chain costs low. By analyzing the key supply chain reports (in the form of supply chain performance management), the company is able to identify the bottleneck in its supply plan and put forward improvement initiatives.

As shown in the mind map for this chapter (see Figure 9.1) we'll discuss various topics related to demand and supply planning reporting such as demand and supply planning data models, the extraction method from SAP APO liveCache, SCOR metrics, and business content activation.

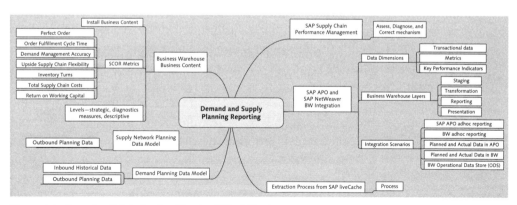

Figure 9.1   Learning Points for the Chapter (Mind Map)

More specifically, we'll discuss the demand and supply planning reporting framework and show how planning data in SAP APO supports the overall process. Besides explaining the data extraction and data model design in SAP APO, the chapter also briefly touches on how SCOR supply chain metrics play an important role in a company's reporting architecture. In addition, you'll find comprehensive information regarding SAP APO integration with SAP NetWeaver Business Warehouse for the staging, extracting, transformation, and reporting processes. We'll also go over the SAP NetWeaver BW data model for demand and supply planning and provide the list of metrics supported in SAP NetWeaver BW business content.

We'll start by understanding how businesses can use the practice of supply chain performance management to adjust forecasting and other metrics, before we get into specific tools.

9.1 SAP Supply Chain Performance Management Overview

In today's competing market environment, manufacturing and distribution companies have increasing requirements to provide better customer service, new products, and quicker delivery of products to their customers. Everyone involved in the supply chain needs to help reduce costs, streamline production, and speed delivery in order to help the company compete and remain profitable. To achieve this goal, companies are turning to supply chain visibility solutions with performance metrics capabilities.

SAP Supply Chain Performance Management is an application that helps companies improve their supply chain effectiveness by focusing on actionable, operational process metrics that impact supply chain performance. The capabilities of the application are build around the industry-recognized Supply Chain Operations Reference model (SCOR, see Chapter 1) metrics, which work on the *Assess, Diagnose, and Correct* mechanism. This mechanism, with the use of key strategic, tactical, and operational reports, helps us to assess whether our supply chain is healthy; then, looking at the reporting trends and patterns, it finds out where the root cause (problem) lies, and finally tries to correct the problem with improvement initiatives.

> **Example**
>
> ABC Technology has recently seen its forecast accuracy downgraded from 65% to a low of 50%, even though its forecasts at a higher aggregation level are good. A task force with the demand planner as process champion revealed that the root cause had been the high forecast errors on some of the strategic items for the company. The manual override forecast had been much higher than the statistical baseline forecast, disjointing the supply plan for serving the customer delivery dates.

Keep in mind that supply chain performance is not just a measurement process. Cross-functional, balanced metrics are necessary, but not sufficient to completely identify the root causes in cases of any metrics that are not performing well. Instead, the SAP Supply Chain Performance Management application is a cycle that consists of the following:

- Identifying the problems
- Understanding the root causes
- Responding to problems with corrective actions
- Continuously validating the data, processes, and actions that are at stake

The application process not only helps the business at the operational level (what is happening now or what has happened), but also looks at the tactical and strategic level on the feasibility of the supply chain plan. The application offers scorecards, dashboards, and analytical reports that the supply chain managers can use to simulate their supply chain.

> **Example**
>
> ABC Technology wants to increase its customer service level from 85% to 90%. By implementing SAP Supply Chain Performance Management, the company will be able to discover the financial costs and operational constraints associated with the increase of customer service. For improving the service level, ABC Technology would need to keep higher safety stock to fulfill customer demand on time. Keeping higher safety stock will result in higher inventory holding costs and financial reporting.

SAP Supply Chain Performance Management takes some of the input data from SAP SCM for metrics calculations. This application helps you manage, monitor, and measure the performance of your company's supply chain. It also provides supply chain executives with a holistic view of their entire supply chain, which includes planning, sourcing, manufacturing, operations, and logistics. The application allows organizations not only to measure and monitor various supply chain metrics, but more importantly, to understand the correlation between these metrics and how changing one metric impacts the others in a positive or negative way.

Figure 9.2 shows how SAP Supply Chain Performance Management integrates different functions to provide the required metrics at a strategic level.

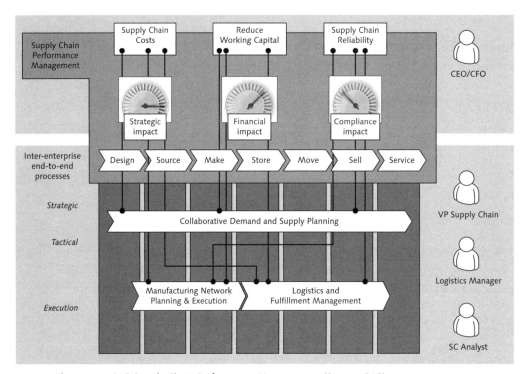

Figure 9.2 SAP Supply Chain Performance Management (Source: SAP)

SAP Supply Chain Performance Management loads relevant data from heterogeneous data sources via flat file and extracts and aggregates it in an SAP NetWeaver BW-based data model. The data can then be analyzed via a rich Internet application–style web client. Companies that implement the application should benefit from gaining overall visibility and enhanced collaboration across their supply chain, increased supply chain flexibility and responsiveness, and overall improved process efficiency. SAP Supply Chain Performance Management provides the following capabilities:

▶ **Strategy management**
Develop and define supply chain strategy and manage, monitor, and measure its progress

▶ **Impact analysis**
Understand the relationship among metrics and their impact on each other

▶ **What-if analysis**
Simulate different business scenarios

▶ **Operational analysis**
Provide end-to-end visibility into all supply chain functions and perform root-cause analysis

Having looked at the an overview of SAP Supply Chain Performance Management, let's look in the next section at how SAP APO and SAP NetWeaver BW are integrated to provide seamless reporting for business communities to make any supply chain corrective decisions to resolve issues at the correct time intervals.

9.2 SAP APO and SAP NetWeaver BW Integration

SAP APO works with two BW systems. The first BW system is built within the SAP SCM system and is primarily used for data staging purposes. This internal BW system not only helps in loading the historical sales orders into SAP APO InfoCubes and planning areas, but also extracts planning data from SAP liveCache for reporting purposes. The second BW system is a separate SAP NetWeaver BW system connected to SAP SCM, and is used for supply chain analytical reporting purposes and storing historical sales orders.

In this section, we'll first discuss basic data dimensions in SAP APO, and then the different staging layers in the internal BW system within SAP SCM that is used to extract data from planning areas. Finally, we'll explain various business scenarios in which SAP APO and SAP NetWeaver BW integrate to provide reporting capabilities to business users.

9.2.1 Data Dimensions in SAP APO

The planning data from SAP APO is used in three different data dimensions, as shown in Figure 9.3.

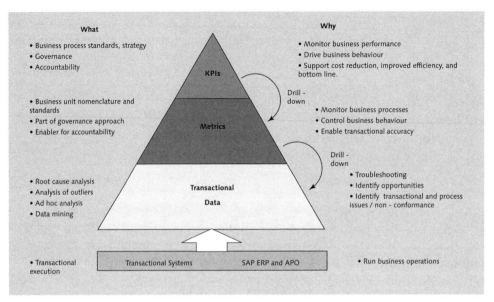

Figure 9.3 Building Blocks for Planning Data Aggregation

▶ **Transactional data**

The transactional data comes in the form of planning data and execution data. The planning data is converted to the execution data for the short-term horizon. The transaction data in SAP APO primarily exists in the areas of order management (sales orders and deliveries), warehouse storage (stocks and stock transport orders), procurement (purchase orders and purchase requisitions), and manufacturing (planner orders and production orders). This data supports the transactions lifecycle and helps in fixing any operational issues. For example, any change in delivery dates from a supplier can be analyzed early enough to inform the customer regarding the possible delay of their orders.

▶ **Metrics**

This information helps control the business's performance and identify the root cause of any problem in the supply chain. For example, a business can improve its forecast accuracy for demand planning. The metrics consists of collective data measurement of the original plan and what actually occurred during the execution. The metrics are primarily operationally related, for example, order fill rate (percentage of orders shipped against the customer orders). The operational metrics (for example, critical stockouts and fill rate) are generated routinely, while the tactical and strategic metrics (for example, demand planning accuracy and manufacturing adherence) are viewed once a month in the sales and operations planning meeting.

▶ **Key performance indicators (KPIs)**

KPIs help monitor business performance and identify process improvement initiatives to support cost reduction, improved efficiency, and the financial bottom line. An example of a KPI for a business is the measurement of the supply chain cost, which is a cumulative measure of logistics, warehouse, transportation, and manufacturing costs. The business can monitor its overall supply chain and identify which area is contributing to higher costs.

9.2.2 SAP NetWeaver Business Warehouse Layers

Understanding SAP NetWeaver Business Warehouse (BW) layers is critical for data staging. By defining different layers, we can track what sort of data (i.e., filtered or unfiltered), resides in each layer for any data reconciliation. The formation of different layers becomes important for demand and supply planning reports due to the fact that the data is consolidated from different sources. In this situation, data accuracy plays an important role for accurate reports. The four SAP NetWeaver Business Warehouse layers used for data modeling are:

1. Staging

2. Transformation

3. Reporting

4. Presentation

As Figure 9.4 shows, the first layer is data Extraction and Staging. Here, planning data is extracted from the source system (such as SAP liveCache) with minor or no transformation performed.

The second layer is the Transformation layer; here, business rules that are enriched with additional attributes are input into the extracted planning data. The additional attributes can be input from the customer or material master (for example, customer group or material group).

The third layer is the Reporting layer. This provides the foundation for the business to create reporting queries.

The last layer is the Presentation layer, which consists primarily of the reports and queries available for business users to analyze and monitor business performance. The first three layers can be automated via the BW process chain, while the last layer can be broadcast to the user community on an as-needed basis.

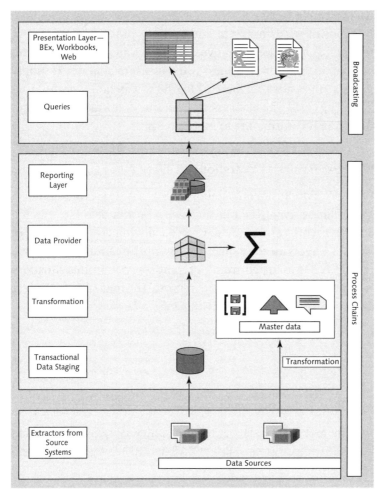

Figure 9.4 SAP NetWeaver BW Layers: Staging, Transformation, Reporting, and Presentation

Example

ABC Technology uses SAP ERP for execution and SAP APO for planning. For reporting purposes, some important transactional information, such as stock, sales orders, and deliveries, is extracted from SAP ERP, and planning transactional information, such as purchase requisitions, forecasts, and planned orders are extracted from SAP APO. In this scenario, the SAP NetWeaver BW layer plays an important role in extracting the data from the two source systems (SAP ERP and SAP APO) in a raw form to the staging area. The data is then further transformed with material master and customer attributes or other routines (for example, a change to the common planning unit of measure) and parked in the transformation layer. The data is then moved to the reporting layer in the form of virtual cubes. The virtual cube can extract one form of data from an SAP ERP InfoCube and another form of data from an SAP APO InfoCube and consolidate them.

All these steps are performed in the background using a BW process chain. Once in the reporting layer, the data is broadcast for the business users create queries and then passed to presentation layers for analysis.

9.2.3 Integration Scenarios

Next, let's look at the different SAP APO and SAP NetWeaver BW integration scenarios that can be implemented.

Scenario 1

The first scenario is the ad hoc reporting scenario in SAP APO to pull the SAP live-Cache directly and display it in the report, as shown in Figure 9.5. In this model, SAP APO planning data is read directly from the SAP liveCache, and no data is stored in the SAP remote cube. When the user calls the query or reports, the business users get the current planning situation directly. There is no data staging to the SAP NetWeaver BW system. This scenario is not recommended for large reporting purposes due to possible impact on SAP liveCache performance issues.

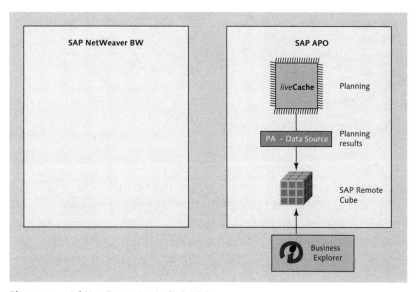

Figure 9.5 Ad Hoc Reporting in SAP APO

Note

Further SAP NetWeaver BW configuration on data extraction is shown later in Section 9.3.

Scenario 2

The second integration scenario, again, is ad hoc reporting, but performed in the SAP NetWeaver Business Warehouse system instead of SAP APO, as shown in Figure 9.6. As in the first scenario, the data is extracted on a real-time basis from SAP liveCache and reported in the SAP NetWeaver BW query or report on the current planning situation.

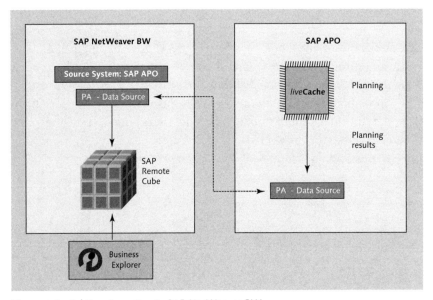

Figure 9.6 Ad Hoc Reporting in SAP NetWeaver BW

Scenario 3

The third integration scenario involves the comparison of planned and actual data for metrics purposes, as shown in Figure 9.7. The reporting comparison can be performed via two virtual cubes (remote cube and multicube) taking one portion of the data from SAP NetWeaver Business Warehouse and the other portion from SAP APO planning data. The historical data is sent to SAP APO for statistical forecasting.

ABC Technology has a monthly process whereby it takes a monthly forecast snapshot and then measures the forecast accuracy with the actual sales orders after one month.

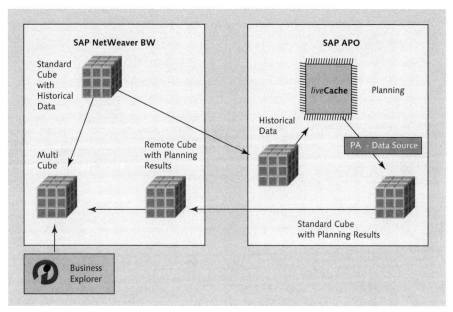

Figure 9.7 Actual and Planning Data Comparison Reporting—Part I

Another example is the quarterly comparison of planning data on a rolling basis. A snapshot is taken every quarter and stored in SAP NetWeaver BW. This snapshot data is then compared with current SAP APO planning data after three months. Since the remote cube cannot read the planning data from SAP liveCache directly, the planning data is extracted to standard cube in the SAP APO landscape as a staging layer.

Scenario 4

The fourth integration scenario also involves the comparison of planned and actual planning data, as shown in Figure 9.8. The only difference between this scenario and the third scenario is that the standard cube that extracted the planning data from SAP liveCache resides in the NetWeaver Business Warehouse system. The other design elements are similar to the third integration scenario. The company may use this scenario over the third scenario to avoid any performance problems in SAP APO.

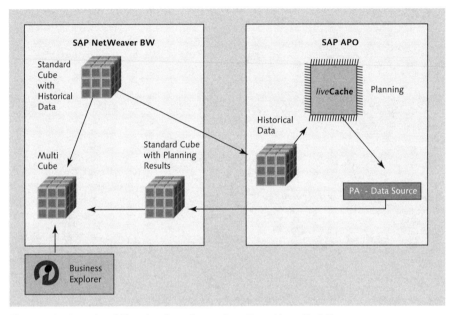

Figure 9.8 Actual and Planning Data Comparison Reporting—Part II

Scenario 5

The fifth integration scenario introduces SAP NetWeaver BW Operational Data Store (ODS) into the design, as shown in Figure 9.9. The ODS replaces the standard cube for storing the extracted planning data from SAP APO. The ODS extracts and stores the data at the document level and stores the data in a de-normalized transparent table format.

ODS plays an important role in handling the changed or duplicate records with change logs. The ODS covers all SAP NetWeaver BW ODS tables. It therefore consists of consolidated data from several InfoSources on a detailed (document) level in order to support the document analysis. You can run this analysis directly on the contents of the ODS table or from an InfoCube query into an ODS query by means of a drill down. In the context of the ODS, the Persistent Staging Area (PSA) makes up the first level, and the ODS table makes up the second level. Therefore, the first level consists of the transaction data from the source system, and the second level consists of the consolidated data from several source systems and InfoSources.

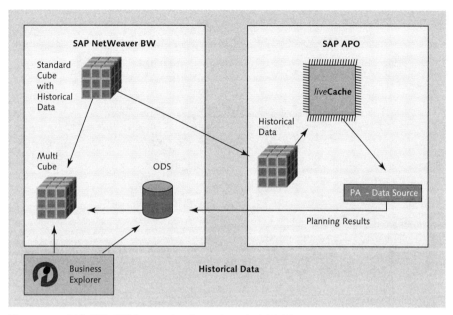

Figure 9.9 SAP APO-BW Integration Scenario with ODS Object

Next, we'll look at the technique by which planning data is extracted from SAP liveCache.

9.3   Extraction Process from SAP APO liveCache to SAP NetWeaver BW

As explained in Section 9.2, the SAP SCM system has an internal BW system, which serves to extract the relevant planning data from SAP liveCache and send the data to SAP NetWeaver Business Warehouse for reporting purposes. In this section, we'll highlight the data extraction process performed by SAP SCM's internal BW system.

9.3.1   Generate DataSource Export

The DataSource indicates the source structures and becomes the mechanism that the system uses to extract data from SAP liveCache. This concept is similar to SAP ERP, in which we use logistics information structure (LIS) to extract the planning data. The DataSource needs to be generated for each APO Demand and Supply Planning area from which we want to extract the data.

465

Follow these steps to generate your export DataSource:

1. Execute Transaction /SAPAPO/SDP_ADMIN and identify your planning area. Click header menu path EXTRAS • GENERATE DATASOURCE, as shown in Figure 9.10, step ❶.

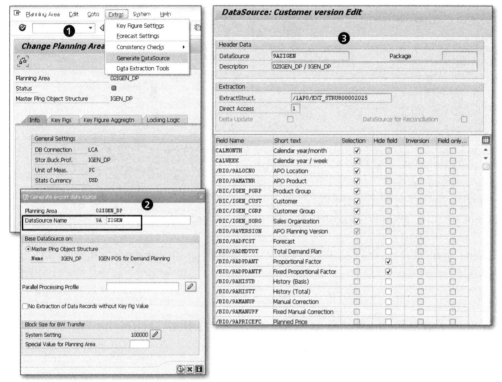

Figure 9.10 Steps for Generating Export DataSource for SAP APO Planning Area

2. In the following pop-up screen, input your DataSource name and click EXECUTE, as shown in step ❷.

3. The extract structure for the DataSource will be created where you select and hide the key figures. Click SAVE after making any modification, as shown in step ❸.

4. After the export DataSource is created, we need to test the extraction process. Again, access Transaction /SAPAPO/SDP_ADMIN and select the same planning area. For the specified planning area, click header menu path EXTRAS • DATA EXTRACTION TOOLS, as shown in Figure 9.11, step ❶.

5. The DP/SNP Data Extraction screen is shown next, which can also be accessed via Transaction /SAPAPO/SDP_EXTR. Input your generated DataSource for the planning area and click Test DataSource, as shown in step ❷. This screen also gives the option to display, repair, or delete the existing DataSource.

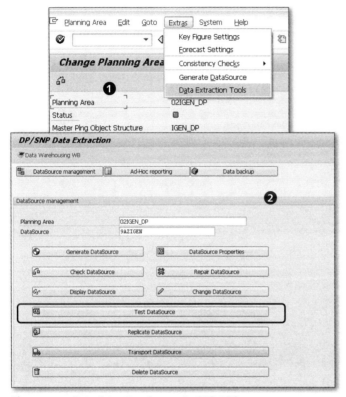

Figure 9.11 Data Extraction Process in SAP APO

6. The next screen is the BW extractor, which can also be called from Transaction RSA3. Input the active version and select Execute, as shown in Figure 9.12, step ❶.

7. The data extraction can be viewed by clicking the ALV grid icon in the BW extractor screen, as shown in step ❷.

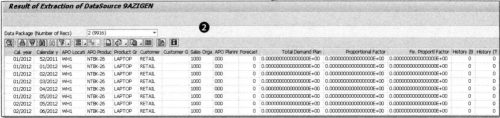

Figure 9.12 SAP APO Data Extraction from the BW Extractor

Tips & Tricks

You may find it useful to research more details on SAP APO/BW extraction with the following SAP Notes:

▸ SAP Note 428147: Consulting note for SNP planning area extraction

▸ SAP Note 373756: Data extraction from a planning area

▸ SAP Note 420927: Data extraction of selected key figures

▸ SAP Note 386735: DP: Extract data to an IC with delta update

▸ SAP Note 383906: DP 3.0: Data extraction—memory problems/COM error

▸ SAP Note 376727: Auxiliary key figures in SNP planning areas

▸ SAP Note 374534: Generated export DataSource not visible

8. Next, you need to replicate the export DataSource in the BW Administrator Workbench (Transaction RSA1) to make it available to other source systems. Execute Transaction /SAPAPO/SDP_EXTR and select REPLICATE DATASOURCE.

9. Create an export DataSource for the APO-SNP planning area based on different aggregates. Access Transaction /SAPAPO/SDP_ADMIN and choose the menu path EXTRAS • GENERATE DATASOURCE. When we generate the DataSource for the APO-SNP planning area, we will be given an option to select the aggregate, as shown in Figure 9.13. Unlike with APO-DP, we can create multiple DataSources based on APO-SNP aggregates.

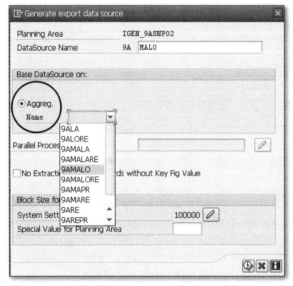

Figure 9.13 APO-SNP Aggregate Selection while Generating DataSource

The most common APO-SNP aggregates for reporting are 9AMALO for product location combination, 9AMALA for product transportation lane combination, and 9ALORE for location resource combination. For an APO-SNP aggregate, only the key figures assigned to it can be extracted. You can see which key figures are assigned to an aggregate in Transaction /SAPAPO/MSDP_ADMIN on the KEY FIGURE ASSIGNMENT tab page for the relevant planning area. For the generation of an export DataSource for an APO-SNP aggregate, only the key figures assigned to this aggregate are taken into account.

Existing APO-SNP Aggregates

Below is the list of the standard APO-SNP aggregates provided for better indexing of data and faster access from SAP liveCache.

- ▶ 9AAC   (9AACTNAME)
- ▶ 9AACPR   (9AACTNAME, 9APPMNAME)
- ▶ 9ALA   (9ATRNAME)
- ▶ 9ALO   (9ALOCNO)
- ▶ 9ALORE   (9ALOCNO, 9ARNAME)
- ▶ 9AMA   (9AMATNR)
- ▶ 9AMALA   (9AMATNR, 9ATRNAME)
- ▶ 9AMALARE   (9AMATNR, 9ARNAME, 9ATRNAME)
- ▶ 9AMALO   (9ALOCNO, 9AMATNR)
- ▶ 9AMALORE   (9ALOCNO, 9AMATNR, 9ARNAME)
- ▶ 9AMAPR   (9AMATNR, 9APPMNAME)
- ▶ 9AMARE   (9AMATNR, 9ARNAME)
- ▶ 9APR   (9APPMNAME)
- ▶ 9ARE   (9ARNAME)
- ▶ 9AREPR   (9APPMNAME, 9ARNAME)

Business users will also find the ability to run an ad hoc query out of the SAP APO planning area on an as-needed basis using SAP Business Explorer (BEx). In many business situations, the planner would like to extract the latest planning data from the SAP APO application for either analysis or reporting purposes. The functionality of ad hoc extraction helps them to perform this task. This was the first SAP APO-BW integration scenario we discussed in Section 9.2, where we used the SAP APO remote cube capability to extract the data from SAP liveCache.

Once we have created a remote cube, the InfoProvider is linked with the generated APO-SNP DataSource, which will extract the data from SAP liveCache. An example is shown from the BW Administrator Workbench in Figure 9.14, whereby the various APO-SNP remote cubes are created based on the generated DataSource by aggregates.

Note

The steps for creating the InfoCube are similar to what we discussed in Chapter 4, Section 4.2.

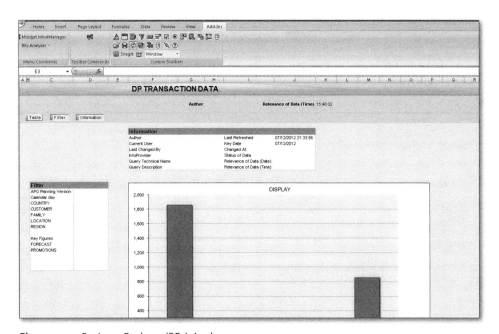

Modeling		InfoProvider	Tech. Name	M..	Execute Func...	Display Tree	O...	Object Information
•	InfoProvider	▶ SCM225 Group 00	SCM225		Change			
•	InfoObjects	▶ USER20	USER20		Change			
•	InfoSources	▶ SALES	SALES		Change			
•	DataSources	▼ SNP Remote Cube Reporting	SNP_REPORT		Change			
•	Source System	▼ SNP REMOTE CUBE (MALA)	SNP_RPT5	=	Manage			
•	Open Hub Desti	▼ SNP_REPORT / 9AMALA	9ASNP_REPORT5		Change	InfoSources		
•	Find	▼ from SNP_REPORT / 9AMALA for SCM Client 800	9ASNP_REPORT5 ...		Change			
•	Favorites	• SNP_REPORT / 9AMALA	9ASNP_REPORT5		Change	DataSources		APOCLNT800
		▶ SNP REMOTE CUBE (MALARE)	SNP_RPT6	=	Manage			
		▶ SNP REMOTE CUBE (MARE)	SNP_RPT7	=	Manage			
		▶ SNP REMOTE CUBE (RE)	SNP_RPT4	=	Manage			
		▶ SNP Remote Cube (LORE)	SNP_RPT1	=	Manage			
		▶ SNP Remote Cube (MALO)	SNP_RPT2	=	Manage			
		▶ SNP Remote Cube (MALORE)	SNP_RPT3	=	Manage			

Figure 9.14 SAP SCM BW Administrator Workbench

9.3.2 Create a Query

The next step is to create a query in BEx using Transaction RRMX. BEx can then be called in Microsoft Excel, where the query builder resides. BEx is seen as an add-in to the Microsoft Excel application. Using the query builder functions, we can link the InfoProvider from where the data will be pulled. Figure 9.15 shows an example of the query builder, which pulls the data from the SCM/BW InfoCube.

Figure 9.15 Business Explorer (BEx) Analyzer

You can technically validate the query results with Transaction /SAPAPO/SDP_EXTR. As Figure 9.16 shows, click the AD-HOC REPORTING option and enter the virtual provider. Next, click the START QUERY MONITOR button and input the query that you created earlier in BEx. The query can be run interactively here, as well, to validate the technical design.

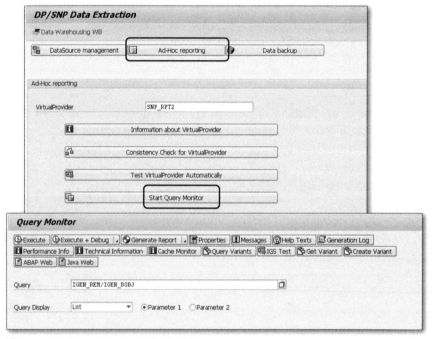

Figure 9.16   Query Monitor in SAP APO

Now that we've walked through the data extraction process of planning data from SAP liveCache for both the demand and supply planning areas, we'll now look at various data model designs to technically flow data across various applications.

9.4   Demand Planning Data Model

A *data model* consists of identifying the source of the data and making it available at the target system. The other primary reason to use a data model in demand planning is to design data staging flow for BW reports or queries. The design of the data model should encompass both the inbound and the outbound flows, if applicable. The business benefit lies in the overall understanding of the data model, which helps in the data reconciliation process and improves standardization of the overall technical architecture. The solution designer should properly design and draft the data model for each business user reporting requirement before starting work in the system.

The SAP APO data model for demand planning consists of inbound and outbound data flows. The first flow (inbound) loads the historical sales orders, which the demand planning functionality uses to calculate statistical forecasting. The second flow (outbound) consists of the extracted final consensus demand plan from SAP APO for reporting purposes.

9.4.1 Flow 1: Historical Data Load (Inbound Flow)

From a business process viewpoint, one of the demand planning requirements is to extract the historical data from SAP ERP and stage it via SAP NetWeaver Business Warehouse to make it available in SAP APO. To accomplish this from a technical architecture perspective, the first flow consists of SAP ERP, SAP NetWeaver BW, and SAP APO applications. The sales orders, deliveries, and returns can be extracted using Logistics Information System (LIS) in SAP ERP.

As Figure 9.17 shows, the logistics (LO) cockpit serves as the mechanism for pulling the sales orders and delivery transaction data from the SAP ERP system, which is loaded in the ODS at the document level. Before transferring the data to the standard cube, it might be transformed with unique business upload logic. The data may also be enriched by additional master data attributes not captured in the document level. This can be any product or customer hierarchy master data.

> **Example**
>
> Figure 9.18 shows a business example from ABC Technology, whereby only transactions relevant to SAP APO are filtered before loading into the standard cube. Instead of loading the complete dataset, the business would like to filter the data. Some examples of filters are material type (finished goods), MRP type (external planning), or order types. The figure shows that the check is first on the sales order types and then on the material type (for example, finished goods) before looking at the MRP type (example relevant to SAP APO for planning).

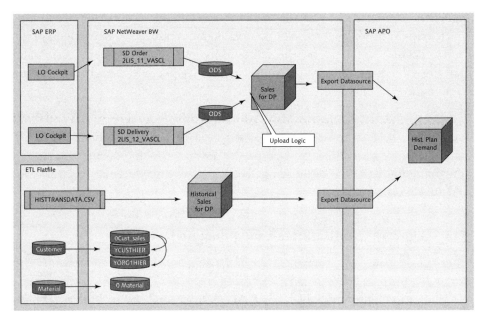

Figure 9.17 Upload Logic Example from SAP ERP to SAP NetWeaver BW

Figure 9.17 shows the master data also being transferred from SAP ERP to SAP NetWeaver BW on a routine basis. You can see an alternative way of loading the historical data via the extract transform load (ETL) flat file mechanism. This method is an alternative to the one discussed earlier on extracting the historical sales orders from the SAP ERP system directly. The flat file option provides the business user the flexibility to cleanse the history offline before directly loading into an SAP APO application.

The replicated DataSource transfers the data from SAP NetWeaver BW to the SAP APO internal BW standard cube. Once in SAP APO, the data is transferred from the internal BW system to the SAP APO planning area (SAP liveCache) using standard report /SAPAPO/RTSINPUT_CUBE. The data transfer is usually coordinated using the BW process chain in the background.

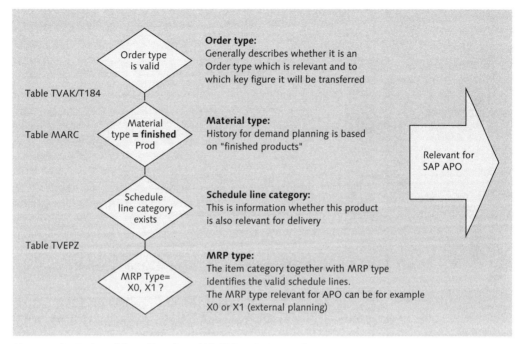

Table TVAK/T184

Order type:
Generally describes whether it is an Order type which is relevant and to which key figure it will be transferred

Table MARC

Material type:
History for demand planning is based on "finished products"

Relevant for SAP APO

Table TVEPZ

Schedule line category:
This is information whether this product is also relevant for delivery

MRP type:
The item category together with MRP type identifies the valid schedule lines.
The MRP type relevant for APO can be for example X0 or X1 (external planning)

Figure 9.18 Technical Data Flow from SAP ERP to BW to APO

9.4.2 Flow 2: Data Extraction (Outbound Flow)

The second technical flow is data extraction from the SAP APO planning area (SAP liveCache) into the SAP NetWeaver BW system. The generated DataSource for the APO-DP area is replicated to the SAP NetWeaver BW system. As Figure 9.19 shows, the data is transferred to ODS, and then to standard cube. The BW reports can be generated from this cube. Additional provisions are taken to archive the data to a different cube for planning data backup on a monthly basis.

Having looked at the demand planning data model for both the inbound and outbound process flows to SAP APO, we'll now look at the supply planning data model on how the data can be designed to provide a reporting platform.

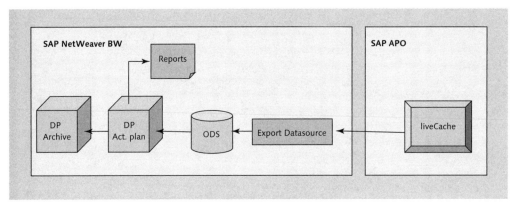

Figure 9.19 Extraction of APO-DP Data from SAP APO to BW

9.5 SAP APO Supply Network Planning Data Model

The data model for Supply Network Planning (APO-SNP) is similar to what we discussed for APO-DP. The planning data (outbound) is extracted from the SAP APO planning area and stored in SAP NetWeaver BW for both reporting and archiving (backup) purposes. The only difference between APO-DP and APO-SNP is that the data is stored in the form of aggregates for APO-SNP, which helps with proper indexing and better performance in accessing planning data from SAP liveCache. The generated DataSource for APO-SNP are in aggregate form (for example, 9AMALO and 9AMALA). Based on the planning area key figure definition on planning area aggregates (see Figure 9.13 for details), not all the key figures of the APO-SNP planning area will be available in a single DataSource.

As Figure 9.20 shows, two replicated DataSources in the form of 9AMALO and 9AMALA are extracted into the ODS and then to the standard cubes. Extraction of planning data in the form of aggregates helps with system performance. Instead of accessing the complete database, the aggregates serve as an index in accessing the planning data more quickly and making it available for reporting or other planning purposes. You can also define a multi-cube for further reporting out of these two standard cubes. A similar strategy is formed to archive the APO-SNP planning data into separate standard cubes on a weekly or monthly basis.

476

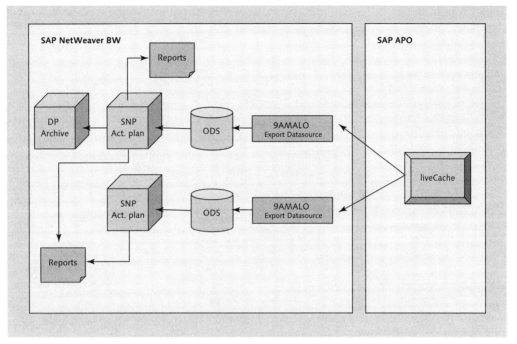

Figure 9.20 Extracting APO-SNP Data from SAP APO to BW

Note on System Upgrades

You need to de-initialize the APO-SNP planning area during the upgrade process; otherwise you risk the loss of all time series data in the APO-SNP planning area. An alternative solution would be to design a BW cube data model for loading all the time series key figure data before upgrade and then re-importing it after the system upgrade process.

9.6   SAP NetWeaver BW Business Content

SAP NetWeaver Business Warehouse provides business content for standard industry reports. The business content delivers a preconfigured set of roles and tasks that are relevant information models. These information models include all the technical objects, such as workbooks, queries, info sources, data sources, InfoCubes, key figures, characteristics, update rules, and extractors.

However, there isn't much SAP NetWeaver BW business content available for APO-DP or SNP. Most of the supply chain reports are built by individual companies directly in SAP NetWeaver BW based on their unique business rules and requirements. A few good standard reports that are available in SAP NetWeaver BW include forecast accuracy, global inventory, and global capacity.

9.6.1 Access Standard Business Content

You can access standard business content in the BW Administrator Workbench (more details on this transaction in Chapter 4, Section 4.2) by executing Transaction RSA1 under the BI content functional area. As Figure 9.21 shows, the BI content has three screens. The first screen (❶) is where you determine the view of the objects either by object types or other options. Selecting MY OBJECT TYPE provides flexibility to identify the SAP NetWeaver BW query or InfoProvider you want to activate. The middle screen (❷) is where you select the objects you want to activate. The last screen (❸) provides different installation settings and also contains the overview of the objects you have selected.

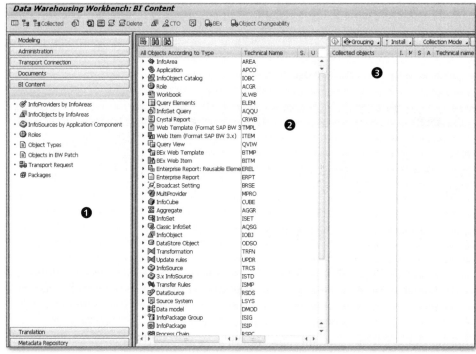

Figure 9.21 Business Content Screens

9.6.2   Install Standard Business Content

Let's go over the different steps to install the standard business content.

Identify Business Content Object Type

First, identify the business content object by object type. As Figure 9.22 shows, we want to activate the forecast accuracy query (forecast vs. actual sales). By using SELECT OBJECT (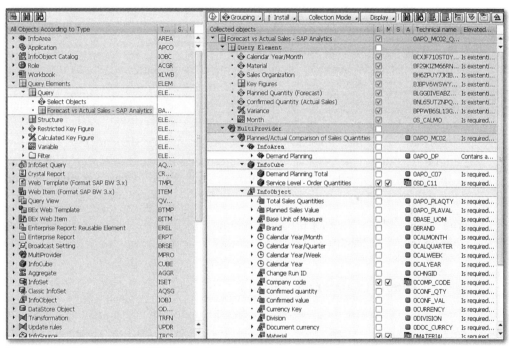), you can select the query you want to install. The user accesses this screen using Transaction RSA1 and clicking the BI CONTENT path in left screen. The query is then further located by clicking the QUERY ELEMENTS option.

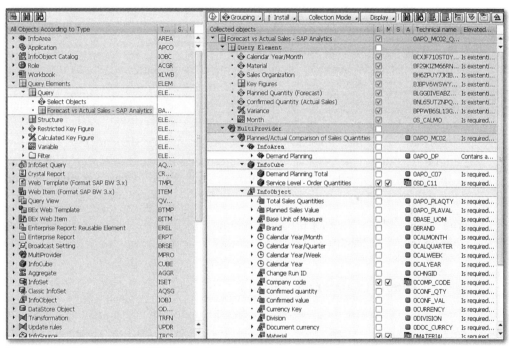

Figure 9.22   Collection of All BW Objects for a Standard Query Activation

Grouping

The next step is grouping, which is performed by dragging and dropping the object from the left side to the right side in Figure 9.22. Before performing this activity, make sure to select whether you want to collect all the associated objects on the data model automatically or manually. The automatic option is the default setting.

Also, some of the objects may be single source (SAP NetWeaver BW) dependent, while others may have multiple source system (SAP SCM and SAP NetWeaver BW) dependency. The use of business content helps in this equation because the multiple-system (for example, SAP SCM and SAP NetWeaver BW) objects can be packaged to make a specific business object (for example, reporting InfoCube) work. Also, most of the contents are already built, and the user just has to activate the collected objects and see if the content output provides the result output.

During the grouping, an option is provided to select the source system linked with the objects. The example in Figure 9.22 shows all the collected objects when the query is selected for activation.

Install and Activate

The last step is to install and activate the standard business content once all the required SAP NetWeaver BW objects are collected. You can execute the installation and activation directly from the SAP NetWeaver BW administrator workbench by using the INSTALL icon, as shown in Figure 9.22. The installation process can start once we have transferred all the collected SAP NetWeaver BW objects. During the installation, all tables, objects, structures, programs, and dependent components will be activated. The installation process can be simulated to identify any errors using INSTALL in simulation mode. Other options are to install in the background and transport request creation.

The Supply Chain Council provides standard metrics for business performance measurement under SCOR. Let's look at this in next section.

9.6.3 Supply Chain SCOR Metrics

The Supply Chain Operation Reference (SCOR) model offers the possibility to model a company's business processes. Companies can leverage existing predefined metrics to form their business scorecard. This scorecard can be at both the operational and executive levels for better monitoring of business performance.

SCOR provides performance metrics, which the company can associate as characteristics. As Figure 9.23 shows, the SCOR metrics provide measurement in all process areas of planning, sourcing, manufacturing, inventory management, and customer delivery. The measurement can be at the strategic, tactical, or operational level.

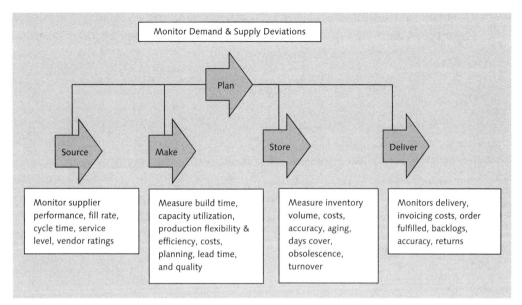

Figure 9.23 SCOR Metrics to Monitor Business Processes

The five performance attributes measured in SCOR are:

▶ **Supply chain agility**
This attribute gives information about whether and how fast a supply chain responds to demand/supply market changes.

▶ **Supply chain responsiveness**
This attribute provides information about the speed at which a supply chain provides its product to the customer.

▶ **Supply chain asset management**
With the help of this attribute, a supply chain can be analyzed in terms of effectiveness in managing assets for demand satisfaction.

▶ **Supply chain cost**
All costs incurred along supply chain processes are taken into the calculation.

▶ **Supply chain reliability**
The attribute looks at the performance of product delivery (correct product, correct place, and correct time).

SCOR metrics consist of three levels. (Currently SCOR has 570 metrics in version 9.0.) These metrics are defined in such a way that the company has diverse control and easy access to information needs.

9.6.4 Level 1

Level 1 contains high-level strategic metrics. These metrics may cross multiple business processes along the supply chain, as they do not relate to one core processes of SCOR Level 1. These metrics are suitable for the management level to monitor business performance. Figure 9.24 shows the classification of Level 1 metrics grouped under customer-facing and internal-facing. Customer-facing is primarily focused towards measuring external business partners (for example customers) while internal-facing is relevant to measure internal business process (manufacturing, for example).

In the following subsections, we'll explore the seven key SCOR scorecard metrics that help in translating company strategic goals into measurable targets, measuring effectiveness across end-to-end business processes, and proactively identifying bottlenecks and pin-pointing root causes.

1: Perfect Order Fulfillment

A *perfect order* is defined as an order that meets all of the following five standards:

▶ An order is considered complete if the products ordered are the products provided and the quantities provided match the quantities ordered (percentage of orders delivered in full).

▶ An order is considered on time if the location, specified customer entity, and delivery time are met upon receipt (delivery performance to customer by commit date).

▶ An order is considered in perfect condition if the product delivered has no manufacturing or packaging errors and is accepted by the customer (perfect condition).

▶ An order is considered to have shipment transaction accuracy if all the shipment documentation related to the order is accurate, complete (with the correct price and quantity) and on time (shipment transaction accuracy).

▶ An order is considered to have EDI transaction accuracy if the customer-facing EDIs mentioned in the list run error-free (EDI 859, 855, and 810) (EDI transaction accuracy).

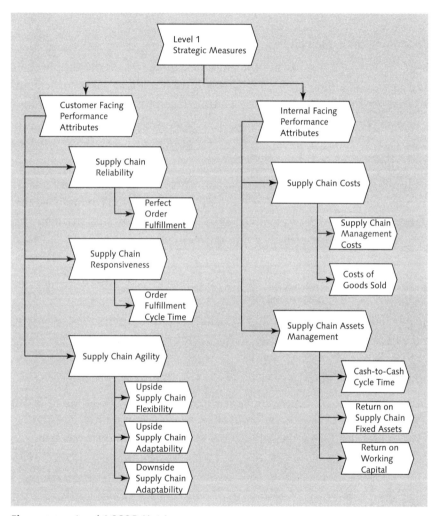

Figure 9.24 Level 1 SCOR Metrics

2: Order Management Cycle Time

Order fulfillment cycle time is defined as the time taken from customer authorization of a sales order to customer receipt of the product. The major segments of time include order entry, manufacturing, distribution, and transportation.

3: Demand Management Accuracy

Demand management accuracy is a measure (as a percentage) of how accurately sales figures are forecasted. Mean Absolute Percentage Error (MAPE) is the industry-wide accepted tool to measure supply chain forecast accuracy.

4: Upside Supply Chain Flexibility

Upside supply chain flexibility measures the amount of time it takes the supply chain to respond to an unplanned increase in demand from forecast without incurring service or cost penalty. It measures the total time taken (in days) from generating the manufacturing order to its shipment.

5: Inventory Turns

Inventory turns measure how many times the company inventory is sold or replaced during a financial year. Since inventory (both finished goods and components) has low liquidity, a high inventory turnover ratio would indicate that the company is using its inventory assets well. It is the ratio of cost of goods sold to average inventory.

6: Total Supply Chain Management Cost

Total supply chain management cost measures controllable and uncontrollable costs associated with the plan, source, make, deliver, and return supply chain processes.

7: Return on Working Capital

Return on working capital is a measurement comparing the depletion of working capital (cash in hand) to the generation of sales over a given period. The metrics provide some useful information about how effectively a company is using its working capital to generate sales.

9.6.5 Level 2

Level 2 metrics are diagnostics metrics. They identify the root cause in the supply chain where corrections are required with proactive action. These metrics are important for business owners who own a particular end-to-end function in the company. Some of the metrics are represented in percentage form (for example, what percentage of orders was fulfilled today). An example is shown in Figure

9.25, illustrating how the supply chain metric in Level 1 depends on various Level 2 metric calculations.

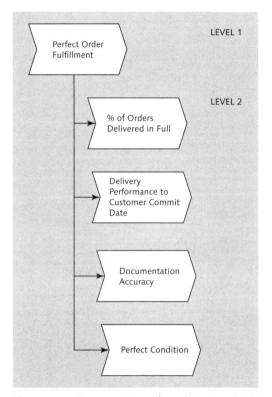

Figure 9.25 Decomposition of Level 1 to Level 2 Metrics

9.6.6 Level 3

Level 3 metrics contain the configuration metrics and are more descriptive. One example is the number of occurrences in which excessive inventory is returned and followed. These metrics enable SCOR users to define improvement opportunities and follow implementation of identified actions. An example is shown in Figure 9.26, in which the Level 2 metrics are decomposed to Level 3 metrics.

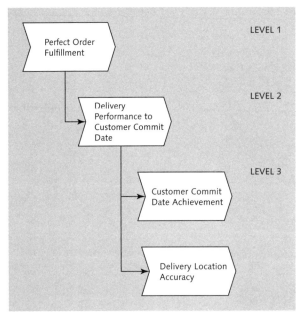

Figure 9.26 Decomposition of Level 2 to Level 3 Metrics

Example

ABC Technology currently uses numerous Excel spreadsheets and gathers information from different sources to manage its reporting needs. With the implementation of SAP APO, it hopes to streamline its demand and supply planning–related metrics and KPIs to better manage its business. With the integration of SAP APO and SCOR, it has selected a few metrics and KPIs to build operational scorecards and one executive scorecard.

9.7 Summary

SAP APO plays a pivotal role in providing a subset of demand and supply planning data. The chapter introduces supply chain performance management and highlights various SAP NetWeaver BW integration scenarios with SAP SCM for reporting purposes. The chapter also explained how data is extracted from SAP APO and explained the steps to implement standard business content and SCOR.

The next chapter focuses on the SNP optimizer. This planning engine attempts to deliver the most cost-effective plan by balancing demand with supply chain penalties.

This chapter focuses on performing supply chain optimization with the SNP optimizer functionality. We'll explain the mathematical model concept and provide insight on how to set up the SNP optimizer for your business.

10   SNP Optimizer

SAP APO provides the SNP optimizer, which is one of the SNP planning engines that can be used to resolve complex supply chain situations using a mathematical linear programming concept. The optimization is based primarily on the supply chain cost model and has the core objective of minimizing the business's costs. The SNP optimizer searches through all feasible plans to produce the most optimal solution based on a set of decision variables and constraints that have been defined by the business. The SNP optimizer makes sourcing decisions based on optimization-based planning. This means that it uses cost as a basis for deciding the following:

▶ Which products are to be produced, transported, procured, stored, and delivered and in which quantities (product mix)

▶ Which resources and which production process models (PPMs) or production data structures (PDSs) to use (technology mix)

▶ The dates and times for production, transportation, procurement, storage, and delivery

▶ The locations for production, procurement, storage, and delivery and the source and destination locations for transportation

As shown in the mind map for this chapter (see Figure 10.1) we will be discussing the optimization concepts and the optimizer cost parameters and profiles required to set up the optimization equation in APO-SNP.

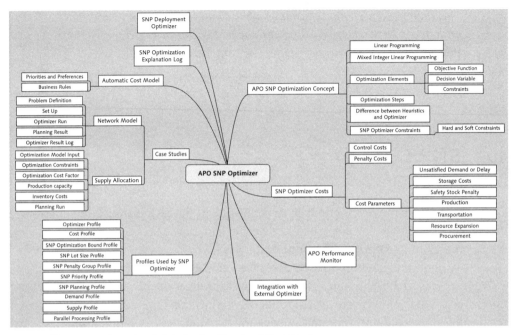

Figure 10.1 Learning Points for the Chapter (Mind Map)

We'll explain how different cost factors influence the business's planning results. The chapter will highlight the profiles and master data setup requirement to solve a specific business problem. We'll also quickly overview some additional topics, such as monitoring the system's performance and integrating third-party optimizers into SAP APO.

10.1 SNP Optimization Concept

APO-SNP uses linear programming concepts to determine the cost optimization model. Linear programming (LP, or linear optimization) is a mathematical method for determining a way to achieve the best outcome (such as maximum profit or lowest cost) in a given mathematical model for some list of requirements represented as linear relationships. Linear programming is a technique for optimizing linear objective functions, subject to linear equality and linear inequality constraints.

The feasible region is defined by a convex polyhedron, which is defined by the intersection of finite half spaces. The linear programming algorithm finds a point in the polyhedron where this function has the smallest (or largest) value, if such mathematical point exists.[1]

A mixed-integer programming (MIP) problem is another linear programming part in which some of the decision variables are constrained to have only integer values (whole numbers such as -1, 0, 1, 2, and so on) as the optimal solution. The use of integer variables greatly helps in solving complex supply chain optimization problems. Figure 10.2 shows an example of the mathematical linear programming in which the convex polyhedron area (area ❶) is defined for finding the optimal solution point for the linear programming problem. The x and y are the decision variables for the equations.

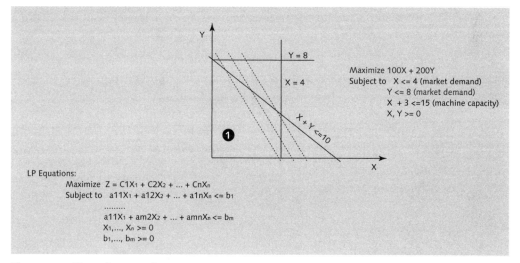

Figure 10.2 Linear Programming

The SNP optimizer is based on LP and mixed integer linear programming (MILP) using ILOG's CPLEX as the optimization engine. The model feeding the CPLEX engine in SAP APO is SAP's intellectual property, closely owned and controlled by SAP Development Lab.

The goal of an optimization problem is to find the combination of independent variables that optimizes the given objective function while satisfying constraints. Costs are the coefficients in the objective function in the mathematical equation.

---

1 Bernd Gärtner and Jiří Matoušek, *Understanding and Using Linear Programming* (Berlin: Springer, 2006).

There are three parts, or elements, of the optimization problem, which are managed in linear programming:

- **Objective function**
  This is the business goal that the decision maker is trying to achieve (e.g., minimize total cost or maximize profit). A question that might be asked is: What is the SNP optimizer trying to achieve? This might translate, for example, into a simple mathematical equation; *Maximize {Revenue – Transportation Costs – Inventory Holding Costs – Penalties}*

- **Decision variables**
  These are the unknowns that would affect the outcome (e.g., production date and quantity). What does the SNP optimizer control? Some examples are which plant we manufacture and ship the products to, lot size, and lead time parameters.

- **Constraints**
  Constraints are physical and logical limitations (e.g., demand, material availability, and resource capacity). A question that the decision maker might ask is: What will constitute an acceptable optimizer solution? One example is work center capacities. The defined constraints can be hard or soft. Hard constraints are restrictions that are difficult to change (for example, resource capacity), while soft constraints offer flexibility (for example, safety stock). Violations of these constraints are translated into cost penalties.

10.1.1 SNP Optimization Steps

From a technical perspective, SNP optimization happens in three steps:

1. **Data collection**
   Master and transactional data are read from the SAP APO database and SAP liveCache and formatted into an input file. The input file is sent to the optimizer server.

2. **Optimization**
   The SNP optimizer runs a C++ mathematical program that runs on the optimization server. The output from the optimization is formatted into the output file.

3. **Results created in SAP liveCache**
   The result of the optimization planning run is created in SAP liveCache.

Figure 10.3 shows the optimization planning run results with the input file and output file logs. The transaction for accessing the SNP optimizer explanation log is Transaction /SAPAPO/SNPOPLOG.

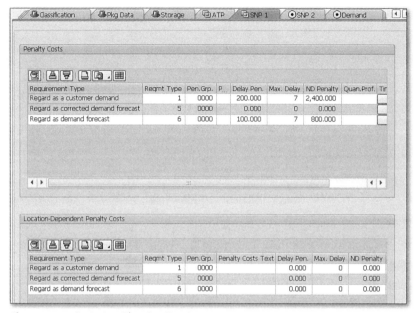

Figure 10.3 Optimizer Planning Run Log

10.1.2 Differences between Heuristics and Optimizers

While designing SNP optimizer, it is important to understand the difference between heuristics and the optimizer. The simplest SNP algorithm, SNP heuristics, uses lot sizing and lead time calculation and yields an unconstraint plan. On the other hand, the SNP optimizer creates a finite plan but requires extensive master data maintenance. Some of the mathematical differences between heuristics and the optimizer are shown in Table 10.1.

Heuristics	SNP Optimizer
Based on a requirement that is calculated and directed (i.e., produces the solution based on a rules-based approach)	Produces the optimal solution by creating a path between every node and selecting the path that produces the lowest cost

Table 10.1 Difference between SNP Heuristics and Optimizer Planning Engines

Heuristics	SNP Optimizer
Generally specifies a starting state and/or a goal state	Arbitrarily selects any node from the network as the starting state
Produces a feasible solution that is not necessarily the optimal solution	Produces an optimal solution that achieves the objective of the optimization problem
Applied to problems that specify how an acceptable solution is derived	Applied to problems that do not specify how an acceptable solution is derived

Table 10.1 Difference between SNP Heuristics and Optimizer Planning Engines (Cont.)

10.1.3 SNP Optimizer Constraints

During the SNP optimization run, the system considers hard and soft constraints. The planning run searches through all feasible plans to find the most optimal and cost-effective plan.

The feasibility of a solution will involve due date constraint violations or safety stock constraint violations to find the optimal plan. Due dates and safety stock are soft constraints, which are restrictions that you can assign violation costs to. The optimizer only proposes a plan that will violate soft constraints during its creation of the most cost-effective plan. Hard constraints, in turn, reflect the actual capacity constraint, which we cannot change. An example of a hard constraint is production or resource capacity limits per day. Table 10.2 lists some examples of soft and hard constraints, which are factored in the SNP optimization run.

Hard Constraints	Soft Constraints
▶ Production capacities ▶ Transportation capacities ▶ Handling capacities ▶ Storage capacities ▶ Shelf life ▶ Material availability ▶ Calendar ▶ Duration of activities ▶ Discrete production lot size ▶ Discrete transportation lot size	▶ Safety stock ▶ Due dates (demand) ▶ Resource expansion

Table 10.2 Hard and Soft Constraints in SNP Optimization

The SNP optimization planning run can be performed either in the APO-SNP planning book or via Report /SAPAPO/RMSNPOPT in the background. Per the normal planning cycle, it is recommended that the business user run the optimization in background jobs. However, the user can execute the optimizer for a small selection of products directly in the APO-SNP planning book, as well. The planning book option is also good for performing analysis or simulation runs because the optimization results are not published until the result is saved in the planning book.

Now that you have an understanding of what the SNP optimizer is, we'll introduce ABC Technology's business case.

Example

ABC Technology recently acquired a competitor company that manufactures and distributes computer servers to various markets in the United States. Due to its complex supply chain in demand and supply combination possibilities with the integration of the new company, ABC Technology wants to implement the APO optimizer to perform linear programming calculations for feasible optimal plan proposals.

ABC Technology is challenged with two supply chain topics. The first is the transportation network model. The newly acquired company has two manufacturing facilities, and both can fulfill all the eight to ten customer dealer networks from where ABC Technology distributes its products. The second challenge is resource allocation. The manufacturing facility is now not always able to meet production goals, which sometimes means that there is a supply constraint situation. ABC Technology has to prioritize the demand allocation to the supply based on its profit margin.

Using the SNP optimizer linear programming technique, ABC Technology plans to resolve these two constraints in the supply chain. One of the key inputs to the SNP optimizer is cost maintenance, which will help to generate correct planning results.

In the next section, you'll see how the various costs are maintained in SAP APO for the SNP optimizer.

10.2 SNP Optimizer Costs

During supply chain modeling of a network, ABC Technology will need to determine various supply chain cost factors to determine the optimization objective. The defined costs can be either control costs (for example, production costs for computer servers) or penalty costs (for example, not achieving the delivery date

493

promised to the customer). The overall goal of the optimizer is to minimize costs, taking into consideration the various defined priorities (for example, demand type—sales orders versus forecast). For ABC Technology's scenario, the company would like to prioritize sales orders first and then the forecast.

Table 10.3 shows how the cost factors can influence the optimizer planning output and requirements for the proper definition of costs during modeling. The majority of the costs are interdependent in the model.

Cost Definition	OptimizerTechnical View
Higher non-delivery penalty	Results in forced production
Higher relative storage costs	Results in moving products from one location to another ahead of requirements
Higher delay costs	Results in controlling lateness/early building scenarios
Maximum delay	Used to control number of days demand fill can be delayed
Transportation costs	Used to prioritize the source location
To increase priority of a manufacturing location	Decrease the production cost defined in PPM/PDS
To ensure meeting inventory target	Increase the safety stock violation penalty
To perform site sourcing priority	Reduce the transportation cost from the preferred site and vary the relative transportation costs across sites
To use stock before build	Increase the storage costs
To meet delivery date early	Increase the delay costs and reduce the storage costs
To meet delivery date late	Decrease the delay costs and increase the storage costs Increase maximum delay allowed
To reduce stock	Increase the storage costs

Table 10.3 SNP Optimizer Costs Influencing Results

Let's now look at various master data for cost maintenance.

10.2.1 Unsatisfied Demand or Delay

We need to define cost penalties in SAP APO for not satisfying or delaying customer demand. There are two defined parameters that can be maintained to be either global- or location-dependent. The latter takes precedent if both are maintained. The cost parameters that are maintained for unsatisfied demand or delay are as follows:

▶ The minimum cost parameter for demand required by the optimizer is penalty for non-delivery (ND), which is the cost per base unit of demand not satisfied. If this parameter is set to zero, the optimizer will not satisfy any demand.

▶ The *delay penalty* is another cost parameter, which is defined as the cost per day that a unit of demand is delivered late. If the APO-SNP planning run is performed in buckets, the system calculates the cost per day in buckets. In the master data, we maintain the maximum number of allowed delay days along with the delay penalty field.

The master data is maintained in the SNP1 tab in product master data Transaction /SAPAPO/MAT1. As Figure 10.4 shows, ABC Technology plans to maintain its cost parameters at the global level with sales orders having higher penalties than forecast. Per business rules, the cost penalty for not fulfilling customer orders is three times more than the normal forecast.

You maintain the demand priorities in Transaction /SAPAPO/PBSTDOBJ (see Figure 10.5) The prioritization is based on demand type of sales orders (DEM_KU), additional forecast (DEM_P1), and forecast (DEM_P2) key figures maintained by different levels (1 to 3), as seen in the figure.

You can transfer the product unit cost to one of the additional fields in the product master, which can be used further for different cost calculations. The product unit cost can be moving average price and transferred during the CIF with enhancement (you can find additional details on CIF enhancements in Chapter 16, Section 16.4). Using the product unit cost, we can define the non-delivery penalty and penalty cost. Primarily, the non-delivery cost is higher than the production (PPM) cost. The cost penalties for demand are viewed in the ET_DEMCLTIM (Demand Classes) optimizer input log. The optimizer input log provides all the parameters that go in the linear programming calculation as input. The parameters are either taken from the master data or logically calculated.

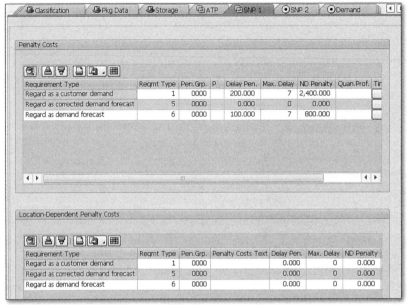

Figure 10.4 SAP APO Product Master for Demand Penalty Cost Maintenance

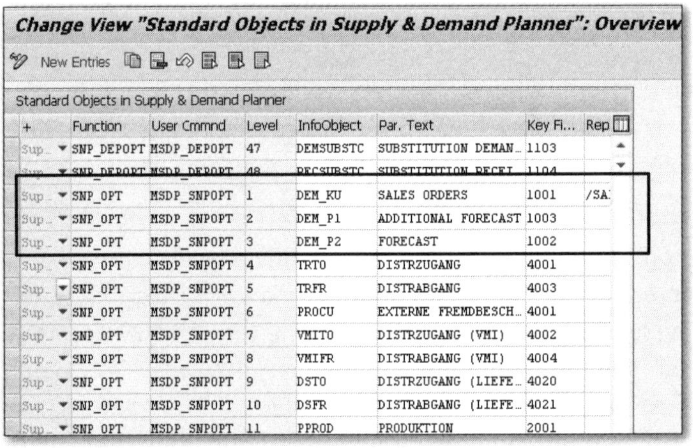

Figure 10.5 Demand Priorities for SNP Optimizer

10.2.2 Storage Costs

ABC Technology uses storage costs to control the inventory level and prevent any unnecessary buildup of materials or products. The storage costs for holding excess inventory need to be balanced with the penalty for violating the safety stock target. You can define the cost as storage cost per unit of inventory per day or storage cost per unit of inventory per time bucket.

To define and control the cost, go to the SAP APO product master (Transaction /SAPAPO/MAT1) in the PROCUREMENT tab, as shown in Figure 10.6, and access the storage cost indicator field COSTH in table /SAPAPO/SNPOPT. If the COSTH value is maintained as *X*, the calculation of storage costs will be *storage costs × ending inventory × number of days* in the bucket. If the COSTH value is maintained " " (blank), then the calculation only factors *storage costs × ending inventory*.

In the optimizer input log, storage costs are viewed in segment ET_LOCMAT− Storage costs (HCOST).

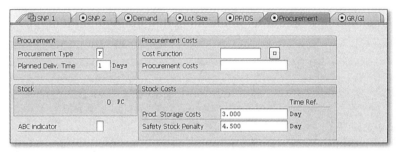

Figure 10.6 Product Storage Cost

10.2.3 Safety Stock Penalty

The safety stock penalty cost is used as a trigger by ABC Technology to hold more safety stock inventory. The penalty cost must be greater than the inventory holding cost. To maintain the safety stock penalty, access the SAP APO product master (Transaction /SAPAPO/MAT1) in the PROCUREMENT tab, as shown in Figure 10.6. In the optimizer input log, safety stock penalty is viewed in segment ET_LOCMAT− Safety Stock Penalty (SSPEN).

As with the storage cost, the penalty is calculated per planning bucket.

> **Note**
>
> The calculation is *safety stock cost of the bucket = safety stock cost on the product master ×
> percentage violation × number of days in the bucket*. The percentage violation = *(target stock
> level – ending inventory)/ target stock level*.
>
> For example: if safety stock penalty is 4.5, target stock level is 50, ending inventory is
> 20, and there are 7 days in the planning bucket, then the safety stock penalty is 4.5 ×
> (50-20)/50 × 7. In general, safety stock cost is higher than the production cost.

10.2.4 Production

The production cost is maintained in SAP APO PPM/PDS. The production cost
is maintained in an SNP PPM single-level variable cost field, as shown in Figure
10.7. For example, if the production cost entered in PPM is $10 and the output
component is 100 units, then the cost that can be interpreted is $10 per 100 units.

ABC Technology uses PDS instead of PPM in SAP APO. The costs can be maintained
in SAP ERP Transaction PDS_MAINT, and then Transaction CURTO_CREATE in SAP
ERP can be used to transfer the cost parameters. Now with SCM 7.0, EHP2, the
business user can maintain the SNP header data (for example, costs) directly in SAP
APO using PDS maintain Transaction /SAPAPO/CURTO_EDIT.

> **Tips & Tricks**
>
> SAP also provides BAPI BAPI_PDSSRVAPS_SAVEMULTI (PDS_HEAD parameter) for
> designing PDS cost maintenance.

Figure 10.7 shows the cost function maintained in PPM. The cost function is used
by the SNP optimizer to calculate the costs of procurement, production, or transportation of varying product quantities that have been defined in intervals using the
maintenance functions. We can maintain the cost function in the product location
master, transportation lane, and PPM/PDS.

Another way of maintaining the production cost can be the difference of bill of
material costs between input and output components. The production cost calculation would be the difference of {bill of material qty × product unit cost} between
all input and output components. In the optimizer input log, production cost is
viewed in segment ET-PROMO.

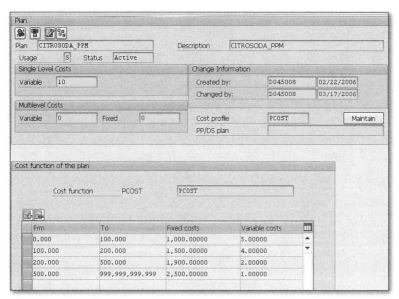

Figure 10.7 Production Cost Maintenance in PPM

10.2.5 Transportation

The relative transportation cost is defined in the SAP APO transportation lane. In the optimizer input log, transportation cost is viewed in segment ET-ARCMAT (field: TCCOST). As with the PPM, we can maintain the cost function in the transportation lane using Transaction /SAPAPO/SNPCOSF.

ABC Technology defines the transportation cost by maintaining either at means of transport or at product-specific means of transport, as shown in Figure 10.8. If both costs are maintained, the product specific means of transport is taken into calculation consideration.

> **Note**
>
> Transportation cost is calculated as [{mileage-based cost × number of miles} + unit-based costs] × number of units transported.

While performing the SNP optimizer run in discrete mode, we need to activate the transportation cost function. In the optimizer input log, the cost function is displayed in the ET_TRANCOS section.

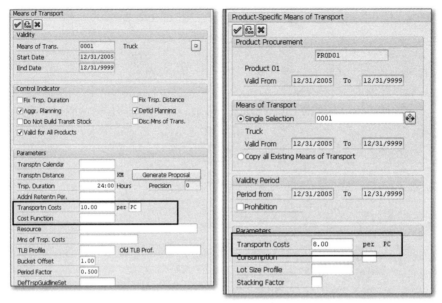

Figure 10.8 Transportation Costs Maintained in SAP APO Transportation Lane

10.2.6 Resource Expansion

In business situations when the resource capacity (production, storage, transportation, and handling) needs to be expanded due to an increase in demand, the additional increment resource cost is factored by the SNP optimizer. The cost is maintained in the SAP APO resource master, via Transaction /SAPAPO/RES01.

We start by defining two capacity variants. Capacity Variant 1 will have the base capacity (eight hours), while the extended capacity (12 hours) will be assigned to Capacity Variant 2. Any capacity more than the baseline of eight hours will cost more, which can be extended up to 12 hours, as defined in Variant 2. The cost in the resource is defined on the quantity/rate definition, as shown in Figure 10.9. The active variant is then extended with Capacity Variant 2 in the GENERAL tab of the resource master.

> **Note**
>
> In the resource master, if the bucket definition is selected as FROM CONTINUOUS CAPACITY in the SNP BUCKET CAPACITY tab, then you cannot see the resource in the CAP.VAR. QTY tab in capacity variants. The bucket definition should be X-MAINTAIN for capacity variant quantity maintenance.

Figure 10.9 Resource Cost Maintenance

Qty/Rate Definition	Valid to	Planne...	Number of P...	Period Type	Bucket Capacity	Unit	Costs
	12/31/9999						
DEF_01_77	12/31/9999	ZAP	1	Day	8	H	1,000.000
DEF_02_77	12/31/9999	ZAP	1	Day	10	H	1,200.000

In the optimizer input log, resource cost is viewed in segment ET-RESFAMC (Field: INPEN).

10.2.7 Procurement

The *procurement cost* is the incremental cost of procuring a product from a supplier that is not part of the SAP APO supply chain. The procurement cost can be defined as a variable per unit cost or with a cost function.

> **Note**
>
> Overall, all the costs described in Sections 10.2.1 through 10.2.7 can be maintained via Transaction /SAPAPO/CSNP.

The optimizer issues a warning message if the procurement cost is greater than the cost of not satisfying the demand of a specific material. As with PPM and the transportation lane, we can define cost function in the procurement master data. In the optimizer input log, the procurement cost is viewed in segment ET-LOCMAT (Field: FCOST). The cost function is displayed in the ET_PROCCOS segment.

The procurement cost is defined as a variable per unit cost or with a cost function maintenance. Figure 10.10 shows the SAP APO product master data PROCUREMENT tab, where we can maintain either a fixed procurement cost or incremental cost functions.

Figure 10.10 Procurement Cost Maintenance

The cost function is only effective with the discrete solver with the procurement cost function defined as active in the optimizer cost profile. The cost function has to start with zero units. Procurement cost is also used as the cost for discarding inventory if inventory exceeds the maximum shelf life. This cost is displayed in the ET_LOCMAT section (WASTE field).

10.3 Profiles Used by the SNP Optimizer

The SNP optimizer result is heavily influenced by the various profile definitions. The profiles with further control parameters dictate how the optimizer will perform the optimization run. This section outlines various profile definitions used by the optimizer during the optimization run. Some of the important profiles are explained further in detail with the ABC Technology business case study.

The two most important profiles used are the *optimizer profile* and *cost profile*. The profiles are maintained in menu path SUPPLY NETWORK PLANNING • ENVIRONMENT • CURRENT SETTINGS • PROFILES. A summary of various profiles used in the SNP optimizer is listed in Table 10.4.

Profile	Description
Optimizer profile	This profile is used to specify the linear programming method to be used and the supply chain constraints to be considered during the optimization run. Different profiles can be set based on the constraints we want to model based on the business operating model. This profile can also be maintained when we perform SNP interactive planning from the planning book.
Cost profile	This profile maintains the different supply chain cost weighing factors we want to factor in for the linear programming objective function. We can specify which hard and soft constraints we want to prioritize more with weighing factors. This profile can also be maintained when we perform SNP interactive planning from the planning book.

Table 10.4 SNP Optimizer Profiles

Profile	Description
SNP optimization–bound profile	This profile is used if you want to benchmark with any of the previous optimizer planning runs and limit the variations in the planning results. This might hold where the business wants to limit any major changes in the short term but allow for re-planning in the medium- to long-term horizon. This profile can also be maintained when we perform SNP interactive planning from the planning book.
SNP lot size profile (transportation lane)	We maintain this profile in the product-specific means of transport section of the transportation lane. The business requirement might be to propose shipments based on the minimum, maximum, and rounding transportation lot sizes. To use this profile, we have to select the discrete optimization option in the SNP optimizer run.
SNP penalty cost group profile	This profile is used to prioritize the customer demand in the planning run. The business requirement might be that we want to serve a group of customers to whom we want to offer a high customer service level first. As the SNP optimizer searches for a solution based on lowest costs, we can influence the prioritization of demands by assigning high penalty costs for non-delivery or delay to the high priority customers. If we want to create a profit-oriented plan that considers both the costs and the revenue, we can specify the actual prices of the products as the penalty costs for non-delivery of the products. The forecast needs to be released as descriptive characteristics from APO-DP to SNP.
SNP priority profile	You use this profile to define the product decomposition and resource decomposition. Using the decomposition, we can group the product and resource that needs to be planned first.
SNP planning profile	This profile is maintained in the IMG for global parameter settings to be used by different SNP planning methods. This profile needs to be maintained for the background jobs variant.

Table 10.4 SNP Optimizer Profiles (Cont.)

Profile	Description
Demand profile	In the demand profile, we specify how the system calculates demand via the *forecast horizon* (demand types) and *demand horizons* (in conjunction with category groups in Customizing). The profile is maintained in the product location master data.
Supply profile	In the supply profile, we specify how the system calculates supply via the production horizon and supply horizon.
Parallel processing profile	This is primarily a technical profile used to process the background jobs more quickly by running in parallel servers.

Table 10.4 SNP Optimizer Profiles (Cont.)

Consultant Tip

The SNP optimizer runs based on deterministic business rules defined in the profiles. The profiles govern the SNP optimizer planning result and require the solution designer to properly understand each setting in the profile. The optimizer profile and the cost profile are the two important profiles where the solution designer models the supply chain constraints, priorities, and the business objective the optimization will try to solve.

Also, depending on the business scenarios and constraints to be modeled, different optimizer profiles can be designed and saved for the optimization run. For example, let's say we want shelf life to be considered for specific product family for which we define specific parameter settings in the optimizer profile.

Additionally, instead of selecting all the supply chain costs, we might only want to optimize specific cost parameters (for example, transportation cost for the distribution network). The profile definitions require multiple iterations and fine-tuning until the desired result is reached from the optimization planning run.

Now that you have an understanding of how the SNP optimizer works and the different ways it can be set up, we'll look at a few different business requirements that ABC Technology has that will necessitate different uses of the optimizer.

10.4   Case Study Scenario: Network Model

ABC Technology needs to resolve its factory distribution network problem, which consists of two manufacturing sites serving five different customers, as shown in

Figure 10.11. Either facility can fulfill any requirement from the customers. The network model has two manufacturing plants from which it distributes computer servers to five customers. At the start of every week, customers send an order to the plant for some number of units of servers, which is then dispatched from the appropriate plant to the customers.

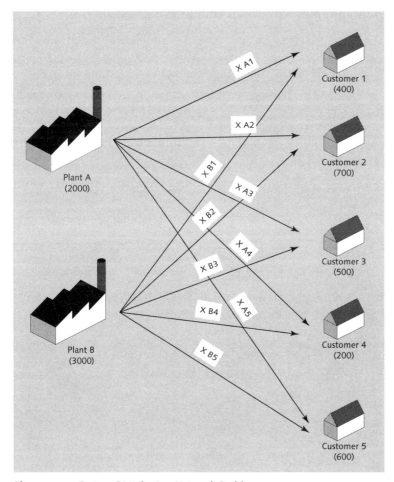

Figure 10.11 Factory Distribution Network Problem

Business Requirement

The plant would like to optimize its distribution flow to minimize the distribution cost of the whole operation.

For example, suppose that at the start of a given week, the plant has 2000 units of servers at Plant A and 3000 units of servers at Plant B. The customers require 400, 700, 500, 200, and 600 units of servers, respectively. ABC Technology needs to decide which plant should supply which customer.

10.4.1 Identifying Variables for a Graphical Representation

We will use a graphical representation to present this problem in a diagram. The starting point for the user is to formulate the mathematical problem in the form of the linear programming equation. This will help the user in defining the various parameters, profiles, and master data settings for setting up the SNP optimizer model. Follow these steps:

1. Identify the decision variables. Let the manufacturing plants be called A and B and call the customers 1, 2, 3, 4, and 5.

   Let X_{NM} be the number of server units to be transported from plant N (N= A, B) to customer M (M = 1, 2, 3, 4, 5).

2. We will make a few assumptions:

   ▸ There is a fixed transportation cost per unit of servers.

   ▸ There is no penalty cost of over-supplying a customer.

   Table 10.5 provides the transportation cost matrix (dollars per unit of server) for shipping products from one location to another.

Shipping from Manufacturing to Customer	A	B
Customer 1	$2	$3
Customer 2	$4	$1
Customer 3	$5	$3
Customer 4	$2	$2
Customer 5	$1	$3

Table 10.5 Transportation Cost Matrix (Dollars per Unit of Server)

3. Identify the objective function:

   Minimize $(2XA1 + 4XA2+ 5XA3+ 2XA4 +1XA5 + 3XB1 + 1X B2 + 3XB3 + 2XB4 + 3XB5)

4. Identify constraints on variables:

   The supply of servers at Plant A is 2000, units and the total amount transported from Plant A is given in terms of the decision variables by XA1 + XA2+ XA3+ XA4 +XA5. Since this cannot exceed supply, we have the constraints: XA1 + XA2+ XA3+ XA4 +XA5 ≤ 2000. Similarly, considering the supply at B gives:

   ▸ XB1 + X B2 + XB3 + XB4+ XB5 ≤ 3000

5. The demand for servers at Customer 1 is 400 units, and the amount delivered there in terms of the decision variables is XA1 + XB1. Since this must satisfy the demand, we have the constraint:

   ▸ XA1 + XB1 ≥ 400 (Customer 1)

   ▸ XA2 + XB2 ≥ 700 (Customer 2)

   ▸ XA3 + XB3 ≥ 500 (Customer 3)

   ▸ XA4 + XB4 ≥ 200 (Customer 4)

   ▸ XA5 + XB5 ≥ 600 (Customer 5)

6. The final constraints are the logical non-negatively restrictions:

   XA1 + XA2+ XA3+ XA4 + XA5 + XB1 + X B2 + XB3 + XB4+ XB5 ≥ 0

The mathematical equation helps the user in defining the capacity constraints in the supply chain and objective function for the optimization run.

10.4.2 Running the SNP Optimizer with Constraints

After the constraints are formulated, you run the SNP optimizer to produce the optimal solution. The optimizer utilizes its underlying logic to reveal the best combination of results based on the constraints to produce the optimal solution, which in this scenario minimizes the distribution costs of the whole operation.

Let's see how we can model this business scenario in the SNP optimizer by maintaining the costs in the product master and transportation lane.

Maintain Costs

As Figure 10.12 shows, we maintain the transportation cost in each of the transportation lanes (Transaction /SAPAPO/SCC_TL1) for common transportation duration. Also, the non-delivery penalty is maintained high in the product master data (Transaction /SAPAPO/MAT1), allowing the system to optimize the best feasible plan.

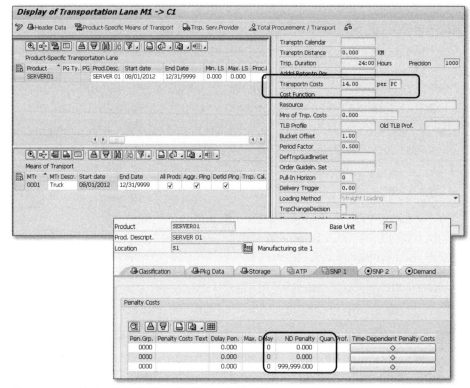

Figure 10.12 Master Data Settings for Network Model

Perform Interactive Optimizer Planning Run

Next, we perform an interactive optimizer planning run to locate the most feasible solution. The interactive optimizer planning run can be performed in the following three steps:

1. Load the products in the planning book and call the SNP optimizer.

2. Confirm the optimizer and cost profile parameters and execute the SNP optimization.

3. Analyze the SNP optimization result.

Let's go over each of these steps in detail in the following subsections.

Step 1

In the first step (see Figure 10.13), all the products in the supply chain model that need to be within the scope for the optimization are loaded into the SNP interactive planning book. The user then triggers the SNP optimizer interactive screen by click-ing the `Optimizer` icon. This will take the user to a new screen where the optimizer and cost profiles are defined.

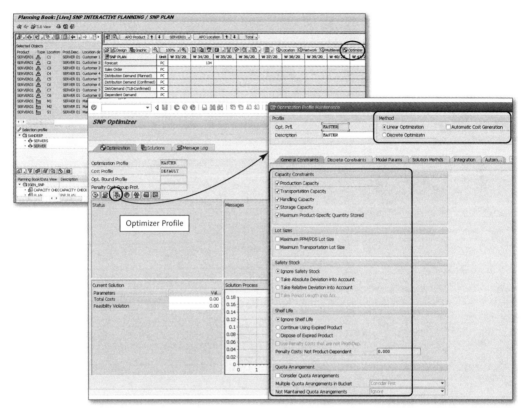

Figure 10.13 SNP Optimizer Interactive Screen

Step 2

Figure 10.13 shows the optimizer screen, and highlighted is the optimizer profile. In the optimizer profile, we have defined the optimization method in the form of linear programming. The optimizer profile has many tabs; the GENERAL tab is where we define the supply chain constraints to be considered. Any changes made to the optimizer profile need to be saved before executing the optimizer run.

There are three primary methods for solving continuous linear optimization prob-lems with the optimizer:

- ▶ Primal simplex method
- ▶ Dual simplex method
- ▶ Interior point method

All three methods arrive at the same optimal solution. The main difference in the application of these methods is the runtime. A good measure for the application is running all three methods and benchmarking on a test scenario because the optimal choice of the method depends mainly on the structure of the supply chain and less on the given input data. The method selection is defined in the SOLUTION METHOD tab in the optimizer.

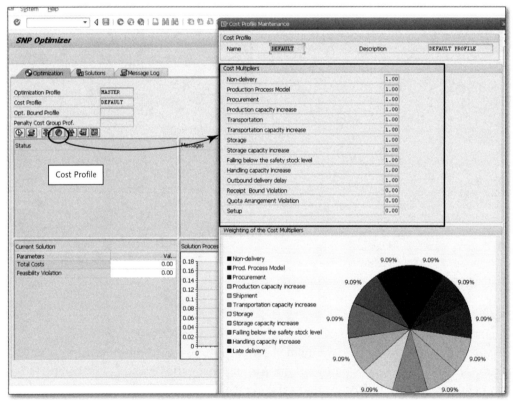

Figure 10.14 SNP Cost Profile

Also defined in the optimizer screen is the cost profile (see Figure 10.14). In the cost profile, we define the weighing factor for the hard and soft constraints. The weighing factor defines which supply chain constraints (hard/soft) we would like the SNP optimizer to emphasize more. The solution designer needs to put emphasis on more important criteria (example constraints) rather than less important criteria's in the supply chain. Therefore, never put weight on all criteria. Also, for different criteria, the same integer number signifies the same weight.

The SNP optimizer is started by pressing the EXECUTE icon. Take note that, as the optimization considers both cost and duration, the duration needs to be considered as costs to be able to compare both units (e.g., in APO-SNP, one APO dollar corresponds to one second). During the optimization, the key factors that are considered are the following:

- Valid transportation lanes
- Lead times
- Transportation capacity
- Transportation cost
- Handling capacity
- Handling cost
- Production capacity
- Production cost
- Storage capacity
- Storage cost
- Time stream (location master data)
- Lot sizing (minimum, maximum, and rounding value)
- Scrap
- Alternate resources
- Demand violation penalty costs
- Safety stock violation penalty costs
- Procurement costs
- Shelf life
- Cost multipliers
- Location-specific products
- Demand profile
- APO-SNP demand profile

▶ APO-SNP supply profile

▶ Fixed PPM resource consumption

Once the optimizer starts, it gives various progress statuses on the steps while locating the feasible point (see Figure 10.15). The optimizer provides the solution log in terms of the cost, which for our scenario, is primarily for transportation.

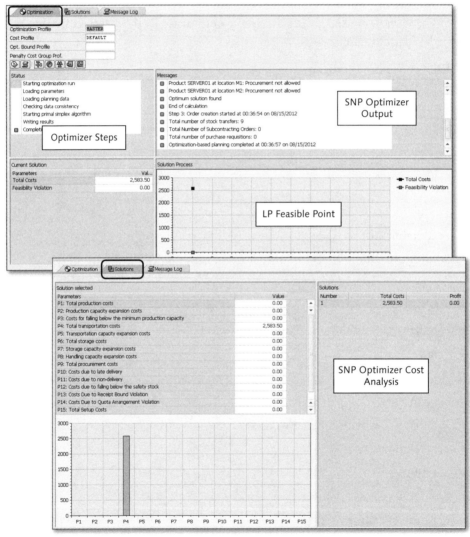

Figure 10.15 SNP Optimizer Planning Result

The other option available is the discrete optimization, for which we have to maintain the discrete constraints settings, as shown in Figure 10.16. The method is used when we want the planning result as an integer value or have business rules for transportation, production, and procurement ordering or shipping units.

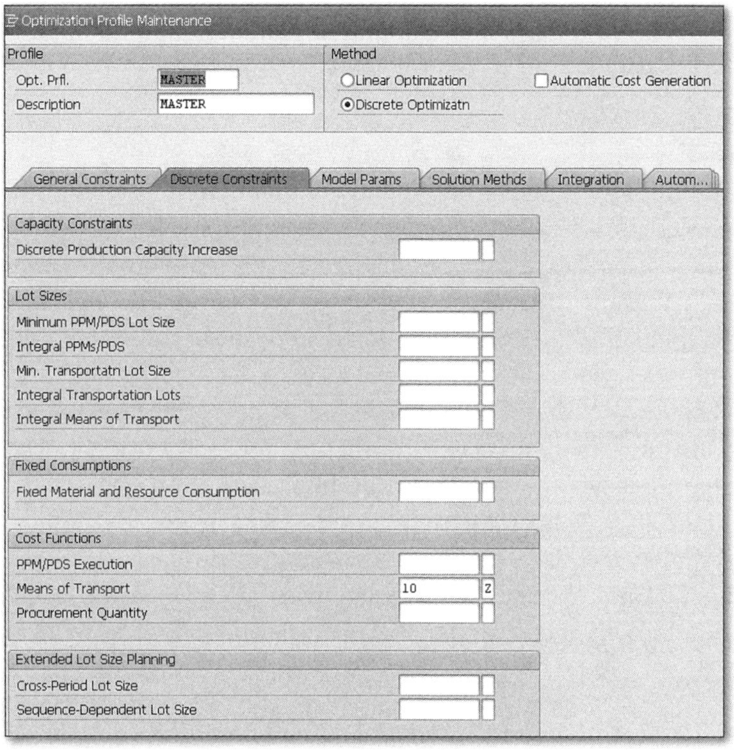

Figure 10.16 Discrete Optimization

In a discrete optimization scenario, the problem is not continuous (that is, discrete) in APO-SNP, when the model contains:

▶ Discrete lot sizes for PPMs/PDSs (in integers)

▶ Discrete means of transport

▶ Discrete capacities for transportation or production

▶ Minimum lot sizes for transportation or PPMs/PDSs

- Piecewise linear cost functions for transportation, production, or procurement
- Fixed PPM/PDS resource consumption

Discrete optimization problems arise when the variables occurring in the optimization function can take only a finite number of discrete values.

Another important tab is the SOLUTION METHODS tab (see Figure 10.17), where we define the decomposition and the aggregated planning setting (if applicable). Take note of the following sections in the screen:

- DECOMPOSITION
  The primary focus of decomposition is reducing the optimizer planning run runtime and memory requirements of optimization. Both time decomposition and product decomposition are techniques that can be used with both continuous and discrete optimization. Using decomposition, the user has a flexible tool for balancing the tradeoff between optimization quality and required runtime. The time decomposition speeds up the optimizer solution process by dividing the source problem into a series of sub-problems. These sub-problems are then solved sequentially. In general, the quality of the solution is lower than when using the SNP optimizer without time decomposition. On the other hand, the product decomposition speeds up the solution process by building groups of products. The complete model solves one product group at a time according to both the time interval and selected product window size (see Figure 10.17).

- VERTICAL AGGREGATED PLANNING
  To reduce the size of the model to be optimized, the optimizer can plan only on the location product group level defined in the hierarchy master data. In the hierarchy master data, we define both the location and product hierarchies. These data are then used to generate the product-location hierarchy. You also must define the PDS or PPMs for the product groups and create the PDS or PPM hierarchy in the hierarchy master. If you set the product aggregation indicator in the SNP optimizer profile, the products are automatically aggregated into the respective groups for planning, and disaggregated after planning has completed.

- HORIZONTAL AGGREGATED PLANNING
  This essentially allows you to plan a subset of your supply chain. You can limit the products or locations that are taken into account during the optimization run.

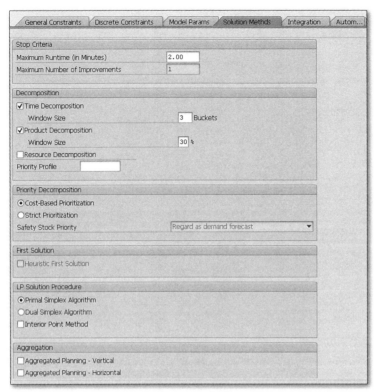

Figure 10.17 SNP Optimizer Solution Method

Step 3

Once the optimizer run is performed in the background, the business users want to evaluate the planning output. SAP APO offers the SNP optimizer log (Transaction /SAPAPO/SNPOPLOG) and explanation of SNP result (Transaction /SAPAPO/ OPTEXPLAIN) tools to evaluate the results.

In the results log, the planner will view input logs and output logs. The input logs are the parameters input to the SNP optimizer, while the output log is the planning result from the SNP optimization run. As Figure 10.18 shows, for example, we have transportation cost in the output log derived from the input log. This helps the business users to better interpret the optimizer planning output.

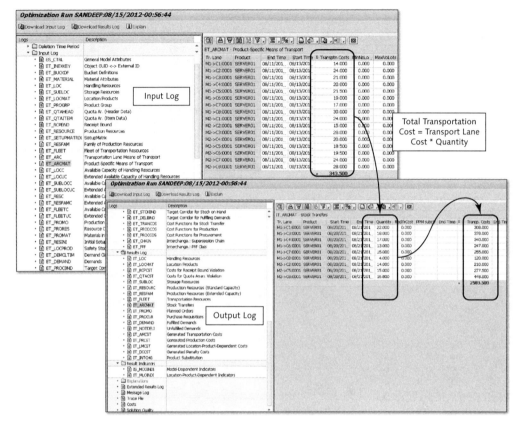

Figure 10.18 SNP Optimizer Result Log

We'll now discuss a different model. In the earlier example, we had defined the mathematical equation in the form of cost modeling to input as master data for defining the various constraints. However, this method is not always practical and may lead to incorrect derivations of penalty costs. To combat this, SAP provides an automatic cost model generation for defining the constraint optimization model.

10.5 SNP Optimizer: Automatic Cost Model

The automatic cost model in the SNP optimizer provides an alternative to the traditional cost maintenance exercise to make the SNP optimizer work. The automatic cost model uses business logic to determine the cost factors for the optimizer run. The SNP optimizer can work even though we do not maintain any non-delivery penalty costs. The automatic cost model uses the priorities (for example production and transportation) to determine the costs. The automatic generation of the cost model consists of the following factors:

- Storage costs
- Production (PPM/PDS) costs
- Product-specific transport costs
- Procurement costs
- Safety stock penalty
- Non-delivery penalty
- Late delivery penalty

Example

In many business situations, it is hard to gather cost parameter details for the SNP optimizer. An automatic code model offers an opportunity in the form of defining the supply chain constraints and priorities for translation into cost modeling. ABC Technology plans to use the automatic cost generation while defining its optimizer profile.

10.5.1 Priorities and Preferences

The objective of the automatic cost model is to translate some of the business rules into simple rules of priorities or preferences. The priorities are defined in terms of simple master data maintenance for both demand and supply:

- The sourcing or supply priorities are the transportation lane priority and production priority (defined in PPM/PDS). If both the transportation and production priorities are maintained, the system takes the preference over production priority. Figure 10.19 shows both priorities maintained in PPM and transportation lane. (A priority of 0 is the highest priority.)

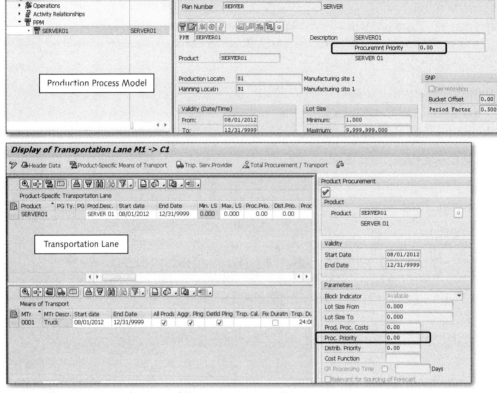

Figure 10.19 Production and Transportation Lane Priority

▶ The demand priorities are classified basically in the demand priority class, where we can define which demand elements (e.g., sales orders and forecasts) take higher priority in the optimizer run. Also, we can maintain individual location product priorities in the master data. The automatic cost model derives the on-time and late delivery costs for all three demand categories: customer demand (sales orders), corrected forecast, and forecast. The safety stock violation cost is also factored in, if required. Besides the demand class, we also maintain the product priority in the product location SNP2 tab. We can define the priority from 0 to 255. The value 1 represents the highest priority, whereas 255 is the lowest priority. If you enter the value 0 or no value, the system equates this with priority 255. The business can segment its products based on ABC classification definition.

10.5.2 Business Rules

Based on the business rules, we can define whether we want to prioritize the demand class first and then the location product, or vice versa. These two options are shown in Figure 10.20 in the previous section.

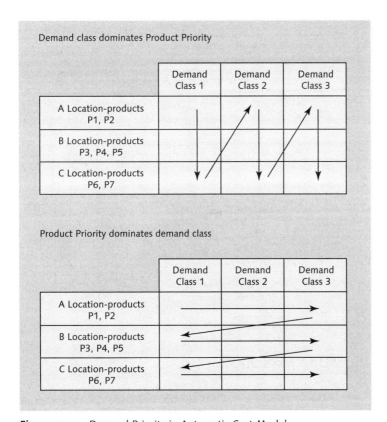

Figure 10.20 Demand Priority in Automatic Cost Model

As Figure 10.21 shows, you maintain the product priority in the SNP2 tab. Also shown is the optimizer profile with the automatic cost generation checked. In the AUTOMATIC COST GENERATION tab, we need to maintain the demand class priority as well as the prioritization method for demand class versus product.

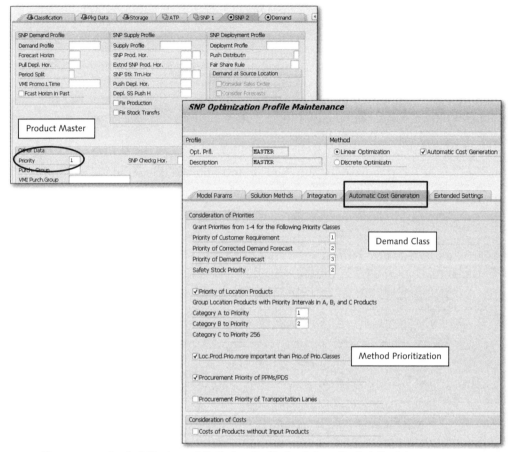

Figure 10.21 Product Master and Optimizer Profile for Automatic Cost Model

10.6 SNP Optimization Explanation Log

The explanation tool for the SNP optimization provides a detailed explanation of the optimization planning result. The business user can choose the *explanation goal*, which is the level where more information and precision of information is required. The user can navigate to the SNP optimization explanation log using Transaction /SAPAPO/OPTEXPLAIN. As Figure 10.22 shows, the user can get high-level and detailed analysis of the SNP optimization result. The analysis is broken down into capacity and penalty cost (for example, order proposals breakdown), allowing the user to understand and interpret the proposal results well.

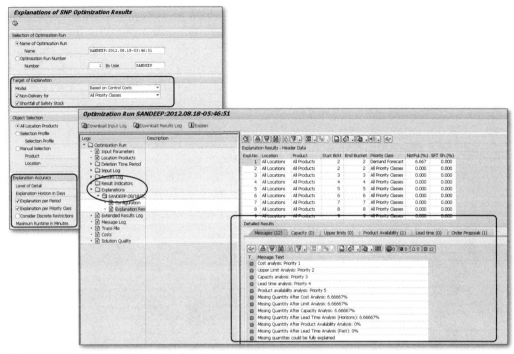

Figure 10.22 SNP Optimization Explanation Log

10.7   Case Study Scenario: Supply Allocations

ABC Technology's manufacturing environment consists of many activities constantly competing with machine capacity resources and finished goods inventory availability at the distribution centers. Due to manufacturing capacity limits, the available supply is sometimes unable to fulfill all the market demands. This requires proper allocation of supply so that the distribution plan meets the company's business targets. ABC Technology can resolve this issue by using the SNP allocation optimizer. The allocation optimizer helps provide decisions related to the following questions:

▶ How much each manufacturing facility produces

▶ How much to sell

▶ How much to store in inventory

At a high level, the SNP optimization tries to match supply and demand in the best possible way for ABC Technology and its customers. Different supply chain constraints can be input into the optimizer to generate a feasible plan. For example, one of the business requirements is for the optimizer to look at the customer contract validity dates and priority class in the input model. The goal of the ABC Technology optimization is to maximize the revenue minus the transportation and inventory holding costs. The SNP optimizer calculates the penalty cost for not meeting the target delivery dates.

10.7.1 Optimization Model Input

As Figure 10.23 shows, the various inputs in the form of master data and transaction data to the optimization model are the supply chain model cost maintenance, demand forecast, and production forecast. The SNP optimizer identifies the most feasible solution to distribute the supply (production) among different customers.

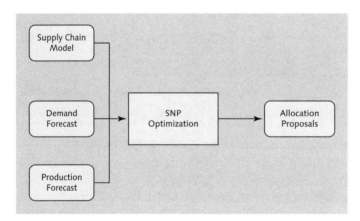

Figure 10.23 SNP Optimization Model

10.7.2 Optimization Constraints

One of the modifications required for SNP optimization are the additional constraints of customer contract validity and yearly allocation the business planners would like to consider in the planning run. These data are maintained in SAP APO custom tables, which the SNP optimizer needs to read. This can be possible with technical enhancement on BAdI /SAPAPO/SDP_OPT_LOG.

As Figure 10.24 shows, this BAdI has two methods available to influence any changes in the input log and output log. Using the method ACCESS_INPUT_LOG, the enhancement would be to populate the ET_ARCMAT and ET_CONSTRAINT structures populated from the custom tables.

Business Add-Ins: Display Definition /SAPAPO/SDP_OPT_LOG

→ | 🖉 🖽 🔏 | 🖧 🖧 🖳 🖬 Documentation

| Definition name | /SAPAPO/SDP_OPT_LOG |
| Definition short text | BAdI for Processing Optimizer Input and Result Logs |

Attributes / Interface / FCodes / Subscreens

| Interface name | /SAPAPO/IF_EX_SDP_OPT_LOG |

Method	Description
ACCESS_RESULT_LOG	Access to Results Logs and More
ACCESS_INPUT_LOG	Access to Input Logs and More

Figure 10.24 SNP Optimizer Enhancement

10.7.3 Optimization Cost Factors

ABC Technology sells three different types of hardware servers to its cluster of customers. Not only does the price configuration of each server differ, but the manufacturing capacity is also different. ABC Technology has to balance its overall supply chain costs to sell more units of each individual type of server.

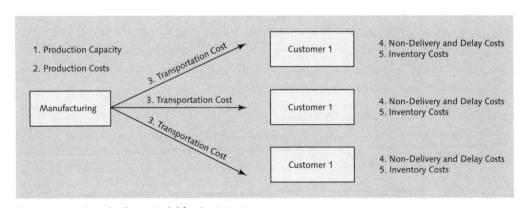

Figure 10.25 Supply Chain Model for Optimization

Figure 10.25 shows the different cost factors that are maintained in the supply chain model. The first one is the production costs maintained in PPM for manufacturing the goods. The second is the transportation costs maintained for shipping the goods from the manufacturing facility to the customers. The third cost is the inventory holding costs if goods are manufactured in advance and kept in the inventory.

The objective function of our business scenario is to perform the following calculation:

Maximize { Revenues – Transportation Costs – Inventory holding Costs – Production Cost – Penalties}

You can maintain the costs in the SNP optimizer in three ways: actual costs, judgmental costs, and high costs. While the actual costs (for example, product unit cost) are valid values, the judgment or high costs are weighing cost factors decided by business users to represent penalties for not achieving the business objectives (for example, not meeting delivery dates on time), or they can represent hard supply chain constraints as well.

10.7.4 Production Capacity Maintenance

Also, we define the production capacity in the manufacturing plant and the non-delivery and delay costs in the customer locations. The latter ensures that the customers' demands are fulfilled based on priority and capacity availability. Let's see the maintenance of this master data in SAP APO.

Figure 10.26 shows the different prices (maintained in delay cost) and the common non-delivery costs maintained. A max delay period is also defined to fulfill all the customer demands. Using Transaction /SAPAPO/QUAN, we can also maintain quantity-based penalty costs to prioritize larger orders.

Next we maintain the production capacity in the resource master data using Transaction /SAPAPO/RES01. We maintain the production cost in the PPM per output unit. Figure 10.27 shows the maintenance of these two master data. Unlike SNP heuristics, the optimization run creates a finite schedule plan, so maintenance of capacity is important for the capacity.

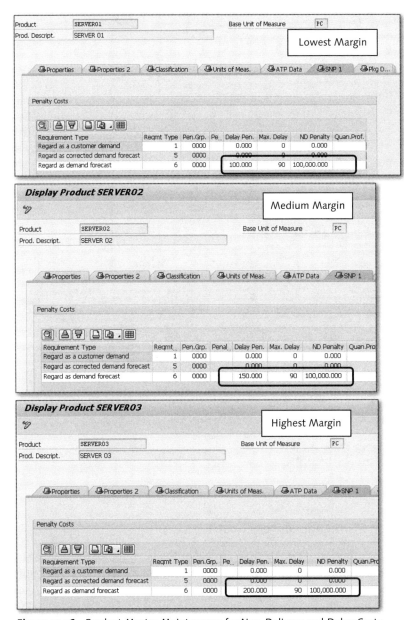

Figure 10.26 Product Master Maintenance for Non-Delivery and Delay Costs

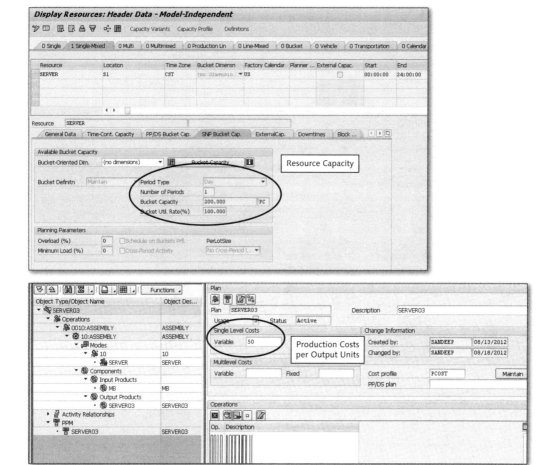

Figure 10.27 Resource Capacity and Production Cost Maintenance

10.7.5 Maintain Storage Inventory Costs

Last, we also maintain the storage inventory costs in the product master data PRO-CUREMENT tab (Transaction /SAPAPO/MAT1) and the transportation costs per unit in the transportation lane master data (Transaction/SAPAPO/SCC_TL1), as shown in Figure 10.28.

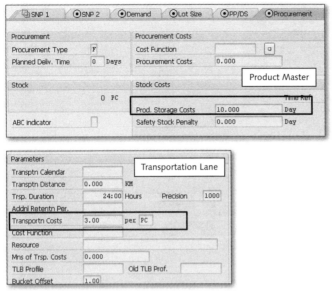

Figure 10.28 Inventory Storage and Transportation Costs Maintenance

10.7.6 Testing

For our business scenario testing, let's assume we have received the same demand for all three servers across from all three customers. Figure 10.29 shows the forecast of 500 units received for each bucket. Currently, the capacity is 1000 units per week, so the demand fulfillment will take 14 weeks to fulfill all three weeks' demand of 4500 units per week. Take note that we have maintained the maximum accepted delay lead time as 90 days. Beyond this limit, the SNP optimizer will not propose any production.

10.7.7 Planning Run

The SNP optimization planning run (see Figure 10.29) results in calculation of all the defined costs and proposal of a production plan in the manufacturing site. As Figure 10.30 shows, the production plan is proposed first for products that will generate more profit margin than subsequent products following a similar pattern. The production utilization is 100% for all weeks until all demands are fulfilled.

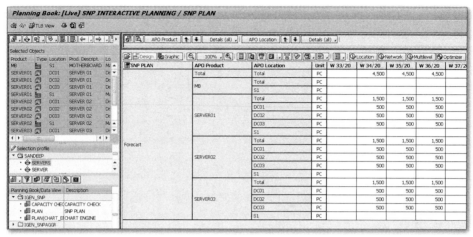

Figure 10.29 Demand Forecasts for Optimizer Input

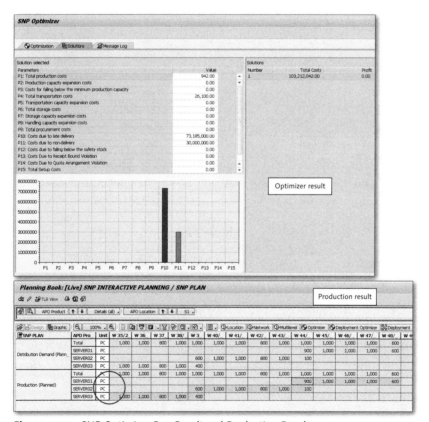

Figure 10.30 SNP Optimizer Run Result and Production Results

Also, Figure 10.31 shows the allocation proposals to three customers, taking into consideration the transportation and inventory holding costs.

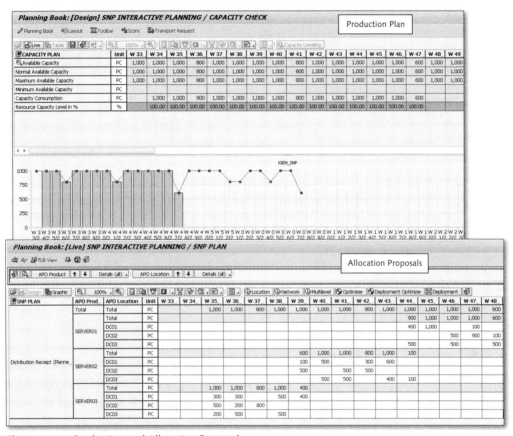

Figure 10.31 Production and Allocation Proposals

While the SNP optimizer primarily formulates the replenishment and production plan, the distribution plan requires an additional planning run in the form of *SNP deployment*. We'll explain the use of the SNP deployment optimizer to create a constraint distribution plan in the next section. Using the deployment optimizer, ABC Technology is able to plan not only its execution shipments but also project the shortages and surpluses due to supply chain constraints in various time buckets.

10.8   SNP Deployment Optimizer

The SNP deployment optimizer is used for creating a distribution plan in the supply chain network. The deployment optimizer takes all the input from the production plan or other receipts to calculate the available-to-deploy (ATD) quantity. The SNP optimizer, using the deployment optimizer profile, determines how the ATD quantity needs to be distributed to the destination locations. The deployment optimizer considers the following factors:

▶ Distribution rules (such as fair share and push rules), if the available product receipt quantities exceed or fall below the demand

▶ Supply chain costs defined in the supply chain model, such as transportation costs, storage costs, and penalties for non-delivery

▶ Supply chain constraints, such as transportation capacity, storage capacity, and transportation lot sizes

The deployment (distribution plan) concept is similar to what we learned in Chapter 5, Section 5.4, with the only exception being that the deployment optimizer can consider the lowest costs as well as the demand during the optimization. Figure 10.32 shows the deployment options, with options available for supply shortage or supply surplus. The pull/push deployment horizon can be maintained either in the product master or directly in the deployment profile.

After running the deployment optimizer, we can see the deployment plan in the distribution demand or receipt (confirmed) key figure. Figure 10.33 shows the deployment result where the allocation proposals to the customers are different than the earlier SNP optimization planning run. These results are different because in SNP optimization, we focus on the entire production, replenishment, and procurement plan, while the deployment optimization is primarily for the distribution plan. The most feasible plan is proposed, generating the lowest costs.

The performance of the SNP optimizer needs to be closely monitored as the supply chain model changes. SAP APO provides functionality in the form of the APO Performance Monitor to constantly pulse check the hardware parameters to ensure that the background optimization is using the correct system resources and that the batch jobs are being completed on time.

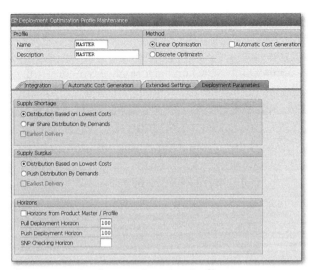

Figure 10.32 Deployment Optimizer Profile

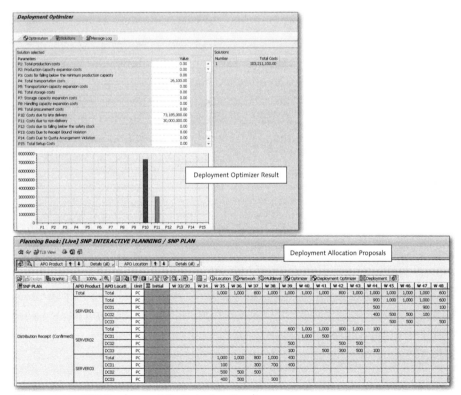

Figure 10.33 SNP Deployment Optimization Result

10.9 The APO Performance Monitor

The APO Performance Monitor (Transaction /SAPAPO/PERMON) is a tool provided to collect information about the application usage and performance. It helps to diagnose whether there are any critical issues in the different application components. The monitor, with historical data records, provides a benchmark to identify any abnormal running in the SAP APO application. Traditionally, we use Transaction ST14 in the SAP ERP and SAP SCM systems to collect important business data (for example, the number of objects in the MRP run), but this transaction does not provide any information on runtime or memory allocation.

Monitoring the SNP application is important to scaling any increase in supply chain model size, monitoring the volume of SAP liveCache orders, and allocating peak memory while running the background process chain during the planning weekly cycle.

The APO Performance Monitor helps to decompose the usage of the SNP optimization planning results into a database, SNP optimizer, and SAP liveCache usage.

Figure 10.34 shows the APO Performance Monitor showing different characteristics of the SNP optimization planning run. The result shows the optimization runtime, allocated address space, and log file director and also gives the memory consumption. With this transaction, we can also view the SNP log files by clicking the LOG DISPLAY icon. The button DETAIL<>OVERVIEW displays the runtime details and provides additional information on data read time, optimizer engine duration, and time for order creation. Lastly, by clicking the glass icon, we can view the APO Performance Monitor. The result has three sections:

▶ VERSION INFORMATION specifies the number of master data objects.

▶ DETAILS ABOUT INTERNAL MODEL OF OPTIMIZER shows the number of variables and constraints used in the optimizer model.

▶ ORDERS STATISTICS OF SNP OPTIMIZER shows the number of orders created.

Now we know about the SNP optimizer within SAP APO, but you may run into a situations where there's and external optimizer that may need integration with SAP APO. This topic is briefly explained in the following section.

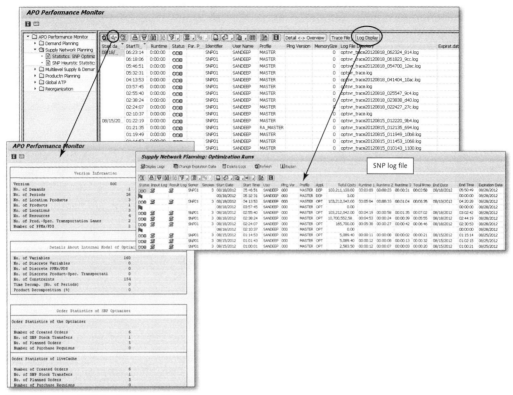

Figure 10.34 APO Performance Monitor

10.10 Integration of External Optimizers to SAP APO

Different industries require a specific type of optimization (for example, steel or paper) where the standard optimizer may not yield the desired results. In this scenario, the company may opt to use the industry-specific optimizer to be integrated with the SAP landscape. External optimizers can be integrated into the SAP APO component by the following options:

▶ Connection of an external optimizer using Business Application Programming Interfaces (BAPIs)

▶ Integration of an external optimizer in SAP APO using the Extension Workbench (APX)

If an external optimizer designed by the manufacturer for connection to the SAP APO component is used, the interface configuration required is specified to the external optimizer. However, if an external optimizer (for example ILOG components) that is not designed with a connection to the SAP APO component is used, then SAP RFC, BAPI technology, MS ActiveX, OCX technology, and ABAP programming is required to integrate the external optimizer with SAP APO.

APX (see Figure 10.35) integrates external optimizers with SAP APO and is able to access the dataset on the database server and in SAP liveCache. The external (customized) optimizer becomes an integral component of SAP APO. Hence, the external optimizer can then store the results of an optimization run in the SAP APO component's dataset, which eliminates the need for a separate database. APX offers such functionality as the following:

▶ Ability to integrate and call the external optimizer directly from the SAP APO component.

▶ Control of communication between the SNP optimizer server and frontend by the SAP APO component.

▶ Transfer of application-specific, optimizer-specific data and system information when the optimizer is being called.

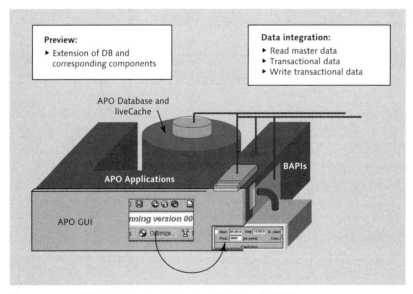

Figure 10.35 APO Optimization Extension Workbench (APX)

▸ Extension options using BAdIs.

▸ Ability of the customizing function for the APX in the SAP APO component to enable the user to save a small amount of fixed data, e.g., customized data, on the optimization algorithm or the runtime.

Standard BAPIs or an RFC connection can be used to transfer data when additional constraints or target figures are introduced to external optimizers that are not considered by the SAP APO component's standard optimizer.

10.11   Summary

Optimization is the application of mathematical models based on a set of decision variables and constrains to reveal the best possible combination of results as measured by a goal. This chapter demonstrated how, with the use of mathematical linear and mixed integer programming, the complex supply chain model can be provided with feasible solutions. This chapter showed how we can program linear programming for two different supply chain models in the form of a factory distribution model and resource allocation in the SNP optimizer. In the optimizer view, a plan is feasible when it satisfies all the supply chain model constraints that are set in the SNP optimizer profile.

This chapter explained different cost factors and how they can be used to reflect the supply chain optimization business case. SAP APO provides an automatic cost model whereby the business can define demand and supply prioritization or preferences to derive on the costs. The chapter also highlighted the use of the deployment optimizer for creating the distribution plan.

The next chapter focuses on a third SNP planning engine—Capable-to-Match (CTM)—which provides capabilities in demand and supply matching and considers demand and supply prioritization during the planning run. The chapter provides an overview of CTM capabilities, customization, and master data setup.

Capable-to-Match is a commonly used planning engine that takes into consideration business rules around demand and supply priorities. This chapter gives an overview of CTM capabilities, customization and master data setup to make the functionality work.

11 Demand and Supply Matching with Capable-To-Match

SAP APO provides a tool called Capable-to-Match (CTM, also known as a rules-based algorithm) that works on demand and supply priorities while creating a feasible capacity constrained plan. Businesses can best use CTM when they need to create a process of supply allocation where many products share the same resource pool.

As shown in the mind map for this chapter (see Figure 11.1) we will be covering CTM as a planning algorithm to perform demand and supply matching. The various topics covered in the chapter will touch on CTM concepts, customization, master data, planning run, and closes with a CTM case study of how a petrochemical company implemented CTM to support its business objectives.

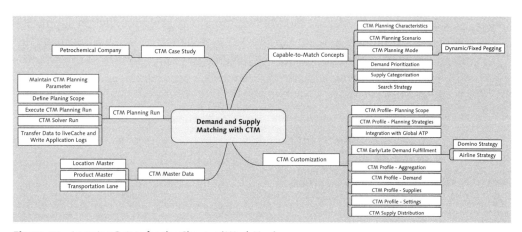

Figure 11.1 Learning Points for the Chapter (Mind Map)

11.1 Capable-to-Match Concept

Capable-to-Match (CTM) planning is an alternative to the optimization-based or heuristics-based planning methods of SAP APO Supply Network Planning. CTM is a planning solver engine that matches prioritized customer demands and forecasts sequentially against feasible supplies in the network, with the current component availability and production capacities being taken into account (multi-level). The CTM planning run is based on constraint-based propagation techniques that plan the first feasible solution, which does not have to be the optimal solution for subsequent demands.

In the following sections, we'll outline the concept behind CTM planning scenarios, dynamic and fixed pegging, demand prioritizations, supply categorization, and search strategy.

11.1.1 CTM Planning Characteristics

CTM executes a multi-level, rules-based, finite, iterative planning run of individual demands. The planning run prioritizes demands and receipts via rules. This approach suits companies with a business operating model that calls for different priorities in terms of demand type and customer and product priorities. Since CTM is order based, after the planning run, the business user can trace the relevant receipts and supplies for each demand.

CTM considers individual production and distribution levels simultaneously and explodes the bill of materials (BOM) to determine feasible production supplies in the network considering global capacities. The planning does not support detailed scheduling strategies such as sequence-dependent setup activities or the synchronization of multi-activity resources but considers quota arrangement master data for stock transfer proposals.

11.1.2 CTM Planning Scenario

Let's look at the CTM planning scenario to better understand how CTM fulfills a demand element. The scenario is explained in three steps, as shown in Figure 11.2:

❶ A high-priority sales order is coming into the distribution center. The distribution does not have any physical stock to fulfill the customer orders. The requirement is propagated along to the next level to Production Plant 1. This is defined by the transportation lane, where the sourcing priority for the scenario of multiple sources can be maintained.

❷ Production Plant 1 checks capacity and finds no capacity for the customer-requested data that is found. The requirement is next propagated along to Production Plant 2.

❸ Production Plant 2 has enough inventory to fulfill the demand. A stock transfer is created from Production Plant 2 to the distribution center.

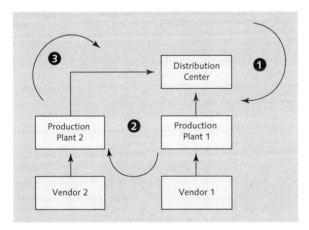

Figure 11.2 CTM Planning Scenario

During the planning run, CTM uses constraint-based heuristics to conduct multi-plant checks of production capacities and transportation lead time and capacity based on predefined supply categories and demand priorities. The CTM planning run is performed in the CTM engine, which matches the prioritized demands to the available stock and receipts.

Figure 11.3 shows the functioning of the CTM engine whereby the primary inputs are the supply chain model (master data), demand elements prioritization, and supply categorization. During the planning run, CTM performs a search strategy to peg individual demand elements with the supply elements going from one location to the next.

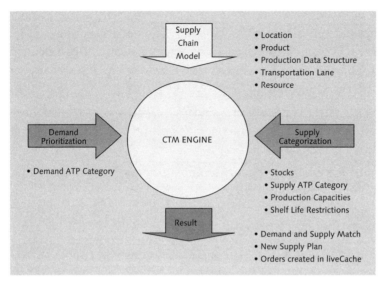

Figure 11.3 CTM Engine

11.1.3 CTM Planning Modes

The planning method in CTM determines which orders need to be included in the CTM planning run based on the pegging relationship in the order net. There are two types of pegging relationship available: dynamic and fixed (see Figure 11.4).

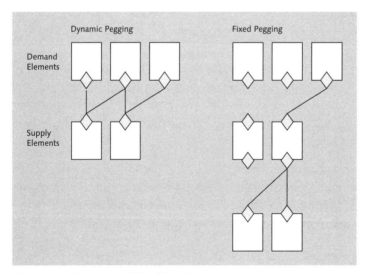

Figure 11.4 Dynamic and Fixed Pegging Concept

Dynamic pegging is a function with which the system automatically links requirements for a location product with suitable stocks or receipts for the location product. If there is any change in the next planning run, the system creates new dynamic pegging to create new requirement and receipts relationships.

On the other hand, *fixed pegging* is used if we want to fix the assignment of a stock or receipt elements to a requirement. A fixed assignment is retained if there is change in the document. For example, when you use fixed pegging, the assignment of a sales order item to a receipt element remains stable. Moreover, the component assignments can be kept stable over multiple levels. In other words, components that are assigned to an order via fixed pegging cannot be consumed by other competing orders from the planning perspective in SAP APO. This means that it is easier to keep the confirmation date that you have given to your end customer.

11.1.4   Demand Prioritization

Businesses often like to prioritize their current demand based on the order category or demand due dates. For example, the customer sales order carries more priority than the demand forecast or safety stock. This sequencing of the demand element is important during the CTM run. If no priorities are set, prioritization occurs on a first-come, first-served basis by the due date. Using demand prioritization, the business user can determine the criteria to be used during the CTM planning by sorting and sequencing the demand elements for CTM to plan.

An example of demand prioritization (see Figure 11.5) is a scenario in which the sort can be carried out according to customer (location) priority, product priority, order type, demand due date, and demand selection. Using order selection, the user can specify to the CTM planning engine which demand elements to consider: sales orders, stock transport orders, order reservations, or forecasts, and what the demand sequence should be. The user can simulate the settings and check the results. The sort-within criteria can be descending, ascending, or user defined.

11.1.5   Supply Categorization

All receipt and stock elements are categorized before the CTM planning run. The receipt elements are grouped and can be assigned to supply categories. Alternatively, different supply limits are defined for the supply categories. The supply limits can be defined for each location, product, or location product combination. In this way, you select the stock categories that determine how inventory can be processed during the planning run.

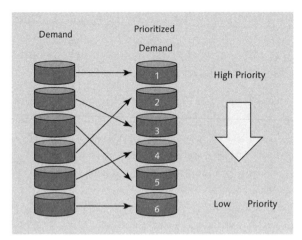

Figure 11.5 Demand Prioritization in CTM

The business user can also define whether safety stock needs to be built or target days' supply and inventory limits need to be used. As with the demand prioritization, the user can simulate stock categorization and check the results before the planning run. At the start of the planning run, the stock in the stock categories is classified as normal or surplus stock, and the search strategy defines the order in which the stock categories should be searched. Figure 11.6 shows the grouping of the supply category as inventory target, normal, and surplus available for each location product combination.

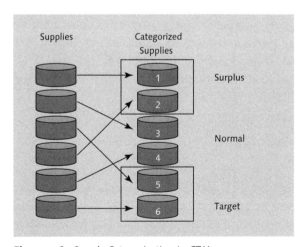

Figure 11.6 Supply Categorization in CTM

11.1.6 Search Strategy

The search strategy defines the sequence in which demand and supply are matched. It also determines whether the CTM planning run should create production receipts elements. One of technique CTM uses to determine the sourcing location is including priority in the APO transportation lane master data or, alternatively, using quota arrangement master data with a sourcing percentage and validity dates. The search strategy is done location by location.

You can see an example of this search strategy by working through the different supply category in the following steps: distribution of excess stocks, production with free capacity, and normal supply toward meeting the inventory target.

Now that we have a good understanding of what CTM does, let's look at the actual steps to set up this tool in the SAP system.

11.2 CTM Customization

The CTM profile is the primary location where we define the planning parameters and also perform the planning run. The CTM profile works along with global settings during the CTM planning run. Let's look at the different settings that need to be defined in the CTM profile before the planning run. Access the CTM profile via Transaction /SAPAPO/CTM.

11.2.1 CTM Profile: Planning Scope

We define the planning version, master data selection, order selection (demand and supply), and CTM time stream on the PLANNING SCOPE tab (Figure 11.7). The planning version can be either an active or simulation version. The advantage of working on a simulation version is that the business user can analyze the planning result before publication to the execution SAP ERP system.

The master data selection defines the planning scope for the CTM run and needs to include all the master data objects (location product, transportation lanes, and PDS/PPM). If we have a business scenario in a petrochemical company in which a stock transfer needs to be created between the source and target location, both the location products need to be maintained with the transportation lane. Similarly, for the PDS/PPM, all bill of material (BOM) components need to be included for CTM to generate the external procurement proposals.

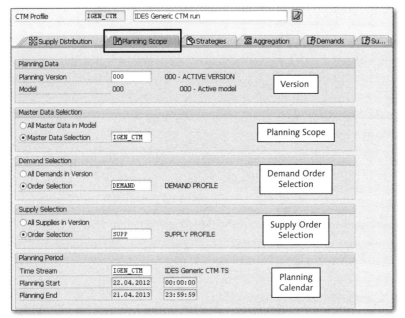

Figure 11.7 CTM Profile: Planning Scope

The master data selection is maintained in Transaction /SAPAPO/CTMMSEL. Here, we maintain the active model and all the location products in scope (see Figure 11.8), which includes both finished and raw materials. Include the entire supply chain network, which needs to be part of the planning run. The network is represented by the transportation lanes across source and destination locations.

Next, maintain all the relevant transportation lanes and the manufacturing PDS/ PPM master data in the EXTERNAL PROCUREMENT and IN-HOUSE PRODUCTION tabs. CTM offers a master data consistency check via Transaction /SAPAPO/CTM01, which is a useful tool to identify any master data errors.

Also built within the planning scope is the order selection option if the business would like to consider only specific demand and supply elements. The order selection is maintained in Transaction /SAPAPO/CTMORDSEL. Figure 11.9 shows an example for the demand and supply ATP categories that need to be included in the planning scope.

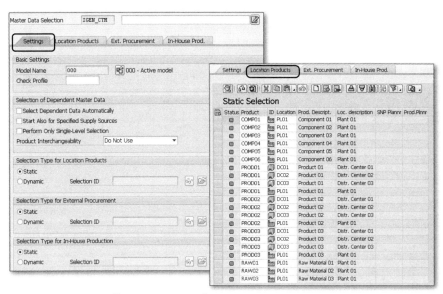

Figure 11.8 CTM Profile: Master Data Selection

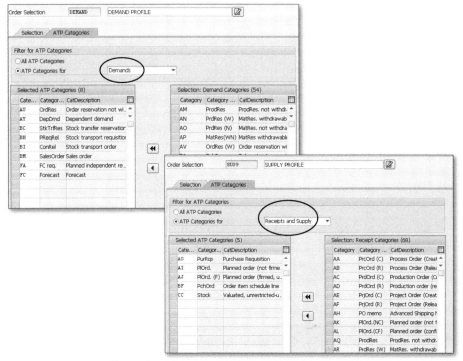

Figure 11.9 CTM Profile: Order Selection

Lastly, in the planning scope, we maintain the CTM time stream calendar. This is maintained in Transaction /SAPAPO/CTMTSTR. Figure 11.10 shows an example of the CTM time stream, where the relative dynamic date selection will be picked by CTM during the planning run from today's date through the next 365 days.

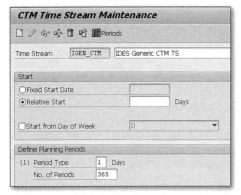

Figure 11.10 CTM Profile: Time Stream Calendar

11.2.2 CTM Profile: Strategies

In the STRATEGIES tab settings, we define various planning parameters; for example, what kind of planning mode we want to execute, fixed/dynamic pegging, forward/backward scheduling, consider shelf life, global available-to-promise (global ATP), and rules-based planning. Also in the CTM global setting customization, we define demand fulfilment rules. The global settings are defined in Transaction /SAPAPO/CTMCUST. Figure 11.11 shows the combination of the CTM profile and global settings related to the planning strategies.

There are three options available in CTM under planning mode:

▶ ORDERS WITHOUT PEGGING
If you choose this strategy, CTM will plan only those orders that are not pegged to others. In this mode, CTM does not delete any pegged production orders, fixed or dynamic. Pegged orders are simply ignored and not included in planning. In the case of partially pegged orders, the pegged ones are ignored and the rest included.

▶ ORDERS WITHOUT FIXED PEGGING
If you choose this strategy, CTM plans all orders that are not attached to others by fixed pegging and ignores all those that are. No orders are deleted.

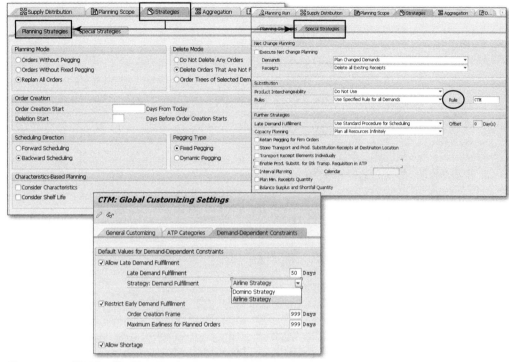

Figure 11.11 CTM Profile: Planning Strategies

▶ RE-PLAN ALL ORDERS

If you choose this strategy, CTM deletes all production orders that are not fixed, along with any corresponding pegging relationships. If an order and its pegging relationship are both fixed, no change will occur. How fixed orders are dealt with depends on whether or not an order and its related orders are in a fixed pegging relationship. Fixed relationships are not touched. Orders in dynamic pegging relationships, on the other hand, are re-planned.

11.2.3 CTM Integration with Global ATP

We can also integrate global ATP for the rule-based product substitution during the CTM run. If rules are defined, we can substitute a similar manufacturing product to fulfil the customer demand. For the configuration of CTM, to define the parameter values, follow the path: IMG • ADVANCED PLANNING AND OPTIMIZATION • SUPPLY CHAIN PLANNING • MULTILEVEL SUPPLY AND DEMAND MATCHING • MAKE SETTINGS FOR RULES-BASED PLANNING. (The resulting screen is shown in Figure 11.12.)

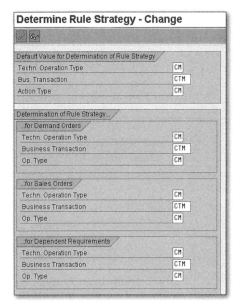

Figure 11.12   CTM Configuration for Rules-Based ATP Check

The master data steps for our business scenario consist of maintaining the global ATP rule maintenance and condition table while maintaining the CTM profile, as shown in Figure 11.11.

Rule Maintenance

The global ATP rule maintenance specifies the business rule for the product substitution, while the condition table connects the product with the rule for the global ATP check. In the CTM profile, we mention rules-based planning for the supply planning run in determining the correct destination location. You can access this step via Transaction /SAPAPO/RBA04. Maintain the rule with a location product substitution (shown in Figure 11.13). Create a user-defined rule, and then under LOCATION PRODUCT SUBST., maintain the primary products and co-products that need to be substituted.

Maintain Rule Condition Table

Access this step via Transaction /SAPCND/AO11 and maintain the rule condition table (shown in Figure 11.14). In the rule condition table, assign the product with the rule created in the prior step.

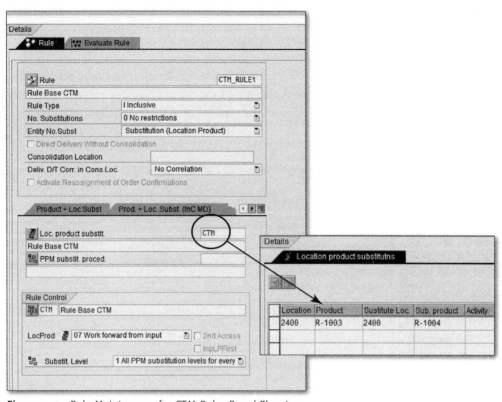

Figure 11.13 Rule Maintenance for CTM Rules-Based Planning

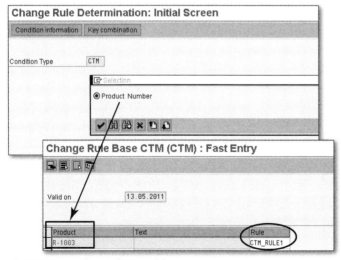

Figure 11.14 Rule Condition Table

Simulate Run

Now that the configuration and the master data are complete, you can start the simulation run. The simulation run provides a good indication that the master data rule is picked. After the rule is picked, the item substitution should also occur for the supply shortage scenario. As Figure 11.15 shows, the simulation run displays the substituted item as a supply element for the primary product demand (requirement).

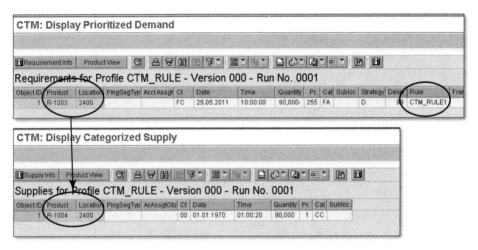

Figure 11.15 CTM Simulation for CTM

11.2.4 CTM Early/Late Demand Fulfilment

The business does not want any demand to be fulfilled late, but allowing lateness allows a demand to be considered even if it can't be satisfied on time so that the customer can be informed how late the demand will be satisfied and to estimate the capacity requirements.

There are settings in CTM global settings, as shown in Figure 11.11, where we can maintain the maximum earliness/lateness for the demand. There is a maximum earliness setting that controls how early a receipt can be created to satisfy a demand. Likewise, there is a maximum lateness setting that controls how late a receipt can be created to satisfy a demand. Allowing maximum earliness enables pre-building of inventory to meet planned shutdowns and inventory policies, which may happen more than a year into the future.

Let's look at a business example for a petrochemical company (case study discussed in Section 11.5) to better understand this concept. Figure 11.16 shows sample data for forecast and production capacity, along with three business scenarios. Based on the maintained earliness/lateness data, the CTM result will vary. If maximum early and late are both maintained at zero days, the Scenario 1 forecast for Month 2 remains unfulfilled. Again, if maximum early is thirty days and late is zero days, the demand in Scenario 2 for Month 2 is fulfilled by Month 2 production capacity. Lastly, if the maximum early is zero days and late is 30 days, the demand in Scenario 3 is fulfilled by Month 3 production capacity.

Demand	Month 1	Month 2	Month 3	Month 4
Forecast		100	100	
Scenario 1		50	100	
Scenario 2	50	50	100	
Scenario 3		50	100	50
Production Capacity	50	50	100	50

Figure 11.16 CTM Earliness/Lateness Example

In the configuration, we can also maintain two strategies for late demand fulfilment:

▶ **Domino strategy**
If the first demand is late to be fulfilled, all the subsequent demands would be fulfilled late.

▶ **Airline strategy**
If a demand can't be met on time, its fulfillment is postponed, and subsequent demants are prioritized and fulfilled before it.

You can perform the configuration by following menu path SPRO • ADVANCED PLANNING AND OPTIMIZATION • SUPPLY CHAIN PLANNING • MULTILEVEL SUPPLY AND DEMAND MATCHING • CAPABLE-TO-MATCH • DEFINE GLOBAL VALUES AND DEFAULT VALUES. Inside the configuration, under the DEMAND-DEPENDENT CONSTRAINTS tab, we select ALLOW LATE DEMAND FULFILLMENT and define the strategy (airline or domino) along with the number of days that late demand fulfilment is allowed.

11.2.5 CTM Profile: Aggregation

CTM supports the aggregating planning concept explained in Chapter 7, Section 7.2. In this way, the detailed supply plan will be aggregated (see Figure 11.17) by running a separate CTM planning run for the production location hierarchy. This hierarchy is created via maintenance of location and product hierarchy.

> **Example**
>
> If all the demand is aggregated at the production plant, once the resource capacity leveled, the plan can be disaggregated to the location product level.

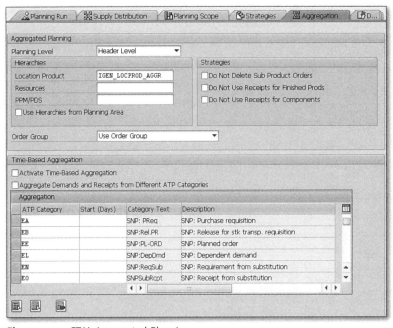

Figure 11.17 CTM Aggregated Planning

11.2.6 CTM Profile: Demand

We define the demand prioritization either by directly inputting the ATP category or using the backorder processing (BOP) sort profile. As Figure 11.18 shows, we can maintain the demand prioritization sequence via configuration path IMG • Advanced Planning and Optimization • Supply Chain Planning • Multilevel

SUPPLY AND DEMAND MATCHING • DEMAND PRIORITIZATION • DEFINE SORT PROFILE. Alternatively, we can include the ATP categories directly in the profile.

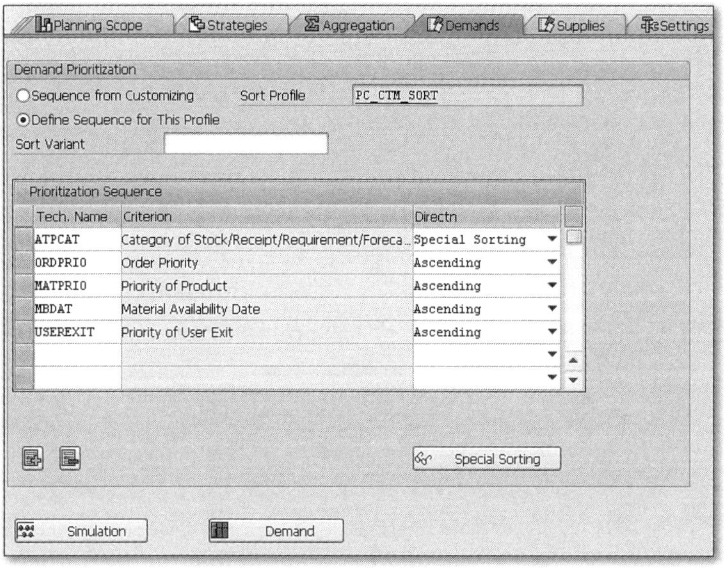

Figure 11.18 CTM Profile: Demand Prioritization

The figure shows the special sorting for the ATP category if we have more than one demand element (for example, sales orders, deliveries, forecasts, stock transfer requirements, etc). The special sorting is also defined in the configuration path IMG • ADVANCED PLANNING AND OPTIMIZATION • SUPPLY CHAIN PLANNING • MULTILEVEL SUPPLY AND DEMAND MATCHING • DEMAND PRIORITIZATION • DEFINE SPECIAL SORTING.

Another available feature is the catalog field USEREXIT, which allows the flexibility for inputting any business-specific logic. For example, the company wants to sequence based on the plant production date and subtract the demand requested date from the transportation lane lead-time to derive the production date. This calculation can be achieved by using function module /SAPAPO/MSDP_MD_SOS_GET to identify the longest lead time sourcing and enhancement APOBO020 using function module EXIT_/SAPAPO/SAPLBOP_SORT_020. The user exit is triggered by adding the field category USEREXIT to the CTM profile, as seen in Figure 11.18. A simulation option is given to see how CTM has sequenced the demand elements per the current definitions in the CTM profile.

11.2.7 CTM Profile: Supplies

In the SUPPLY tab of the CTM profile, we can define how the receipt elements can be grouped and assigned to supply. As Figure 11.19 shows, the business users can define safety stock, target days of supply, and inventory limits. Different supply limits can also be defined for each location, product, or location product combination.

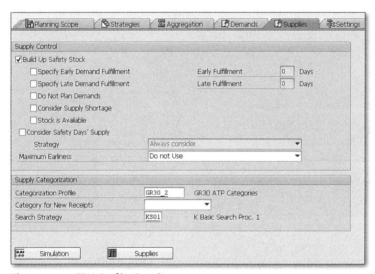

Figure 11.19 CTM Profile: Supplies

Figure 11.20 shows the configuration of the categorization profile (maintained in Transaction /SAPAPO/CTMSCPR), where different supply limits—normal, target, and excess—are classified. In this way, the stock is categorized based on how it will be processed before the planning run. The CTM supply categories are maintained in Transaction /SAPAPO/SUPCAT. Also defined with supply categorization is the search strategy, which defines the order in which the stock categories should be searched.

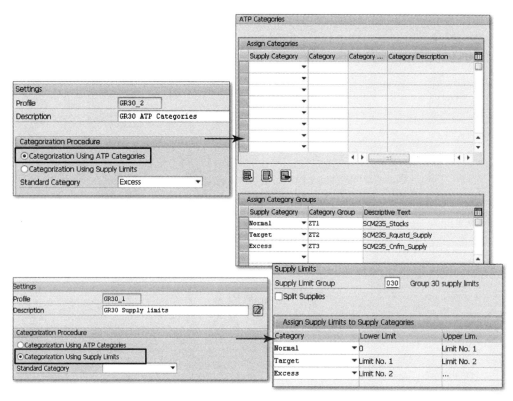

Figure 11.20 CTM Profile: Supply Categorization

11.2.8 CTM Profile: Settings

In the SETTINGS tab, we have three sections: BASIC SETTINGS, MASTER DATA SETTINGS, and TECHNICAL SETTINGS (see Figure 11.21).

▶ In BASIC SETTINGS, define whether the CTM should generate APO-SNP or PP/DS orders or define an alert profile, and whether we should transfer the CTM results to SAP ERP. This allows the business the flexibility to validate the result in SAP APO before publication to the SAP ERP system for execution. If the supply network is complex and there are many warehouses, it is recommended to use the CTM result as APO-SNP (bucket-oriented planning), while if the network is small and the primary focus is on manufacturing the plant, we can select PP/DS (continuous planning).

▶ The MASTER DATA SETTINGS define the different planning parameters that need to be considered or ignored during the CTM planning run.

▶ The TECHNICAL SETTINGS defines via various actions if there are any missing master data. We also define here how the CTM planning run logs need to be written in the database. Since the CTM logs are so large, a routine batch job via report /SAPAPO/OM_REORG_DAILY needs to be periodically set to clear the old logs.

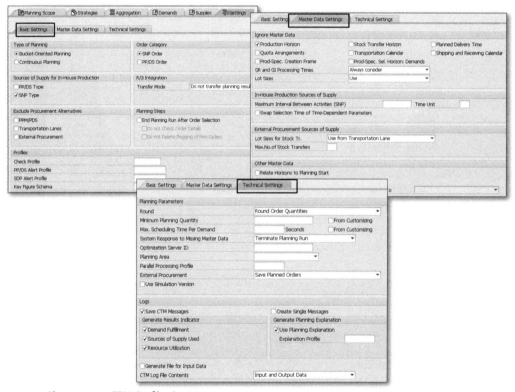

Figure 11.21 CTM Profile: Settings

11.2.9 CTM Supply Distribution

CTM Supply Distribution, also maintained in the CTM profile, provides functionality to move the excess supplies to the target locations even when there are no net requirements from the locations. You can include the supply distribution in the CTM planning by saving the profile as variant during the planning run. The functionality can also be executed separately via Transaction /SAPAPO/CTM10. Master data in the form of outbound quota arrangements needs to be maintained for pushing the un-pegged supplies, for example, from manufacturing locations to distribution centres. The supply distribution functionality has the feature of repositioning your inventory at a better stocking location from where the company can generate sales.

After we've maintained the CTM profile for the planning run, the next activity is to maintain the CTM master data, which we explain next.

11.3 CTM Master Data

CTM requires a set of master data to make sourcing and manufacturing decisions during the planning run. The common set of master data is based on prioritization. We can define priorities in three different master data:

▶ **Location master (Transaction /SAPAPO/LOC3)**
Defined in the GENERAL tab, the location priority can be used during supply shortage situations in which CTM prioritizes which locations need to supplied first. Characteristic LOCPRIO needs to be defined as sort criteria on the demand prioritization.

▶ **Product master (Transaction /SAPAPO/MAT1)**
Similar to location, the product priority can be defined for shortage situations. The priority is defined in the SNP2 tab of the product master. Characteristic MATPRIO needs to be defined as sort criteria on the demand prioritization.

▶ **Transportation lane (Transaction /SAPAPO/TL1)**
The procurement priority (defined in means of transport) in the transportation lane can be used for sourcing decisions. The transportation lane identifies the most economical sourcing location based on this priority where there are no capacity issues. (The highest is zero.) If quota arrangement master data is maintained, it takes more precedence over transportation lane master data. Unlike quota arrangements, priorities do not split the demands in pre-defined percentages, but rather work in sequential search of satisfying demand.

Besides priorities, other master data planning parameters (for example, the lot size) are also used by the CTM run. Quota arrangement (explained in Chapter 4, Section 4.7.7) and production data structures (explained in Chapter 4, Section 4.7.5) are also used in the CTM planning run. The CTM time stream calendar can be maintained in Transaction /SAPAPO/CTMTSTR by specifying the period type.

Additionally, from SAP SCM 7.0 Enhancement Pack 1, we can perform aggregated planning in the CTM run. The functionality provides automatic aggregation in the CTM run. As Figure 11.22 shows, we can maintain the aggregated planning settings in the CTM profile under the AGGREGATION tab. In this tab, we select the planning run applicable for aggregated planning and maintain the hierarchy master data (Resource, PPM/PDS, and Location Product). Also shown in the figure is report /SAPAPO/CTMDISAGGR, which displays the CTM planning result disaggregated from the header product level to the detailed SKU level.

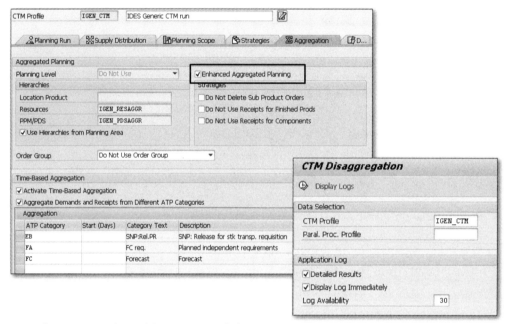

Figure 11.22 Enhanced CTM Aggregated Planning

11.4 CTM Planning Run

The steps for the CTM planning run are performed as follows (see Figure 11.23):

❶ **Maintain CTM planning parameters**
The profile can be maintained in Transaction /SAPAPO/CTM. The CTM profile is where all the planning parameters reside for the CTM run. This includes defining the planning version and horizon, CTM calendar timestream, demand prioritization, and supply categorization.

❷ **Define planning scope**

The planning scope is also defined within Transaction /SAPAPO/CTM. The master data selection is added as part of the planning scope in the CTM profile.

❸ **Execute CTM planning run**

The CTM planning run is next interactively started from Transaction /SAPAPO/CTM or in the background from Transaction /SAPAPO/CTMB. The demand elements are sorted based on demand prioritization. The supply elements are searched next to match (pegging) with the demand elements.

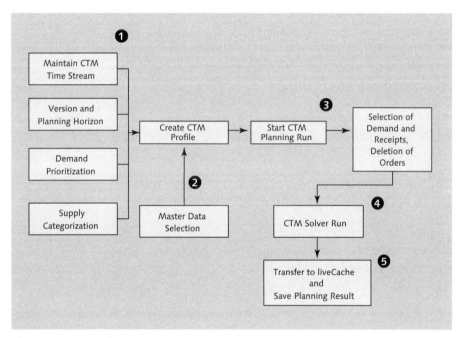

Figure 11.23 CTM Planning Run Steps

❹ **CTM solver run**

The solver performs a rule-based, cross-plant constraint planning, taking into account both material and capacity constraint in the network. CTM uses an order-based planning method, which allows the system to peg the orders created with the individual demand fulfilled. The CTM solver run is logged in Transaction /SAPAPO/OPT11.

❺ **Transfer results to SAP liveCache and write application logs**

The CTM planning results are transferred back to SAP liveCache, where orders are created and deleted. A result log is also written, showing all the earlier steps performed during the planning run. The planning result is saved in SAP live-Cache and can be analyzed in the PP/DS product view, in the graphic planning board, in the interactive APO-SNP planning book or in the Supply Chain Viewer. The CTM planning run application log is written in Transaction /SAPAPO/CTMAPLOG.

11.5 CTM Case Study

This section provides a case study of a petrochemical company using CTM for its supply and distribution planning process. The petrochemical supply chain is complex. Some of the industry characteristics are as follows:

▶ The industry is highly asset intensive.

▶ The supply chain can account for up to 70% of overall cost.

▶ Highly specialized business processes encourage fragmentation.

▶ The industry is typically non-linear in nature.

▶ Supply chain optimization at a strategic and operational level is seen as a competitive advantage in the industry.

The supply chain consists of upstream and downstream activities. The upstream activities focus on exploration, production, trading, and transport of feed stock to the refineries, while the downstream activities focus on the distribution and marketing of all the products coming out of the refined feed stock.

Figure 11.24 provides a glimpse of the supply chain distributed based on business activities. Due to material and capacity constraints on the crude oil, the company uses CTM to manage the demand prioritization with the available crude oil supply.

The other reasons for the company to use CTM are to prioritize its customer base and because CTM provides the opportunity to prioritize its production of products that generate high sales and revenue growth. CTM provides complete, multi-level pegging for the organization to keep track of its order fulfilment performance.

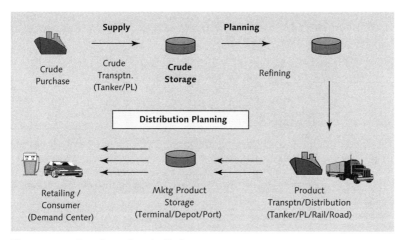

Figure 11.24 Petroleum Supply Chain

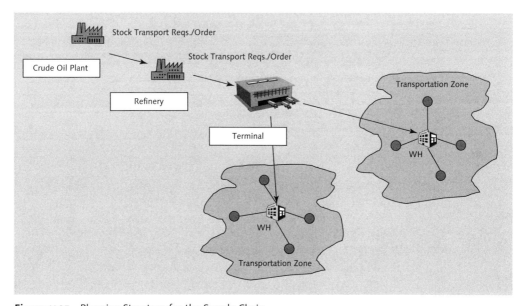

Figure 11.25 Planning Structure for the Supply Chain

As Figure 11.25 shows, the supply chain planning structure for the company consists of multi-tier planning. The company performs planning in the following logical business process steps:

1. The company clusters its customers based on transportation zone. The transportation zone represents a virtual grouping of customers who are all served by

specific warehouses. The sales orders from customers are captured in these warehouses and form the basis for forecasting.

2. The warehouses are then internally replenished from terminals based on the market demand that uses a market pull strategy.

3. The terminal receives the chemical products from the refinery and stores the majority of downstream feed stock.

4. The refinery is where the bulk and base oil are produced out of crude oil. It balances the product mix with bulk oil stock availability.

5. The crude oil plant does the exploration and pumps the available crude oil stock to the refineries.

The demand forecast and sales orders are placed in the warehouse, defined by transportation zones. The first CTM run searches for available inventory at the warehouse or the terminal, which are the replenishing points for the warehouse. If no inventory is found, the next CTM run places the demand at the refineries. The demand element is matched with the production plan of the bulk product. The crude oil exploration plant performs push production of the crude oil into the refinery. The refinery is where various balancing of demand and supply is performed.

11.6   Summary

CTM executes multi-level, finite-based planning for your supply chain. By setting up business priorities, the planner can influence the sequence of demand and selection of sourcing opportunities.

An understanding of fixed pegging is required to evaluate CTM planning results. Besides planning on priorities, CTM also performs order-based planning to explode the bill of material at manufacturing locations to peg the components with finished goods. Overall, CTM meets the objective of constrained planning in both the distribution network and production planning process.

The next chapter focuses on inventory planning and optimization in SAP APO and explains a framework for designing inventory models in SAP APO.

Here we explain how inventory modeling can be performed in SAP APO to optimize your supply chain, and introduce methodology and tools for effective management.

12 Inventory Planning and Optimization with SAP APO and SAP ERP

Before we start our discussion on planning and optimization, let's begin with the definition of *inventory*: it's the material stored in warehouses that's waiting to be processed or in transit. It can be represented as a flow into the system, remaining for a specific time and then flowing out. The *inventory level* is defined as the difference between the inventory flowing relative rate in and flowing relative rate out of a facility, as shown in Figure 12.1. The inventory can be either manufactured or procured from the supplier and usually has a lead time from planning to physical stock availability. Once in stock, the system calls it *inventory on hand*. In business situations when sales orders are greater than the inventory (shortages), there is the possibility of taking customer orders as backorders to be fulfilled at a later time. If the company policy is not to take any backorders, then these become lost sales. Variability and uncertainty factors also need to be taken into account in inventory system design.

Inventory planning and optimization is critical for any business to ensure that the products are shelved in the right place at the right time. Inventory planning is defined as a calculation of optimal quantity at the correct ordering time, taking into account supply chain constraints. Inventory optimization involves balancing the inventory level to fulfill customer orders, while at the same time keeping the financial interest on inventory holding costs low. Businesses are constantly challenged with product shortages or surpluses in the supply chain while maintaining the balance with the customer service level. Some of the symptoms of poor inventory planning that companies might encounter include low service levels, excessively slow moving inventory, high expedite costs, manual planning processes, and a general lack of faith in the plan. Furthermore, these types of planning processes do not scale well with growing SKU counts, extended sourcing models, and longer lead times.

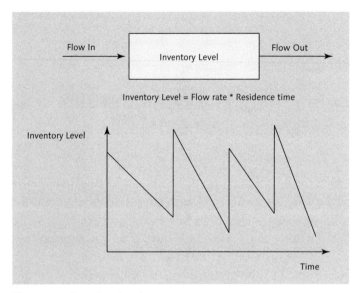

Figure 12.1 Inventory Level

To counter these potential problems, we want to perform inventory planning and optimization in SAP ERP and SAP SCM with the objective of providing inventory models with calculated time-phase inventory plans. Proper inventory planning helps to reduce supply chain variability and reduces any unwanted expediting costs in production and transportation. Unlike with SAP ERP, the benefits of using inventory optimization in SAP APO include precise mathematical calculations to take the guessing out of planning materials stock. SAP APO provides basic and advanced inventory methods with the option of time-dependent safety stock maintenance. This allows the business to adjust its inventory levels during the course of the year.

As shown in the mind map for this chapter (see Figure 12.2) we will be discussing inventory optimization with SAP APO and SAP ERP. The chapter commences with discussion on various inventory optimization concepts and then deep dives into the inventory analysis methodology. The chapter then discusses on how we design efficient inventory control system using SAP ERP and SAP APO.

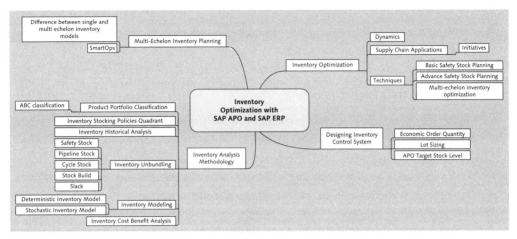

Figure 12.2 Learning Points for the Chapter (Mind Map)

We'll continue to use ABC Technology to show you how to build an inventory analysis methodology for setting up correct inventory levels at network locations. We'll explain different inventory models and provide techniques and tools that you can use to identify how much inventory needs to be ordered, and identify the trigger points when the inventory needs to be procured. We'll also briefly introduce the multi-echelon concept and how SAP partner programs can help you with inventory optimization.

12.1 Inventory Optimization

Inventory optimization means balancing a company's inventory to meet customer demand. Using a range of tools and techniques, inventory optimization balances a company's inventory level with the customer service level to reach the overall objective of a company's working capital reduction. Besides inventory reduction, the optimization also offers opportunities in various business scenarios in which the company is tasked to implement a postponement strategy, increase service levels without increasing inventory, adjust inventory levels per product family, consolidate manufacturing or distribution operations, or source products from overseas with high lead-time. The benefits of inventory optimization include a reduction in inventory, customer satisfaction, fewer stockout situations, improved sales, and reduced obsolescence inventory.

In the following sections, we'll go over some of the applications that inventory optimization can be applied to. First, however, we'll see the dynamics of inventory optimization working in a system.

12.1.1 Dynamics

Every company interested in pursuing inventory optimization needs to understand the market dynamics' affect on inventory optimization. To avoid stock out situations, most companies hold inventories at a level much higher than the required optimal level. This stock holding region is shown in Figure 12.3. By slowly moving inventory to the optimal stock curve, the opportunities lie not only in the inventory reduction, but also in improvement in the customer service level. Here, an inventory turn reduction of five can improve the service level from 95% to 97% while keeping the inventory at optimal level. Industry benchmark figures show a reduction of 5–10% of inventory, which translates to 1–2% improvement in the customer service level. This brings us to the question: If the opportunities are there, why are many companies not yielding these benefits?

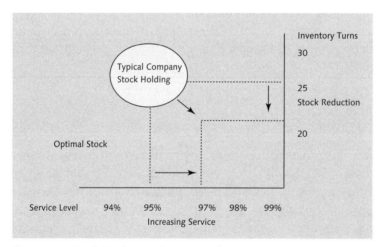

Figure 12.3 Stock Level versus Service Level

There are many reasons why companies have not been able to move in this direction. The primary reason is the uncertainty in demand and supply situations not factored into the inventory level calculation. Another factor is the failure to unbundle the inventory into different types (for example, safety stock, cycle stock, pre-build stock).

Let's look at an example in which ABC Technology maintains the same inventory method in the form of safety days' supply across all its product groups (desktops, laptops, and monitors). This approach doesn't guarantee any protection to the company, as different products have different sales patterns. As you can see in Figure 12.4, since the inventory holding patterns are all different across product groups or products, there will be critical stock out situations and obsolescence risks with some products holding high inventory levels.

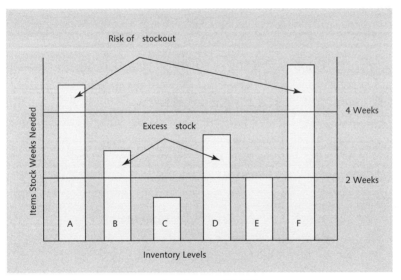

Figure 12.4 Common Inventory Level across All SKUs

Traditionally, ABC Technology has been using an SAP ERP system that has user-defined fields for inventory parameters. In other words, the SAP ERP system is relying on users to specify the safety stock, reorder points, and minimums and maximums.

Inventory optimization is a better practice because it has mathematical algorithms to plan a service-level goal for each SKU. SAP APO software takes into account the service-level goals, demand volatility, and lead-time variability for each specific SKU to optimize the inventory levels. The output of this planning is an enhanced inventory planning process that reduces excess inventory and improves the service-level performance for SKUs with stockout occurrences. This scientific approach to inventory planning, taking into account the demand and supply volatilities, product lead time, and service level definition, has produced significant benefits. Companies often claim a 15–30% reduction in inventory with a 10–25% increase in service level within the first year.

12.1.2 Supply Chain Applications

You can apply inventory optimization in many application areas in the supply chain. Some of the techniques and initiatives that ABC Technology is planning to deploy across the supply network in an effort to reduce inventory are as follows:

▸ **Transportation network**
Using correct transportation modes and cost structures, ABC Technology is able to keep optimal safety stock in its warehouse to fulfill customer orders. ABC Technology, for its distribution of customer orders, runs nightly line-hauls to replenish consolidated orders and requirements across the network, keeping its inventory lean at branch distribution centers. Another example is direct delivery from the ABC Technology manufacturing center or the supplier to the end customers.

▸ **Lot size optimization**
By synchronizing the use of the common lot size parameters in planning, ABC Technology's production batch run can be the same as the transportation shipment quantities. The lot size needs to be defined per the ordering or producing batch lot size to gain synergy in stock holding.

▸ **Common component planning**
Many finished goods require the same components for manufacturing or assembly. By consolidating the component planning, ABC Technology can negotiate better sourcing contracts and plan better inventory.

▸ **Postponement**
The concept of postponement revolves around delaying the final production closest to the true customer demand. This avoids any excessive building of inventory where the sales are unpredictable. This strategy is widely used by ABC Technology to combine the common components used in different product

groups. The assembly of the finished goods is only done based on different customer sales orders with the use of these common components.

▶ **Risk pooling**[1]

Risk pooling suggests that demand variability is reduced if the company aggregates demand across locations because as demand is aggregated across different locations, it becomes more likely that high demand from one customer will be offset by low demand from another. This reduction in variability allows a decrease in safety stock and therefore reduces average inventory. For ABC Technology, working in the centralized distribution system, the warehouse serves all customers, which leads to a reduction in variability measured by either the standard deviation or the coefficient of variation. The critical points of ABC Technology's risk pooling strategy are:

   ▶ Centralized inventory saves safety stock and average inventory in the system.

   ▶ When market demands are negatively correlated, the higher the coefficient of variation, the greater the benefit obtained from centralized systems—that is, the greater the benefit from risk pooling.

▶ **Sourcing policies**

With better reviews of strategic policies, ABC Technology looks at various sourcing options with lower costs and supply flexibility. Negotiating with a supplier at the strategic level helps ABC Technology reduce its annual inventory costs.

▶ **Manufacturing batch run**

ABC Technology performs planning with the correct inventory lot size, which ensures that the manufacturing resources are running at the capacity required to gain economies of scale.

Implementing the Initiatives

To implement these initiatives, ABC Technology first needs to define an inventory policy. Inventory policies help companies to define *when to order, how many to order,* and *from what source.* Table 12.1 outlines the elements for developing an inventory policy. While developing the policies, the company needs to describe the demand, lead time, product volume, planning horizon, costs, and customer service level per their business operating model.

---

1   Simchi-Levi, D, P. Kaminsky, and E. Simchi-Levi. *Designing and Managing the Supply Chain* (2nd Edition). (New York, NY: McGraw-Hill, 2002)

Key Elements	Driving Factors

Demand	▶ Deterministic
	▶ Random
	   ▶ Forecasting techniques (exponential smoothing, trend, and trend and seasonality)
	   ▶ Variability

Lead time	▶ Deterministic ▶ Random (distribution) ▶ Supplier reliability
Number of products in warehouse	▶ Constraints on space ▶ Constraints on number of orders per year
Planning horizon	▶ One period ▶ Infinite
Costs	▶ Ordering (transportation, information technology, and stocking) ▶ Setup (in a production system) ▶ Holding (taxes and insurance, maintenance, obsolescence)
Customer service level	Different service levels (90%, 95%, 99%, etc.)

Table 12.1 Driving Factors for Formulating Inventory Policy in Company

12.1.3 Techniques

SAP APO offers different tools and techniques for inventory planning in the area of inventory optimization. Depending on the business requirements and product characteristics, different inventory methods can be used to define ABC Technology's inventory targets. The techniques can be broadly classified into three groups:

▶ **Basic safety stock planning**
Defined for single product and locations, the safety stock calculations are driven by parameters (i.e., fixed safety stock quantity and days of supply) entered by business users in either SAP ERP or SAP APO master data. The safety stock planning is integrated in the APO-SNP planning run, and values can be either static or time dependent.

▶ **Advanced safety stock planning**
This statistical method uses demand variability, supplier lead time variability, and service level for calculating the time-dependent safety stock. This method considers one location at a time and is available in SAP APO.

▶ **Multi-echelon inventory optimization** (offered as an SAP Partner Product from SmartOps, *www.smartops.com*)
The goal of the algorithm here is to balance the inventory level and customer service. The technique plans the complete network simultaneously (multiple DC layers and manufacturing sites) to minimize the total inventory cost. The application uses non-linear optimization and stochastic algorithm techniques and supports the risk pooling concept. We'll discuss this topic in more detail in Section 12.4.

We'll now move on to show you how ABC Technology can perform inventory analysis to build an initiatives roadmap for inventory optimization.

12.2 Inventory Analysis Methodology

Inventory analysis is important for ABC Technology to formulate inventory strategies according to product characteristics. In this section, we define a methodology to perform inventory analysis across the company's product portfolio. Figure 12.5 provides a framework wherein each product or product group is decomposed to study its historical pattern, and inventory is un-bundled to provide its fit into the inventory strategy quadrant and potential inventory models in SAP APO.

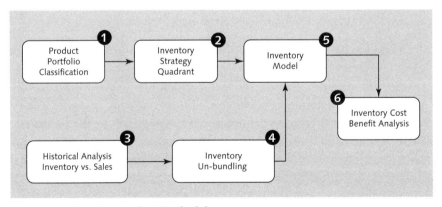

Figure 12.5 Inventory Analysis Methodology

At the end of this methodology, an inventory cost benefit analysis is performed to evaluate the various stock norms proposed for the inventory models. The cost of inventory holding is benchmarked with the historical sales orders.

> **Note**
>
> Since SAP ERP performs the inventory execution, some of the activities reports need to be pulled from the SAP ERP system via standard transactions or reports.

The overall goals of performing the inventory analysis to do the following:

▶ Formulate an inventory model that has less demand and supply variability

▶ Improve the company's inventory turnover (inventory turnover = cost of goods sold (COGS)/average inventory at value)

▶ Ensure stock availability to avoid any stock out situations and ensure the optimal inventory level

▶ Analyze dead stock in inventory for reduction opportunities

Now, let's look at the six steps that are shown in Figure 12.5 for performing inventory analysis.

12.2.1 Product Portfolio Classification (ABC Analysis)

The first step for inventory analysis is to perform product portfolio classification, which is also known as *ABC analysis*. ABC analysis helps us to put emphasis on "where the value is." By focusing efforts on higher value inventory, ABC Technology can assign proper resources to attain the optimum inventory levels, reduce inventory costs, and increase customer satisfaction.

When ABC analysis is applied to an inventory situation, it highlights the importance of finished goods items and the level of controls placed on a specific product. By dividing a company's inventory into different classifications—A, B, C—the inventory manager can focus on the products that account for the majority of the inventory. The definition of ABC materials is defined by the importance of the product to finance (margin) and sales (sales hits). Based on the ABC classification, the material's inventory impact is seen on the company's inventory cost. The adaptation of Pareto's Law of the vital few and trivial many follows a pattern:

- ▶ **A:** Inventory accounts for about 20% of the items and 80% of the dollar usage.

- ▶ **B:** Inventory accounts for about 30% of the items and 15% of the dollar usage.

- ▶ **C:** Inventory accounts for about 50% of the items and 5% of the dollar usage.

These defined percentages are approximate and will vary from company to company. Normally the ABC classifications are based upon annual dollar usage, but other criteria can be used, such as transaction usage, unit cost, or lead times. Figure 12.6 shows that 20% of ABC Technology's products generate 80% of their overall revenue.

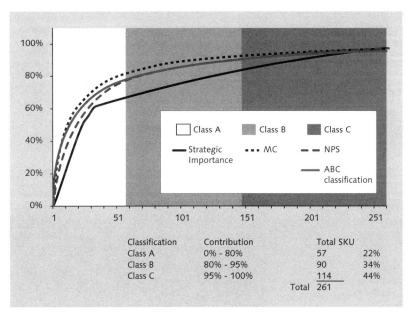

Figure 12.6 ABC Classification for Product Portfolio

You can perform ABC analysis in SAP ERP via menu path INFORMATION SYSTEMS • LOGISTICS • INVENTORY MANAGEMENT • MATERIAL • ABC ANALYSIS, and then select Transaction MC40 (Total Analysis) or MC41 (Ranking List). Transaction MC40 is based on the historical consumption, while Transaction MC41 is based on future requirements.

While running the report (see Figure 12.7), we can define the percentage of the usage to generate a list of the products that are consumed in high volume and quantities. The ABC analysis result can also be viewed using the cumulative frequency curve. This curve can be shown for absolute values or percentages. The cumulative frequency curve shows information about the relative concentration of materials. Displayed on the x-axis are the number of materials (or the number of materials in percentages), and on the y-axis are the cumulated usage/requirements values (or values in percentages). The graph provides a good overview of how great a proportion of the total usage value/total requirements value is concentrated in just a few materials.

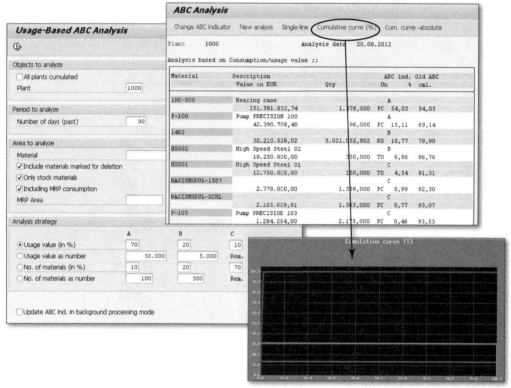

Figure 12.7 ABC Inventory Analysis Report in SAP ERP

Inventory Stock Policies for ABC Classification

The stocking policy differentiates between key product models (high volume/high margin or low margin) and settings of the product service levels. The combination of high/low volume and margin is isolated by using the Pareto Principle, or the 80/20 rule.[2] Thus, high volume would mean that the product comprises 80%

---

2 Juran, J. M and J. Defeo. *Juran's Quality Control Handbook* (6th Edition). (New York, NY: McGraw-Hill, 2010)

of the total volume for profit margin, while the rest of the products fall into the low category. Similarly, high margin products comprise 80% of the total integral income from operations (IFO) generated (in absolute terms), while the rest of the products fall into the low margin category. The combination of high/low volume and high/low margin is then mapped into the inventory stocking policies quadrant, as explained in the next sub-section.

12.2.2 Inventory Stocking Policies Quadrant

Based on the ABC analysis, we can identify an inventory stocking policies quadrant. The quadrant will help ABC Technology to cluster its products for strategic direction on inventory policies. In the representation, the *y*-axis is the volume and the *x*-axis the margin. As shown in Figure 12.8, we can break down the volume and margin further into high/low and form four quadrants.

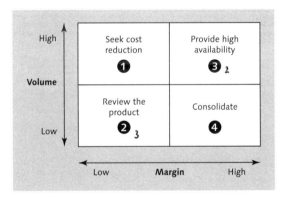

Figure 12.8 Stocking Policies

Next, we can define different strategies for these four quadrants:

► **Quadrant ❶: Seek cost reduction**
As these products have high volume, they are in frequent demand. However, they are also low in profit contribution, and the priority should be to re-examine the costs to see if there is any scope for enhancing the margin.

► **Quadrant ❷: Provide high availability**
These products are frequently demanded and more profitable than the rest. We should provide the highest level of service on these items (by increasing the

customer service level to 98–99% to adjust the stock norm), thus ensuring the highest availability.

▶ **Quadrant ❸: Review the products**
Products in this category should be regularly appraised and maybe even deleted (unless they are strategic) from the range, as they do not contribute to profits and are slow movers. To calculate the stock norm, the customer service level for this category can be set to a minimum.

▶ **Quadrant ❹: Consolidate**
As these products are highly profitable and sell only low volumes, we should not ship them in container loads or include them in direct shipments from the factory, but rather consolidate them with other items and ship from a local warehouse.

	Customer Service Level (Average Percentage Based on Quadrant)	Sales Plan Reliability (Average Percentage Based on Quadrant)	Supply Plan Reliability (Average Percentage Based on Quadrant)	Planning Policy	Local Consolidation
Quadrant ❶: Seek Cost Reduction	95%	95%	95%	Monthly	Local warehouse
Quadrant ❷: Provide High Availability	99%	95%	95%	Weekly	Local warehouse
Quadrant ❸: Review the Product	90%	95%	95%	Monthly	Factory
Quadrant ❹: Consolidate	98%	95%	95%	Monthly	Local warehouse

Table 12.2 Planning Policies Based on Product Characteristics

The business planner can collaborate with the product manager to identify the different planning parameters and policies. Table 12.2 shows an example in which, based on product characteristics, the four quadrants are defined with different service levels and planning frequencies.

The next exercise is to understand the inventory historical pattern compared with the actual sales.

12.2.3 Inventory Historical Analysis

By studying its historical inventory pattern, ABC Technology can identify whether it's holding high or low inventory levels. The study is primarily done by mapping the historical inventory level with the actual sales. The company can also map the historical sales, stocks, stock policies, and actual stock cover to better understand the actual unused buffers or risk situations.

We'll now discuss a few different types of reports that you can use to monitor your stock during this step.

Perform Inventory Historical Analysis

The inventory historical analysis can be performed in SAP ERP via menu path LOGISTICS • LOGISTICS CONTROLLING • LOGISTICS INFORMATION SYSTEMS • STANDARD ANALYSES • STOCKS • DOCUMENT EVALUATIONS, and then select Transaction MC40 (Total Analysis) or MC42 (Coverage/Usage). Transaction MC42 is based on historical usage, while Transaction MC43 is based on future requirements.

As you can see in Figure 12.9, we might have a situation when the company is holding excessive inventory levels; we now have opportunities to reduce the total inventory to save money and space.

On the other hand, we might have a situation like Figure 12.10 shows, when the inventory level is not sufficient and the company experiences various stock out situations. In this scenario, the company would like to increase its inventory holding to avoid stock out situations.

The standard SAP report *range of coverage* (Transaction MC42) provides stock information in relation to the demand. This is rather a key figure that is calculated by the system based on requirements and stock. It provides information on how the stock evolution is seen for specific average daily requirements. It is calculated as *current stock/average usage/day*.

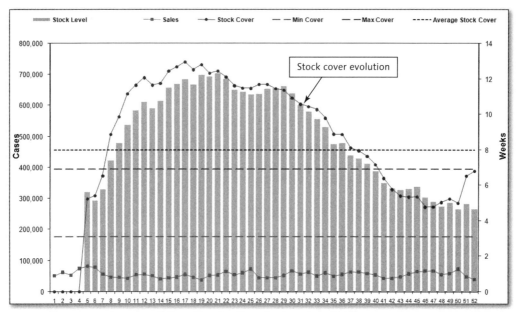

Figure 12.9 Inventory Pattern Showing Excessive Inventory Holding

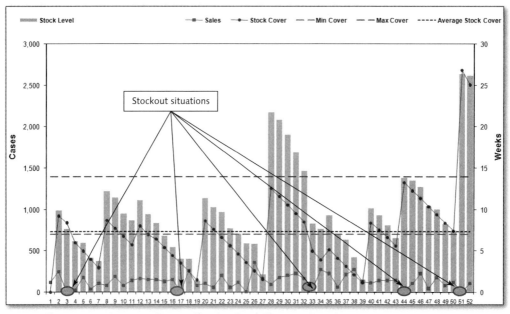

Figure 12.10 Inventory Pattern Showing Stock Shortage Situations

Figure 12.11 shows how the report can be generated by defining the date range in the report selection screen and selecting the STOCK LEVEL in the DETAILED DISPLAY option in SAP ERP, which displays the average inventory coverage over a period of time. By reviewing the graphical display for the top materials, we will get an indication of whether the company is holding inventory at the correct level.

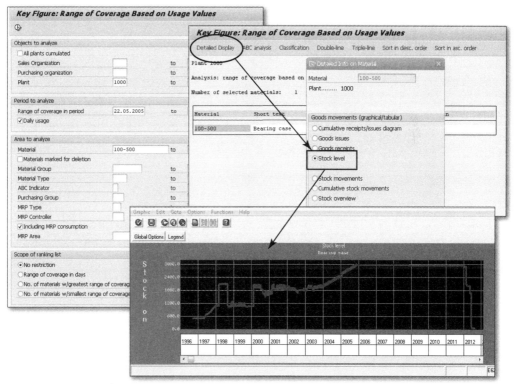

Figure 12.11   Range of Coverage

The other reports available in SAP ERP that are important for inventory analysis are INVENTORY TURNOVER and DEAD STOCK.

Inventory Turnover

The inventory turnover report tells us how the average inventory is consumed and calculated as a ratio of average cumulative usage to average stock level. The inventory turnover report can be performed in SAP ERP via menu path LOGISTICS • LOGISTICS CONTROLLING • LOGISTICS INFORMATION SYSTEMS • STANDARD ANALYSES •

STOCKS • DOCUMENT EVALUATIONS, and then select Transaction MC44. Figure 12.12 shows the inventory turnover calculation in SAP ERP.

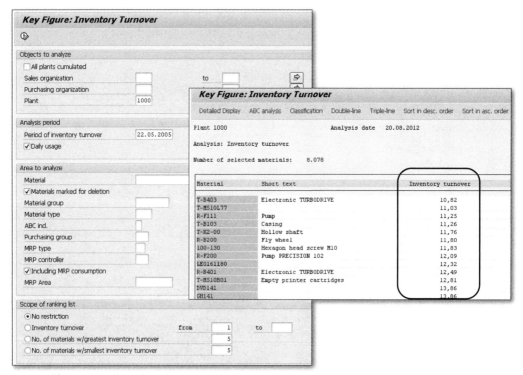

Figure 12.12 Inventory Turnover

The *inventory turnover ratio* is a common measure of the firm's operational efficiency in the management of its assets. Minimizing inventory holdings reduces overhead costs and, hence, improves the profitability performance of the enterprise. Ideally, the inventory turnover ratio would be calculated as units sold divided by units on hand. This ratio should be compared against industry averages. A low turnover implies poor sales and, therefore, excess inventory. A high ratio implies either strong sales or ineffective buying.

> **Note**
>
> Transaction MC46 in SAP ERP identifies the slow-moving items that identify the last period of consumption for each material.

Dead Stock

Another inventory measurement is *dead stock,* which is defined by the inventory level that is being consumed, but stock level never dips below a certain level of inventory. The dead stock report can be performed in SAP ERP via menu path LOGISTICS • LOGISTICS CONTROLLING • LOGISTICS INFORMATION SYSTEMS • STANDARD ANALYSES • STOCKS • DOCUMENT EVALUATIONS, and then select Transaction MC50. Figure 12.13 shows the SAP ERP dead stock report, which allows business users to review the products for which inventory can be reduced.

Key Figure: Dead Stock				

Detailed Display   ABC analysis   Classification   Double-line   Triple-line   Sort in desc. order   Sort in asc. order

```
Plant 1000                          Analysis date   22.08.2012

Analysis: Dead stock

Number of selected materials:    8.084

Dead stock value      1.550.730.664,59  EUR
```

Material	Short text	Dead stock value	%	cum.%
1310	Wood Set # 20	1.000.000.000,00 EUR	64,49 %	64,49 %
GTS-14001	Fire fighting vehicle	115.184.700,00 EUR	7,43 %	71,91 %
1316	Welding Set	24.000.000,00 EUR	1,55 %	73,46 %
1315	Steel Rail 140 Lb/Yd 60'	8.000.000,00 EUR	0,52 %	73,98 %
1319	Standard Joint Bar 136 Lb/Yd	8.000.000,00 EUR	0,52 %	74,49 %
P-100	Pump PRECISION 100	7.065.118,08 EUR	0,46 %	74,95 %
100-500	Bearing case	6.160.074,48 EUR	0,40 %	75,35 %
T-FUC01	Flatscreen MS 1460 P	4.044.200,00 EUR	0,26 %	75,61 %

Figure 12.13 Dead Stock Report

12.2.4 Inventory Un-Bundling

The next step is to decompose the inventory in the SAP SCM system into different categories to highlight what quality of inventory the company is holding. The information source may be available as different key figures in the SAP APO planning book or may need further analysis. The main categories of inventory are shown in Figure 12.14, where we can un-bundle inventory into the following:

▸ **Safety stock**
Inventory kept on hand to allow for the uncertainty of demand and supply in the short term. The level of safety stock is controllable in the sense that this investment is directly related to the desired level of customer service (that is, how often customer demand is met from stock).

▸ **Pipeline stock**
Inventory that is in transit or on quality inspection. This gives us a picture of the product lead time and how much inventory remains on the road or water at any given time.

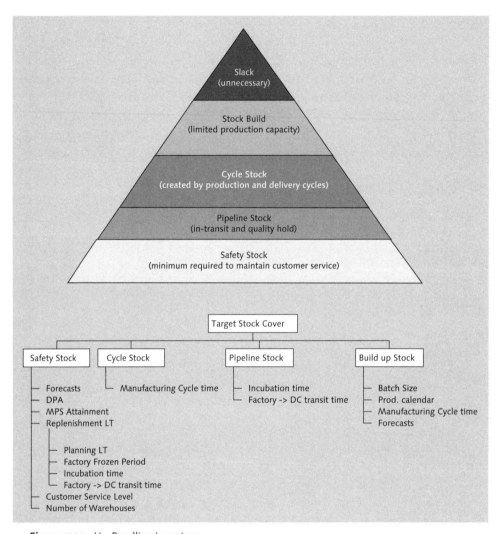

Figure 12.14 Un-Bundling Inventory

▶ **Cycle stock**

Cycle inventories result from an attempt to produce or source in batches rather than one unit at a time. The amount of cycle stock depends on how frequently orders are placed. This can be determined by senior management, which can specify the desired trade-off between the cost of ordering and the cost of having cycle stock on hand.

582

► **Stock build**

Inventory build-up in order to deal with any sales and marketing promotional event (Fourth of July, summer sales, promotions, strikes, etc.) during which the rate of supply is likely to be lower than the rate of demand. This inventory is also held to combat any capacity issues leading to the peak sales season.

► **Slack**

This inventory is primarily dead stock and stock idling without any consumption.

Figure 12.15 shows a further graphical representation of the additional manufacturing of goods that serve as pre-build inventory. This pre-build inventory is then consumed by the sales in the subsequent periods. A typical inventory consumption graph is shown in the lower end of Figure 12.15, which shows the safety stock as the minimum stock level and cycle stock based on the replenishment cycle.

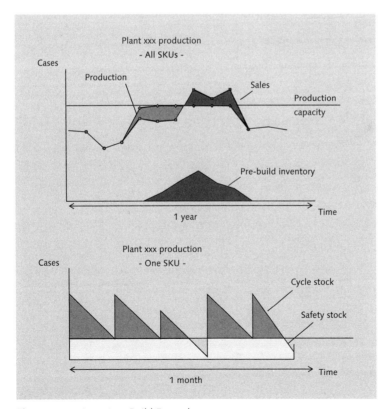

Figure 12.15 Inventory Build Example

Table 12.3 lists the inventory drivers for different types of inventories.

Inventory Element	Key Drivers
Manufacturing stocks	▸ Supplier reliability ▸ Manufacturing processes ▸ Reliability and quality of output
Cycle stocks	▸ Manufacturing and shipping economics ▸ Minimum order sizes throughout supply chain
Safety stocks	▸ Demand variability ▸ Forecasting inaccuracy ▸ Delay in receiving data ▸ Lead time to re-order ▸ Service level required (driven by cost of service failure) ▸ Supply variability
Pipeline stocks	▸ Transport times ▸ Transport costs (which preclude some modes of transport)

Table 12.3 Drivers for Inventory

Let's look at some of the calculations that can be derived by calculating in the APO-SNP planning book:

▸ The pipeline stock can be calculated by adding the quality release time and average transit time. The average lead time can be calculated based on the last x number of goods receipt.

▸ The safety stock can be calculated based on different safety stock methods identified (basic and advanced).

▸ The cycle stock can be calculated based on the minimum lot size calculated either by economical order quantity (EOQ) lot size or production batch size. The maximum of the production cycle and batch lot size is taken into the cycle stock calculation.

12.2.5 Inventory Modeling

The concept of *inventory modeling* is to provide a mathematical equation or formula for the firm to determine economic order quantity and frequency of ordering products to ensure that goods are flowing to the customer without any delay. There are different industry inventory models available, which we will discuss next. We'll also provide an example of SAP APO safety stock supporting the concept. The selection of the inventory model is done based on business requirements.

The Deterministic Inventory Model

The inventory pattern in this method is relatively constant and stable. The inventory is withdrawn from the warehouse at an even rate and lot size. The model (see Figure 12.16) is good for the items that have a fast-moving, stable demand pattern (no trend, seasonality, or promotions) and a stable lead time. We can model this using the SAP APO basic safety stock planning, which takes the lot size and lead time parameters into account during the calculation.

> **Note**
>
> SAP APO manual static safety stock planning methods, such as safety days or safety stock, will support this inventory, which was introduced earlier in Chapter 6, Section 6.1.1.

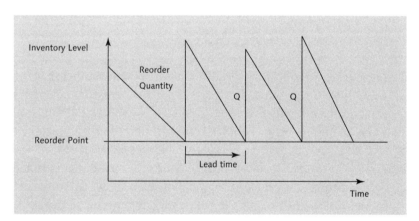

Figure 12.16 Deterministic Inventory Model

Stochastic Inventory Model

This inventory model balances demand and supply, taking into consideration a certain amount of uncertainty. Two examples for the demand stochastic model are the reorder point and reorder quantity function. The model assumes that the inventory level is observed at all times. When the inventory level declines to a specified reorder point, an order is placed for the lot size. The order arrives to replenish the inventory after a lead time. Figure 12.17 shows an example in which the new inventory is ordered once existing inventory reaches the reorder point and then, based on the lead time, the new inventory will be received at later dates. This concept can be supported by manual, time-dependent safety stock planning methods, as explained earlier in Chapter 6, Section 6.1.2.

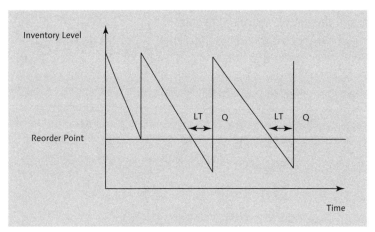

Figure 12.17   Inventory Model Using Reorder Point Lot Size Policy

Another stochastic inventory model is to use the inventory position rather than the inventory level as an indicator, as shown in Figure 12.18. The inventory position is the inventory level plus the quantity on order (comparable with SAP ERP function "Additional External Requirements in Reorder Point Planning" in Customizing of MRP type VB). In the earlier method, the inventory level crosses the reorder point at the same time as the inventory position, and the same order pattern is obtained using either measure. Using the inventory position, however, allows two orders to be placed in quick succession, thus keeping the inventory under control. Using the inventory position in this manner allows us to drop the requirement that the lot size be very much greater than the average demand during the lead time. This method is also supported by the SAP APO advanced safety stock method using demand and supply variability. The safety stock was explained in Chapter 6, Section 6.1.3.

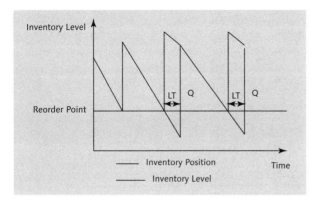

Figure 12.18 Inventory Position Model

You can also use the *periodic review policy,* in which the inventory level is only observed at specific intervals. As Figure 12.19 shows, the inventory is replenished after a fixed cycle, irrespective of the current inventory level. This method, also called the *reorder cycle*, is supported by the SAP APO advanced safety stock planning method, as explained in Chapter 6, Section 6.1.3.

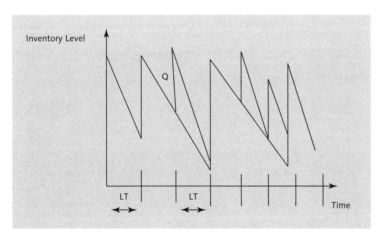

Figure 12.19 Reorder Cycle Inventory Model

Another dimension to look at is the demand stability versus the lead time. A quadrant is shown in Figure 12.20, which maps the different SAP APO safety stock planning methods that best suit the demand and lead time variability factor. While the statistical safety stock method is a good fit for a model with stable demand, the manual static and time-dependent method is good for a model with unstable demand.

587

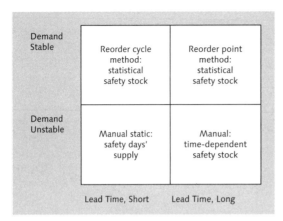

	Lead Time, Short	Lead Time, Long
Demand Stable	Reorder cycle method: statistical safety stock	Reorder point method: statistical safety stock
Demand Unstable	Manual static: safety days' supply	Manual: time-dependent safety stock

Figure 12.20 Inventory Methods Quadrant

12.2.6 Inventory Cost-Benefit Analysis

One of the important aspects of inventory analysis, and the last step as shown in our methodology, is to come out with a cost-benefit analysis for any inventory reduction initiative. This is important because any company needs to be aware of quantifiable benefits that can be generated. Some of the key benefits for businesses are:

▸ Higher customer service levels with optimized inventory levels

▸ Optimized warehouses utilization

▸ Increased direct deliveries and decreased transfer between warehouses

▸ Lower working capital and higher return of capital

Example

ABC Technology has determined that there are three primary areas where the reductions can be seen due to better inventory planning and optimization. These three areas are:

▸ **Overall reduction in inventory (impacting balance sheet)**
Achieved by better inventory visibility in the supply chain, identifying any bottleneck issues early, improving the delivery schedule to customer orders, and with overall reduction in cycle time, resulting in lower safety stock.

▸ **Reduction in inventory carrying cost (impacting P&L)**
Achieved with ongoing reduction in costs associated with financing, storage, handling, insurance, obsolescence, and damage.

> ▶ **Reduction in labor expenses (impacting P&L)**
> With better inventory visibility and a single source, the users are able to spend less time in consolidating information and tracing inventory information.

Figure 12.21 provides an example of ABC Technology's inventory reductions over a three-year time horizon. The reductions are assumed at 30% for Year 1, followed by 50% in Year 2, and then neutralizing at 20% in Year 3. Assuming ABC Technology's net worth is $3 billion, cost of goods sold is $1.75 billion, and standing inventory is $500 million, the company holds 104 days of inventory (calculated using formula days of *inventory = inventory/(COGS/365)*). With better inventory planning and optimization, let's assume ABC Technology reduces the days of inventory from 104 days to 102 days. This two-day reduction can itself reduce 1.92% of overall inventory.

With all these assumptions and two days' inventory reduction in the supply chain, Figure 12.21 provides the gross benefits ABC Technology can yield over the course of three years. Take note that the reduction in inventory carrying costs is calculated using the assumption that inventory carrying charges are 10% of actual inventory. Also, as an example, the labor expense reductions are derived using $1.5 million for the labor value associated with the tracking and tracing of shipments.

	Yearly Total				Cumulative Effect		
	Year 1	Year 2	Year 3		Year 1	Year 2	Year 3
Gross Benefit							
Balance sheet (capital reduction)							
Reduction in inventory	2.877	4.795	1.918		2.877	7.672	9.59
Subtotal balance sheet benefit	2.877	4.795	1.918		2.877	7.672	9.59
Expense Reductions							
Reductions in inventory carrying							
cost	0.288	0.767	0.959		0.288	1.055	2.014
Labor expense reduction	0.009	0.023	0.029		0.009	0.032	0.061
Subtotal P & L benefit	0.297	0.79	0.988		0.297	1.087	2.075
Total Gross Benefit	3.174	5.585	2.906		3.174	8.759	11.665
Figures in $USD millions							

Figure 12.21 Projections Due to Inventory Reduction

Overall, ABC Technology projects that the three-year effect of reducing inventory by two days will result in over $11.5 million in savings, with a net present value of $8.5 million.

12.3 Designing an Inventory Control System

Now that you understand the financial benefits of better inventory planning, we'll explain how to design inventory control systems. A good inventory control system requires two important parameters for setting inventory levels in SAP APO: *how much* inventory to order and *when* the inventory needs to be ordered. These two parameters are paramount factors that the business user needs to consider while designing the inventory system and make up the three sections dealing with order quantity and lot sizing, which we'll discuss next.

12.3.1 Economic Order Quantity

The first parameter revolves around the order quantity. Many companies use the *economic order quantity (EOQ)* while defining the order quantity. EOQ is defined as the optimal quantity of orders that minimizes total variable costs required to order and hold inventory. The EOQ is determined by the total cost curve, which is a combination of the inventory holding costs and procurement cost graph.

> **Note**
>
> The EOQ calculation is not available as a standard functionality of SAP APO, but forms a part of SAP SPP (Service Parts Planning). However, the concept of EOQ can be implemented in SAP APO with the use of master data maintenance and APO macros defining the formulas, which we discuss later in this section.

Figure 12.22 shows how the EOQ graph can be decomposed into three components, as follows:

▶ The first cost graph (linear) is the inventory carrying costs, or the costs associated with holding inventory. These costs increase as you hold more and more inventory. Some of the examples linked with these costs are keeping inventory on hand, interest, insurance, taxes, theft, obsolescence, and storage costs.

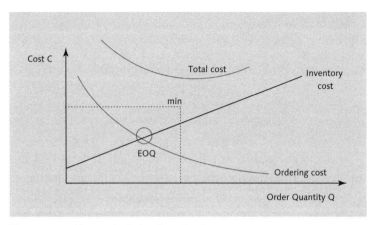

Figure 12.22 Economic Order Quantity Curve

▶ The second cost graph is the order processing costs, also known as the procurement costs. The costs decrease as the order quantity increases. Each event of ordering has certain additional costs (administration, handling) associated with it. For example, a certain amount of paperwork needs to be filled out and people need to be contacted and told how much to order. When the inventory comes in, it has to be inspected and then stocked. Then the invoices need to be processed, as well.

▶ The two costs are added to reflect the total variable costs associated with the order quantity. This new graph is called the *total cost curve*. By looking at the minimum cost per unit on the graph, we can determine what is the proper order quantity, or EOQ. The total cost is represented by the following formula:

$$TC(Q) = PR + \frac{CR}{Q} + \frac{PFQ}{2}$$

Total Cost = Purchase Cost + Order Cost + Holding Costs[3]

Where:

▶ P = Purchase cost per unit

▶ R = Forecasted monthly usage

▶ C = Cost per order event (not per unit)

---

3   Hax, AC and D. Candea. *Production and Inventory Management* (Englewood Cliffs, NJ: Prentice-Hall, 1984)

▶ Q = The number of units ordered

▶ F = Holding cost factor

The result of the differentiation of the formula leads to final EOQ formula:

$$Q^* = \sqrt{\frac{2CR}{PF}} = \sqrt{\frac{2CR}{H}}$$

Implementing EOQ in SAP APO means that you must maintain the ordering and holding costs in SAP APO product master data Extras tab as one of the user-definable attributes. These attributes can then be used in the SAP APO macro to calculate the EOQ key figure. Once the EOQ is calculated, we need to add this custom key figure to the SAP APO target stock level key figure.

The calculation of the EOQ also needs to factor in the lot size. If the EOQ is greater than the vendor minimum lot size, we will use the EOQ, and if the EOQ is less than the vendor minimum lot size, we will use the first rounded lot size that is closer to the EOQ. Various lot sizing procedures available in SAP APO are used during the ordering process. This is discussed in the next section.

12.3.2 Lot Sizing

SAP APO product master data offer various lot sizing procedures that need to be maintained for the correct ordering quantity to be proposed during the planning run. The master data are primarily maintained in SAP ERP, and then transferred via CIF to the SAP APO product master.

There are three basic groups of lot sizing procedures: static, periodic, and optimum. Each of the groups has multiple members, allowing for more options. Besides the maintenance of the lot sizing procedure, we will also optionally (based on procedure) need to maintain the minimum, maximum, and rounding lot size parameters as input to the procedures. Let's walk through some examples to understand the lot sizing procedures and parameters.

Static Lot Sizing Procedures

The static lot size procedures are mainly the exact lot sizing, fixed lot sizing, and replenish to maximum to maximum stock level. The definition of the lot sizing procedure is done at the material plant combination in the SAP ERP material master

(Transaction MM02), MRP 1 tab view. In this view, under FIELD LOT SIZE, we define the various procedures based on business rules.

Lot-for-Lot

The lot sizing procedure is the lot-for-lot (exact size) that takes the demand and proposes supply based on the minimum or maximum lot sizing procedure. The lot size field in SAP ERP for this scenario is defined as exact lot size (EX) and then transferred via CIF to SAP APO as a lot-to-lot procedure in the SAP APO product master. As you can see in Figure 12.23, the demand is spread across many weeks, but due to the minimum lot sizing parameters, the supply is proposed for intervals requiring the minimum lot size quantity.

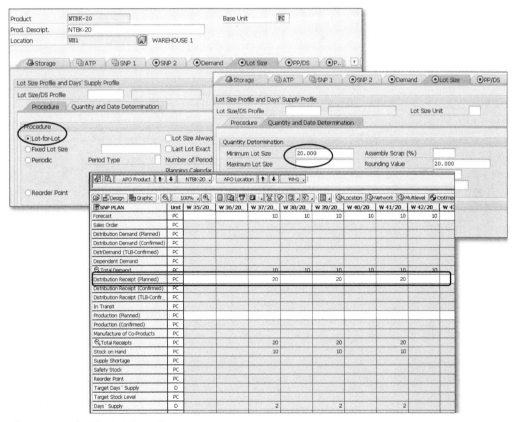

Figure 12.23 Lot-for-Lot Procedure

In many business scenarios, we maintain the minimum and rounding lot sizes simultaneously. A minimum lot size can be a vendor minimum, which needs to be ordered, or a production batch lot size for manufacturing. The lot size is the complete shortage quantity required to satisfy the demand.

Fixed Lot Size

The next procedure is the fixed lot size, where the ordering quantity from the vendor needs to be of fixed lot size. The lot size field in SAP ERP for this scenario is defined as EX and then transferred via CIF to SAP APO as a fixed lot procedure in SAP APO product master. Figure 12.24 shows an example in which the fixed lot size parameter proposes supply based on the procedure.

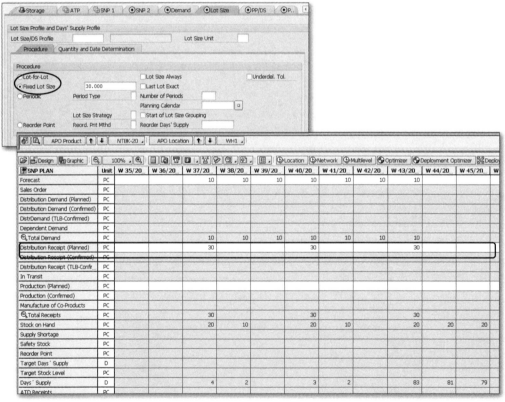

Figure 12.24 Fixed Lot Sizing

Unlike the earlier exact lot size procedure, the total requirement quantity proposed by the system to cover the shortage is divided into the number of fixed quantities as maintained in the master data. For example, if we have shortage quantities of 1,000 units, and the fixed lot size is defined as 200 units, then the system will propose five orders (planned or purchase requisitions) to cover the shortages.

Similarly, if we have maintained the lot size field in SAP ERP as replenish to maximum stock level (HB), along with the maximum stock level field, it is transferred via CIF as a fixed lot size procedure into SAP APO. In this scenario, the system creates orders to fill it to the maximum stock level.

Periodic Lot Sizing Procedures

Periodic lot sizing procedures are defined by daily lot sizing (lot size value = TB), monthly lot sizing (lot size value = MB), and weekly lot sizing (lot size value = WB) in SAP ERP. The requirements that lie for a specific period are all grouped together, and the availability date for the proposal would be the start date of the first requirement in the period.

Period Lot Sizing

The third lot sizing procedure is the period lot sizing defined by the lot size field in SAP ERP and transferred to SAP APO as a period lot size in SAP APO product master. The period type (i.e., daily, weekly, or monthly) dictates how we would like the supply proposals. The period type can be hourly, daily, weekly, monthly, or a different period of your choosing. Also defined within the period lot sizing procedure can be planning calendar, number of horizons, and/or period factors. Period factors are defined as points in the time in a defined period when the system is to create the availability dates of receipt elements. This field only applies to period lot sizing procedures.

Figure 12.25 shows an example in which a three-week period is defined in the SAP ERP lot size field (configured for three-week buckets) and transferred to the SAP APO product master. The supply planning proposal is created per this definition. This method is a good choice if we want to cumulate the demand for all the period types and raise a single proposal (for example, ordering from a vendor once a month).

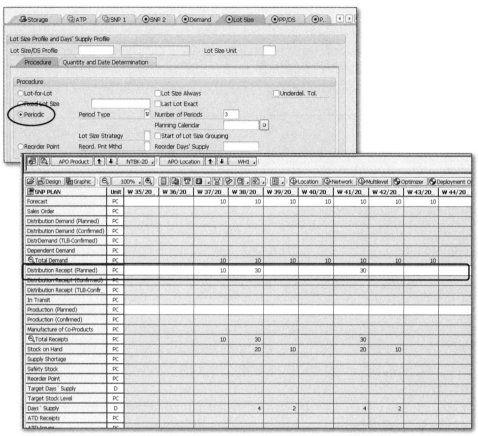

Figure 12.25 Periodic Lot Sizing Procedure

Optimum Lot Sizing Procedures

These lot sizing procedures deal with the concept of economical lot sizing, namely the Groff lot sizing method (lot size value = GR) and part period balancing (lot size value = SP).

Reorder Point

The last lot sizing procedure is the reorder point, which can be defined in both a static and time-dependent fashion. There are two methods defined here, which are *reorder stock* and *reorder supply*. The reorder stock is defined in the form of reorder point quantity, while the reorder supply is defined in the form of days of supply. We can also tell the system to pick the maximum of the two methods.

In the example shown in Figure 12.26, we have defined the safety stock procedure to read the reorder days' supply master data in the product master, which is maintained as three days. The setup is done both in SAP ERP by defining the lot size field as reorder point planning, and then with some additional maintenance in the SAP APO product master LOT SIZE tab. After the planning run, as you can see in the figure, the system proposes a supply proposal to keep the days' supply at three days. This means that the ending inventory at each bucket is sufficient for three days of future demand. The reorder days' supply is defined as the number days for which the current stock and the planned receipts of a material should last to cover the demand that exists at the time of planning.

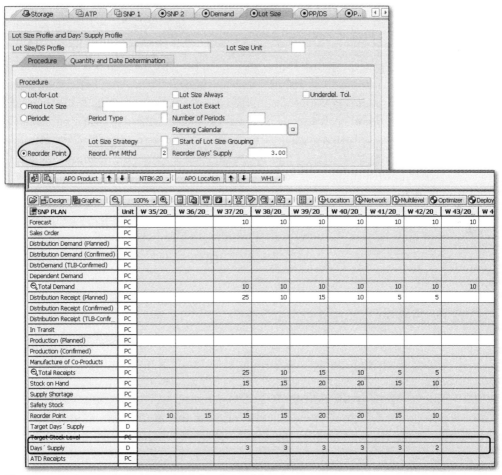

Figure 12.26 Reorder Point Using the Safety Days of Supply

If we are using EOQ with the Groff Procedure in SAP ERP, we would be using the EOQ to calculate the fixed number of period requirements to include in each order. The period order quantity will be equal to EOQ divided by average period usage.

Since most of the company migrating from SAP ERP to SAP APO for planning uses MRP concepts in the SAP ERP system, we need to understand how the different MRP procedures correlate with SAP APO inventory methods. We have two main MRP procedures:

▸ **Consumption-based planning**
This planning procedure is based on consumption of material stock and can be based on past or current historical consumption levels or forecast values. In this scenario, most of the demand components (i.e., sales orders and reservations) are not relevant to the planning process. A good example of this method is the re-order point, at which the planning of material is triggered when the inventory falls below the reorder table. All the MRP types in SAP ERP (i.e., manual and automatic reorder points) can be easily modeled in SAP APO using advanced safety stock planning with the concept re-order point planning (MRP Type V1/ V2, VM) method. Advanced safety stock, along with the planning strategy definition, is explained in Chapter 6, Section 6.1.3. The forecast-based consumption planning (MRP Type = VV) in SAP ERP can be mapped with the statistical safety stock planning method.

▸ **Materials requirement planning**
This planning procedure uses all demand and supply elements to generate the most optimal plan. An APO-SNP algorithm performs this function with the use of a planning engine and lot sizing strategy defined in the SAP APO product master.

12.3.3 SAP APO Target Stock Level

The *target stock level* is an important key figure in the APO-SNP planning figure that helps to answer our second inventory control system parameter of when the inventory needs to be ordered. You can modify the key figures in SAP APO Macro workbench (Transaction /SAPAPO/ADVM) per business requirements to define the stock level for which we would like to propose the supply plan. The stock level serves as the trigger point for placing the order either to the external vendor or internally to the manufacturing location. Per the standard key figure definition, the target stock level equals the calculated safety stock. To complete our EOQ calculation, we can add the EOQ to the safety stock to reach the target stock level.

You can see the relationship between the safety stock and EOQ in Figure 12.27. The increased EOQ leads to a lower effective service level and less safety stock. On the other hand, the decreased EOQ leads to greater effective service level and higher safety stock level.

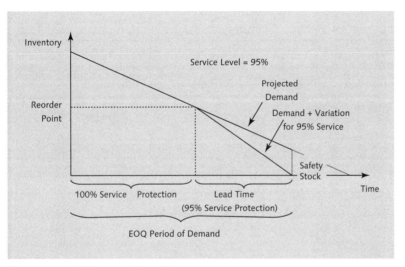

Figure 12.27 EOQ versus Safety Stock

Figure 12.28 shows an example in which the safety stock is seen as the minimum target stock level, and after the planning run, the proposed supply plan closing inventory equals the target stock level.

The overall objective of the inventory control system is to look at the overall fill rate versus total inventory value. Figure 12.29 shows the economical optimal operating curve with the fill rate and the inventory value. As you can see in the figure, a good inventory policy should be in the section where the curve has a flat slope, i.e., the right-hand side of the knee of the curve. This will tell the business that the customer orders are being filled on time with stable inventory levels.

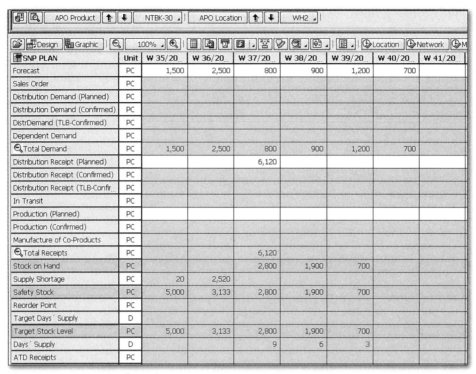

Figure 12.28 Target Stock Level

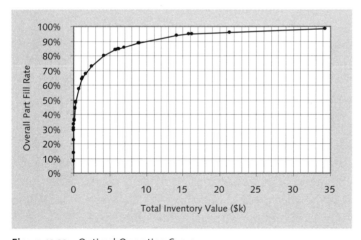

Figure 12.29 Optimal Operating Curve

12.4 Multi-Echelon Inventory Planning

Companies that store inventories in multi-tier locations encounter constant challenges in keeping inventory at the right place at the right time. The distribution model may consist of up to three tiers of locations: regional distribution centers (RDC), distribution centers (DC), and branches. While the regional distribution center stores all the product classes, the branch may only store fast-moving class A products. These networks with multi-tier locations are termed *multi-echelon networks*. A multi-echelon distribution offers many improvement opportunities for inventory optimization in terms of transportation, warehouse, and storage costs. The complexity of the modeling lies in the multiplicities of inventory drivers and synchronization of locations in the echelon.

Figure 12.30 shows the difference between the single and multi-echelon models where the lead time and demand are key inputs to the inventory driver in the setting inventory level at each location.

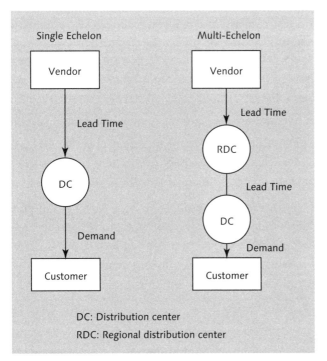

Figure 12.30 Comparison between Single- and Multi-Echelon Models

In the single echelon, the business planner can adjust his inventory levels as he has clear visibility on the customer demand and also on the supplier lead time variability. This becomes a challenge in the multi-echelon model as the visibility of demand, both up and down, becomes difficult. The regional distribution center is unable to predict the customer demand from the distribution center, and except the lead time, the distribution center has no clear visibility on incoming supplies at the regional distribution center. Also, the bullwhip effect comes into picture on any fluctuations of demand and supply situations since each location develops its worn demand. Since the focus is on an individual echelon, there is a possibility the network costs remain unevaluated. Therefore, the key benefits of implementing a multi-echelon model are inventory visibility, reduced bullwhip effect, and improved forecasting and customer service with shorter cycle times.

SAP APO offers a distribution resource planning (DRP) approach that does not fully suffice the inventory optimization objective in the multi-tier distribution model. The multi-tier locations are replenished purely based on net requirements. Also, the safety stock is calculated at individual nodes.

SAP provides a partner solution from SmartOps to address some of the complexity of the supply chain. Per the current SAP solution map, SmartOps can be seamlessly integrated with SAP ERP and SAP SCM applications to reap the benefits of inventory optimization in a multi-tier network. The definition of SAP Enterprise Inventory Optimization by SmartOps is as follows:

> *Determining detailed optimal and visible inventory targets across the supply chain that drive successful planning and replenishment in an ongoing manner for every item at every location across time, resulting in lower aggregate working capital with equal or better customer service and lower supply chain costs.*

The overall goal of the Enterprise Inventory Optimization by SmartOps solution is inventory optimization, as shown in Figure 12.31, where the solution captures any changes in demand at the network level, accounts for all lead time and lead time variability in the supply chain, monitors the bullwhip effect on the supply chain, synchronizes order strategies, and offers differentiated service levels based on product selling patterns.

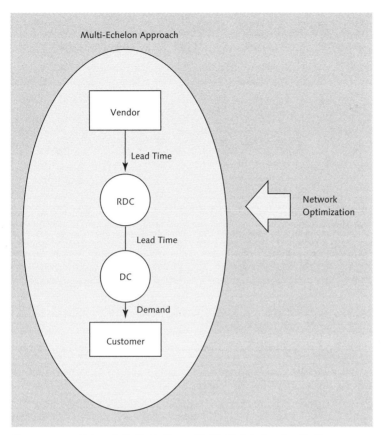

Figure 12.31 Network Optimization with Multi-Echelon Application

Table 12.4 shows the difference between the SAP APO DRP approach and the Industry EIO solution.

Key Areas	SAP APO – DRP Approach	Multi-Echelon Inventory Optimization (MEIO)
Optimization objective	Calculation based on replenishment rules across the network	Customer service goal based on lowest inventory costs

Table 12.4 Difference between SAP APO—DRP Approach and Multi-Echelon Inventory Optimization[4]

---

4   Calvin Lee, Evant Inc., Multi-Echelon Inventory Optimization, 2010

Key Areas	SAP APO – DRP Approach	Multi-Echelon Inventory Optimization (MEIO)
Demand forecasting	Individual forecasting at echelon based on historical sales pattern	Forecast based on lowest echelon primary demand, along with demand variations
Lead times	Supplier lead time with variations	Models all lead times, along with variability
Bullwhip effects	Ignored	Measures and accounted in replenishment calculation
Network visibility	Downstream visibility, along with immediate upstream visibility	Complete network visibility and taken as rules in the replenishment program calculation
Order synchronization between echelons	Ignored	Possible modeling option
Differentiated customer service	Not possible	Possible to set different customer service with allocation rules
Cost implication between echelons	Not possible	Possible modeling option

Table 12.4 Difference between SAP APO—DRP Approach and Multi-Echelon Inventory Optimization (Cont.)

The SAP Enterprise Inventory Optimization option by SmartOps provides complete visibility into different inventory types at different supply chain nodes, as shown in Figure 12.32. The option also offers what-if capabilities to identify and quantify supply chain improvement opportunities and provides the correct mechanism for the product mix inventory levels, giving a clear picture of products that may require inventory reviews and corrections, as shown in Figure 12.32. The SmartOps option comes with the standard SAP connector and a library of BAPIs, which extract input data from SAP master data and also provide an interface to feed inventory targets to SAP ERP-MM and SAP SCM-APO.

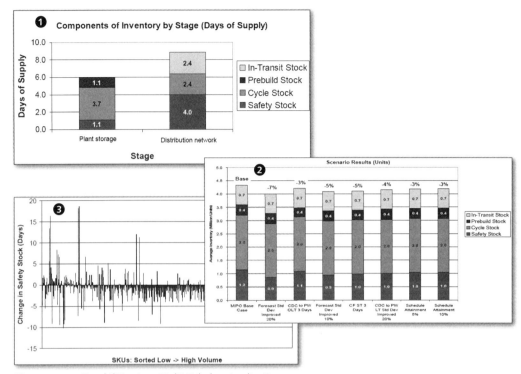

Figure 12.32 Capabilities in a Multi-Echelon Application

12.5 Summary

This chapter provided an overview of what inventory optimization and methodology for effective inventory analysis entail. Two of the key elements in the methodology are the inventory modeling and design of the inventory model system for the product or product family. The second section of the chapter focused on designing an inventory control system that revolves around identifying the correct ordering quantity and trigger point for ordering inventory. The chapter closes with a brief overview of multi-echelon models and support of SAP partner-provided solution capabilities.

The next chapter shows how SAP APO supports a characteristics-based planning process for industries in which variant planning is a common business requirement. Characteristics-based forecasting allows companies to forecast products with different attributes and manufacture them using modern forecasting methods and production techniques.

Characteristics attributes are important for supply chain planning in some industries. In this chapter, we'll provide an overview of the characteristics-based planning functionality and its other integration aspects.

13 Characteristics-Based Planning in SAP APO

Companies are now adopting the market pull-driven concept of reducing their inventory levels and providing flexibility to the customer to design their end-product configuration. This concept allows the customer to place their orders based on specific product characteristics (e.g., color) that best suit their requirements. The characteristics concept refers to a company providing its customer selection criteria (e.g., color of a product) to use when purchasing a product.

Real-time integration between the manufacturing shop floor and the order-promising business process is fast becoming a necessity for industries using characteristics-based planning. Industries that use characteristics-based planning range from automotive, chemical, mills (e.g., metal and paper), engineering, and construction to high-tech (e.g., PC manufacturing) industries. The motivation in these industries requires the customer order ATP check to trigger the manufacturing process. This concept holds true for ABC Technology, from which the custom desktop customer expects the delivery date based on their order specifications. The manufacturer faces a unique challenge in matching demand and supply with the business objective of maximizing the yield and revenue.

As shown in the mind map for this chapter (see Figure 13.1) we'll discuss various topics for modeling characteristics-based planning in SAP APO. We'll cover the customization, master data, business scenario testing scenario with the help of our ABC Technology case study and explain how to integrate characteristics into its planning, forecasting, and supply planning.

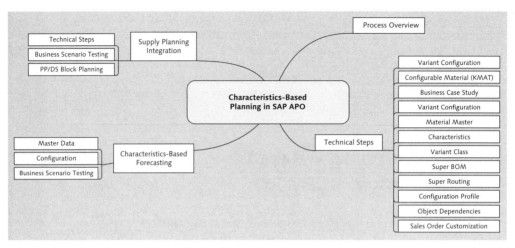

Figure 13.1 Learning Points for the Chapter (Mind Map)

13.1 Characteristics-Based Planning Process Overview

Characteristics-based planning consists of the integration of characteristics-based forecasting, production planning, and material availability check. SAP APO provides functionality in the form of global available-to-promise (global ATP) for the multilevel ATP check method. The multilevel ATP check method can be designed for ABC Technology that engages in multilevel assembly for configured products (e.g., laptops). This method is useful for ABC Technology where the assembly items are stocked and only when customer sales order is received the assembly items are assembled for the final product. The method checks the availability of the components (via BOM explosion of the primary product) before committing to the delivery date of the order. SAP APO uses the global ATP multilevel ATP process to check the component availability before confirming the delivery date for the customer orders. Figure 13.2 illustrates the planning process integrated with the availability check when the customer order is received, and the process steps are as follows:

❶ Characteristics-based forecasting (CBF) provides demand planning for the configurable custom desktop product. The forecast is based on historical sales orders and then released to SAP APO PP/DS at the configurable product characteristics level. SAP APO PP/DS creates a master production schedule plan as well as a procurement plan for the assembly/component products.

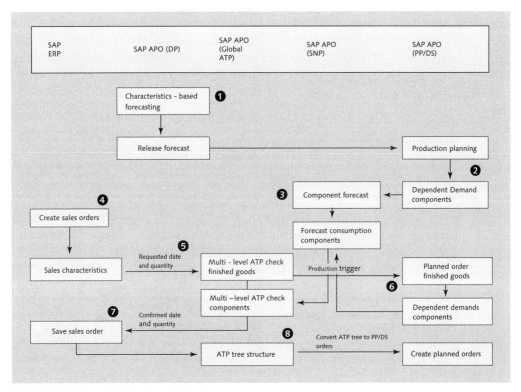

Figure 13.2 Characteristics-Based Planning

❷ Production planning (PP) explodes the bill of materials (BOM) for the components by which the dependent demands are transferred to APO-SNP as a forecast (i.e., planned independent requirement). The forecast for the component becomes the basis for the production or procurement plan

❸ If the sales orders are placed, the forecast of the component is consumed by the dependent demands of the components. To enable this process, make sure that you've checked the ASSEMBLY PLANNING indicator within the product master DEMAND tab (Transaction /SAPAPO/MAT1).

❹ Once the customer sales orders are created with characteristics (variant configuration) in SAP ERP, the multilevel ATP check is triggered.

❺ The multilevel ATP triggers the production plan for finished goods with the requested date and quantity. The PP/DS production data structure (PDS) explodes the BOM and, internally, a simulated planned order is created.

❻ The dependent demand for the components is passed back to the multilevel ATP to check the component inventory availability. The components can have separate check instruction and check control defined to separate the scope of check between the configurable product and the assembly products.

❼ The customer sales orders are confirmed based on the results of the component availability check. The object dependency factors are considered as constraints during the process.

❽ Once the sales order is saved in SAP ERP, no planned orders are immediately created, but an ATP tree structure is created in the background and stores all the simulated planned order information based on the sales order confirmation dates. Depending on the PP/DS HORIZON maintained in the product location master data or PP/DS global setting customization, the ATP tree structure is converted to receipt planned orders. The planned orders are created with the properties CHECKED AND FIRMED and ATP category AL.

> **Note**
>
> When using multilevel ATP, please consider SAP Note 455421, which explains possible limitations.

Now that you understand the planning process for characteristics-based planning, we'll walk through the various configuration and master data steps to set this up in the SAP system.

13.2 Characteristics-Based Planning Technical Steps

Industries such as high-tech, consumer electronics, engineering, and automotive use the characteristics concept to minimize the amount of effort it takes to create and maintain a high volume of master data. This provides supply chain transparency and the ability to improve forecasting on components and the configurable end product. The main driver for these industries is that planning is performed at the end product level as well as at detailed component levels.

> **Note**
>
> There are two primary concepts in SAP APO: characteristics-dependent planning (CDP) and variant configuration (VC). The CDP is used for manufacturing the planning of products using characteristics. The products are configurable in SAP ERP with the process of consumption occurring when the requirements (i.e., sales orders) and receipts (i.e., planned orders and purchase requisitions) elements are matched.
>
> VC, on the other hand, is useful if the company has a large number of components with different permutations and combinations while making the finished product. The concept of VC avoids the creation of large master data sets. This lesson focuses on the SAP ERP–integrated VC concept.

The basic planning runs as a two-step process:

1. The first step is the consolidation of the forecast on the configurable finished product level (SAP material type KMAT), also known as *independent forecasting*.

> **KMAT (Configurable Materials)**
>
> Configurable materials represent materials that contain a large number of variants. An example of configurable materials is computers, which can have different combinations of motherboard, CPU, desktop, keyboard, etc., to form different end products. The MATERIAL IS CONFIGURABLE indicator is already set for this material type in Customizing for the MATERIAL MASTER in the activity DEFINE ATTRIBUTES OF MATERIAL TYPES.
>
> A material master record of this material type contains sales data, but not purchasing data.

2. The second step in the process is to configure a forecast on the finished product level and break it down to an assembly or component level represented by characteristics value of the object dependency. This step is commonly known as *attach rate planning*.

Now let's look at various configuration and master data for setting up characteristics-based planning. To aid the explanation of these complex topics in the subject, we will use the ABC Technology business case study, which is explained next.

13.2.1 Business Case Study

Characteristics-based planning is commonly used in high-tech industries that have complex product structures with many characteristics. The business example we will use in this chapter is ABC Technology, which receives customers' orders based on various custom specifications. The company primarily manufactures custom desktop computers with different specification for external casing, hard disk capacity, keyboard, and motherboard (CPU and RAM processors). Figure 13.3 shows the configuration, in which the four assemblies serve as important components for taking customer orders, planning, and stock availability.

ABC Technology receives all these components from different suppliers with different lead times. To manage the market demand, the company keeps optimal inventory of these various parts, besides routine procurement. During the customer order, the delivery date is promised based on the assembly/component stock availability or procurement lead time of the component from the suppliers.

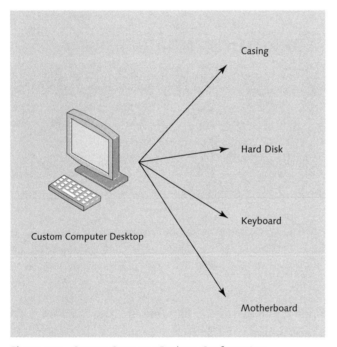

Figure 13.3 Custom Computer Desktop Configuration

The planning for ABC Technology is driven by the variant configuration concept, which is explained in the next section.

13.2.2 Variant Configuration

As we mentioned, characteristics-based planning supports variant configuration. Variant configuration allows the customer or sales personnel to put together specifications based on their needs and to ensure that the company has the production and availability of these specifications. Variant configuration has the following features:

▶ You do not need to create separate material master data for each variant configuration.

▶ Super BOM and super routing is enough to represent all possible manufacturing variants and operations.

▶ You can react with more flexibility to customer demands.

▶ Collaboration (i.e., information exchange) increases among sales, engineering, and production functional areas.

From a technical point of view, the process is set up mainly in SAP ERP (where most of the master data comes from CIF) and only very little in SAP APO, e.g., by choosing the VC configuration scheme. Still, the entire planning process, the evaluation and conversion, takes place in SAP APO.

You need to maintain configuration in SAP APO at the system client level for specifying the variant configuration settings for SAP ERP and SAP APO integration. The configuration path in SAP SCM is IMG • SCM BASIS • MASTER DATA • CLASSIFICATION AND CONFIGURATION • DEFINE CONFIGURATION SCHEMA. In the configuration, we select VARIANT CONFIGURATION as the default setting.

For variant configuration support, a material with different product characteristics called a *configurable material* is created. These materials are created with material type KMAT or given the indicator CONFIGURABLE in the material master record (BASIC DATA VIEW 2) in Transaction MM01. Figure 13.4 shows the structure for the KMAT configurable material, whereby the material is connected with various master data objects: class, configuration profile, super BOM, super routing, and pricing.

In the next section, we'll take a look at some of the important master data elements that affect both SAP ERP and SAP APO.

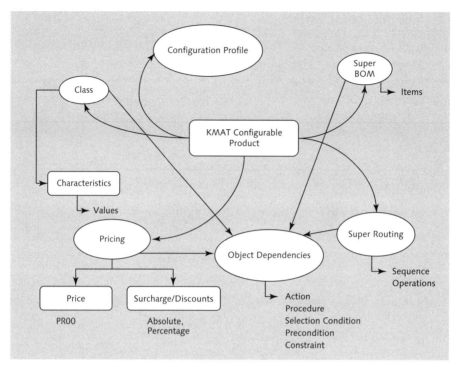

Figure 13.4 Configurable Product Structure

13.2.3 Material Master

There are a few things you'll need to alter in the material master, if it has characteristics that can be chosen by the customer.

Access the material master via Transaction MM02. To configure the different characteristics for a material, you need to check the MATERIAL IS CONFIGURABLE box in the BASIC DATA VIEW 2 tab.

The other area of interest is the strategy group in the MRP 3 tab. The strategy group connects strategy and requirement type/class, which defines the behavior of requirements in planning. Here, you need to extend the variant configuration to the requirement class and type in SAP ERP, as shown in Figure 13.5. The example shows requirement class 046 mapped with the requirement class and requirement type KEK. The configuration path in SAP ERP is IMG • SALES AND DISTRIBUTION • BASIC FUNCTION • AVAILABILITY CHECK AND TRANSFER OF REQUIREMENTS • TRANSFER OF REQUIREMENTS. In the customization, maintain the configuration is applicable for the requirement class. Then assign the requirement class (example, 046) to the requirement type (example, KEK), as shown in the figure.

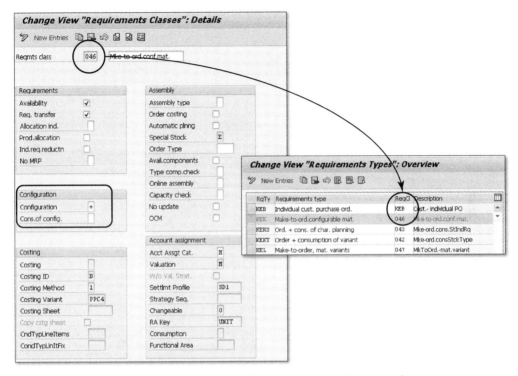

Figure 13.5 Requirement Type and Requirement Class in SAP ERP for Variant Configuration

Next, maintain the strategy and strategy group in the customization to map, requirement type, and requirement class. The configuration path in SAP ERP is IMG • PRODUCTION PLANNING • DEMAND MANAGEMENT • PLANNING STRATEGY • DEFINE STRATEGY or DEFINE STRATEGY GROUP. As Figure 13.6 shows, the strategy group and strategy are connected with the material master data maintenance.

1. Start by maintaining the strategy with the requirement type and mandatory configuration (step ❶).

2. Next, assign the strategy to the strategy group (step ❷).

3. Assign the strategy group in the material master data using Transaction MM02 (step ❸).

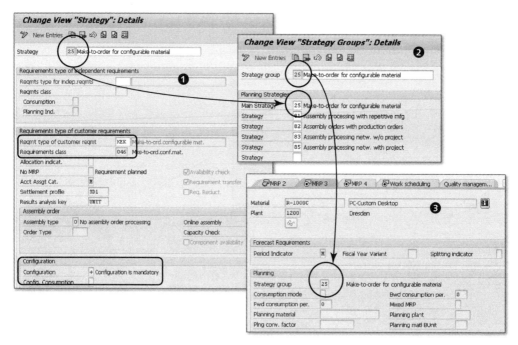

Figure 13.6 Strategy and Strategy Group in SAP ERP

Figure 13.7 shows the various relations and interdependencies among the master data objects. The figure shows how the configurable item BOM is linked with the class and characteristics values. The figure shows the overall schematic layout how the KMAT material is linked with the class and characteristics. The KMAT material, in turn, has the super BOM with different components (i.e., variant materials) containing the characteristics values from the class.

13.2.4 Characteristics

Characteristics are used to define the feature or specifications of a configurable material. The relevant characteristics are maintained in SAP ERP using Transaction CT04. The characteristics can be further transferred to SAP APO via the CIF integration model. For ABC Technology's business scenario, we maintain separate characteristics for casing, hard disk, keyboard, and motherboard. For each characteristic (accessed via Transaction CT04), we need to maintain all possible freely definable values under the VALUES tab, as shown in Figure 13.8. The example shows various combinations of motherboards that ABC Technology offers as options during custom customer requests.

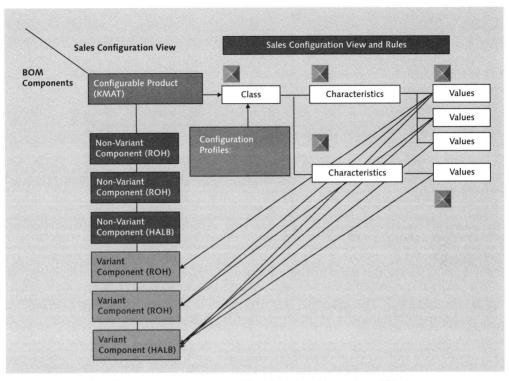

Figure 13.7 Configurable Item Structure in SAP ERP with Various Master Data Objects

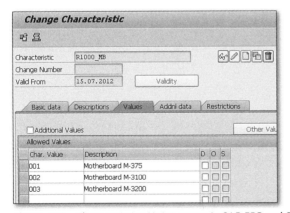

Figure 13.8 Characteristics Maintenance in SAP ERP and SAP APO

To enable the system to use characteristics for a configurable material, follow these steps in SAP ERP:

1. Access Transaction MM02.

2. Assign the material to class type 300 (variant).

3. Choose the CLASSIFICATION tab in the material master.

4. Maintain the characteristics values for the material.

The characteristics are transferred to SAP APO from SAP ERP using the CIF. The integration model is created/activated in Transaction CFM1 and then generated using Transaction CFM2.

13.2.5 Variant Class

The *variant class* is used to hold, or contain, the characteristics that describe the configurable material. An example would be desktop outer color, which would be class in this case (for example, characteristics values of red, blue, or gray). The class type determines which object types can be classified.

Example

For our ABC Technology case study, we will use class type 300, which is for variants. Class 300 is used in variant configuration if the class has a class type that supports variant configuration.

In Customizing for classification in SAP ERP, the VARIANT CLASS TYPE indicator must be set for the class type. The configuration path is IMG • CROSS APPLICATION COMPONENTS • CLASSIFICATION SYSTEM • CLASSES • MAINTAIN OBJECT TYPES AND CLASS TYPES.

Figure 13.9 shows the class for ABC Technology whereby all the characteristics for casing, hard disk, keyboard, and motherboard are maintained in both SAP ERP and SAP SCM.

Another characteristics variable condition (VARCOND) is used to capture any ad hoc characteristics not in standard customer ordering. The variant class is transferred to SAP APO from SAP ERP using the CIF. The integration model is created/generated in Transaction CFM1 and then activated using Transaction CFM2.

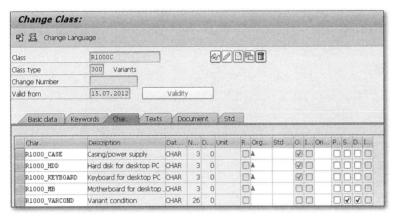

Figure 13.9 Variant Class Maintenance

13.2.6 Super BOM

A *super BOM* contains all the components (both variant and non-variant parts) that are needed to produce any variants of the configurable product. The advantage of using a super BOM is that there is no need to create a separate material number for each characteristics combinations. One configurable material will cover all the variants.

You can access the BOM via Transaction CS01. Figure 13.10 shows an example for ABC Technology whereby the entire BOM is input into the configurable product. The super BOM contains any component that would potentially be needed to produce any variant of the finished product. In the sales order, the user decides which components are actually used for their individual variant. A simulation of the configuration can be performed in SAP ERP using Transaction CU50 without actually creating any sales orders.

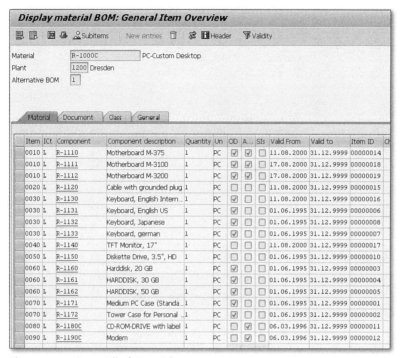

Figure 13.10 Super Bill of Material

13.2.7 Super Routing

A *super routing* contains information on the production process for all variants of a product. Instead of creating routing for each variant of a product, you can create operations for one routing, or a "super routing." You can also maintain object dependencies for sequences, operations/sub operations, and production resource/tool assignments in super routing.

The advantage of creating super routing is that there is no need to create separate routings, as one configurable material will cover all variants. You can access the routing master data via Transaction CA01. Figure 13.11 shows an example in which the routing for the configurable product has two routing variant operations, 40 and 45, for the CPU assembly process. The BOM and routing are then combined in the production version. The production version transaction is Transaction C223, whereby the routing and BOM combination are input at the configurable product level, checked for consistency, and saved (shown in the second screen in Figure 13.11).

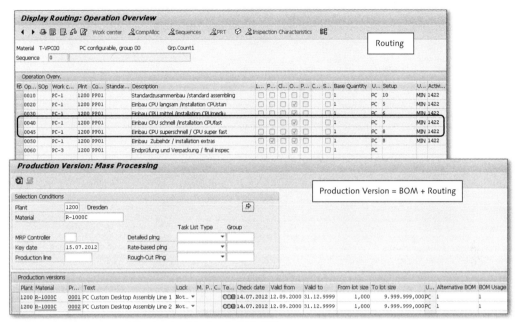

Figure 13.11 Routing and Production Version in SAP ERP

The production version is then transferred to SAP APO via CIF. You create/generate the integration model in Transaction CFM1 and then activate it using Transaction CFM2. The production version is mapped to SAP APO production data structure (PDS) or production process model (PPM) master data.

13.2.8 Configuration Profile

The configuration profile controls the configuration process when sales orders are being created and defines the central settings that are mandatory for the object. As part of configuration, you can define the screen layout and hide some of the characteristics values that are defined during characteristics creation using this profile via Transaction CU43 (see Figure 13.12) in SAP ERP.

Here you can see that ABC Technology has edited the configuration profile for its custom desktops in Transaction VA01, used for creating customer sales orders. When placing their order, the customer will be prompted to enter all the characteristics values that are defined here (e.g., casing, keyboard, hard disk, motherboard, etc.) as shown in the figure.

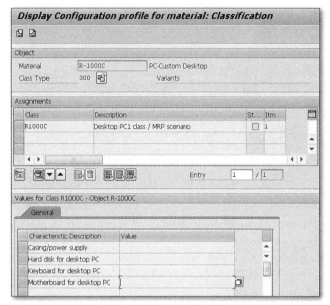

Figure 13.12 Configuration Profile Definition in SAP ERP

13.2.9 Object Dependencies

You can use object dependencies to restrict the combinations of characteristics options and select the correct BOM components and operations to produce a variant. The following functions are performed by object dependencies:

- Describe the interdependence between the characteristics and characteristics values
- Control which components are selected from a BOM and which operations are selected from a task list
- Change the values of fields in BOM items and operations during configuration

Figure 13.13 shows the object dependencies syntax example in SAP ERP with possible different pricing structure based on different computer case configuration. The object dependencies are maintained in the configuration profile (explained in Section 13.2.8) using Transaction CU43.

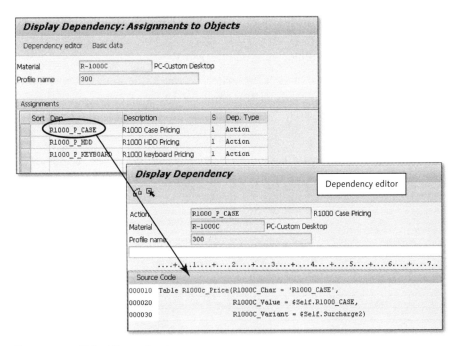

Figure 13.13 Object Dependencies

Note

For more details on this subject, refer to the second edition of *Variant Configuration with SAP* by Uwe Blumöhr, Manfred Münch, and Marin Ukalovic (SAP PRESS, 2011).

13.2.10 Customizing Sales Orders

An additional configuration is required in SAP ERP for the sales orders that take variant configuration material in their customer orders. You first need to link the sales order type with the item category to switch on variant configuration. Figure 13.14 shows the configuration steps and the material master data maintenance.

❶ Follow the customization path IMG • SALES AND DISTRIBUTION • SALES • SALES DOCUMENT ITEM • DEFINE ITEM CATEGORIES. Maintain the item category for variant matching in the BILL OF MATERIAL/CONFIGURATION section. The relevant settings need to be maintained for the configuration strategy and material variant action, as shown in the figure.

❷ Follow the customizing path IMG • Sales and Distribution • Sales • Sales Document Item • Assign Item Categories. Here, you assign the sales order type with the variant configuration item category.

❸ The third step is optional: assign the material type to the item category group before the material master data maintenance. If this configuration is not maintained, the system will default the item category group for customer sales orders from the material master, per the next step.

❹ The final step is to maintain the item category group in the SAP ERP material master in the Basic Data View 1. This will be automatically populated in the Sales Org 2 tab, as well.

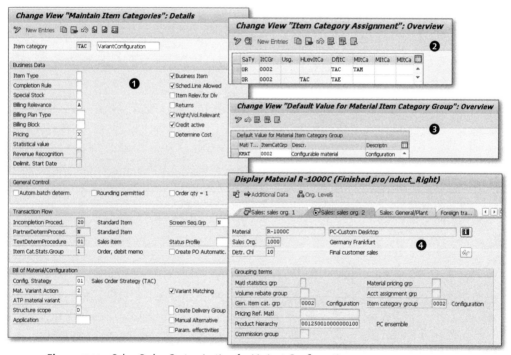

Figure 13.14 Sales Order Customization for Variant Configuration

13.3 Characteristics-Based Forecasting

The business process of characteristics-based planning is supported by *characteristics-based forecasting*, which is a functionality in SAP APO Demand Planning that is used to forecast products with different attributes as well as perform the BOM explosions for the assembly or components.

In our ABC Technology business scenario, we can correlate the custom desktop to be manufactured based on different specifications that the customer provides for hard disk, casing, keyboard, and motherboard. These characteristics, in turn, have unique defined values. Figure 13.15 shows the general CBF flow whereby the forecast is created and then released to PP/DS based on characteristics. As shown in the figure, the demand plan is released, which triggers the BOM explosion, which in turn calls the dependent requirement for the components. The components are procured or manufactured and then assembled.

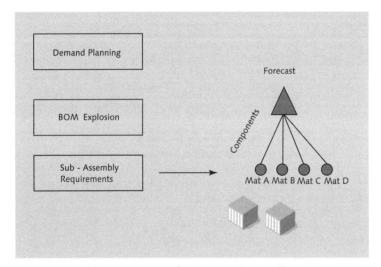

Figure 13.15   Characteristics-Based Forecasting Process Flow

In the following sections, we'll show you how ABC Technology activates characteristics-based planning and basic configuration steps and then maintains the master data required for performing characteristics-based forecasting (CBF).

13.3.1   Activate Characteristics-Based Planning

To activate the CBF in SAP APO Demand Planning to support the functionality, check the CHARSTC BASED FORECASTING indicator at the basic planning object structure (accessed via Transaction /SAPAPO/MSDP_ADMIN), as shown in Figure 13.16. Add three characteristics—9AMV_PROF (CBF Profile), 9MV_ROW (Char. Based forecast), and 9MV_TAB (CBF Table)—to the planning object structure for enabling CBF functionality. Based on the planning object structure, we can create planning areas for the addition of key figures.

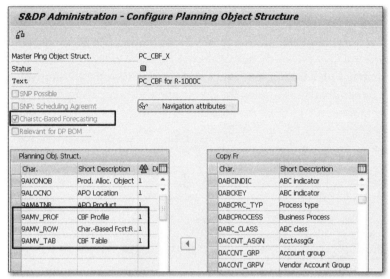

Figure 13.16 Characteristics-Based Forecasting Planning Object Structure

13.3.2 CBF Master Data

Characteristics-based forecasting requires a combination of different master data maintenance: linking tables and maintenance, as shown in Figure 13.17.

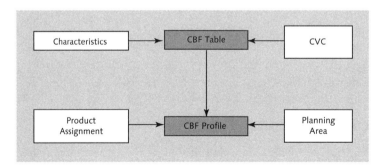

Figure 13.17 Characteristics-Based Forecasting Master Data

The three primary master data tables are CBF profile, CBF table, and characteristics value combination (CVC). These three data elements help in the forecasting process and subsequent release of the forecast to SAP APO PP/DS. The CBF profile assigned to the configurable product is maintained in the CBF profile and consists of CBF table and characteristics value. The forecasting is done on these characteristics values and is also relevant for the ATP check and forecast consumption process. Let's now briefly describe each of these master data objects and how to maintain them.

1. **CBF table (Transaction /SAPAPO/IPM01)**
   The characteristics table is a planning object that contains all the characteristics combinations (keyboard, hard disk, motherboard, etc.). As Figure 13.18 shows, the characteristics are assigned to the CBF table directly in step ❶. Any new characteristics can be added on the right side of the screen.

2. **CBF profile (Transaction /SAPAPO/IPM01)**
   The planning profile contains characteristics tables for a configurable material. As Figure 13.18 shows, step ❷, the valid characteristics combination for a custom desktop, is generated for a particular configurable item. To maintain the profile, follow these five steps:

   ▸ Create the CBF profile.

   ▸ Assign the planning area to the CBF profile.

   ▸ Activate the CBF profile.

   ▸ Assign the CBF table.

   ▸ Optionally remove CVCs from the CBF table as necessary.

> **Note**
>
> The CBF profile needs to be created before the CVC maintenance.

3. **Characteristics value combination (CVC) (Transaction /SAPAPO/MC62)**
   The CVC defines the combinations by which the configurable product can be forecast and planned. Figure 13.19 shows the generated CVC, whereby the three characteristics defined in the master planning object structure are automatically populated to the CVC during the creation process based on the CBF profile and CBF table defined definitions.

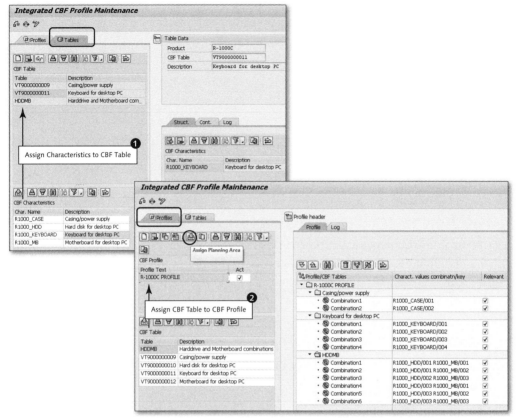

Figure 13.18 CBF Profile Maintenance in APO-DP

Display Existing Characteristic Combinations

24 Data records selected for Planning Obj. Struct.: PC_CBF_X

Prod. Allo	APO Location	APO Product	CBF Profil	Char.-Base	CBF Table
PC_ATP_CTO	1200	R-1000C	25	1	3247
PC_ATP_CTO	1200	R-1000C	25	1	3249
PC_ATP_CTO	1200	R-1000C	25	1	3255
PC_ATP_CTO	1200	R-1000C	25	2	3247
PC_ATP_CTO	1200	R-1000C	25	2	3249
PC_ATP_CTO	1200	R-1000C	25	2	3255
PC_ATP_CTO	1200	R-1000C	25	3	3249
PC_ATP_CTO	1200	R-1000C	25	3	3255
PC_ATP_CTO	1200	R-1000C	25	4	3249
PC_ATP_CTO	1200	R-1000C	25	4	3255
PC_ATP_CTO	1200	R-1000C	25	5	3255
PC_ATP_CTO	1200	R-1000C	25	6	3255

Figure 13.19 Characteristics Value Combination for CBF Process

13.3.3 Planning Book Design

To aid in characteristics-based forecasting, the business users in ABC Technology use two planning books to plan the configurable product and assembly products. They use the first planning book to plan the configurable product, which is also called *independent forecasting*. The configurable product-generated forecast becomes the basis for the assembly planning, which is also called *attach rate planning*.

Business Process Steps

The business process steps are as follows (shown in Figure 13.20):

❶ The configurable product (KMAT) forecasting is performed based on historical sales orders. The business planner reviews the plan and makes any adjustments on outliers. The forecast is based on the proportional factors of the characteristics sold in the past. The proportional factors define the percentage of historical sales that can be used during the forecast disaggregation to the individual characteristics levels.

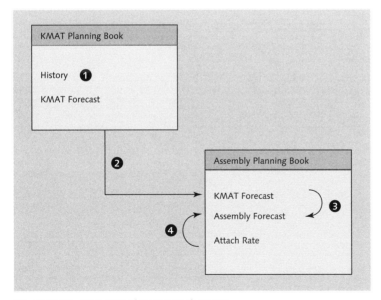

Figure 13.20 SAP APO Planning Book Design

❷ The KMAT forecast is transferred to the second component planning book for attach rate planning.

❸ A macro is used to copy the KMAT forecast to the assembly forecast at the product location level.

❹ The business planner maintains the *attach rate* based on current market demand and sales and marketing inputs. The attach rate defines the proportional factor for the characteristics combinations (keyboard, hard disk, casing, etc.). Once the attach rate is finalized, the proportional ratio is used for assembly forecast recalculation. This becomes the final plan, which will be released to supply planning.

Technical Steps

The planning book created via Transaction /SAPAPO/SDP8B in the earlier steps can include multiple data views. The data view defines which key figures are visible to the business planners for which characteristics combinations. As Figure 13.21 shows, additional CBF characteristics are automatically assigned in the planning book.

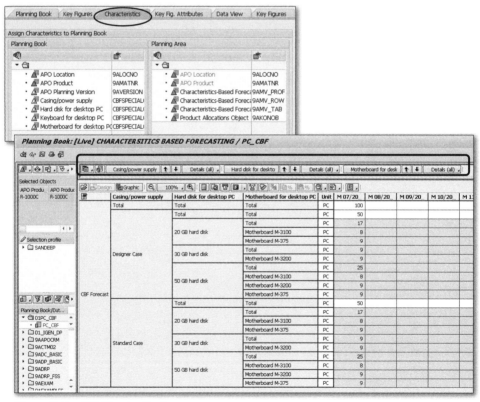

Figure 13.21 CBF Planning Book

Access Transaction /SAPAPO/SDP8B by following menu path EDIT • ASSIGN PLAN-
NING AREA to link the planning book with the planning area that you created in
Section 13.3.1. In this manner, the planning book inherits the characteristics and
key figures.

The business users can visualize the attach rate (allocations) in the SAP APO planning book, as shown in Figure 13.21. As seen in the figure, the planning book
displays the units for two finished desktop products with different characteristics
values (for example, different motherboard configurations).

> **Note**
>
> To find out more about how to transfer historical data (SAP ERP to SAP NetWeaver BW)
> for CBF, refer to SAP Note 304265.

13.3.4 Descriptive Characteristics

The concept of *descriptive characteristics* is used for planning by specific characteristics at the supply planning level. By default, the supply planning is performed at
the product and location levels, but in many business scenarios, there is need for
additional attributes (for example, customer number or customer group), which
help the business to not only prioritize the plan but also allocate the supply to these
customers, taking into account different business rules.

Primarily, a combination of product and location is used to send the forecast from
APO-DP to APO-SNP and PP/DS. In today's business environment, that use of
descriptive characteristics allows the business to release a forecast more on the
characteristics level than the product and location levels for detailed planning.
For example, a forecast may be released to supply planning for specific customers characteristics. Sales orders from other customers will, in turn, not be able to
consume these forecasts.

> **Example**
>
> For ABC Technology, the sales orders need to be prioritized, and the descriptive charac-
> teristics will be used for forecast consumption (since the sales orders contain all the key
> characteristics) and assembly planning. The forecast is created with attach rate planning
> detailed characteristics, which now allows SAP APO PP/DS to plan production and
> procurement properly.

To set up descriptive characteristics, you need to configure the consumption group. The customization path is IMG • Supply Chain Planning • Demand Planning • Basic Settings • Consumption • Maintain Consumption Group. As Figure 13.22 shows, maintain all the characteristics for our example (casing, hard disk, keyboard, etc.) under the Consumption Group. These characteristics are populated in the DP Char. Assignment tab on the right side (populated based on the DP Planning area), which you need to transfer to the left side to the Consumption Group tab.

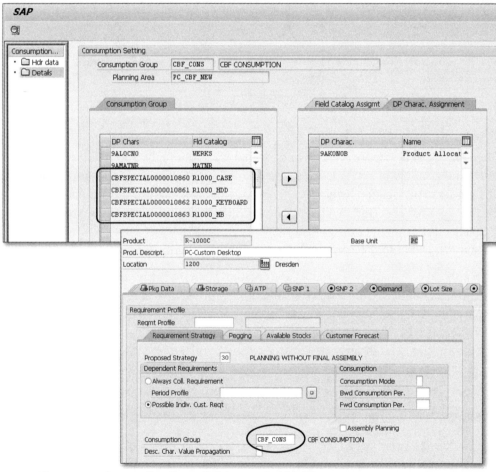

Figure 13.22 Consumption Group Maintenance in APO-DP

Then, access the product master data via Transaction /SAPAPO/MAT1 to maintain the consumption group in the Demand tab, as shown in Figure 13.22.

13.3.5   Demand Planning Release

Once the forecasting is performed in demand planning, the unconstrained demand needs to be released to supply planning for capacity and material availability planning. The demand planning is released to supply planning using Transaction /SAPAPO/MC90. As Figure 13.23 shows, the consumption group is maintained in the release transaction (step ❶). After the forecast release, the forecast is seen in the PP/DS Transaction /SAPAPO/RRP3 with the descriptive characteristics, as seen in the figure (step ❷). You can visualize the characteristics by clicking the Charac-teristics icon ( ).

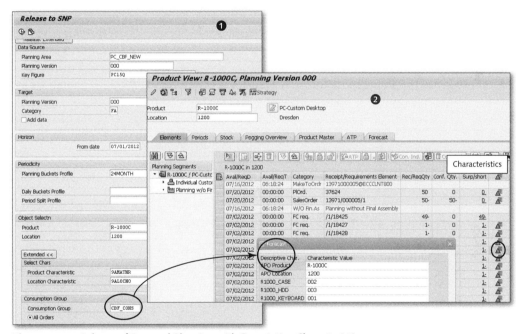

Figure 13.23   Release of Demand Planning with Descriptive Characteristics

Now that we've seen the characteristics-based forecasting process, let's look at supply planning integration.

13.4 Supply Planning Integration

Supply planning is required for the capacity planning and replenishment process based on CBF demand. Once the constrained supply plan is created, ABC Technology would like to check how much supply deviation there is from the original demand forecast. The business benefit is for the planners to take any other proactive steps well in advance to meet customer sales orders.

The supply planning integration in the characteristics-based planning requires the use of SAP APO Production Data Structure. The production version (routing and BOM) is transferred via CIF to SAP APO in the form of the Production Data Structure (PDS) or Production Process Model (PPM). Using the PDS is mandatory for the integration of object dependencies from SAP ERP.

The syntax of the object dependencies as displayed in the PDS is slightly different from SAP ERP, as you can see in Figure 13.24. The PDS structure contains the configuration tab with applicable values for that material. We also observe the object dependencies for some of the component materials in the figure. As with the object dependencies check in SAP ERP, it is possible to simulate the impact of a configuration within the PDS display via Transaction /SAPAPO/CURTO_SIMU.

It is important to know that object dependencies are not CIF-transferred as an object, but their impacts and consequences are interpreted by SAP APO. Figure 13.24 shows the PDS structure of the custom desktop (configurable product) with BOM components and characteristics values (keyboard, casing, hard disk, etc.) for the components.

13.4.1 Business Scenario and Technical Steps

Let's look at ABC Technology, where the sales order characteristics values are transferred to SAP APO. Based on these characteristics values that are provided by the customer (keyboard, hard disk, casing combinations, etc.), the components are checked for availability. When the customer creates the sales order (as shown in Figure 13.25), the sales order requests the characteristics value assignment for the component items.

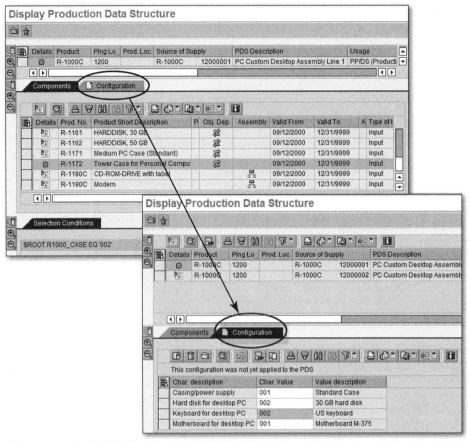

Figure 13.24 Production Data Structure in SAP APO

The sales order item category is TAC (variant configuration), as configured in the earlier SAP ERP strategy object configuration (see Figure 13.6). During the sales order processing, the finished good (and components) availability check is done with the multilevel ATP check, and the corresponding planned order is created in SAP APO.

The RECEIPTS CHARS and REQUIREMENTS CHARACTERISTICS for pegged elements are shown in the PEGGING OVERVIEW tab in the SAP APO PRODUCT VIEW screen of Transaction /SAPAPO/RRP3 (Figure 13.26). You can see the characteristics valuation for the planned order and sales order by clicking the green triangle icons. The confirmation of the configurable product is based on the component availability dates.

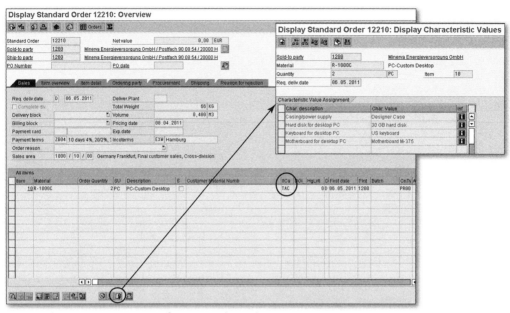

Figure 13.25 Variant Configuration Sales Order Creation in SAP ERP

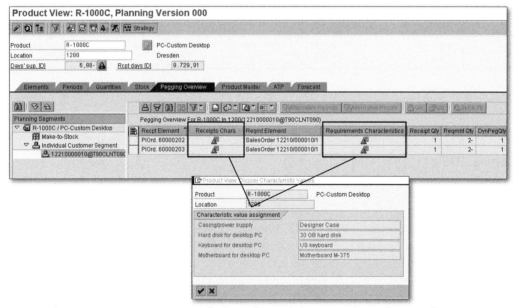

Figure 13.26 Pegging Overview of Sales Orders and Planning Orders with Same Characteristics Value

The planned order details are shown in the CONTEXT FOR PLANNED ORDER screen shown in Figure 13.27 (accessed via Transaction /SAPAPO/RRP3). Along with the displayed planned order details, click the CONTEXT button for more drill-down details. All the dependent demands of the component element are shown pegged with the corresponding receipt elements. If you increase the sales order quantity, an additional planned order is generated in the next planning run.

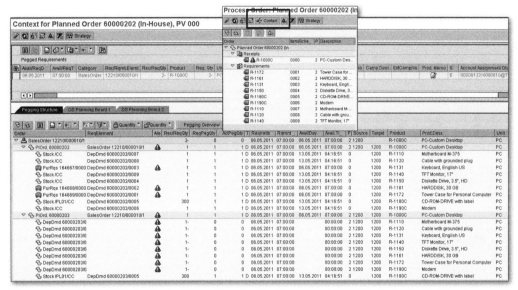

Figure 13.27 Planned Order Context View Showing the Component BOM Explosion in Multilevel ATP

13.4.2 Block Planning Integration

SAP APO PP/DS block planning helps in reducing the manufacturing changeover time, and results in a program with orders having similar characteristics (motherboard, casing, hard disk, and keyboard) are grouped together, allowing optimization of the resources. The blocks are planned to minimize the setup duration when the product configuration is changed (e.g., change of motherboard assembly). The integration here focuses on proper bucketing of the customer orders based on characteristics to match with the production cycle. This in turn improves the production efficiency and reduces the setup (i.e. changeover) time in the manufacturing process.

Example

ABC Technology uses the concept of *blocks*, where the blocks are defined as resource availability periods for similar product characteristics. The blocks here are defined in terms of a grouping of similar characteristics values (for example, a 20-GB hard disk) for the production cycle. Instead of making all the products randomly, to gain production efficiency, ABC Technology consolidates and schedules the production per the hard disk and motherboard similar combination.

For example, the production cycle runs for the 20-GB hard disk first, then the 40-GB and 60-GB hard disk products. This reduces the setup and machine changeover times. Once the forecast is released based on the descriptive characteristics combination, it falls on the adjustable defined blocks in APO PP/DS.

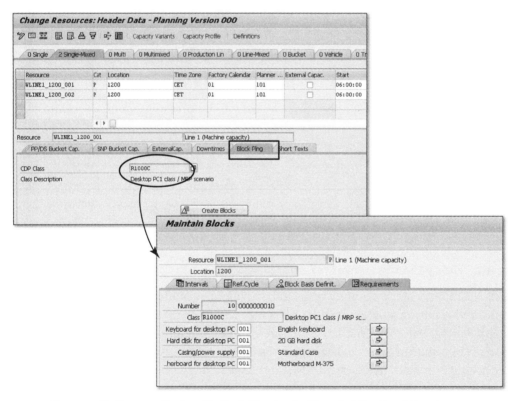

Figure 13.28 Resource Master with Block Planning for Characteristics-Based Planning

The block basis definition (see the screen in Figure 13.28, which is accessed via Transaction /SAPAPO/MC01_BBD) has a unique name and is the quantity of all characteristics requirements for the class on which the block is based. It enables the user to define several similar blocks of the same type at the same time. Several of these block basis definitions, together with a duration, form a reference cycle.

Additionally, the block planning schedules maintenance is required in the SAP APO resource master data, as shown in Figure 13.28. In the RESOURCE MASTER • BLOCK PLNG tab, input the CDP CLASS and BLOCK BASIS DEFINITION, which we defined earlier. The block reference cycle intervals are maintained by inputting the date interval when the different blocks would be scheduled. You can manually adjust the blocks per the resource capacity loads.

13.5 Summary

Characteristics-based forecasting allows companies to forecast products with different attributes and manufacture them using modern forecasting methods and production techniques. The usage of characteristics-based planning allows the companies to be in a competitive position, have shorter delivery times, and improve customer satisfaction. This chapter provided an overview of characteristics-based planning and characteristics-based forecasting. Using ABC Technology's business scenario of a custom desktop manufacturer, the chapter provided configuration and master data steps for setting up variant configuration to support characteristics-based planning.

The next chapter shows how SAP APO supports industry solutions. Using a business case example of an Apparel and Footwear (AFS) company, it provides an overview of the SAP APO functionalities that support the industry.

This chapter explains the integration of SAP APO with an SAP industry solution. Follow along with the processes as we demonstrate the steps with a case study that integrates the apparel and footwear industry with SAP APO for supply chain planning.

14   SAP Industry Solution Example with SAP APO

SAP provides more than 25 industry-specific ERP solutions tailored to address the business processes of specific industries, such as the auto, oil, and gas industries. The business processes are mapped in an SAP solution map that's created by user groups, partners, and SAP development teams.

In this chapter, we'll put ABC Technology on the backburner and take the Apparel and Footwear (which we'll refer to as AFS) industry as an example. This industry has specific characteristics, such as a shorter product lifecycle, product variety, volatile and unpredictable demand, and long and inflexible supply processes. The purpose of this chapter is to describe an example that shows how SAP APO can be used with industry-specific solutions as an integrated solution for the demand and supply planning process.

As shown in the mind map for this chapter (see Figure 14.1), we'll introduce you to the specific characteristics that make the AFS industry a prime candidate for integration with SAP APO. You'll see how the integration provides motivation for making SAP APO relevant with the industry solution to address that specific industry's business requirements and needs. We'll first go over a brief overview on the business process flow and then walk through master and transactional data integration in the AFS solution. You'll see additional information on the APO-DP seasonal and APO-SNP aggregated planning function, which supports AFS industry requirements. A brief overview is also given of the enhancement package approach by SAP to implement enhancements in a modular fashion.

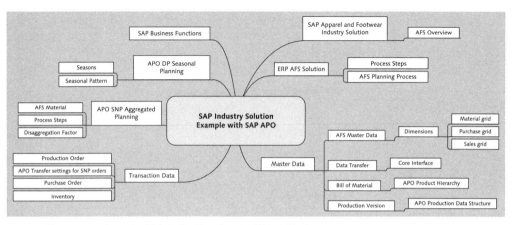

Figure 14.1 Learning Points for the Chapter (Mind Map)

14.1 SAP Apparel and Footwear (AFS) Industry Solution

In the AFS industry, companies have to cope with seasonal fluctuation, proliferation of design variations, volatile demand (making forecasting process difficult), stock shortages, and price wars. Figure 14.2 shows the ecosystem of the AFS industry. As you can see in the figure, the business model uses external subcontractors and manufacturers (mills) for the production process. This practice of outsourcing raises a challenge for the industry to monitor its lead times and delivery dates to receive products in the warehouse.

Similarly, the AFS company has to manage fluctuating market demand coming from retailers and catalog and internet sales. These external factors, both upstream and downstream, put the AFS company in a challenging position to balance both market demand and supply constraints.

AFS companies are increasingly coordinating internal and external supply chains. Thus, these companies are shifting from manufacturing and moving toward planning, controlling, and monitoring goods movement in the supply chain. Companies can better adjust their practices and meet their needs by using the SAP Apparel and Footwear solution, which provides the following benefits:

▶ Flexible user interface design, in that the screens for the business user manual entry can be designed per business user requirements for the order entry process

▶ Credit card processing facilitated by the process which includes accepting in-store and web credit card payments

642

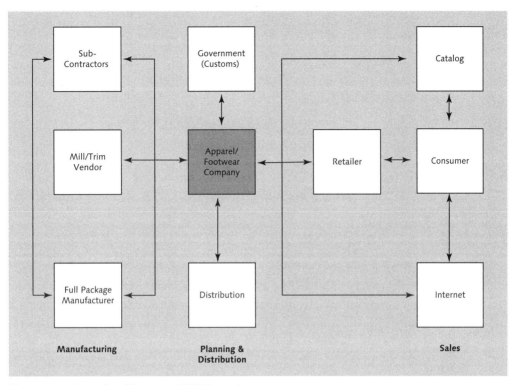

Figure 14.2 Apparel and Footwear (AFS) Ecosystem

▸ Better management of rush sales orders with sales orders, allocation, and delivery all done in the same step to give the order to the warehouse for picking

▸ Better management of value-added services (e.g., performing additional packaging) requested during order taking

▸ Concept of *mark for* modeled for the direct customer delivery option, which is a practice used in the retail industry wherein the consolidated shipment is cross-docked to smaller satellite warehouses

Some of the highlights of SAP Apparel and Footwear solution are:

▸ It helps you to manage the supply chain from procurement to finished goods delivery. The solution provides both manufacturing and outsourcing processes, which can be implemented at the global scale.

▸ The solution is able to manage custom regulations and quota rules for fulfilling customer orders. The solution also provides automatic order scheduling and backorder processing and supports pricing discounts and rebates on customer orders.

▶ It's able to manage a high volume of SKUs with flexible data maintenance. The master data structure is three-dimensional and can represent color, quality, and size at the SKU level.

We'll now look at the SAP Apparel and Footwear solution integrated with SAP ERP and SAP APO, as well as some solution–specific definitions.

14.2 SAP ERP (AFS Extension): Integrated Solution Overview

To have a better idea of what the integrated solution consists of, we've provided an example of the technical architecture (see Figure 14.3) perspective on how SAP APO provides the demand and supply planning elements to the overall AFS solution. The integration of SAP ERP (with the AFS extension, a means of installing an industry solution to activate the AFS functionalities) with SAP SCM (APO) is done via Core Interface (CIF). Both master data and transactional data are exchanged via CIF.

> **Note**
>
> SAP OSS Note 983640: SAP ERP AFS 6.0 add-on installation provides more information on the AFS extension installation.

In the SAP SCM system, APO-DP performs the seasonal planning and releases the plan to APO-SNP. In turn, APO-SNP is able to calculate the company's medium- to long-term planning and provides a distribution, procurement, and manufacturing plan.

In SAP ERP, AFS MRP considers the short-term horizon and plans procurement and manufacturing, including the subcontracting process. Once the goods are in inventory, the allocation run provides prioritization of the customer orders, which are subsequently delivered.

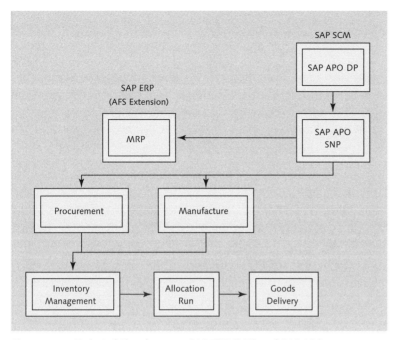

Figure 14.3 Technical Flow between SAP ERP (AFS) and SAP APO

In the following sections, we'll go into further details regarding the high-level process steps that you need to organize the integrated solution, as well as SAP Apparel and Footwear planning information. Starting in Section 14.3, we'll discuss the technical integration steps.

14.2.1 Process Steps

The integrated solution consists of planning, execution, and finance, as shown in Figure 14.4. The process steps are:

❶ The supply chain planning process team performs forecasting based on historical sales orders and the seasonal pattern defined in SAP APO. The forecast is then released to manufacturing. The seasonal forecasting drives the vendor procurement before the retail orders are captured. The seasonal demand allows the buyer to send the purchase order based on material lead times. In some scenarios, the retailers also place orders well in advance of the season to ensure the material inventory and lock early discounts via advertisements (for example, catalog sales). This entire process, from forecasting to ordering, is covered in the SAP ERP (AFS extension) integration solution.

❷ The manufacturing process calculates the net requirements and provides the constraint capacity plan to the allocation process. Also, input is provided to the procurement for buying long lead time raw materials from the vendors. The manufacturing process primarily consists of the outsourcing process. All transactions in SAP ERP (AFS extension) are performed via subcontracting orders for both material and service procurement with the vendor.

❸ The allocation run is an AFS-specific process of allocation of stocks to the customer requirements based on business rules. This situation arises when the customer has placed orders well in advance and the confirmed dates are based on material lead times. However, when the dates come close, there might be a scenario of demand-supply imbalance, and the allocation process determines the prioritization of physical stock distribution to the open customer orders. The allocation process consists of selection of requirements (customer orders), grouping, and sorting (to determine the priorities). The allocation can run on first in-first out (FIFO) or equal distribution rules whereby the stocks follow the fair share rule based on demand. Other criteria, such as customer type, partial/complete deliveries, and order/delivery dates, can also be input as customer parameters to define the allocation logic. The output of the allocation is then released to the manufacturing or distribution process to create deliveries to fulfill customer orders.

❹ Another important process in AFS is third-party processing, or the direct shipment scenario. The process consists of delivering the goods directly to the customer from the supplier or vendor. All the information is available at the SKU level from the purchase orders linked with the sales orders. These direct delivery items are termed accessories in SAP ERP (AFS extension). In a scenario in which there are bulk or consolidated orders, the vendor delivers goods to the AFS company, which then physically distributes to the customer. Goods the vendor ships to the company before customer delivery are termed *third-party items*.

❺ The procurement process involves running MRP for material procurement from the vendor and supplying the components to subcontractors for manufacturing. SAP ERP (AFS extension) also provides a vendor capacities function to book the vendor resources well in advance.

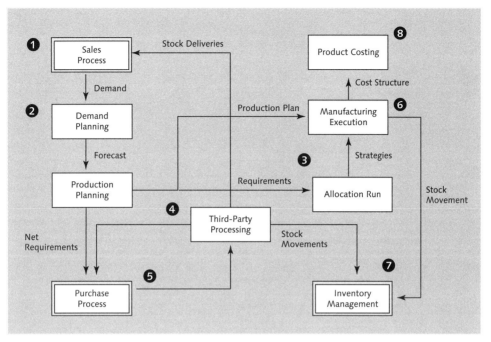

Figure 14.4 Integrated SAP ERP (AFS) Solution Overview

❻ The execution process yields the finished goods materials, which can be distributed to retailers. A portion of the manufacturing process might involve the subcontracting process, as well. The routing master data in SAP ERP (AFS extension) defines manufacturing processes, such as cutting, embroidering, and sewing.

❼ The stocks are updated in the inventory management system either via the manufacturing or subcontracting (third-party processing) business process.

❽ Product costing helps a company know the costs incurred by its products in order to successfully manage its product portfolio. The product cost accounting business process calculates the cost of goods manufactured (COGM) or cost of goods sold (COGS), broken down by each step of the production process.

Figure 14.5 shows the AFS master data and business process supported by the SAP ERP and SAP SCM systems. We've included specific AFS master data (for example, material grids, season, etc.) and processes (for example, allocation run) that are built to support AFS business requirements. Some of these will be explained in the coming sections.

647

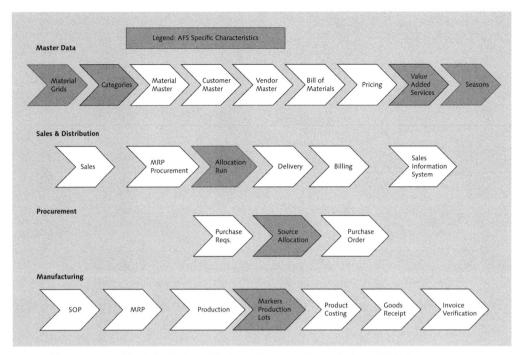

Figure 14.5 AFS Master Data and Business Processes Supported in SAP ERP

14.2.2 AFS Planning

As Figure 14.6 shows, the planning process involves different data exchanges between the SAP ERP (AFS extension) and SAP SCM systems. The figure shows the use of seasonal demand planning, along with APO-SNP aggregated planning functionalities. From the master data perspective, the dimensions, grids and categories are mapped into CIF to transform into a hierarchy structure in SAP APO master data. The forecast is transferred as planned independent requirements from APO-DP.

APO-SNP performs planning at two levels: header and sub-header. The header planning at the SKU level consists of sourcing and capacity planning, while the sub-header consists of forecast consumption, netting, and quantity calculations. The APO-SNP aggregated planning is supported by different APO-SNP planning engines (heuristics, optimizer, and CTM). The output of the APO-SNP planning run, in the form of planned orders and purchase requisitions, is interfaced (CIF) to SAP ERP (AFS extension). The execution process in SAP ERP (AFS) converts purchase requisitions into purchase orders or planned orders into production orders, which are interfaced (CIF) back to SAP APO.

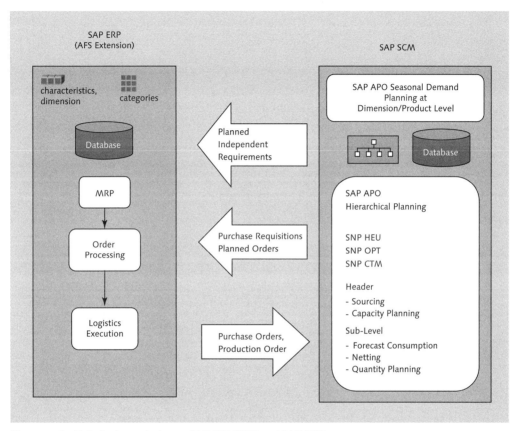

Figure 14.6 Data Exchange between SAP ERP (AFS) and SAP APO

14.3 Master and Transactional Data Integration

In this section, we'll go over the steps you need to follow to maintain your SAP ERP (AFS extension) master data and enable the system to transfer the data from SAP ERP to SAP SCM via CIF.

14.3.1 Maintain Master Data

Dimensions in SAP ERP (AFS extension) are defined as characteristics with characteristics group name /AFS/SAP-D. You can maintain the relevant characteristics values (for example, T-shirt sizes) in SAP ERP Transaction CT04. The dimensions can be numeric or alphanumeric.

Once the dimensions are maintained, maintain the material grid using Transaction J3AH. A *material grid* is a data construct that allows the business user to enter dimensions information for the material. The dimensions within the grid represent the attributes of the product (for example, color, size, and style). Up to three dimensions can be maintained in a specific grid. There are three types of material grids:

- **Master grid**: part of the material master
- **Purchase grid**: a subset of the master grid
- **Sales grid**: a subset of the master grid

You can maintain the purchase and sales grids specifically to the vendor and customer. The segmentation in SAP ERP (AFS extension) is maintained via *categories*. Categories provide additional information to specify or characterize your product. Some examples of categories are customer segment, quality, and country of origin.

Once the master data are created, you're ready to transfer AFS material data to SAP APO using the Core Interface (CIF).

14.3.2 Data Transfer from SAP ERP to SAP APO

Before you can transfer any data, you need to run two reports (SKU variant and material class assignment to AFS material) in SAP ERP (AFS extension). These reports help map the dimensions during the transfer. You can find the reports by choosing SAP menu path LOGISTICS • AFS INTERFACES • CREATE SKU VARIANT PER AFS MATERIAL/CREATE MATERIAL CLASS ASSIGNED TO AFS MATERIAL. Here, you can generate and activate the CIF integration model further to transfer the AFS material. SAP Tables /AFS/NDIF_XREF and /AFS/NDIFRDUPD are populated with valid entries to be transferred (via CIF) after running these reports.

Once the tables are populated, we can perform the CIF transfer using integration model transactions CFM1 and CFM2. Figure 14.7 shows the data transfer of AFS material with dimensions, size, and color. The example shows that the SKU level (T-shirt) is transferred as aggregated product in SAP APO. The dimensions of color (grey and red) and size (small, medium, and large) are then further constructed at the item level in SAP APO, under the hierarchy of the SKU item.

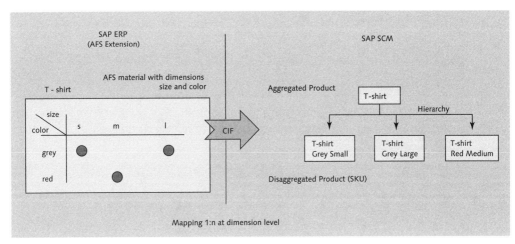

Figure 14.7 Data Transfer of AFS Material into SAP APO

14.3.3 Bill of Materials Construct in SAP ERP (AFS Extension)

The next important master data step is the bill of material (BOM) construct in SAP ERP Transaction CS01. There are two types of BOM maintained in SAP AFS: *standard* (with pre-pack option) and *assortment*.

▶ The standard BOM consists of AFS materials and component materials. The pre-pack (for example, a golf pack consisting of a shirt, pants, and a cap) is a set of predefined combinations of size and quantity in BOM. The header material may have the master grid different than the component grids. Some of the components may also have their individual BOM assembly. All items maintained in BOM are MRP-relevant.

▶ You can create an assortment BOM based on a company's sales promotions, whereby the customer requests for grouping of two or more finished products in the form of a set. This is similar to the concept of phantom assembly in SAP ERP. The header material in this case doesn't have a master grid, but the components will have their own individual, defined grids.

Figure 14.8 shows an example of a BOM, in which the SAP ERP (AFS extension) BOM is transferred as a product hierarchy master data in SAP SCM (APO) system.

The example shows that the T-shirt and fabric are created based on the maintained characteristics and dimensions. In the CIF integration model, we can select which AFS need to be planned in SAP APO and the other components directly in SAP ERP (AFS extension) via the MRP process.

> **Note**
>
> The CIF integration model selection usually is not arbitrary. (If you have multilevel structures, you need to make sure that all the SAP APO products are planned first to have the dependent requirements as prerequisites for the MRP in AFS). The relevant planning run jobs need to be properly organized to make this process work smoothly.

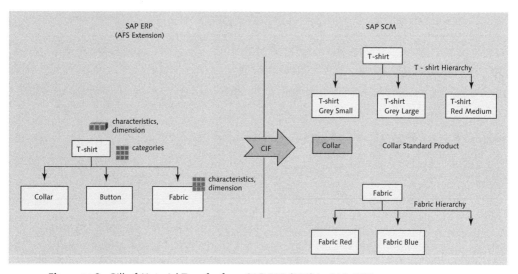

Figure 14.8 Bill of Material Transfer from SAP ERP (AFS) to SAP APO

You combine the BOM and the routing in SAP ERP (AFS) to form a production version via Transaction C223. The production version is transferred from SAP ERP (AFS extension) to SAP APO as a production data structure (PDS) for both the aggregated product and the other SKU defined in the dimensions. Figure 14.9 shows an example of the PDS structure formation in SAP APO. For each material dimensions combination (SKU) in SAP ERP (AFS extension), there is one PDS created in SAP APO.

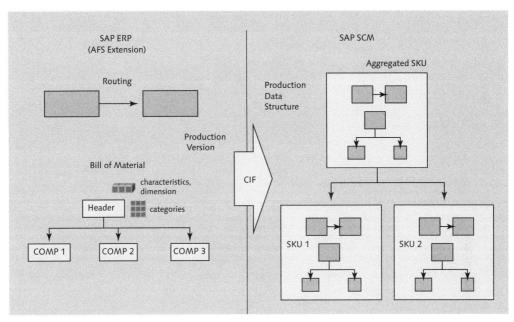

Figure 14.9 Production Data Structure in SAP APO for AFS Material

The automatic transfer of master data creates three hierarchies in SAP APO: product hierarchy, location product hierarchy, and PDS hierarchy, which are mandatory master data for AFS functionality to work with the APO-SNP aggregated planning feature.

14.3.4 Transactional Data Integration

The transactional data integration between SAP ERP (AFS extension) and SAP APO follows the concept of grouping orders based on header material. Figure 14.10 shows an example of the integration of planned orders, which are transferred to SAP ERP (AFS extension) and converted to production orders during execution, which is then transferred back to SAP APO.

APO-SNP will create planned orders for each location product for all sub-products. An *order group* will collect all the sub-product planned orders that have the same header product for the same time bucket. When the order is transferred to SAP ERP (AFS extension) at the sub-product level, the planned orders are merged to create one planned order in SAP ERP (AFS extension) at the AFS material level. The planner will convert the planned orders to production orders in SAP ERP (AFS

653

extension). While sending the conversion back to SAP APO, the grid information is used to split the production order into sub-levels before SAP APO is updated.

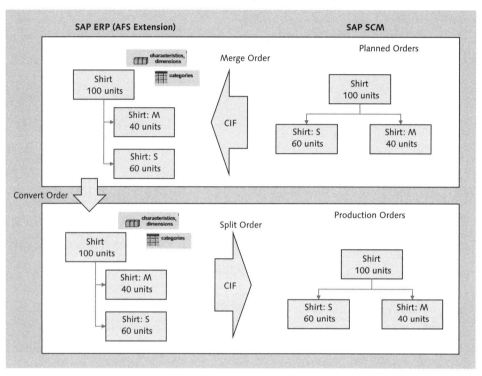

Figure 14.10 Transactional Order Integration between SAP ERP (AFS) with SAP SCM (APO)

You can set the APO-SNP order transfer at either the header or sub-order level. This way, you can control whether you want to publish the SAP APO planning result for only header products or both header and sub-order products to the SAP ERP system. This is controlled in customization in menu path IMG • ADVANCED PLANNING AND OPTIMIZATION • SUPPLY CHAIN PLANNING • SUPPLY NETWORK PLANNING • BASIC SETTINGS • CONFIGURE TRANSFER TO OLTP SYSTEMS. Figure 14.11 shows this setting.

Once the purchase requisitions are transferred to SAP ERP via the above setting in SAP APO, it can be displayed in Transaction ME52N. Figure 14.12 shows an example of a purchase requisition, in which the AFS materials are grouped under the same header material in the SAP ERP (AFS extension) document. The various characteristics of the AFS materials are shown as line items.

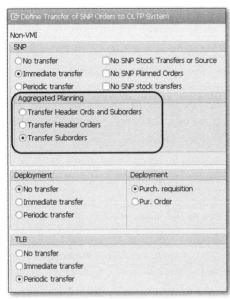

Figure 14.11 Transfer Setting for APO-SNP Orders

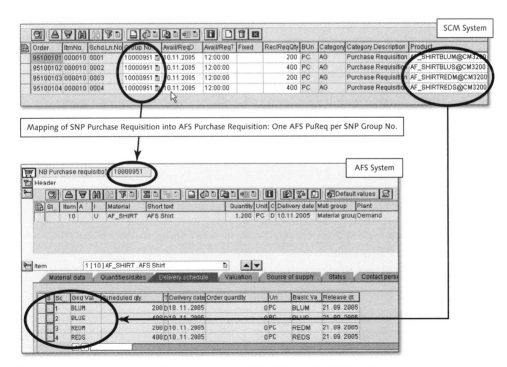

Figure 14.12 Purchase Requisitions Grouping in SAP APO and SAP ERP (AFS)

As with the purchasing document, the inventory can also be displayed in the form of product hierarchy in both the SAP ERP stock requirement list and the SAP APO planning book. Figure 14.13 shows another example of how the inventory is seen as both aggregated and disaggregated in the SAP APO planning book under different product/location combinations, while in the SAP ERP (AFS) system (stock overview, Transaction MMBE) it is seen as two different batch characteristics for the same AFS material.

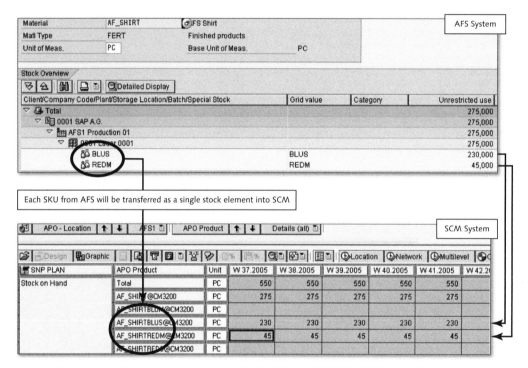

Figure 14.13 Physical Inventory View in SAP APO and SAP ERP (AFS Extension)

Now that we've looked at the master data integration between SAP ERP and SAP APO for the AFS solution, we'll next go over the demand and supply planning functionality embedded within the AFS solution.

14.4 SAP APO Solution for AFS Using Aggregated Functionality

SAP APO aggregated planning forms the pivotal functionality for integrating the AFS solution with SAP APO business processes. Aggregated (or hierarchical) planning forms a planning concept whereby the demand and supply plans are created at the product family level instead of individual variant products. For example, instead of planning at individual shirts with various color or size variations, the planning is done at the family shirt level. The requirements and inventory are also consolidated at the upper hierarchical level.

SAP defines *aggregation* as, "an approach to simplify a problem structure by temporal and/or logical grouping of data and decision variables. This means the grouping of similar objects to a common generic object."

The functionality of seasonal planning (APO-DP) and aggregated APO-SNP supports the planning of AFS in an integrated way with SAP AFS, as shown earlier in Figure 14.6. The key features in SAP APO supporting the aggregation concept in both APO-DP and SNP are:

▶ Individual demand planning seasons for apparel and footwear with region variables with multiple characteristics, which allows you to slice and dice the data per the business requirements

▶ Demand planning by different planning years along with the calendar year

▶ Aggregated and disaggregated functionality in APO-SNP, which includes forecast consumption and forecast netting

▶ Order grouping functionality between the header and sub-product levels

In the following sections, we'll explain the demand and supply functions using the aggregated planning concepts. While APO-DP uses the aggregation on seasons per characteristics, the APO-SNP performs planning at a higher product family or AFS material.

14.4.1 Demand Planning: Seasonal Functionality

Once defined, the seasons are seen as aggregates of weekly or monthly buckets mapped into seasons. We can define the seasons per characteristics, meaning that we can define multiple seasons based on the product group/characteristics, for example. The business user can define the seasonal year to view the consolidated picture. The maintenance of seasons per seasonal patterns is done by the business user in Transaction /SAPAPO/SDP_SEASON. We explained how to set up demand planning seasonal functionality in Chapter 6, Section 6.3; refer to that part of the book for more detailed steps.

Figure 14.14 shows an example in which the business can have two seasonal patterns that are different for different products or product groups in the same calendar year. This flexibility helps the company to plan different seasons for different product groups. If the company is trading different brands, they can define individual seasons based on their yearly strategic sales and marketing plans.

Figure 14.14 Seasonal Pattern Definition in SAP APO

Technical Limitations

The seasonal planning functionality is not available in the APO-SNP planning area or APO-DP planning area with BOM and characteristics-based forecasting (CBF) functionality switched on. Also, for technical reasons, the seasonal planning functionality can only be performed on key figures that are based on SAP liveCache time series.

14.4.2 SAP APO Supply Network Planning: Aggregated Functionality

The APO-SNP aggregated function fully supports specific AFS industry business requirements. With this functionality, a business is able to perform sourcing and capacity planning with an AFS material (for example, a shirt) and then perform detailed planning at the SKU level (for example, shirt/blue color/small size). The business will also be able to plan at different planning levels and aggregate/disaggregate to maintain consistent data. It can perform forecast consumption and netting at the detailed SKU level.

Process Steps

In the AFS environment, the APO-SNP aggregated functionality allows business users to perform an APO-SNP planning run at the aggregated level by defining hierarchies for product, location, and production resource as master data for APO-SNP planning engines. The process steps for setting up SNP aggregated functionality in the AFS environment are as follows:

1. **Define the aggregated planning objects.**
   First, the business identifies whether to perform aggregates at the product, location, or resource level.

2. **Define the relationships between aggregated objects and detailed objects.**
   Once the aggregated level is defined, form the hierarchy master data in the system. We showed in Section 14.3 how the various SAP ERP (AFS extension) and SAP APO master data can be integrated to support the planning process. The location, production data structure (PDS), and resource hierarchies are created in this step by CIF transfer.

3. **Generate aggregated transactional data based on the definition of aggregated master data.**
   APO-SNP offers the functionality of grouping orders, as explained in Sections 14.1 to 14.3, which allows the system to group orders across multiple location products created by APO-SNP hierarchical planning and disaggregation. This capability allows the orders to be merged when transferring data to SAP AFS and then merging when transactional data comes back from the SAP ERP system. Order group information is displayed in interactive planning and stored persistently in SAP liveCache. Storing the transactional data at the detailed level allows for proper forecast consumption from customer sales orders and also proper netting calculation at the detailed level.

   SAP provides Transaction /SAPAPO/SNP08 to perform single-level demand and supply mapping for forecast netting calculation. If the netting is done at the header level, the receipts and requirements quantities are matching, but there might be mismatch on the variants at the detailed level. Using the transaction, we can perform proper netting at the detailed level before planning at the aggregated level.

4. **Perform safety stock planning at aggregated level.**

   Prior to the APO-SNP planning run, perform the safety stock evaluation at the detailed level. You can define the safety stock parameters (i.e., lead time, service level, and safety stock method) for safety stock calculations in the hierarchy master data via Transaction /SAPAPO/RELHSHOW. Figure 14.15 shows an example of hierarchy maintenance with safety stock.

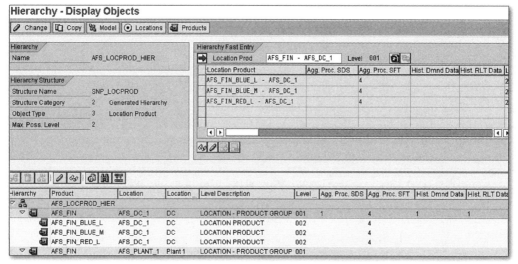

Figure 14.15 Aggregated Safety Stock Planning Parameter in Hierarchy Master Data

5. **Perform supply network planning based on aggregated master and transactional data.**

   All the APO-SNP planning engines—heuristics, Capable-to-Match (CTM), and optimizer—are supported by aggregated APO-SNP functionality. The APO-SNP planning run generates replenishment, distribution, and production plans for the medium- to long-term horizon at the AFS material (header) level. The resource capacity can also be viewed at the header level, and capacity leveling can be performed at the aggregated resource level. The business planner has the option of changing the plan at both the header and sub-product levels using the *network aggregation* and *location aggregation* functions in the APO-SNP interactive planning book. Figure 14.16 shows the CTM planning profile using the aggregated planning hierarchies, order group, and planning level definition. The CTM profile can be accessed using Transaction /SAPAPO/CTM.

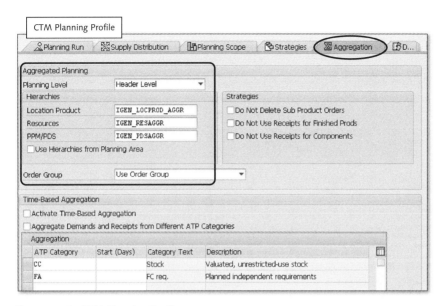

Figure 14.16 CTM Planning Profile

6. **Disaggregate planning result to detailed level (optional).**

The APO-SNP aggregated plan can now be further disaggregated based on business rules. Using the SNP LOCATION DISAGGREGATION and NETWORK DISAGGREGATION functions, the planner can manipulate the transaction orders at the sub-product detailed level. SAP provides resource disaggregation functionality (see Figure 14.17). The MINIMAL RESOURCE CONSUMPTION option selects the PDS with the minimum resource variable consumption rate per output quantity relative to open capacity. A new order with the maximum capacity is created in this scenario. This functionality can be accessed via Transaction /SAPAPO/SNP09 for APO-SNP resource disaggregation. SAP also provides BAdI /SAPAPO/SDP_DIS-AGRES for defining any customer-specific business rules for disaggregation.

Disaggregation Factor

Another important functionality in APO-SNP planning disaggregation is the use of the quota, or key figure, for defining the *disaggregation factor*. The factor is used to split the allocated supply in the constraint supply business situation. The original design of SAP APO has the disaggregation factor based on the demand key figure of lower levels. You can maintain the quota allocation either in the hierarchy master data or in the APO-SNP time-dependent planning time series key figure. The quota allocation can also be automatically transferred from the SAP ERP (AFS) distribution profile data construct via CIF. You can define in the horizon whether to use the demand or quota allocation.

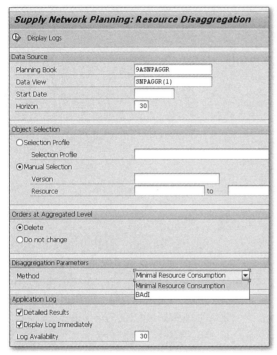

Figure 14.17 Resource Disaggregation

Figure 14.18 shows the hierarchy master data (Transaction /SAPAPO/RELHSHOW) and the APO-SNP disaggregation program (Transaction /SAPAPO/SNP06) to define whether to use the quota or APO-SNP time-dependent time series key figure value to disaggregate the plan from the AFS material to the SKU detailed levels. You can use the HORIZON FOR METHOD COMBINATION field to combine both the quota and time-dependent key figure methods.

Last, we'll take a quick look at how the various functionalities are implemented with the enhancement package modular concept.

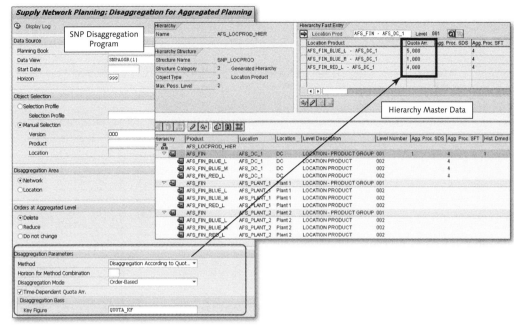

Figure 14.18 Disaggregation Methods for APO-SNP Plan

14.5 SAP Business Function

SAP has taken a new approach to deploying innovate solutions to its customers. Instead of continuing to upgrade to higher version, SAP now offers new functionalities in the form of *enhancement packages*. With each new enhancement package, SAP provides new functionalities, which the customer can opt to implement if they match their requirements. The implementation of these new functionalities is done via the *business function*. The business function is accessed via Transaction SFW5 in both the SAP ERP and SAP SCM systems.

The business function works on the Switch Framework customizing concept. The business function construct comes with some differences between SAP ERP and SAP SCM. While the business function in SAP ERP is organized by industry solutions, this concept is not there in SAP SCM. There is only one Switch Framework in SAP SCM, which buckets all the new functionalities. Figure 14.19 shows the business function in the SAP ERP and SAP SCM systems. To activate the business function, select it and click the ACTIVATE CHANGES icon on the top.

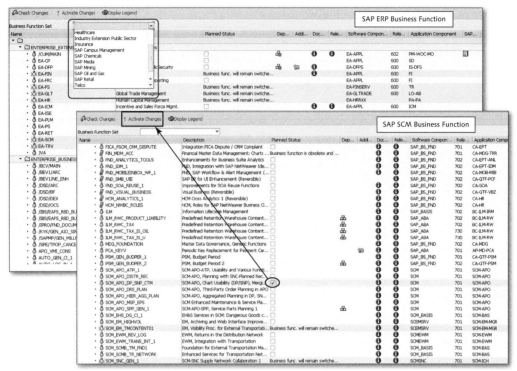

Figure 14.19 SAP ERP and SAP SCM Business Functions

14.6 Summary

SAP's industry solutions play a major role in delivering additional functionalities to meet the unique industry business requirements to companies that have already implemented the SAP ERP system. In this chapter, we used SAP AFS to show how the complexity of the industry can be matched by the integrated solution of SAP ERP (via the AFS extension) and SAP APO. The chapter provided a brief overview of the business process flow, and then went through master and transactional data integration in AFS.

The next chapter provides the technical concepts for monitoring and maintaining the SAP APO system. The chapter also touches on SAP SCM system upgrade activities, authorization, and CIF concepts.

This chapter explains the operational technical concepts within SAP APO and highlights the best practices for monitoring and maintaining productive SAP APO environments.

15   Technical Concepts in SAP APO

Understanding some key technical areas in SAP APO is important to run the system smoothly. Many companies implement SAP APO in stages or only scope one specific module in order to meet individual business requirements. This calls for possible interfaces with existing legacy applications, and understanding the technique for integrating SAP APO with non-SAP application becomes important.

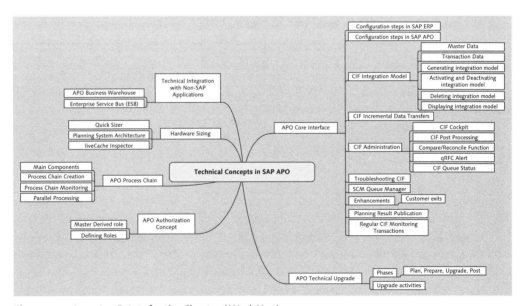

Figure 15.1   Learning Points for the Chapter (Mind Map)

As shown in the mind map for this chapter (see Figure 15.1) we'll be discussing various technical concepts in SAP APO. We explain how to set up the APO Core

Interface (CIF), which is the backbone needed to integrate the SAP ERP and SAP APO systems. We'll then move on to talk about the current releases of SAP SCM and how that impacts your system upgrades. You'll also learn about other important technical subjects, such as authorization, process chain for batch jobs, upgrade activities, and a few important tools for calculating available space in your system.

First, we'll explain the technical details that are involved in setting up the CIF.

15.1   APO Core Interface

The APO Core Interface (CIF) is the communication layer to be applied to SAP ERP to enable an exchange of data between SAP APO and SAP ERP. CIF forms a part of the SAP ERP plug-in, ensuring compatibility between different SAP ERP components installed in a single system. Using a remote function (RFC) technology, CIF provides the following:

▶ Integration models to specify which master and transaction data need to be exchanged between the SAP ERP and SAP SCM systems

▶ Techniques for initial, incremental, or real-time data transfers between the SAP ERP and SAP SCM systems

▶ Error-handling alerts and monitoring to ensure data transfer consistency between execution (SAP ERP) and planning systems (SAP SCM)

▶ Synchronous communication mode for real-time online updates between SAP ERP and SAP APO (e.g., global ATP)

▶ Asynchronous communication mode for processing data in the background between SAP ERP and SAP APO (e.g., APO-SNP)

Communication between SAP ERP and APO is based on the asynchronous transfer technique *queued Remote Function Call* (qRFC). This technique is used in the integration of SAP APO with an SAP ERP system, both for the initial data supply and incremental supply (data flow from SAP ERP to SAP APO) and for the publication of planning results (data flow from SAP APO to SAP ERP). The function calls are buffered in the sending system and executed asynchronously in the same sequence in which they were called. This serialization is controlled by the use of identical queue names and is required to assure consistency. Saved function calls are used.

The use of outbound queues enables the processing of saved function calls to rerun without generating inconsistencies after problems are corrected. The system automatically combines the multiple qRFCs into a *logical unit of work* (LUW), whereby one LUW on the sender side results in one LUW on the receiver side.

In the following sections, we'll go over the configuration steps in SAP ERP and SAP APO to set up CIF communication between the two systems.

15.1.1 CIF Configuration Steps

Setting up and running distributed SAP ERP applications is based on Application Link Enabling (ALE) technology. ALE involves the exchange of messages with consistent data retention in linked SAP ERP systems, controlled by the business. Because data is distributed between systems, you need to identify each system within a network. The *logical system* is used for this purpose and serves as the identity for the application running on that specific server. Various applications that run on a common database are grouped together in a logical system. The logical system is set up by an SAP Basis team.

As an example, let's say that a company has global and regional SAP ERP systems that are connected with one SAP SCM system. In this scenario, we have to integrate master and transactional data from different logical systems referencing the same object in SAP APO. For this purpose, a *business system group* (BSG) helps integrate different physical systems into a super-ordinate logical unit. BSG is commonly used for setting up SAP ERP-APO communication via CIF and is also used in distributed system landscapes. The setup is done by the SAP Basis team. A mapping structure for maintaining and activating *user enhancements* may also be required.

Table 15.1 lists important configuration steps in SAP ERP for setting up CIF communication between SAP ERP and SAP APO.

Steps	Transaction	Remarks
Define logical systems for SAP ERP and SAP APO.	SALE or BD54	Set up different logical systems for communication. For example, communication between SAP ERP and SAP SCM, SAP CRM, or SAP NetWeaver BW.

Table 15.1 Configuration Steps in SAP ERP for the Core Interface

Steps	Transaction	Remarks
Assign SAP ERP client to logical SAP ERP.	SCC4	Before two or more systems can communicate with each other, the technical coupling between them must be set up. The target address for the data transfer is determined during the setup of an RFC destination in SAP ERP. The name of the corresponding RFC destination must be identical to the name of the logical target system (SAP APO). One RFC destination is required for each target client (e.g., 001).
Define SAP APO release.	NDV2	The table controls the downward compatibility of the CIF.
Set target system and queue type.	CFC1	To enable the successful setup of communication between SAP ERP and SAP APO, the appropriate SAP SCM target system for this data channel must be installed in the definition of the RFC destination.
Define RFC connection to SAP APO.	SM59	Connection is defined to the source system via a communication user (CPIC) with proper authorization.
Register inbound queues.	SMQR	Register for CF* queues communication flow.
Register outbound queues.	SMQS	Register for CF* queues communication flow.
Define transfer parameters.	CFC2	Detailed error messages are stored in the destination system's application log.
Filter and select block size.	CFC3	Parameters: block sizes for initial transfer (setting).

Table 15.1 Configuration Steps in SAP ERP for the Core Interface (Cont.)

Similar configuration activities are required in the SAP APO system for the CIF communication between SAP ERP and SAP APO, which are detailed in Table 15.2.

Steps	Transaction	Remarks
Define the logical system for SAP ERP and SAP APO.	SALE or BD54	
Assign the SAP APO client to the logical SAP APO system.	SCC4	
Define the BSG.	/SAPSAP APO/C1	It is recommended that the SAP APO system be assigned to the same BSG as the logical system or SAP ERP instances that contain the master data server.
Assign the logical system for SAP APO and SAP ERP to BSGs.	/SAPAPO/C2	To provide for correct communication on the SAP APO side as well, every source system (SAP ERP) must be assigned to a BSG. (A BSG can consist of one or more source systems.) This means that the current BSG must be linked to at least one SAP ERP source system.
Define the RFC connection to SAP ERP.	SM59	The connection is defined to the source system via a communication user (CPIC) with proper authorization.
Register inbound queues.	SMQR	Register for CF* queues communication flow.
Register outbound queues.	SMQS	Register for CF* queues communication flow.
Define transfer parameters.	/SAPAPO/C4	Display/set user parameters (debugging, logging).
Define runtime information.	/SAPAPO/CP3	Object-specific setting for publication.
Define distribution per publication type.	/SAPAPO/CP1	Define the publication object (planning result) per location (plant) and logical system.
Generate and publish the distribution definition.	/SAPAPO/CP2	Generation and deletion of distribution definitions.

Table 15.2 Configuration Steps in SAP APO for the Core Interface

15.1.2 CIF Integration Models

Now that you've set up CIF in the system, you need to enable CIF integration models for setting up a communication channel between the SAP ERP and SAP SCM systems. There are three primary types of integration models: *master* (for example, material master), *transactional* (for example, purchase requisitions), and *customizing objects* (for example, ATP customizing). The integration models define the scope of the master data and transactional data objects we want to transfer between SAP ERP and SAP SCM. One of the prerequisites to setting up CIF communication between SAP ERP and SAP SCM is the activation of a business transaction event (BTE) by maintaining entry ND-APO or NDI via Transaction BF11 or FIBF.

The datasets (master and transactional) required for SAP APO are selected in the integration model. The structure of the integration model is important for performance reasons. It is recommended that you keep separate integration models for master data and transaction data. Also, depending on the data volume set, create one model per master and transactional data object type.

> **Example**
>
> ABC Technology has multiple locations in the supply chain network. For easier maintenance and troubleshooting, it has decided to create/maintain one integration model for each master data object (for example, material master per plant) and also integration models for each of the transaction data (for example, inventory per plant) objects. In this way, any error failures for a specific plant do not affect other plants' integration models.

The integration model is set up in two steps:

1. *The generation* step selects the object based on the selection criteria. Filter selection restricts the object volume further. This step is performed in Transaction CFM1.

2. *The activation* step transfers the data across the systems. This step is performed in Transaction CFM2.

Table 15.3 lists all the important transactions you will need to set up in the CIF integration model.

Steps	Transaction	Remarks
Create the integration model.	CFM1	No change integration model is available. Use the same variant to make object changes and save the variant. The model needs to be regenerated to include the new objects.
Activate the integration model.	CFM2	
Search objects for CIF models.	CFM5	Filter object search.
Change the transfer for master data.	CFP1	
Delete the integration model.	CFM7	Deactivated integration models are not automatically deleted.
Transfer master data online.	CFC5	Online delta transfer of master data.
Transfer the production process model (PPM).	CFP3	Online delta transfer of PPM.
Display application logs.	SLG1	Display entries in the application log (outbound from SAP ERP).
Display application logs.	CFG1	Display entries in the application log (inbound to SAP ERP).
Delete entries in application logs.	CFGD	Periodic deletion of entries in application logs.
Adjust Target-System-Ind. settings in CIF for master data change transfers in SAP ERP.	CFC9	Used for indicating periodic or real-time change transfer of master data objects from SAP ERP.

Table 15.3   Lists of Transaction Codes Relevant to CIF in SAP ERP

For master data integration models, we recommend grouping the following objects in a single integration model and activating them in the sequence we've outlined for data consistency:

1. ATP customizing: here we transfer SAP ERP MRP elements as ATP elements in SAP SCM.

2. Product allocation customizing: here we can transfer SAP ERP product allocation customizing objects to SAP SCM.

3. Plants (plants + DCs)

> **Note**
>
> The default setting for CIF is to transfer all the plants into SAP APO as a production plant type unless it is defined as DC in SAP ERP customizing menu path PRODUCTION • DISTRIBUTION REQUIREMENT PLANNING • BASIC SETTINGS • MAINTAIN ASSIGNMENT OF NODE TYPE-PLANT. We can also change the location type in SAP APO using report /SAPAPO/ CHANGE_LOCTYPE.

4. Charactersitics and classes

5. Material master + classes and classification (if the material master classification also needs to be transferred)

6. MRP areas + material master for MRP area

7. Availability check

8. Customers

9. Vendors

10. Work centers

11. Production data structure/production process model

12. Scheduling agreements, purchasing info records, and contracts

> **Note**
>
> During the activation of the material master integration model, the system blocks the material master record to include the indicator in MARC-APOKZ. If for any situation the material master was being created by a business user during the activation, the model will still be activated, but the indicator will not be set. To correct this inconsistency, always run report RAPOKZFX via Transaction SE38; otherwise, no transaction data will be transferred for these materials. This report can also be scheduled with other routine CIF reports (e.g., RIMODGEN, RIMODA2, and RIMODDEL) and batch jobs.
>
> SAP Notes 201516, 335771, 397919, and 424927 provide more information.

You should also group and activate the transaction data integration model as follows:

1. Stocks (for the scenario of consignment, stocks of the same integration model should contain both the stock and customer/vendor locations)

2. Sales orders (includes sales orders, deliveries, scheduling agreements, quotations, and customer requirements)

3. Purchase orders and purchase requisitions

4. Production/process orders + planned orders

5. Production campaign (can also be activated together with production/planned orders but never before the latter)

6. Manual reservation and planned independent requirements

7. Shipments

Next, we'll discuss several reports that allow you to activate and maintain the integration model for optimal performance. Some of these reports are run on routine nightly batch jobs, allowing you to capture any changes in the master data (i.e., addition or deletion) in the integration models.

Generating Integration Model (Report RIMODGEN)

This report is used to filter objects (master and transaction data) that we want or do not want to include in the integration model. As Figure 15.2 shows, there are three sections we need to maintain to define the objects selection for the integration model in Transaction CFM1:

❶ Select the object (PDS in our example).

❷ Define the material selection. (For example, we have selected all materials in Plant 1000 that are externally planned X0 MRP type.)

❸ You can use further restrictions on the type of the object (for example, SNP PDS) we want to transfer. Once defined, the generation of the integration model is done in a two step process: first by saving the variant for the integration model and second by generating the integration model.

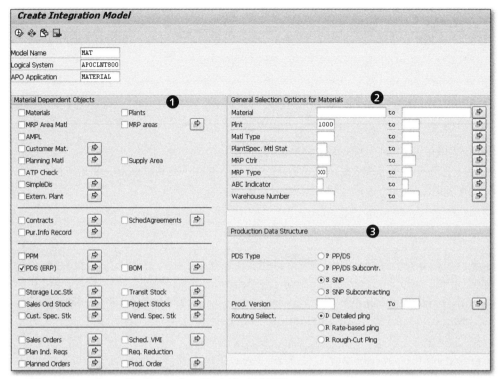

Figure 15.2 Generating Integration Model in SAP ERP

Activating and Deactivating the Integration Model (Report RIMODAC2)

By activating the integration model, you're able to transfer data from SAP ERP to SAP APO. You can activate the model using either Transaction CFM2 or report RIMODAC2.

Once the model is activated, the initial data transfer is performed automatically. For any subsequent changes in the integration model, it is advisable to deactivate the integration model first and then activate the integration model to include the delta changes in the model. A particular master data can only be active in a single integration model for consistency reasons.

In the report, check the IGNORE FAULTY QUEUE ENTRIES indicator to avoid complete failure of the variant processing.

Deleting Integration Model (Report RIMODDEL)

Inactive integration models and versions should routinely be deleted using report RIMODDEL.

Displaying Integration Model (Report RIMODOUT)

This report can be used to display active generated integration model. The models are displayed in alphabetical order.

Finding Filter Object (Report RIMODSRH)

This report is used to identify which master data objects are active in which integration models.

15.1.3 CIF Incremental Data Transfer

The initial data supply loads planning-relevant data from the SAP ERP system to SAP APO. This applies to both master data and transaction data. The initial supply is always performed sequentially. When you activate an integration model for master data the first time, an initial data transfer takes place. All changes to the master data after the initial data transfer can be transferred immediately after the change. It is also possible to record the changes made to the master data and send them routinely via a batch job.

To send the changes via a batch job, you have to evaluate and transfer change recordings (see Figure 15.3) of the integration model using Transaction CFP1 (report RCPTRAN4). In this way, we are transferring the collected change pointers for the master data changes.

The master data change transfer is also governed by settings defined in Transaction CFC9. In this transaction (see Figure 15.4), we can define whether the transfer is sent periodically via a batch job or immediately. SAP recommends the use of BTE TRANSFER, IMMEDIATELY as the setting for Transaction CFC9.

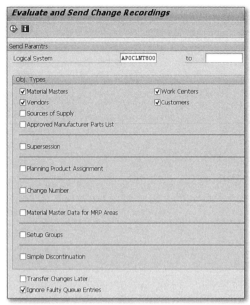

Figure 15.3 Master Data Change Transfers in SAP ERP

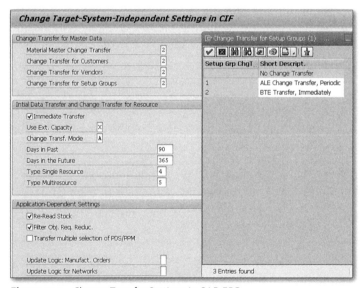

Figure 15.4 Change Transfer Settings in SAP ERP

The term *recording* used earlier is achieved technically via ALE change pointers. The change pointers for master data transfers need to be activated in SAP ERP. The change pointer refers to the collection of the changes done on the master data. To collect the changed data, follow these steps:

1. Define the change pointer number range via Transaction BDCP.

2. Define the master data objects for change pointers in Transaction BD50. The important message types to be activated are CIFMAT (material master), CIFCUS (customer), CIFVEN (vendor), and CIFSRC (source of supply).

3. Maintain Transaction BD52 with the table/fields details per message type. This will trigger the change pointer for the transfer.

The initial data transfer of transaction data is performed via the APO CIF, similarly to what happens with the master data. This is usually followed automatically by the incremental data transfer between SAP ERP and SAP APO for transaction data objects that are members of an active integration model. This means that new transaction data or changes to existing transaction data are transferred automatically.

> **Note**
>
> There is no similar Transaction CFC9 concept like master data in SAP APO.

For the transaction data of the APO-SNP, you can specify in Customizing whether a real-time or periodic retransfer is to be performed. To set this up, follow SAP APO IMG menu path ADVANCED PLANNING AND OPTIMIZATION • SUPPLY CHAIN PLANNING • SUPPLY NETWORK PLANNING • BASIC SETTINGS • CONFIGURE TRANSFER TO OLTP SYSTEMS.

The SAP APO transaction data objects are not generally identical to those of the SAP ERP system. The system transfers various SAP ERP transaction data into SAP APO as orders that differ by ATP category. Planned independent requirements can only be transferred via CIF from the SAP ERP system to SAP APO. The transfer of planned independent requirements from SAP APO into the SAP ERP, which you need if you only perform demand planning in SAP APO, must be triggered from APO-DP in SAP APO using a separate Transaction /SAPAPO/REL_TO_OLTP.

To publish transaction data from SAP APO into SAP ERP, maintain the distribution definitions for all the plants and object types. The maintenance is done via Transaction /SAPAPO/CP1, and generation via Transaction /SAPAPO/CP2. As Figure 15.5 shows, we maintain the transactional data to be published to SAP ERP per location along with the logical system definition of the target SAP ERP system.

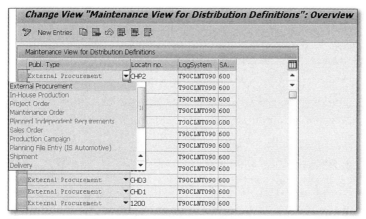

Figure 15.5 Distribution Definitions in SAP APO

15.1.4 CIF Administration

An important part of working with the CIF is dealing with the administration of master and transactional data flow between the SAP ERP and SAP SCM systems. This section highlights different mechanisms (i.e., tools) in CIF to identify the CIF errors. Monitoring how the master and transactional data queues are successfully processed between SAP ERP and SAP APO requires you to understand the error that has been encountered. Two forms of errors are possible during the communication:

▸ **Communication errors**
For example, network errors or a nonexistent RFC destination

▸ **Application errors**
For example, program errors, locking of objects, missing master data for transactional data, and non-posting of data to the target system

Table 15.4 lists all the necessary CIF-related transactions in SAP APO for monitoring and routine processing of master and transaction data.

Action	Transaction	Remarks
Monitor the CIF queues using the CIF cockpit.	/SAPAPO/CC	CIF cockpit is a container for CIF background jobs, qRFC, and CIF comparisons.

Table 15.4 CIF Processing Transactions in SAP APO

678

Action	Transaction	Remarks
Rectify the SAP ERP and SAP APO transaction data inconsistencies.	/SAPAPO/CCR	CIF Delta Report to detect transactional data inconsistencies that can be corrected by suitable measures.
Monitor CIF using queue manager.	/SAPAPO/CQ	SAP SCM Queue Manager to manage the inbound and outbound queues in SAP APO.
Trigger CIF queue alert when the queue is struck.	/SAPAPO/CW	qRFC monitoring for outbound queues.
Run consistency report between SAP liveCache and the database.	/SAPAPO/OM17	Inconsistencies may occur if the SAP APO database data or the SAP liveCache data can no longer be completely restored due to system crashes or inappropriate backup strategies. Because there is currently no logging for APO-DP data, inconsistencies can still occur in this area following a recovery. To check the external consistency between the SAP APO database and SAP liveCache and to set it up again, if necessary, use this transaction.
Display outbound application logs.	SLG1	Display entries in the application log (outbound from SAP APO).
Display inbound application logs.	/SAPAPO/C3	Display entries in the application log (inbound to SAP APO).
Delete application logs.	/SAPAPO/C6	Routine deletion of application logs.
Monitor outbound queues processing.	SMQ1	qRFC monitor (outbound queue).
Monitor inbound queues processing.	SMQ2	qRFC monitor (inbound queue).

Table 15.4 CIF Processing Transactions in SAP APO (Cont.)

In the following subsections, we'll discuss the different APO-CIF tools that help you perform the steps in Table 15.4.

CIF Cockpit

The CIF cockpit is a central monitoring in SAP APO for various CIF functions. The cockpit can be accessed via Transaction /SAPAPO/CC, where various information related to SAP APO and the SAP ERP system can be found. The basic information found for both SAP APO and SAP ERP is as follows:

▶ **SAP APO**

General information, CIF background jobs, entries in application logs, qRFC, post-processing records, CIF transfer setup, and CIF comparison/reconciliation of transaction data

▶ **SAP ERP**

General information, CIF background jobs, entries in application logs, superfluous filter objects, inconsistent APO indicators, CIF transfers, qRFC, post-processing records, integration model consistency, performance of each application

Figure 15.6 shows the CIF cockpit functionality where the SAP application support user can access all the above information by clicking the MONITORING section on the left side of the screen. The results are shown on the right side of the screen, as seen in the figure. Beside the MONITORING section, there is also a SETTINGS section, which shows the current technical setups.

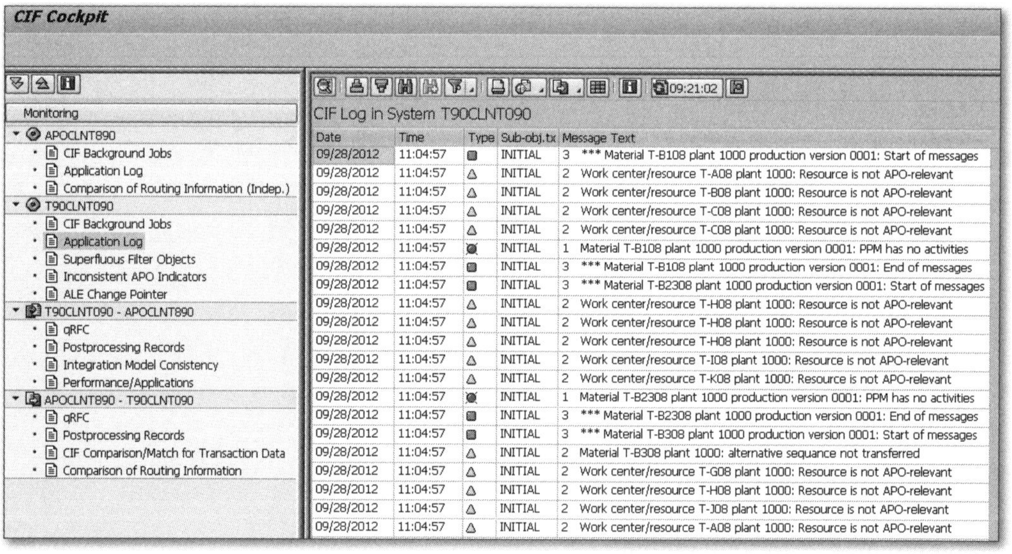

Figure 15.6 CIF Cockpit in SAP SCM

CIF Post-Processing

The earlier CIF concept was that all CIF queues must be processed strictly in sequence in order to prevent inconsistencies. In the case of a queue error, subsequent entries would typically queue behind the blockage and wait for it to be cleared. This causes a large number of queue errors and the need for constant monitoring to delete/ reprocess queues.

Since SAP APO version 4.1, there is a new concept of *post processing*. If the new functionality is switched on, the serialization of CIF queues becomes less strict. Error queues for transaction data no longer go into the CIF queue as before (SMQ1, SMQ2), but are logged as a "post processing error" visible in a separate transaction. This post-processing record does not prevent the transfer of subsequent LUWs. When the post-processing record is processed, the system re-reads the current state of the relevant object, rather than the state at the time it was first sent. Therefore, it is not a problem that the various queues have been processed out of sequence.

The CIF post-processing functionality is only available for ongoing transactional data transfers (e.g., orders and stocks). It does not apply to master data transfers or initial loads—these continue to be handled as before with the old CIF queue transactions.

The settings to activate the CIF post-processing are done via Transaction /SAPAPO/ C2. Change the ERR. HNDLG setting for the APO system and the linked SAP ERP systems to POSTPROCESSING FOR ERRORS, NO SPLITTING OF LUWS.

You can access CIF post-processing via Transaction /SAPAPO/CPP to analyze any CIF errors. You can set up the CIF Post Processing Alert Report (/SAPAPO/CIF_POST-PROC_ALERT) if the CIF administrator wants to be alerted if there are any new errors flowing to the CIF post-processing database.

Compare/Reconcile Function

The compare/reconcile function (report /SAPAPO/CIF_DELTAREPORT3) within CIF is used to maintain transaction data consistency between the SAP ERP and SAP APO systems. The inconsistencies can occur due to application errors or the deletion of orders that did not replicate to the other system. The process is executed in two steps:

1. Comparing the two systems on the selected data objects
2. Manually reconciling transaction data between the two systems

The report is usually run routinely to ensure that the planning run output is correct in SAP APO. The comparison is performed between the SAP ERP database and SAP liveCache systems in SAP APO. The overall process is performed in three screens, as shown in Figure 15.7:

❶ Access report /SAPAPO/CIF_DELTAREPORT3 and identify the transaction data objects that need to be reconciled. Input the corresponding SAP ERP system and the plant location and execute the report.

❷ The second screen shows a report that identifies the number of inconsistencies for each transaction document type (purchase orders, sales orders, etc.).

❸ Perform manual reconciliation by highlighting the row(s) and sending the orders to SAP ERP, or vice-versa, or deleting the orders in SAP APO. The nature of each error is identified by the error code. The administrator should log these errors, their causes, and the corrective action performed.

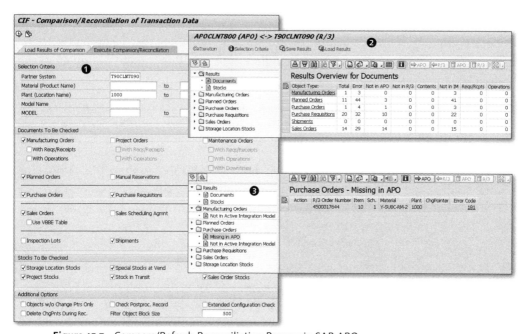

Figure 15.7 Compare/Refresh Reconciliation Process in SAP APO

qRFC Alert

Another commonly used report is /SAPAPO/RCIFQUEUECHECK (qRFC alert), which triggers an alert for any qRFC errors between the SAP ERP and SAP SCM systems.

The data transfer between SAP ERP and SAP APO is performed in asynchronous mode, and the user might not be immediately informed if there are any application errors. This report monitors all the outbound queues from SAP APO and queues of logical SAP ERP–connected system to give a proactive notification in case of any errors. Transaction /SAPAPO/CQ (SCM Queue Manager) is another important location to locate the error (explained in the "SCM Queue Manager" section).

Logical Unit of Work

As we discussed, the system automatically combines the multiple qRFCs into a *logical unit of work* (LUW), whereby one LUW on the sender side results in one LUW on the receiver side. The two SAP functions that monitor the data transfer between SAP ERP and SAP APO are the qRFC monitor and application log:

▶ **qRFC monitor** to monitor errors

  ▶ SAP ERP: Transaction codes SMQ1 and SMQ2 for inbound and outbound queues

  ▶ SAP APO: Transaction codes SMQ1 and SMQ2 for inbound and outbound queues

▶ **Application log** to perform error analysis

  ▶ SAP ERP: Transaction CFG1 to display entries of application log

  ▶ SAP APO: Transaction /N/SAPAPO/C3 to display entries of application log

Troubleshooting

If the queue cannot be processed, this could be due to a number of reasons, including connection errors (here, you'll see a status of CPICERR) and errors caused by the application (status SYSFAIL). In addition, if necessary, the user can stop and start specific queues with Transaction SMQ1.

While in the case of CPICERR the data can usually be transferred successfully after correcting the problem simply by executing the function call again, application errors require intensive analysis. Under some exception conditions, the function call in the target system (for example, an inconsistency in transaction data due to master data errors) never runs correctly, and the entry must be deleted from the queue to enable transfer of the data following it. This may result in inconsistencies that can be corrected by suitable measures. Which measures are called for depends on the exact problem. One possibility is the comparison/refresh function (SAP APO Transaction /SAPAPO/CCR).

Example

To ensure data consistency between the SAP ERP and SAP SCM system, the ABC Technology IT team regularly runs the transactional data reconciliation check between the two systems. The majority of the failures found are due to incorrect or missing master data. ABC Technology has designed a process flow to re-direct these business-related errors to the data stewards responsible for the area.

Table 15.5 shows the various queue names used in the SAP ERP and SAP SCM communication.

Queue	Explanation
CF_ACD_LOAD	Initial data load
CFSTK*	Stocks
CFPO*	Purchase orders and purchase requisitions
CFPLO*	Planned orders/production orders
CFSLS*	Sales orders
CFRSV*	Manual reservations
CFCNF*	Confirmations
CFPIR*	Planned independent requirements
CFMAT*	Requirement reduction independent requirements
CFPCM*	Production campaigns
CFCLA*	Master data classes
CFCHR*	Master data characteristics
CFSHP*	Transportation
CFCUVT*	Planning tables

In online transfers, * stands for the number of purchase orders, sales orders, and so on; in incremental data transfers of master data, * stands for the material number.

Table 15.5 Queue Channel between SAP ERP and SAP APO

When SAP ERP or SAP APO is taken out of service, the CIF queues should be stopped to reduce CIF queue errors.

SAP APO programs that are suggested in this scenario to stop and restart the CIF communication between SAP ERP and SAP SCM include the following:

Prior to System Shutdown	Action
/SAPAPO/CIFSTOPQUEUES	Lock CIF outbound queues in connected SAP ERP system
/SAPAPO/CIF_QIN_STOPQUEUES	Lock CIF Inbound queues in connected SAP system
After System Startup	**Action**
/SAPAPO/CIF_QIN_STARTQUEUES	Unlock CIF Inbound queues in connected SAP system
/SAPAPO/CIFSTARTQUEUES	Unlock CIF outbound queues in connected ERP system

Possible Queue Statuses

Depending on the way a LUW is processed, an inbound queue, outbound queue, or table ARFCRSTATE (status table of the LUWs in the tRFC/qRFC target system) can have different statuses. Table 15.6, Table 15.7, and Table 15.8 explain the various statuses based on the queue definition.

Outbound Queue	The Following Statuses can be Displayed in SMQ1
READY	The queue is ready for transmission. (This status should only be a temporary status. However, this status can also be a permanent status when a queue was locked manually via SMQ1 or via a program and then unlocked without being activated at the same time. This queue must be activated explicitly.)

Table 15.6 Outbound Queues Status and Their Meanings

Outbound Queue	The Following Statuses can be Displayed in SMQ1
RUNNING	The first LUW of this queue is currently being processed. (If a queue in this status hangs for more than 30 minutes, this might mean that the work process responsible for sending this LUW has terminated. In this case, you can activate this queue again. Note that activating a queue in status RUNNING might cause an LUW to be executed several times if this LUW is processed in the target system at that time. We therefore recommend a waiting time of at least 30 minutes before you activate the queue again.)
EXECUTED	The first LUW of this queue is processed. (The system waits for a qRFC-internal confirmation from the target system before further LUWs are processed. If a queue in this STATUS hangs for more than 30 minutes, this might mean that the work process responsible for sending this LUW has terminated. In contrast with status RUNNING, this current LUW has definitely been executed successfully. You can activate this queue again without problems. The qRFC Manager will automatically delete the LUW already executed and send the next LUW.)
SYSLOAD	At the time of the qRFC call, no DIALOG work processes were free in the sending system for sending the LUW asynchronously. (A batch job for subsequent sending has already been scheduled [see SAP Note 319860 for more detail].)
SYSFAIL	▶ A serious error occurred in the target system while the first LUW of this queue was executed. (The execution was interrupted. When you double-click this status, the system displays an error text. You can find additional information on this error in the corresponding short dump in the target system [ST22].) ▶ No batch job is scheduled for a repetition, and the queue is no longer processed. (To solve the problem, you need information from the affected application. Refer to Note 335162 for the special error text, CONNECTION CLOSED.)

Table 15.6 Outbound Queues Status and Their Meanings (Cont.)

Outbound Queue	The Following Statuses can be Displayed in SMQ1
CPICERR	During the transmission or processing of the first LUW in the target system, a network or communication error occurred. (When you double-click this status, the system displays an error text. You can find additional information on this error in the syslog [SM21], the trace files dev_rd or dev_rfc*. Depending on the definition in SM59 for the destination used, a batch job is scheduled for subsequent sending. Status CPICERR might also exist in the following cases, although no communication error occurred: a qRFC application finds out that an LUW cannot be processed any further due to a temporary error in the application and therefore calls function module RESTART_ OF_BACKGROUNDTASK in order to prompt the qRFC Manager to cancel the execution of this LUW and to repeat this LUW later in accordance with the specification in SM59. In this case, qRFC simulates a communication error with the text COMMAND TO TRFC/QRFC: EXECUTE LUW ONCE AGAIN. If this error occurs very often, you must contact the corresponding application.)
STOP	On this queue (status: STOP) or a generic queue (for example, BASIS_*), a lock was set explicitly (SMQ1 or programs). Note that the qRFC never locks a queue in its processing. After having informed the corresponding application, you can unlock and activate this queue using SMQ1.
WAITSTOP	The first LUW of this queue has dependencies to other queues, and at least one of these queues is currently still locked.
WAITING	The first LUW of this queue has dependencies to other queues, and at least one of these queues contains other LUWs with higher priorities.
NOSEND	LUWs of this queue (status: NO SEND) are never sent, but picked up by a special application. These queues are only used internally at SAP (SAP NetWeaver BW or SAP CRM during communication with mobile clients).
NOSENDS	During status NO SEND, the qRFC call, the application at the same time determines that the current LUW should not be sent immediately. This is used to debug the execution of a LUW in the target system.

Table 15.6 Outbound Queues Status and Their Meanings (Cont.)

Outbound Queue	The Following Statuses can be Displayed in SMQ1
WAITUPDA	The current LUW was executed in a transaction that also contains update functions. Therefore, this LUW may only be sent after the update has been successfully completed. If this status is retained for more than a couple of minutes, go to SM13 and check whether an update termination has occurred. After successful subsequent posting, this LUW is automatically restarted. You can reset this status from qRFC Monitor SMQ1 and activate the queue again. Note that this might cause inconsistencies in the application data between the two systems. CAUTION: If you are using 4.0x, 4.5x, 4.6A, or 4.6B and an update module with type "collective run" exists, this might cause this status due to an error in the kernel. The queue also hangs in this case. This error has already been corrected with a kernel patch (see SAP Note 333878).
ARETRY	During LUW execution, the application has diagnosed a temporary problem and has prompted the qRFC Manager in the sending system via a specific qRFC call to schedule a batch job for a repetition on the basis of the definition in SM59.
ANORETRY	During the LUW execution, the application has found a serious error and prompted the qRFC Manager via a specific qRFC call to cancel processing of this LUW. To solve the problem, information from the affected application is required.
MODIFY	Processing of this queue is locked temporarily because of the LUW data being modified.

Table 15.6 Outbound Queues Status and Their Meanings (Cont.)

Inbound Queue	Statuses that can be Displayed in SMQ2
READY	The queue is ready for transmission. (This status should only be a temporary status. However, this status can also be a permanent status if a queue was locked manually via SMQ2 or via a program and then unlocked without being activated at the same time, for example. This queue must be activated explicitly.)

Table 15.7 Inbound Queues Status and Their Meanings

Inbound Queue	Statuses that can be Displayed in SMQ2
RUNNING	The first LUW of this queue is currently being processed. (If a queue in this status hangs for more than 30 minutes, this might mean that the work process responsible for sending this LUW has terminated. In this case, you can activate this queue again. Note that activating a queue in status RUNNING might cause an LUW to be executed several times if this LUW is processed in the target system at that time. We therefore recommend a waiting time of at least 30 minutes before you activate the queue again.)
SYSFAIL	A serious error occurred in the target system while the first LUW of this queue was executed. The execution was interrupted. (When you double-click this status, the system displays an error text. You can find additional information on this error in the corresponding short dump in the target system [ST22].)
	No batch job is scheduled for a repetition, and the queue is no longer processed. (To solve the problem, you need information from the affected application. Refer to Note 335162 for the special error text CONNECTION CLOSED.)
CPICERR	During transmission or processing of the first LUW in the target system, a network or communication error occurred. (When you double-click this status, the system displays an error text. You can find additional information on this error in the syslog [SM21], the trace files dev_rd or dev_rfc*. Depending on the registration of this queue [SMQR] a batch job is scheduled for repetition. Refer to Note 369524 for the error text SAP ERP LOGON FAILED.)
	Status CPICERR might also exist in the following cases although no communication error occurred: an qRFC application finds out that an LUW cannot be processed any further due to a temporary error in the application and therefore calls function module RESTART_OF_BACKGROUNDTASK in order to prompt the qRFC Manager to cancel the execution of this LUW and to repeat this LUW later in accordance with the specification in SM59. (In this case, qRFC simulates a communication error with the text COMMAND TO TRFC/QRFC: EXECUTE LUW ONCE AGAIN. If this error occurs very often, you must contact the corresponding application.)

Table 15.7 Inbound Queues Status and Their Meanings (Cont.)

Inbound Queue	Statuses that can be Displayed in SMQ2
STOP	On this queue or a generic queue (for example, BASIS_*), a lock was set explicitly (SMQ2 or programs). Note that the qRFC never locks a queue in its processing. After having informed the corresponding application, you can unlock and activate this queue using SMQ2.
WAITSTOP	The first LUW of this queue has dependencies to other queues, and at least one of these queues is currently still locked.
WAITING	The first LUW of this queue has dependencies to other queues, and at least one of these queues contains other LUWs with higher priorities.
ARETRY	During LUW execution, the application has diagnosed a temporary problem and has prompted the qRFC Manager in the sending system via a specific qRFC call to schedule a batch job for a repetition on the basis of the registration in SMQR.
ANORETRY	During the LUW execution, the application has found a serious error and prompted the qRFC Manager via a specific qRFC call to cancel processing of this LUW. To solve the problem, information from the affected application is required.
MODIFY	Processing of this queue is locked temporarily because of the LUW data being modified.

Table 15.7 Inbound Queues Status and Their Meanings (Cont.)

Table ARFCRSTATE	Statuses Displayed via SE16
EXECUTED	The respective LUW is completely executed in the target system. (The system waits for a tRFC/qRFC-internal confirmation from the sending system before this entry is deleted.)
HOLD	The respective application has processed this LUW in parts and wants to prevent this LUW from being repeated in the case of later network or communication errors (see SAP Note 366869 if there are many entries with this status).

Table 15.8 Table ARFSTATE Statuses and Their Meanings

Table ARFCRSTATE	Statuses Displayed via SE16
WCONFIRM	During an LUW execution, the application has prompted the tRFC/qRFC Manager to set status HOLD. If the LUW execution has already been completed but this application has not yet signalized the logical LUW end, and if the tRFC/qRFC-internal confirmation from the sending system has been received, then this LUW receives status WCONFIRM. If the respective application informs the tRFC/qRFC Manager about the logical LUW end, then this entry is deleted (see SAP Note 366869 for more details).

Table 15.8 Table ARFSTATE Statuses and Their Meanings (Cont.)

15.1.5 Troubleshooting CIF

There can be many reasons that data is inconsistent between the SAP ERP and SAP APO systems. The starting point for troubleshooting the CIF is CIF Delta Inconsistency Report /SAPAPO/CIF_DELTAREPORT3. This report only handles the transactional data mismatch between the SAP ERP and SAP SCM system. Once we run the report and still see inconsistencies, the errors are logged in the qRFC monitor. To use the qRFC monitor, follow these steps:

1. Access Transaction SMQ1 or SMQ2 to view the queues, as shown in step ❶ of Figure 15.8.

2. To find more details of any inconsistencies or errors in the queues, select the queues, as shown in step ❷. In this step, we can see the queue status and interpret the cause, as explained earlier in Table 15.6, through Table 15.8. In our example, the queue status is showing SYSFAIL, which primarily occurs due to some functional error or missing integration model in the SAP ERP system.

3. Double-click the queue to drill into step ❸. This view shows the possible error that's causing the queue to be struck.

4. Next, click the queue name or status. Once the queue is double-clicked in step ❸, we arrive at step ❹, shown in Figure 15.9. This view provides the detailed breakdown on the mapping and how the structures from SAP APO are passed into SAP ERP, or vice-versa.

5. Alternatively, double-clicking the status error leads us to step ❺ which is the application log for the CIF. The application log (Transaction /SAPAPO/C3) provides a detailed explanation of where the failure occurred.

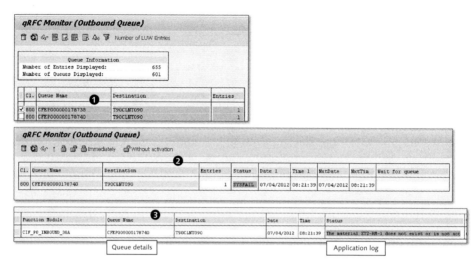

Figure 15.8 Steps in Troubleshooting CIF Errors

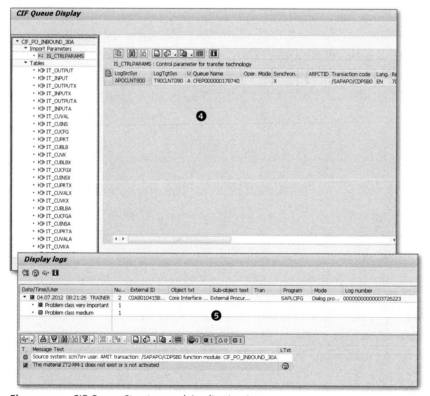

Figure 15.9 CIF Queue Structure and Application Log

Note: Logical System Assignment

There might be scenarios when the CIF integration models are created with a logical system assignment in a development environment. After transporting the integration model variants, the logical system assignment must be changed to the relevant, new, logical system (for example, production or quality) using program RCIFVARIANTCHANGE.

SCM Queue Manager

There can be situations when we encounter both master data and transactional data errors. For example, while publishing the purchase orders from the TLB to SAP ERP, we might get errors due to missing parameters in SAP ERP master data (for example, purchase info record/lot size range are different). This will require correcting the master data and activating the queue again for re-process. SCM Queue Manager, accessed via Transaction /SAPAPO/CQ, is a user-friendly tool that monitors both the inbound and outbound queues. This transaction is widely used by application support users for effectively troubleshooting any CIF failures.

As Figure 15.10 shows, the SCM Queue Manager results screen consists of a navigation window with a tree structure (left window) and a main window. In the tree structure, the systems that have been checked are represented as root nodes, and the individual object types as branches.

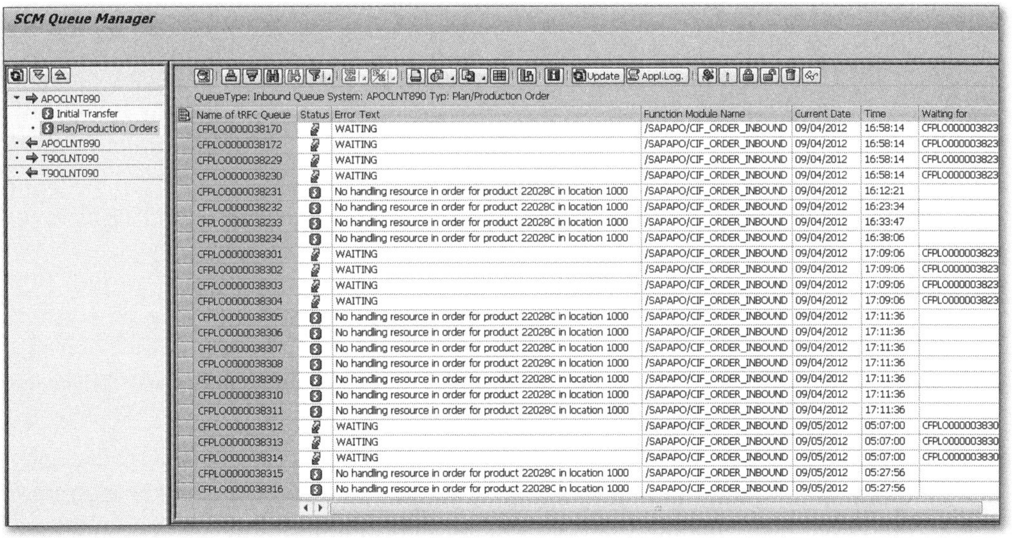

Figure 15.10 SCM Queue Manager

Table 15.9 lists the queue STATUS that tells us what is currently happening for each data object. Once the master data is corrected, the user can action the queue by pressing the ACTIVATE icon (📶) directly from the SCM Queue Manager. Alternatively, they can go to inbound/outbound queue monitors (Transaction SMQ1/ SMQ2) by clicking the 🐝 icon.

Status Icon	Status Description
✅	No queues with errors
💾	Queues are recorded
🛑	Queues manually stopped
ⓢ	Queues with errors
📝	Queues are being processed
🐝	Queue is waiting for another queue to be processed

Table 15.9 SCM Queue Manager Status Symbols

15.1.6 Customer Exits

Enhancements refer to custom code that's added to SAP ERP objects to include additional custom functionalities to meet business requirements that are not supported in standard SAP ERP functionality. Different types of enhancements can be implemented. The common ones are source code modifications (user exits), customer exits, Business Add-Ins (BAdIs), business transaction events (BTEs), screen enhancements, and menu exits.

An example of a CIF enhancement would be the requirement of transferring additional material master data from SAP ERP to SAP APO to influence planning results or global ATP allocation determination. SAP recommends SAP ERP to be the master data system and the CIF enhancement for any additional master data maintenance (for example, an MRP controller in SAP ERP material master mapping with APO-SNP or production planner in the SAP APO product master) so the supply chain planners do not have to manually maintain the master data in the SAP SCM system. This can be easily achieved by using EXIT_SAPLCMAT_001 during the CIF outbound from SAP ERP to SAP APO. Similarly, EXIT_/SAPAPO/ SAPLCIF_PROD_001 is available in CIF inbound.

The list of available CIF enhancements can be accessed by using Transaction SMOD (as shown in Figure 15.11), which lists all available user exits provided by SAP ERP and SAP APO. The enhancement can be further implemented by using Transaction CMOD for creating a project and assigning the enhancement to your project. Another way for the technical programmer to identify the user exits is to identify the function module (FM) in Transaction SE37.

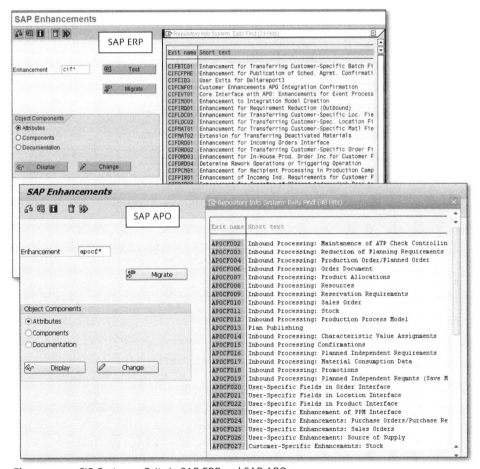

Figure 15.11 CIF Customer Exits in SAP ERP and SAP APO

15.1.7 Publication of Planning Results

There are two ways we can publish the planning result from SAP APO to SAP ERP. The first method is the direct publication used by SAP APO PP/DS for real-time publication of planning run results. The other method commonly used by APO-SNP is the periodic transfer. For the periodic transfer setting, we can define (customization explained earlier in Section 15.1.3) which planning result we want to send periodically to SAP ERP (for example, APO-SNP deployment or TLB). This offers the opportunity to the business users to review the result and make adjustments before publication to SAP ERP for execution. The periodic transfer is scheduled routinely via report /SAPAPO/RDMCPPROCESS or Transaction /SAPAPO/C5 (see Figure 15.12).

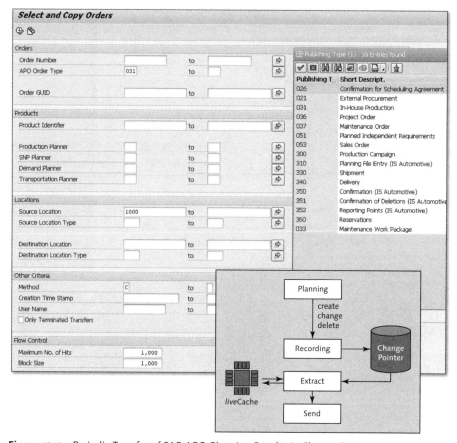

Figure 15.12 Periodic Transfer of SAP APO Planning Result via Change Pointers

15.1.8   Regular CIF Monitoring Transactions

Table 15.10 lists the monitoring transactions[1] that need to be performed by the SAP Basis and Application team to maintain control of the system.

Monitoring Object	Transaction/ Report	Monitor Frequency	Monitoring Activity or Error Handling Procedure
SAP APO report /SAPAPO/RCIF QUEUECHECK The report ensures that emails are sent in case of CIF errors.	SM37	Daily	Check if job is running as scheduled. If the report is not scheduled on a regular basis, schedule it to run every 15 minutes.
APO: Mail sent by /SAPAPO/RCIF QUEUECHECK	SO01 (or responsible email system)	Every 15 minutes	Verify email and apply handling procedure described in email text
APO report /SAPAPO/RCIF INQUEUECHECK The report ensures that emails are sent in case of CIF inbound queue errors.	SM37	Daily	Check if job is running as scheduled. If the report is not scheduled on a regular basis, schedule it to run every 15 minutes.
APO: Mail sent by /SAPAPO/RCIF INQUEUECHECK.	SO01 (or responsible email system)	Every 15 minutes	Verify email and apply error handling procedure described in email text

Table 15.10   Core Interface (CIF) Monitoring Transactions

---

1   SAP SCM—CIF Best Practices

Monitoring Object	Transaction/ Report	Monitor Frequency	Monitoring Activity or Error Handling Procedure
APO: SCM queue manager. This transaction enables you to check all qRFC queues on the local SAP APO and all connected SAP ERP systems.	/SAPAPO/CQ		Check if red or yellow queue indicators are displayed. /SAPAPO/CQ can be used instead of or in addition to SMQ1 and SMQ2 (which is much more user friendly).
SAP ERP: Monitor qRFC outbound queues.	SMQ1	Use /SAPAPO/ RCIFQUEUE CHECK for sending errors by email.	
APO: Monitor qRFC outbound queues.	SMQ1	Use /SAPAPO/ RCIFQUEUE CHECK for sending errors by email.	
SAP ERP: Monitor qRFC inbound queues.	SMQ2	Use /SAPAPO/ RCIFINQUEUE CHECK for sending errors by email.	
APO: Monitor qRFC inbound queues.	SMQ2	Use /SAPAPO/ RCIFINQUEUE CHECK for sending errors by email.	
SAP ERP application log	CFG1	At least daily	Check if there are very important logs (flagged red) or important logs (flagged yellow).

Table 15.10 Core Interface (CIF) Monitoring Transactions (Cont.)

Monitoring Object	Transaction/ Report	Monitor Frequency	Monitoring Activity or Error Handling Procedure
APO application log	/SAPAPO/C3	At least daily	Check if there are very important logs (flagged red) or important logs (flagged yellow).
SAP ERP reports RIMODGEN and RIMODAC2 (two steps in one job). These reports generate and activate integration models, respectively.	SM37	Daily	Check if the job is running as scheduled. If the report is not scheduled as provided by Application Support, schedule it accordingly.
SAP ERP report RAPOKZFX This report detects and corrects inconsistencies between material master and integration models.	SM37	Daily	Check if the job is running as scheduled. If the report is not scheduled on a regular basis, schedule it to run once a day.
Output of report RAPOKZFX	SP01	Daily	Check for material/ plant combinations where the correction of APOKZ was not carried out (this is due to lock problems). If errors are reported, determine why material is locked (for example, an update on material master or stock) and rerun job when the lock is released.

Table 15.10 Core Interface (CIF) Monitoring Transactions (Cont.)

Monitoring Object	Transaction/ Report	Monitor Frequency	Monitoring Activity or Error Handling Procedure
SAP ERP report RCIFIMAX This report detects and corrects inconsistencies between integration models and the runtime version. The runtime version is a representation of the table of the active integration model in a form that is optimized for the online transfer to SAP APO. In the runtime version, all active integration models are stored in an optimized form for each object type (for example, stocks) and target system. Using the runtime version helps improve the performance. Once activated, the report needs to be scheduled regularly to check for any inconsistencies.	SM37	Daily	Check if the job is running as scheduled. If the report is not scheduled on a regular basis, schedule it to run once a day.
Output of report RCIFIMAX	SP01	Daily	Check for items listed and reconcile inconsistencies by using the generation option of report RCIFIMAX.

Table 15.10 Core Interface (CIF) Monitoring Transactions (Cont.)

Monitoring Object	Transaction/ Report	Monitor Frequency	Monitoring Activity or Error Handling Procedure
APO report /SAPAPO/CIF _DELTAREPORT3 This report checks the consistency between SAP ERP and SAP APO transactional data and allows correction.	SM37	Daily	Check if the job is running as scheduled. If the report is not scheduled on a regular basis, schedule it to run daily.
Output of APO report /SAPAPO/ CIF_DELTAREPORT3	SP01	Daily	Check for objects reported to be missing either in SAP APO or in SAP ERP.
Reconciliation of inconsistencies	/SAPAPO/CCR	If errors are reported by /SAPAPO/CIF _DELTAREPOR Transaction in background	Check for inconsistent objects and execute the transfer of objects on the respective tab strip.
APO report /SAPAPO/CIF_ POSTPROC_ALERT This report ensures that e-mails are sent in case CIF error handling generates post-processing records.	SP01	Daily	Check if the job is running as scheduled. If the report is not scheduled on a regular basis, schedule it to run every 15 minutes.

Table 15.10 Core Interface (CIF) Monitoring Transactions (Cont.)

Monitoring Object	Transaction/ Report	Monitor Frequency	Monitoring Activity or Error Handling Procedure
APO: Mail sent by /SAPAPO/CIF_ POSTPROC_ALERT	SO01 (or responsible email system)	Every 15 minutes	Verify e-mail and apply error handling procedure described in email text (post-processing).
Post-processing of CIF error handling	/SAPAPO/CPP	If errors are mailed by /SAPAPO/CIF_ POSTPROC_ ALERT	Determine the error cause (verify application log) and correct the error. Re-transfer objects.
APO Core Interface Cockpit /SAPAPO/CC. This transaction enables an overview of all CIF-related activities in the SAP APO and the connected SAP ERP system(s).	/SAPAPO/CC		/SAPAPO/CC can be used as a central entry point for checking all CIF-related activities and enables a detailed analysis and correction by branching to the corresponding transactions listed above. All checks/monitoring activities have to be performed as specified, starting from the cockpit.

Table 15.10 Core Interface (CIF) Monitoring Transactions (Cont.)

15.2   SAP APO Technical Upgrade: Functional Activities

As of SAP SCM release 7.0, the software has many added functionalities. The development of new features was based on customer feedback and new market capability offering in the area of supply chain planning. SAP offers a maintenance cycle for all its application versions, after which no support is provided. The maintenance cycle and the new functionality offering become the main drivers for companies to upgrade to the new version. The current version (as of this book's publication) is SAP SCM 7.0 with Enhancement Pack 2.

Starting with SAP ERP 6.0 release, SAP introduced the concept of *enhancement packages* with business functions. Instead of repackaging the complete suite, enhancement packages are offered as a business function that requires activation via Transaction SFW5. Enhancement packages are optional packages that enable companies to easily take advantage of SAP's ongoing innovations in specific functional areas. Companies can deploy the enhancements in a modular fashion by activating only the new features and technical improvements they want to use to add the most value to their businesses.

The prerequisite for companies seeking to upgrade to SAP SCM 7.0 is that their present landscape should be at least SAP APO 4.1. There is no direct upgrade path from SAP APO 3.1 through SAP SCM 7.0. While upgrading to SAP SCM 7.0, the internal SAP NetWeaver Business Warehouse (BW) is also upgraded from version 3.5 to 7.0.

The technical upgrade process is always challenging and requires a fair bit of planning and regression testing to ensure that the current business processes are not impacted. The upgrade process is broken into four main phases, as shown in Figure 15.13.

A typical system landscape will have sandbox (used for prototyping new functionalities), development (build solution), quality (testing and training), and production (operational usage). The upgrade process starts with sandbox to gauge the effort and time it requires for technical upgrade and regression testing. The technical upgrade in each environment will undergo four phases, as shown in Figure 15.13:

▶ **Plan**
  Primary planning starts two weeks before the upgrade and involves project planning in all the tasks to reduce the system downtime and ensure that the upgrade process runs smoothly.

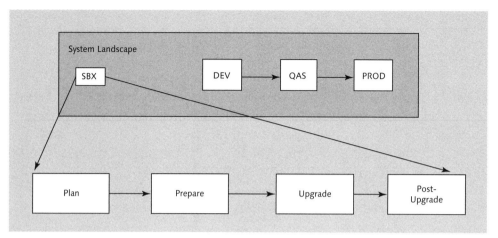

Figure 15.13 Technical Upgrade Phases

▶ **Prepare**
The prepare phase involves running checks during business operations to identify any system abnormalities in advance of the actual upgrade process.

▶ **Upgrade**
The physical technical upgrade process involves various technical stages.

▶ **Post upgrade**
The follow-up activities to bring back the operational system and perform data consistency across the SAP ERP and SAP SCM systems.

To facilitate the upgrade process, SAP provides a workbench via Transaction /SAPAPO/OM_LC_UPGRADE_70 (see Figure 15.14), which guides the technical administrator through the four upgrade phases we just explained.

Besides these activities, there are some additional functional activities that need to be performed in each phase, which we'll discuss in the following sections.

15.2.1 Plan Phase

In this phase, the business users are recommended to upgrade the SAP GUI to 720 with the highest patch level.

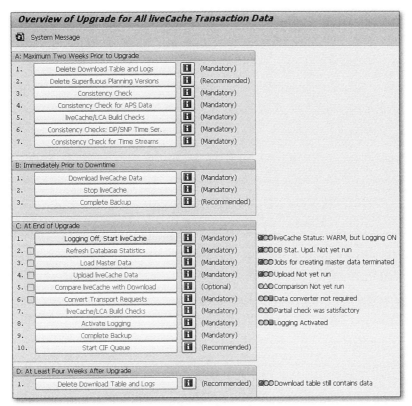

Figure 15.14 Upgrade Workbench for SAP liveCache Data

On the functional side, the solution designer can check the macro compatibility by running report /SAPAPO/ADV_UPGRADE_50 to check how many planning book macros have the compatibility checked. The macro compatibility needs to be unchecked for the new SAP SCM 7.0 functionality after the upgrade.

Make sure to prepare a list of transports for any bug fixes/corrections in the production environment.

15.2.2 Prepare Phase

The preparation phase involves backing up critical data and stopping the batch jobs and CIF communication between the SAP ERP and SAP SCM systems.

- ▶ **APO-DP activities:**
  - ▶ De-initialize the promotions (Transaction /SAPAPO/PROMOTION_UPDATE_30)
  - ▶ Back up time series data in backup cube as a contingency measure
  - ▶ De-initialize APO-DP planning area (Transaction /SAPAPO/MSDP_ADMIN)
  - ▶ Stop all APO-DP batch jobs
- ▶ **SAP NetWeaver BW activities:**
  - ▶ Back up all the active InfoCubes for the planning data
  - ▶ Check that DataSources are all active
  - ▶ Check that the DataSource is replicated in both source and target systems
  - ▶ Make sure that the InfoSource/transfer rules are active
  - ▶ Make sure that the InfoPackages are updated with your own data
  - ▶ Check that the update rules include start routine to delete zero values
  - ▶ Perform at least one data loading (execution of InfoPackage) for every backing up cube
- ▶ **APO-SNP activities:**
  - ▶ Perform initial load for master data integration model
  - ▶ Back up time series in backup cube as contingency measure
  - ▶ De-initialize APO-SNP planning area (Transaction /SAPAPO/MSDP_ADMIN)
  - ▶ Stop all APO-SNP batch jobs and take a snapshot of batch job processing time from Transaction ST13
  - ▶ Clear any inbound or outbound queue entries using Transactions SMQ1/SMQ2
  - ▶ Stop CIF queues via report /SAPAPO/CIFSTOPQUEUES

15.2.3 Upgrade Phase

The Basis team performs the technical upgrade and progresses that the functional team needs to validate the result. The Basis team needs to run report /SAPAPO/DELETE_LC_ANCHORS after booting up SAP liveCache for the first time in the upgraded system.

15.2.4 Post-Upgrade Phase

Once in the upgraded system, there are many functional steps that need to be performed; for example, ensuring that the technical data objects are consistent, activating various planning objects, restarting the CIF communication, and performing batch jobs. Make sure that the following activities are completed:

- ▶ **APO-DP activities**:
  - ▶ Run Transaction RSA1 (BW Administrator). If there are any BW errors, begin by running program RSDG_IOBJ_ACTIVATE to activate InfoObjects.
  - ▶ Run program RSDG_CUBE_ACTIVATE to activate all InfoCubes
  - ▶ Activate all planning object structures in Transaction /SAPAPO/MSDP_ADMIN. If you get an error mentioning that the planning object structure is not valid, run report /SAPAPO/TS_D_OBJECTS_COPY to rectify the situation.
  - ▶ Initialize all APO-DP planning areas and create time series objects
  - ▶ Upload SAP liveCache data. If the load is not successful, load the time series data from the backup InfoCubes using program /SAPAPO/RTSINPUT_CUBE
  - ▶ Run various consistency checks using programs: /SAPAPO/TS_LCM_CONS_CHECK, /SAPAPO/TS_PSTRU_CONS_CHECK, and /SAPAPO/TS_LCM_REORG
  - ▶ Activate promotions using Transaction /SAPAPO/MP42
  - ▶ Run program /SAPAPO/RMDP_FCST_LC_UPGRADE to update all the phase in-phase out, lifecycle planning data
  - ▶ Validate that all macros are active in macro workbench /SAPAPO/ADVM; if not, run program /SAPAPO/ADV_MACRO_REGENER
  - ▶ Schedule APO-DP background jobs
- ▶ **SAP NetWeaver BW activities:**
  - ▶ Perform planning area extraction via the BW extractor using Transaction RSA3
  - ▶ Activate all source systems in the BW Administrator Workbench
  - ▶ Replicate BW data sources in the upgraded system. Run program RS_TRANSTRU_ACTIVATE_ALL after replication.
  - ▶ Run program /SAPAPO/TS_PAREA_EXTR_DS_CHECK to remove any data source inconsistencies

- **APO-SNP activities:**

  - Execute /SAPAPO/OM17 for planning version "000" with the PRODUCT-LOCATION COMBINATION flag checked. If any inconsistencies are displayed, click CORRECT ALL INCONSISTENCIES.

  - Run OM17 again to ensure that all inconsistencies have been corrected.

  - Activate all planning object structures in Transaction /SAPAPO/MSDP_ADMIN. If you get an error mentioning that the planning object structure is not valid, run report /SAPAPO/TS_D_OBJECTS_COPY to rectify the situation.

  - Initialize all APO-SNP planning areas and create time series objects.

  - Execute program /SAPAPO/TS_LCM_PAREA_CHANGE: Time Series Update. It determines if key figure descriptions in the SAP APO database are consistent with the key figure descriptions in SAP liveCache (version 000).

  - Upload SAP liveCache data. If the load is not successful, load the time series data from the backup InfoCubes using program /SAPAPO/RTSINPUT_CUBE.

  - Run various consistency checks using programs: /SAPAPO/TS_LCM_CONS_CHECK, /SAPAPO/TS_PSTRU_CONS_CHECK, and /SAPAPO/TS_LCM_REORG

  - Stop CIF queues via report /SAPAPO/CIFSTARTQUEUES.

  - Generate and activate integration models for both transactional and master data.

  - Run CIF delta reconciliation report /SAPAPO/CIF_DELTAREPORT3.

  - Clear any inbound or outbound queue entries using Transactions SMQ1/SMQ2.

  - Schedule APO-SNP background jobs.

> **Note: Analysis and Repair of SAP NetWeaver BW Objects**
>
> Use Transaction RSRV to correct any unknown inconsistencies in SAP NetWeaver BW objects or in the database.

A good source to get the installation and upgrade guides is in the SAP Service Marketplace (*service.sap.com*). The navigation path for guides is shown in Figure 15.15. On service marketplace, under business suite, SAP SCM Server, you find the installation and upgrade guides with the release and upgrade information.

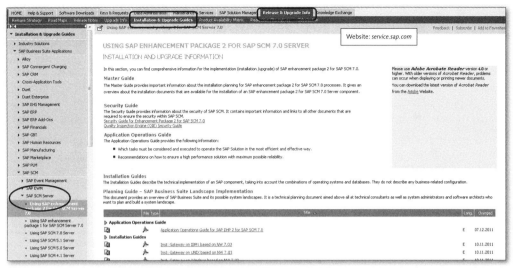

Figure 15.15 Service Marketplace for Installation and Upgrade Guides

15.3 SAP APO Authorization Concept

Setting up the correct level of authorization is important for users to get access to the transactions and data objects for doing their daily operational work. The users in SAP APO are not only the business users but also the application support users and the communication RFC users between SAP SCM and other SAP components and applications (for example, SAP ERP, SAP NetWeaver BW, and SAP CRM).

The authorization concept in SAP APO is different from SAP ERP. Not only do the business roles need to be mapped to the SAP transaction, but the authorization objects need to be properly aligned, as well. The complexity lies in that the supply chain organization will have business users with different levels of authorization and different responsibilities (for example, by product group). This is defined by segregation of duties (SOD) definitions in the company.

A good way to start on authorization in SAP APO is to look at the generic single and composite roles provided in SAP APO for demand and supply planning in Transaction PFCG. Composite roles consist of multiple single roles to serve business process activities. Figure 15.16 shows the single and composite roles that are available.

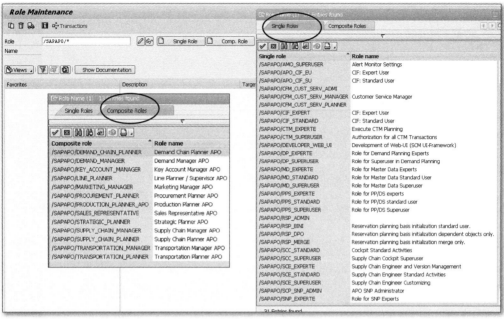

Figure 15.16 SAP Generic Single and Composite Roles for SAP APO

15.3.1 Master-Derived Role Concept

Another important concept for SAP APO roles is the *master-derived role concept,* where the solution is being rolled out in many geographical countries in the form of a template design. In the master role, the authorization values are maintained, and the roles for different regions (for example) are derived from the master role. The organizational level values for different sites like location and sales organization are maintained in the derived roles. This makes the maintenance of roles easier, since any authorization level change has to be done only in the master role, and the child (derived) roles can adapt the changes by master role generation. The master-derived role definitions can be found in the AGR_DEFINE table via Transaction SE16.

15.3.2 Defining Roles

There are two steps in defining roles in SAP APO. The first step is to map the transactions to the business roles. The second step is to define authorization objects to the business roles. Figure 15.17 shows an example of the various authorization objects assigned to the roles. This SAP security measure can restrict authorization for different users by maintaining the values for these authorization objects.

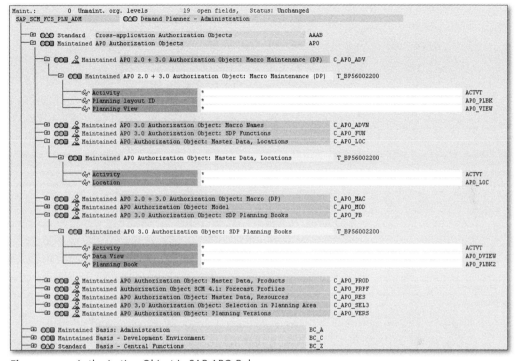

```
Maint.:        0  Unmaint. org. levels        19  open fields,   Status: Unchanged
SAP_SCM_FCS_PLN_ADM                  Demand Planner - Administration

      Standard   Cross-application Authorization Objects              AAAB
      Maintained APO Authorization Objects                           APO

           Maintained APO 2.0 + 3.0 Authorization Object: Macro Maintenance (DP)   C_APO_ADV

              Maintained APO 2.0 + 3.0 Authorization Object: Macro Maintenance (DP)   T_BP56002200

                   Activity                 *                                                           ACTVT
                   Planning layout ID       *                                                           APO_PLBK
                   Planning View            *                                                           APO_VIEW

           Maintained APO 3.0 Authorization Object: Macro Names               C_APO_ADVN
           Maintained APO 3.0 Authorization Object: SDP Functions             C_APO_FUN
           Maintained APO Authorization Object: Master Data, Locations        C_APO_LOC

              Maintained APO Authorization Object: Master Data, Locations      T_BP56002200

                   Activity                 *                                                           ACTVT
                   Location                 *                                                           APO_LOC

           Maintained APO 2.0 + 3.0 Authorization Object: Macro (DP)          C_APO_MAC
           Maintained APO Authorization Object: Model                        C_APO_MOD
           Maintained APO 3.0 Authorization Object: SDP Planning Books        C_APO_PB

              Maintained APO 3.0 Authorization Object: SDP Planning Books      T_BP56002200

                   Activity                 *                                                           ACTVT
                   Data View                *                                                           APO_DVIEW
                   Planning Book            *                                                           APO_PLBK2

           Maintained APO Authorization Object: Master Data, Products         C_APO_PROD
           Maintained Authorization Object SCM 4.1: Forecast Profiles         C_APO_PRFF
           Maintained APO Authorization Object: Master Data, Resources        C_APO_RES
           Maintained APO 3.0 Authorization Object: Selection in Planning Area C_APO_SEL3
           Maintained APO Authorization Object: Planning Versions             C_APO_VERS

      Maintained Basis: Administration                              BC_A
      Maintained Basis - Development Environment                    BC_C
      Standard   Basis - Central Functions                          BC_Z
```

Figure 15.17 Authorization Object in SAP APO Role

For example, there might be a business requirement to restrict the planning book by a characteristics value that is not available in the authorization object. Only one authorization check for the object version (C_APO_VERS), products (C_APO_PROD), and locations (C_APO_LOC) can be performed in APO-DP for selections in the standard system. In SAP APO-SNP, you can check the object version (C_APO_VERS), products (C_APO_PROD), locations (C_APO_LOC), location products (C_APO_PROD), resources (C_APO_RES), and transportation lanes (C_APO_TLAN).

Additional authorization checks, in particular for other characteristics of the selection (for example, sales organizations in APO-DP), are not provided in the standard system. You can run these using the user exit for authorizations. With this user exit or the BAdI method SELECTION_CHECK (BAdI /SAPAPO/SDP_SELECTOR), you can, for example, force a user to make a selection for a certain characteristic.

> **Note: SAP APO Security-Related SAP Notes**
>
> The most commonly used SAP Notes related to SAP APO authorization are:
>
> - 400434: Authorizations in APO Demand Planning
> - 727839: Authorization role for the SAP SCM - SAP ERP integration
> - 1464451: Authorizations in APO Master Data
> - 724095: SDP Selector: Authorization check for location products
> - 700659: Security Guide: mySAP Supply Chain Management
> - 627983: Addition BAdI /SAPAPO/SDP_FCSTAUTH
> - 436400: Enhancement user exit authorizations for data view

15.4 SAP APO Process Chain

A *process chain* is an SAP NetWeaver BW technique that has been widely adapted by companies that have implemented SAP APO. The advantage of using a process chain is that the dependencies of multiple jobs or conditional steps can be easily defined as a part of the batch schedule sequence. The process chain can be triggered by external events, and the monitoring becomes easier since it is GUI-based.

An SAP APO process chain helps us to design the daily, weekly, and monthly planning cycles in the form of SAP APO functions (for example, forecasting and heuristics calculations) performed in background batch jobs. The use of the background jobs provides automation in performing planning tasks per business requirements. Many companies run background jobs to support their monthly and weekly planning cycles. Some examples of background jobs are running statistical forecasting and running an SNP heuristics planning run. Also, in the scenario of processing a large volume of data, the planner can trigger the background job manually and analyze the output. Background jobs can be created and scheduled either using Transaction SM36/SM37 or via a process chain using Transaction RSPC.

In the following sections, we'll discuss the main components that make up a process chain and then walk through the technical steps that explain how to create and monitor a process chain.

15.4.1   Main Components

An SAP APO process chain has two main components:

▶ **Process type**

The *process type* is defined as activities performed to execute a specific module: APO-DP or APO-SNP. Besides module-specific types, there are also general process types; for example, the ABAP program or conditional elements (such as AND, OR), which can group multiple branches of the process chain to form a logical sequence chain. Figure 15.18 shows an example of the process chain interactive screen with process types, which can be dragged and dropped to the right side of screen to form a logical process chain.

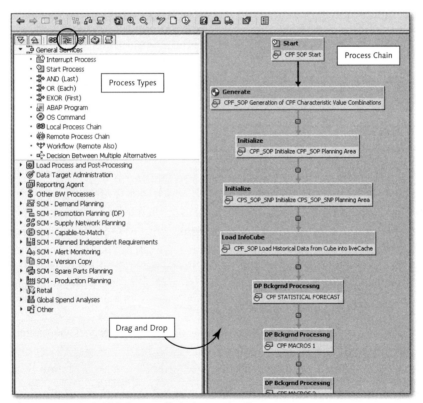

Figure 15.18   SAP APO Process Chain Interactive Screen

▶ **Process variants**
Process variants are defined as process steps in the process chain. For example, running a heuristics network in the background, we can have two process steps, or variants. The first process type can be for running an SAP liveCache consistency check, while the second process type can be used for running the SNP heuristics program.

15.4.2 Create the Process Chain

The steps for creating a process chain are simple. Before you start, always draft the sequence of the process steps on piece of paper. Let's create an example: we want to create a process chain for running the APO-SNP planning cycle. The process steps need to be running consistency checks, deleting the last APO-SNP planning result, running SNP heuristics, and running the APO-SNP deployment run. The steps for creating the process chain are as follows:

1. Using Transaction RSPC, go to the Process Chain Maintenance screen. Click the Create icon and enter the process chain name and description. We recommend that the description represent the SAP APO module and purpose the process chain is trying to achieve (for example, APO-SNP daily planning cycle). The system will prompt you to define a START process variant. In the START field, define the scheduling date/time.

2. The next step is to identify the process types, which will form the part of the process chain. As Figure 15.19 shows, we have identified four process types that will form part of the process chain. Take note that since APO-SNP doesn't have the transactional deletion activity listed in its node, we can use the ABAP program directly. To begin, drag and drop the process type to the right side (❶)—the system will prompt you to define the variant (❷) and nominate the variant (❸). Perform these steps for all four programs.

3. The next step is to connect all the process types into a logical process sequence. To connect the two objects, use the pencil cursor to mark the first object and drop a line to the second object. The system will prompt you for an action task, indicating that the second job should be executed with various permutation options, such as only when the first job runs successfully, runs with an error, or a combination of either successful and errors. Figure 15.20 shows the prompt asking whether the successor job needs to be performed only after the first job completes with various status options.

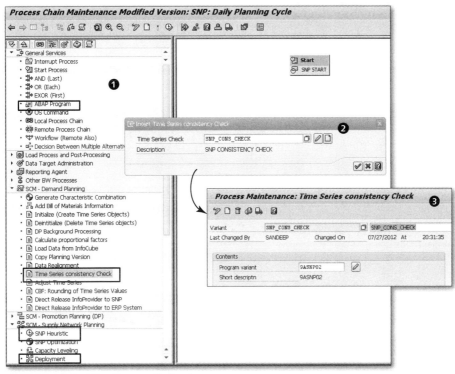

Figure 15.19 Building Process Chain—I

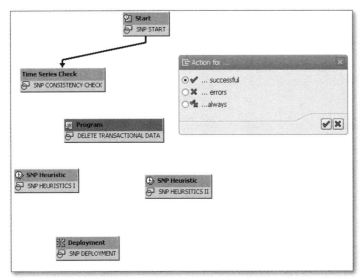

Figure 15.20 Building Process Chain—II

4. Now define any conditional statement in the process chain. For example, Figure 15.21 shows that we run the SNP heuristics jobs in parallel and only perform the SNP deployment planning run once both the SNP heuristics jobs are complete. This is achieved by inserting a conditional statement (for example, AND, OR, etc.) between the various functions.

5. Another available option is to issue a notification if a particular process type fails during the processing. As Figure 15.21 shows, right-click the process type to create a notification and mechanism for distribution (for example, email to distribution list).

6. The final step is to save the process chain and perform a consistency check by clicking the CONSISTENCY icon (🔧). If the consistency check is passed, activate and schedule the process chain (menu path PROCESS CHAIN • ACTIVATE AND SCHEDULE).

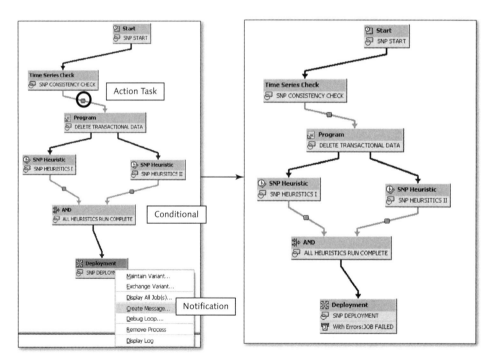

Figure 15.21 Building Process Chain—III

15.4.3 Process Chain Monitoring

Since the majority of SAP APO batch jobs run in the background in the form of a process chain, some form of monitoring is required in the backend to ensure all the jobs are completed successfully as per their average historical run-time. Process chain monitoring provides the mechanism of monitoring the process chain on exceptions. Some of the transactions for monitoring the process chain are RSPCM and ST13. In the latter transaction, enter the tool name as BW-TOOLS and execute. The report provides the status and processing runtime for each process chain. The following are different status codes shown in the Process Chain Monitor (Transaction RSPCM):

▶ **Red**
The process variant was cancelled by the system or that it completed with errors. A notification can be tagged for important jobs in the process chain.

▶ **Yellow**
The process variant is still active and that the process is not complete.

▶ **Green**
The process variant completed without any errors. This status can sometimes be misleading, as the job might have errors shown in the application log (Transaction SLG1) even though the job completed successfully.

▶ **Gray**
The process variant has not yet run. These variants are run after the yellow status is complete. This state occurs only when the job is active and still processing.

15.4.4 Parallel Processing

Another consideration on the background jobs is the parallel processing of the jobs. Parallel processing utilizes multiple application servers during the process chain run and ensures that the job is completed with an efficient runtime. This method is ideally used when we have a large volume of data processing.

The parallel processing parameters are defined in Transaction /SAPAPO/SDP_PAR. In this transaction, we define the application, indicate the number of maximum application servers the process can use, and indicate the block size.

ABC Technology's demand planning process has 100,000 CVCs, and we can use 15 servers at a time. We can define the block size as 100000/15 = 6700. A large block size reduces the database operation but leads to higher memory utilization.

It is recommended to monitor the workload processes in Transaction SM50 after making the setting changes.

15.5 Hardware Sizing using Quick Sizer

Quick Sizer is a tool that helps in determining whether there are enough hardware and application server resources in the SAP SCM system to handle the SAP APO expected workload. This check is important and needs to be scheduled routinely to prevent any severe performance problems that can be caused by underestimating the hardware requirements. The input to Quick Sizer involves some basic master and transactional data volumes from SAP APO and SAP ERP. You can access the Quick Sizer tool online via *service.sap.com\quicksizer*.

Figure 15.22 shows an example sizing framework on planning system architecture, which affects the overall sizing parameters in the SAP SCM system. The two primary variables in sizing any system are the data and the process. The data provides us with the volume and structures that will be used in interactive and batch processing. The process defines the SAP APO functionality that the business is currently using in the design. The more functionalities the business uses, the more processing will be recorded in the system during interactive and batch jobs. All four parameters of data, process, batch, and interactive planning impact the CPU usage in the system. Besides CPU, the SAP APO architecture also has database, application, and SAP liveCache components that need to be calculated.

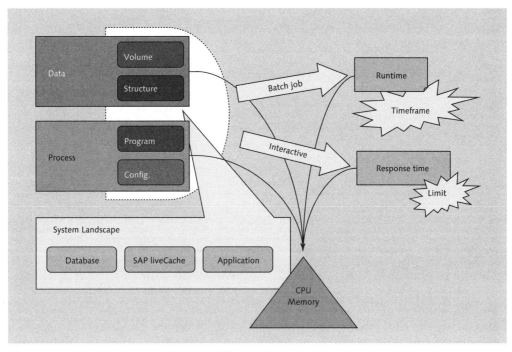

Figure 15.22 Planning System Architecture Affecting Sizing

The Quick Sizer for SAP SCM (see Figure 15.23) provides a questionnaire (provided in the SAP Service Marketplace) for both demand planning and supply planning. The demand planning questions primarily focus on the number of characteristics combinations, users, and planning areas, as well as peak time. The characteristics combination initial calculation is challenging since it is not a straight multiplication of characteristics in the planning object structure, but requires the user to define the product and customer hierarchy for better estimation. APO-SNP is primarily concerned with the number of product-location combinations, resources, and various transactions that impact the processing time of supply planning processes.

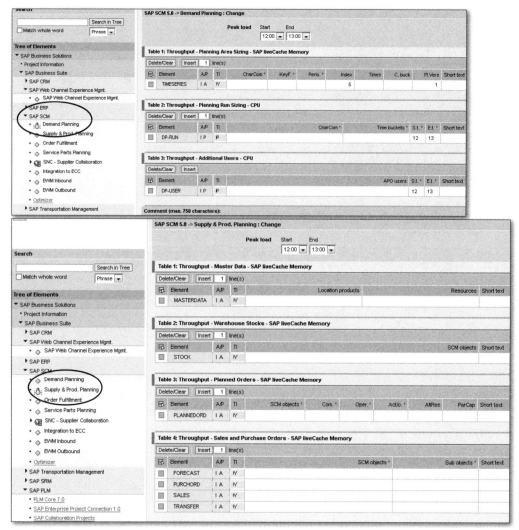

Figure 15.23 Quick Sizer Questionnaire for SAP APO

To complete the Quick Sizer questionnaire, SAP provides the SAP liveCache inspector program in Transaction /SAPAPO/OM_LVC_OBJECTS (see Figure 15.24), which primarily calculates the SAP liveCache memory requirements. We'll go over the different views you can see in the figure here:

▶ The OVERVIEW segment outputs the net memory requirement for each planning version. For sizing purposes, we take only the active version into account. The total number of time series is determined by the number of characteristics combinations and the number of key figures.

► In the ORDERS section, the number of orders for each object type and the average number of items per order are output. The output occurs for each planning version. In addition, the master data is issued. The total number of location products includes all pegging areas stored in the SAP liveCache.

► In the PLANNING AREAS section, the time bucket profile and the number of key figures for each planning area are issued. Those active planning areas are relevant for high memory requirements, which have a certain number of time buckets and a number of time series key figures and relevant planning objects.

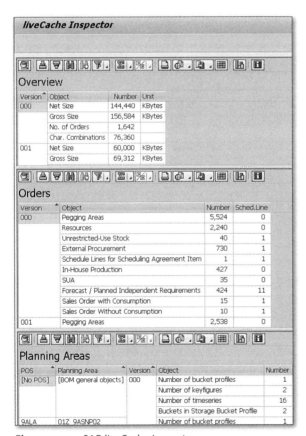

Figure 15.24 SAP liveCache Inspector

Based on the Quick Sizer questionnaire as input parameters, the output yields results in various hardware parameter requirements (see Figure 15.25), such as CPU, disk, memory, and input/output resource categories based on throughput numbers and the number of users working on the SAP APO application. This provides the SAP infrastructure and architecture team some baseline of the hardware requirement for the SAP SCM system supporting SAP APO functions.

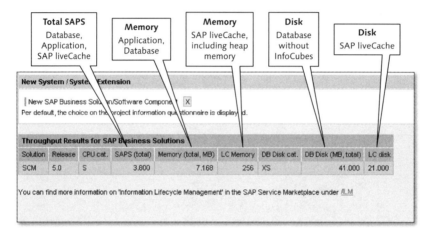

Figure 15.25 Quick Sizer Result Screen

15.6   Technical Integration with Non-SAP Applications

In many SAP APO solution implementations, the design will integrate with non-SAP applications based on the planning scope. For example, there might be a scenario when SAP APO is used for the demand planning business process only while the supply planning is still performed in legacy applications, or vice-versa. The company might put forward a roadmap for implementing the SAP APO solution in phases. The planning integration might involve SAP ERP or another ERP system, as well.

A different business scenario could be collaborative planning, whereby the business partners exchanges files via a business to business (B2B) interface. The files can be received in XML format and will need middleware for posting in the SAP SCM system.

In the following sections, we'll discuss a few different technologies you can use to integrate SAP APO with non-SAP applications.

15.6.1 SAP APO Business Warehouse

The most common method for interfacing internal planning data is seen via the SAP APO internal Business Warehouse (BW) component. This is the BW system within the SCM system. The business uses the SAP NetWeaver Application Server's in and out directory to exchange the files via an automated process. Figure 15.26 shows an example of inbound and outbound exchanges via the internal SAP APO BW system. In this example, the customer sales orders are routinely loaded into the BW InfoCube, which then transfers the data to the SAP APO planning area for planning. Once planning is performed, the data is extracted into either Operational Data Store (ODS) or InfoCube providers and dispatched via the open hub service.

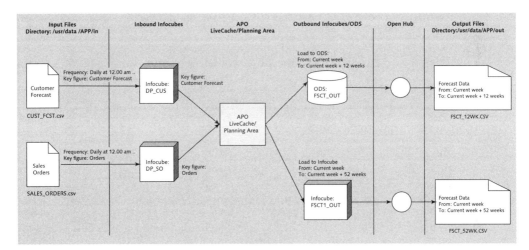

Figure 15.26 Interface Design Using SAP NetWeaver BW

The BW open hub service enables you to distribute data from an SAP NetWeaver BW system into external data marts, analytical applications, and other applications. With this, you can ensure controlled distribution toward several systems.

The central object for the export of data is the InfoSpoke. With the evolution of the open hub service, SAP NetWeaver BW becomes the hub of an enterprise data warehouse. The distribution of data becomes clear through central monitoring for both inbound and outbound exchanges. Any BW objects, such as InfoCubes, ODS objects, or InfoObjects (attributes or texts), can serve as open hub data sources. We can select database tables or flat files as open hub destinations. Both a full and a delta mode are available as the extraction mode.

15.6.2 Enterprise Service Bus

The other technology that is commonly used for exchanging the data with business partners uses an enterprise service bus (ESB). An ESB is a software architecture model used for designing and implementing the interaction and communication among mutually interacting software applications. An example of an ESB is the SAP process integration (PI, formerly known as XI) system. SAP PI is a tool that enables you to implement cross-system processes. It's used to connect various ERP/legacy systems from different vendors (non-SAP and SAP) using different versions and implemented across different programming languages (e.g., Java, ABAP, and so on). SAP PI is based on an open architecture and uses open standards (in particular, those from the XML and Java environments) and offers services that are essential in a heterogeneous and complex system landscape. A brief list of the services is as follows:

▶ Modeling and design of messages, transformations, and cross-component integration processes

▶ Configuration options for managing collaborative processes and message flow

▶ Runtime for message and process management

▶ Adapter engine for integrating heterogeneous system components

▶ Central monitoring for monitoring message flow and processes

▶ Support for internal company and cross-company scenarios

The technique that can be used in the interface is Business Application Programming Interface (BAPI). BAPI is a set of interfaces to object-oriented programming methods that provides access to processes and data in business application systems like SAP APO and SAP ERP. For specific business requirements like uploading transactional data or routine master data, BAPIs are implemented and stored in the SAP APO system as remote function call (RFC) modules. BAPIs can also be triggered using the LSMW method. Using Transaction BAPI in the SAP APO system, we can view all the available objects that can be implemented (see Figure 15.27). Besides uploading master and transaction data, there is a BAPI for updating the SAP APO planning books, as well. However, this method is not real time and is scheduled in the background in the form of the data subscription/publication model.

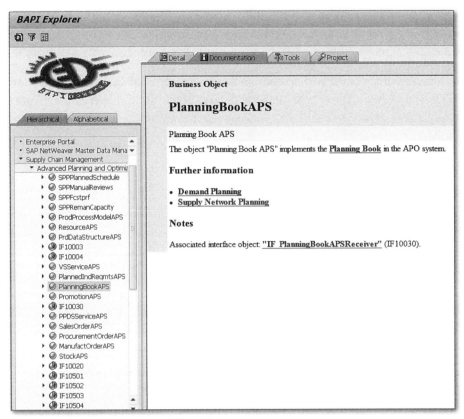

Figure 15.27 BAPI Repository in SAP APO

15.7 Summary

In this chapter, we discussed several of the more technical concepts that exist when working with SAP APO, including maintenance and upgrades. We first discussed the CIF, which keeps the master data and transactional data synched near real time between the execution and planning systems. You learned how to set up CIF and monitor and troubleshoot errors.

This chapter lists the stages of the upgrade process and some of the key functional activities that need to be performed to bring the system back to its original state. Both the APO-DP and APO-SNP functionalities depend on the process chain for scheduling background jobs to support daily, weekly, and monthly planning activities. The chapter highlighted the steps for setting up a process chain and how we can monitor it. The chapter also touched on how we can use Quick Sizer for hardware sizing exercises to ensure good system performance. The chapter closes out by showing some techniques for integrating SAP APO with non-SAP applications.

The next chapter provides the more technical concepts of the data conversion process in SAP APO. The chapter also touches on how different technical enhancements can be performed in the SAP APO system to suit business requirements not provided by standard functions.

Because standard SAP APO functions may not support all the technical requirements of a specific business or industry, technical enhancements are required. Data conversion forms an integral part of SAP APO implementation to migrate master data models into the new system.

16 Data Conversion and Technical Enhancements

Data conversion is an important activity in any SAP APO project to extract, transform, and load data objects (such as master data) from legacy applications into new SAP APO applications. Every SAP implementation requires good data to be loaded into the new system, and may need enhancements to help enable business requirements that aren't supported by native SAP functionalities.

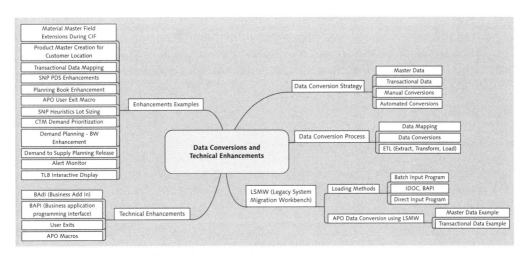

Figure 16.1 Learning Points for the Chapter (Mind Map)

As shown in the mind map for this chapter (see Figure 16.1) we'll discuss two technical concepts in this chapter. As we first discuss data conversion activities performed during an SAP APO project, we'll provide a step-by-step guide to creating a legacy system migration workbench (LSMW) object in SAP APO, which is the primary tool used in data conversion.

We'll then discuss how different complex business requirements can be supported via technical enhancements in either SAP ERP or SAP APO, when standard functionality isn't supported by native SAP APO functions. Before the development work begins, the solution team needs to prepare the functional specifications for the report, interface, conversion, enhancement, forms, and workflow (RICEFW) objects. These objects are required to fit together with the configuration items to provide complete business requirements.

We'll first go over a comprehensive discussion of what data conversion means in terms of SAP APO as it should be understood by a project team.

16.1   Data Conversion Strategy for SAP APO

Data conversion consists of activities to provide initial master data and/or transactional data from legacy application for new SAP application, enabling the company to perform its business processes smoothly when it goes live with the new SAP application. There can be two business situations when the company is implementing SAP APO with SAP ERP integration or another legacy ERP application. For the first scenario, the majority of the master and transactional data will be interfaced from SAP ERP via the CIF with additional SAP APO-specific master data loads to be performed directly in SAP APO. For the second scenario, the data conversion (master and transactional data) will play a vital role in integration, not only during the cutover period, but also on an ongoing basis after the go-live phase to support the supply chain planning activities.

The data can be categorized into two forms: *master data* and *transactional data*. Examples of master data are SAP APO transportation lanes, SAP APO resources, and SAP APO quota arrangements. Since master data doesn't change, it can be loaded in an earlier part of cutover activities. Transactional data are records performed during the completion of business processes. Transactional data are dynamic and usually loaded in the last stage of cutover so that the current business activities have less of an impact on the implementation of the new system. Historical data also forms a part of the transactional data loaded into the system (for example, historical sales orders, which form the basis of the forecasting process in SAP APO).

There are two types of conversions or data loads:

▶ **Manual data conversion**
Manual data loads are typically items that require a limited number of entries into the system and can be manually entered with no tool automation process. In the manual data load, it is difficult to justify the time and effort in coding, testing, and automating the conversion process. An example is SAP APO table maintenance to influence any CIF enhancements.

▶ **Automated data conversion**
This data conversion primarily involves loading a large volume of data. Legacy data is formatted into a temporary database or data files, validated, transformed (if necessary), and loaded into the system. Automated conversion requires clear business rules to define the loading process. Companies can either use standard SAP-delivered utilities, such as legacy system migration workbench (LSMW), IDOC/ALE, eCATT, or BAPI, or develop custom conversion programs using the ABAP programming language.

Once you've decided which type of conversion is best for your situation, you can move on to deciding the data conversion process, which provides a framework for documenting the scope, effort, and steps that are required to successfully perform each conversion. The conversions are identified during the blueprint or design phase of the SAP APO project.

16.1.1 Data Conversion Process

Figure 16.2 shows a typical example of the data conversion process, consisting of initial data gathering, writing functional specifications, and going through the validation process, whether manual or automatic conversion is required. You can see that the data cleansing process is also defined and may consist of the process of fixing duplicate records, cleansing, and mapping. Once the conversion process is defined, the unit and integration process is performed, along with the pre-production data conversion exercise, before the final cutover execution in the production environment. Any errors or bugs identified in the testing phase are fixed, and the testing is performed successfully. Once the data conversion is loaded into the production environment, a reconciliation process occurs to validate the data accuracy, and the process is signed by the functional owner.

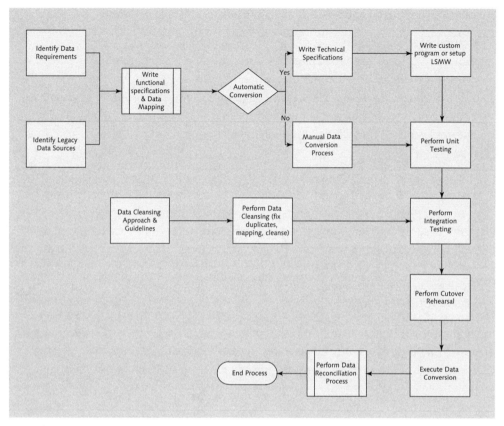

Figure 16.2 Data Conversion Process

16.1.2   Data Mapping and Cleansing

The build phase within the data cleansing process involves data mapping and data cleansing, which form important components.

Data mapping is done to translate the legacy application fields and business rules into the SAP APO structure. Mapping needs to be performed prior to any development of the conversion program. The mapping also addresses how the missing data fields will be identified and what form of transformations will be required, along with the verification process.

Data cleansing aims to convert an accurate form of data from legacy into the SAP APO application. The process analyzes application data to verify that data are correct, complete, consistent, and convertible. The process involves filtering valid data records, identifying and correcting inaccurate data records at the source, avoiding duplicate records, and reformatting and standardizing data so that it can be converted. Data cleansing is critical to the success of any SAP APO implementation since the application is data centric. The data forms part of the modeling exercise in the system and if not set up correctly, the business processes will not operate as designed. Ideally, data needs to be cleansed in the source or in a staging area.

Example

As part of data mapping and data cleansing, ABC Technology needs to perform the ETL (extract, transform, and load) process. The ETL process consists of extracting the raw data from their legacy application and performing data mapping as per SAP data standards. Once the raw data is cleansed and mapped with SAP data fields, the loading process is performed. The loading process creates the master data and/or transactional data in the SAP system.

Figure 16.3 shows an example of an extract, transform, and load (ETL) process, where the data is extracted from the legacy application and staged into tables formatted for loading into SAP tables. The example shows two ETL process for initial validation and then direct loading into the SAP tables using the LSMW utility.

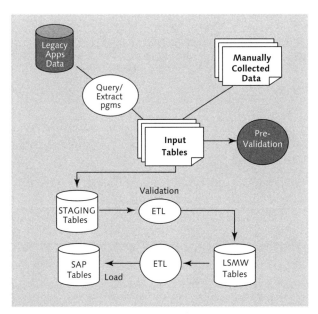

Figure 16.3 Extract, Transform, Load (ETL) Process

LSMW is a widely accepted tool for data conversion and is shown as a utility example for SAP APO data conversions in the next couple of sections.

16.2 Introduction to the Legacy System Migration Workbench (LSMW)

The Legacy System Migration Workbench (which we'll refer to as LSMW) is an SAP tool that supports a single or periodic data transfer from a legacy application to a new SAP application. The core function of LSMW is that it imports the legacy data from a PC spreadsheet or sequential files. LSMW converts data from its original (legacy system) format to the target (SAP APO) format and loads the data using the batch or direct input technique, or BAPI and Intermediate Documents (IDocs) technique.

The main advantage of using LSMW as a data conversion tool is that it forms a part of SAP APO and is therefore platform independent. LSMW offers a wide range of data conversion techniques (e.g., fixed values, translation, ABAP coding) and uses conversion programs that are automatically generated from conversion rules. The tool also provides user guidance into the different data migration steps. No extensive ABAP knowledge is needed (main conversion techniques at the push of a button). For complex conversions, individual ABAP coding can be added.

LSMW consists of various loading methods; see the following list for the main techniques used in the data conversion process:

- **Batch input program (SAP screen)**
  - SAP standard program
  - Custom-developed program
  - LSMW recording
  - Transaction recording to generate a batch input program in the background
  - Flat target structure (no header position constellations with a variable amount of positions)
- **IDOCs/BAPIs (function module – object-oriented)**
  - BAPI
  - SAP standard IDocs
  - Custom-developed extensions on IDocs

SAP APO Data Conversion Using LSMW | **16.3**

▶ **Direct Input Program (direct table update)**

   ▶ SAP standard program

   ▶ Custom-developed program

Figure 16.4 shows how LSMW works: the conversion program using the field mapping and conversion rules generate the input file for loading in the foreground or background. The transfer program can trigger different loading mechanisms.

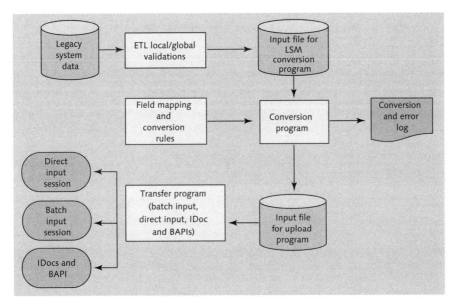

Figure 16.4 LSMW Loading Process

In the next section, we'll go over the steps for creating an LSMW loading structure for two cases: first for SAP APO master data (location) and second for transaction data (sales orders). The master data example uses the batch recording mechanism, while the transaction data example shows the use of the BAPI mechanism.

16.3 SAP APO Data Conversion Using LSMW

In this section, we'll learn how to set up LSMW. To start the activity, call SAP APO Transaction LSMW. In the initial screen click CREATE and maintain the following values:

► PROJECT
An ID with a maximum of 10 characters to name your data transfer project. If you want to transfer data from several legacy systems, you may create a project for every legacy system.

► SUBPROJECT
An ID with a maximum of 10 characters that is used as a further structuring attribute.

► OBJECT
An ID with a maximum of 10 characters to name the business object.

Once you've maintained the values and clicked the EXECUTE button, LSMW offers an interactive process guide to help you complete the process. Figure 16.5 shows the initial screen for the LSMW transaction for setting up the project and the steps for setting up the LSMW structure.

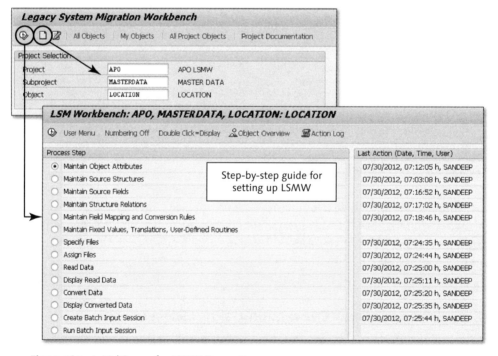

Figure 16.5 Initial Screen for LSMW Transaction

16.3.1 Loading Master Data

After you've maintained the information on the initial workbench screen, the program will show you a list of steps, which are indicated by the radio buttons in the LSM WORKBENCH screen. We'll explain each of the steps in the following list, along with manual and system processes.

1. MAINTAIN OBJECT ATTRIBUTES

   Select the object type and import technique. Define the following fields:

   ▶ OBJECT: Object name and description

   ▶ OWNER: By naming the owner after your user ID, you can display this later on in the initial screen under MY OBJECTS.

   ▶ DATA TRANSFER: Choose whether data transfer is one time or periodic. In the case of periodic transfers, files cannot be read from the frontend. This adds processing step FRAME PROGRAM FOR THE PERIODIC DATA TRANSFER.

   ▶ FILES NAMES: Flag whether the file names are system dependent (this gives you the chance to enter file names per system ID later).

   ▶ OBJECT TYPES: Select the object type and import technique.

   If neither a standard batch input program, standard direct input program, nor an IDoc is available for a data object, you can create a new object using the recording function of the LSMW. However, in cases when a standard program is available, it may make sense to use the recording function in order to reduce the number of target fields. Figure 16.6 shows that once we have maintained the object type, we can perform the recording by menu path GOTO • RECORDING OVERVIEW. The screen will prompt us for a transaction code and request that we perform recording by performing transactions steps. Click SAVE once the recording is completed. Figure 16.6 shows the LSMW object type recording technique and result after the transaction recording. Remember to click the DEFAULT ALL icon after the recording to take the mapping into consideration at later steps.

> **Note**
>
> The recording function records a fixed screen sequence. It cannot be used for migrating data containing a variable number of items or for transactions with dynamic screen sequences. Also, it is possible to create a recording via Transaction SHDB, generate a program out of this recording, adopt the program to your needs, and register the program for use in LSMW.

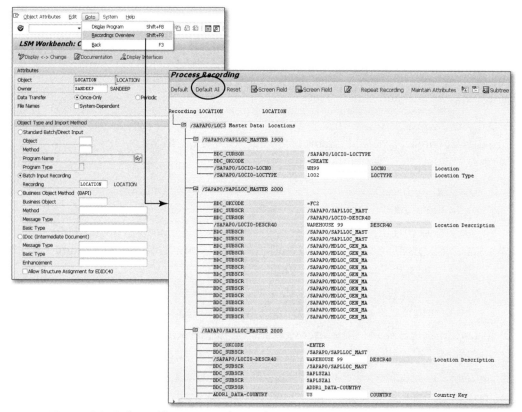

Figure 16.6 Defining Object Type and Recording Overview

2. MAINTAIN SOURCE STRUCTURES

   Define the structures of the object with its name, description, and hierarchical relationships.

3. MAINTAIN SOURCE FIELDS

   In this step, the fields are created and maintained for the structures defined in the earlier step. Figure 16.7 shows the source fields and source structure that are maintained.

4. MAINTAIN STRUCTURE RELATIONS

   The structural relationships define the relationships between source and target structures. The possible target structures are defined during the selection of the object type and the import technique.

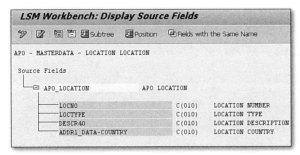

Figure 16.7 Mapping Source Fields to Source Structure

5. MAINTAIN FIELD MAPPING AND CONVERSION RULES

Assign source fields to target fields and define how the field contents will be converted. All fields of all target structures, which you selected in the previous step, will be displayed. For each target field, we define the field description, assigned source fields (if any), rule types (fixed value, translations, etc.), or any coding. Figure 16.8 shows how we can perform auto-mapping on the source and target fields using menu path EXTRAS • AUTO-FIELD MAPPING.

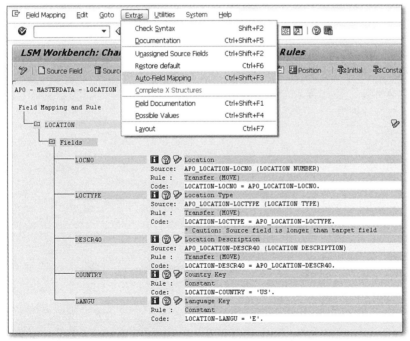

Figure 16.8 Maintaining Field Mapping and Conversion Rules

6. SPECIFY FILES

Describe all files to be used in the form of legacy data on the PC and/or SAP server. Select the TABULAR option based on the text file format, as shown in Figure 16.9.

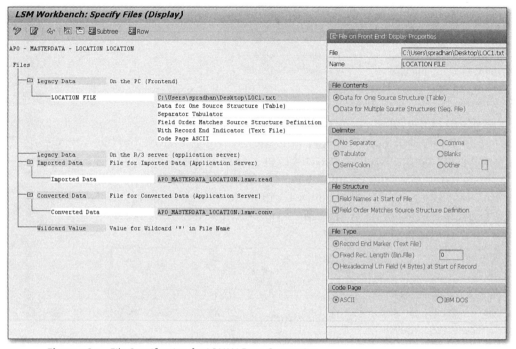

Figure 16.9 File Specification for LSMW Data Conversion

7. ASSIGN FILES

Assign defined files to the source structures.

8. READ DATA

In this step, the system reads the input file for loading. The file might be stored in an SAP application server file path.

9. DISPLAY READ DATA

In this step, you can display all or a part of the read data in table form.

10. CONVERT DATA

In this step, we convert the input data file from source to target structures.

11. DISPLAY CONVERTED DATA

In this step, you can display all or a part of the converted data in table form, as shown in Figure 16.10. Validate whether the conversion has occurred properly per the fields mapping.

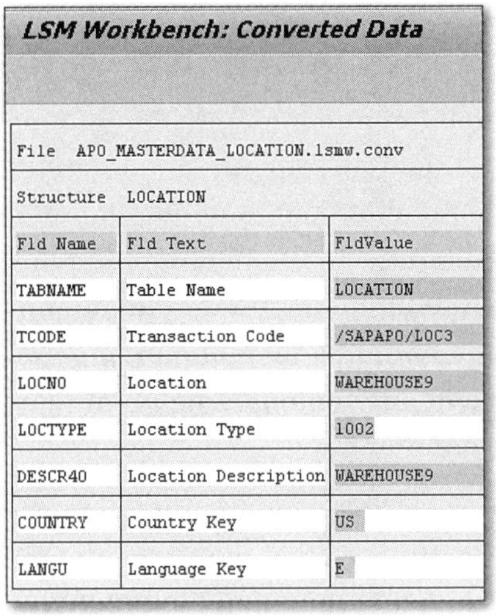

LSM Workbench: Converted Data

File   APO_MASTERDATA_LOCATION.lsmw.conv

Structure   LOCATION

Fld Name	Fld Text	FldValue
TABNAME	Table Name	LOCATION
TCODE	Transaction Code	/SAPAPO/LOC3
LOCNO	Location	WAREHOUSE9
LOCTYPE	Location Type	1002
DESCR40	Location Description	WAREHOUSE9
COUNTRY	Country Key	US
LANGU	Language Key	E

Figure 16.10 Converted Data Format

12. CREATE BATCH INPUT SESSION

In this step, the standard batch input program belonging to the object is directly called. The name of the file with the converted data is already proposed. The batch input sessions to be generated are named after the LSMW object.

13. RUN BATCH INPUT SESSION

The program goes to SAP standard Transaction SM35. However, only the batch input sessions for the selected object are displayed. Figure 16.11 shows the batch input session, which is ready to be processed. By clicking the PROCESS icon, we can perform the data conversion activity in either the background or foreground.

This step concludes our first example of loading master data.

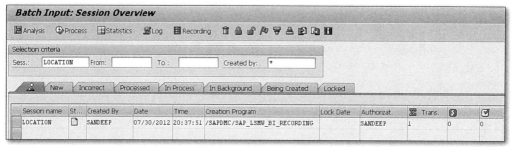

Figure 16.11 Batch Input File

16.3.2 Converting Transactional Data

Our next example is for transactional data in the form of sales orders. In this sample business scenario, the SAP ERP system hasn't been implemented, and a legacy application is used to interface with SAP APO. The transactional data needs to be integrated into SAP APO for planning calculations.

In this example, instead of the recording feature, we will use the standard BAPI function for creating sales orders. For this scenario, we need the IDoc inbound processing customization. IDocs were developed for exchanging messages between different systems. Since it is a standard interface to the SAP applications, this technique can also be used for transferring data.

To perform this, we need to perform some pre-settings, and preparations are required. For a summary of these requirements, see SETTINGS • IDOC INBOUND PROCESSING in the LSMW workbench, as shown in Figure 16.12.

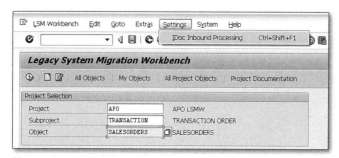

Figure 16.12 IDoc Inbound Processing Setting for LSMW

The first requirement is a file port for the file transfer. If required, create a port of the file type FILE via MAINTAIN PORTS—position the cursor on FILE and click CREATE. You should be in change mode. Maintain the following settings.

Port	LSMW
Name	Legacy System Migration Workbench
Version	3 (IDocs record types SAP Release 4.x)
Outbound file	Please enter a (dummy) physical directory and a file name, i.e. 'filelsmw'

Additionally, in Transaction LSMW, you can specify a transactional RFC (tRFC, previously named as asynchronous RFC port). This port is required: if you do not want to create a file during data conversion but submit the data in packages directly to function module `IDoc_Inbound_Asynchronous`, maintain the following settings.

Port	Value Assigned by the System
Version	3 (IDocs record types SAP Release 4.x)
RFC destination	Name of the SAP system
Name of port	Legacy System Migration Workbench

Finally, define or select a partner number by maintaining the following settings.

Partner number	LSMW
Partner type	US
Partner status	A (active)
Type	US
Language	EN
Person in charge	Your user ID

Next, click the ACTIVATE IDOC INBOUND PROCESSING button, as shown in Figure 16.13.

IDoc Inbound Processing: Preparatory Measures

Project	APO

IDoc Inbound Processing

File port	LSMW	Maintain Ports
tRFC port		
Partn.Type	US	Maintain Partner Types
Partner No.	LSMW	Maintain Partner Numbers
	Activate IDoc Inbound Processing	
	Workflow Customizing	

Figure 16.13 IDoc Inbound Processing Customization

Confirm with YES (to be done once for each system). Also verify WORKFLOW CUS-TOMIZING (to be done once for each system). The following entries of the workflow runtime system should be marked with a green check mark to post the file success-fully, as shown in Figure 16.14.

▶ Workflow administrator maintained

▶ Workflow RFC destination completely configured

▶ Generic decision task classified completely

▶ Sending to objects and to HR objects is active

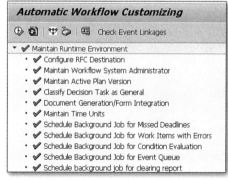

Figure 16.14 LSMW Workflow Customization

For sales order (transaction data), we need to specify the object type that will be the BAPI method, as shown in Figure 16.15. The majority of the steps for setting up sales order LSMW are similar to the master data.

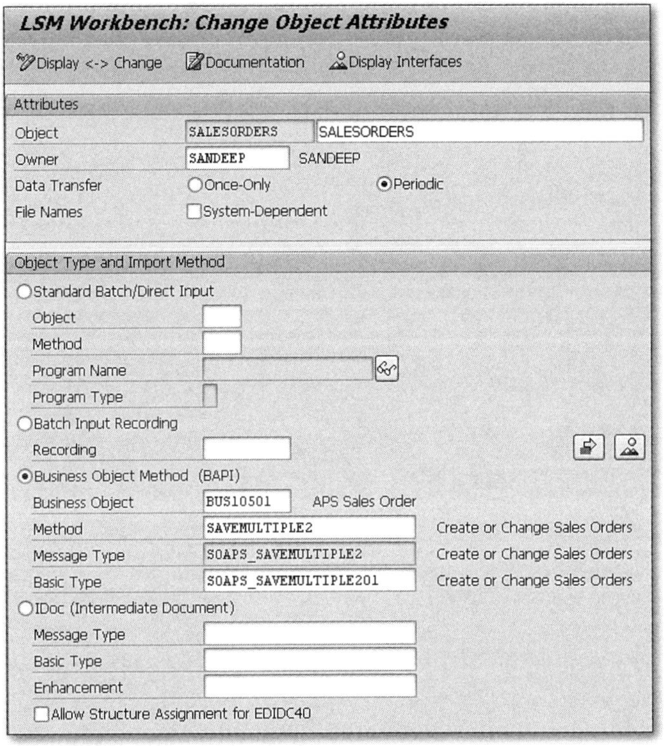

Figure 16.15 BAPI Method for Sales Orders Periodic Load

The only other minor difference is setting up the structure relationship for mapping where the different BAPI segments need to be mapped. The BAPI will have some mandatory fields, which need to be filled up, as shown in Figure 16.16.

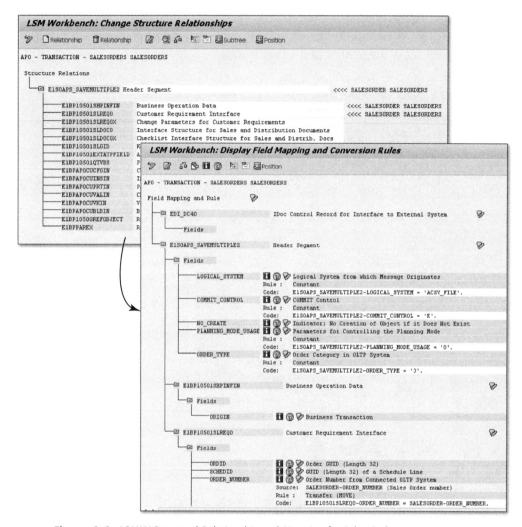

Figure 16.16 LSMW Structural Relationship and Mapping for Sales Orders

16.3.3 Importing Data with IDocs

Data stored in a file by means of the IDocs technique is generally imported in two steps. You can call these steps in Transaction LSMW (LSM Workbench). We maintain the IDoc details (i.e., message type, basic type, and enhancements) under the first menu path of MAINTAIN OBJECT ATTRIBUTES:

1. **Start IDoc generation**

   First, the file of the converted data is read. The information packages contained are stored in the SAP database in the IDocs format. The read data is, however, not stored in the database of the corresponding application. The system assigns a number to every IDoc. Then, the file of the converted data is deleted.

2. **Start IDoc processing**

   The IDocs created in the first step are submitted to the corresponding application program. This application program checks the data and posts it in the application's database, if applicable.

In situations when the LSMW needs to be used more than once and is nominated to be used as the interface for loading the files routinely parked in application server, SAP provides program /SAPDMC/SAP_LSMW_INTERFACE, which can be scheduled as a background job.

16.4 Technical Enhancements in SAP APO

In many situations, a business will require enhancements because standard software functionality won't meet its business requirements. In this section, we'll demonstrate how specific business requirements can be achieved via modification on both the SAP ERP and SAP SCM systems.

The technical modifications that you can use in SAP SCM include BAdIs, BAPI, user exits, and macros, per the technical developer decision:

▶ BAdIs are object-oriented enhancement programming techniques used in the enhancement of runtime objects like production data structure (PDS). The BAdI enhancement technique differentiates between enhancements that can be implemented only once and enhancements that can be used actively by any number of customers at the same time. In addition, BAdIs can be defined according to filter values. This allows you to control the add-in implementation and make it dependent on specific criteria (for a specific production plant, for example).

▶ A Business Application Programming Interface (BAPI) is used to process any external system–provided data in the form of a function module. For example, when the new CIF material is transferred from SAP ERP, the function module (BAPI) is processed in SAP SCM side to post the data into SAP tables.

- ▶ SAP provides the user exit enhancement object type to make any modifications before the data is posted.

- ▶ Macros play an important role in the SAP APO planning book calculations. Macros are used in the planning book not only for doing simple calculations, creating alerts, changing colors, and triggering pop-ups for cell values below threshold, but also for complex business scenarios. For complex calculations, SAP provides the provision of writing routine code in the form of a macro function unavailable in standard macros.

You'll find a high-level overview of sample enhancements; we'll first explain the selected business scenarios and requirements, and then discuss how the relevant system can be enhanced to meet the business needs. The idea of this section is show you the techniques of possible technical enhancement possibilities to address specific business requirements.

16.4.1 Business Scenario 1: Material Master CIF

The CIF is used to transfer the material master data from SAP ERP to the SCM system. SAP provides standard mapping of fields between the two systems. After the CIF has transferred the standard fields, SAP APO has to maintain additional fields to support the business process.

Let's say that a business wants to populate SAP APO-SNP planner code with an SAP ERP purchasing group or MRP-maintained controller. Alternatively, it wants to read the standard price and lot size values from SAP ERP info record while populating the SAP APO location product master. These requirements aren't maintained by standard functionality; instead, you can use an enhancement to include additional fields or any alterations required in the standard CIF mapping. SAP provides CIF enhancements for master data that can be used to transform the data during the transfer.

Enhancement Solution

As Figure 16.17 shows, the CIF enhancement occurs during the data transfer from SAP ERP to the SAP SCM system. For our business scenario, SAP provides CIF user exit EXIT_SAPLCMAT_001, which can be enhanced to transform the SAP APO field during the transfer.

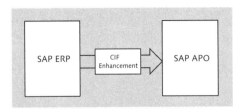

Figure 16.17 CIF Enhancement during the Data Transfer from SAP ERP to SAP APO

The technique for writing functional specifications (to be given to the technical developer for coding) is to provide the CIF user exit name along with CIF structure and fieldname mapped with an SAP ERP table name and field. (An example is shown in Table 16.1.) This mapping can then be coded in the user exit program provided by SAP.

Structure	Fieldname	Description	SAP TABLE	SAP FIELDNAME	Mapping Conversion
CIF_MATLOC	PLANNR_ SNP	Purchasing group	MARC	EKGRP	Material plant combination
CIF_MATKEY	ATT02	Material status	MARA	MSTAE	Material

Table 16.1 Example for CIF Enhancement Mapping

Figure 16.18 shows how to locate the CIF structure within the function module and look at the available fields that can be mapped. In our example, under the function module `EXIT_SAPLCMAT_001`, the structure `CIF_MATLOC` is shown, which has all the SAP APO 216 fields that can be mapped.

16.4.2 Business Scenario 2: SAP APO Product Master Creation

While building a supply chain model in SAP APO, we sometimes need to extend the SAP APO product location master data to customer or vendor locations. For example, vendor managed inventory (VMI) modeling in SAP APO requires maintaining the product master for customer locations directly in SAP APO since this material master data for the technical material master does not exist in SAP ERP. Since the material master in SAP ERP is not maintained for customer or vendor locations, we need an enhancement to auto-create this master data in SAP APO.

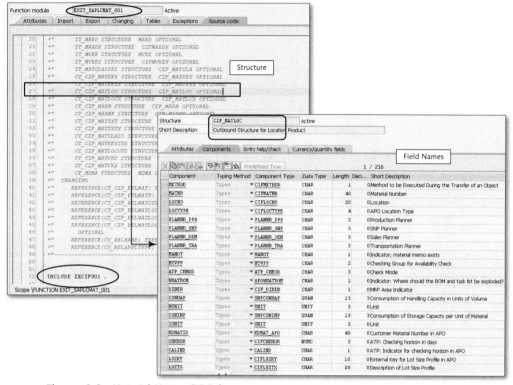

Figure 16.18 Material Master CIF Enhancement

Enhancement Solution

Since the target system here is SAP APO, it is recommended that the logic be written on SAP APO user exit. The enhancement logic can be written in two ways:

▶ Copy the data from one location to the vendor or customer location.

▶ Use a standard BAPI to create product location master data in SAP APO.

The user exit in the SAP APO side for the product master is EXIT_/SAPAPO/SAP-LCIF_PROD_001. Also, the BAPI that is available in SAP APO to create master data is BAPI_PRDSRVAPS_SAVEMULTI2. The prerequisite for this enhancement to work is that the vendor or customer location is transferred first via CIF.

Next, during the material master transfer, we need to pass some field identifier to indicate which material vendor/customer location is valid. Figure 16.19 shows the SAP APO CIF user exit mapping, where the master data is checked before the new record is created. For example, we can read the valid SAP ERP info record master data for the active vendor, which supplies the material.

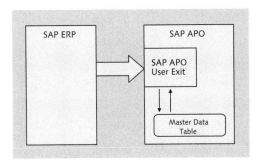

Figure 16.19 Mapping SAP APO CIF User Exit

Then, on the SAP APO user exit, we can include the following sample pseudo code logic: In the SAP APO product master user exit, `EXIT_/SAPAPO/SAPLCIF_PROD_001` do the following:

1. Check if structure `IT_MATKEY` field ATT04 (vendor number) exists in table /SAPAPO/LOCMAP.

2. If `NO`, exit the logic.

3. If `YES` (SAP APO table, check if the product/vendor master exists in table /SAPAPO/MATLOC)

4. If `YES`, skip to the next record in CIF.

5. If no master data exist in the table for the product/vendor location combination, use `BAPI_PRDSRVAPS_SAVEMULTI2` (or copy the complete structure and extend to vendor location) to create location product (vendor) master data in SAP APO. Change some of the default values, such as procurement type or pull/push deployment horizon during the master data creation.

> **Note: Debugging CIF**
>
> During the development, we often need to debug the CIF enhancement. To achieve this, we need to change some of the settings. In SAP APO Transaction /SAPAPO/C4, provide your SAP user name and RFC CPIC (communication user) to switch on the debugging mode. Also, in SAP ERP side Transaction CFC2, change the username to debugging mode. In this mode, a queue will be registered in Transaction SMQ1 or SMQ2 where you can select the debug LUW option to trigger the function module.

16.4.3 Business Scenario 3: Transaction Data Mapping

In some specific scenarios, the business may not want to include specific transaction data (for example, returns) in SAP APO for planning. There might be another situation in which the transaction data of one plant needs to be mapped to another location. To make adjustments to these sorts of transformations on the transactional data, you will need to use enhancements.

Enhancement Solution

You can change the transactional data by user exit in either SAP ERP or SAP APO. For example, with the SAP APO TLB publication for VMI sales orders to SAP ERP, we want to nominate the ERP sales orders type to be used. Besides changing the transaction data user exit, we will also need to adjust the CIF delta reconciliation report on the new business rule. In the following list, we've provided the user exits in SAP APO and SAP ERP that can be used to change the logic.

Transaction Data User Exit in SAP APO

- APOCF011 EXIT_/SAPAPO/SAPLCIF_STOCK_001: Inbound processing: Stock
- APOCF004 EXIT_/SAPAPO/SAPLCIF_ORD_001: Inbound processing: Production orders and planned orders
- APOCF013 EXIT_/SAPAPO/SAPLCIF_ORD_002: Outbound processing: Production orders and planned orders (before send user exit)
- APOCF006 EXIT_/SAPAPO/SAPLCIF_PU_001: Inbound processing: Purchase order documents
- APOCF010 EXIT_/SAPAPO/SAPLCIF_SLS_001: Inbound processing: Sales and distribution document

Transaction Data User Exit in SAP ERP for the Publication Types:

- CIFORD03: Change Order Data
  To change orders that are transferred from SAP APO to SAP ERP in ERP inbound queue
- CIFORD01: Change Object Type and Order Data
  To change order data that is transferred from SAP APO to SAP ERP and is already in SAP ERP format in the ERP inbound queue
- PPAPO002: Influence Order Data after the Transfer from SAP APO
  To influence the data that was transferred from SAP APO to SAP ERP for a manufacturing order before it is transferred to the SAP ERP manufacturing order

- ▶ PPAPO008: Override Order Type for Planned Order Conversion
  To manually influence the order type of a manufacturing order generated by conversion from SAP APO (customer exit EXIT_SAPLCOXT_002)
- ▶ PPAPO004: Re-Explode BOMs for Planned Order Conversion
  To force the re-explosion of a BOM (customer exit EXIT_SAPLCOXT_001)
- ▶ PPAPO009: Add Components and Items
  To run own checks when components are added to a manufacturing order from SAP APO
- ▶ PPAPO007: Override Checkbox Fields for Manufacturing Orders, SAP APO, and SAP ERP
  To override checkbox fields for manufacturing orders on transfer from SAP APO to SAP ERP
- ▶ CIFPUR01 (enhancement for the transmission of customer-specific purchase order fields)
  To change purchasing data from purchase requisitions, POs, scheduling agreement schedule lines (OLTP scheduling agreement), and confirmations/shipping notifications (for SAP APO and OLTP scheduling agreements)
- ▶ CIFPUR02 (enhancement PO interface—inbound)
  To change PO data from SAP APO before a purchase requisition, scheduling agreement schedule line, or a PO is created in the OLTP system

Figure 16.20 shows an example in which the stock CIF user exit is called in the SAP APO side, which does look up at custom table to perform the relevant mapping.

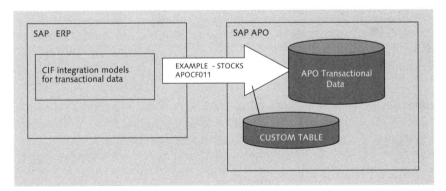

Figure 16.20 Transaction Data CIF Enhancement Mapping

To create an add-on project from within the ABAP Workbench menu, choose UTILITIES • ENHANCEMENTS • PROJECT MANAGEMENT (TRANSACTION CMOD).

Figure 16.21 shows the steps performed in Transaction CMOD. Within the transaction, a name for an enhancement project is APOCF011 (❶). Then, different enhancements can be assigned to this project. Assign SAP enhancements APOCF011 to an enhancement project. If you select COMPONENTS and then DISPLAY (❷), you are able to change the source. By double-clicking the included ZXCIFUSERU15 (❸), you can include your custom logic code. Activate the project in order for the enhancements you maintained to become effective (❹).

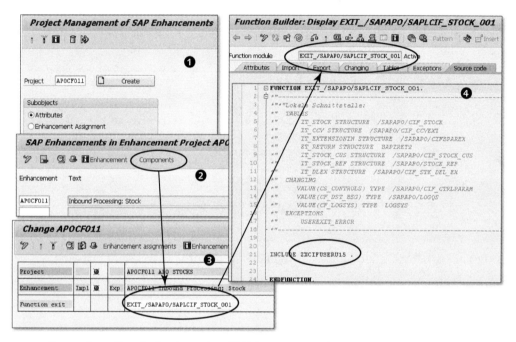

Figure 16.21 Steps for Implementing CIF Enhancements in SAP APO

The transaction data are reconciled using the CIF delta report 3 and Transaction /SAPAPO/CCR. Any changes on the transactional mapping also include changes on the CIF delta report reconciliation between SAP ERP and SAP APO.

You also need to implement BAdI /SAPAPO/CIF_DELTA3 with similar logic as for the transaction data. This will ensure that the expected transaction data is consistent with the SAP ERP during the CIF delta reconciliation process. One example is when the stocks are mapped to different locations in SAP APO during the CIF transfer. A similar logic needs to be implemented in the CIF delta report to avoid any SAP ERP–SAP SCM reconciliation failures when the report is run routinely.

16.4.4 Business Scenario 4: APO-SNP PDS Modification

APO-SNP is used to calculate the master production schedule and rough-cut capacity plan. The key master data used is APO-SNP production data structure (PDS), which contains the entire bill of material and all the routing information. However, the standard APO-SNP PDS sometime does not fulfill the complex modeling requirement to calculate the proper master production schedule. In these cases, the SNP optimizer uses production cost, which needs to be maintained in PDS. The maintenance of costs (single level, variable, and fixed for APO-SNP) is possible with SAP ERP Transaction PDS_MAINT. This transaction will also be available in SAP SCM 7.02, locally within the PDS maintenance (as part of the PDS header). Also, the bucket consumption in PDS needs to be enhanced to ensure that the APO-SNP and PP/DS planned orders have consistent operation lead times.

Enhancement Solution

The production master data can be represented either by SNP PPM or SNP PDS. The SNP PDS structure can be directly created in SAP APO via CIF from SAP ERP, unlike PPM, which needs to be converted from PP/DS PPM in SAP APO. SAP recommends using PDS over PPM because SAP's future development will be done only on PDS.

Most of the enhancement required for PDS can be achieved by implementing BAdI /SAPAPO/CURTO_SNP. As Figure 16.22 shows, there are various methods (for example, bucket consumption and costs) that can be implemented. Additional business logic can be written in the form of code for the method to achieve the result.

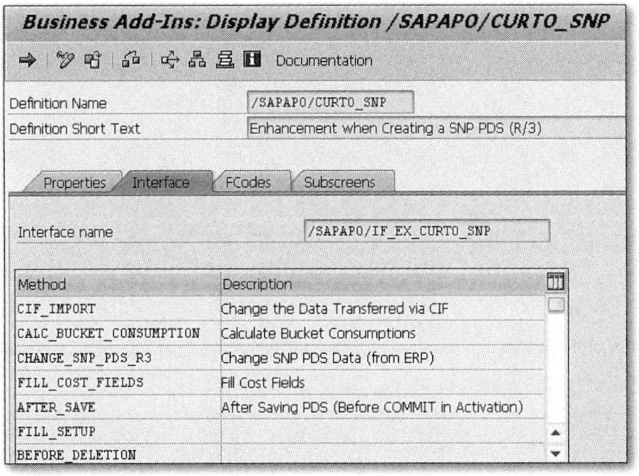

Figure 16.22 SNP PDS Enhancement BAdI

16.4.5 Business Scenario 5: APO-SNP Planning Book Modifications

The APO-SNP planning book is the user interface for the demand and supply planning process. Depending on the business, the characteristics that are available in the APO-SNP planning book selection profile are sometimes not sufficient to define the complete planning level that the business users want to plan. Therefore, you'll need to implement an enhancement in the APO-SNP planning book selection profile.

You can also use an enhancement to sort the sequence of products displayed in the planning book. The standard interface will automatically show products by ascending product number. With the use of an enhancement in the APO-SNP planning book pivot sorting, you can plan Class A products first within the same product family before working on Class B and C products.

Enhancement Solution

For the APO-SNP planning book, we can use BAdI /SAPAPO/SDP_SELECTOR and method INIT_OBJECT_LIST to include the master data field we want as additional characteristics in the selection profile.

The other useful BAdI for making changes on the interactive planning is /SAPAPO/SDP_INTERACT. For our business scenario, we can modify the changes in method GET_KEYF_SPECIALS to read some sort criteria from the SAP APO product master data.

16.4.6 Business Scenario 6: SAP APO User Exit Macro

An example of a business scenario might be where SAP NetWeaver BW performs average lead-time calculation, which needs to be updated in the SAP APO product location master. There is no direct provision for such an update, so we need an enhancement to update the product master once the data is populated in the planning book.

Enhancement Solution

The user exit macro enhancement is a two-step process: gather all the technical information and then code the routine. The first step is to create a user exit macro in Transaction /SAPAPO/ADVM. As Figure 16.23 shows, note the technical details of the macro. The ID LAYOUT field contains the technical ID of the planning book, and the ID VIEW field contains the technical ID for the data view.

Next, under menu path EDIT • BOOK INFORMATION, note the technical information of the planning book and data view to be used, as shown in Figure 16.24.

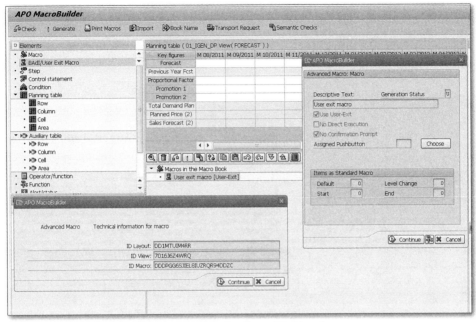

Figure 16.23 Configuring User Exit Macro in the Macro Workbench

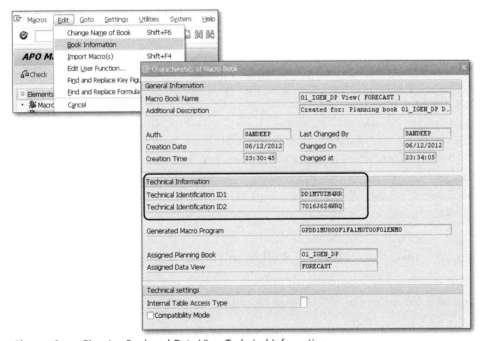

Figure 16.24 Planning Book and Data View Technical Information

The last part of technical information gathering is the technical object name for the key figure and the characteristics. Using Transaction /SAPAPO/SDP8B, note the technical field name under the KEY FIGURES AND CHARACTERISTICS tab, as shown in Figure 16.25.

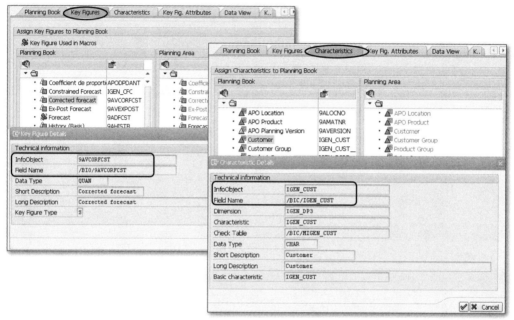

Figure 16.25 Characteristics and Key Figure Technical Information

Next, under Transaction CMOD, we need to create a project and include enhancement object APODM005. As Figure 16.26 shows, function module EXIT_/SAPAPO/SAPMMCP6_005 is available for this object. This function module has the INCLUDE PROGRAM, where you can write the user exit code for the task that you want the macro to perform. Double-click the function module EXIT_ /SAPAPO/SAPMMCP6_005 to access this code. The INCLUDE program ZXDMUSERU05 contains the ABAP code in which you can code your user exit routine for your macro.

16.4.7 Business Scenario 7: SNP Heuristics Lot Sizing

SNP heuristics is a repair-based planning engine in SAP APO that uses lot size for calculation. In the repair-based situation, the heuristics attempts to find the best solution to correct any demand and supply imbalance (for example, supply shortages). In some business situations, the lot sizing method, along with the safety days, needs to be factored during the planning calculation. The SNP heuristics does not provide this feature and needs enhancement.

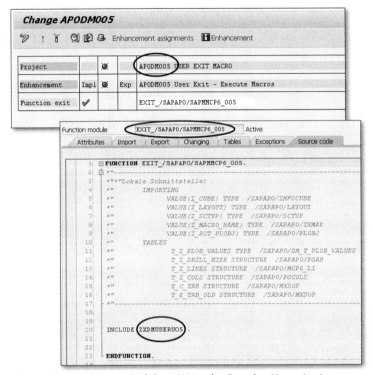

Figure 16.26 Function Module to Write the Complex Macro Logic

Enhancement Solution

SAP provides BAdI /SAPAPO/SNP_PERIO_LS, which can be used to influence the SNP heuristics run. The BAdI is called several times for the same product when executing SNP heuristic for a product. The BAdI is called for each planned receipt (planned orders, purchase requisitions) that is placed for the product.

The big difference is that when the BAdI is called for the first time, the table CT_REPL is modified over the whole horizon. These changes also remain for the later calls. Therefore, this modification of CT_REPL happens only once (during the first call). In CT_REPL in the field REORD, the BAdI highlights the buckets in which it has calculated a supply element with a certain key.

16.4.8 Business Scenario 8: CTM Demand Prioritization

In the business situation when CTM is used as the planning engine, we need to define the demand prioritization. The demand prioritization can be defined based on demand type, delivery dates, and other business rules. In some business scenarios, not all the available fields support the business requirement. An enhancement is done on the SAP APO sort profile to input the additional rules.

Enhancement Solution

SAP provides a user exit field in the CTM sort profile, which can be used as an enhancement. As Figure 16.27 shows, we can include the UserExit field in the sequence and implement project APOBO020. The function module EXIT_/SAPAPO/ SAPLBOP_SORT_020 provides the Include function to add custom logic.

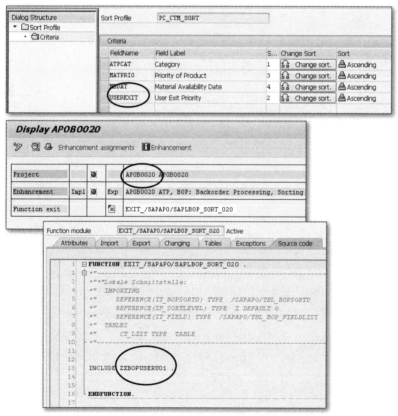

Figure 16.27 CTM Demand Prioritization User Exit

16.4.9 Business Scenario 9: Demand Planning with SAP NetWeaver BW

Sales orders in SAP ERP are processed in a different unit of measure (UOM) that customer orders. The sales orders are interfaced via SAP NetWeaver Business Warehouse as historical demand to calculate future forecast. APO-DP is done at a single planning unit of measure, as defined in the planning area customization. An enhancement is required to translate the customer sales order UOM to the default APO-DP planning book UOM.

Enhancement Solution

A routine can be written in the SAP NetWeaver BW component within SAP SCM to convert the customer sales orders UOM to the planning UOM. This modification is done in Transaction RSA1 as a part of update rule while transferring the data from the communication structure to the InfoCube. The routine can read the base and alternative unit of measure from table /SAPAPO/MARM. Figure 16.28 shows the rule type of routine defined for the key figure where the changes can be made.

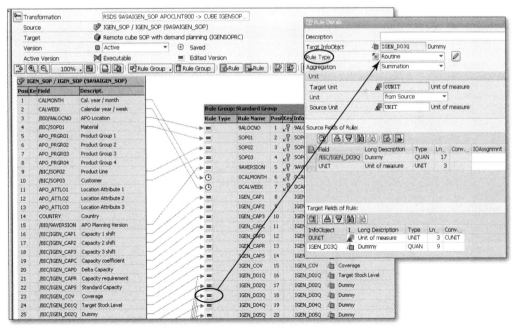

Figure 16.28 SAP NetWeaver BW Routine to Convert UOM

16.4.10 Business Scenario 10: Demand Planning to Supply Planning Release

The planning levels for demand and supply planning may differ. In demand planning, different characteristics can be modeled to formulate demand planning, while the supply planning plans at the product location level. In business situations in which we find additional complex requirements, we need an enhancement during the demand plan release to supply network planning.

Enhancement Solution

SAP APO provides function module EXIT_/SAPAPO/SAPLAPO_EXIT_001, where we can input complex logic on the demand plan release. This function module forms part of enhancement APODM017. The interface structure of this exit includes an internal table SCHEDULE_LINE_TAB, where the demand can be assigned to the appropriate ATP category.

16.4.11 Business Scenario 11: Alert Monitor

The Alert Monitor in SAP APO is a component that's used by a business as a central monitoring tool for any planning exceptions. In many scenarios, the business would like to add additional attributes in the alert monitor to address specific business scenarios. SAP provides the flexibility of adding the customer-specific fields to the Alert Monitor in SAP APO.

Enhancement Solution

SAP APO provides BAdI /SAPAPO/AM_ALERTLIST (method MODIFY_ALERTLIST), which can be enhanced to add the additional attributes.

16.4.12 Business Scenario 12: TLB Interactive Display

The TLB is used for building rough-cut load shipment for execution. In many business scenarios, the planner has to consider additional attributes (for example, transportation group and ABC indicator) while building the shipment load. SAP provides flexibility in adding the customer-specific fields to the TLB interactive screen for better usability.

Enhancement Solution

SAP APO provides BAdI `/SAPAPO/TLB_DISP_CHG`, which can be enhanced to add additional attributes in the TLB interactive screen. The structure /SAPAPO/MSDP_TLBEDIT_STR needs to be appended before the use of the BAdI.

16.5 Summary

Before the development work begins on the SAP APO project, it is very important to understand all solution gaps and properly classify them as a report, interface, conversion object, enhancement, form, or workflow. This chapter focused on conversion object and enhancement possibilities in SAP APO. Data conversion activities are imperative for project success and need to be properly planned and executed.

This chapter showed how we can use the LSMW tool to migrate the legacy data to the SAP APO application. LSMW supports loading both master and transactional data. The chapter also provided sample enhancements, which can be implemented to support complex business requirements. The enhancements are required to support SAP native functionality to fully meet the business requirements.

17   Conclusions and Outlook

The demand and supply planning process deals with balancing unconstrained market demand with constrained supply chain and formulating operational, tactical, and strategic plans for the company. SAP Advanced Planning & Optimization (SAP APO) is a user-decision support tool that supports the demand and supply planning process. The chapters in this book outlined the capabilities of SAP APO Demand Planning (APO-DP) and Supply Network Planning (APO-SNP) in providing robust functions to meet demand and supply planning business requirements in an evolving global environment. The business benefits of improved demand and supply planning using SAP APO can include enhanced revenue, reduction in costs, and improvement in asset management. These benefits are achieved with better forecast accuracy, inventory availability for orders, and proper utilization of the company's supply chain resources (e.g., manufacturing and transportation).

With the advancement of SAP Supply Chain Management (SCM) in the areas of business processes and technology, SAP APO provides functionality to forecast, purchase, manufacture, and distribute product in order to satisfy customer demand. There are two factors that make SAP APO one of the top-tier Advanced Planning and Scheduling (APS) tools:

▶ The first is its support of demand and supply planning business process decomposition (Chapter 2), which can further be traced down to Supply Chain Council's Supply Chain Operation Reference (SCOR) model. The supply chain operation reference model (Chapter 1) provides leading practices for a company's sales and operations planning definitions and supply chain metrics. The adoption of these definitions in SAP APO demonstrates its dedication in defining best practices for business processes within IT tools.

▶ The second factor is the ability of the tool to model the supply chain to solve basic and complex optimization demand and supply planning problems. There are two aspects on solving these problems: the analytical system algorithms to propose the best feasible demand and supply plan based on current market situation and the ability of the business planners to analyze, correct, and endorse the plan for execution. The human factor can never be ignored in the whole demand and supply planning process. For this reason, any business process improvement initiatives should address people, process, and tool/technology (Chapter 3) as part of change management.

The empowerment of the business user to use the APO DP/SNP tool really depends on the system design and understanding. The business user can learn and master the tool by taking a building block approach. The first step for the business user and solution designers is to put forward a basic demand and supply planning process (Chapters 4 and 5). The basic planning addresses the weekly/monthly planning cycle leading to the company's sales and operations planning process. The business user should be able to navigate, make adjustments on plan, and perform interactive forecasting and supply planning in SAP APO during this process. Once the basic planning understanding is mature, the business users and solution designer can take the planning to the next week with the introduction of some advanced functionalities (Chapters 6 and 7) available in APO-DP/SNP. The purpose of advanced features (for example, promotion planning, subcontracting, aggregated planning, etc.) is to build on the basic planning foundation and provide solutions for complex business scenarios. Taking this two-step approach (basic and advanced) will increase business user effective adoption of the SAP APO tool.

This book shows how, using SAP APO collaborative planning (Chapter 8), companies can gain synergy and reduce cycle time in fulfilling customer orders, resulting in lower inventory levels. Demand and supply planning reporting (Chapter 9) generates important information for business performance monitoring and helps companies to track their sales and operations planning decisions. Reporting plays an integral role in closing the loop between planning and execution.

We learned in this book how different SAP APO functionalities within the APO-DP and APO-SNP modules provide different supply chain modeling options. Starting with forecast modeling (Chapter 4) on the demand side, the business has the option of selecting different optimization engines (i.e., heuristics, optimizer, or CTM) based on business rules. The heuristics algorithm (Chapter 5) is intended to solve certain planning problems in an analytic and reproducible way without necessarily finding the optimal solution. The optimizer (Chapter 10) focuses on cost-based optimization, while CTM (Chapter 11) works based on demand and supply priorities.

Also embedded within the supply chain modeling is inventory planning and optimization (Chapter 12) for defining inventory models for your products. Designing an inventory control system that revolves around identifying the correct ordering quantity and locating the trigger point for ordering inventory is critical for any inventory management process. This book also provides real-life business examples in the form of characteristics-based industries (automotive, high tech, mills, chemical, etc.) and industry solutions (apparel and footwear) for which SAP APO provides a complete, end-to-end planning solution (Chapters 13 and 14).

The last section of this book covers the IT concepts in the form of Core Interface (CIF), which provides the communication platform between the SAP ERP and SAP SCM systems (Chapter 15). This book also discusses a dozen examples of technical enhancements (Chapter 16) for managing different business scenarios to close the SAP APO functionality gap to support the business requirements. Data forms a critical element for planning result output, and in many times is forgotten until the time the functionality moves into the production environment. This book describes the data conversion and cleansing methodology (Chapter 16), which requires the same priority as other project activities during the implementation and post-implementation phases of any SAP APO project.

By understanding the content we have covered in this book and carefully walking through the examples we have provided, you will now have a strong base understanding of APO-DP and APO-SNP functions and will be able to design, customize, and implement solutions based on any organization's requirements.

Future Outlook

The future outlook for both the business process (demand and supply planning) as well as the technology (SAP APO) seems bright and evolving. SAP has taken a new approach to deploying innovate solutions to its customers. Instead of continuing to upgrade to higher versions, SAP now offers new SAP APO functionalities in the form of enhancement packages. With each new enhancement package, SAP provides new functionalities, which the customer can opt to implement if they match their business requirement.

Recent years have also seen SAP developing Rapid Deployment Solutions (RDS) in the form of packaged solutions to accelerate implementation times with fixed investment costs. Currently, SAP offers RDS in 14 (as of October 2012) different areas in supply chain management, of which demand planning and sales and operations planning are some examples. Another area for supply chain practitioners interested in the demand and supply planning area will be SAP Sales and Operations Planning Powered by HANA. SAP HANA is marketed by SAP as the next wave of in-memory computing technology and represents an information appliance strategy whereby all key supply chain planning data is readily available on an SAP HANA platform, avoiding the need to access various SAP SCM business suites to consolidate planning data. Customers should view HANA applications as an alternative to the classic SAP NetWeaver Business Warehouse form of storing planning and decision-support data.

Appendices

A   Resources

Bremmer, Ian. *The J Curve: A New Way to Understand Why Nations Rise and Fall* (New York, NY: Simon and Schuster, 2007)

Chidhambaram. *A Supply Chain Transformation Methodology*, Industrial Engineering Conference paper (Wichita State University, 2002)

Harrison, Terry P., Hau Leung Lee, and John J. Neale. *The Practice of Supply Chain Management* (Medford, MA: Springer, 2008)

Hax, A.C. and D. Candea. *Production and Inventory Management* (Englewood Cliffs, NJ: Prentice-Hall, 1984)

Juran, J. M and J. Defeo. *Juran's Quality Control Handbook* (6th Edition). (New York, NY: McGraw-Hill, 2010)

Kotter, John. "Leading Change" Harvard Business Review, March 2011

Lee, H., V. Padmanabhan, and S. Whang. *"The Bullwhip Effect in Supply Chains,"* Sloan Management Review, Spring 1997, 93-102.

Narahari, Y. and S. Biswas. Indian Institute of Science whitepaper, Supply Chain Management (2000)

Simchi-Levi, D, P. Kaminsky, and E. Simchi-Levi. *Designing and Managing the Supply Chain* (2nd Edition). (New York, NY: McGraw-Hill, 2002)

Tague, Nancy R. *The Quality Toolbox*. (Milwaukee, WI: ASQ *Quality* Press, 2004)

Viney, David. *The J-Curve Effect, Observed in Change* (*http://www.viney.com/DFV/intranet_portal_guide/during/business_change_management.html*)

B   List of Acronyms

Following is a list of acronyms used throughout this book.

Acronym	Definition
AFS	Apparel and Footwear
ALE	Application Link Enabling
APO	Advanced Planning & Optimization
APS	Advanced Planning and Scheduling
ATD	Available-to-deploy
B2B	Business-to-business
BAdI	Business Add-In
BAPI	Business Application Programming Interface
Bex	Business Explorer
BI	Business intelligence
BOM	Bill of material
BSG	Business system group
BTE	Business Transaction Event
BW	Business Warehouse
CBF	Characteristics-based forecasting
CDP	Characteristics-dependent planning
CFM	Customer Forecast Management
CIF	Core Interface
CLPBID	Collaborative Transportation Planning
CLPPROMCAL	Collaborative Promotion Planning
CLPSDP	Collaborative Supply and Demand Planning
COGS	Cost of goods sold
CPFR	Collaborative Planning, Forecasting, and Replenishment

Acronym	Definition
CRM	Customer Relationship Management
CTM	Capable-to-Match
CVC	Characteristic value combination
DB	Database
DC	Distribution centers
DP	Demand planning
DRP	Distribution requirement planning
EDI	Electronic Data Interchange
EIO	Echelon Inventory Planning
EOQ	Economical order quantity
ERP	Enterprise resource planning
ESB	Enterprise Service Business
ET	Error total (ET)
ETL	Extract transform load
FGI	Finished goods inventory
FIFO	First in first out
FM	Function module
Global ATP (GATP)	Global available-to-promise
GUI	Graphical user interface
ICF	Internet Communication Framework
ICM	Internet Communication Manager
IFO	Income from operations
ITS	Internet transaction server
JIT	Just in time
JSA	Joint service agreement
KMAT	Configurable material type

Acronym	Definition
KPI	Key performance indicator
LIS	Logistics Information System
LP	Linear programming
LSMW	Legacy System Migration Workbench
LTL	Less than truck load
LUW	Logical unit of work
MAD	Mean absolute deviation
MAPE	Mean absolute percentage error
MIP	Mixed-integer programming
MLR	Multiple linear regression
MPE	Mean percentage error
MRP	Material requirements planning
MSE	Mean square error
ND	Non-delivery
NPI	New product introduction
ODS	Operational data store
OMS	Object memory system
PDS	Production data structures
PFN	Product Forecast Notification
PI	Process integration
PIR	Planned independent requirement
PP	Production planning
PP/DS	Production planning and detailed scheduling
PPM	Production process models
PSA	Persistent staging area
QI	Quality inspection

Acronym	Definition
QM	Quality management
qRFC	queued Remote Function Call
RDBMS	Relational Database Management System
RDC	Regional distribution center
RFC	Remote function call
RICEFW	Report, Interface, Conversion, Enhancement, Forms, and Workflow
RLT	Replenishment lead time
RMSE	Square root of mean square error
S&OP	Sales and operations
SAP PI	SAP Process Integration
SAP SPP	SAP Service Parts Planning
SCC	Supply Chain Cockpit
SCE	Supply Chain Engineer
SCM	Supply Chain Management
SCOR	Supply Chain Operation Reference
SCP	Supply chain planning
SCPM	Supply chain performance management
SKU	Stock-keeping unit
SLED	Shelf life expiration date
SNP	Supply Network Planning
SOD	Segregation of duties
SSL	Secure sockets layer
TLB	Transport Load Builder
TSDM	Time Series Data Management
UOM	Unit of measure
USAT	User acceptance testing

Acronym	Definition
VARCOND	Variable condition
VC	Variant configuration
VMI	Vendor managed inventory
VSM	Value stream mapping
WACC	Weighted average cost of capital
Web AS	Web Application Server

C   The Author

Sandeep Pradhan is an SAP solution architect in the supply chain management field and has more than 17 years of professional experience. He specializes in supply chain application advisory services and has achieved results by helping clients understand, architect, select, and implement the SAP supply chain solutions required to run their businesses.

In his various roles (project manager, solution architect, functional consultant, supply chain manager), he has been responsible for providing thought leadership in supply chain strategy, business processes transformation, technology architecture, and business integration. He has worked on numerous full lifecycle SAP APO-Demand Planning and Supply Network Planning implementations from the discovery phase through the implementation phase.

Sandeep holds an MBA from Monash University, Australia, and is also author of the book *Implementing and Configuring SAP Event Management* (SAP PRESS, 2010) and co-author of *Global Available-to-Promise with SAP: Functionality and Configuration* (SAP PRESS, 2011).

You can contact Sandeep Pradhan at *spradhan13@gmail.com.*

Index

U

- Connect your business process needs with Materials Management in SAP

- Learn MM configuration steps and identify potential areas for customization

- Explore case studies, real-world examples, and best practices

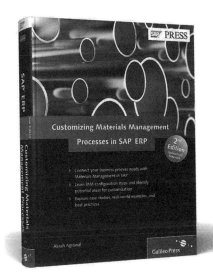

Akash Agrawal

Customizing Materials Management Processes in SAP ERP

If you need to familiarize yourself with Materials Management (MM) customization or connect MM business processes to your SAP system, this book is for you. You'll gain a thorough understanding of the key processes for materials management, and learn how to customize SAP ERP to support your business. This new and expanded edition includes a new chapter on Batch Management and MRP, additional step-by-step configuration instruction, as well as extended customer examples throughout.

556 pp., 2. edition 2012, 69,95 Euro / US$ 69.95
ISBN 978-1-59229-415-2
www.sap-press.com

Galileo Press

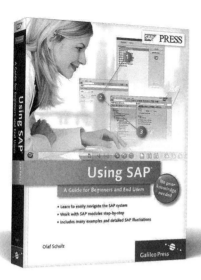

- Learn to easily navigate the SAP system

- Work with SAP modules step-by-step

- Includes many examples and detailed SAP illustrations

Olaf Schulz

Using SAP

A Guide for Beginners and End Users

This book helps end users and beginners get started in SAP ERP and provides readers with the basic knowledge they need for their daily work. Readers will get to know the essentials of working with the SAP system, learn about the SAP systems' structures and functions, and discover how SAP connects to critical business processes. Whether this book is used as an exercise book or as a reference book, readers will find what they need to help them become more comfortable with SAP ERP.

388 pp., 2012, 39,95 Euro / US$ 39.95
ISBN 978-1-59229-408-4
www.sap-press.com

Interested in reading more?

Please visit our website for all new
book and e-book releases from SAP PRESS.

www.sap-press.com